# Lecture Notes in Computer Science　　13053

More information about this subseries at http://www.springer.com/series/7412

Nicolas Tsapatsoulis · Andreas Panayides ·
Theo Theocharides · Andreas Lanitis ·
Constantinos Pattichis · Mario Vento (Eds.)

# Computer Analysis of Images and Patterns

19th International Conference, CAIP 2021
Virtual Event, September 28–30, 2021
Proceedings, Part II

Springer

*Editors*
Nicolas Tsapatsoulis ⓘ
Cyprus University of Technology
Limassol, Cyprus

Theo Theocharides ⓘ
University of Cyprus
Nicosia, Cyprus

Constantinos Pattichis ⓘ
University of Cyprus
Nicosia, Cyprus

CYENS Centre of Excellence
Nicosia, Cyprus

Andreas Panayides ⓘ
University of Cyprus
Nicosia, Cyprus

Andreas Lanitis ⓘ
Cyprus University of Technology
Limassol, Cyprus

CYENS Centre of Excellence
Nicosia, Cyprus

Mario Vento ⓘ
University of Salerno
Salerno, Italy

ISSN 0302-9743          ISSN 1611-3349   (electronic)
Lecture Notes in Computer Science
ISBN 978-3-030-89130-5          ISBN 978-3-030-89131-2   (eBook)
https://doi.org/10.1007/978-3-030-89131-2

LNCS Sublibrary: SL6 – Image Processing, Computer Vision, Pattern Recognition, and Graphics

This Springer imprint is published by the registered company Springer Nature Switzerland AG
The registered company address is: Gewerbestrasse 11, 6330 Cham, Switzerland

# Preface

Welcome to the proceedings of the 19th International Conference on Computer Analysis of Images and Patterns (CAIP 2021), which took place during September 28–30, 2021. The CAIP series of biennial international conferences is devoted to all aspects of computer vision, image analysis and processing, pattern recognition, and related fields. Previous conferences were held in Salerno, Ystad, Valletta, York, Seville, Münster, Vienna, and Paris, amongst other places. Due to the ongoing COVID-19 pandemic, CAIP 2021 was held as a virtual conference, but the organizing committee were dedicated to offering the best possible online experience.

The scientific program of the conference consisted of plenary lectures and contributed papers presented in a single track. A total of 129 papers were submitted to CAIP 2021, which were reviewed in a single-blind process with at least two reviewers per paper. A total of 87 papers were accepted. The program featured the presentation of these papers organized into the following 15 sessions:

Session 1: 3D Vision I
Session 2: 3D Vision II
Session 3: Biomedical Image and Pattern Analysis I: Segmentation
Session 4: Biomedical Image and Pattern Analysis II: Segmentation and Classification
Session 5: Biomedical Image and Pattern Analysis III: Disease Diagnosis
Session 6: Deep Learning I: Classification
Session 7: Deep Learning II: Classification
Session 8: Deep Learning III: Image Processing and Analysis
Session 9: Machine Learning for Image and Pattern Analysis
Session 10: Feature Extraction
Session 11: Object Recognition
Session 12: Face and Gesture
Session 13: Guess the Age Contest
Session 14: Biometrics, Cryptography and Security
Session 15: Segmentation and Image Restoration

CAIP 2021 featured a contest on "Guess the Age: Age Estimation From Facial Images with Deep Convolutional Neural Networks" organized by Antonio Greco, University of Salerno, Italy. In addition, the CAIP 2021 program included distinguished plenary and keynote speakers from academia and industry who shared their insights and accomplishments as well as their vision for the future of the field. Moreover, CAIP 2021 included three tutorials as follows:

Tutorial 1: Discovering Patterns in the Road from Genotype to Phenotype
Tutorial 2: Video Summarization for Unpaired Videos
Tutorial 3: Large Scale Video Analytics.

We want to express our deepest appreciation to all the members of the CAIP 2021 organizing committee and Technical Program Committee, as well as all the reviewers, for their dedication and hard work in creating an excellent scientific program. We want to thank all the authors who submitted their papers to CAIP 2021, and all of those who presented and shared their work. Finally, we would like thank all the participants for taking part in the conference.

We hope that you enjoyed this exciting and memorable event, and we look forward to meeting in person at the next CAIP!

October 2021

Constantinos Pattichis
Andreas Lanitis
Nicolas Tsapatsoulis
Andreas Panayides
Theo Theocharides
Mario Vento

# Organization

## General Chairs

| | |
|---|---|
| Constantinos S. Pattichis | CYENS and University of Cyprus, Cyprus |
| Andreas Lanitis | CYENS and Cyprus University of Technology, Cyprus |
| Nicolai Petkov | University of Groningen, The Netherlands |

## Program Chairs

| | |
|---|---|
| Nicolas Tsapatsoulis | Cyprus University of Technology, Cyprus |
| Andreas Panayides | University of Cyprus, Cyprus |
| Theo Theocharides | KIOS and University of Cyprus, Cyprus |
| Mario Vento | University of Salerno, Italy |

## Local Organizing Committee

| | |
|---|---|
| Constantinos S. Pattichis | CYENS and University of Cyprus, Cyprus |
| Constandinos Mavromoustakis | IEEE Cyprus Section and University of Nicosia, Cyprus |
| Alexis Polycarpou | IET Cyprus Local Network and Frederick University, Cyprus |
| Toumazis Toumazi | Cyprus Computer Society, Cyprus |

## Steering Committee

Mario Vento (Chair CAIP 2019)
Gennaro Percanella (Co-chair CAIP 2019)
Michael Felsberg (Chair CAIP 2017)
Nicolai Petkov (Permanent Member)

## Awards Chair

| | |
|---|---|
| Xiaoyi Jiang | University of Münster, Germany |

## Contests Chairs

| | |
|---|---|
| Christos Loizou | Cyprus University of Technology, Cyprus |
| Yannis Avrithis | Inria Rennes-Bretagne Atlantique, France |

## Tutorials Chairs

| | |
|---|---|
| Gennaro Percannella | University of Salerno, Italy |
| Kleanthis Neokleous | CYENS, Cyprus |

## Workshops Chairs

| | |
|---|---|
| Nicola Strisciuglio | University of Twente, The Netherlands |
| Melinos Averkiou | CYENS, Cyprus |

## Student Activities Chairs

| | |
|---|---|
| Andreas Aristeidou | University of Cyprus, Cyprus |
| Sotirios Chatzis | Cyprus University of Technology, Cyprus |

## Industry Liaison Chairs

| | |
|---|---|
| Alessandro Artusi | CYENS, Cyprus |
| Zenonas Theodosiou | CYENS, Cyprus |

## Publicity Chairs

| | |
|---|---|
| Alessia Saggese | University of Salerno, Italy |
| Klimis Ntalianis | University of West Attica, Greece |

## Publicity Committee

| | |
|---|---|
| Nikolas Papanikolopoulos | University of Minnesota, USA |
| Andreas Spanias | Arizona State University, USA |
| Marios S. Pattichis | University of Mexico, USA |
| Stefanos Kollias | NTUA, Greece |
| Andreas Stafylopatis | NTUA, Greece |
| Xiaoyi Jiang | University of Münster, Germany |
| Enrique Alegre Gutiérrez | University of Leon, Spain |
| Alessia Saggese | University of Salerno, Italy |

## Program Committee

| | |
|---|---|
| Andreas Lanitis | CYENS and Cyprus University of Technology, Cyprus |
| Andreas Panayides | University of Cyprus, Cyprus |
| Constantinos S. Pattichis | CYENS and University of Cyprus, Cyprus |
| Nicolai Petkov | University of Groningen, Netherlands |
| Theo Theocharides | KIOS and University of Cyprus, Cyprus |
| Nicolas Tsapatsoulis | Cyprus University of Technology, Cyprus |
| Mario Vento | University of Salerno, Italy |

# Additional Reviewers

| | |
|---|---|
| Ioannis Anagnostopoulos | University of Thessaly, Greece |
| Yannis Avrithis | Inria Rennes-Bretagne Atlantique, France |
| Athos Antoniades | Stremble Ventures Ltd, Cyprus |
| Zinonas Antoniou | University of Cyprus, Cyprus |
| Andreas Aristidou | University of Cyprus, Cyprus |
| Aristos Aristodimou | University of Cyprus, Cyprus |
| Alessandro Artusi | CYENS, Cyprus |
| Christodoulou Christodoulos | University of Cyprus, Cyprus |
| Christoforos Christoforou | University of Cyprus, Cyprus |
| Adrian-Horia Dediu | SuperData Bucharest, Romania |
| Constantinos Djouvas | Cyprus University of Technology, Cyprus |
| Anastasios Doulamis | NTUA, Greece |
| Basilis Gatos | National Center for Scientific Research "Demokritos", Greece |
| Enrique Alegre Gutiérrez | University of Leon, Spain |
| Xiaoyi Jiang | University of Münster, Germany |
| Minas Karaolis | University of Cyprus, Cyprus |
| Efthyvoulos Kyriacou | Frederick University, Cyprus |
| Christos Kyrkou | KIOS Research and Innovation Center, Cyprus |
| Christos Loizou | Cyprus University of Technology, Cyprus |
| Alberto Marchisio | Technical University of Viennna, Austria |
| Costas Neocleous | Cyprus University of Technology, Cyprus |
| Andreas Neokleous | University of Cyprus, Cyprus |
| Kleanthis Neokleous | CYENS, Cyprus |
| Marios Neofytou | University of Cyprus, Cyprus |
| Athanasios Nikolaidis | Technological Educational Institute of Serres, Greece |
| Klimis Ntalianis | University of West Attica, Greece |
| Maria Papaioannou | University of Cyprus, Cyprus |
| Marios S. Pattichis | University of New Mexico, USA |
| Gennaro Percannella | University of Salerno, Italy |
| Ioannis Pratikakis | Democritus University of Thrace, Greece |
| Benjamin Risse | University of Münster, Germany |
| Alessia Saggese | University of Salerno, Italy |
| Zenonas Theodosiou | CYENS, Cyprus |
| Mario Vento | University of Salerno, Italy |

**Organized and Sponsored by**

**Co-organized and Co-sponsored by**

**Technically Co-sponsored by**

**Endorsed by**

# Contents – Part II

## Object Recognition

## Face and Gesture

**Guess the Age Contest**

**Biometrics, Cryptography and Security**

**Segmentation and Image Restoration**

# Contents – Part I

## Machine Learning

# Machine Learning

# Deep Learning Based Automated Vickers Hardness Measurement

Ehsaneddin Jalilian$^{(\boxtimes)}$ ⓘ and Andreas Uhl ⓘ

Department of Computer Science, University of Salzburg, Jakob-Haringerstraße 2,
Salzburg, Austria
{ejalilian,uhl}@cs.sbg.ac.at

**Abstract.** Automated Vickers hardness measurement remains to be a
challenging task due to the difficulties associated with Vickers indentation detection and complex specimen surface defects. Typical image
processing methods fail to detect the indentations in specimens possess-
ing rough and noisy surfaces, distorted indentation shapes, or cracks. We
propose a robust deep learning based model for accurate automated Vickers hardness measurement in this work. A Fully Convolutional Neural
network (FCN) is chosen to accurately localize and segment the Vickers
indentations. A set of liner curves are then fitted to the boundary pixels data extracted from the output segmentations. The initial positions
of the indentation vertices are estimated as the cross-sectional point of
adjacent boundaries to each indentation vertex. A complimentary segmentation module then is used to refine the target regions, and accurate
indentation vertices positions are then calculated applying further geometric processing steps. The accuracy of the model is compared to known
algorithms from the literature and results are presented. The evaluation
is conducted on two significant indentation image databases with 150
and 216 highly varying images.

**Keywords:** Vickers hardness measurement · Deep learning

## 1 Introduction and Related Work

Vickers hardness testing is a technique used for examining the resistance of
the surface of solid specimens such as metals, ceramics, or polymers. In this
method hardness testing machines called durometers apply a pyramidal diamond
indenter with an angle of 136° between opposite faces on the specimen surface,
with measurable load and time period. The Vickers hardness (VH) is the quotient
obtained by dividing the applied force load (F) by the square area of indentation:

$$VH = \frac{1}{g} \frac{2\,F sin\frac{136°}{2}}{d^2},\tag{1}$$

where $d$ is the mean of the diagonal length of the indentation, and $g$ is the
acceleration of gravity (see Fig. 2 for an illustration). Manual inspection and

© Springer Nature Switzerland AG 2021
N. Tsapatsoulis et al. (Eds.): CAIP 2021, LNCS 13053, pp. 3–13, 2021.
https://doi.org/10.1007/978-3-030-89131-2_1

measurement of indentations is time consuming and very interpretive [11]. Computer-assisted hardness testing systems have been developed to address these issues and also to provide more accurate measurements. Accurate detection and localization (segmentation) of the indentations in the Vickers images is the most crucial step for correct measurement of the indentation dimensions. In fact, the indentations vary significantly in terms of: size, location, rotation, brightness, contrast and texture characteristics in the corresponding images. On the other hand, the target specimens normally have noisy surfaces which contain cracks, sparkles and other industrial distortions. The computational methods proposed so far for automatic indentation detection and measurement fail to perform well in certain groups of images depending on the techniques applied. Thresholding algorithms [10,11] easily get misled by the global distribution of the background (specimen surface) pixels which contribute extensively to the threshold level computation (see Figs. 1a and e for an example). Long overtures, speckles, and break lines that cross through edges or that emit from vertices may disturb the reconstruction algorithms as used in the edge detection approaches [2,8]. Figures 1b, c and d show example images and their corresponding outputs (Figs. 1f, g and h) using a Sobel edge operator. Also, lack of significant markers, or rough specimen surface, or industrial defects may cause the Axes projection algorithms [11] to fail to detect the significant differences (which correspond to the indentation region) in such images. Template matching methods [2,3] are computationally expensive and their matching mechanism is very sensitive to the orientation of the indentation, structural discrepancies and artifacts on the specimen surface. Active-contour algorithms [4] generally require parameters that are distribution dependent and very hard to generalize. Benefiting from the recent advancements in deep learning technology, Tanaka et al. [12] used two CNN modules separately to detect the bounding-box surrounding the Vickers indentation, and the left indentation vertex positions. In fact the feasibility of this model is very restricted as two separate training sessions, and thus

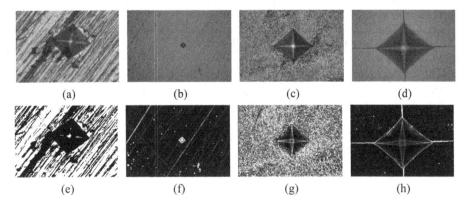

(a)          (b)          (c)          (d)

(e)          (f)          (g)          (h)

**Fig. 1.** Sample indention images (first row), and their output segmentations using adaptive threshold (e, f), and Sobel edge detection algorithm (g, h)

two training datasets along with their corresponding manual ground-truths are required to initialize the system. The authors further used physical deviation (in terms of $\mu m$) measure (instead of pixel-wise measurement as used in other related research) to evaluate the model performance, and thus it is difficult to validate their results against other commonly used algorithms.

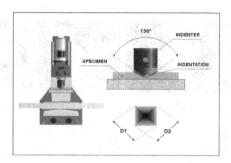

**Fig. 2.** Durometers and Vickers indention hardness test schematics

This study aims to leverage the power of deep learning networks within a simple and viable framework to propose a robust and simplified automated Vickers indentation measurement model. In particular, a powerful semantic segmentation Fully Convolutional Neural Network (FCN) with strong emphasis on boundary pixel preservation is chosen to perform the challenging task of Vickers indentation region detection and segmentation. The Vickers indentation boundary information obtained in this stage then is used as the basis to fit (four) linear curves to the indentation edges. The initial Vickers indentation vertices positions are approximated, at the sub-pixel level, computing the cross-sectional points of the adjacent curves. A Region Of Interest window (ROI) is defined around each vertex position, and the target regions are further refined to extract the actual indention vertices using an adaptive segmentation module. The vertices final positions then are calculated utilizing a geometry-based technique. The robustness and accuracy of the model is verified on samples that differ substantially in terms of indention shape, size, type, and distribution of the noises.

## 2  Methodology

As we already mentioned, the key challenging step in automatic Vickers indentation testing is localization and segmentation of the indentation in the images. So, we selected to handle this task utilizing a segmentation CNN, as the models proved to provide superior performance in wide variety of application, specially in complicated and challenging segmentation tasks [6,7].

### 2.1  Indentation Segmentation Using Convolutional Neural Network

As a key criteria, the network needed to possess very strong profile in preserving boundary pixels data, as later the detected boundary data is used as the input for estimating the initial indention vertices' positions. We selected the RefineNet [9] to accomplish this task, as the network is already proven to enable high-resolution prediction, and at the same time to preserve the boundary information. We used an ADAM optimizer with learning rate of 0.0001, executing 40,000 iterations to train the network[1].

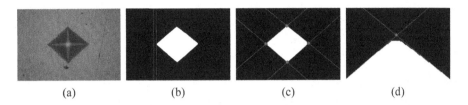

(a)              (b)              (c)              (d)

**Fig. 3.** A sample input image (a), its corresponding output segmentation (b), the curves fitted to the indention four edge points (c), and an initial vertex position specified (d).

## 2.2 Edge Extraction and Initial Indention Vertex Position Estimation

The FCN outputs provide the input data to extract the indentation edge points information. In this way, we first refine the output segmentations by extracting the biggest segmentation profile (by size), thereby removing the false-positive outliers, in the output segmentations. All connected objects in the output masks are found, and their sizes are calculated (pixel-wise) to find the biggest one. Then, the indentation contour points are extracted [5] and a first degree polynomial curve is fitted into each indentation boundary point utilizing a least-squares criterion. The actual indentions' shapes are not fully squared and the edges have rather concave profile, which bend towards the inside as we move along the edges from vertex points toward the middle of the edges. To this extent, we considered an estimate (50%) of uncertainty values (based on the standard deviation of the edge points) to be added to the estimated curve positions. This compensated for the nonlinearity property of the edges and found (by experiment) to improve the algorithm precision notably. The intersection point of the crossing curves $L_1$ and $L_2$ with the line segments defined as $(x_1\ y_1), (x_2\ y_2)$ and $(x_3\ y_3), (x_4\ y_4)$ then are calculated to determine the initial coordinates of the indentation vertices $(V_{x,y})$:

$$V_x = \frac{(x_1y_2 - y_1x_2)(x_3 - x_4) - (x_1 - x_2)(x_3y_4 - y_3x_4)}{(x_1 - x_2)(y_3 - y_4) - (y_1 - y_2)(x_3 - x_4)}$$

$$V_y = \frac{(x_1y_2 - y_1x_2)(y_3 - y_4) - (y_1 - y_2)(x_3y_4 - y_3x_4)}{(x_1 - x_2)(y_3 - y_4) - (y_1 - y_2)(x_3 - x_4)}.$$

(2)

Figure 3 demonstrates a sample input image (3a), its corresponding output segmentation (3b), the curves fitted (3c), and an initial vertex estimated (3d).

[1] https://github.com/eragonruan/refinenet-image-segmentation.

## 2.3  Precision Improvement

To this extent, we leveraged the segmentation power of the FCN to get the challenging task of indentation positioning and segmentation accomplished. We also
estimated (or rather predicted) the initial indentation vertices positions based
on the information obtained in this stage. However, the actual vertex information did not contribute much to these initial estimations. This was mainly due to
the fact that corner region pixels went missing in the output segmentations (see
Fig. 3d). Missing corner pixels is a general segmentation issue and is not specific
to the CNN-based segmentation models. So, in the next step we considered to
extract the actual missing vertex pixels, and further process this information
to improve the initial vertices position estimations. For this, first we defined a
region of interest (ROI) window with size $40 \times 40$ around each initial vertex position. The typical background (specimen surface) distortions already mentioned
are minimized or even not existing in such limited region, and vertex features
are fairly differentiable from the background pixels. Close inspection of the ROI
images (Figs. 4a, b) and their outputs segmentations (Figs. 4c, d) reflected this
fact properly too. Therefore, we chose to utilize Otsu's adaptive clustering algorithm to segment the ROI region into the foreground (corresponding to the
indentation corner pixels) and the background (corresponding to the specimen
surface pixels). To perform the clustering, the algorithm maximizes inter-class
($w$) variance (which is equivalent to minimizing the intra-class variance):

$$\sigma_w^2(t) = \omega_0(t)\omega_1(t)\left[\mu_0(t) - \mu_1(t)\right]^2 . \tag{3}$$

The class probability $\omega_0(t)$ and $\omega_1(t)$ are computed from the $L$ bins of the
histogram:

$$\omega_0(t) = \sum_{i=0}^{t-1} p(i) , \quad \omega_1(t) = \sum_{i=t}^{L-1} p(i), \tag{4}$$

and the class means $\mu_0(t)$, and $\mu_1(t)$, are calculated as:

$$\mu_0^2(t) = \sum_{i=1}^{t} [i - \mu_1(t)]^2 \frac{P(i)}{w_1(t)'} , \quad \mu_1^2(t) = \sum_{i=t+1}^{I} [i - \mu_2(t)]^2 \frac{P(i)}{w_2(t)}. \tag{5}$$

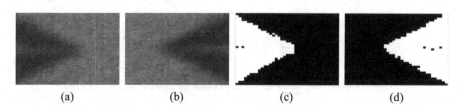

|        (a)        |        (b)        |        (c)        |        (d)        |

**Fig. 4.** A Sample right (a) and left (b) ROI images and their corresponding output
segmentations (c, a), using the complementary segmentation module

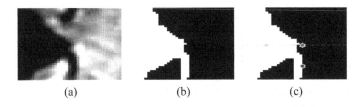

**Fig. 5.** A sample ROI with connected defect (a) and its corresponding output segmentation (b), where the initial vertex point (blue mark) is corrected (red mark), considering the vertex central gravity (green mark) in the output (c). (Color figure online)

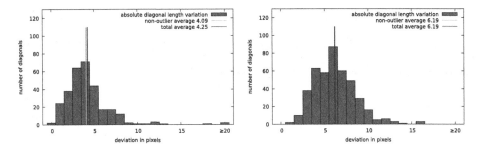

**Fig. 6.** Histogram of the maximum deviation for the manual measurements in DA (left) and DB (right) respectively

As it can be seen in the output results (Figs. 4c, d), the vertex regions are effectively separated from the background. The straight-forward approach to specify the vertex position in the output segmentations is to find the coordinate of the most extreme pixels located at the tip of the segmented indentation corner region. However, locating such a pixel ought not to be a trivial task. In some cases the defects in the surface (grooves or holes) are connected to the indentation corner regions (see an example in Fig. 5). While the target vertex pixel is assumed to be a single pixel located at the tip of the segmented area (see Fig. 4c), yet it turned out in certain cases to have linear shape (formed from two or more pixels) in some. To address these issues, we decided to calculate the horizontal coordinate of the vertex point based on the "central gravity" of the segmented area. So, we calculated the centroid ($C_{x,y}$) of the segmented area [1] as follows:

$$C_{\mathrm{x}} = \frac{1}{6\,A} \sum_{i=0}^{n-1} (x_i + x_{i+1})\,(x_i y_{i+1} - x_{i+1} y_i)$$
$$C_y = \frac{1}{6\,A} \sum_{i=0}^{n-1} (y_i + y_{i+1})\,(x_i y_{i+1} - x_{i+1} y_i),$$

(6)

Where the area $(A)$ of the polygon containing the segmented area is defined as:

$$A = \frac{1}{2} \sum_{i=0}^{n-1} (x_i y_{i+1} - x_{i+1} y_i). \qquad (7)$$

We also calculated the vertical coordinate of the vertex point, averaging the top-left and top-right pixels' vertical coordinates of the polygon containing the segmented area. As illustrated in Fig. 5, this approach enables us to effectively filter out the connecting outliers affect, and at the same time allows us to compute the actual coordinates of the vertex in case of vertices having a linear shape.

## 3   Experimental Framework

We used two Vickers hardness indentation databases to carry out our experimental studies which has been used in previous work [2,3]. Each database contains a substantial number of images (DA: 150, DB: 216) at a resolution of 1280 × 1024 pixels, which were captured directly in production operation environments. Images contain one Vickers micro-indentation with severe variation in the size, location and rotation of the indentation, the texture of the specimen surface, and the overall focus and contrast of the picture. We utilized an annotation tool to generate the manual ground-truths of indentation images required to train the FCN network. The indentation regions were marked (in the corresponding binary ground-truth mask), fitting a square-shaped polygon (manually) to each indention region. We requested multiple testing experts to generate the diagonal measurement manual ground-truths, and the vertices manual ground-truths. Figure 6 shows a histogram of the maximum deviation for the manual measurements for the databases DA and DB respectively, which can be considered as a human baseline for the desired quality of automatic hardness measurement algorithms.

## 4   Experiments and Results

We selected representatives of indentation detection algorithms from Sect. 1, as well as the proposed model as described in Sect. 2 to be evaluated against the two indentation image databases described in Sect. 3. To evaluate our model, first we trained the FCN network on the images in the databases. We applied a 2-fold cross evaluation training scheme for the network. For this, we partitioned each database into two equal parts, and then trained and tested the network alternatively on each database partition. Doing so, we tested the networks on all samples in each database without overlapping the training and testing sets. After obtaining the output segmentations for each database, we applied the measurement pipeline as explained in Sect. 2 to the output segmentations. Results were compared to the median of the manual measurements and presented in terms of two averages errors: the overall average errors (reflecting the algorithm robustness and accuracy), and the non-outlier average error in which the errors exceeding 20 pixels are inhibited (reflecting the algorithm precision). Likewise, we evaluated the other algorithm representatives on the databases as well (i.e. we have taken their accuracy results from [3]). Table 1 lists the algorithms together with the results obtained in these experiments. The axes projection algorithm evaluated here differs from the original proposal [11], as Otsu's algorithm is used to determine the threshold level for the binarization step as well as to determine the threshold level for the indentation detection in the x- and y-projection. Furthermore, all images were rotated by 45° based on the requirements of the algorithm.

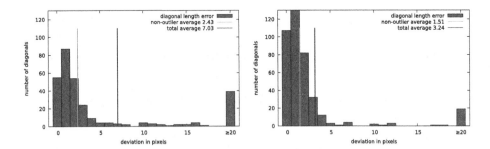

**Fig. 7.** Deviation of the diagonal lengths from the ground-truths for the database DA (left) and DB (right) respectively

**Table 1.** Diagonal indentation measurement results for different algorithms along with the corresponding manual measurements

| Measure | Average Diagonal Error (pixels) | | Non-outlier Average Diagonal Error (pixels) | |
|---|---|---|---|---|
| Database | DA | DB | DA | DB |
| Axes projection [11] | 62.01 | 48.04 | 8.49 | 8.18 |
| Vertex template matching [2] | 10.01 | 4.65 | 4.13 | 4.24 |
| Edge template matching [2] | 14.16 | 5.37 | 4.18 | 4.96 |
| Edge tracing [2] | 13.73 | 5.61 | 4.15 | 4.97 |
| Ray sweeping [2] | 24.58 | 14.70 | 12.03 | 12.09 |
| Three-stage template matching [3] | 8.75 | 4.77 | 2.96 | 2.90 |
| Ours | 7.03 | 3.24 | 2.43 | 1.51 |
| Manual measurements | 3.12 | 4.28 | 3.06 | 4.30 |

Considering the primary measurement errors (non-outlier average diagonal errors), the proposed model shows superior performance in comparison with the other algorithms on both databases (2.43 pixels for DA and 1.51 pixels for DB). The results proved to be very precise on both databases as they are even better than the average manual measurements. Furthermore, considering the average diagonal measurements errors (7.03 pixels for DA and 3.24 pixels for DB), the model delivers a robust performance as well, and proves to deal better with hard cases compared to the other algorithms (see Fig. 7 for the corresponding error graphs). Among the other algorithms representatives, the three-stage template matching algorithm shows better results (in terms of both measurement errors) compared to the others. The axes projection and ray sweeping algorithms result in a vast number of outliers, and generally do not deliver promising results. The vertex and the edge template algorithms however perform better (than the two previous algorithms), stil worse compared to the proposed one.

In addition to the evaluation of the accuracy of diagonal length measurements, we also examined the positional error of the indentation vertices for the proposed model. Examination of the vertex errors is not necessary for the sole computation of the hardness value of a specimen but has significance in imitating the manual hardness measuring process where measurement lines are attached to the indentation in the image. Such measurement lines are likewise welcome in automated measurements to enable verification and monitoring of the operation. Minimal positional errors of the indentation vertices are therefore demanded to ensure good visual feedback. Figure 8 shows the histogram of the deviation of vertex positions from the ground-truths for both databases, where the non-outlier average error is 3.89 and 3.04 pixels for the DA and DB databases, respectively. The deviation is computed according to the procedure described in Sect. 3. Figure 9 shows examples of problematic cases where the model does not yield promising results. For both problem cases, the first step

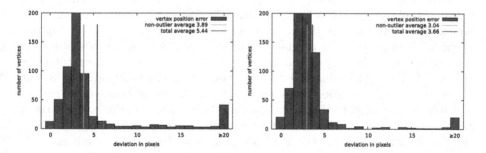

**Fig. 8.** Deviation of vertex positions from the ground-truths for the database DA (left) and DB (right) respectively

(a)　　　　　　　　(b)　　　　　　　　(c)

**Fig. 9.** Examples of problematic cases where the model does not yield good results

of the model, which is the indentation localization and segmentation, failed and generated false indentation boundaries that misled all the following steps. In particular, Fig. 9a shows a segmentation defect (underestimation) on both the upper-right and the lower-right indentation boundaries which placed the indentation vertices' initial positions quite far from the actual vertices positions, as well as the ROI windows. This of course is due to the FCN segmentation error, and needed to be analyzed from this point of view. The significance of Figs. 9b and c are however quite questionable, because the indentations completely lack contrast to the surrounding. This violates the structural features learned by the FCN, and thus the indention region is just guessed by the network here.

## 5    Conclusion

The proposed deep learning based model showed superb results for automatic Vickers indentation measurement in the Vickers images. The FCN network enabled us to successfully perform the challenging task of indentation localization and segmentation, specially in hard cases where indentation profiles are distorted by rough specimen surface, sparkles, and low contrasts. The segmentation network delivered reliable input data to the secondary segmentation module where indentation vertices positions were extracted. The accuracy of the predicted vertex positions were further improved applying a geometric improvement technique, and thereby the model delivered the results that were superior to all studied competing algorithms in terms of both the exactness of the measured diagonal lengths and the robustness. The size of the databases enabled the calculation of statistics, which give quantitative predictions about the viability of an algorithm when deployed. It is also shown that the precision of the proposed algorithm is even better than manual measurements performed by operators and thus lays beyond the scope of human measurement variations. The accuracy of the model was highly influenced by the network segmentation performance. So, enhancing the segmentation accuracy specially in the indentation corner regions will diffidently mitigate the segmentation related errors as those discussed in Sect. 4. The key competences of the proposed algorithm are its robustness to the size, location and rotation of the indentation in the images as well as to the brightness conditions of the images, and the resistance against surface defects. Moreover, simplicity of the techniques applied, and absence of tunable parameters, makes it a practical module for Vickers indention measurement.

## References

1. Bourke, P.: Calculating the Area and Centroid of a Polygon. Swinburne University of Technology 7 (1988)
2. Gadermayr, M., Maier, A., Uhl, A.: Algorithms for microindentation measurement in automated Vickers hardness testing. In: Tenth International Conference on Quality Control by Artificial Vision, vol. 8000, p. 80000M (2011)

 3. Gadermayr, M., Maier, A., Uhl, A.: Robust algorithm for automated microindentation measurement in Vickers hardness testing. J. Electron. Imaging **21**(2), 021109 (2012)
 4. Gadermayr, M., Maier, A., Uhl, A.: Active contours methods with respect to Vickers indentations. Mach. Vis. Appl. **24**(6), 1183–1196 (2013)
 5. Hert, S., Schirra, S.: 2D convex hulls and extreme points. In: CGAL User and Reference Manual. CGAL Editorial Board, 5.2.1 edn. (2021)
 6. Jalilian, E., Uhl, A.: Iris segmentation using fully convolutional encoder–decoder networks. In: Bhanu, B., Kumar, A. (eds.) Deep Learning for Biometrics. ACVPR, pp. 133–155. Springer, Cham (2017). https://doi.org/10.1007/978-3-319-61657-5_6
 7. Jalilian, E., Uhl, A.: Finger-vein recognition using deep fully convolutional neural semantic segmentation networks: the impact of training data. In: Proceedings of the IEEE 10th International Workshop on Information Forensics and Security, pp. 1–8, Hong Kong (2018)
 8. Jiand, Y., Xu, A.: A new method for automatically measurement of Vickers hardness using thick line Hough transform and least square method. In: International Congress on Image and Signal Processing, pp. 1–4. IEEE (2009)
 9. Lin, G., Milan, A., Shen, C., Reid, I.: RefiNenet: multi-path refinement networks for high-resolution semantic segmentation. In: Proceedings of the IEEE Conference on Computer Vision and Pattern Recognition, pp. 1925–1934 (2017)
10. Dominguez-Nicolas, S.M., Wiederhold, P.: Indentation image analysis for Vickers hardness testing. In: International Conference on Electrical Engineering, Computing Science and Automatic Control, pp. 1–6. IEEE (2018)
11. Takao, S., Tadao, K.: Development of an automatic Vickers hardness testing system using image processing technology. IEEE Trans Ind. Electron. **44**(5), 696–702 (1997)
12. Tanaka, Y., Seino, Y., Hattori, K.: Automated Vickers hardness measurement using convolutional neural networks. Int. J. Adv. Manuf. Technol. **109**(5), 1345–1355 (2020). https://doi.org/10.1007/s00170-020-05746-4

# *ElasticHash*: Semantic Image Similarity Search by Deep Hashing with Elasticsearch

Nikolaus Korfhage[(✉)], Markus Mühling, and Bernd Freisleben

Department of Mathematics and Computer Science,
University of Marburg, Marburg, Germany
{korfhage,muehling,freisleb}@informatik.uni-marburg.de

**Abstract.** We present *ElasticHash*, a novel approach for high-quality, efficient, and large-scale semantic image similarity search. It is based on a deep hashing model to learn hash codes for fine-grained image similarity search in natural images and a two-stage method for efficiently searching binary hash codes using Elasticsearch (ES). In the first stage, a coarse search based on short hash codes is performed using multi-index hashing and ES terms lookup of neighboring hash codes. In the second stage, the list of results is re-ranked by computing the Hamming distance on long hash codes. We evaluate the retrieval performance of *ElasticHash* for more than 120,000 query images on about 6.9 million database images of the OpenImages data set. The results show that our approach achieves high-quality retrieval results and low search latencies.

**Keywords:** Deep hashing · Similarity search · Elasticsearch

## 1 Introduction

Query-by-content approaches based on feature representations that are learned by deep convolutional neural networks (CNNs) have greatly increased the performance of content-based image retrieval systems. However, state-of-the-art methods in the field of semantic image similarity search suffer from shallow network architectures and small data sets with few image classes in the training as well as in the evaluation phases. Few image classes in the training phase lead to poor generalizability to query images with unknown content in the evaluation phase, i.e., a more fine-grained modeling of the image content is required. Thus, high accuracy for arbitrary search queries, fast response times, and scalability to millions of images are necessary to meet many users' needs both in scientific and commercial applications.

In this paper, we present *ElasticHash*, a high-quality, efficient, and scalable approach for semantic image similarity search based on the most popular enterprise full-text search and analytics engine Elasticsearch[1] (ES). ES processes

---

[1] https://www.elastic.co..

© Springer Nature Switzerland AG 2021
N. Tsapatsoulis et al. (Eds.): CAIP 2021, LNCS 13053, pp. 14–23, 2021.
https://doi.org/10.1007/978-3-030-89131-2_2

queries very fast due to inverted indices based on Lucene[2], scales to hundreds of servers, provides load balancing, and supports availability and reliability. Apparently, the properties of ES are not only desirable for full-text search, but also for semantic image similarity search. Furthermore, integrating image similarity search into ES allows multi-modal queries, e.g., combining text and images in a single query. The contributions of the paper are as follows:

- We present *ElasticHash*, a novel two-stage approach for semantic image similarity search based on multi-index hashing and integrate it via terms lookup queries into ES.
- We present experimental results to show that *ElasticHash* achieves fast response times and high-quality retrieval results at the same time by leveraging the benefits of short hash codes (better search times) and long hash codes (higher retrieval quality). To the best of our knowledge, we provide the first evaluation of image similarity search for more than 120,000 query images on about 6.9 million database images of the OpenImages data set.
- We make our deep image similarity search model, the corresponding ES indices, and a demo application available at http://github.com/umr-ds/ ElasticHash.

The paper is organized as follows. In Sect. 2, we discuss related work. Section 3 presents *ElasticHash*. In Sect. 4, we evaluate *ElasticHash* on the OpenImages data set in terms of search latency and retrieval quality. Section 5 concludes the paper and outlines areas for future work.

## 2   Related Work

Deep learning, in particular deep CNNs, led to strong improvements in content-based image similarity search. With increasing sizes of the underlying image databases, the need for an efficient similarity search strategy arises. Since high-dimensional CNN features are not suitable to efficiently search in very large databases, large-scale image similarity search systems focus on binary image codes for quantization or compact representations and fast comparisons rather than full CNN features.

Recently, several deep hashing methods were introduced [2,4,6,15,21,23,25]. Many of them employ pairwise or triplet losses. While these methods often achieve state-of-the-art performance on their test data sets, they are not necessarily suitable for very large data sets and fine-grained image similarity search based on thousands of classes. Existing deep hashing methods are often trained using small CNNs that usually cannot capture the granularity of very large image data sets. Often, CNN models like AlexNet [12] are used as their backbones, and they are usually evaluated on a small number of image classes [4,6,22,25] (e.g., a sample of 100 ImageNet categories [4], about 80 object categories in COCO [14], NUS-WIDE [5] with 81 concepts, or even only 10 classes as in MNIST or CIFAR). Additionally, the image dimensions in CIFAR and MNIST are very

---

[2] https://lucene.apache.org.

small ($32 \times 32$ and $28 \times 28$, respectively) and thus not sufficient for image similarity search in real-world applications. Many approaches are trained on relatively small training data sets (e.g., 10,000–50,000 images [3,4,15]). In addition, there are no standardized benchmark data sets, and each publication uses different splits of training, query, and database images, which further complicates a comparison of the methods. Furthermore, training from scratch can be prohibitively expensive for large data sets. We observed that for large data sets with a high number of image classes, a transfer learning approach that combines triplet loss and classification loss leads to good retrieval results. To the best of our knowledge, *ElasticHash* is the first work that presents a deep hashing model trained and evaluated on a sufficiently large number of image classes.

The currently best performing approaches for learning to hash image representations belong either to product quantization (PQ) methods [8,9] and methods based on deep hashing (DH) [6,23]. Amato et al. [1] present PQ approaches that transform neural network features into text formats suitable for being indexed in ES. However, this approach cannot match the retrieval performance of FAISS [9]. Therefore, we focus on deep hashing that in combination with multi-index hashing (MIH) [17] can circumvent exhaustive search in Hamming space and achieve low search latency while maintaining high retrieval quality.

*ElasticHash* is related to other image similarity search methods integrated into ES. For example, FENSHSES [16] integrates MIH into ES and has a search latency comparable to FAISS. The method works efficiently for small radii of the Hamming ball and relatively small data sets (500,000 images). Small hamming radii, however, often produce too few neighbors for a query [17]. MIH like FENSHSES is thus not suitable for our scenario of large-scale image retrieval in ES with long binary codes (256 bits), where we require sub-second search latency on a data set of about 7 million images. Furthermore, we solve the shortcomings of FENSHSES using only a subset of bits rather than the whole hash codes to perform our MIH-based coarse search. While other works extend ES for image similarity search by modifying the Lucene library [7], our approach is seamlessly integrated into ES without modifying its code base.

## 3    *ElasticHash*

*ElasticHash* consists of several components as shown in Fig. 1: a deep hashing component, an ES cluster, and a retrieval component. The deep hashing component is realized as a web service using Tensorflow Serving where the integrated deep hashing model is applied to images and the corresponding binary codes are returned. In the first phase, the binary codes are extracted from the database images in the indexing phase using the deep hashing component and stored into the ES cluster. After initially building the index, the retrieval component handles incoming query images and visualizes the retrieval results. For this purpose, the binary codes are extracted from the query images using the web service, the corresponding ES queries are assembled and sent to the ES cluster that returns the final list of similar images. The entire similarity search system can be easily deployed for production via Docker.

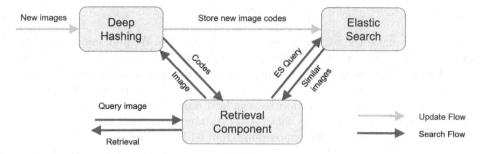

**Fig. 1.** Overview of the workflows for image similarity search in ES.

The deep hashing model is described in more detail in Sect. 3.1, including the training strategy and network architecture. In Sect. 3.2, the ES integration is presented.

### 3.1  Deep Hashing Model

We now describe our deep hashing model and how it is used to extract both short and long hash codes.

The model training consists of two phases that both use ADAM as the optimization method. First, an ImageNet-pretrained EfficientNetB3 [19] model is trained on a data set with a larger number of classes in order to obtain a more fine-grained embedding. In contrast to the original ImageNet dataset, it contains all ImageNet classes with more than 1000 training images and all classes of the Places2 [24] data set, which results in a total number of classes of 5,390. The model is trained with cross-entropy loss on a Softmax output. After two epochs of training the final layer with a learning rate of 0.01, all layers are trained for another 16 epochs with a learning rate of 0.0001.

In the second phase, the classification model's weights are used to initialize the deep hashing model. This model includes an additional 256-bit coding layer before the class output layer with *tanh* activation and 256 outputs. This model is trained for 5 epochs with a learning rate of 0.0001. It is trained on the same data set as before, however, by combining cross-entropy loss on the output and hard triplet loss [18] on the coding layer.

With the classification loss

$$\mathcal{L}_c = \sum_{i=1}^{K} y_i \log p_i \tag{1}$$

for $K$ classes with labels $y_i$ and predictions $p_i$, and the triplet loss

$$\mathcal{L}_t = max(d(a,p) - d(a,n) + \gamma, 0) \tag{2}$$

for Euclidean distance $d$ between the 256-dimensional output of the coding layer for anchor image $a$ and positive example $p$ and between $a$ and a negative example $n$, respectively, the combined loss function is given by:

$$\mathcal{L} = \alpha\mathcal{L}_c + \beta\mathcal{L}_t, \tag{3}$$

where we set margin $\gamma = 2$ and weights $\alpha = 1$ and $\beta = 5$. We first sample a batch of size $b = 128$ images from a uniform distribution of the classes. This batch is used for both computing the classification loss and generating $b$ hard triplets. To make the similarity search more robust, we used heavy data augmentation in both phases, which in addition to standard augmentation methods includes inducing JPEG compression artifacts. After training, the model generates 256-bit codes. These codes can be decomposed into four 64-bit codes for fast computation of Hamming distance on long integers. However, using codes of this length on a corpus of about 10 million images is too expensive, even when using multi-index hashing. We therefore extracted 64-bit codes from the original 256-bit codes to perform the filtering on shorter codes and thus smaller Hamming ball radii. To extract the 64 most important bits from the 256-bit codes, we first partition the 256-bit codes into four partitions by applying the Kernighan-Lin algorithm [10] on the bit correlations. From each of the four decorrelated partitions, we then take the first 16 bits to compose 64-bit codes.

### 3.2   Integration into ES

Before describing our image similarity search integration into ES, we will shortly review MIH in Hamming space [17]. The idea of MIH is based on the following observation: for two binary codes $h = (h^1, ..., h^m)$ and $g = (g^1, ..., g^m)$ where $m$ is the number of partitions, $h^k$ and $g^k$ are the $k^{th}$ subcodes and $H$ is the Hamming norm, the following proposition holds:

$$\|h - g\|_H \le r \Rightarrow \exists k \in \{1, ..., m\} \; \|h^k - g^k\|_H \le \left\lfloor \frac{r}{m} \right\rfloor \tag{4}$$

For the case of 64-bit codes that are decomposed into $m = 4$ subcodes, this means that a code is in a Hamming radius $r < 12$ if at least one of the subcodes has a distance of $d \le \lfloor \frac{r}{m} \rfloor = 2$ from the query subcode. The performance of MIH can be increased if the subcodes are maximally independent of each other [20], especially for shorter codes [16]. Thus, after training a deep hashing model, the bit positions should be permutated accordingly.

The ES index used for retrieval contains four short codes (f_0 - f_3) and four long subcodes (r_0 - r_3) for each image. The short codes are used for MIH and efficiently utilize the reverse index structure of ES and are thus separated into four subcodes of type "keyword". The long codes are also separated into four subcodes in order to allow fast computation of Hamming distances for values of type long.

An additional index is used for fast lookup of neighboring subcodes within the retrieval query. The neighbors index does not change once it has been created and merely serves as an auxiliary index for term queries. It requires pre-computing all nearest neighbors for all possible 16-bit subcodes. Thus, the index of neighbors contains $2^{16}$ documents. The document id corresponds to the unsigned integer representation of a 16-bit subcode and can therefore accessed within a term query. It contains a single field "nbs" that is assigned to a list of all neighboring 16-bit codes within a Hamming radius of $d$ of the corresponding query subcode. Since this index basically works as a lookup table, it could also be realized somewhere else, i.e., not as an ES index. However, integrating the lookup table this way eliminates the need for external code and enables fast deployment of the whole system. All documents representing all possible 16-bit subcodes are inserted according to the query in Listing 1.1.

```
POST /nbs-d2/_doc/<16 bit subcode>
{ "nbs" : [ <d2 neighbors of 16 bit subcode> ] }
```

**Listing 1.1.** Query for adding an entry to neighbor lookup index.

In this stage, MIH is realized by querying the additional index of neighbors for fast neighbor lookup. Even with MIH, using the full code length of the deep hashing model trained for 256-bit codes is too expensive for larger databases. We therefore limit the code length for the filtering stage to 64-bit codes. To obtain a sufficiently large set of candidate hash codes in the first stage, we need to search within a Hamming ball with a correspondingly large radius. We set $d = 2$, which will return at least all codes within $r = 11$ of a 64-bit code. In our setting with $d = 2$, this results in 137 neighbors per subcode, i.e., 548 neighbors in total.

In ES, we realize MIH by using a terms lookup. It fetches the field values of an existing document and then uses these values as search terms (see Listing 1.1). In contrast to putting all neighbors into the query, using a dedicated index for subcode neighbors has the advantage that the retrieval of neighboring subcodes is carried out within ES. Thus, the query load is small, and no external handling of neighbor lookup is necessary.

In the second stage, all codes obtained by MIH are re-ranked according to their Hamming distance to the long code. To compute the Hamming distance of the 256-bit code, the Painless Script in Listing 1.2 is applied to each of the four subcodes.

```
POST _scripts/hd64
{ "script": { "lang": "painless",
  "source": 64-Long.bitCount(params.subcode^doc[params.field].value) } }
```

**Listing 1.2.** Query for adding a Painless Script.

The query in Listing 1.3 combines the MIH step as a filter with a term query and the re-ranking step as an application of the painless script from Listing 1.2 on the filtered retrieval list.

## 4  Experimental Evaluation

To determine the search latency and retrieval quality of *ElasticHash*, we evaluate three settings for using the binary hash codes generated by our deep hashing model for large-scale image retrieval in ES: (1) short codes, i.e., 64 bits for both filtering and re-ranking, (2) long codes, i.e., 256 bits for both filtering and re-ranking, and (3) *ElasticHash*, i.e., 64 bits for filtering, 256 bits for re-ranking. Settings (1) and (2) are similar to the MIH integration of Mu et al. [16].

```
GET /es-retrieval/_search
{ "query": {
"function_score": {
 "boost_mode": "sum",   "score_mode": "sum",
 "functions": [ ..., {
  "script_score": {
   "script": { "id": "hd64",
    "params": {
     "field": "r_<i>",
     "subcode": <64 bit subcode for re-ranking> } } }, "weight": 1 }, ... ],
"query": {
  "constant_score": {
   "boost": 0.
   "filter": {
    "bool": {
     "minimum_should_match": 1,
     "should": [ ..., {
      "terms": {
       "f_<j>": {
       "id": "<16 bit subcode for lookup>",
       "index": "nbs-d2",
       "path": "nbs" } } }, ... ] } } } }, } } }
```

**Listing 1.3.** Query for performing two-stage similarity search.

To evaluate our approach, we use OpenImages [13], which is currently the largest annotated image data set publicly available. It contains multi-label annotations for 9.2 million Flickr images with 19,794 different labels and is partitioned into training, validation, and test data set. On the average, there are 2.4 positive labels for the training split, while the validation and test splits have 8.8. As our database images we use all training images being available when downloading the data set, i.e., 6,942,071 images in total. To evaluate the retrieval quality, we use all downloaded images from the OpenImages test and validation set as query images (121,588 images in total). From these images, we draw a sample of 10,000 images to measure the search latencies for the three different settings.

The quality of the retrieval lists is evaluated using the average precision (AP) score, which is the most commonly used quality measure in image retrieval. The AP score is calculated from the list of retrieved images as follows:

$$AP(\rho) = \frac{1}{|R \cap \rho^N|} \sum_{k=1}^{N} \frac{|R \cap \rho^k|}{k} \psi(i_k), \text{with} \quad \psi(i_k) = \begin{cases} 1 & \text{if } i_k \in R \\ 0 & \text{otherwise} \end{cases} \quad (5)$$

where $N$ is the length of the ranked image list, $\rho^k = \{i_1, i_2, \ldots, i_k\}$ is the ranked image list up to rank $k$, $R$ is the set of relevant documents, $|R \cap \rho^k|$ is the number of relevant images in the top-$k$ of $\rho$ and $\psi(i_k)$ is the relevance function. We consider an image as relevant, if it has at least one label in common with the query image. To evaluate the overall performance, the mean AP score is calculated by taking the mean value of the AP scores over all queries.

**Fig. 2.** Top-10 retrieval results for (a) short codes, (b) long codes, and (c) *ElasticHash* for the same query image (first on the left); green: relevant result; red: irrelevant result. (Color figure online)

## 4.1 Results

We first evaluate the search latency for the queries. Next, we compare the retrieval quality in terms of AP. The experiments were performed on a system with an Intel Core i7-4771 CPU @ 3.50 GHz and 32 GB RAM.

**Table 1.** Retrieval quality in terms of mean AP for different thresholds of $k$ on 121,588 query images.

| Top $k$ | 10 | 25 | 50 | 100 | 250 | 500 | 1000 |
|---|---|---|---|---|---|---|---|
| Short | 87.94 | 86.08 | 84.44 | 82.54 | 79.41 | 76.44 | 72.86 |
| Long | 95.35 | 94.72 | 94.23 | 93.71 | 92.90 | 92.09 | 90.95 |
| *ElasticHash* | 95.21 | 94.48 | 93.90 | 93.22 | 92.02 | 90.61 | 88.42 |

**Table 2.** Search latencies for ES queries (ms) with standard deviation for different thresholds of $k$ on 10,000 query images.

| Top $k$ | | 10 | 25 | 50 | 100 | 250 | 500 | 1000 |
|---|---|---|---|---|---|---|---|---|
| Short | $\mu$ | 23.09 | 23.98 | 24.45 | 25.58 | 28.38 | 33.09 | 42.20 |
| | $\sigma$ | 4.74 | 4.65 | 4.70 | 4.72 | 4.86 | 5.20 | 6.07 |
| Long | $\mu$ | 111.83 | 111.58 | 111.99 | 113.05 | 116.77 | 121.98 | 132.60 |
| | $\sigma$ | 16.50 | 16.58 | 16.72 | 16.54 | 17.04 | 17.13 | 17.99 |
| *ElasticHash* | $\mu$ | 36.12 | 36.75 | 37.28 | 38.17 | 40.88 | 45.73 | 55.23 |
| | $\sigma$ | 7.80 | 7.96 | 7.81 | 7.89 | 7.93 | 8.12 | 8.64 |

Table 1 shows that for a $k$ up to 250 there is no notable decrease in retrieval quality when employing *ElasticHash* rather than using the long codes for both stages. Figure 2 shows examples of the top-10 retrieval results for the three settings. It is evident that the retrieval quality of *ElasticHash* is similar to using long codes, and both are superior to using short codes. On the other hand, Table 2 indicates that the average retrieval time only slightly increases compared to using short codes for both stages. This suggests that *ElasticHash* is a good trade-off between retrieval quality and search latency. Although our deep hashing model was trained on 5,390 classes, but almost 20,000 classes occur in the validation data set, high AP values are achieved for *ElasticHash*.

## 5   Conclusion

We presented *ElasticHash*, a novel two-stage approach for semantic image similarity search based on deep multi-index hashing and integrated via terms lookup queries into ES. Our experimental results on a large image data set demonstrated that we achieve low search latencies and high-quality retrieval results at the same time by leveraging the benefits of short hash codes (better search times) and long hash codes (higher retrieval quality).

There are several areas for future work. For example, it would be interesting to investigate how many classes are necessary to obtain a high degree of generalizability. Furthermore, our loss function could be adapted to multi-label image data. Finally, we plan to extend our approach to achieve intentional image similarity search [11] using ES.

**Acknowledgements.** This work is financially supported by the German Research Foundation (DFG project number 388420599) and HMWK (LOEWE research cluster Nature 4.0).

## References

1. Amato, G., Bolettieri, P., Carrara, F., Falchi, F., Gennaro, C.: Large-scale image retrieval with Elasticsearch. In: The 41st International ACM SIGIR Conference on Research and Development in Information Retrieval, pp. 925–928 (2018)
2. Cao, Y., et al.: Binary hashing for approximate nearest neighbor search on big data: a survey. IEEE Access **6**, 2039–2054 (2017)
3. Cao, Z., Long, M., Wang, J., Yu, P.S.: Hashnet: deep learning to hash by continuation. In: Proceedings of the IEEE International Conference on Computer Vision, pp. 5608–5617 (2017)
4. Cao, Z., Sun, Z., Long, M., Wang, J., Yu, P.S.: Deep priority hashing. In: Proceedings of the 26th ACM Internationl Conference on Multimedia, pp. 1653–1661 (2018)
5. Chua, T.S., Tang, J., Hong, R., Li, H., Luo, Z., Zheng, Y.: NUS-WIDE: a real-world web image database from National University of Singapore. In: Proceedings of the ACM International Conference on Image and Video Retrieval, pp. 1–9 (2009)
6. Erin Liong, V., Lu, J., Wang, G., Moulin, P., Zhou, J.: Deep hashing for compact binary codes learning. In: Proceedings of the IEEE Conference on Computer Vision and Pattern Recognition, pp. 2475–2483 (2015)

7. Gennaro, C., Amato, G., Bolettieri, P., Savino, P.: An approach to content-based image retrieval based on the Lucene search engine library. In: Lalmas, M., Jose, J., Rauber, A., Sebastiani, F., Frommholz, I. (eds.) ECDL 2010. LNCS, vol. 6273, pp. 55–66. Springer, Heidelberg (2010). https://doi.org/10.1007/978-3-642-15464-5_8

8. Jegou, H., Douze, M., Schmid, C.: Product quantization for nearest neighbor search. IEEE Trans. Pattern Anal. Mach. Intell. **33**(1), 117–128 (2010)

9. Johnson, J., Douze, M., Jégou, H.: Billion-scale similarity search with GPUs. IEEE Trans. Big Data **7**(3), 535–547 (2021). https://doi.org/10.1109/TBDATA.2019.2921572

10. Kernighan, B.W., Lin, S.: An efficient heuristic procedure for partitioning graphs. Bell Syst. Tech. J. **49**(2), 291–307 (1970)

11. Korfhage, N., Mühling, M., Freisleben, B.: Intentional image similarity search. In: Schilling, F.-P., Stadelmann, T. (eds.) ANNPR 2020. LNCS (LNAI), vol. 12294, pp. 23–35. Springer, Cham (2020). https://doi.org/10.1007/978-3-030-58309-5_2

12. Krizhevsky, A., Sutskever, I., Hinton, G.E.: ImageNet classification with deep convolutional neural networks. Adv. Neural Inf. Process. Syst. **25**, 1097–1105 (2012)

13. Kuznetsova, A., et al.: The open images dataset V4. Int. J. Comput. Vis. **128**(7), 1956–1981 (2020). https://doi.org/10.1007/s11263-020-01316-z

14. Lin, Lin, et al.: Microsoft COCO: common objects in context. In: Fleet, D., Pajdla, T., Schiele, B., Tuytelaars, T. (eds.) ECCV 2014. LNCS, vol. 8693, pp. 740–755. Springer, Cham (2014). https://doi.org/10.1007/978-3-319-10602-1_48

15. Liu, H., Wang, R., Shan, S., Chen, X.: Deep supervised hashing for fast image retrieval. In: Proceedings of the IEEE Conference on Computer Vision and Pattern Recognition, pp. 2064–2072 (2016)

16. Mu, C.M., Zhao, J.R., Yang, G., Yang, B., Yan, Z.J.: Fast and exact nearest neighbor search in hamming space on full-text search engines. In: Amato, G., Gennaro, C., Oria, V., Radovanović, M. (eds.) SISAP 2019. LNCS, vol. 11807, pp. 49–56. Springer, Cham (2019). https://doi.org/10.1007/978-3-030-32047-8_5

17. Norouzi, M., Punjani, A., Fleet, D.J.: Fast search in hamming space with multi-index hashing. In: 2012 IEEE Conference on Computer Vision and Pattern Recognition (CVPR), pp. 3108–3115. IEEE (2012)

18. Schroff, F., Kalenichenko, D., Philbin, J.: FaceNet: a unified embedding for face recognition and clustering. In: Proceedings of the IEEE Conference on Computer Vision and Pattern Recognition, pp. 815–823 (2015)

19. Tan, M., Le, Q.: EfficientNet: rethinking model scaling for convolutional neural networks. In: International Conference on Machine Learning, pp. 6105–6114 (2019)

20. Wan, J., Tang, S., Zhang, Y., Huang, L., Li, J.: Data driven multi-index hashing. In: 2013 IEEE International Conference on Image Processing, pp. 2670–2673 (2013)

21. Wang, J., Zhang, T., Song, J., Sebe, N., Shen, H.T.: A survey on learning to hash. IEEE Trans. Pattern Anal. Mach. Intell. **40**(4), 769–790 (2018)

22. Wang, J., Kumar, S., Chang, S.F.: Semi-supervised hashing for large-scale search. IEEE Trans. Pattern Anal. Mach. Intell. **34**(12), 2393–2406 (2012)

23. Wang, J., Liu, W., Kumar, S., Chang, S.F.: Learning to hash for indexing big data - a survey. Proc. IEEE **104**(1), 34–57 (2015)

24. Zhou, B., Lapedriza, A., Khosla, A., Oliva, A., Torralba, A.: Places: a 10 million image database for scene recognition. IEEE Trans. Pattern Anal. Mach. Intell. **40**(6), 1452–1464 (2017)

25. Zhu, H., Long, M., Wang, J., Cao, Y.: Deep hashing network for efficient similarity retrieval. In: Proceedings of the AAAI Conf. on Artificial Intelligence,. vol. 30 (2016)

# Land Use Change Detection Using Deep Siamese Neural Networks and Weakly Supervised Learning

Indrajit Kalita[1](✉), Savvas Karatsiolis[2], and Andreas Kamilaris[2,3]

[1] Indian Institute of Information Technology Guwahati,
Guwahati 781015, Assam, India
[2] CYENS Center of Excellence, Nicosia, Cyprus
{s.karatsiolis,a.kamilaris}@cyens.org.cy
[3] Department of Computer Science, University of Twente, Enschede,
The Netherlands

**Abstract.** A weakly supervised change detection method is proposed for remotely sensed multi-temporal images, by utilizing a Siamese neural network architecture. The architecture of the Siamese network is a combination of two multi-filter multi-scale deep convolutional neural networks (MFMS DCNN). Initially, the Siamese network is trained by utilizing the image-level semantic labels of the image pairs in the dataset. The features of the image pairs are obtained using the trained network to generate the difference image (DI). Then, a combination of the PCA and the K-means algorithms has been used to produce the change map for the pair of images. Experiments were carried out using two remotely sensed image datasets. The weakly supervised method proposed in this paper offers better results in comparison to both weakly supervised- and unsupervised-based state-of-the-art models and techniques.

**Keywords:** Change detection · Weakly supervised · Siamese network · Convolutional neural network

## 1 Introduction

The massive volume increase of collected images from satellites and unmanned aerial vehicles, together with the remarkable success of Deep Neural Network (DNN) in computer vision applications, enabled the remote sensing community to develop a plethora of interesting earth observation-related applications. Aerial imagery contains spectral, spatial, and temporal information, which is valuable for the monitoring of different ecosystems and for planning tasks like crop surveillance, deforestation control, soil and water contamination monitoring, biogeochemical cycle monitoring, global heat mapping [18] etc. Moreover, landscape change detection (CD) is a critical task whose results are valuable for many policy-making mechanisms. For example, the outcomes of CD can be utilized to identify illegal changes, evaluate disasters [5] and set goals for

© Springer Nature Switzerland AG 2021
N. Tsapatsoulis et al. (Eds.): CAIP 2021, LNCS 13053, pp. 24–35, 2021.
https://doi.org/10.1007/978-3-030-89131-2_3

mitigating climate change [19]. Manual landscape CD monitoring is expensive, time-consuming and infeasible to perform on a large scale, due to the massive volume of data required and the large size of monitored areas.

## 2  Related Work

CD approaches are categorized into two classes: ones that apply post-classification comparison [22] and ones that apply post-comparison analysis [7,17]. The former class focuses on classifying temporal images of the same region, followed by pixel-by-pixel comparison. The success of these methods depends on the classification strategy. The latter class of methods focuses on estimating a difference-image (DI) by considering multi-temporal images of the same area. The DI produced is used to acquire a feature map to distinguish regions of change over regions of no change. Thus, the quality of the DI is critical for achieving good performance. The features of the DI can be extracted by techniques involving image arithmetics [7] and transformations [17]. The acquired features can be evaluated using strategies such as thresholding, clustering [7], and Markov random fields [2].

DNNs extract robust features from complex input samples and thereby utilize the rich information contained in images. This is especially helpful for large-scale remotely sensed datasets [13]. Under this scenario, a DNN-based CD approach provides better performance on remotely sensed high-resolution images [1,16,21]. DNN based CD methods can be categorized as unsupervised [16], fully supervised [21] and weakly supervised approaches [1]. Liu et al. [16] developed an unsupervised CD algorithm using the pre-trained U-net architecture. Similarly, De et al. [12] also explored the U-net architecture under the unsupervised scenario. Moreover, Cao et al. [6] proposed a deep belief network (DBN) technique for improving the quality of the DI using the SPOT5 multispectral images. Due to the lack of labels, it is difficult to achieve a detailed CD map using the unsupervised scheme. As a result, the fully supervised learning approaches employ labeled information (ground truth) for enhancing the CD performance [10,21]. Under this scenario, Zhan et al. [21] propose a contrastive loss-based supervised Siamese network to obtain the change and unchanged regions in an aerial image using the SZTAKI dataset [2]. Ji et al. [10] explore the Mask R-CNN and the U-net architecture for the identification of building changes using very high-resolution datasets [11]. Still, identifying pixel-level change patterns in the fully supervised system is tedious, inefficient, and expensive. This stresses the importance of exploring CD methods that minimize labelling costs by introducing image-level labels instead of pixel-level ones. Under this scenario, a supervised CD model can be trained based on high-level annotations that indicate whether two images depict land change or not. This is known as a *weakly supervised scheme* [1,14]. Andermatt et al. [1], proposed a weakly supervised CD approach using a U-net based Siamese architecture. Similarly, Khan et al. [14] have used a pre-trained DNN in conjunction with a directed acyclic graph (DAG) to learn patterns of change from image-level labelled training data. The majority of the weakly supervised schemes mentioned above focus on pre-trained models. However, the datasets used to pre-train the models are very different from the targeted CD datasets. Therefore, the performance of these models is low. To address this issue, *this work explores a weakly supervised CD method learned from scratch under a post-comparison analysis framework.*

## 3   Methodology

The proposed CD approach is based on a multi-filter multi-scale (MFMS) [9] DNN, used as the feature extractor of a Siamese model [21]. The co-registered images are first preprocessed with histogram matching and then passed through the Siamese model. The Siamese model has been trained from scratch using the image-level labels only. After, the features of the two images (captured at different times) obtained using the trained Siamese network are used to estimate the DI. Finally, the PCA and the K-Means algorithms are applied to the DI, to produce the CD maps. Features are extracted at different resolutions and then processed to obtain the CD maps for the images captured at two different timestamps. A final stage processes the CD maps and determines which pixels in the images depict land change. Figure 1 illustrates the overall technique.

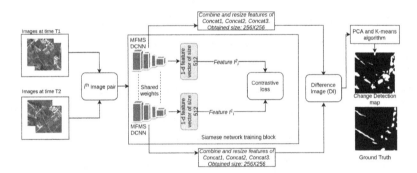

**Fig. 1.** The architecture of proposed change detection model. The Concat1, Concat2, and Concat3 layers are displayed in Fig. 2

### 3.1   Multi Filter Multi-scale Deep Convolutional Neural Network

The MFMS DNN combines the features learned at multiple levels of the architecture, motivated by [9]. The effectiveness of this strategy relies on the fact that the model builds representations at different resolutions. The proposed architecture applies convolution-batch normalization-activation (CBA) layers and down-sampling (max-pooling) layers to create multi-scale feature maps (see Fig. 2). We discriminate between intermediate max-pooling layers and the max-pooling layers applied at the input by naming the latter down-sampling (DS) layers. This distinction stresses the purpose of each unit since the intermediate max-pooling layers aim at reducing the dimensionality of the feature maps while the down-sampling layers aim at producing multi-scale feature maps. We use three down-sampling units (DS1, DS2, DS3) as shown in Fig. 2. The DS1 unit down-samples the input while the DS2 and DS3 units apply further dimensionality reduction and extend the model's multi-scale processing. Similar to [9], various kernel sizes are used for the convolution operations in the CBA layers. The ReLU activation function is used to introduce non-linearities to the model. The outputs of the DS units are also processed by CBA layers to create multi-scale feature maps from various image resolutions. Concatenation operations (Concat1, Concat2, Concat3) fuse the distinct feature maps at different levels of the architecture and the average pooling (AP) operation is applied after the last CBA unit (CBA9). Finally, the generated features are combined using a dense layer. The proposed MFMS architecture constitutes the backbone of the Siamese model described in Sect. 3.2.

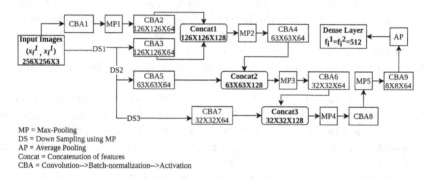

MP = Max-Pooling
DS = Down Sampling using MP
AP = Average Pooling
Concat = Concatenation of features
CBA = Convolution-->Batch-normalization-->Activation

**Fig. 2.** The architecture of the MFMS DCNN model used in the Siamese network

## 3.2   Siamese Neural Network

Siamese networks are models that use instances of the same DNN and share the same architecture and weights, as shown in Fig. 1. The primary objective of the network is to map the features of similar samples closer to each other and the features corresponding to dissimilar samples far apart. Accordingly, a dataset used for training a Siamese model is grouped into pairs of similar or dissimilar samples: pairs of similar samples are labelled as one and the pairs of samples from different classes are labelled as zero. During training, the Siamese model extracts the features of each sample in an image pair and outputs two one-dimensional vectors. Then, the difference between the two vectors is measured using some distance metric and an optimizer minimizes this distance if the features belong to images of the same class and maximize it if the features belong to images of different classes. In the proposed approach, the datasets are prepared (i.e. paired) according to the following two conditions:

1: The paired images share the same geographical region at two different times.
2: The paired images depicting land change are labelled as zero and paired images not depicting land change are labelled as one.

This kind of labelling enables the model to operate in a weakly supervised mode, identifying the exact pixels corresponding to land change without strong supervision, i.e., without explicitly providing a label for each pixel that identifies a change or not. Instead, we just feed the model with weak supervisory information regarding which image pairs depict land change. Concretely, the proposed Siamese model tackles the CD task in a weakly supervised fashion mainly because:

1) It is trained using image-level labels instead of pixel-level labels.
2) It uses a multi-scale DNN architecture which is very efficient on the specific task.

The features of each image are computed as a 512-D vector and the contrastive loss function ($L_{cons}$) [8] is applied on the two extracted feature vectors (shown in Eq. 2). $L$ represents the label of image pair $i$, $D_w$ is the Euclidean distance between the features of the pair (defined in Eq. 1) and $m$ is the desirable margin between image pairs that depict land change and thus have a zero label.

After training the Siamese network, the feature maps of the architecture are used to calculate the differential feature map between the images in the pair. The three concatenation layers (Concat1, Concat2, and Concat3 as shown in Fig. 2) are up-scaled to form a $256 \times 256$ feature map for every image. Then, the Euclidean distance between the two feature maps is calculated. This provides the differential feature map (i.e. DI), which is a 2D representation of the difference between the two images in a pair. The DI holds the necessary information to identify the regions of change in an image pair (see Sect. 3.3).

$$D_w = \|f_i^1 - f_i^2\| \tag{1}$$

$$L_{cons} = (L)\frac{1}{2}(D_w)^2 + (1 - L)\frac{1}{2}\{\max(0, m - D_w)\}^2 \tag{2}$$

### 3.3   Generation of Change Detection Maps

To obtain the CD maps from a DI, we use a technique inspired by Celik *et al.* [7], based on the PCA and the K-means algorithms. Initially, the PCA is applied to every non-overlapping patch of the DI to obtain its eigenvector space. Then, the eigenvector space is projected on the overlapping patches to produce the feature vector space, which is then divided into two clusters via the K-means algorithm. The cluster with the least number of indexes (data points) is considered as the change class because the number of changed pixels in a pair of images is generally much smaller compared to the number of unchanged pixels. In contrast to Celik *et al.*, we use Euclidean distance to calculate the DI between the image representations obtained by the Siamese model, instead of the absolute difference between the two images.

# 4    Experimental Setup

## 4.1    Datasets' Description

The effectiveness of the proposed methodology was tested on two very high resolution (VHR) remotely sensed image datasets.

**SZATAKI AirChange Benchmark Dataset:** A CD dataset consisting of three parts: SZADA, TISZADOB, and ARCHIVE [2]. SZADA is used to evaluate the performance of the model, comparing with related work. We use the 43 multi-temporal images between the years 2000 and 2005. The sizes of the training images are $952 \times 640$ (30 images) and $640 \times 952$ pixels (12 images). An image of size $784 \times 448$ is used to test the model. According to the dataset's description, the changed pixels' annotation of the images has been provided by an expert. During training, the 42 images are divided into patches of size $256 \times 256 \times 3$, and the *change/no change*-depicting image pairs are identified based on the annotations of the images. An image pair gets a label one if its images depict no land change and zero if the images depict land change. A total of 253 image patches are collected for training. Sample images are shown in Fig. 3.

**Aerial Image Change Detection (AICD) Dataset:** AICD is a synthetic change detection dataset [3], used to compare the performance of the proposed model with other state-of-the-art approaches trained with weak supervision. The dataset contains 1000 images (500 image pairs) and each image is $600 \times 800 \times 3$ pixels. Each image contains only one change object (one structure). During training, images are divided into patches of size $256 \times 256 \times 3$ and the *change/no change*-depicting image pairs are identified based on the ground truth label of the corresponding images. In total, 630 image pairs depict changed structures and 2370 depict no land change.

(a)                          (b)                          (c)

**Fig. 3.** Sample images from the SZADA dataset. (a, b) Training image pair, (c) corresponding ground truth information.

## 4.2 Model Adaptation and Parameter Setting

The proposed MFMS CNN comprises 9 CBA layers, 8 max-pooling layers (including DS1, DS2, and DS3), 1 average pooling layer, and 1 dense layer. The number of filters in the CBA layers is 64, whereas the size and stride of each filter are $3 \times 3$ and 1 respectively. The window size and stride of the max-pooling layers are $3 \times 3$ and 2 respectively. For average pooling, the window and stride are $2 \times 2$ and 2 respectively. Both the CBA and the dense layers use the ReLU activation function. The initial images of size $256 \times 256 \times 3$ are down-sampled to $128 \times 128 \times 3$, $64 \times 64 \times 3$ and $32 \times 32 \times 3$ by the DS1, DS2 and DS3 units respectively. The Concat1 layer merges the feature maps generated by CBA2 and CBA3. Here, the size of each feature map for both cases is $126 \times 126 \times 64$. Similarly, the Concat2 and Concat3 layers combine the feature maps of size $63 \times 63 \times 64$, $63 \times 63 \times 64$ computed by CBA4 and CBA5, as well as $32 \times 32 \times 64$, $32 \times 32 \times 64$ computed by CBA6 and CBA7 respectively. The dense layer computes an output of size 512 based on a flattened input of size $8 \times 8 \times 64$. The MFMS CNN extracts a 512-D feature vector ($f_i^j$) for each image at the input, where $i$ is the index of the image and $j \in 1, 2$ is the reference time of image acquisition reflecting images T1 and T2. This means that for each image pair $i$ (consisting of images $x_i^1, x_i^2$), the model calculates two feature vectors ($f_i^1$, $f_i^2$), each having a size of 512. Moreover, the margin $m$ of the contrastive loss is set to 6 (set empirically). Finally, the Adam [15] optimizer with a learning rate of 0.001 is used. The model was trained for 120 iterations with a batch size of 256.

## 5   Results

**Evaluation Measures:** The precision ($p$), recall ($r$), and F-measure ($f$) (harmonic mean of $p$ and $r$ corresponding to the changed class) have been used to compare the result of the proposed method with state-of-the-art unsupervised approaches. Accuracy and mean intersection over union ($mIOU$) have been considered to compare with weakly supervised approaches. These measures are considered as the standard ones in literature [1,14]. We acknowledge the unfairness of comparing our weakly supervised method with state-of-the-art unsupervised methods. However, we believe there is some value in this comparison because of the significantly less effort required to produce the weak labels compared to the effort required to produce the pixel-level change maps. We do not claim that our approach is superior to unsupervised methods nor do we suggest that we adapt the comparison as a head-to-head apposition of methods operating under the same regime. However, we note that significant performance improvement on the CD task can be achieved with minimal effort, by incorporating image-level labels.

**Table 1.** Comparison of the two unsupervised methods (U-A [16], U-B [4]) with the proposed scheme (WS-C). Results are in percentages.

| Model | Precision | Recall | F-measure |
|-------|-----------|--------|-----------|
| U-A   | 27.2      | 56.1   | 36.6      |
| U-B   | 19.2      | 48.7   | 27.5      |
| WS-C  | **43.2**  | **66.9** | **52.5** |

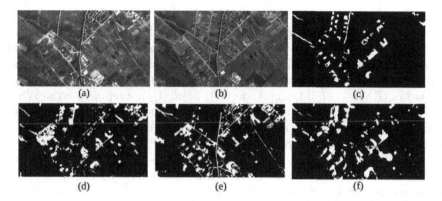

**Fig. 4.** Comparisons on the SZADA dataset. (a, b) Test image pair, (c) ground truth maps, (d) results obtained using U-A [16], (e) results of U-B [4], and (f) results obtained using the proposed method (WS-C).

**Analysis of Results Using the SZADA Dataset:** The values for $p$, $r$, and $f$ for the proposed approach and other state-of-the-art approaches are listed in Table 1. Here, the performance of the proposed methodology is compared with two unsupervised state-of-the-art schemes: Liu *et al.* [16] (U-A in Table 1) and S3VM [4] (U-B in Table 1). The results indicate that the performance of the proposed model (WS-C in Table 1) is significantly better than the two unsupervised schemes (U-A and U-B). In this regard, the proposed method outperforms the scheme U-A by a margin of ≈16%, ≈10%, and ≈15% in terms of $p$, $r$, and $f$, respectively. Similarly, the proposed approach surpasses the scheme U-B by a margin of ≈24%, ≈18%, and ≈25% in terms of $p$, $r$, and $f$ respectively. Figure 4 shows example visual outputs of different methods on the SZADA dataset.

**Table 2.** Comparison of the two weakly supervised methods (WS-A [14], WS-B [1]) with the proposed scheme (WS-C). Results are in percentage.

| Model | Accuracy | mIOU |
|-------|----------|------|
| WS-A | 99.1 | 71 |
| WS-B | 99.2 | 70.3 |
| WS-C | **99.5** | **74.3** |

**Analysis of Results Using the AICD Dataset:** The results obtained using the proposed model are compared with those obtained using two other weakly supervised state-of-the-art CD techniques [1,14]. Here, the results obtained using the proposed approaches (WS-C in Table 2) and the two state-of-the-art approaches (Khan *et al.* [14] and Andermatt *et al.* [1]) are represented as WS-A, and WS-B, respectively in Table 2. It is observed that the proposed approach outperforms WS-A by a margin of 0.4% and 3.3% in terms of accuracy and $mIOU$ respectively. Similarly, the proposed approach achieves a higher performance of 0.3% and 4% in terms of accuracy and $mIOU$ respectively compared to WS-B. Figure 5 shows some example generated results obtained with the proposed method on the AICD dataset.

**Table 3.** Comparison of the two base methods (Base-1 [7], Base-2) with the proposed scheme (WS-C). Results are in percentages.

| Model | Precision | Recall | F-measure |
|-------|-----------|--------|-----------|
| Base-1 | **46.5** | 41.9 | 44.2 |
| Base-2 | 39.6 | 65.3 | 49.3 |
| WS-C | 43.2 | **66.9** | **52.5** |

### 5.1   Ablation Analysis of the Proposed Model

In this experiment, the proposed model is decomposed to its distinct components (Siamese network and PCA + K-means), performing the CD task separately on each component. In this way, we can assess the contribution of each component. The plain Siamese network is tested by replacing the PCA + K-means processing stage with a threshold on the computed DI. Specifically, we use the OTSU threshold [20] and report the performance by performing CD on the test set. We call this approach as *Base-2* in Table 3. Accordingly, we use the PCA + K-means on the DI computed directly from the images as suggested by [7] and not on the DI computed by the Siamese model. We call this method *Base-1* in Table 3. The experiments are carried out using the SZADA datasets. The results shown in Table 3 suggest that the proposed approach (WS-C in Table 3) outperforms the two schemes (Base-1 and Base-2) in terms of recall and F-measure scores. However, in terms of precision, the Base-1 strategy surpasses the proposed scheme. Thus, the proposed (complete) model incorporates the PCA + K-means technique on the DI and significantly improves the recall score of the results at the cost of a small decrease in the precision score.

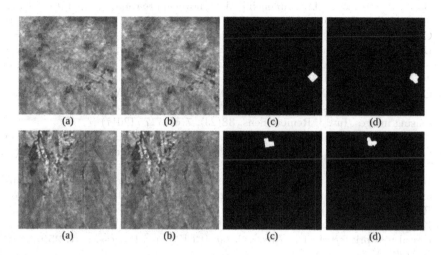

**Fig. 5.** Sample images of AICD dataset and their ground truth as well as the generated change map. (a, b) Test image pair, (c) corresponding ground truth information, (d) results obtained using proposed method (WS-C).

## 6   Conclusions

In this work, a weakly supervised change detection model is proposed for analyzing remotely sensed multi-temporal images. An MFMS CNN Siamese network is trained using the image-level labels of image pairs and not the pixel-level labels adding flexibility and removing complexity from tackling the task. The proposed model achieves huge improvements as compared to the unsupervised approaches by incorporating simple image-level labels. Moreover, it enhances the state-of-the-art weakly-supervised performance on the AICD dataset.

**Acknowledgment.** This project has received funding from the European Union's Horizon 2020 Research and Innovation Programme under Grant Agreement No 739578 and the Government of the Republic of Cyprus through the Deputy Ministry of Research, Innovation and Digital Policy.

## References

1. Andermatt, P., Timofte, R.: A weakly supervised convolutional network for change segmentation and classification. arXiv preprint arXiv:2011.03577 (2020)

2. Benedek, C., Szirányi, T.: Change detection in optical aerial images by a multilayer conditional mixed Markov model. IEEE Trans. Geosci. Remote Sens. **47**(10), 3416–3430 (2009)

3. Bourdis, N., Marraud, D., Sahbi, H.: Constrained optical flow for aerial image change detection. In: International Geoscience and Remote Sensing Symposium, pp. 4176–4179. IEEE (2011)

4. Bovolo, F., Bruzzone, L., Marconcini, M.: A novel approach to unsupervised change detection based on a semisupervised SVM and a similarity measure. IEEE Trans. Geosci. Remote Sens. **46**(7), 2070–2082 (2008)

5. Brunner, D., Lemoine, G., Bruzzone, L.: Earthquake damage assessment of buildings using VHR optical and SAR imagery. IEEE Trans. Geosci. Remote Sens. **48**(5), 2403–2420 (2010)

6. Cao, G., Wang, B., Xavier, H., Yang, D., Southworth, J.: A new difference image creation method based on deep neural networks for change detection in remote-sensing images. Int. J. Remote Sens. **38**(23), 7161–7175 (2017)

7. Celik, T.: Unsupervised change detection in satellite images using principal component analysis and $k$-means clustering. IEEE Geosci. Remote Sens. Lett. **6**(4), 772–776 (2009)

8. Hadsell, R., Chopra, S., LeCun, Y.: Dimensionality reduction by learning an invariant mapping. In: Computer Society Conference on Computer Vision and Pattern Recognition (CVPR), vol. 2, pp. 1735–1742. IEEE (2006)

9. Hu, J., Chen, Z., Yang, M., Zhang, R., Cui, Y.: A multiscale fusion convolutional neural network for plant leaf recognition. IEEE Signal Process. Lett. **25**(6), 853–857 (2018)

10. Ji, S., Shen, Y., Lu, M., Zhang, Y.: Building instance change detection from large-scale aerial images using convolutional neural networks and simulated samples. Remote Sens. **11**(11), 1343 (2019)

11. Ji, S., Wei, S., Lu, M.: Fully convolutional networks for multisource building extraction from an open aerial and satellite imagery data set. IEEE Trans. Geosci. Remote Sens. **57**(1), 574–586 (2018)

12. de Jong, K.L., Bosman, A.S.: Unsupervised change detection in satellite images using convolutional neural networks. In: International Joint Conference on Neural Networks (IJCNN), pp. 1–8. IEEE (2019)

13. Kalita, I., Roy, M.: Deep neural network-based heterogeneous domain adaptation using ensemble decision making in land cover classification. IEEE Trans. Artif. Intell. (2020). https://doi.org/10.1109/TAI.2020.3043724

14. Khan, S.H., He, X., Porikli, F., Bennamoun, M., Sohel, F., Togneri, R.: Learning deep structured network for weakly supervised change detection. arXiv preprint arXiv:1606.02009 (2016)

15. Kingma, D.P., Ba, J.: Adam: A method for stochastic optimization. arXiv preprint arXiv:1412.6980 (2014)

16. Liu, J., et al.: Convolutional neural network-based transfer learning for optical aerial images change detection. IEEE Geosci. Remote Sens. Lett. **17**(1), 127–131 (2019)

17. Liu, J., Gong, M., Qin, K., Zhang, P.: A deep convolutional coupling network for change detection based on heterogeneous optical and radar images. IEEE Trans. Neural Netw. Learn. Syst. **29**(3), 545–559 (2016)

18. Meher, S.K., Kumar, D.A.: Ensemble of adaptive rule-based granular neural network classifiers for multispectral remote sensing images. IEEE J. Sel. Top. Appl. Earth Obs. Remote Sens. **8**(5), 2222–2231 (2015)

19. Mubea, K., Menz, G.: Monitoring land-use change in Nakuru (Kenya) using multi-sensor satellite data (2012)
20. Otsu, N.: A threshold selection method from gray-level histograms. IEEE Trans. Syst. Man and Cybern. **9**(1), 62–66 (1979)
21. Zhan, Y., Fu, K., Yan, M., Sun, X., Wang, H., Qiu, X.: Change detection based on deep Siamese convolutional network for optical aerial images. IEEE Geosci. Remote Sens. Lett. **14**(10), 1845–1849 (2017)
22. Zhong, P., Wang, R.: A multiple conditional random fields ensemble model for urban area detection in remote sensing optical images. IEEE Trans. Geosci. Remote Sens. **45**(12), 3978–3988 (2007)

# AMI-Class: Towards a Fully Automated Multi-view Image Classifier

Mahmoud Jarraya[1], Maher Marwani[1], Gianmarco Aversano[2], Ichraf Lahouli[1(✉)], and Sabri Skhiri[2]

[1] EURANOVA TN, Les berges du lac, Tunisia
{mahmoud.jarraya,maher.marwani,ichraf.lahouli}@euranova.eu
[2] EURANOVA BE, Mont-Saint-Guibert, Belgium
{gianmarco.aversano,sabri.skhiri}@euranova.eu

**Abstract.** In this paper, we propose an automated framework for multi-view image classification tasks. We combined a GAN-based multi-view embedding architecture with a scalable AutoML library, DeepHyper. The proposed framework is able to, all at once, train a model to find a common latent representation and perform data imputation, choose the best classifier and tune all necessary hyper-parameters. Experiments on the MNIST data-set show the effectiveness of our solution to optimize the end-to-end multi-view classification pipeline.

## 1 Introduction

In real-world, multi-view images are quite common and are often complementary which make them exploited in various computer vision applications such as medical applications, [1], surveillance [2,3] and agriculture [4]. Multi-view representation learning is concerned with the problem of learning common (latent) representations of multi-view data, usually by either aligning or fusing view-specific latent features. One popular approach, called multi-view embedding (MVE), is to project these views in a common latent space which can then be used to solve several machine learning tasks. However, the remaining challenge is how to deal with missing views. Mapping different views to a common latent space, instead of concatenating, facilitates the process of data imputation. Typical techniques include kernel-based methods such as Deep Canonical Correlation Analysis (DCCA) [5] or non-negative matrix factorization (NMF)-based methods [6]. However, these two kinds of techniques suffer from several limitations, mainly complexity, inefficiency to scale with large scale databases and wastefulness to compensate for missing views due to regularization and added constraints [7] which makes them less attractive. Recently, generative models such as VAEs [8] or GANs [9] have gained popularity in this field [7,10] because of their ability to map any given distribution to a target one (e.g. the distribution of the missing data) and their effectiveness in narrowing the difference between the distributions of different views [11]. For instance, the implementation of a multi-modal adversarial representation network (MARN) with an

© Springer Nature Switzerland AG 2021
N. Tsapatsoulis et al. (Eds.): CAIP 2021, LNCS 13053, pp. 36–45, 2021.
https://doi.org/10.1007/978-3-030-89131-2_4

attention mechanism has led to state-of-the-art performance for click-through rate prediction [12]. For these reasons, the present work proposes a GAN-based architecture for MVE, inspired by [7,10], that is able to impute missing views.

From a machine learning (ML) perspective, we have recently seen the emergence of frameworks, called AutoML, that automate the whole pipeline, starting from the feature extraction to the model deployment. AutoML attempts to solve either Neural Architecture Search (NAS) problem or a Combined Algorithm Selection and Hyper-parameter tuning (CASH) problem, i.e. find the best configuration for a ML program, within limited computational budget [13]. For image classification tasks, we do not want to rely only on deep neural architectures as DL techniques represent only a subset of machine learning methodologies and some classic classifiers such as K-nearest neighborhood might perform well with certain datasets. Thus, in this paper, we will focus on resolving the CASH problem. The optimization process over an algorithm's hyper-parameters can be black-box (e.g. random-search, grid-search or model-based) or multi-fidelity [14]. Despite the increasing research efforts in AutoML [15,16], there are still several open challenges such as scalability, data preparation, choice of optimization techniques and multi-modality of data [13]. For instance, Auto-Sklearn [15] introduced meta-learning and ensemble methods to improve the performance of vanilla SMAC [17] optimization, however it is built on Scikit-Learn which makes it unsuited to multi-modal/view data. However, as far as we know, even the recent autoML frameworks such as DeepHyper [18] or VEGA [19] can not handle multi-view datasets.

Through this work, we propose a multi-view CASH solver, called AMI, at its basic definition (i.e. what classifier to select and what are the adequate hyper-parameters values). Indeed, the main contributions of this work are (1) the implementation of a modified version of a GAN-based MVE architecture for the visual feature extraction and data imputation based on [7] (2) the MVE model's integration in the mono-modal autoML framework i.e. DeepHyper [18], resulting in an end-to-end pipeline that can be optimized all at once using an asynchronous Bayesian Optimization technique. Consequently, the best architecture for feature extraction from the multi-view images and their embedding in a common latent space and the best classifier are all selected with their optimal hyper-parameters.

## 2  Proposed Methodology

Our solution consists of two main components: the first one ensures the MVE while the second one solves the classification task within a CASH problem by integrating the MVE model architecture within DeepHyper.

### 2.1  Notations

For the sake of clarity, we start by formalising the input data to be used for the rest of the paper. The multi-view data is represented by:
$$\mathbf{X} = \left\{ \mathbf{X}^{(1)}, \mathbf{X}^{(2)}, \cdots, \mathbf{X}^{(V)} \right\} \text{ where } \mathbf{X}^{(v)} = \left\{ x_1^{(v)}, x_2^{(v)}, \cdots, x_N^{(v)} \right\} \in \mathbf{R}^{N \times d_v} \forall v \in$$

$[1, V]$, $V$ is the number of views, $N$ is the number of samples, and $d_v$ is the feature dimension of $v$-th view. $d$ is the feature dimension of the common latent space. Besides, since our data might have missing views that need to be imputed, we split our data into 2 subsets: paired data $\left\{x^{(1)}, x^{(2)}, \cdots, x^{(V)}\right\}$, in which all views exist, and unpaired data, $\left\{x'^{(1)}, x^{(2)}, \cdots, x'^{(V)}\right\}$, in which at least one view is missing. We denote by $r \in [0, 1]$ the missingness ratio as the percentage of the samples with missing data according to the total number of samples $N$ (e.g. if $r = 0.1$ so 10% of the samples have at least one missing view). We denote by $\mathcal{Y}$ the labels space and each $x_i^{(v)} \forall v \in [1, V]$ and $\forall i \in [1, N]$ is associated to $y_i \in \mathcal{Y}$.

## 2.2   MVE Component

**Architecture.** The purpose of this component, denoted by $\mathcal{M}$, is to derive a representative feature vector in a common latent space of the multi-view input data. This can be achieved by relying on an adapted version of the architecture proposed in [7] where we have removed the clustering layer, changed the fusion one and forced the alignment between the view-specific feature vectors. The MVE component architecture consists of four networks:

*Encoder* $\{E_v\}_{v=1}^{V}$: $R^{d_v} \rightarrow R^d$.
$V$ encoders, projecting each input view $X^{(v)}$ to a corresponding view-specific subspace through many stacked convolution-batch normalization-ReLu layers. Each encoder outputs a $d$-dimensional vector $Z^{(v)}$.

*Fusion* $F$: $R^{d \times V} \rightarrow R^d$.
The intuition from the fusion network is to capture the shared semantics of the multiview data from the resulting $V$ view-specific representation vectors. It takes the output of the encoders and derives the target feature vector through a fully connected layer.

*Decoder* $\{G_v\}_{v=1}^{V}$: $R^d \rightarrow R^{d_v}$.
Each $G_v$ has a mirrored architecture to the $E_v$. It takes a vector from the common sub-space and generates the corresponding view. It acts both as decoder and a generator.

*Discriminator* $\{D_v\}_{v=1}^{V}$: $R^{d_v} \rightarrow \{0, 1\}$.
Each $D_v$ takes a sample from its corresponding view distribution, which can be either the generated view $\tilde{x}_i^{(v)}$ by $G_v$ or the real view $x_i^{(v)}$, and outputs the probability for this sample to be real, using a stack of convolution-batch normalization-LeakyReLu layers and a final *sigmoid* activation.

**Objective Function.** The objective function we tend to optimize includes two terms; one to train the AE networks, and the other for the GANs networks.

*Auto-Encoder loss:* The purpose is that the multi-view feature vector is representative enough and holds the cross-view information. The reconstruction loss is defined as follow:

$$L_{rec} = \Sigma_{v=1}^{V}\|X^{(v)} - G_v(Z_v)\|^2 \tag{1}$$

with $Z_v$ being the latent vector of the $v$-th view. Each decoder $\{G_v\}_{v=1}^{V}$ has to generate its corresponding view from a sample $\{z^{(v)}\}_{v=1}^{V}$ of view-specific latent space. However, we want to fuse those into a common latent space. Thus, we also minimize the distance between the different $\{z^{(v)}\}_{v=1}^{V}$ using the following alignment loss:

$$L_{align} = \Sigma_{v=1}^{V}\Sigma_{v'>v}^{V}\|E_v(X^{(v)}) - E_{v'}(X^{(v')})\|^2 \tag{2}$$

Therefore, the final Auto-Encoder loss is:

$$L_{AE} = L_{rec} + a * L_{align} \tag{3}$$

with $a \geq 0$ being a hyper-parameter. This loss is used to train $\{E^{(v)}\}_{v=1}^{V}$, $\{G^{(v)}\}_{v=1}^{V}$ and $F$, differently from [7] where a different loss is used to $F$. During the first few epochs when minimizing Eq. (3), the fusion layer $F$ is not used. The views are reconstructed by the decoders, which take the resulting vector from the fusion operation of $\{Z^{(v)}\}_{v=1}^{V}$. Therefore, the training of the MVE component as Auto-Encoder on minimizing $L_{AE}$ is not enough in the case of unpaired data where the fusion can not be realized. To tackle this, we refine the model by means of adversarial training.

*Adversarial Training Loss:* We employ this loss to train the GANs' part of the model, which is composed of the decoders $\{G_v\}_{v=1}^{V}$ and the discriminators $\{D_v\}_{v=1}^{V}$. The goal of $\{G_v\}_{v=1}^{V}$ is to fool $\{D_v\}_{v=1}^{V}$ by producing realistic images from vectors from common space distribution while the goal of $\{D_v\}_{v=1}^{V}$ is to distinguish whether the input is real or generated (fake). The GAN loss is expressed as follow:

$$L_{GAN} = \Sigma_{v=1}^{V}[\log D_v(X^{(v)}) + \log(1 - D_v \circ G_v(Z_v))] \tag{4}$$

In fact, the generators learn to map a given latent vector to a sample from its target distribution. Yet, the generated sample should be paired with the existing one. Therefore, we add the cycle loss defined in Eq. (5).

This way, $\{G_v\}_{v=1}^{V}$ are trained also on imputing data from the existing one.

$$L_{cyc} = \Sigma_{v=1}^{V}\Sigma_{v'\neq v}^{V}\|X^{(v)} - G_v \circ E_{v'} \circ G_{v'} \circ E_v(X^{(v)})\| \tag{5}$$

Also, the final adversarial training loss is:

$$L_{AT} = L_{cyc} + L_{GAN} \tag{6}$$

*Total Loss:*

$$L = \lambda_{AE} L_{AE} + \lambda_{AT} L_{AT} \tag{7}$$

**Implementation.** We employ a two-stage training procedure where we first pre-train the AE networks on paired data, and then we train all the model components on both paired and unpaired data.

*Step 1* : The paired data is loaded to $\{E_v\}_{v=1}^V$ to get $V$ vectors in the latent space. First, these vectors are passed directly to their corresponding $\{G_v\}_{v=1}^V$ to reconstruct the input. This way, thanks to Eq. (2), the different vectors are forced to be close to each other in the latent spaces. Then, after a portion $\phi$ of the total number of epochs, the $V$ vectors are fused by $F$ before being passed to $\{G_v\}_{v=1}^V$. Finally, we update the networks by Eq. (3).

*Step 2* : We train $\mathcal{M}$ on all the data. In the case of paired data, the input is projected by $\{E_v\}_{v=1}^V$ to the latent space, and regenerated by $\{G_v\}_{v=1}^V$. These fake views with the real ones are passed to the discriminator then to compute the adversarial loss with Eq. (4) . When encountering unpaired data, we take one of the one existing view each time, project it to the latent space and input the resulting vector to the generator corresponding to the missing view to perform the imputation. Therefore, we compute the cycle consistency loss (5). Finally, we update all the model's parameters by Eq. (7).

### 2.3   Multi-view CASH Solver AMI

**Architecture.** DeepHyper [18] is a scalable package for hyper-parameter search, with a generic interface between an asynchronous model-based search method (AMBS) using Bayesian Optimization (BO) ideas (a dynamically updated surrogate model that tries to learn the relationship between the hyper-parameter configurations and their validation errors), and parallel task execution engines. DeepHyper offers: a portable workflow system for parallel, asynchronous evaluations of hyper-parameter configurations at HPC scale; the use of AMBS which has proved to be superior to batch-synchronous methods [18]; a flexible and generic interface that allows for easy extension to a multi-modal framework as DeepHyper is not tied to any ML libraries that can only work on a single node. Besides, as this work combines DeepHyper with a flexible multi-modal embedding model, the problem of data preparation is solved by tuning the hyper-parameters of this model. At First, we have the MVE component's hyper-parameters. This includes: $\mathcal{M}$ HP (AE number of layers, common latent space's dimension $d$, $\phi$ etc.) and the training HP (batch size, learning rate, number of epochs, etc.). In the other hand, we have a set of hyper-parameters related to the classification problem. We also introduced classification model as a categorical hyper-parameter. Therefore, the hyper-parameters of the whole pipeline are optimized simultaneously using the AMBS technique of DeepHyper. The classification accuracy is the objective that we tend to maximize. We illustrate our proposed architecture in Fig. 1.

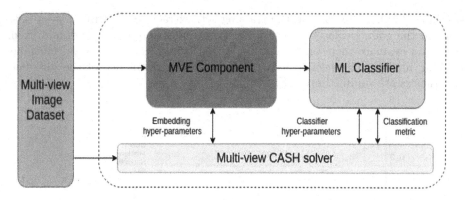

**Fig. 1.** Proposed end-to-end multi-view CASH Solver AMI

**Implementation.** First, we split the data into train and validation, we define the search space $\zeta$ and the objective function we tend to optimize and also the budget (i.e. max number of iterations of the optimization process). Then, at the beginning of each iteration and based on the previous iterations objective, a new configuration $c$ from $\zeta$ is sampled. We pick $\mathcal{M}$ HP from $c$, train it and extract the multi-view data representation for both train and validation in the latent space. After that, we train the selected classifier on the obtained vectors and compute the accuracy on the validation set. Finally, we save the weights of the trained $\mathcal{M}$ whenever a new best objective is achieved. At the end of the process, in addition to the returned best configuration, we obtain a file containing the different configurations associated with their objective.

## 3 Experiments and Results

In order to validate the aforementioned methodology, we first validate the GAN-based MVE architecture for a classic classification task using the MNIST dataset. To get the multi-view aspect, we are considering the original digits' images as the first view while we compute the corresponding edge images to simulate the second view like done in [7,10]. Secondly, we aim to prove that the use of DeepHyper can solve the CASH problem by substituting the work of an expert data-scientist and offering the best configuration of the MVE architecture and of the classifier at once.

### 3.1 MVE Component Validation

We quantitatively test the robustness of the MVE component to deal with missing data by measuring the classification accuracy with respect to different missingness ratios. Indeed, we run $\mathcal{M}$ five times with the same configuration except for the missing data proportion $r$ in training and testing sets. At each run, we step up $r$ by 0.2, train $\mathcal{M}$ on the training set, extract the features representations in the common latent space for both training and testing sets and then train and evaluate them on the multi-classification task using several machine learning models. The results of the classification performance of the different experiences are summed up in Fig. 2.

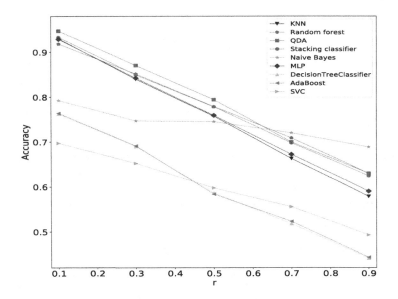

**Fig. 2.** Classification accuracy w.r.t the missingness ratio $r$.

Despite the fact that the classifiers have not been tuned, most of them achieved more than 92% of accuracy when $r$ is at its least value. However, this metric drops linearly when $r$ increases which gives an insight on how the missing data could affect the MVE model. From these preliminary results, We can also notice that, in the worst case (i.e. $r = 0.9$), the accuracy didn't get lower than 0.4 while it exceeds 0.6 with most of the classifiers. Also, these classifiers perform somehow similarly. Thus, we can not determine which is the best one especially if they have not been tuned yet. As a result from the foregoing, the use of a CASH solver is a crucial step.

### 3.2  CASH Solver Validation

We are checking if AMI can substitute data-scientist interventions and solve the CASH problem by offering the best configuration of the MVE architecture and of the classifier at once. First, we test its effectiveness to automatically tune the hyper-parameters and select the best classifier in a simultaneous way. To achieve that, we design the search space by integrating hyper-parameters from the MVE component and also a bunch of classifiers with their specific hyper-parameters.

Then, we let DeepHyper explore, exploit and evaluate the sampled configuration by measuring its classification accuracy ($r$ is fixed to 0.1). The accuracy results of the exploration process done by DeepHyper are exposed in Fig. 3.

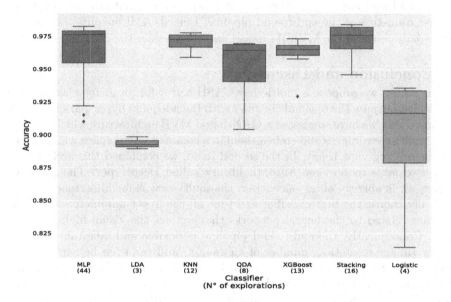

**Fig. 3.** AMI explorations for solving the CASH problem.

We notice that, despite the large search space, AMI has examined favorable, if not the best, configurations for the most of the classifiers. Also, the more explored classifiers, the better it performs. For instance, MLP and the Stacking classifier achieved more than 98% accuracy, which assert that the optimization process is doing well.

**Table 1.** Classification performance comparison of the 3 best classifiers chosen and tuned by AMI and the same models when they are either non-tuned or extensively-tuned.

| Default-values | Extensive tuning | AMI tuning |
| --- | --- | --- |
| 94.57 | 97.60 | **98.40** |

Table 1 reports a comparison between AMI's solution (MVE+Stacking classifier) with two different MVE models: a default-parameters model (non-tuned one following some parameters given by [7]) and a $\mathcal{M}$ model which has been extensively tuned by a human expert via a trial and error process. The missingness ratio $r$ is 0.1 for the three aforementioned experiments. First, we notice that AMI's returned solution surprisingly outperformed the human-tuned solutions. Second, this solution indicates that the stacking classifier is the best for this classification problem, which is the best classifier found by human tuning. Therefore, we conclude that the way we have configured DeepHyper leads to a reliable tool that can suggest the best classifier and automate the tuning of the hyper-parameters of the end-to-end pipeline. Indeed, AMI outputs the optimal hyper-parameters of the MVE $\mathcal{M}$ model and the ones for the Stacking classifier.

## 4    Conclusion and Discussion

In this paper, we propose a multi-view CASH solver for an image classification task which outputs the optimal classifier with the adequate hyper-parameters. In the first hand, we have suggested a GAN-based MVE architecture which takes as input multi-view images and embed them in a common latent space while imputing the missing view if any. In the second hand, we combined this architecture with a scalable mono-view AutoML library called DeepHyper. The proposed framework is able to, all at once, train the multi-view embedding model, automatically choose the best classifier and tune all the hyper-parameters including the ones related to the neural networks that extract the visual high-level features. Consequently, the end-to-end pipeline is flexible and adaptable to data variety (image resolution, number of views etc.) and can even be extensible to other modalities such as text or audio. In future works, we aim to let DeepHyper choose between several MVE techniques such as graph-based or kernel-based. We also tend to support supplementary autoML features such as data pre-processing (e.g. data cleaning, data augmentation), to support meta-learning to benefit from prior knowledge (e.g., a warm-start could be valuable in reducing the optimization process time) and also support NAS, to further parameterize the neural-based components.

## References

1. Khan, H.N., Shahid, A., Raza, B., Dar, A., Alquhayz, H.: Multi-view feature fusion based four views model for mammogram classification using convolutional neural network. IEEE Access **7**, 165724–165733 (2019)
2. Wang, L., Ding, Z., Tao, Z., Liu, Y., Fu, Y.: Generative multi-view human action recognition. In: Proceedings of the IEEE International Conference on Computer Vision, pp. 6212–6221 (2019)
3. Bai, Y., Tao, Z., Wang, L., Li, S., Yin, Y., Fu, Y.: Collaborative attention mechanism for multi-view action recognition, arXiv preprint arXiv:2009.06599 (2020)
4. Mishra, P., Herrmann, I., Angileri, M.: Improved prediction of potassium and nitrogen in dried bell pepper leaves with visible and near-infrared spectroscopy utilising wavelength selection techniques. Talanta **225**, 121971 (2021)
5. Sun, Z., Sarma, P., Sethares, W., Liang, Y.: Learning relationships between text, audio, and video via deep canonical correlation for multimodal language analysis. In: Proceedings of the AAAI Conference on Artificial Intelligence (2020)
6. Rai, N., Negi, S., Chaudhury, S., Deshmukh, O.: Partial multi-view clustering using graph regularized NMF. In: 2016 23rd International Conference on Pattern Recognition (ICPR), pp. 2192–2197 (2016)

7. Wang, Q., Ding, Z., Tao, Z., Gao, Q., Fu, Y.: Generative partial multi-view clustering (2020)
8. Ainsworth, S.K., Foti, N.J., Fox, E.B.: Disentangled VAE representations for multi-aspect and missing data, arXiv preprint arXiv:1806.09060 (2018)
9. Creswell, A., White, T., Dumoulin, V., Arulkumaran, K., Sengupta, B., Bharath, A.A.: Generative adversarial networks: an overview. IEEE Signal Process. Mag. **35**(1), 53–65 (2018)
10. Creswell, A., White, T., Dumoulin, V., Arulkumaran, K., Sengupta, B., Bharath, A.A.: VIGAN: missing view imputation with generative adversarial networks. In: 2017 IEEE International Conference on Big Data (Big Data), pp. 766–775. IEEE (2017)
11. Li, Y., Yang, M., Zhang, Z.: A survey of multi-view representation learning. IEEE Trans. Knowl. Data Eng. **31**(10), 1863–1883 (2019)
12. Li, X., et al.: Adversarial multimodal representation learning for click-through rate prediction. In: Proceedings of the Web Conference, April 2020
13. Yao, Q., et al.: Taking human out of learning applications: A survey on automated machine learning, arXiv preprint arXiv:1810.13306 (2018)
14. Elshawi, R., Maher, R., Sakr, S.: Automated machine learning: state-of the-art and open challenges, arXiv preprint arXiv:1906.02287 92019)
15. Feurer, M., Eggensperger, K., Falkner, S., Lindauer, M., Hutter, F.: Auto-sklearn 2.0: The next generation, arXiv preprint arXiv:2007.04074 (2020)
16. Thornton, C., Hutter, F., Hoos, H.H., Leyton-Brown, K.: Auto-WEKA: combined selection and hyperparameter optimization of classification algorithms. In: Proceedings of the 19th ACM SIGKDD international conference on Knowledge discovery and data mining, pp. 847–855 (2013)
17. Hutter, F., Hoos, H.H., Leyton-Brown, K.: Sequential model-based optimization for general algorithm configuration. In: Coello, C.A.C. (ed.) LION 2011. LNCS, vol. 6683, pp. 507–523. Springer, Heidelberg (2011). https://doi.org/10.1007/978-3-642-25566-3_40
18. Balaprakash, P., Salim, M., Uram, T.D., Vishwanath, V., Wild, S.M.: DeepHyper: asynchronous hyperparameter search for deep neural networks. In: 2018 IEEE 25th International Conference on High Performance Computing (HiPC) (2018)
19. Wang, B., et al.: VEGA: Towards an end-to-end configurable AutoML pipeline, arXiv preprint arXiv:2011.01507 (2020)

# How Realistic Should Synthetic Images Be for Training Crowd Counting Models?

Emanuele Ledda[2], Lorenzo Putzu[1]([✉])(iD), Rita Delussu[1](iD), Andrea Loddo[1,2](iD), and Giorgio Fumera[1](iD)

[1] Department of Electrical and Electronic Engineering, University of Cagliari,
Cagliari, Italy
{lorenzo.putzu,rita.delussu,andrea.loddo,fumera}@unica.it
[2] Department of Mathematics and Computer Science,
University of Cagliari, Cagliari, Italy
e.ledda7@studenti.unica.it

**Abstract.** Using synthetic images has been proposed to avoid collecting and manually annotating a sufficiently large and representative training set for several computer vision tasks, including crowd counting. While existing methods for crowd counting are based on generating realistic images, we start investigating how crowd counting accuracy is affected by increasing the realism of synthetic training images. Preliminary experiments on state-of-the-art CNN-based methods, focused on image background and pedestrian appearance, show that realism in both of them is beneficial to a different extent, depending on the kind of model (regression- or detection-based) and on pedestrian size in the images.

**Keywords:** Crowd counting · Synthetic training images

## 1 Introduction

Crowd counting is a computer vision task consisting of estimating the number of people in a given image or video. It has recently attracted increasing interest for its potential security-related applications, in particular to video surveillance [13,18]. This task is still challenging due to issues such as perspective distortions, scale variations, illumination variations, background complexity, and occlusions. Early approaches based on full-body or body part (e.g., head) detection are effective only on small and sparse crowds with limited occlusions, whereas regression-based approaches (mapping from low-level image features to crowd count) can be effective also on dense crowds [13]. Notable performance improvements have been reported by more recent methods based on Convolutional Neural Networks (CNNs) [18], which are nevertheless affected by the above mentioned issues, although usually to a lower extent. In particular, such issues arise in cross-scene scenarios, i.e., when a crowd counting model is deployed to target scenes different from the ones used for training [24].

© Springer Nature Switzerland AG 2021
N. Tsapatsoulis et al. (Eds.): CAIP 2021, LNCS 13053, pp. 46–56, 2021.
https://doi.org/10.1007/978-3-030-89131-2_5

Another issue is the requirement of a representative training set of manually annotated crowd images. This is even more demanding for CNN-based methods, that require head point annotations. Some authors proposed to address it using *synthetic* training images, e.g., through computer graphics tools or Generative Adversarial Networks (GAN) [4,5,17,19]. This solution presents several advantages, chiefly the possibility of automatically annotating images, enabling the construction of large training sets; it also allows to control several factors such as image perspective, background and illumination, as well as crowd size and the position of people in the scene. Existing work attempt to generate *realistic* images, in particular in terms of camera style and colours [8,10,19]. However, it would be interesting to investigate what *kind* and what *degree* of realism are most beneficial to crowd counting effectiveness. For instance, how useful is it to realistically reproduce image background, illumination conditions, pedestrian appearance, etc., relatively to each other? And, "how much" realistic should they be? Answering this question is not straightforward, since several factors may influence the effectiveness of synthetic training images, including the specific crowd counting model used. This work aims at making a first step toward investigating the above issue. This problem has recently been addressed in the context of other computer vision tasks [6,7,15]. In particular, it was found that the kind and degree of realism required by different tasks (e.g., object instance detection vs object class detection and semantic segmentation) may be different [6].

To limit the complexity of our preliminary investigation, we consider a *scene-specific* scenario with a single target (testing) camera view, i.e., a fixed perspective and background, which are assumed to be known during the design phase (at training time) and focus on the influence of *background* and *pedestrian appearance*. To this aim, we experimentally compare the crowd counting accuracy attained using as the training set real images of the target scene with the one attained by synthetic replicas of the *same* images, characterised by the same number and position of pedestrians, and by different, increasing degrees of realism in terms of background and pedestrian clothing appearance. To generate synthetic images we used the computer graphics engine Blender. We carry out the above comparison using three representatives, state-of-the-art CNN-based models, and five benchmark data sets. Our preliminary results seem to generally confirm the benefit of realistically reproducing scene background and show that even a limited degree of realism in pedestrian appearance may be sufficient, especially when pedestrian size (in pixel) is small. Some differences also emerge depending on the kind of crowd counting model used.

## 2 Related Work

**Crowd Counting Methods.** State-of-the-art methods use CNN models and follow two main approaches: regression-based (mapping an input image to its density map, from which the people count can be easily obtained) and detection-based (locating pedestrians' heads and counting them). **Regression-based**

**methods** can in turn be categorised depending on the main addressed issue: scale variations [14,21,26,27], influence of the background [11,22] and perspective variations [23]. *Scale variations* were addressed in [27] through a multi-scale and multi-level feature aggregation network architecture. Preliminary feature maps (extracted by VGG-16 backbone) are further processed to extract scale variation information and to discriminate the importance of each feature map. Then, these maps are aggregated and fed into a density regression module that estimates the final density map. In [26] a Multi-Column CNN (MCNN) based on filters of different size was proposed. During training, each column is trained separately on a large data set, then they are jointly fine-tuned on the target data set; the outputs of all the columns are finally merged into the estimated density map. The BL+ architecture [14] uses a VGG-16 backbone and a Bayesian loss; in contrast to the other works, head point annotations are used not to build the ground-truth density map, but to handle scale variations. In [21] a multi-scale GAN was proposed. The generator uses a multi-scale fully convolutional network to produce realistic density maps by extracting features at different scales. The discriminator is trained to distinguish real density maps from generated ones. Other works focus on mitigating *background influence*. A self-attention mechanism was proposed to this aim in [11]. Feature maps extracted by a backbone are fed into a module that preserves image resolution. A self-attention mechanism is used to extract high-level features. Preliminary and refined feature maps are combined to obtain the final density map. In [22] a mask guided GAN was proposed. The mask generator (based on mask-RCNN) separates the pedestrian image from the background. The original image and the corresponding mask are fed into an encoder-transformer-decoder structure which estimates the density map. The estimated people count is obtained by a regression module that takes as input only the encoder-transformer output. *Perspective distortions*, as well as variations of crowd distribution, are addressed in [23] through a granular computing network. First, a splitting ratio is learnt to subdivide the image into two parts. Then, each part is processed by a model that computes the corresponding density map. The corresponding people counts are then obtained and summed up. **Detection-based methods** In [20] a self-training network was proposed for object detection and counting; a detection network based on ResNet-50 and a decoder module are used to extract high-resolution feature maps to estimate the object centre point and size, using a non-uniform kernel. The Locate, Size and Count (LSC) model [16] is composed of three parts. The first two aim at extracting features and detecting (through a bounding box) pedestrian heads at different scales. The last part consists of a loss module, which is replaced in the testing phase by a prediction fusion module that also removes wrong bounding boxes from prediction maps. In [12] a detection and a regression networks are combined. A regression-detection model is trained to transform a density map into a localisation and a scale maps. A detection-regression model is also trained to compute the opposite transformation. The training phase consists of two stages: first, transformation models are learnt by using a source data set;

then, pre-trained models are fine-tuned using unlabelled target data through self-supervision.

**Synthetic Training Images for Crowd Counting.** Some works proposed to use synthetic images to train CNN-based crowd counting models [1,8,10,19]. In [8] a scene-specific scenario is considered, and synthetic training images are generated in several steps: *i)* the background of the target scene is extracted by a subtraction algorithm; *ii)* pedestrians are extracted by subtracting the background image; *ii)* a realistic background is generated by changing illumination and adding noise; *iv)* the region of interest is defined; *v)* synthetic images are generated by adding pedestrians on the region of interest. A scene-specific scenario is also considered in [5], where pedestrian images collected from the Web are placed on a background image of the target scene. In [10] a synthetic training set was generated through a computer graphics tool, merging background images from different data sets and pedestrians extracted from other data sets. The model is pre-trained on ImageNet and fine-tuned on the synthetic images. In [1] synthetic images that focus on structure information are generated following similar steps used to generate ground truth density maps, and a two-branch network is used: one branch is trained on synthetic images, the other one on real images using a synthetic-guided loss aimed at learning features similar to the ones extracted from synthetic images. The model of [19] consists of a spatial fully connected layer network (SFCN) using a ResNet-101 network as a backbone. Synthetic images are generated using the Grand Theft Auto V (GTA 5) video game and transformed into photo-realistic ones using GANs. SFCN is pre-trained on synthetic images and fine-tuned on real target images.

# 3   Motivations and Goal of This Work

The effectiveness of crowd counting models depends on several characteristics of the training and testing data, such as background, illumination, perspective and scale. Work exploiting synthetic training images (see Sect. 2) attempt to generate *realistic* images through either relatively simple methods, such as superimposing pedestrian images on a background image of the target scene [5], or more sophisticated ones based on GANs and style transfer techniques [19]. In this context, it is interesting to understand whether and how increasing the realism of different image components affects the accuracy of crowd counting models. For instance, how useful it is to realistically reproduce image background, perspective, illumination conditions, and pedestrian clothing appearance, and "how much" realistic do they need to be? This work aims at making the first step toward this direction for the crowd counting task.

Given that several other factors beside the ones mentioned above may affect crowd counting accuracy, including crowd spatial distribution and pedestrian appearance variability, in this preliminary work, we chose to focus only on a few of them, trying to minimise the influence of the other ones. To this aim, we considered a scene-specific scenario characterised by a single target camera view, with a given perspective map and region of interest (ROI) which are known at training time. This allows one to train a crowd counting model on synthetic images having the same perspective and ROI as the target scene. We then investigated the effect of different degrees of realism in reproducing two specific factors: the **background** of the target scene and pedestrian **clothing appearance**. To this aim, we used several single-scene benchmark data sets. For each of them, we generated synthetic images reproducing each training image, with the same perspective, ROI, and spatial location of pedestrians (we exploited head point annotations available in benchmark data sets), while we varied image background and pedestrian clothing appearance. To analyse the influence of realistically reproducing the background of the target scene, we generated synthetic images either with a uniform, "unrealistic" background or with the real background image of the target scene. To analyse the influence of pedestrian appearance, we generated synthetic pedestrians using 3D human models either with a uniform, "unrealistic" body colour or with different colours simulating realistic clothing patterns (although not the same as in the real images). More precisely, we generated three distinct sets of training images corresponding to three basic, increasing degrees of realism in terms of scene background and pedestrian appearance: **SET0**: pedestrians with uniform neutral colour, over a background with a uniform colour: this allows us to assess the effectiveness of reproducing only the perspective of the target scene and pedestrians' position (see Fig. 1, second column); **SET1**: pedestrians with uniform neutral colour superimposed on a background image of the target scene: this allows us to assess also the benefit of realistically reproducing the background (see Fig. 1, third column); **SET2**: pedestrians with various clothing appearance patterns superimposed on a background image of the target scene: this allows us to evaluate also the benefit of realistically reproducing clothing appearance (see Fig. 1, fourth column). To generate synthetic images, we use the API of the computer graphics engine Blender[1]. The detailed image generation procedure is described in Sect. 4.

Based on the above setting, we evaluated and compared crowd counting accuracy attained on *real* testing images of each data set using the original, *real* training images, and using our synthetic replicas for each of the above degrees of realism. To this aim, we used state-of-the-art CNN-based models representative of the different approaches mentioned in Sect. 2.

## 4   Synthetic Image Generation

According to Sect. 3, for each real training image $I$ with head point annotations, our aim is to generate a synthetic image $S$ with the same perspective, containing 3D human models in the same spatial locations of pedestrians in $I$. Human models are drawn either with a uniform, neutral colour (SET0 and SET1) or with different colours mimicking clothing patterns (SET2); then, they are superimposed either on a uniform background (SET0) or on a real background image of the target scene (SET1 and SET2). This requires: (i) a **background image** of the target scene not including pedestrians nor other non-static objects (e.g.,

---

[1] https://www.blender.org/.

cars), (ii) the **ROI** in the form of a binary mask to define the image region where synthetic pedestrians can be placed (to avoid inconsistent occlusions with static scene objects), and (iii) the **perspective map** of the target scene (available together with the benchmark data sets, see Sect. 5.1), which is necessary to compute the following camera parameters: position and rotation of the camera with respect to the ground, and focal length.

**Computing the Projection Map.** After refining the head point annotations, the projection map is obtained through their geometric transformation. This requires defining the spatial region where the pedestrians are placed; to this aim, for the sake of simplicity, we assume that all pedestrians have the same height of 1.7 m and that the scene ground is flat. This allows us to find the *head plane*, an imaginary plane parallel to the ground and intersecting pedestrians' heads. We exploit the camera parameters to obtain their exact positions by projecting the annotations onto the head plane and by subtracting the assumed height of 1.7 m from the $z$ coordinate.

**Reproducing and Rendering the Scene.** We used the Blender API to automate the pipeline of generating the desired synthetic images from the corresponding projection maps: (1) The camera setting is reproduced in the simulated environment, in terms of focal length, position and rotation with respect to the ground, by adding a virtual camera with the same set-up as in the real image. (2) The background image of the target scene is used as a background rendering image (except for SET0). (3) The projection map of the crowd is used to add the 3D human models to the scene. To simulate clothing appearance, we assigned pseudo-random colours to jumpers, pants, shoes and hair of each pedestrian.

# 5   Experimental Evaluation

In the following we describe the benchmark data sets, the experimental set-up and the obtained results.

## 5.1   Data Sets

To improve generalisation capability, recent crowd counting data sets are multi-scene, and each image comes from a different scene. Only a few benchmark data sets contain a sufficient number of manually annotated training and testing images from the same camera view, as required by our experiments: Mall [3], UCSD [2] and PETS [9]. Although also Shanghai World Expo 2010 [18] includes videos from fixed camera views, only 120 frames per video (one per 30 s, out of one hour) are manually annotated, making it unsuitable for our purposes. Despite the chosen data sets contain small crowds (at most 53 people per image), they are very challenging due to lighting variations, perspective distortions and severe occlusions. **Mall** contains 2,000 frames with a size of 640 × 480 pixels, collected from a single surveillance camera in a shopping mall, with 31 people per frame on average. As in previous work [13,18] we split the data set into

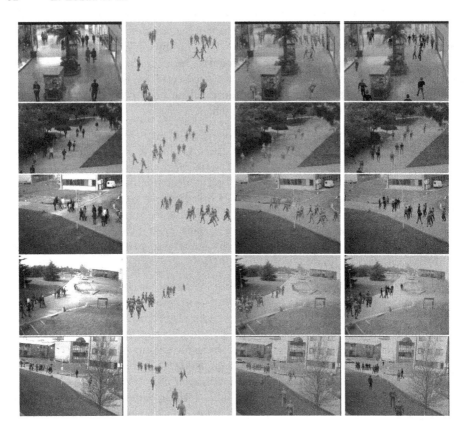

**Fig. 1.** Examples of real training images from the considered data sets (1st column, from top to bottom: Mall, UCSD, PETSView1, PETSView2, PETSView3) and of the corresponding synthetic images in SET0, SET1 and SET2 (2nd to 4th column).

600 training, 200 validation and 1,200 testing images. **UCSD** has been collected with a low-resolution camera in a pedestrian walkway at a university campus. As in recent work [13,18], we used a subset of 2,000 frames with a size of $238 \times 158$ pixels (containing on average 25 people per frame) and split them into 600, 200 and 1,200 training, validation and testing frames, respectively. **PETS2009** is a benchmark for several visual surveillance tasks [9] and is composed of different video sequences acquired with various cameras at different times and under diverse illumination and shading conditions. We used them to create three single-scene data sets named PETSview1, PETSview2 and PETSview3, by grouping the frames from the first three camera views [5]. Each of them contains 1,229 frames of size $576 \times 768$, with 25 people per frame on average. We split each set into 361, 128 and 740 frames for training, validation and testing, respectively. We used the head point annotations provided in [25], since they are not included in the original data set. Figure 1 shows some examples of real and synthetic images from each data set.

**Table 1.** MAE and RMSE attained on real testing images of five data sets by the crowd counting methods trained on real and synthetic (SET0, SET1 and SET2) images.

| | Training set | Testing set (target scene) | | | | | | | | | |
|---|---|---|---|---|---|---|---|---|---|---|---|
| | | Mall | | UCSD | | PETSview1 | | PETSview2 | | PETSview3 | |
| | | MAE | RMSE | MAE | RMSE | MAE | RMSE | MAE | RMSE | MAE | RMSE |
| MCNN | Real | 5.33 | 6.17 | 2.3 | 2.84 | 6.2 | 7.86 | 4.23 | 5.08 | 4.18 | 5.13 |
| | SET0 | 25.69 | 26.32 | 16.06 | 17.49 | 31.05 | 32.71 | 30.3 | 31.93 | 27.79 | 28.29 |
| | SET1 | 24.82 | 25.65 | 10.43 | 11.31 | 27.97 | 30.07 | 27.52 | 29.15 | 24.57 | 25.12 |
| | SET2 | 23.49 | 23.97 | 2.82 | 3.61 | 23.62 | 25.57 | 22.07 | 23.71 | 20.42 | 21.66 |
| BL+ | Real | 2.18 | 2.74 | 2.5 | 3.57 | 3.75 | 5.12 | 5.8 | 6.57 | 4.72 | 5.61 |
| | SET0 | 62.07 | 62.23 | 8.12 | 9.04 | 78.13 | 78.32 | 83.71 | 84.06 | 71.9 | 72.09 |
| | SET1 | 29.63 | 30.15 | 3.53 | 5.0 | 22.29 | 24.84 | 24.87 | 27.47 | 29.51 | 30.28 |
| | SET2 | 23.55 | 24.0 | 3.64 | 5.14 | 12.82 | 15.62 | 17.23 | 19.75 | 21.61 | 22.17 |
| LSC | Real | 2.33 | 2.97 | 9.96 | 10.79 | 4.89 | 6.39 | 20.79 | 22.69 | 16.18 | 17.31 |
| | SET0 | 6.47 | 8.03 | 32.08 | 32.80 | 5.75 | 7.23 | 8.50 | 10.76 | 44.97 | 46.88 |
| | SET1 | 31.53 | 32.06 | 15.01 | 16.10 | 23.33 | 25.42 | 22.93 | 24.94 | 30.66 | 31.07 |
| | SET2 | 25.52 | 26.03 | 5.0 | 6.07 | 13.88 | 16.29 | 17.62 | 19.90 | 20.27 | 20.95 |

## 5.2 Experimental Set-Up

We selected three representative CNN-based models among the ones whose source code was available and fully functional: MCNN [26], BL+ [14] and LSC [16]. LSC is detection-based, whereas MCNN and BL+ are regression-based (see Sect. 2); however, MCNN and BL+ differ significantly in terms of structure and design. MCNN has an ad-hoc multi-column architecture created from scratch, while BL+ has a single column architecture based on a VGG-19 backbone. Furthermore, BL+ uses a Bayesian loss function designed to directly exploit head point annotations, while MCNN uses a common mean square error (MSE) loss function between the estimated and ground truth density map; the latter is computed using Gaussian kernels of fixed size.

For each data set we trained each crowd counting model (using the hyper-parameters suggested in the respective papers) on the original, real training images and on the synthetic training sets SET0, SET1, and SET2. We then evaluated the corresponding performance on real testing images using two common metrics, Mean Absolute Error (MAE) and Root Mean Square Error (RMSE), computed between the true and estimated people count over all testing images.

## 5.3 Results

Table 1 reports the results of our experiments. The main observation is that, as expected, the performance of all the considered crowd counting methods improved as the degree of realism of the synthetic training set increased (from SET0 to SET2), even if with very different trends, with some exceptions. Specifically, synthetic images produced worse results than real ones, except for SET2 on the UCSD data set (for all models) and for the LSC model trained on SET0 on Mall and PETSview2.

Except for UCSD (discussed below), MCNN and LSC achieved lower improvements than BL+ for increasing degrees of realism. However, BL+ often performed poorly on SET0. On the other hand, LSC shows some exceptions to the above trend, because it reached a very good accuracy in three out of five data sets by merely training it on SET0, even outperforming real training data for PETSview2; however, it achieved a worse performance on SET1 and SET2 on these data sets. This behaviour may depend on the fact that, being LSC a detection-based method, it may produce an effective model even when trained on images containing only pedestrians, with no background.

Consider now the results on UCSD. Besides the fact that BL+ achieved a much better performance than MCNN and LSC even on SET0, all three models achieved comparable performances to the ones obtained on real training images, when trained on SET2. This is not surprising since the size of pedestrians in UCSD is smaller than in the other data sets (see Fig. 1), and therefore the corresponding synthetic images look relatively more similar to real ones.

To sum up, in the considered scene-specific scenario, our preliminary results show that: *i)* using a realistic background (from SET0 to SET1) is beneficial to regression-based crowd counting models, whereas its usefulness is not clear for detection-based ones; *ii)* a more realistic clothing appearance (from SET1 to SET2) is clearly advantageous; *iii)* regression-based methods show qualitatively different behaviour than detection-based ones with respect to synthetic training images' characteristics; *iv)* the smaller the size of pedestrians (in pixels), the lower the degree of realism in their appearance required to obtain an effective model, as one may expect (see the results on UCSD); this may also imply that synthetic images should be more beneficial for scenes with larger crowds.

## 6  Conclusions

Recent work shows that using synthetic training images is a promising direction also for the crowd counting computer vision task. In this work, we made a first step toward analysing whether and to what extent realistically reproducing two specific factors, scene background and pedestrian appearance, is beneficial to crowd counting accuracy for representative, state-of-the-art CNN-based models. We found that a certain degree of realism in both factors seems beneficial, and that the performance improvement also depends on the kind of model (either regression- or detection-based) and on pedestrian size (in pixels). As interesting directions for further work, aimed at developing guidelines for generating effective synthetic training images for crowd counting, we envisage a more fine-grained analysis of scene background (e.g., by also evaluating synthetic backgrounds), finer clothing details and other pedestrian attributes and illumination variations, as well as perspective variations; the analysis of the latter factor can be useful for cross-scene scenarios where the target scene is unknown during system design.

# References

1. Cao, Z., Shamsolmoali, P., Yang, J.: Synthetic guided domain adaptive and edge aware network for crowd counting. Image Vis. Comput. **104**, 104026 (2020)
2. Chan, A.B., Liang, Z.S.J., Vasconcelos, N.: Privacy preserving crowd monitoring: counting people without people models or tracking. In: CVPR, pp. 1–7 (2008)
3. Chen, K., Loy, C.C., Gong, S., Xiang, T.: Feature mining for localised crowd counting. In: BMVC, pp. 1–11 (2012)
4. Chen, Y., Zhu, X., Gong, S.: Instance-guided context rendering for cross-domain person re-identification. In: ICCV, pp. 232–242 (2019)
5. Delussu, R., Putzu, L., Fumera, G.: Investigating synthetic data sets for crowd counting in cross-scene scenarios. In: VISIGRAPP, pp. 365–372 (2020)
6. Dvornik, N., Mairal, J., Schmid, C.: On the importance of visual context for data augmentation in scene understanding. IEEE TPAMI **43**(6), 2014–2028 (2021)
7. Dwibedi, D., Misra, I., Hebert, M.: Cut, paste and learn: surprisingly easy synthesis for instance detection. In: ICCV, pp. 1310–1319 (2017)
8. Ekbatani, H.K., Pujol, O., Seguí, S.: Synthetic data generation for deep learning in counting pedestrians. In: ICPRAM, pp. 318–323 (2017)
9. Ferryman, J., Shahrokni, A.: Pets 2009: dataset and challenge. In: IEEE International Workshop on PETS, pp. 1–6 (2009)
10. Ghosh, S., Amon, P., Hutter, A., Kaup, A.: Pedestrian counting using deep models trained on synthetically generated images. In: VISIGRAPP, pp. 86–97 (2017)
11. Liu, Y.-B., Jia, R.-S., Liu, Q.-M., Zhang, X.-L., Sun, H.-M.: Crowd counting method based on the self-attention residual network. Appl. Intell. **51**(1), 427–440 (2020). https://doi.org/10.1007/s10489-020-01842-w
12. Liu, Y., Wang, Z., Shi, M., et al.: Towards unsupervised crowd counting via regression-detection bi-knowledge transfer. In: ACM Multimedia, pp. 129–137 (2020)
13. Loy, C.C., Chen, K., Gong, S., Xiang, T.: Crowd counting and profiling: methodology and evaluation. In: Ali, S., Nishino, K., Manocha, D., Shah, M. (eds.) Modeling, Simulation and Visual Analysis of Crowds. TISVC, vol. 11, pp. 347–382. Springer, New York (2013). https://doi.org/10.1007/978-1-4614-8483-7_14
14. Ma, Z., Wei, X., Hong, X., Gong, Y.: Bayesian loss for crowd count estimation with point supervision. In: ICCV, pp. 6141–6150 (2019)
15. Movshovitz-Attias, Y., Kanade, T., Sheikh, Y.: How useful is photo-realistic rendering for visual learning? In: Hua, G., Jégou, H. (eds.) ECCV 2016. LNCS, vol. 9915, pp. 202–217. Springer, Cham (2016). https://doi.org/10.1007/978-3-319-49409-8_18
16. Sam, D.B., Peri, S.V., Sundararaman, M.N., et al.: Locate, size and count: Accurately resolving people in dense crowds via detection. TPAMI (2020)
17. Shang, C., Ai, H., Zhuang, Z., et al.: Improving pedestrian detection in crowds with synthetic occlusion images. In: ICME, pp. 1–4 (2018)
18. Sindagi, V., Patel, V.M.: A survey of recent advances in CNN-based single image crowd counting and density estimation. Pattern Recognit. Lett. **107**, 3–16 (2017)
19. Wang, Q., Gao, J., Lin, W., Yuan, Y.: Learning from synthetic data for crowd counting in the wild. In: CVPR, pp. 8198–8207 (2019)
20. Wang, Y., Hou, J., Hou, X., Chau, L.: A self-training approach for point-supervised object detection and counting in crowds. IEEE Trans. IP **30**, 2876–2887 (2021)
21. Yang, J., Zhou, Y., Kung, S.: Multi-scale generative adversarial networks for crowd counting. In: ICPR, pp. 3244–3249. IEEE Computer Society (2018)

22. Yao, H., Wan, W., Li, X.: Mask guided GAN for density estimation and crowd counting. IEEE Access **8**, 31432–31443 (2020)
23. Yu, Y., Zhu, H., Wang, L., Pedrycz, W.: Dense crowd counting based on adaptive scene division. Int. J. Mach. Learn. Cybern. **12**(4), 931–942 (2020). https://doi.org/10.1007/s13042-020-01212-5
24. Zhang, C., Li, H., Wang, X., Yang, X.: Cross-scene crowd counting via deep convolutional neural networks. In: CVPR, pp. 833–841 (2015)
25. Zhang, Q., Chan, A.B.: Wide-area crowd counting via ground-plane density maps and multi-view fusion CNNs. In: CVPR, pp. 8297–8306 (2019)
26. Zhang, Y., Zhou, D., Chen, S., Gao, S., Ma, Y.: Single-image crowd counting via multi-column convolutional neural network. In: CVPR, pp. 589–597 (2016)
27. Zhu, F., Yan, H., Chen, X., Li, T., Zhang, Z.: A multi-scale and multi-level feature aggregation network for crowd counting. Neurocomputing **423**, 46–56 (2021)

# Unsupervised Recognition of the Logical Structure of Business Documents Based on Spatial Relationships

Louisa Kessi[1,2](✉), Frank Lebourgeois[1,2], and Christophe Garcia[1,2]

[1] Université de Lyon, CNRS, Lyon, France
{louisa.kessi,franck.lebourgeois,
christophe.garcia}@liris.cnrs.fr, l.kessi@orpalis.com
[2] INSA-Lyon, LIRIS, UMR5205, 69621 Lyon, France

**Abstract.** This paper presents the very first unsupervised and automatic system which can recognize the logical structure of business documents without any models or prior information about their logical structure. Our solution can process totally unknown new models of documents. We consider the problem of recognition of logical structures as a problem of detection, because we simultaneously have to localize and recognize the logical function of blocks of text. We assume that any document is composed of parts from several other models of documents. We have proposed a part-based spatial model suited for partial voting. Our proposed model presents the concept of Spatial Context (SC) as a spatial feature, which locally measure the distribution of spatial information around a point of reference. Our method is based on a Gaussian voting process providing a robust mechanism to detect elements of any logical structure. Our solution is suited for non-rigid structures and works well with a reduced number of images. This excellent property is not shared by the supervised approaches, especially methods based on neuronal networks.

**Keywords:** Unsupervised recognition · Spatial relation · Voting · Logical structure recognition · Business documents

## 1 Introduction and Context

The main objective of this work is the automatic reading of business documents. In the Document Image Analysis (DIA) domain, it is a direct application of the recognition of the logical structure of documents. In contrast to the layout analysis of documents named physical structure that study the documents' appearance, the recognition of the logical structure aims to localize and recognize the logical function of text blocks. It is one of the most challenging problems in DIA because of the causality dilemma between recognition and localization. There is only a limited number of research on the recognition of the logical structure of documents and only very few studies concerning business documents. All previous works in logical structure recognition use supervised approaches applied on homogeneous documents with structures known a priori and that have a very standardized

© Springer Nature Switzerland AG 2021
N. Tsapatsoulis et al. (Eds.): CAIP 2021, LNCS 13053, pp. 57–72, 2021.
https://doi.org/10.1007/978-3-030-89131-2_6

predetermined rigid model. The systems developed by means of this research can only process documents with a model. They are not applicable to business documents.

Today companies have numerous suppliers and customers that exchange a great number of commercial documents. Each year, millions of companies go bankrupt and disappear; simultaneously almost the same number of new companies are created. Each company creates its own model of documents with a specific layout and logical structure because there is no regulation to design a model of business documents. Manual processing of all ingoing and outgoing documents is too expensive. Large and medium-sized companies need automatic solutions to process their business documents on a daily basis. The automatic processing of administrative documents is an important business that generates large profits for private companies. Most existing commercial solutions are systems based on rules or templates for each model of business document. Software based on templates requires manual modelization of each type of document. For new or unknown types of documents, an operator must define the location and the label of each metadata to read. The conception of a document model is time consuming and expensive work. Some companies provide an annotation tool to costumers so that they design the new models by themselves. The new models are shared among the costumers, which is a kind of crowdsourcing solution. Systems based on rules try to generalize the modelization of several different models of documents and can process some of documents having different layouts and structures. But these rule-based systems cannot outperform the software based on templates.

Research in this field rallied much later than research in the field of automatic recognition of characters. Indeed, the characterization of the different structures of a document presents various difficulties. Some OCR software maintains the physical structure and preserves the typography and the organization of documents, but the function of blocks of text and thus the logical structure cannot be analyzed. Today, there is no commercially available structure recognition system that is completely automatic.

The business documents are so heterogeneous that it becomes impossible to modelize millions of templates, for each company or administration. Our proposed work aims to develop an automatic system which can read any business or administrative document without a model of these documents. It is one of the more challenging developments in DIA.

This paper is organized as follows: Sect. 2 presents the related state of the art in the domain of the logical structure recognition. Section 3 details our proposal and the new concepts we have introduced. Section 4 describes a novel spatial feature; we have called "Spatial Context". Section 5 introduces the Gaussian voting mechanism and the final decision stage. The last section gives the results on a database of real invoices.

## 2 State of the Art

Most of related works about logical structure recognition has been introduced between 1990 and 2010. Specific session about logical structure recognition has existed in the ICDAR until recently. The sessions "Segmentation and Layout Analysis" of the last ICDAR do not concern the logical structure understanding. A specific Workshop DLIA

(Document Layout Interpretation Analysis) introduced during ICDAR99 has disappeared. Only a very small number of previous works concerns business documents. We split the related works into four categories:

**Data-Driven Approaches:** Usually, they analyze the layout by using rules, grammars, or heuristics in order to retrieve the tabular structure of the document [1–5]. Few papers concern business documents. In [6] Klein used the headers of the tables as the first solution for locating tables. Furthermore, header extraction works only if similar headers exist in a header database related to the extraction system. [7] proposed to localize tables using a grammar (EPF) and an associated analyzer. Moreover, its major disadvantage lies in the fact that the user must himself formalize the grammar relating to the type of documents before starting the information extraction.

**Model-Driven Approaches:** These systems are based on a model of the document to extract information. The model can be built automatically or manually [8–16]. The work presented in [13, 14] uses keywords, and other areas of interest such as logos and horizontal and vertical lines, in the context of manual document modeling. All these elements are extracted manually. The proposed final model is a labeled and oriented graph. However, the ability to generalize this system is not really demonstrated. The tests established on 138 documents are insufficient to aspire to a generalization. In addition, if a completely new invoice case arises and the information in the knowledge bases does not cover this specific case, it becomes very difficult to find an interpretation of this invoice. This is because each keyword is analyzed independently of the others. Esser et al. [7] builds a database of absolute positions of fields for each template. The work proposed in [15, 16] aimed to develop a system of recognition of heterogeneous documents from observations already memorized. The modeling of the structure of a document is performed from the text obtained by OCR and the relative position of the textual fields between them. The model is generated semi-automatically from keyword and pattern structures described in a spatial relationship graph. The modeling and recognition system uses the Case Reasoning (RpC) mechanism. However, this system is not suitable for the process of totally unknown new models of documents not registered in the database. Very few papers report quantitative results about logical structure recognition [17–22] on various documents like patents, newspapers, books, magazines, scientific papers, table of contents.

**Deep Learning-Driven Approaches:** [41] concerns only web wrappers and not the logical structure of invoices for the digitized business document recognition. The analysis of Web page is easier because it is OCR errors free. They recognize only one metadata: the field "price". The authors doubt about their ability to recognize a second metadata. The works of [42–44] are however not applicable in our task as we do not have access to the representation of source markup for the documents we process.

Information extraction from business documents for problematics like named entity recognition and relation extraction take advantage from recent advances in deep learning [31, 35–37, 47], however, these techniques are not directly applicable to our task on logical structure recognition. [38–40, 46] didn't deal with the logical structure recognition (i.e. the logical function of text blocks) but the layout analysis (description of the layout in terms of figure, table, section, caption, list paragraph) which is a different problem. Layout analysis can use the visual appearance (font style and size, color, alignments, texture...) to recognize the components of the layout. For the logical structure of invoices, we must use the spatial relationships between text blocks.

Commercial systems exists but they are limited to regular documents having a layout that rarely change. For unknown document, each company design its own documents and create a new layout (color, logo, fonts, style…) for their business documents.

**Industrial Known Systems:** The works of DocuWare [34] and the work by ITESOFT [29] require the creation of a database of templates in order to extract keywords and positions for each field. A template based system and a rule-based approach for unknown documents which are not recognized by the models is processed using heuristic and machine learning classifiers. The work of smartFIX [30] uses a manually programed rules for each template. ABBYY FlexiCapture [33] processes business documents and can extract data from forms. Some manual checking of data is done before the import into business databases. ReadSoft [32] Match zones from templates designed by users (for free!). For each new document, a user modelize manually a template which is shared automatically to the other users in the world. A manual verification mechanism reduces the recognition errors. CloudScan [31] is an invoice analysis system using recurrent neural networks. The authors takes a PDF file as the input and extract the words and their positions. Each line is analyzed as a vector of n-grams which limit the accuracy. A contextual features based on the closest four entities and an Long Short-Term Memory (LSTM) is used for classification.

# 3  Proposal

We describe the high-level stages of a more complex system which process automatically business document. The low level processing stages (separation between added text and preprinted text, color segmentation, layout extraction, character restoration) have already been published [48–51]. We introduce new concepts and make several assumptions during the development of the final stages of our recognition system:

- We assume that any document with an unknown model can be recognized by using parts of the logical structures of other known documents. We introduce a part by part recognition approach and a part-based model of the structure of documents which can recognize the logical structure of any document without a model of this document.
- We introduce the concept of micro-structure suited for the recognition part-by-part of any document. We define a micro-structure all pairs of text blocks that have a logical link. For business documents, most of the logical text blocks to detect, called "metadata", are mostly associated with a label called "caption" which are vertically or horizontally aligned. We define a micro-structure by the pairs of text blocks (*Caption → Metadata*) with → which describes the spatial relation between the caption and the metadata to retrieve. ("Due date" → 13/02/2018) ("Total Net" → "*135,00€*") ("VAT → *19,6%*") are some example of micro-structures. The class of possible caption is given by the matching of the OCRresults into a dictionary of all possible captions

found in business documents in Europe. Spatial horizontal or vertical alignment is also an important feature which links the metadata and its caption.

- We claim that an unsupervised system is better suited for this problem than a supervised approach. Millions of new models of business documents are created each year, and supervised approaches must be retrained each time a single new model is introduced or deleted. This explains our choice to focus our work only on an unsupervised approach which allows to add new models without a retraining.
- The recognition of the logical structure of a document is not possible without taking the spatial relation into account as the main feature. We introduce the concept of Spatial Context (SC) as a spatial feature, which describes the relative positions of metadata or caption in a Neighborhood around each word of interest.
- We introduce an original voting process in the spatial space that allows to localize and recognize a researched metadata and its logical function. The voting process is a statistical unsupervised approach which accumulates concordant information according to different parameters. Voting approaches has already been used in computer vision to find straight lines [23] shapes [24, 25], arbitrary lines [26], objects detection [27, 28]. This approach is well-known to be robust to noise and missing information due to the partial occultation of an object. For our application, a recognition system based on voting is an unsupervised approach that does not require any training and can manage part-based models and spatial mutual information into a single scheme.

## 4 Spatial Contexts

We define the Spatial Context ($SC$) of a neighborhood $N$ centered into a point C, the pairs of text block $E_i$ and a vector $\vec{U}_i$ which define the spatial relation between $E_i$ and the center $C$ of the neighborhood. Because the spatial structure of a document essentially varies horizontally and vertically, $\vec{U}_i$ is expressed in Cartesian coordinates ($dx,dy$) (1) (Fig. 1).

$$SC_{N(C)} = \left\{ \left( E_i, \vec{U}_i \right) E_i \in N(C) \ \vec{U}_i = \overrightarrow{CE_i}, \right\} \tag{1}$$

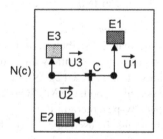

Fig. 1. A Spatial Context (SC).

We propose a novel spatial structure model and replace a classical spatial structure (Fig. 2a) by a set of Spatial Contexts which describe locally the neighboring elements

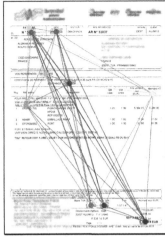  

*a) Classical structure model*    *b)Part-based Spatial Structure*

**Fig. 2.** Comparison between classical spatial model and our part-based spatial structure.

of the structure (Fig. 2b). This model allows to analyze a spatial structure part-by-part and reduce the structure complexity.

We introduce two types of spatial contexts:

- Metadata to Captions Spatial Context (MCSC)
- Metadata to Metadata Spatial Context (MMSC)

Because the documents may have different sizes and different resolutions, we normalize all positions of text block by dividing all coordinates by the size of the image. During the detection process, we multiply all coordinates by the size of the current image. This normalization guarantees that the spatial relations are always suited to the current document, whatever its size.

### 4.1  Metadata to Captions Spatial Context (MCSC)

The Metadata to Captions Spatial Context $MCSC_k$, centered on the metadata $M_k$ from the logical class $n°k$, measures the spatial distribution of the possible captions described by the words $W_i$ which are vertically or horizontally aligned with $M_k$ and belonging to the lexical dictionary of captions of class $n° k$ (2). With a window size of 50% of the size of the image to define the neighborhood, the MCSC is a local spatial feature suited for body part processing and part-by-part recognition.

It is the main information that must be used first during the recognition step. But the MCSC may be empty if there is no word $W_i$ found in the neighborhood of the metadata $n°k$, with the lexical class k. In this case, the metadata $n°k$ cannot be recognized with only this spatial context.

$$MCSC_k = \left\{ W_i. = \begin{pmatrix} W_i.x \\ W_i.y \end{pmatrix}, \vec{U}_i = \overrightarrow{M_k W_i} = \begin{pmatrix} W_i.x - M_k.x \\ W_i.y - M_k.y \end{pmatrix} / f(W_i) = k, \ W_i \rightarrow M_k \right\}$$

(2)

$$W_i \rightarrow M_k \Leftrightarrow \{W_i \text{ is aligned to the metadata } M_k\}$$

$$f(W_i) = \{\text{Lexical Class of the word } n°i \ W_i\}$$

## 4.2 Metadata to Metadata Spatial Context (MMSC)

The Metadata to Metadata Spatial Context ($MMSC_k$) measures the spatial distribution with the other $i^{th}$ metadata $M_i$ which appear in the neighborhood $N(M_k)$ centered on $M_k$ (3). The MMSC must be used after the prior localization of metadata by using the MCSC. This spatial context assumes that the metadata make statistically recurrent micro-structures. Voting by using the MMSC will reinforce the correct prior detection of the metadata and reduce false detections.

$$MMSC_k = \left\{ M_i = \begin{pmatrix} M_i.x \\ M_i.y \end{pmatrix}, \vec{U}_i = \overrightarrow{M_k M_i} = \begin{pmatrix} M_i.x - M_k.x \\ M_i.y - M_k.y \end{pmatrix} / M_i \in N(M_k), \ i \neq k \right\}$$

(3)

## 5 Voting and Detection Stages

For the recognition of the logical structure of documents, we use a 2-dimensional voting space defined by the parameters $(xc, yc)$ coordinate which localize the metadata to detect. The structure of business documents is based on very few text blocks. The voting process for the recognition of the logical structure of documents is achieved part-by-part and not model by model. We have a 2D-pool for each metadata to retrieve.

After several experiments, we chose a pool with a variable size that depends on the size of the document. The reduction factor $\alpha$ is also important for the precision of the localization of the text blocks to detect. After several experiments on our image database, the optimal choice of the reduction factor $\alpha$ equals 16. This value makes sense because it approximately corresponds to the average height of characters and text lines with 400 dpi of resolution. We quantify the parameters $(xc, yc)$ into $W \times H$ bins with $W = \text{ImageWidth}/\alpha$ and $H = \text{ImageHeight}/\alpha$. We introduce the Gaussian voting which consists to vote spatial Gaussian functions instead of using a classical variation of parameters generally apply during voting process (Fig. 3). A classical vote of dirac functions, followed by a smoothing of the pool by a Gaussian function in order to detect local maxima in the pools, doesn't work in our case.

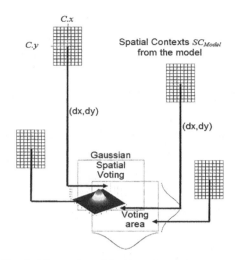

**Fig. 3.** Illustration of the Gaussian voting process

We choose to use four different voting processes into four different pools:

- Voting by using Metadata position
- Voting by using Metadata to Captions Spatial Context
- Voting by using the metadata format
- Voting by using Metadata to Metadata Spatial Context

These four voting processes are complementary. Metadata aligned with a caption can be detected by using their relative positions' possibilities, the spatial relations with their captions, the spatial relations with the other metadata, and the metadata format. The metadata that are not described by a caption are detected by using the metadata's possible position, the metadata format and the possible relationships between the other metadata.

### 5.1   Voting by Using Metadata Position

We use the relative position for a preliminary vote in order to coarsely localize each metadata $M_k$ within the image. For each model from the training, we sum the Gaussian function with high standard deviation values $\sigma x = 0.4 \times W$ and $\sigma y = 0.2 \times H$ because the localization of the metadata by using their relative position is imprecise. We sum the 2D Gaussian function for all $(a,b)$ within the limits of the pool $H \times W$ (4). The 2D Gaussian function has a width two times larger than its height because the positions of text blocks in documents vary more horizontally than vertically.

$$Pool[k][a][b]+ = \sum_{MMSC_k} \sum_{a=xc-3\sigma x}^{a=xc+3\sigma x} \sum_{b=yc-3\sigma y}^{b=yc+3\sigma y} e^{-\frac{(a-xc)^2}{2\times\sigma x^2} - \frac{(b-yc)^2}{2\times\sigma y^2}} \qquad (4)$$

$$(a, b) \in [0..W - 1] \times [0..H - 1] \ (xc, yc) = (M_k \cdot x, M_k \cdot y)$$

## 5.2 Voting by Using the Metadata to Captions Spatial Context

The Metadata to Captions Spatial Context $n°k$ ($MCSC_k$) allows the detection of the metadata $M_k$ from the possible captions localized by the words $W_i$ with the lexical class of the captions of the metadata $n°k$ and aligned with $M_k$. We also use a Gaussian function with small standard deviations $\sigma y = TextHeight/2$ and $\sigma x = \sigma y \times 2$ that depend on the text height of the word $W_i$. For each word $W_i$ which potentially is a caption having the lexical class of the metadata $n°k$, for each $MCSC_k$, we compute all possible positions of the metadata $(xc,yc)$ by using the word position $W_i$ and the vectors $-\overrightarrow{U_i}$. Then for each $(a,b)$ coordinate in the limits of the pool, we sum the Gaussian function values (5).

$$Pool[k][a][b]+ = \sum_{Wi} \sum_{MCSC_k} \sum_{\bar{U}_i} \sum_{a=xc-3\sigma x}^{a=xc+3\sigma x} \sum_{b=yc-3\sigma y}^{b=yc+3\sigma y} e^{-\frac{(a-xc)^2}{2\times\sigma x^2} - \frac{(b-yc)^2}{2\times\sigma y^2}} \tag{5}$$

$$(a, b) \in [0..W - 1] \times [0..H - 1] \; Lexical \; Class(W_i) = k$$

$$(xc, yc) = (W_i \cdot x - U_i \cdot dx, \; W_i \cdot y - U_i \cdot dy)$$

The voting applied for document structure recognition has a very low complexity in comparison to the voting for object detection in the computer vision domain. The voting process is fast because there are only 2 parameters in a 2D spatial pool and a reduced number of words.

## 5.3 Voting by Using the Metadata Format

Most of the metadata are described by a format or a regular expression. Among all formats, we only selected 4 regular expressions or formats of metadata that match the 10 metadata to detect.

- **Date:** DOCDATE, DUEDATE
- **Number:** DOCNBR, ORDERNBR, DELIVNBR
- **Amount:** TOTAMT, NETAMT
- **Percentage:** TAXRATE

The format of a word W is detected by the regular expression regex(W) or by heuristics if regex() fails. We start a vote around all words $W_i$ that have a regular expression or a format compatible with the metadata to detect. Like the other voting stages, we use a Gaussian function with small standard deviations $\sigma y = TextHeight/2$ and $\sigma x = \sigma y \times 2$ (6).

$$Pool[k][a][b]+ = \sum_{Wi} \sum_{a=xc-3\sigma x}^{a=xc+3\sigma x} \sum_{b=yc-3\sigma y}^{b=yc+3\sigma y} e^{-\frac{(a-xc)^2}{2\times\sigma x^2} - \frac{(b-yc)^2}{2\times\sigma y^2}} \tag{6}$$

$$FormatOfMetadata(W_i) = k$$

$$(xc, yc) = (W_i \cdot x, \ W_i \cdot y)$$

DOCTYPE, CURRENCY, TAXRATE have no votes because there is no text format for these metadata. These metadata will be detected in the voting stage by MCSC or MMSC.

## 5.4 Voting by Using the MMSC

Voting with the MMSC requires the coarse localization of each metadata with previous voting stages. For each metadata class $k_1$, for each local optima in position $(xc, yc)$ with a normalized value $Pool2[k1][xc][yc]/Max\{Pool2[k1]\}$ superior to a threshold $\varepsilon$, and for all metadata class $k_2$ different from $k_1$, we sum the Gaussian weights around position $(xc, yc)$ (7). These coordinates are deduced from the spatial relation between the metadata $k_1$ and the metadata $k_2$ contained in the $MMSC_{k1}$ and the possible position of the metadata of $k_1$ localized by $(xc, yc)$. To avoid interference we analyze pool2, which is a copy of the original pool. We use small standard deviations $\sigma y = TextHeight/2$ and $\sigma x = 2 \times \sigma y$. The threshold $\varepsilon$ is fixed to a very high value with $\varepsilon = 0.9$. A vote is started for each local maximum value of the pool superior to 90% of the absolute highest value of the pool. This important step predicts the possible positions of the metadata from previous votes.

$$Pool[k2][a][b]+ = \sum_{k1=0}^{k1<NM} \sum_{\substack{Optima \\ Pool2[k1]}} \sum_{\substack{k2=0 \\ k1 \neq k2}}^{k2<NM} \sum_{a=xc-3\sigma x}^{a=xc+3\sigma x} \sum_{b=yc-3\sigma y}^{b=yc+3\sigma y} e^{-\frac{(a-xc)^2}{2\times\sigma x^2} - \frac{(b-yc)^2}{2\times\sigma y^2}}$$

$$(xc, yc) = argmax\{Pool2[k1][x]\big[y\big]/$$
$$Pool2[k1][xc]\big[yc\big] > \varepsilon \times Max\{Pool2[k1]\}\} \tag{7}$$

## 5.5 Detection Stage

We have 10 metadata to retrieve from the logical structure [DOCDATE, DOC-NBR, TOTAMT, NETAMT, DOCTYPE, CURRENCY, DUEDATE, ORDERNBR, DELIVNBR, TAXRATE]. The description of the metadata is given in the Table 1. Figure 4 shows the pools contents for the 10 metadata in the same order of the list and for the 4 voting stages in the order of the description.

These pools have been computed from the image of the invoice Fig. 6. The four voting stages vote in the same pool for each of the 10 metadata to detect (Fig. 5).

The detection stage builds a map "Classmap" of possible metadata locations from the 10 final pools. For each coordinate $(x,y)$ in the image, we compute the list of classes of metadata having normalized pool values that exceed a threshold $\gamma = 0.7$ (8). Each word in position $(x,y)$ from the document is automatically detected with the metadata returned by non empty values of $ClassMap[x][y]$. If the word overlaps several metadata in the $ClassMap$, we select the metadata that are found more frequently inside its bounding

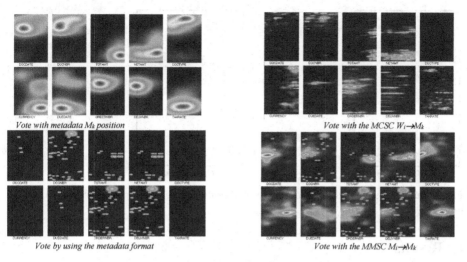

Vote with metadata $M_k$ position          Vote with the MCSC $W_i{\rightarrow}M_k$

Vote by using the metadata format          Vote with the MMSC $M_i{\rightarrow}M_k$

**Fig. 4.** Pools for the 10 metadata and the 4 voting stages

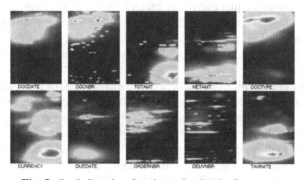

**Fig. 5.** Pools Results after the voting by the four stages

box. The word is also detected if its format *(IsaNumber(), IsAdate(), IsAnAmount()...)* is compatible with the detected metadata.

$$ClassMap[x][y] = \underset{k=1..NbrOfMetadata}{AllArgMax} \left\{ \frac{Pool[k][x/\alpha][y/\alpha]}{\underset{(i,j)}{Max}\{Pool[k][j][i]\}} > \gamma \right\} \qquad (8)$$

$$(x, y) \in [0..ImageWidth] \times [0..ImageHeight]$$

Figure 6 shows the maxima of the combination of the pools from the 4 voting stages and the ground truth. Seven metadata are correctly detected *(DOCTYPE, TOTAMT, TAXRATE, CURRENCY, DELIVRNBR, DUEDATE, DOCDATE)* and three metadata are not correctly detected *(ORDERNBR, DOCNBR, NETAMNT)*.

DOCDATE

DOCNBR

TOTAMT

NETAMT

DOCTYPE

CURRENCY

DUEDATE

ORDERNBR

DELIVNBR

TAXRATE

*ClassMap[x][y] γ=70%*                              *Ground truth*

**Fig. 6.** Superposistion of the maxima of the combination of the pools $> \gamma$ compare to the ground truth.

## 6   Results

The company which grants this work provides a database of 474 annotated invoices. We cut the database into two equal parts, 237 images for the conception of the part-based structure and 237 different images for the evaluation. We found 228 different templates for 474 images. Most of the templates are represented by only one or two images. Only ten templates are represented by a dozen of images in average. For that, our base is very heterogeneous.

It is absolutely impossible to train a supervised method with only a few hundred samples. But for an unsupervised detection system a knowledge database can be generated with a small number of samples. Because several metadata are repeated several times in different places in the document, the operator arbitrarily chooses only one text block for each metadata. Unfortunately, the same operator can choose different text blocks for the same metadata and the same model of document. Therefore, this database is difficult to use for the construction of a reliable knowledge database even for an unsupervised detection system. Moreover, it impacts the evaluation of the system because the text block chosen by the operator for each metadata may be different from those detected by our system (Fig. 7).

Because the ground truth contains, for each class of metadata, only one text block chosen randomly and not all occurrences of the same metadata, our results will be under evaluated. The database also shows a unknown number of annotation errors. We consider the errors negligible for the evaluation.

The results (Table 1) are encouraging if we consider that they are under evaluated by the annotation of the ground truth and the arbitrary choice of only one sample among several occurrence of repeated metadata.

Our detection system is completely unsupervised and works well with a reduced number of images. Several hundred of images from hundreds of different models of invoices are sufficient to build a good knowledge of all spatial relationships. This excellent property is not shared by the supervised approaches, especially methods based on neuronal networks that require from thousands to millions of images for their training. Moreover, our system is highly scalable and perfectible by adding new images from

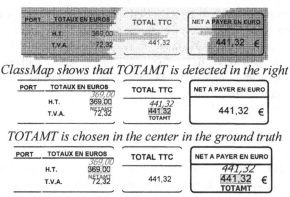

*ClassMap shows that TOTAMT is detected in the right*

*TOTAMT is chosen in the center in the ground truth*

*TOTAMT is falsely detected by the evaluation system*

**Fig. 7.** Example of metadata correctly detected but considered as wrongly detected

**Table 1.** Results of the logical structure recognition on invoices

| Label | Description | Detection rate | Nbr of objects |
|-------|-------------|----------------|----------------|
| DOCDATE | The date of the document | 74,56% | 228 |
| DOCNBR | The document number | 85,46% | 227 |
| TOTAMT | The total amount after taxes | 93,69% | 222 |
| NETAMT | The net amount | 88,88% | 225 |
| DUEDATE | The date of payment | 82,77% | 180 |
| DOCTYPE | The type of document | 76,54% | 226 |
| ORDERNBR | The order number | 90,82% | 229 |
| DELIVNBR | The delivery number | 92,18% | 64 |
| CURRENCY | The currency of the amount | 68,49% | 219 |
| TAXRATE | The tax rate applied | 74,52% | 212 |
| **TOTAL** | | **82,79%** | **2032** |

numerous other models of invoices. The more images and models of invoices that are provided to the system, more performant the detection will be. This property is explained by the robustness of the partial voting. The classes of metadata {DOCDATE, DOCTYPE, CURRENCY, TAXRATE} are the more difficult to detect, which is explained by the fact that they are not always associated with a caption.

Unfortunately we cannot compare ourselves directly to the works described as the datasets used are not publicly available and the evaluation methods are different. It is also difficult to compare our self to other industrial works for the same reason. It is also hard to create our own dataset due to privacy restrictions. We sincerely believe that such a dataset if exists in the future will contribute to advance the domain significantly.

However, all previous works use supervised approaches to recognize documents with a rigid logical structure, which never change spatially. These approaches are trained on the specific models of each document to read. In contrast to existing systems for business documents, our recognition rate is absolutely given without any heuristics, post-processing steps and contextual enhancements. The results confirm the several assumptions we made at the beginning of the work Sect. 3.

# 7 Conclusion

Structure recognition is an emerging field that is beginning to break into effective and sufficiently generic platforms. If we consider the same time scale that has been needed to develop OCR into an unmarked industrial product, the development of document-structure recognition software will require many years of research. However, the need for automatic recognition of structures is increasingly urgent in the face of current digitization projects. Difficult problems remain to be solved. The modeling and recognition of the logical structure remains the Achilles' heel of recognition systems.

At present, each system developed in public or private laboratories operates on specific documents, with structure that is regular, rigid, and is either predictable or already known in advance. Therefore, even today, there are no structure-recognition systems that can automatically decode the structure of any text.

In this paper, we have proposed the very first automatic and scalable system which can recognize the logical structure of business documents without any models or prior information about their logical structure. Our solution can process totally unknown new models of documents. Our detection system can also deal with non-rigid structures.

We have proposed *a part-based spatial model suited for partial voting*. Our proposed model introduce the concept of Spatial Context (SC) as a spatial feature, which describes the relative positions of metadata or caption in a Neighborhood around each word of interest. We have introduced two different types of SC: *the Metadata to Captions Spatial Context (MCSC) and the Metadata to Metadata Spatial Context (MMSC)*. The MCSC memorizes the spatial relation between possible captions detected by the lexical classification of words and the metadata to detect. The MMSC measures the spatial relations between neighboring metadata.

We introduce an original and robust Gaussian voting process in the spatial space that allows to localize and recognize automatically a researched metadata and its logical function. Our voting process is robust against missing information, OCRerrors and annotation errors. Our detection system is completely unsupervised and is working well with a much-reduced number of images. This excellent property is not shared by the supervised approaches, especially methods based on neuronal networks.

In future works, we want to explore other applications in DIA of our part-based model of detection.

**Acknowledgement.** This work was granted by ITESOFT and LIRIS Lab from INSA-LYON for the project DOD.

# References

1. Srihari, N., et al.: Name and address block reader system for tax form processing. In: ICDAR, pp. 5–10 (1995)
2. Mao, J., et al.: A system for automatically reading IATA flight coupons. In: ICDAR97, pp. 153–157 (1997)
3. Cesarini, F., et al.: Trainable table location in document images. In: ICPR (3), pp. 236–240 (2002)
4. Gatos, B., Danatsas, D., Pratikakis, I., Perantonis, S.J.: Automatic table detection in document images. In: Singh, S., Singh, M., Apte, C., Perner, P. (eds.) ICAPR 2005. LNCS, vol. 3686, pp. 609–618. Springer, Heidelberg (2005). https://doi.org/10.1007/11551188_67
5. Coüasnon, B., et al.: Dmos, a generic document recognition method: application to table structure analysis in a general and in a specific way. In: IJDAR, pp. 111–122 (2006)
6. Klein, B., et al.: Three approaches to "industrial" table spotting. In: ICDAR, pp. 513–517 (2001)
7. Coüasnon, B., et al.: DMOS, It's your turn! In: 1st International Workshop on Open Services and Tools for Document Analysis. ICDAR17
8. Mao, J., et al.: A model-based form processing sub-system. In: ICPR (1996)
9. Ting, A., et al.: Business form classification using strings. In: ICPR 96, p. 690
10. Héroux, P.: Etude de méthhodes de classification pour l'identification automatique de classes de formulaires. In: CIFED (1998)
11. Duygulu, P.: A hierarchical representation of form documents for identification and retrieval. IJDAR 5(1), 17–27 (2002)
12. Ishitani, Y., et al.: Model based information extraction and its application to document images. In: DLIA (2001)
13. Cesarini, F., et al.: INFORMys: A Flexible Invoice-Like Form-Reader System. In: IEEE PAMI, pp. 710–745 (1998)
14. Cesarini, F., et al.: Analysis and understanding of multi-class invoices. IJDAR 6(2), 102–114 (2003)
15. Hamza, H., et al.: Incremental classification of invoice documents. ICPR, pp. 1–4 (2008)
16. Hamza, H., et al.: Application du raisonnement à partir de cas à l'analyse de documents administratifs. Nancy2 University, France (2008)
17. Tateisi, Y., et al.: Using stochastic syntactic analysis for extracting a logical structure from a document image. In: ICPR, pp. 391–394 (1994)
18. Belaïd, Y., et al.: Form analysis by neural classification of cells. In: DAS, pp. 58–71 (1998)
19. Tsuji, Y., et al.: Document recognition system with layout structure generator. In: Proceedings of the MVA (1990)
20. Yamashita, A., et al.: A model based layout understading method for the document recogntion system. In: ICDAR, pp. 130–138 (1991)
21. LeBourgeois, F., et al.: Document understanding using probabilistic relaxation: application on tables of contents of periodicals. In: ICDAR, pp. 508–512 (2001)
22. Lebourgeois, F.: Localisation de textes dans une image 'a niveaux de gris. In: CNED 1996, pp. 207–214
23. Hough, P.V.C.: Method and means for recognizing complex patterns, U.S. Patent 3,069,654, December 18 (1962)
24. Duda, R.O. et al.: Use of the Hough transformation to detect lines and curves in pictures. Commun. ACM 72, 11–15
25. Ballard, et al.: Generalizing the Hough transform to detect arbitrary shapes. Pattern Recogn. 13(2), pp. 111–122 (1981)

26. Medioni, G., et al.: 3-D structures for generic object recognition. In: ICPR, pp. 1030–1037 (2000)
27. Opelt, A., Pinz, A., Zisserman, A.: A boundary-fragment-model for object detection. In: Leonardis, A., Bischof, H., Pinz, A. (eds.) ECCV 2006. LNCS, vol. 3952, pp. 575–588. Springer, Heidelberg (2006). https://doi.org/10.1007/11744047_44
28. Leibe, B., et al.: Robust object detection with interleaved categorization and segmentation. Int. J. Comp. Vis. **77**(1–3), 259–289 (2008)
29. Rusinol, M., et al.: Field extraction from administrative documents by incremental structural templates. In: ICDAR, pp. 1100–1104 (2013)
30. Dengel, A.R., Klein, B.: smartFIX: a requirements-driven system for document analysis and understanding. In: Lopresti, D., Hu, J., Kashi, R. (eds.) DAS 2002. LNCS, vol. 2423, pp. 433–444. Springer, Heidelberg (2002). https://doi.org/10.1007/3-540-45869-7_47
31. Palm, R.B., et al.: Cloudscan-a configuration-free invoice analysis system using recurrent neural networks. In: ICDAR, pp. 406–413 (2017)
32. https://www.kofax.com/-/media/Files/Datasheets/EN/ps_kofax-readsoft-invoices_en.pdf
33. https://www.abbyy.com/media/16413/fcadminguide0.pdf
34. Schuster, D., et al.: Intellix – end-user trained information extraction for document archiving. In: ICDAR, pp. 101–105 (2013)
35. Liyuan, L., et al.: On the variance of the adaptive learning rate and beyond. In: ICLR (2020)
36. Katti, A.R., et al.: Chargrid: towards understanding 2d documents. In: EMNLP, pp. 4459–4469 (2018)
37. Zhao, X., et al.: CUTIE: learning to understand documents with convolutional universal text information extractor (2019)
38. Denk, T.I., et al.: Bertgrid: Contextualized embedding for 2d document representation and understanding. CoRR,abs/1909.04948 (2019)
39. Xiaojing, L., et al.: Graph convolution for multimodal information extraction from visually rich documents. In: NAACL, pp. 32–39 (2019)
40. Majumder, B.P., et al.: Representation learning for information extraction from form-like documents. In: ACL, pp. 6495–6504 (2020)
41. Gogar, T., Hubacek, O., Sedivy, J.: Deep neural networks for web page information extraction. In: IFIP AIAI (2016)
42. Cai, D., Yu, S., Wen, J.-R., Ma, W.-Y.: Block-based web search. In: SIGIR, pp. 456–463 (2004). Yu et al. 2003
43. Yu, S., et al.: Improving pseudo-relevance feedback in web information retrieval using web page segmentation. In: WWW, pp. 11–18 (2003)
44. Zhu, J., et al.: Simultaneous record detection and attribute labeling in web data extraction. In: KDD, pp. 494–503 (2006)
45. Lample, et al.: Neural architectures for named entity recognition. In: NAACL, pp. 260–270 (2016)
46. Yang, X.: Learning to extract semantic structure from documents using multimodal fully convolutional neural networks. In: CVPR (2017)
47. Peng, N., Poon, H., Quirk, C., Toutanova, K., Yih, W.-T.: Cross-sentence N-ary relation extraction with graph LSTMs. Trans. Assoc. Comput. Linguist. **5**, 101–115 (2017)
48. Kessi, L., Lebourgeois, F., Garcia, C.: An efficient new PDE-based characters reconstruction after graphics removal. In: ICFHR, pp. 441–446 (2016)
49. Kessi, L., Lebourgeois, F., Garcia, C.: An efficient image registration method based on modified nonlocal-means - application to color business document images. VISAPP (1), pp. 166–173 (2015)
50. Kessi, L., Lebourgeois, F., Garcia, C., Duong, J.: AColDPS - robust and unsupervised automatic color document processing system. In: VISAPP (1), pp. 174–185 (2015)
51. Kessi, L., Lebourgeois, F., Garcia, C.: AColDSS: robust unsupervised automatic color segmentation system for noisy heterogeneous document images. EPS (2015)

# Feature Extraction

# The Method for Adaptive Material Classification and Pseudo-Coloring of the Baggage X-Ray Images

Krzysztof Dmitruk[1]($\boxtimes$) (ID), Marcin Denkowski[1] (ID), Paweł Mikołajczak[2] (ID), and Emil Benedykciuk[1] (ID)

[1] Institute of Computer Science, Maria Curie Sklodowska University, Lublin, Poland
`krzysztof.dmitruk@umcs.pl`
[2] State School of Higher Education, Chełm, Poland

**Abstract.** Baggage X-ray scanners are one of the most widely used tools for maintaining mass security. Baggage scanners use the same operating principle as their medical counterparts, but the task entrusted to the scanner operator is different from that of the doctor. The scanner operator's task is to find if there are any dangerous objects in the X-ray image. The operator has to evaluate the shape and kind of material of the scanned objects within a few seconds. Therefore, there is a need for algorithms and methods that analyse such images. This paper presents the dual-energy X-ray scan image segmentation algorithm Adaptive Horizontal Material Classification (AHMC) that classifies materials into multiple classes. The effect is obtained by clusterization of the two-dimensional histograms of low and high energy images using the sliding window method. On the basis of those histograms, local material classes are created. As a result, local classes are combined into global ones, corresponding to the specific material. Our experiments show that the proposed method achieves performance on the same level in comparison to the standard semi-automatic lookup table based methods, but due to its ability to create any number of material classes that every object in an image is made of, outperforms these methods and act as an initial instance segmentation. The generated segmentation is then used in an innovative pseudo-colorization algorithm for X-ray scans.

**Keywords:** X-ray imaging · Histogram analysis · Image segmentation · X-ray material classification

## 1 Introduction

Conventional X-ray inspection scanners acquire images measuring the number of photons that are suppressed when passed through the scanned object. Such scanner has a fan shaped, collimated X-ray beam whose absorption is measured by a line of detectors, and the image derived from the degree of absorption is produced. Typical scanner use a Dual energy technique (DEXA) that allows

N. Tsapatsoulis et al. (Eds.): CAIP 2021, LNCS 13053, pp. 75–87, 2021.
https://doi.org/10.1007/978-3-030-89131-2_7

obtaining two different images of the same object for two different energies. In theory it should allow to classify the object on the basis of its atomic number. However the tests showed that the objects thickness has a major impact on the classification, particularly in the places where there are many different kinds of materials at a given point. The use of the average energy ratio obtained from the dual-energy scan images is widely discussed in [19]. In our previous paper [7,8] this ratio was used in lookup table pseudo-coloring method of X-ray scan images. Considering the results obtained in this paper, as well as the more profound research presented by Kolkoori et al. [15], this method does not allow achieving good classification of materials the with atomic number $Z \leq 10$, which are the dominant part of the organic material class. Summarizing, the limitation of the dual energy systems is that it only provides an indication of the effective atomic number as an integrated effect throughout the scanned object. Moreover, common scanner detectors work at the 16-bit depth resolution. Such a resolution is beyond the ability of a human sight because, although the average human eye is able to distinguish up to 720 shades of grey in the comparative study, only 8–16 shades are absolutely perceived [14]. In most cases, the resulting images are displayed using a linear color map (LCM) – commonly called pseudo-coloring, thresholding or normalization in the selected range. The purpose of pseudo-coloring is to mark pixels with colors corresponding to material classes. The industrial standard is the classification of the image pixels into 3 possible classes: organic (orange), inorganic (green) and metals (blue). The example of such color map and the colored scan are shown in Fig. 1. All these solutions are incorporated into the commercial baggage scanners constructed in cooperation with Arida Systems. However, these methods require participation of the scanner operator which extends the time of scan analysis. Therefore, there is a need to facilitate recognition of objects and materials through the automatic analysis.

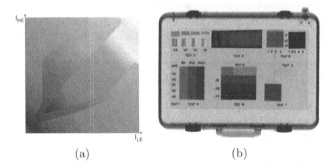

(a)                                        (b)

**Fig. 1.** (a) Two-dimensional Intensity Color Map (ICM) (color lookup table) which maps low $I_{LE}$ and high $I_{HE}$ energy to a proper color. (b) The effect of coloring using LUT mapping from (a). (Color figure online)

In this paper, an Adaptive Horizontal Material Classification (AHMC) method is introduced. In the opposite to the standard material methods that classify materials to one of four or six categories, we propose an adaptive method that is capable of differentiating each material that a scanned object is made of. As a result, we can create an initial instance segmentation for each material class found in the image.

The presented method is not intended to be used for segmentation only but to colorize the image for visual distinction of materials. To propose a full segmentation method, the issues with class boundaries prediction have to be dealt with. It is not possible to determine these boundaries globally due to the X-ray beam hardening effect which causes the linear attenuation coefficient to be dependent on the material thickness.

## 2   Related Work

Attempts at automatic analysis of the Dual energy X-ray images have been made for many years. Alvarez and Macovski were pioneers in this field. They proposed an approximation of the attenuation equations by the second-order power series of two variables and achieved the coefficients using the generalized Newton-Raphson iterative method [2]. Chuang and Huang in [6] proposed direct approximation of polynomials of the inverse of double energy equations with a calibration process. Another method of solving attenuation equations was the lookup table procedure implemented by Kalender mentioned in [12]. However, this paper mostly concerns medical applications with a limited number of materials (tissues). There are also papers describing object recognition in scans based on a combination of shape and absorption [18,20]. On the other hand, there are many machine learning approaches discussed in the literature. The efficient classification of X-ray images method is proposed by Seong-Hoon Kim [13] where the random forest classifier was applied to achieve a fast and accurate classification task. According to the authors, the testing results show that the proposed method improves accuracy, especially the speed for either training or testing. The random forests methods were customized for a large variety of tasks in computer vision, even for X-ray imaging problems [17]. In our previous work [4] classification process is achieved by using random forest classifier and a supervised multi-class classifier based on the support vector machine for classifying X-ray images. We also tried a deep learning solution based on a convolutional network to classify materials in DEXA images [5]. However, machine learning methods require generation of a very large number of training samples for each hardware copy. There are some workarounds for this problem, like in [22], but it may be impractical on a larger scale. Thus, based on the experience gained from the development of the scanner devices we made a decision to develop a non-learning method that will be capable of easy and quick fine tuning to a specific scanner hardware.

In recent years there has been carried out some research in automated inspection of X-ray images of airport baggage [1,9,10,16,21] and cargo [3,11] but much of that focused on object detection, not on the material classification.

# 3  Proposed Method

## 3.1  Method Overview

The main idea of the method is to divide input X-ray image, consisting of two channels: (1) low energy ($I_{LE}$) and (2) high energy ($I_{HE}$) values, into overlapping blocks. For each block, two dimensional histogram of the values in the low energy image ($I_{LE}$) and high energy image ($I_{HE}$) is created. The histograms are clustered to isolate value aggregates or divide larger aggregates if they are irregular. The pixels in the $I_{LE}$ and $I_{HE}$ images corresponding to these aggregates form local material classes. Local classes are combined into global classes if they contain the same or very similar pixels in the areas where they overlap. A weight determining the pixel distance from the aggregate center in the histogram is assigned to each pixel. The pixels with larger weight have a greater impact on the class merge. Global classes are the final result of the algorithm. A general flow diagram showing the following steps of the method is presented in Fig. 2.

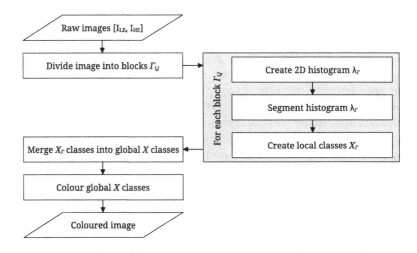

**Fig. 2.** General flow chart showing the steps of the method.

The idea of segmentation based on the histogram analysis came from the observations made when implementing the pseudo-coloring method [7].

## 3.2  Algorithm

**Local Histograms.** The pixel values read from the $I_{LE}$ and $I_{HE}$ images can be written on the quadratic matrix. Let the vertical matrix index denote the pixel value in the $I_{HE}$ and the horizontal one – the value in the $I_{LE}$ image. The values in the matrix indicate the number of pixels with the corresponding values. This matrix will be called the histogram in further considerations. The depth resolution of the input images is 16-bit, but the used histograms are quantized so that the value aggregates form consistent areas. An example of such a histogram is shown in Fig. 3. If the input image contains large uniform areas, the histogram will clearly show aggregates of values. The scanned image of the STP (standard test piece) suitcase shown in Fig. 3(a) meets these conditions.

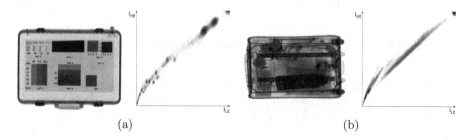

(a)                                                    (b)

**Fig. 3.** Row (a): The scanned image of the STP suitcase and its histogram with the well-defined aggregates. Row (b): The scanned image of the travelling bag including different multiple objects and its histogram (hard to clusterize).

Typical scan images are less uniform and do not undergo easy clustering. The example of such object and their histogram is presented in Fig. 3(b).

The first step of the algorithm is to divide the image into $\Gamma_{i,j}^{(\sigma)}$ blocks – the square image fragments of a fixed size $\sigma$. For a scanner with a resolution of 0.8 mm per pixel, our tests showed the optimal $\sigma$ being 32 or 64. The adjacent blocks contain the common part of the picture. There are defined 3 types of neighbourhood: horizontal (Eq. 1a), vertical (Eq. 1b) and diagonal (Eq. 1c):

$$\Gamma_{i,j}^{(\sigma)}\left(x + \frac{\sigma}{2}, y\right) = \Gamma_{i+1,j}^{(\sigma)}(x, y) \text{ for } x \in [0, \frac{\sigma}{2}) \tag{1a}$$

$$\Gamma_{i,j}^{(\sigma)}\left(x, y + \frac{\sigma}{2}\right) = \Gamma_{i,j+1}^{(\sigma)}(x, y) \text{ for } y \in [0, \frac{\sigma}{2}) \tag{1b}$$

$$\Gamma_{i,j}^{(\sigma)}\left(x + \frac{\sigma}{2}, y + \frac{\sigma}{2}\right) = \Gamma_{i+1,j+1}^{(\sigma)}(x, y) \text{ for } x \in [0, \frac{\sigma}{2}), y \in [0, \frac{\sigma}{2}) \tag{1c}$$

where $i$, $j$ specify the location of the $\Gamma^{(\sigma)}$ block in the $I$ image, and $x$, $y$ specify the pixel position in the $\Gamma^{(\sigma)}$ window. For each block $\Gamma^{(\sigma)}$, the histogram $\lambda_\Gamma$ is generated in the way similar to the global one. Segmentation of regions with aggregated points described here is performed independently for each $\Gamma$ block. Its purpose is to extract aggregates of values and define them as local material classes.

The points in histograms $\lambda_\Gamma$ are segmented using a modified version of hierarchical cluster analysis (HCA). It is an iterative algorithm for dividing a dataset into classes based on a specific metric. For this paper, the Euclidean metric is used in the two-dimensional space $I_{LE} \times I_{HE}$ and the points are weighted by the number of pixels with very similar reading values from histogram $\lambda_\Gamma$. This significantly reduces the number of the initial set, which speeds up the runtime.

**Neighbouring Class Merge.** For the objects and materials that contain more than one block, the corresponding classes from the adjacent blocks must be combined. In addition to the class assignment, each pixel obtains a second value which will be called its weight $W$. The weight metric is the proximity to the cluster and is obtained from the Eq. 2:

$$W_{\gamma_{i,j}^{(\sigma)}}(x,y) = \lambda_{\Gamma_{\frac{i}{2},\frac{j}{2}}^{(\sigma)}(x+\frac{\sigma}{2},y+\frac{\sigma}{2})}^{c}(i,j) \tag{2}$$

where the histogram values $(i,j)$ correspond to the pixels $(x+\frac{\sigma}{2}, y+\frac{\sigma}{2})$ in the block $\Gamma_{\frac{i}{2},\frac{j}{2}}^{(\sigma)}$. As a result of splitting the image into $\Gamma_{(i,j)}^{(\sigma)}$ blocks (see Eqs. 1a–1c), each pixel will lie in four blocks (except the blocks at the edges of the image which are neglected in this step and all subsequent ones). It is possible to define a common segment for four adjacent blocks (Eq. 3):

$$\gamma_{\Gamma_{\frac{i}{2}+k,\frac{j}{2}+l}^{(\sigma)}A}^{(\sigma)}(x,y) = \Gamma_{\frac{i}{2}+k,\frac{j}{2}+l}^{(\sigma)}(x+(1-l)\frac{\sigma}{2}, y+(1-k)\frac{\sigma}{2}) \tag{3}$$

for $x \in 0,1,...,\frac{\sigma}{2}$ and $y \in 0,1,...,\frac{\sigma}{2}$, where $(k,l) \in (0,1)$. This means that every $\gamma_{i,j}^{(\sigma)}(x,y)$ pixel is described using exactly four local $X_\Gamma(i)$ classes – each from another block $\Gamma^{(\sigma)}$ (see Fig. 4). For each pixel there is assigned a maximum weight value of the four classes this pixel belongs to which is described by Eq. 4:

$$W(2i+x, 2j+y) = \max(W_{\gamma_{\Gamma_{\frac{i}{2},\frac{j}{2}}^{(\sigma)}A}}(x,y), ..., W_{\gamma_{\Gamma_{\frac{i}{2}+1,\frac{j}{2}+1}^{(\sigma)}D}}(x,y)) \tag{4}$$

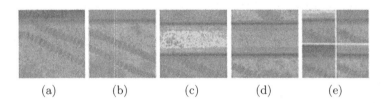

(a)          (b)          (c)          (d)          (e)

**Fig. 4.** The $S_\Gamma$ segmentation for four (a–d) adjacent $\Gamma^{(\sigma)}$ blocks. Image (e) shows their common $\gamma$ segment. The colors in each image are selected independently of the others.

As $X(i)$ classes can only be constructed based on the adjacent $\Gamma^{(\sigma)}$ blocks, for the final result it is necessary to create global classes which will be denoted as $\Xi(i)$. Combination of local classes $X_\Gamma(j)$ into the global classes $\Xi(i)$ is done using two non-directed graphs: weighted $G_t$ with $\omega$ as the weight and non-weighted final graph $G$. The vertices of both graphs represent all found classes $X_\Gamma(j)$. The edges between them are created based on the number and weight of their common pixels. In $G_t$, edges are created between every two $X(i), X(j)$ classes that have at least one common point in the image. The $\omega$ weight defined for each of these edges initially equals 0. The pixels are sorted by $W$ in the decreasing order. Then the algorithm iterates over all points. In the single iteration step, the weight $W(x, y)$ of the analysed pixel $(x, y)$ is added to the weight $\omega_{X(i),X(j)}$ if this pixel belongs simultaneously to the classes $X(i)$ and $X(j)$ (Eq. 5):

$$\omega'_{X(i),X(j)} = \omega_{X(i),X(j)} + W(x, y) \text{ if } (x, y) \in X(i) \wedge (x, y) \in X(j) \qquad (5)$$

If, after completing the iteration step, $\omega'_{X(i),X(j)} > 0$ weight of the edge between the classes $X(i)$ and $X(j)$ is positive, the edge between these two classes is established in the final graph $G$. If there is an edge in $G_t$ between the classes $X(i)$ and $X(j)$, but the pixel being analysed is in $X(i)$ and not in $X(j)$, the weight $W(x, y)$ of the analysed pixel $(x, y)$ is subtracted from the weight $\omega_{X(i),X(j)}$ (Eq. 6):

$$\omega'_{X(i),X(j)} = \omega_{X(i),X(j)} - W(x, y) \text{ if } (x, y) \in X(i) \wedge (x, y) \notin X(j) \qquad (6)$$

The previously established edges between the classes $X(i)$ and $X(j)$ in the $G$ graph are not broken even if the corresponding edges in the $G_t$ graph obtain a negative value. Owing to this approach, pixel classes with a comparable weight can be combined while the points of low weight will not disconnect the previously connected sub-graphs of the $G$ graph.

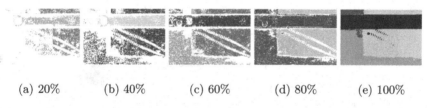

(a) 20%        (b) 40%        (c) 60%        (d) 80%        (e) 100%

**Fig. 5.** Progress of the iterative class linking algorithm in the subregion of the sample image. The classes $\Xi(i)$ are distinguished by the color. The results are shown for 20, 40, 60, 80, 100% of linked points.

The steps of the presented algorithm are displayed in Fig. 5. The result of this algorithm are global classes $\Xi(i)$ equivalent to the consistent sub-graphs of the $G$ graph. These classes are displayed in Fig. 6.

## 3.3  Pseudo-Coloring

From the scanner operator's point of view, binary images mapping pixels to classes are not very helpful. The expected result is an easy-to-interpret, colored image, allowing the materials to be easily distinguished. To achieve this, for each $\Xi$ class, its Intensity Color Map (ICM) is built.

Because the segmented $\Xi$ classes have histograms that occupy only a small part of the $I_{LE} \times I_{HE}$ space we can assign a specific color gradient in the HSV color model to each class. HSV is a color model that separates luminance (Value)

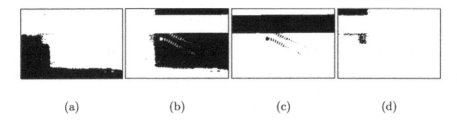

(a)          (b)          (c)          (d)

**Fig. 6.** The $\Xi(i)$ classes resulting from segmentation.

from its chromatic components (Hue and Saturation) so that it is more closely aligned with the way human eyes perceive colors. The hue (H) component for the $\Xi$ class is taken from the ICM from the position of the mean value of the histogram of that class. All points in the $\Xi$ class histogram are surrounded by a bounding box and the lower-left point is assigned the HSV value (H, S = 1.0, V = 0.1), and the upper-right point is (H, S = 1.0, V = 0.9). The value (V) component for each ICM point is directly proportional to the number of intensity points in the $\Xi$ class histogram at that point on the map. Examples of such ICM gradients are shown in the Fig. 7.

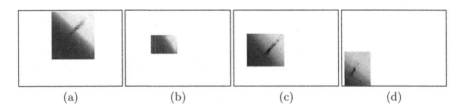

(a)          (b)          (c)          (d)

**Fig. 7.** Examples of Intensity Color Maps (ICM) created for different $\Xi$ classes along with the points used to create them. Each class uses a separate gradient and does not depend on the others.

### 3.4   Evaluation Metrics

The quality of classification problem of the proposed method was evaluated using two standard, common metrics: Precision (PPV) and Recall (TPR) defined as follows:

$$PPV = \frac{\text{true positives}}{\text{true positives} + \text{false positives}} \tag{7}$$

$$TPR = \frac{\text{true positives}}{\text{true positives} + \text{false negatives}} \tag{8}$$

The quality of the segmentation was assesed by Dice Sorensen Coefficient (DSC) defined by:

$$DSC = \frac{2 \cdot \text{true positives}}{2 \cdot \text{true positives} + \text{false positives} + \text{false negatives}} \tag{9}$$

## 4   Experimental Results

**Experimental Setup.** A series of experiments was performed on the full-scale prototype of the customs inspection system developed and manufactured by the Arida Systems Sp. z o.o. The applied X-ray tube was XRB160P from Spellman. It has an anode made of tungsten set on the 30° angle and the X-ray window filtered by the 4 mm layer of aluminium. It was set to operate with 160 kVp voltage and 0.7 mA current. The detector strip was built of eight X-Card 0.8-128DE detection cards from DT. Spatial resolution of each card was 0.8 mm per pixel. The widths of all acquired images were 1024 pixels and the height depended on the scanning time.

For the tests 12 sets of objects were built to mimic the distribution of bags in public places. These sets were scanned and on each image one particular object was chosen. Due to the characteristics of the algorithm, the selected objects were composed of uniform material. The expert manual segmentation, which separates this object from the background and other objects was performed for each of them. The mask created in this step serves as the ground truth. Afterwards, the results of the manual, expert segmentation were compared with those of two algorithms: (1) the semi-automatic LUT based algorithm and (2) the fully automatic histogram based algorithm described in Sect. 3. Taking advantage of the general application map (see Fig. 1) in the LUT method the results would be skewed by combining multiple objects into one class. To address this, a special LUT version was prepared containing only the material class of the selected object.

**Material Classification Results.** All metrics (Precision, Recall, DSC) used to evaluate the material classification quality for each test set are summarized in the Table 1 for the proposed method as well as for the standard LUT method. All measures show similar results. In most cases, both algorithms achieve very good compliance with the ground truth. It is worth noting that the average DSC value for the proposed method is even higher than for the LUT method: 93.16% to 92.76%, respectively. There is a visible correlation between the low value of similar pixels in the surroundings and the high indicators of segmentation correctness. As expected, there is no relationship between the material class and the correctness of the segmentation, which means the class does not affect the correctness of the segmentation.

**Table 1.** Results obtained for the LUT-based and for the proposed method. Higher numbers are better. Presented values are in %.

| # | LUT-based | | | Proposed method (AHMC) | | |
|---|---|---|---|---|---|---|
| | Precision | Recall | DSC | Precision | Recall | DSC |
| 1 | 93.19 | 95.59 | 94.37 | 89.58 | 91.88 | 90.72 |
| 2 | 99.90 | 99.57 | 99.74 | 99.34 | 99.85 | 99.60 |
| 3 | 92.54 | 97.81 | 95.10 | 89.85 | 98.12 | 93.80 |
| 4 | 99.59 | 95.10 | 97.30 | 96.72 | 97.80 | 97.26 |
| 5 | 97.35 | 98.68 | 98.01 | 91.80 | 99.06 | 95.29 |
| 6 | 100.00 | 95.23 | 97.55 | 99.01 | 98.03 | 98.52 |
| 7 | 53.14 | 54.45 | 53.79 | 62.02 | 74.04 | 67.50 |
| 8 | 100.00 | 95.91 | 97.91 | 96.07 | 99.59 | 97.80 |
| 9 | 72.17 | 97.70 | 83.02 | 77.02 | 93.93 | 84.64 |
| 10 | 99.31 | 98.00 | 98.65 | 99.84 | 95.72 | 97.74 |
| 11 | 99.80 | 97.22 | 98.49 | 93.26 | 99.88 | 96.45 |
| 12 | 99.13 | 99.28 | 99.20 | 97.71 | 99.49 | 98.59 |
| Mean | **92.18** | 93.71 | 92.76 | 91.02 | **95.62** | **93.16** |

For each class, an $\epsilon$ measure of the compliance of absorption of that class with the environment was calculated as the absolut difference between the values of the corresponding pixels outside and inside the class in the image $I_{LE}$. Class edge points where the $\epsilon$ value is less than three arbitrarily set thresholds 0.2, 0.1, 0.05 were counted. Their number is presented in the Table 2 as a percentage of the length of the entire edge.

It is worth to mention that the proposed algorithm is fully automatic while the LUT one was created for specific scanner set.

**Pseudo-Coloring Results.** In the case of a coloring algorithm, it is difficult to propose an objective verification method. The Fig. 8 shows a comparison of coloring with both methods. The results based to the LUT-based method are similar to the images created by scanners currently available on the market. The results obtained with the presented algorithm make it possible to reveal more details in uniform areas. This is done without compromising the result when scanning complex objects with a large number of details. A visible disadvantage, which has not yet been eliminated, is the enhancement of the noise in the image.

**Table 2.** Objects used in the conducted tests along with their characteristics: object name, percentage similarity of surroundings, material class. Similarity of surroundings is defined with ε, which is the percentage of pixels with similar values on the outer and inner contours of the class. The three arbitrary levels of value difference at which a pixel counts towards ε have been fixed at: 0, 2, 0, 1, and 0, 05.

| # | Object name | ε < 0,2 (%) | ε < 0,1 (%) | ε < 0,05 (%) | Material class |
|---|---|---|---|---|---|
| 1 | cork | 62.45 | 42.37 | 5.24 | organic |
| 2 | notebook | 45.66 | 0.12 | 0.00 | organic |
| 3 | soap | 36.76 | 0.00 | 0.00 | organic |
| 4 | plastic bottle | 8.32 | 0.66 | 0.19 | organic |
| 5 | glasses case | 48.08 | 7.58 | 4.78 | nonorganic |
| 6 | clay figurine | 0.00 | 0.00 | 0.00 | nonorganic |
| 7 | clay figurine | 34.6 | 23.04 | 8.65 | nonorganic |
| 8 | spoon | 0.00 | 0.00 | 0.00 | nonorganic |
| 9 | suitcase | 38.77 | 3.82 | 0.94 | metal |
| 10 | thermos | 3.37 | 0.97 | 0.52 | metal |
| 11 | nail clipper | 0.00 | 0.00 | 0.00 | metal |
| 12 | blade | 99.77 | 37.11 | 0.00 | metal |

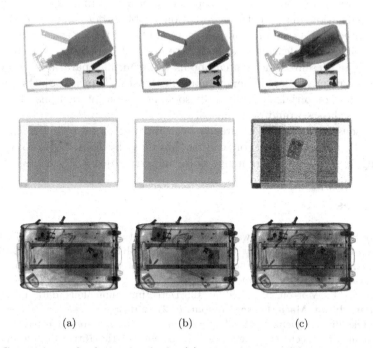

(a)     (b)     (c)

**Fig. 8.** Comparison of coloring methods: (a) original image, (b) coloring with LUT, (c) coloring with the proposed method.

## 5   Conclusions and Future Work

In this paper, we proposed the new adaptive material classification method in X-ray images. We investigated the performance of our proposal with some real X-ray scans and compared to the ground truth data and to the semi-automatic, well-known LUT method. Results have demonstrated the performance of new features and confirmed that this method achieved performance on the same level in comparison to the standard method. But the greatest achievement of our method is the ability to create any number of material classes that every object in an image is made of as opposed to the fixed four (or six) classes in compared methods. It is worth noting that due to these adaptive capabilities our method can be considered as an initial instance segmentation method. The main disadvantage of the proposed method is the high level of noise in the generated pseudo-color images in regions with highly mixed materials.

The proposed algorithm could not be compared with the other methods proposed in the literature as most of them focus on object detection rather than material classification. Significant obstacle is that commercially available baggage x-ray scanners use closed, proprietary algorithms that prevent access to anything but the final colored image, without any material classification information that can be used for comparison. For this reason, only expert segmentation masks were used.

The next stage of our investigations is the recognition of objects in the scans, which we plan to perform using a deep neural network. In contrast to the proposed classification method, the recognition problem does not depend on the hardware used and its calibration parameters. One of the most time-consuming tasks in such machine learning methods is to mark objects in the collected image database. The presented method can be used for initial separation of objects as it is able to return a set of binary material masks. Typical objects are composed of a few materials (usually 1–3) so some user's interactions of selecting and merging classes would be required.

The discussed method has already been introduced into professional usage as a part of a software driver for scanners produced by Arida Systems Sp. z o.o. It is being used among others image adjusting and object detection algorithms.

## References

1. Akçay, S., Breckon, T.P.: Towards automatic threat detection: a survey of advances of deep learning within x-ray security imaging. CoRR abs/2001.01293 (2020)
2. Alvarez, R., Macovski, A.: Energy-selective reconstructions in x-ray computerized tomography. Phys. Med. Biol. **21**, 733–744 (1976)
3. Andrews, J., Morton, E., Griffin, L.: Detecting anomalous data using autoencoders. Int. J. Mach. Learn. Comput. **6**, 21 (2016)
4. Benedykciuk, E., Denkowski, M., Dmitruk, K.: Learning-based material classification in x-ray security images. In: Proceedings of the 15th International Joint Conference on Computer Vision, Imaging and Computer Graphics Theory and Applications - Volume 4: VISAPP, pp. 284–291. INSTICC, SciTePress (2020)

5. Benedykciuk, E., Denkowski, M., Dmitruk, K.: Material classification in x-ray images based on multi-scale CNN. Signal Image Video Process. 1–9 (2021)
6. Chuang, K.S., Huang, H.K.: Comparison of four dual energy image decomposition methods. Phys. Med. Biol. **33**(4), 455–466 (1988)
7. Dmitruk, K., Mazur, M., Denkowski, M., Mikołajczak, P.: Method for filling and sharpening false colour layers of dual energy x-ray images. Int. J. Electron. Telecommun. **62**(1), 49–54 (2016)
8. Dmitruk, K., Denkowski, M., Mazur, M., Mikołajczak, P.: Sharpening filter for false color imaging of dual-energy x-ray scans. SIViP **11**(4), 613–620 (2018)
9. Flitton, G., Breckon, T., Megherbi, N.: A comparison of 3D interest point descriptors with application to airport baggage object detection in complex CT imagery. Pattern Recogn. **46**, 2420–2436 (2013)
10. Hassan, T., Werghi, N.: Trainable structure tensors for autonomous baggage threat detection under extreme occlusion. In: Proceedings of the Asian Conference on Computer Vision (ACCV), November 2020
11. Jaccard, N., Rogers, T., Morton, E., Griffin, L.: Detection of concealed cars in complex cargo x-ray imagery using deep learning. J. X-Ray Sci. Technol. **25**, 323–339 (2017)
12. Kalender, W.A., Perman, W.H., Vetter, J.R., Klotz, E.: Evaluation of a prototype dual-energy computed tomographic apparatus. i. phantom studies. Med. Phys. **13**(3), 334–339 (1986)
13. Kim, S., Lee, J., Ko, B., Nam, J.: X-ray image classification using random forests with local binary patterns. In: 2010 International Conference on Machine Learning and Cybernetics, vol. 6, pp. 3190–3194, July 2010
14. Kimpe, T., Tuytschaever, T.: Increasing the number of gray shades in medical display system-how much is enough? J. Digit. Imaging **20**(4), 422–32 (2006)
15. Kolkoori, S., Wrobel, N., Deresch, A., Redmer, B., Ewert, U.: Dual high-energy x-ray digital radiography for material discrimination in cargo containers. In: 11th European Conference on Non-Destructive Testing (ECNDT 2014), Prague 2014, 6–11 October 2014 (2014)
16. Kundegorski, M., Akcay, S., Devereux, M., Mouton, A., Breckon, T.: On using feature descriptors as visual words for object detection within x-ray baggage security screening. In: 7th International Conference on Imaging for Crime Detection and Prevention (ICDP 2016), p. 6 (2016)
17. Mehta, S., Sebro, R.: Random forest classifiers aid in the detection of incidental osteoblastic osseous metastases in dexa studies. Int. J. Comput. Assisted Radiol. Surg. **14**, 903–909 (2019)
18. Noa, A.G., Reyes, E.B.G.: Image processing methods for x-ray luggage images: a survey (2011)
19. Rebuffel, V., Dinten, J.M.: Dual-energy x-ray imaging: benefits and limits. Insight: Non-Destr. Test. Cond. Monit. **49**, 589–594 (2007)
20. Roomi, M.: Detection of concealed weapons in x-ray images using fuzzy K-NN. Int. J. Comput. Sci. Eng. Inf. Technol. **2**, 187–196 (2012)
21. Wei, Y., Tao, R., Wu, Z., Ma, Y., Zhang, L., Liu, X.: Occluded prohibited items detection: an x-ray security inspection benchmark and de-occlusion attention module. In: Proceedings of the 28th ACM International Conference on Multimedia, MM 2020, pp. 138–146. Association for Computing Machinery, New York (2020)
22. Zhu, Y., Zhang, Y., Zhang, H., Yang, J., Zhao, Z.: Data augmentation of x-ray images in baggage inspection based on generative adversarial networks. IEEE Access **8**, 86536–86544 (2020)

# Sampling of Non-flat Morphology
# for Grey Value Images

Vivek Sridhar[(⊠)] and Michael Breuß

Institute for Mathematics, Brandenburg Technical University, Platz der Deutschen
Einheit 1, 03046 Cottbus, Germany
{sridhviv,breuss}@b-tu.de

**Abstract.** Sampling is a basic operation in image processing. In previous literature, a morphological sampling theorem has been established showing how sampling interacts with image reconstruction by morphological operations. However, while many aspects of morphological sampling have been investigated for binary images in classic works, only some of them have been extended to grey scale imagery. Especially, previous attempts to study the relation between sampling and grey scale morphology are restricted by construction to flat morphological filters. In order to establish a sampling theory for non-flat morphology, we establish an alternative definition for grey scale opening and closing relying on the umbra notion. Making use of this, we prove a sampling theorem about the interaction of sampling with fundamental morphological operations for non-flat morphology. This allows to make precise corresponding relations between sampling and image reconstruction, extending classic results for flat morphology of grey value images.

**Keywords:** Sampling theorem · Mathematical morphology ·
Opening · Closing · Non-flat morphology

## 1 Introduction

Sampling is a basic operation in signal and image processing. The celebrated Nyquist-Shannon sampling theorem relates the bandwidth of a continuous-scale signal to its reconstruction via equidistant sampled values, cf. [12] for an account. Turning to morphological filters, the question arises if the classic sampling theorem has an equivalent, relating sampling with signal or image reconstruction by morphological processes.

Mathematical morphology is a very successful approach in image processing, cf. [6,7,11] for an account. Morphological filters make use of a so called structuring element (SE), characterised by its shape, size and centre location. There are two types of SEs, flat and non-flat [1]. A flat SE basically defines a neighbourhood of the centre pixel where morphological operations take place, whereas a non-flat SE also contains a mask of finite values used as additive offsets. The basic morphological operations are dilation and erosion, where a pixel value is set to

© Springer Nature Switzerland AG 2021
N. Tsapatsoulis et al. (Eds.): CAIP 2021, LNCS 13053, pp. 88–97, 2021.
https://doi.org/10.1007/978-3-030-89131-2_8

the maximum or minimum of the discrete image function within the SE centred upon it, respectively. Many morphological processes of practical interest, like e.g. opening, closing or top hats, can be formulated by combining dilation and erosion. In a seminal work [3], based on previous developments in [1] and related to the work [2], Haralick and coauthors constituted a morphological sampling theorem. Let us elaborate in some detail on the contents of [3]. As an analogon to the bandwidth assumption in classic sampling, the authors of [3] describe how a digital image has to be filtered morphologically before sampling, in order to preserve the relevant information after sampling. Let us emphasize that the filtering amounts there to an idempotent operation, i.e. opening/closing. The work [3] also constitutes to what precision an appropriate morphologically filtered image can be reconstructed after sampling. These aspects are described there for binary and grey scale images, and for both flat and non-flat structuring elements. The work [3] also provides the relationship between filtering morphologically before sampling, and the computationally more efficient method of filtering morphologically on a sampled image, using a sampled structuring element. This is only explained in [3] for binary images, and not for grey scale imagery.

The latter line of work was extended by Heijmans and Toet [5] to the setting of grey scale morphology with flat structuring elements. Let us also elaborate a bit more at this point. While [5] does give some relations between operating morphologically before sampling and operating morphologically on a sampled image with a sampled structuring element for grey value images, there are several limitations. First of all, as indicated the work in [5] is limited to flat structuring elements. Furthermore, there are some inconveniences that arise by the definitions of sampling and reconstruction employed in [5], restricting the approach to dilation/erosion that are not idempotent filters. This has meaningful practical implications, e.g. noise is effectively kept by dilating an image. Reconstruction is also obtained in [5] by dilation. Since dilation is not an idempotent operation, it is seldom used directly as a filter in real world applications, and a corresponding sampling and reconstruction setting as in [5] bears considerable restrictions. Let us also note that the work [5] assumes that the structuring element is already a subset of the sampled domain, i.e. the SE is affected by and acts on only those pixels of the image which are sampled.

**Our Contribution.** As a key feature of our developments we propose a different formulation of grey value opening and closing as employed in [5], relying on the notion of the umbra of an image. Based on this we show how to relate opening and closing in sampled domain and sampling after opening or closing for grey value images, with non-flat structuring elements. One may interpret this result as an extension of the corresponding property for binary images provided in [3].

## 2   Fundamental Morphological Operations

We now recall formal definitions and some fundamental properties of morphological operations.

## 2.1   Morphological Notions for Binary Images

We start with recalling classic notions for binary images, since we may later interpret grey value images as three dimensional binary images, technically. Let $E$ denote the set of integers used to index the rows and column of the image. $E^N$ is an $N$-tuple of $E$. A (two dimensional) binary image $A$ is a subset of $E^2$. That is, if a vector $x \in A \subseteq E$, then the position at $x$ is a 'white' dot, where the default background is black. For sake of generality, we consider the image as $A \subseteq E^N$, $N \in \mathbb{N}$ [1].

**Definition 1.   *Dilation and Erosion, Reflection, Duality.*** *Let $A, B$ be subsets of $E^N$. For $x \in E^N$, the dilation of $A$ by $B$ is defined as*

$$A \oplus B = \{c \in E^N \mid c = a + b \text{ for some } a \in A, b \in B\} = \bigcup_{b \in B} (A)_b \qquad (1)$$

*The erosion of set $A$ by $B$ is defined as*

$$A \ominus B = \{x \mid x + b \in A \text{ for each } b \in B\} = \{x \in E^N \mid (B)_x \subseteq A\} = \bigcap_{b \in B} (A)_{-b}$$
$$(2)$$

*In addition, the reflection of a set $B$ is denoted by $\check{B} = \{x \mid \text{ for some } b \in B,\ x = -b\}$. Moreover, it holds duality in the sense $(A \ominus B)^c = A^c \oplus \check{B}$.*

**Definition 2.   *Opening and Closing, Duality of Opening and Closing***
*The opening of $B \subseteq E^N$ by structuring element $K$ is denoted by $B \circ K$ and is defined as $B \circ K = (B \ominus K) \oplus K$. Analogously, opening is denoted as $B \bullet K = (B \oplus K) \ominus K$. The operations are dual i.e. $(A \bullet B)^c = A^c \circ B$.*

We note that there exist the following alternative definitions of opening and closing which are useful in proofs of various results:

$$\text{Define } B_y = \{z + y \mid z \in B\}, \text{ where, } y \in E^N \qquad (3)$$

$$A \circ B = \{x \in A \mid \text{for some } y,\ x \in B_y \subseteq A\} = \bigcup_{\{y \mid B_y \subseteq A\}} B_y \qquad (4)$$

$$A \bullet B = \{x \mid x \in \check{B}_y \text{ implies } \check{B}_y \cap A \neq \emptyset\} \qquad (5)$$

## 2.2   Morphological Notions for Grey Scale Images

Let $E$ be the set of integers used for denoting the indices of the coordinates. A grey scale image is represented by a function $f : F \to L$, $F \subseteq E^{N-1}$, $L = [0, l]$ (here as a subset of all integers), $N \geq 2$, $l > 0$ is the upper limit for grey value at a pixel in grey scale image; so $N = 3$ and $l = 255$ for two dimensional grey scale images.

Though lattice theory provides a rich framework (refer to [9,10]) for dealing with morphological operators, umbra gives geometric relation between pixels.

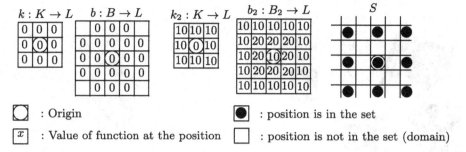

○ : Origin

⬛ : position is in the set

▣ *x* : Value of function at the position

□ : position is not in the set (domain)

**Fig. 1.** The flat structuring elements $k : K \to L$ and $b : B \to L$, the non-flat structuring elements $k_2 : K \to L$ and $b_2 : B_2 \to L$ , and $S$ is the sampling sieve.

Thus, umbra approach provides important and convenient tools to deal with non-flat structuring elements and sampling [1,3]. Using umbra allows us to treat two dimensional grey scale images and filters like three dimensional binary images and filters. We are able to extend many morphological concepts developed for binary images directly to grey scale images.

Our definition of umbra (see Fig. 2) works perfectly for grey scale images, compare [1]. Note that here we are restricting ourselves to discrete non-negative value at discrete positions (pixels). This concept cannot be directly extended to continuous domain or negative values [4,8].

**Definition 3.** *Top Surface.* *Let $A \subseteq E^N$. and $F = \{x \in E^{N-1}|\, for\ some\ y \in E,\ (x,y) \in A\}$. Then the top surface of $A$ is denoted as $T[A]$ and defined as $T[A](x) = \max\{y|\, (x,y) \in A\}$*

**Definition 4.** *Umbra of an Image.* *Let $F \subseteq E^{N-1}$ and $f : F \to E$. The umbra of the image $f$ is denoted by $U[f]$ and is defined as $U[f] = \{(x,y)|\, x \in F\ and\ 0 \le y \le f(x)\}$*

Suppose now $A$ and $B$ are umbras. Then $A \oplus B$ and $A \ominus B$ are umbras. The umbra homomorphism theorem below follows this property.

**Theorem 1.** *Umbra Homomorphism Theorem [1].* *Let $F, K \subset E^{N-1}$ and $f : F \to E$ and $k : K \to E$. Then*

1. $U[f \oplus k] = U[f] \oplus U[k]$
2. $U[f \ominus k] = U[f] \ominus U[k]$

We will employ at some point the following notions.

**Definition 5.** *Reflection of an Image.* *The reflection of a grey scale image $f : F \to E$ is denoted by $\breve{f} : \breve{F} \to E$, and it is defined as $\breve{f}(x) = f(-x)$ for each $x \in \breve{F}$.*

**Definition 6.** *Negative of an Image.* *The negative of a grey scale image $f : F \to E$ is denoted by $-f : F \to E$, and it is defined as $(-f)(x) = l - f(x)$ for each $x \in F$, where $l > 0$ is the upper limit for grey values at a pixel.*

 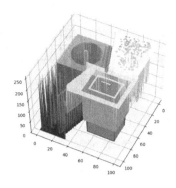

**Fig. 2.** Left: $f : F \to L$ used for examples. Centre: $f|_S$, image sampled using sieve $S$. Right: Visualisation of the corresponding umbra.

**Definition 7. *Dilation for Grey Value Images.*** *Let* $F, K \subseteq E^{N-1}$ *and* $f : F \to E, \ k : K \to E$. *The dilation of* $f$ *by* $k$ *is denoted by* $f \oplus k : F \oplus K \to E$ *and can be computed by* $(f \oplus k)(x) = \max_{u \in K, \, x-u \in F} \{f(x - u) + k(u)\}$.
*We can also write the definition in terms of umbras as* $f \oplus k = T[U[f] \oplus U[k]]$.

**Definition 8. *Erosion for Grey Value Images.*** *Let* $F, K \subseteq E^{N-1}$ *and* $f : F \to E, \ k : K \to E$. *The erosion of* $f$ *by* $k$ *is denoted by* $f \ominus k : F \ominus K \to E$ *and is defined as* $(f \ominus k)(x) = \min_{u \in K} \{f(x + u) - k(u)\}$ *Using the umbra approach, we can define erosion as* $f \ominus k = T[U[f] \ominus U[k]]$.

Let us note that the method to compute $(f \ominus k)(x)$ as given in Definition 8 is valid only for $x$ such that $(x, y) \in U[f] \ominus U[k]$ for some $y$. To extend the definition to all $x \in F \ominus K$, one may define $(f \ominus k)(x) = \max\{0, \min_{u \in K} \{f(x + u) - k(u)\}\}$.

As already mentioned, the operations of opening and closing can easily be extended from binary images to the grey value setting, following the same combination of dilation/erosion as in Definition 2.

**Fig. 3.** Left: $f \ominus k$. Centre Left: $f \circ k$. Centre Right: $f \bullet k$. Right: $f \oplus k$.

Similar to the binary versions, grey scale opening and closing are antiextensive and extensive, respectively ($f \circ k \leq f \leq f \bullet k$, cf. Fig. 3). Both grey scale opening and closing are idempotent (i.e. $(f \circ k) \circ k = f \circ k$ and $(f \bullet k) \bullet k = f \bullet k$) as well as dual operations [9].

Let us now recall the grey scale morphological sampling theorem from [3].

**Theorem 2.** *The Grey Scale Digital Morphological Sampling Theorem.*
Let $F, K, S \subseteq E^{N-1}$, $f : F \to E$ *is the image,* $k : K \to E$ *is the structuring element used for filtering. Let* $K, S$, *and* $k : K \to E$ *satisfy the following conditions:*

I. $S \oplus S = S$
II. $K \cap S = \{0\}$
III. $a \in K_b \Rightarrow K_a \cap K_b \cap S \neq \emptyset$
IV. $k = \check{k}$
V. $k(a) \leq k(a - b) + k(b)$, $\forall a, b \in K$ *satisfying* $a - b \in K$
VI. $k(0) = 0$

*Then,*

I. $f|_S = (f|_S \bullet k)|_S$
II. $f|_S = (f|_S \oplus k)|_S$
III. $f|_S \bullet k \leq f \bullet k$
IV. $f \circ k \leq f|_S \oplus k$
V. *If* $f = f \circ k$ *and* $f = f \bullet k$, *then* $f|_S \bullet k \leq f \leq f|_S \oplus k$
VI. *If* $g = g \bullet k$, $g|_S = f|_S$ *and* $g \leq f|_S \bullet k$ *then* $g = f|_S \bullet k$
VII. *If* $g = g \circ k$, $g|_S = f|_S$ *and* $g \geq f|_S \oplus k$ *then* $g = f|_S \oplus k$

Let us now give some comments on the meaning of the grey value digital morphological sampling theorem at hand of an example, see Fig. 1.

We observe that the sampling sieve $S$ as in the figure will return every second grid point after sampling. The original image and the sampled image can be compared in Fig. 2. Fixing the centre point of the structuring element $k : K \to L$ at the same pixel as the centre of the sampling sieve (in Fig. 1), we see that the range of the structuring element is smaller than the distance between grid points of the sampling sieve. This amounts for a correct sampling and can be used systematically for image reconstructions given in Theorem 2.

## 3  New Extensions

Before discussing sampling, let us introduce the notion of the reflection of the umbra in our setting, and we prove a corresponding monotonicity principle.

**Definition 9.** *Reflection of Umbra. Let* $b : B \to [0, l]$ *be a Grayscale image. The reflection of the umbra of* $b$ *is denoted by* $\tilde{U}[b]$ *defined as* $\tilde{U}[b] = \{(x, a) | -x \in B, l - b(-x) \leq a \leq l\}$.

**Proposition 1.** *Umbra Monotonicity Principle. Let* $f : F \to E$ *and* $k : K \to E$. *If* $F \subseteq K$ *and* $f \leq k$ *then* $\tilde{U}[f] \subseteq \tilde{U}[k]$.

*Proof.*

$$(x, a) \in U[\tilde{f}] \Rightarrow -x \in F \text{ and } l - f(-x) \leq a \leq l$$
$$\Rightarrow -x \in K \text{ and } l - k(-x) \leq l - f(-x) \leq a \leq l$$
$$\Rightarrow (x, a) \in U[\tilde{k}]$$

$\square$

We will make use of the following notion, defined for umbra and its reflection.

**Definition 10. *Translation of an Umbra.*** *Let* $f : F \to E$ *be a Grayscale image and* $y_0 \geq 0$. *Then:*

a. $U[f]_{(x_0, y_0)} = \{(x + x_0, y + y_0) | (x, y) \in U[f]\}$
b. $U[\tilde{f}]_{(x_0, y_0)} = \{(x + x_0, y + y_0) | (x, y) \in U[\tilde{f}]\}$

In our work, we will employ the following alternative definitions of grey scale opening and closing. Our notions rely on the alternative definitions of opening and closing for grey value images as formulated in (4) and (5).

**Proposition 2. *Alternative Definition of Grey Scale Opening / Closing.***

$$f \circ k = T\left[ \bigcup_{\{(x,y) | U[k]_{(x,y)} \subseteq U[f]\}} U[k]_{(x,y)} \right] \quad (6)$$

$$U[f \bullet k] = U[(-((-f) \circ \check{k}))]$$
$$= \left\{ (x, y) \in E^N \mid (x, y) \in U[\tilde{k}]_{(x_0, y_0)} \Rightarrow \left[ U[\tilde{k}]_{(x_0, y_0)} \cap U[f] \neq \emptyset \right] \right\} (7)$$

*Proof.* The alternative definition of opening directly follows Umbra homomorphism theorem and definition of opening for grey value images.

We elaborate here on the last equality, (7), which may represent the most intricate step:

$(x, y) \in U[f \bullet k] = U[(-((-f) \circ k))]$
$\Leftrightarrow$ for any $\alpha > 0$, $(x, l + \alpha - y) \notin U[((-f) \circ k)]$
$\Leftrightarrow$ for any $\alpha > 0$, for any $(x_0, y_0)$, $y_0 \geq 0$ satisfying
$\quad (x, l + \alpha - y) \in U[\check{k}]_{(x_o, y_0 + \alpha)}, U[\check{k}]_{(x_o, y_0 + \alpha)} \nsubseteq U[(-f)]$
$\Leftrightarrow$ for any $\alpha > 0$, for any $(x_0, y_0)$, $y_0 \geq 0$ satisfying
$\quad (x, l + \alpha - y) \in U[\check{k}]_{(x_o, y_0 + \alpha)}, \exists u \in \check{K} : T[U[\check{k}]_{(x_o, y_0 + \alpha)}](u + x_0) > l - f(u + x_0)$
$\Leftrightarrow$ for any $\alpha > 0$, for any $(x_0, y_0)$, $y_0 \geq 0$ satisfying
$\quad (x, l + \alpha - y) \in U[\check{k}]_{(x_o, y_0 + \alpha)}, \exists u \in \check{K} : f(u + x_0) > l - T[U[\check{k}]_{(x_0, y_0 + \alpha)}](u + x_0)$
$\Leftrightarrow$ for any $(x_0, y_0)$, $y_0 \geq 0$ satisfying
$\quad (x, l - y) \in U[\check{k}]_{(x_0, y_0)} \exists u \in \check{K} : f(u + x_0) \geq l - T[U[\check{k}]_{(x_0, y_0)}](u + x_0)$
$\Leftrightarrow (x, y) \in U[\tilde{k}]_{(-x_0, y_0)}$ implies $U[k]_{(-x_0, y_0)} \cap U[f] \neq \emptyset$
i.e. $(x, y) \in E^N \mid (x, y) \in U[\tilde{k}]_{(x_0, y_0)}$ implies $U[\tilde{k}]_{(x_0, y_0)} \cap U[f] \neq \emptyset$

$\square$

## 3.1   Operating on Grey Scale Images in the Sampled Domain

We assume that $S, K \subseteq E^{N-1}$ and $k : K \to E$ satisfies the conditions mentioned in Theorem 2.

The following is the main result of this paper. Theorem 3 provides the relation between opening, closing, sampling and reconstruction of grey value images, where the filter and structuring element can be non-flat.

**Theorem 3.** *Grey Scale Sample Opening and Closing Bounds Theorem.* Let $B = B \circ K$ and $b = b \circ k$, then

I. $(f \circ [b|_S \oplus k])|_S \leq f|_S \circ b|_S \leq ((f|_S \oplus k) \circ b)|_S$

II. $((f|_S \bullet k) \bullet b)|_S \leq f|_S \bullet b|_S \leq (f \bullet (b|_S \oplus k))|_S$

*Proof.* Here we just show the proof of the inequality $f|_S \bullet b|_S \leq (f \bullet (b|_S \oplus k))|_S$. The other inequalities can be shown in a similar way. As will become evident, the proof inherently relies on the developments in this paper.

First, we need to show $(f \bullet b|_S)|_S = f|_S \bullet b|_S$. Let $x \in (F \cap S) \bullet (B \cap S) = (F \bullet (B \cap S)) \cap S$, (compare also [3]).
Clearly, $(f|_S \bullet b|_S)(x) \leq (f \bullet b|_S)(x) = ((f \bullet b|_S)|_S)(x)$, so that $(f|_S \bullet b|_S) \leq ((f \bullet b|_S)|_S)$.

Now we use the alternative definition of closing as from Proposition 2 that we proposed. We show that if $x \in (F \cap S) \bullet (B \cap S) = (F \bullet (B \cap S)) \cap S$ then $(x, ((f \bullet b|_S)|_S)(x)) = (x, (f \bullet b|_S)(x)) \in U[f_S \bullet b_S]$:
$(x, (f \bullet b|_S)(x)) \in U[((f \bullet b|_S)|_S] = U[(f \bullet b|_S)] \cap (S \times E)$
$\Rightarrow \exists (y, y_0) , y_0 \geq 0$ such that $(x, (f \bullet b|_S)(x)) \in U[b|_S]_{(y,y_0)}$ and $U[b|_S]_{(y,y_0)} \cap U[f] \neq \emptyset$
$\Rightarrow x \in (B \check{\cap} S)_y$ and $(B \check{\cap} S)_y \cap F \neq \emptyset$
$\Rightarrow y \in S$ and $(B \check{\cap} S)_y \cap F = (B \check{\cap} S)_y \cap (F \cap S)$
$\Rightarrow U[b|_S]_{(y,y_0)} \cap (S \times E) = U[b|_S]_{(y,y_0)}$
Therefore, $(x, ((f \bullet b|_S)|_S)(x)) = (x, (f \bullet b|_S)(x)) \in U[b|_S]_{(y,y_0)} \cap (S \times E) = U[b|_S]_{(y,y_0)}$ and $U[b|_S]_{(y,y_0)} \cap (S \times E) \cap U[f] = U[b|_S]_{(y,y_0)} \cap U[f|_S] \neq \emptyset$
$\Rightarrow (x, ((f \bullet b|_S)|_S)(x)) \in U[f|_S \bullet b|_S]$
$\Rightarrow (f \bullet b|_S)|_S \leq f|_S \bullet b|_S$
This concludes the first part of the proof.

Now, from [3] we have, $\{[(F \cap S) \bullet K] \bullet B\} \cap S \subseteq (F \cap S) \bullet (B \cap S) \subseteq \{F \bullet [(B \cap S) \oplus K]\} \cap S$. From Umbra Homomorphism Theorem (Theorem 1) and Umbra Monotonicity Principle (Proposition 1), we have $(f \bullet b|_S)|_S \leq (f \bullet (b|_S \oplus k)|_S$, meaning if $\in (F \bullet (B \cap S)) \cap S$, then $\exists (y, y_0) \in E^N, y_0 \geq 0$ such that $(x, (f \bullet b|_S)(x)) \in U[b|_S]_{(y,y_0)}$ and $U[b|_S]_{(y,y_0)} \cap U[f] \neq \emptyset$. Then:
$U[b|_S]_{(y,y_0)} \subseteq U[b|_S \oplus k]_{(y,y_0)}$
$\Rightarrow (x, (f \bullet b|_S)(x)) \in U[b|_S \oplus k]_{(y,y_0)}$ and $U[b|_S \oplus k]_{(y,y_0)} \cap U[f] \neq \emptyset$
$\Rightarrow (x, (f \bullet b|_S)(x)) \in U[(f \bullet (b|_S \oplus k))|_S]$ $(\because x \in S)$
i.e. $f|_S \bullet b|_S = (f \bullet b|_S)|_S \leq (f \bullet (b|_S \oplus k))|_S$     □

Figure 4 demonstrates the interaction of sampling with opening operation. There we have used the non-flat SEs $k_2 : K \to L$ for filtering and reconstruction, and $b_2 : B_2 \to L$ for the opening operation (cf. Fig. 1). The choice of filter $k_2$ satisfies the conditions of Sampling Theorem 2 with respect to the sieve $S$ and also the requirements of Theorem 3, as $B_2 = B_2 \circ K$ and $b_2 = b_2 \circ k_2$. We observe that operation in sampled domain is bounded below by sampling after opening with reconstruction of filter $b_2|_S \oplus k_2$, and bounded above by opening reconstructed image $f|_S \oplus k_2$ with $b_2$.

**Fig. 4.** Left: $(f \circ [b_2|_S \oplus k_2])|_S$. Centre: $f|_S \circ b_2|_S$. Right: $((f|_S \oplus k_2) \circ b_2)|_S$.

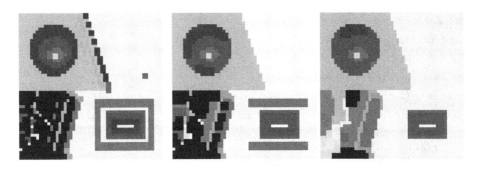

**Fig. 5.** Left: $((f|_S \bullet k_2) \bullet b_2)|_S$. Centre: $f|_S \bullet b_2|_S$. Right: $(f \bullet (b_2|_S \oplus k_2))|_S$.

Figure 5 demonstrates the interaction of sampling with closing operation. In Fig. 5 we employed the non-flat SEs $k_2 : K \to L$ for filtering and reconstruction and $b_2 : B_2 \to L$ for the opening operation (cf. Fig. 1). We observe here that operation in sampled domain is bounded below by closing reconstructed image $f|_S \bullet k_2$ with $b_2$, and bounded above by sampling after closing with reconstruction of filter $b_2|_S \bullet k$.

# 4   Conclusion

In this paper we have extended results from classic works in mathematical morphology, and we have shown in detail how to transfer digital sampling theorems concerned with opening/closing from the binary setting to grey value images. Let us note that it is also possible to extend in a similar fashion other assertions dealing with sampling of dilation/erosion from binary to grey value images. We also conjecture that results can be transferred to colour imagery.

# References

1. Haralick, R.M., Sternberg, S.R., Zhuang, X.: Image analysis using mathematical morphology. IEEE Trans. Pattern Anal. Mach. Intell. PAMI-**9**(4), 532–550 (1987). https://doi.org/10.1109/TPAMI.1987.4767941
2. Haralick, R., Zhuang, X., Lin, C., Lee, J.: Binary morphology: working in the sampled domain. In: Proceedings CVPR 1988: The Computer Society Conference on Computer Vision and Pattern Recognition, pp. 780–791 (1988). https://doi.org/10.1109/CVPR.1988.196323
3. Haralick, R., Zhuang, X., Lin, C., Lee, J.: The digital morphological sampling theorem. IEEE Trans. Acoust. Speech Signal Process. **37**(12), 2067–2090 (1989). https://doi.org/10.1109/29.45553
4. Heijmans, H.: A note on the umbra transform in gray-scale morphology. Pattern Recogn. Lett. **14**(11), 877–881 (1993). https://doi.org/10.1016/0167-8655(93)90151-3
5. Heijmans, H., Toet, A.: Morphological sampling. CVGIP: Image Underst. **54**(3), 384–400 (1991). https://doi.org/10.1016/1049-9660(91)90038-Q
6. Najman, L., Talbot, H.: Mathematical Morphology: From Theory to Applications. ISTE Wiley (2010). https://doi.org/10.1002/9781118600788
7. Roerdink, J.B.T.M.: Mathematical morphology in computer graphics, scientific visualization and visual exploration. In: Soille, P., Pesaresi, M., Ouzounis, G.K. (eds.) ISMM 2011. LNCS, vol. 6671, pp. 367–380. Springer, Heidelberg (2011). https://doi.org/10.1007/978-3-642-21569-8_32
8. Ronse, C.: Why mathematical morphology needs complete lattices. Signal Process. **21**(2), 129–154 (1990). https://doi.org/10.1016/0165-1684(90)90046-2
9. Ronse, C., Heijmans, H.: The algebraic basis of mathematical morphology i. dilations and erosions. Comput. Vis. Graph. Image Process. **50**(3), 245–295 (1990). https://doi.org/10.1016/0734-189X(90)90148-O
10. Ronse, C., Heijmans, H.: The algebraic basis of mathematical morphology: Ii. openings and closings. CVGIP: Image Underst. **54**(1), 74–97 (1991). https://doi.org/10.1016/1049-9660(91)90076-2
11. Serra, J., Soille, P.: Mathematical Morphology and Its Applications to Image Processing. Springer, Dordrecht (2012). https://doi.org/10.1007/978-94-011-1040-2
12. Shannon, C.: Communication in the presence of noise. Proc. IEEE **86**, 447–457 (1998)

# A Multi-scale Line Feature Detection Using Second Order Semi-Gaussian Filters

Baptiste Magnier[(✉)], Ghulam-Sakhi Shokouh, Binbin Xu,
and Philippe Montesinos

EuroMov Digital Health in Motion, Univ. Montpellier, IMT Mines Alès, Alès, France
`baptiste.magnier@mines-ales.fr`

**Abstract.** Among the common image structures, line feature is the extensively used geometric structure for various image processing applications, including the analysis of biomedical image with blood vessels highlighting, graph-shape structures, cracks detection, satellite images or remote sensing data. Multi-scale processing of line feature is essentially required for the extraction of more relevant information or line structures of heterogeneous widths. In this paper, a multi-scale filtering-based line detection approach using second-order semi-Gaussian anisotropic kernel is proposed. Meanwhile, a strategy is introduced to calculate the strength of the observed line feature across the different scales. The proposed technique is evaluated on real images by using their tied hand-labeled images. Finally, the experimental results and comparison of images containing different line feature widths with state-of-the-art techniques have sufficiently supported the effectiveness of our technique.

**Keywords:** Line-feature detection · Multi-scale · Semi-filters · Steerable

## 1 Introduction

Line features represent ridges and valleys in a digital image, they correspond to thin, elongated structures and ridges refer to the valleys of the inverted relief on the image surface, as illustrated in Fig. 1(b). Line feature characterization is the initial step in all aforementioned applications. Amongst the low level image structures, such as, texture, edge, corner or junction, line features is the widely applied structure in the image processing literature. Line structures on multi-scale like ridges or valleys contain determinative information required in image analysis problems, such as, scene understanding, photogrammetry, biomedical [12] and remote sensing data. It is important to have a reliable line detector, especially adapted to different scales. Today, there are many post-processing methods to align segments, group or recognize shapes. These methods are all more effective when the line detector is reliable.

© Springer Nature Switzerland AG 2021
N. Tsapatsoulis et al. (Eds.): CAIP 2021, LNCS 13053, pp. 98–108, 2021.
https://doi.org/10.1007/978-3-030-89131-2_9

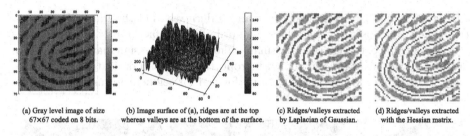

(a) Gray level image of size 67×67 coded on 8 bits.   (b) Image surface of (a), ridges are at the top whereas valleys are at the bottom of the surface.   (c) Ridges/valleys extracted by Laplacian of Gaussian.   (d) Ridges/valleys extracted with the Hessian matrix.

**Fig. 1.** 3D representation of ridges/valleys and their extractions using the Laplacian of Gaussian and Hessian matrix [14], $\sigma = 2.88$, see [13]. In (c)–(d), extracted ridges in red and valleys in green are superimposed on the original image. (Color figure online)

Two parallel step edges construct a line structure, they can be roughly extracted by the Laplacian operator, as in Fig. 1(c). Technically the step or ramp edges correspond to local maxima of the first order derivative [2], while ridges are tied to local maxima of second order derivative in the local analysis of Hessian matrices of an image [5,14]. There exist other techniques to extract line structures, including oriented filters, as presented in the next section.

In this paper, a multi-scale Second Derivative of Semi-Gaussian (SDSG) filtering technique is proposed. The line feature profiles can vary across scale space; they are detected with different filter parameters, whose outputs would be merged latter to create a single edge map. Hence, a function is proposed for the scale fusion considering the desired scale.

## 2  Multi-scale Ridge Extraction: Related Works

Gaussian kernels as well as their derivatives are the widely employed filtering techniques for the processing of low level image structures due to their isotropy, steerability and decomposability properties. The zeroth order Gaussian kernels are used for smoothing and regularization. This section covers the main theoretical principles of multi-scale line-feature extraction in digital images.

### 2.1  Isotropic Filters

For the line-structure detection, several works are based on the eigen-decomposition of the Hessian computed at each image pixel [5,13,14]. The combination of the eigen-values measures the overall strength of the ridge or the valley, as illustrated in Figs. 1(d) and 2(b). In scale space, theoretically, a pioneer work proposed by Lindeberg assumes that a ridge point is defined as a location for which the intensity assumes a local maximum (or minimum for the valleys) in the main principal curvature direction [5]. Considering an image $I_\sigma$ smoothed by a Gaussian of standard deviation $\sigma$, the line-structure measure of the original image $I$ is given by:

$$\mathcal{N}_\gamma(I) = \sigma^{2\gamma} \cdot \left( \left( I_{\sigma,xx} - I_{\sigma,yy} \right)^2 + 4 \cdot I_{\sigma,xy} \right), \tag{1}$$

where $I_{\sigma,xx}$ and $I_{\sigma,yy}$ represent the $x$ and $y$ derivatives of the image $I_\sigma$ respectively, and $\gamma > 0$ is termed as the scale normalization factor.

Bae *et al.* [1] extended the $\gamma$-normalized multi-scale Hessian matrix of Eq. 1 to derive a width-invariant and contrast-proportional second derivative magnitude map. Then a high-level processing is performed for segment formation.

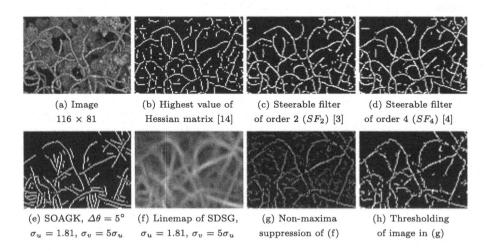

| (a) Image | (b) Highest value of | (c) Steerable filter | (d) Steerable filter |
|---|---|---|---|
| 116 × 81 | Hessian matrix [14] | of order 2 ($SF_2$) [3] | of order 4 ($SF_4$) [4] |

| (e) SOAGK, $\Delta\theta = 5°$ | (f) Linemap of SDSG, | (g) Non-maxima | (h) Thresholding |
|---|---|---|---|
| $\sigma_u = 1.81$, $\sigma_v = 5\sigma_u$ | $\sigma_u = 1.81$, $\sigma_v = 5\sigma_u$ | suppression of (f) | of image in (g) |

**Fig. 2.** Extraction of ridges corresponding of long chains of streptococcus pyogenes infecting grape-like clusters of MRSA biofilm: comparison of mono-scale ridges extractors. Original image source: https://www.nikonsmallworld.com

## 2.2   Oriented Filters for Line Feature Detection

The well-known and popular steerable filters [3,4] are built by linear combination of the direct rotation of the derivatives of the basic isotropic Gaussian. Thereafter, it captures the line structure energy in the direction of the maximum response of the filter. Edge detection techniques using elongated kernels are efficient to correctly detect large linear structures [4,6,11]. The robustness against noise depends strongly on the smoothing parameters of the filter, i.e., the parameter of the filter elongation. Moreover, the elongated filters enable us to capture discontinuous line features, as illustrated in Figs. 2(d)–(e). To extract ridges, the Second-Order Anisotropic Gaussian Kernel (SOAGK) can be applied [6]. Considering the vertical anisotropic Gaussian directed at $\theta = 0°$, its second derivative in the $x$ direction is:

$$\mathcal{G}''_{\sigma_u,\sigma_v,\theta=0}(x,y) = \frac{x^2 - \sigma_u^3}{2\pi\sigma_u^5\sigma_v} \cdot e^{-\frac{1}{2}\left(\frac{x^2}{\sigma_u^2} + \frac{y^2}{\sigma_v^2}\right)}. \tag{2}$$

The choice of $\sigma_v > \sigma_u$ enables to build a narrow filter smoothing mostly in the $y$ direction while enhancing valleys in the $x$ direction. Now, this 2D kernel can

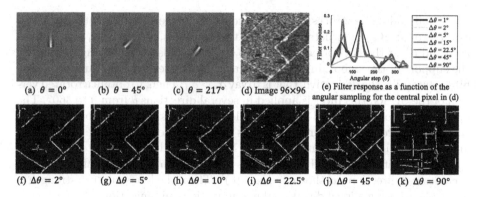

**Fig. 3.** Ridge detection as a function of the angular step $\Delta\theta$, with $\sigma_d = 1.8$, $\sigma_s = 5\sigma_d$, and SDSG responses (clockwise) at a pixel tied to a bended ridge.

be oriented in different directions to capture line structures in the image, see Fig. 2(e). To this end, this anisotropic choice produces a smoothing alongside the ridge/valley, which helps to extract easily elongated features, even disturbed by noise. On the contrary, kernels having parameters $\sigma_v \approx \sigma_u$ are equivalent to a Steerable Filter of order 2 ($SF_2$) [3] and may highlight undesirable features as noise which are interpreted as small, non-elongated ridges [6]. Finally, SOAGK at different scales are applied in [6] to detect the line structures and the combination is done by means of the maximum among the different obtained line-maps.

## 3  Second-Derivative of a Semi-Gaussian Filter (SDSG)

The basic idea of the developed filter is to consider paths (i.e., ridges or valleys) crossing each pixel. Inspired by [10], the proposed technique Second-Derivative of a Semi-Gaussian Filter (SDSG) represents a truncated 2nd derivative of an anisotropic Gaussian which can be steered. It's able to detect bended ridges due to two elongated and oriented filters in two different directions.

### 3.1  Concept of the SDSG

The main idea of SDSG is to "*cut*" the second order anisotropic Gaussian kernel (Eq. 2) using a Heaviside function and, then, steer this filter in all directions around the considered pixel: from 0 to 360°. Hence, the SDSG can be built by combining a vertical semi-Gaussian on the one hand and its horizontal second derivative on the other hand. Mathematically, it is defined by:

1. a semi-Gaussian for the smoothing in the $y$ direction (vertically):

$$\mathcal{G}(\sigma_s, t) = H(t) \cdot e^{\frac{-t^2}{2 \cdot \sigma_s^2}}, \text{ with } \sigma_s \in \mathbb{R}_+^*, t \in \mathbb{R} \text{ and } H \text{ the Heaviside function,}$$

2. a second derivative of a Gaussian in the $x$ direction (horizontally):

$$\mathcal{G}''(\sigma_d, t) = \frac{t^2 - \sigma_d^2}{\sigma_d^4} \cdot e^{\frac{-t^2}{2 \cdot \sigma_d^2}}, \text{ with } \sigma_d \in \mathbb{R}_+^* \text{ and } t \in \mathbb{R}.$$

For signal and image processing, $t$ represents an integer. The Fig. 3(a) shows an example of SDSG, constructed with these two functions, respectively, $\mathcal{G}$ at the vertical and $\mathcal{G}''$ at the horizontal. In order to create an anisotropic (elongated) filter, the support of the smoothing half-filter must be greater than the support of the filter containing the derivative, that is to say $\sigma_s > \sigma_d$. Then, to obtain a rotated version of the SDSG, this filter is applied in several directions $\theta$ from 0 to 360°. The original rotation is centered on the middle of the basis filter; for a better understanding, the rotation center corresponds to the middle of the image in Fig. 3(a), and the SDSG is rotated from this point in Figs. 3(b) and (c). Thereafter, the image convolution with the steered filters allows to compute a derivative information at each desired direction (as shown in Fig. 3(e)). Then, the line structure strength $L$ is calculated using a local directional maximization/minimization:

- addition of the two local maxima regarding ridge detection,
- addition of the two local minima regarding valley detection.

The direction perpendicular to the line structure, called $\vec{\eta}$ is calculated by the bisector between these two local directions (maxima or minima). Then, the line structures can be extracted with non-maxima suppression (NMS) process by deleting local non-maxima in the $\vec{\eta}$ direction, same strategy as in [2]. The Fig. 3(e) illustrates two local maxima tied to the directions of a bended line (here the $\vec{\eta}$ direction is around 90° direction). When the angular step $\Delta\theta$ is well discretized, such a filtering technique allows computing two precise directions of the line structure. The two directions cannot be correctly calculated when the angular step is too spaced ($\Delta\theta > 5°$, Figs. 3(f)–(k)).

In [9], an anisotropic directional filter is implemented considering difference of two half rotating Gaussian filters (DoG mechanism), which can approximate the SDSG filter. Meanwhile, a multi-scale approach has been developed by selecting the maximum response among the scales [9]. Such a normalization function may miss some thin objects, as illustrated in Fig. 5(c)–(d) and next subsection.

## 3.2 Scale Fusion of the SDSG

In one dimension, the $\sigma$ of the Gaussian derivatives depends on the line width of the structures to be detected, as shown in Fig. 4(a)–(b). The SDSG corresponds to a semi-filter. It can be seen as a scan of the projected pixels in all the directions around the considered pixel, illustrated by the signals in Fig. 3(e). When the SDSG is steered in the line feature direction, the $\sigma_s$ parameter allows an elongated smoothing in the line direction, whereas the $\sigma_d$ (tied to the 2nd derivative which is perpendicular to the line) captures the line structure strength. For multi-scale line structure detection, the maximum value among the different filter responses can be selected [9], as in Fig. 4(b). However, it may not be sufficient, especially in real conditions. Consequently, we propose the following improved scale function:

$$\mathcal{F}_\sigma(L) = \left(\sigma^{\frac{1}{\sigma}} + \frac{1}{\sqrt{\sigma}}\right) \cdot L, \tag{3}$$

where $L$ represents the filtered image line structure at scale $\sigma$.

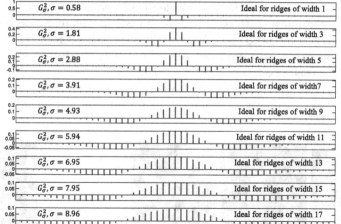

(a) Discrete second derivatives of the Gaussian with different parameters tied to the ridge width

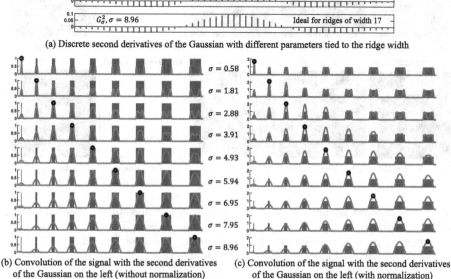

(b) Convolution of the signal with the second derivatives of the Gaussian on the left (without normalization)

(c) Convolution of the signal with the second derivatives of the Gaussian on the left (with normalization)

**Fig. 4.** Ridge highlighting in one dimension (1D) by convolution with different second derivative of Gaussians in (a), detailed in [13]. In (b), ridges are highlighted with the different Gaussian convolutions and (c) takes into account Eq. 3. The original signal containing separated ridges of growing widths: 1, 3, 5....17 is displayed by the blue bars in (b)–(c) while the convolved signals are plotted in orange and the maximum of the signal is displayed by the black circles for each scale $\sigma$, exhibited between (b) and (c). (Color figure online)

This function allows to improve line structure enhancement at the corresponding scale. Its values are always superior than 1, which is efficient for large scales. Thin line features are also well highlighted, as illustrated in Fig. 4(c). Finally, the $\sigma_d$ parameter is considered in the Eq. 3, regarding the SDSG filter, see Fig. 5(h) where thin and large elongated structures are better connected.

The fusion procedure of the multi-scale SDSG can be summarized as follows:
**(i)** Filtering the image with each possible SDSG at different directions $\theta$ and scales (but with same ratio $\frac{\sigma_s}{\sigma_d}$), then compute the line strength $L$.
**(ii)** Retaining the strongest response $L$ after applying the Eq. 3 and its tied direction $\vec{\eta}$ for each pixel.
**(iii)** Suppress non-maxima pixels in the $\vec{\eta}$ direction for the fused image.
The next section presents evaluations and results on real images.

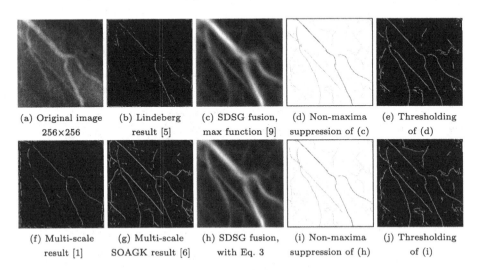

(a) Original image     (b) Lindeberg     (c) SDSG fusion,     (d) Non-maxima     (e) Thresholding
    256×256                result [5]      max function [9]   suppression of (c)      of (d)

(f) Multi-scale      (g) Multi-scale    (h) SDSG fusion,     (i) Non-maxima     (j) Thresholding
    result [1]       SOAGK result [6]     with Eq. 3       suppression of (h)      of (i)

**Fig. 5.** Blood vessel extraction of different widths by non-maxima suppression (NMS) and thresholding in a Magnetic Resonance Angiography image. In (b), (f) and (g), 20% of the highest pixels are preserved while 30% are preserved for (e) and (j). Note that (d) and (i) are inverted images. Here, scales varied between 1.81 and 6.95, see [13].

## 4    Experimental Results and Evaluation

Experiments are carried out on real images. First, a dataset containing fungi images with manually annotated ground truth $G_t$ is used [6]. To evaluate the line feature detection, the *Normalized Figure of Merit* method [7] is employed. Let $D_c$ be the detected contour map of an image. Comparing pixel by pixel $G_t$ and $D_c$, a simple evaluation based on pixel-wise comparison leads to the definition of the following indicators

- True Positive ($TP$), common points of $G_t$ and $D_c$,
- False Positive ($FP$), spurious detected edges of $D_c$,
- False Negative ($FN$), missing boundary points of $D_c$,
- True Negative ($TN$), common non-edge points.

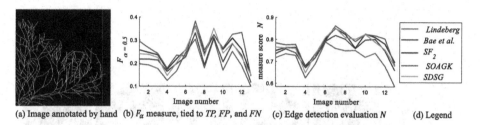

(a) Image annotated by hand   (b) $F_\alpha$ measure, tied to *TP*, *FP*, and *FN*   (c) Edge detection evaluation $N$     (d) Legend

**Fig. 6.** Evaluation of the ridge extraction technique on real images (Fungal images [6]). Detected line structures of image 3 are available in Fig. 7(a).

The normalized $\mathcal{N}$ edge detection evaluation measure is, for $FN>0$ or $FP>0$:

$$\mathcal{N}(G_t, D_c) = \frac{1}{FP + FN} \cdot \left[ \frac{FP}{|D_c|} \cdot \sum_{p \in D_c} \frac{1}{1 + \delta \cdot d^2_{G_t}(p)} + \frac{FN}{|G_t|} \cdot \sum_{p \in G_t} \frac{1}{1 + \kappa \cdot d^2_{D_c}(p)} \right],$$
(4)

where $(\delta, \kappa) \in ]0, 1]^2$ represent two scale parameters [7], $|\cdot|$ denotes the cardinality of a set, and $d_A(p)$ is the minimal Euclidian distance between a pixel $p$ and a set $A$. So, if there are no error, i.e., $FP = FN = 0$, then $\mathcal{N} = 1$. Therefore, the measure $\mathcal{N}$ calculates a standardized dissimilarity score; the closer the evaluation score is to 1, the more the edge detection is qualified as suitable. On the contrary, a score close to 0 corresponds to a poor detection of contours.

The aim here is to get the best contour map in a supervised way. For that, the line features are extracted after a suppression of the local non-maxima, then a threshold by hysteresis is applied to obtain a binary segmentation [2]. Theoretically, to be objectively compared, the ideal contour map of a measure must be a $D_c$ at which the supervised evaluation gets the highest score [7,8]. In addition, from proper binary confusion matrix, the precision ($P_{rec}$) and recall ($R_{ec}$) evaluations are computed, given the overall quality expressed in terms of the $F_\alpha$-measure with $\alpha = 0.5$ allowing a equal penalization between $FN$ and $FP$:

$$F_\alpha = \frac{P_{rec} \cdot R_{ec}}{\alpha P_{rec} + (1 - \alpha) R_{ec}} \text{ with } P_{rec} = \frac{TP}{TP + FP} \text{ and } R_{ec} = \frac{TP}{TP + FN}, \quad (5)$$

The SDSG filter is compared with 4 other multi-scale feature line detection techniques, namely: Lindeberg [5], Bae *et al.* [1], $SF_2$ [3] and SOAGK [6]. Evaluation scores are presented in Figs. 6(b)–(c) for $F_\alpha$ and $\mathcal{N}$ measures respectively. Usually, scores achieved by SDSG are similar to those of the SOAGK, showing the reliability of the proposed filter. Both are better than Lindeberg, $SF_2$ and Bae *et al.* which uses a post processing segment formation. Visually, detections obtained by the SDSG are close to those derived from the SOAGK, excepted that SOAGK creates many straight (small) segments for isolated points, see Fig. 7(a).

In order to interpret the output of the SDSG versus the state of the art techniques for line feature detection and extraction, the comparative tests have been carried out on different real images shown in Fig. 7, including (a) fungal, (b)

106    B. Magnier et al.

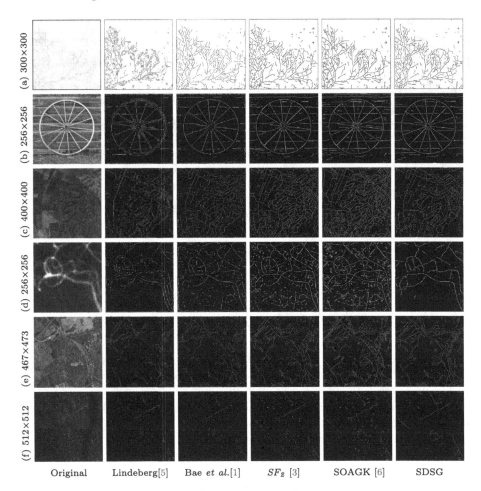

**Fig. 7.** Line-feature extraction on real images with multi-scale filtering methods. The images in (a) correspond to the 3rd image in Fig. 6 in the evaluation. For the images (b)–(f), detected lines correspond to the same percentage of highest pixels after NMS per method, respectively (b) 60%, (c) 50%, (d) 40%, (e) 35%, (f) 5%.

cart wheel picture, (c) satellite image, (d) angiography to detect blood vessels, (e) aerial image, (f) a noisy biomedical image to detect and extract filaments.

Taking into account that the original images are noisy and blurred, the Lindeberg filtering [5] extracted the impure desired lines in spite of non-maxima suppression. The Bae *et al.* [1] output is better visually in extracting finer lines with higher precision because of its segment formation created by the high-level processing. Considering the steerable filter ($SF_2$), it has detected more line features of varied scale. The SOAGK has rather extracted more connected line features, which is considered a strength point in filtering. The SOAGK in general demonstrates good results, particularly for elongated ridges; but too thin blood vessel as filaments and roads are not well detected, while some extracted lines are tripled and blobs are extracted as lines, penalizing this line detector. The proposed SDSG obviously has demonstrated significant result in case of noise suppression. Indeed, visually desired line features as with less or no post processing need for final output, while looking the original images.

The SDSG filter has extracted desirable line features in general, and in particular in Fig. 7 (c) roads (d) blood vessels, (e) large roads and (f) filament without too many undesirable false positive points. Usually, the extracted lines are more pure using the same thresholding ratio, comparing other techniques.

## 5   Conclusion

In this paper a multi-scale filtering approach for line feature detection has been proposed. The proposed approach can be adapted to noisy environments, and is also reliable to detect line feature with heterogeneous types, widths, and prominence. An optimal scale selection function for multi-scale processing is the main contribution of this approach. This approach has been compared to different types of multi-scale filtering methods, including isotropic (using the Hessian matrix) and oriented filters (isotropic or anisotropic). Quantitative and qualitative experiments regarding real images of different types and scales have shown the optimal efficiency and very promising results of the SDSG technique compared with the three major techniques of the state of the art.

Future work will examine the fusion of line feature detection with different ratios of $\frac{\sigma_s}{\sigma_d}$ (described in Sect. 3.1) which will add another dimension to our model. Further evaluations could involve the scales of the detected features, not only the positioning of the detection, as assessed here with $F_\alpha$ measure. The multi-scale responses can also serve as input layer of neural networks in biomedical applications to improve the contrast between line features and background, as explored in [12]. SDSG could bring more improvement in this type of applications.

## References

1. Bae, Y., Lee, W.H., Choi, Y., Jeon, Y., Ra, J.: Automatic road extraction from remote sensing images based on a normalized second derivative map. IEEE GRSL **12**(9), 1858–1862 (2015)
2. Canny, J.: A computational approach to edge detection. IEEE TPAMI **6**, 679–698 (1986)
3. Freeman, W., Adelson, E.H.: The design and use of steerable filters. IEEE TPAMI **13**(9), 891–906 (1991)
4. Jacob, M., Unser, M.: Design of steerable filters for feature detection using canny-like criteria. IEEE TPAMI **26**(8), 1007–1019 (2004). Aug
5. Lindeberg, T.: Edge detection and ridge detection with automatic scale selection. Int. J. Comput. Vis. **30**(2), 117–156 (1998)
6. Lopez-Molina, C., De Ulzurrun, G., Baetens, J., Van den Bulcke, J., De Baets, B.: Unsupervised ridge detection using second order anisotropic gaussian kernels. Sig. Process. **116**, 55–67 (2015)

7. Magnier, B.: Edge detection evaluation: a new normalized figure of merit. In: IEEE ICASSP, pp. 2407–2411 (2019)

8. Magnier, B., Abdulrahman, H., Montesinos, P.: A review of supervised edge detection evaluation methods and an objective comparison of filtering gradient computations using hysteresis thresholds. J. Imaging **4**(6), 74 (2018)

9. Magnier, B., Aberkane, A., Borianne, P., Montesinos, P., Jourdan, C.: Multi-scale crest line extraction based on half gaussian kernels. In: IEEE ICASSP, pp. 5105–5109 (2014)

10. Montesinos, P., Magnier, B.: A new perceptual edge detector in color images. In: Blanc-Talon, J., Bone, D., Philips, W., Popescu, D., Scheunders, P. (eds.) ACIVS 2010. LNCS, vol. 6474, pp. 209–220. Springer, Heidelberg (2010). https://doi.org/10.1007/978-3-642-17688-3_21

11. Perona, P.: Steerable-scalable kernels for edge detection and junction analysis. In: Sandini, G. (ed.) ECCV 1992. LNCS, vol. 588, pp. 3–18. Springer, Heidelberg (1992). https://doi.org/10.1007/3-540-55426-2_1

12. Sanchez, C.F., Ivan, C.A., Arturo, H.A., Martha Alicia, H.G., Sergio Eduardo, S.M.: Automatic segmentation of coronary arteries in x-ray angiograms using multiscale analysis and artificial neural networks. Appl. Sci. **9**(24), 5507 (2019)

13. Shokouh, G.S., Magnier, B., Xu, B., Montesinos, P.: Ridge detection by image filtering techniques: a review and an objective analysis. Pattern Recogn. Image Anal. **31**(2), 551–570 (2021). https://doi.org/10.1134/S1054661821030226

14. Steger, C.: An unbiased detector of curvilinear structures. IEEE TPAMI **20**(2), 113–125 (1998)

# Experimental Analysis of Appearance Maps as Descriptor Manifolds Approximations

Alberto Jaenal, Francisco-Angel Moreno$^{(\boxtimes)}$, and Javier Gonzalez-Jimenez

Machine Perception and Intelligent Robotics group (MAPIR), Department of System Engineering and Automation, University of Malaga, Malaga, Spain
{ajaenal,famoreno,javiergonzalez}@uma.es

**Abstract.** Images of a given environment, coded by a holistic image descriptor, produce a manifold that is articulated by the camera pose in such environment. The correct articulation of such Descriptor Manifold (DM) by the camera poses is the cornerstone for precise Appearance-based Localization (AbL), which implies knowing the correspondent descriptor for any given pose of the camera in the environment. Since such correspondences are only given at sample pairs of the DM (the *appearance map*), some kind of regression must be applied to predict descriptor values at unmapped locations. This is relevant for AbL because this regression process can be exploited as an observation model for the localization task. This paper analyses the influence of a number of parameters involved in the approximation of the DM from the appearance map, including the sampling density, the method employed to regress values at unvisited poses, and the impact of the image content on the DM structure. We present experimental evaluations of diverse setups and propose an image metric based on the image derivatives, which allows us to build appearance maps in the form of grids of variable density. A preliminary use case is presented as an initial step for future research.

## 1 Introduction

Appearance-based localization (AbL) is the task of estimating the pose of a camera directly from the image content, avoiding any explicit representation of the 3D geometrical elements of the scene (typically keypoints and segments). The key assumption supporting AbL is that all the possible images in a given environment, considered as vectors in the image-size dimension space, configure a manifold (the *Image Manifold*) that can be traversed by changing the pose of the camera [2, 4, 6]. Formally, this means that the camera pose, given by $\mathbf{x} = (x, y, \theta)$ for planar motion, articulates the IM.

Working directly with the IM is impractical for a number of reasons, including not only its huge dimensionality, but also because it presents a highly twisted and non-differentiable structure, mostly due to image discontinuities and occlusion

N. Tsapatsoulis et al. (Eds.): CAIP 2021, LNCS 13053, pp. 109–119, 2021.
https://doi.org/10.1007/978-3-030-89131-2_10

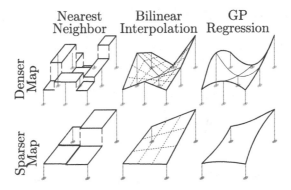

**Fig. 1.** Different approximations of a Descriptor Manifold, using sets of pose-descriptor samples (*appearance maps*, circles) with diverse sampling rates (rows) and descriptor regression methods (columns).

boundaries [17]. The common solution to alleviate these issues is to code the image content with a compact whole-image descriptor that projects the image points into a much lower-dimension and smother space, named the *Descriptor Manifold* (DM).

In this scenario, AbL consists of, given a query image descriptor $\mathbf{d}_q$, estimating the pose of the camera: $\mathbf{x}_q = \phi(\mathbf{d}_q)$. In practice, this equation is not available since it implies knowing the continuous shape of the DM for a given environment. Instead, the DM is represented through a set of samples in the form of descriptor-pose pairs, which is called the *appearance map* ($\mathcal{M}$). Thus, AbL becomes the problem of numerically estimate the relation between descriptors and poses $\hat{\mathbf{x}}_q \approx \hat{\phi}_{\mathcal{M}}(\mathbf{d}_q)$ from the samples of the map. Selecting the adequate samples of the appearance map is key for the precise approximation of the DM, and consequently, for the performance of AbL.

In this paper, we analyze the level of accuracy that can be achieved when approximating the DM with different regression techniques, which is of great interest for tackling AbL. To that purpose, given appearance maps shaped as planar position grids, we compare different approaches for approximating the DM by taking into consideration the following parameters:

- **Sampling density:** the distance between the map samples in the grid, illustrated in Fig. 1 by two maps composed of closer (top row) or further (bottom row) samples.

- **The estimation method:** the technique employed to predict descriptor values at unmapped areas (corresponding to each column in Fig. 1) determines the generalizability of the map, so that those that provide more accurate predictions will ensure better localization performance.

- **The image appearance:** ideally, the map sampling should not be fixed but dependent on the image content (e.g. areas with significant changes, like highly textured zones, or with occlusions, would require a denser sampling). Besides, the estimation method should also be taken into account to reduce the number of samples needed to obtain an optimal map that maximizes the reconstruction accuracy.

Thus, we contribute with an experimental analysis comparing diverse estimation techniques and densities for two different holistic descriptors into a virtual indoor environment, in order to find the best setup regarding both parameters. Additionally, we propose a simple image-based metric to adjust the density of the map, based on the image derivatives. To illustrate this, we also present a use case in a simple setup while further research in more complex scenarios is left for future work.

## 2    Methodology

This section introduces a set of elements that will be employed in the subsequent experimental analysis: the appearance map, the employed state-of-the-art holistic descriptors, the considered metrics and, finally, the estimation methods.

### 2.1    Appearance Map

We define the appearance map $\mathcal{M} = \{(\mathbf{x}_i, \mathbf{d}_i) \,|\, i = 0...M\}$ as the set of pairs composed of an image global descriptor $\mathbf{d}_i \in \mathbb{R}^d$ and the camera pose $\mathbf{x}_i \in SE(2)$ from where the image was captured. Note that these pairs represent the samples of the DM, which are employed to perform interpolation.

### 2.2    Global Descriptor

In this work, we have chosen two of the most employed state-of-the-art Deep Learning-based global descriptors to codify the information in the images.

*VGGNet* [15] is one of the most renowned Convolutional Neural Networks in the literature, whose first convolutional layers hold rich feature maps that have been employed in diverse Computer Vision tasks such as image synthesis [18]. Regarding its perceptiveness, we have employed as holistic descriptor the 4096-sized FC_6 layer from the VGG-16 network.

Also, the *NetVLAD* image descriptor [1] is a 4096-sized descriptor designed for Visual Localization with high performance against radiometric changes, commonly employed in Place Recognition works [13,16].

### 2.3    Metrics

In the presented experiments, given the dimensionality of the applied descriptors, we determine the **cosine similarity** ($CS$) to obtain a normalized measure of the resemblance between a certain estimated descriptor ($\hat{\mathbf{d}}_q$) and the actual observed one ($\mathbf{d}_{gt}$):

$$CS(\hat{\mathbf{d}}_q, \mathbf{d}_{gt}) = \frac{\hat{\mathbf{d}}_q^{\mathsf{T}} \mathbf{d}_{gt}}{||\hat{\mathbf{d}}_q|| \cdot ||\mathbf{d}_{gt}||}. \tag{1}$$

On the other hand, we propose the **mean derivative module** of the image $I$ as a measurement of the image discontinuity content (i.e. the amount of texture, occlusion borders, etc.) for the adaptive sampling of the map:

$$G = \frac{1}{HW} \sum_{}^{H} \sum_{}^{W} ||\nabla I||_2, \tag{2}$$

with $H, W$ being the height and width of the image, respectively.

### 2.4   Evaluated Estimation Approaches

These are the three compared methods that are built from $\mathcal{M}$ for the purpose of estimating descriptor values at unvisited poses. They produce a numerical approximation of the structure of the DM by modelling $\hat{\phi}_{\mathcal{M}}^{-1}$:

- **Nearest Neighbor (NN).** The NN or *piecewise constant* interpolation (left column in Fig. 1) is the counterpart of traditional *Place Recognition* [3,9], which solves AbL by assigning the pose of the nearest descriptor to the query one. NN models the *observational descriptor function* without considering interpolation between the samples of $\mathcal{M}$, assigning to a query location the descriptor of the nearest element of the map (in the pose space).
- **Bilinear interpolation.** Motivated by the linear interpolation of the appearance proposed in [10], we propose a bilinear interpolation method for the descriptor value prediction at unvisited places. We address such interpolation (middle column in Fig. 1) by forming a cell with $Q$ map samples and computing independent bilinear interpolations for each component of the holistic descriptor.
- **Gaussian Process estimation.** Similarly to the authors of [5,7,14], we employ non-parametric Gaussian Process regression [12] to predict descriptor values based on the pose similarity measured by the kernel proposed in [6]. Specifically, we employ a single GP that considers the entire DM, or equivalently, the whole appearance map, as training data for the regression process. However, in order to achieve computational tractability, we implemented the *Subset of Datapoints* approximation [8,12], selecting the $Q$ nearest pairs in pose to the query as training samples for the GP regression.

## 3   Experiments

Here we present three different experiments: the first measures the accuracy of the DM approximation for the three above-described methods within appearance maps of different density, while the two remaining investigate the association between the image content and the DM approximation, using for that our

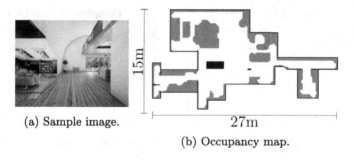

(a) Sample image.                              27m

(b) Occupancy map.

**Fig. 2.** (a) An example image from the UnrealCV *Archinteriors Vol2Scene1* dataset and (b) the occupancy map of the environment.

proposed image-based metric. Note that, pursuing a clearer insight for the experiments, we will suppress the rotational component of the camera pose, gathering images at position grids with the camera pointing to the same direction.

### 3.1 Approximation Accuracy of the Descriptor Manifold

This first experiment aims to study the accuracy achieved when approximating a DM with appearance maps of different densities and the different estimation approaches introduced in Sect. 2.4.

This evaluation has been carried out using images from the UnrealCV *Archinteriors Vol2Scene1* dataset [11] (refer to Fig. 2(a)), where we could gather realistic virtual indoor images at any desired location of the map shown in Fig. 2(b). We have built appearance maps with different densities in this dataset, being the most dense a regular grid with a distance of 0.2 m between samples, from which sparser maps have been built by sub-sampling.

For the training and testing of the DM interpolation, we have also gathered a large subset of images placed at random positions within the environment. A subset of 20% of these samples has been used for GP parameter optimization (unused for the other approaches), and the remaining have been left for measuring the error at those places. Concretely, regarding the bilinear interpolation and the GP regression, we have used the four nearest map samples to the query one (in a square-shaped manner) as known, or training, data for the prediction. Finally, for the GP-based method, as its output is a Gaussian distribution over the descriptor space and not just a descriptor, we have considered the mean of such distribution as the predicted value. We have used the cosine similarity (CS) metric to measure the difference between the real descriptor at a test pose and the estimation provided by each of the three approximation methods: NN, bilinear interpolation and GP-based regression.

Figure 3 shows the experimental results of the mean descriptor estimation accuracy achieved for the VGG (a) and the NetVLAD (b) descriptors by each method in the *Archinteriors Vol2Scene1* dataset, and for maps of different densities. The results have been computed with respect to the distance between the

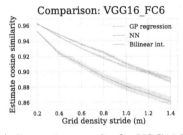
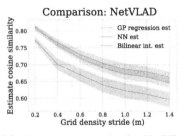

(a) Comparison results for VGG16 FC_6.    (b) Comparison results for NetVLAD.

**Fig. 3.** Descriptor approximation accuracy for different descriptors, employing three different estimation methods in maps with different densities.

grid map samples. In the figure, the line represents the mean value of the CS for each distance and the shaded area represents its variance. As can be seen, the VGG descriptor achieves higher similarity scores and proves to be smoother than NetVLAD, due to the point-of-view invariance of the later. On the other hand, as expected, the comparison between the methods reveals that interpolating between map samples improves the accuracy of the prediction over pure NN, with the bilinear and the GP-based methods achieving similar performance. Indeed, interpolation allows to hold the same approximation accuracy than pure NN for much sparser maps, proving themselves as the most suitable methods for creating smaller maps. Despite the GP employs a more complex regression process, it achieves similar performance than the bilinear method due to the simple conditions of this test. In turn, the advantage of using a GP is that its output can be directly introduced within probabilistic filters, as, unlike the bilinear method, it provides a distribution over the descriptor space and not only an estimated value.

### 3.2 Proof of Concept: The Image Gradient and the Descriptor Variation

This section analyzes how the appearance of the scene affects to the error of the DM approximation. For this, we have built a virtual scene (depicted in Fig. 4d) that contains a ∼12.5 m wall displaying a grayscale scale. Then, we have placed a camera at a $8 \times 5$ m position grid with increments of 0.25 m, and a large set of random positions in between for optimization and testing. Three different images containing variations of the grayscale scale have been used: a striped version, containing edges (Fig. 4a), a continuous gradient covering the full range (Fig. 4b), and a similar gradient but only covering a portion of the grayscale range (Fig. 4c). For this experiment, we have selected the VGG FC_6 descriptor and the GP-based regression method due to the proper performance demonstrated in the previous experiment.

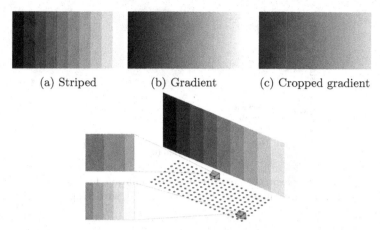

(a) Striped          (b) Gradient          (c) Cropped gradient

(d) Perspective simulation of a camera placed on a position grid (red dots), pointing to a wall containing a grayscale image, in this case the striped version (4a).

**Fig. 4.** The virtual environment for the proof of concept of the image gradient. (Color figure online)

Figure 5 compares, for each of the three variants of the gradient image, the mean cosine similarity achieved by the estimates within maps of variable density. The results demonstrate that the presence of edges, i.e. strong image derivatives, as in the striped image, lead to higher error on the descriptor approximation, suggesting that the DM may effectively hold discontinuities or have a twisted shape that the estimation method is unable to approximate for sparse maps. In turn, descriptors from images with an uniform gradient (a smoothly distributed gradient across the image) are more accurately approximated. Reinforcing this, the cropped gradient (an image with even smaller derivatives) seems to allow an even more precise descriptor approximation. This experiment proves that the image derivatives have impact on the descriptor variation, although it does not seem to be particularly large, considering the range of similarity values. In conclusion, the appearance of the image influences the DM shape and, consequently, the approximation accuracy.

### 3.3 Use Case: Image Derivative-Based Indicator for Appearance Maps

This experiment builds upon the previous proof of concept, proposing the **mean derivative module** metric $G$ in (2) as an indicator of the amount of changes in the image. Knowing this allows us to build an appearance map as a grid with variable density, being sparser in areas with small changes and denser otherwise. Again, we have employed the VGG descriptor and the GP regression method within the virtual scene from Sect. 3.1 depicting the striped image (Fig. 4a).

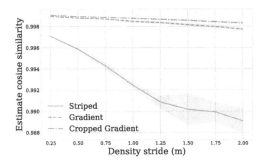

**Fig. 5.** Comparison between the descriptor approximation for the virtual scene of Fig. 4d depicting the three images of Fig. 4, compared with respect to the density of the map.

Specifically, the experiment followed this procedure: i) first, we have started from the most dense grid, with samples 0.25 m apart (see Fig. 6a), and grouped them in *cells* (samples forming a square shape); ii) then, we have computed the mean $G$ of the cell vertices to estimate which of them could be approximated with a more sparse sampling; iii) if the mean $G$ value of four adjacent cells falls below an experimentally chosen threshold, they are merged becoming a 0.5 m-sized cell. This process is iteratively repeated, merging adjacent cells until one of them surpasses the experimental threshold.

The first row of Fig. 6 depicts the spatial distribution of the cosine similarity for maps with different fixed densities: 0.25 m (Fig. 6a), 0.5 m (Fig. 6b), and 1 m (Fig. 6c). The number of samples and the mean similarity value for each map are shown on top. The second row (6d and 6e) presents the spatial distribution of the cosine similarity for two maps obtained after the described merging process, using different $G$ thresholds to achieve maps with different accuracies. The resulting maps achieve comparable precision to the regular grids while reducing the number of samples to ∼80% of the original, suppressing map samples which do no provide valuable information for the descriptor approximation. The samples are distributed with higher density at those regions further away from the virtual wall, since their FoV captures more stripes, hence having higher $G$. Evidently, the presented results stem from a proof of concept, so it is worth noting that the metric $G$ should be employed in combination with other indicators capable of estimating other parameters that affect the appearance of the image in more complex environment, as the depth of the scene or the lighting conditions. In any case, we believe that these results provide insight about the structure of the DM, and will lead to further research on map building for AbL.

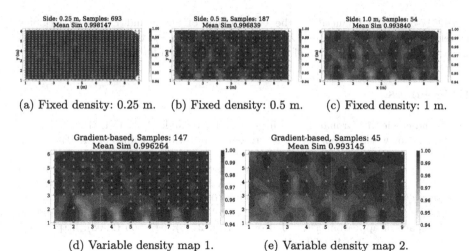

(a) Fixed density: 0.25 m.     (b) Fixed density: 0.5 m.     (c) Fixed density: 1 m.

(d) Variable density map 1.     (e) Variable density map 2.

**Fig. 6.** Spatial distribution of the descriptor approximation accuracy for maps with fixed and variable densities. The wall is situated on the $x$-axis and the camera is pointing towards it.

## 4   Conclusion

This paper has analyzed how a Descriptor Manifold can be approximated by an appearance map (in the form of pose-descriptor pairs) that is optimal for Appearance-based Localization. Concretely, we have investigated three parameters for such maps: their sampling density, the method employed for interpolating between samples, and the image content. Thus, we have first performed an experimental evaluation for three common estimation methods: NN, bilineal interpolation and GP-based regression, in maps with different density. For that, we have measured the accuracy of a set of estimated descriptors at unmapped camera poses, revealing that the bilineal and the GP-based methods perform similarly but with the GP also providing a distribution over the descriptor space, which is particularly suitable for probabilistic localization filters. Regarding the image content, we first performed a proof of concept to validate the idea that the DM shape (and hence the interpolation accuracy) depends on the image content, with smooth areas when the images do not change significantly and twisted ones otherwise. Based on this, we have proposed an image-based metric grounded on its derivative as an indicator of the image *variation*. Then, we have applied it in a use case to build an appearance map as a grid with variable density that significantly reduces the number of samples needed to keep the same accuracy level than a regular grid. These results will be used in further research for mapping applications in order to design optimal maps to accurately perform AbL.

**Acknowledgements.** This research was funded by: Government of Spain grant number FPU17/04512; and under projects ARPEGGIO (PID2020-117057) and WISER

(DPI2017-84827-R) financed by the Government of Spain and European Regional Development's funds (FEDER). We gratefully acknowledge the support of NVIDIA Corporation with the donation of the Titan X Pascal used for this research.

# References

1. Arandjelovic, R., Gronat, P., Torii, A., Pajdla, T., Sivic, J.: NetVLAD: CNN architecture for weakly supervised place recognition. In: Proceedings of the IEEE Conference on Computer Vision and Pattern Recognition, pp. 5297–5307 (2016)
2. Crowley, J.L., Pourraz, F.: Continuity properties of the appearance manifold for mobile robot position estimation. Image Vis. Comput. **19**(11), 741–752 (2001). https://doi.org/10.1016/S0262-8856(00)00108-6
3. Cummins, M., Newman, P.: FAB-MAP: probabilistic localization and mapping in the space of appearance. Int. J. Robot. Res. **27**(6), 647–665 (2008). https://doi.org/10.1177/0278364908090961
4. Ham, J., Lin, Y., Lee, D.D.: Learning nonlinear appearance manifolds for robot localization. In: 2005 IEEE/RSJ International Conference on Intelligent Robots and Systems, pp. 2971–2976. IEEE (2005). https://doi.org/10.1109/IROS.2005.1545149
5. Huhle, B., Schairer, T., Schilling, A., Straßer, W.: Learning to localize with gaussian process regression on omnidirectional image data. In: 2010 IEEE/RSJ International Conference on Intelligent Robots and Systems, pp. 5208–5213. IEEE (2010). https://doi.org/10.1109/IROS.2010.5650977
6. Jaenal, A., Moreno, F.A., Gonzalez-Jimenez, J.: Appearance-based sequential robot localization using a patchwise approximation of a descriptor manifold. Sensors **21**(7), 2483 (2021). https://doi.org/10.3390/s21072483
7. Lopez-Antequera, M., Petkov, N., Gonzalez-Jimenez, J.: Image-based localization using gaussian processes. In: 2016 International Conference on Indoor Positioning and Indoor Navigation (IPIN), pp. 1–7. IEEE (2016). https://doi.org/10.1109/IPIN.2016.7743697
8. Lopez-Antequera, M., Petkov, N., Gonzalez-Jimenez, J.: City-scale continuous visual localization. In: 2017 European Conference on Mobile Robots (ECMR), pp. 1–6. IEEE (2017). https://doi.org/10.1109/ECMR.2017.8098692
9. Lowry, S., et al.: Visual place recognition: a survey. IEEE Trans. Robot. **32**(1), 1–19 (2015). https://doi.org/10.1109/TRO.2015.2496823
10. Maddern, W., Milford, M., Wyeth, G.: CAT-SLAM: probabilistic localisation and mapping using a continuous appearance-based trajectory. Int. J. Robot. Res. **31**(4), 429–451 (2012). https://doi.org/10.1177/0278364912438273
11. Qiu, W., et al.: UnrealCV: virtual worlds for computer vision. In: Proceedings of the 25th ACM International Conference on Multimedia, pp. 1221–1224 (2017). https://doi.org/10.1145/3123266.3129396
12. Rasmussen, C.E.: Gaussian processes in machine learning. In: Bousquet, O., von Luxburg, U., Rätsch, G. (eds.) ML -2003. LNCS (LNAI), vol. 3176, pp. 63–71. Springer, Heidelberg (2004). https://doi.org/10.1007/978-3-540-28650-9_4
13. Sattler, T., et al.: Are large-scale 3D models really necessary for accurate visual localization? In: Proceedings of the IEEE Conference on Computer Vision and Pattern Recognition, pp. 1637–1646 (2017)

14. Schairer, T., Huhle, B., Vorst, P., Schilling, A., Straßer, W.: Visual mapping with uncertainty for correspondence-free localization using gaussian process regression. In: 2011 IEEE/RSJ International Conference on Intelligent Robots and Systems, pp. 4229–4235. IEEE (2011). https://doi.org/10.1109/IROS.2011.6094530
15. Simonyan, K., Zisserman, A.: Very deep convolutional networks for large-scale image recognition. arXiv preprint arXiv:1409.1556 (2014)
16. Thoma, J., Paudel, D.P., Chhatkuli, A., Probst, T., Gool, L.V.: Mapping, localization and path planning for image-based navigation using visual features and map. In: Proceedings of the IEEE Conference on Computer Vision and Pattern Recognition, pp. 7383–7391 (2019)
17. Wakin, M.B., Donoho, D.L., Choi, H., Baraniuk, R.G.: The multiscale structure of non-differentiable image manifolds. In: Wavelets XI, vol. 5914, p. 59141B. International Society for Optics and Photonics (2005). https://doi.org/10.1117/12.617822
18. Zhang, R., Isola, P., Efros, A.A., Shechtman, E., Wang, O.: The unreasonable effectiveness of deep features as a perceptual metric. In: Proceedings of the IEEE Conference on Computer Vision and Pattern Recognition, pp. 586–595 (2018)

# Building Hierarchical Tree Representations Using Homological-Based Tools

Fernando Díaz-del-Río[2], Pablo Sanchez-Cuevas[1], Helena Molina-Abril[3], Pedro Real[2(✉)], and María José Moron-Fernández[1]

[1] Department of Computer Architecture and Technology, University of Seville, Seville, Spain
[2] Research Institute of Computer Engineering (I3US), Seville, Spain
`real@us.es`
[3] Mathematical Institute of the University of Seville (IMUS), Seville, Spain

**Abstract.** A new algorithm for computing the $\alpha$-tree hierarchical representation of a grey-scale digital image is presented here. The technique is based on an efficient simplified version of the Homological Spanning Forest ($HSF$) for encoding homological and homotopy-based information of binary digital images. We create one Adjacency Tree ($AdjT$) for each intensity contrast in a fully parallel manner. These trees, which define a Contrast Adjacency Forest ($CAdjF$), are in turn transversely interconnected by another couple of trees: the classical $\alpha$-tree, and a new one complementing it, called here the $\alpha^*$-tree. They convey the information of the contours and the flat regions of the original color image, plus the relations between them. Using both the $\alpha$ and $\alpha^*$-trees, this new topological representation prevents some classical drawbacks that appear when working with a single tree. An implementation in OCTAVE/MATLAB validates the correctness of our algorithm.

**Keywords:** Alpha-tree · Hierarchical representation · Digital image · Parallelism · Homological spanning forests

## 1 Introduction

Hierarchical image representations describe the content of an image from fine to coarse level through a tree structure, where the nodes represent the image regions at different levels and the edges model the hierarchical relationships among those regions. More concretely, $\alpha$-trees were first introduced to avoid relying on an ordering relation among image pixels (as in Max- and Min- trees). They are based on representing quasi-constant color regions of the original image, by relying on local dissimilarities. This hierarchical representation supports a wide family of image operators on graphs, and its practical usage has been extensively demonstrated.

In this paper we propose a new method to find a semantically correct partition of gray-level or color nD digital images from which several structures, such as Contrast Adjacency Forest, $\alpha$-tree and $\alpha^*$-tree, are directly obtained. Our

© Springer Nature Switzerland AG 2021
N. Tsapatsoulis et al. (Eds.): CAIP 2021, LNCS 13053, pp. 120–130, 2021.
https://doi.org/10.1007/978-3-030-89131-2_11

simplification allows to reduce the computation time by extending the degree of parallelism to every single pixel.

The paper has the following sections. Section 2 summarizes the main related work and Sect. 3 is devoted to recall the machinery and definitions of hierarchical representations. Next, the algorithm for constructing the trees using $HSF$ structures is described in Sect. 4. Finally, conclusions are summarized in Sect. 5. In addition, this section introduces the applications and future research.

## 2   Related Work

Although there are in the literature a wide amount of methods for computing Max and Min trees and other hierarchical representations, results dealing with an efficient construction of $\alpha$-trees are certainly limited. In [3] the authors mainly focus on the computational issues of classical $\alpha$-tree's construction algorithms, and propose various schemes for their efficient computation, using parallelism for modern multicore processor. In [9] a quasi-linear method based on a dedicated Union-Find procedure is proposed. The paper [4] fuses these two approaches. In general, many research papers have addressed computational efficiency of Union-Find procedures, including tuning parallel algorithms for specific computers. Another approach is that of using saliency maps to achieve an efficient construction of the $\alpha$-tree by relying on Khalimsky grids [2]. Recently, some authors have dealt with (memory) efficient $\alpha$-tree computation [5]. Nevertheless, all of them use a classical divide-and-conquer approach, by dividing the original image into strips. The issue is that this division necessarily implies more data dependencies between the strips in which the original image was divided (it makes harder the union-find stage). Thus, a pure parallel approach is not possible. In this respect, none of these methods use the ideal mathematical scenario for promoting parallelism in a natural way, that is, topology. The intrinsic nature of topological properties is essentially qualitative and local-to-global, having the additional advantage that its magnitudes are robust under deformations, translations and rotations. Nevertheless, the results in the literature in that sense are rare, and to our knowledge, no fully parallel computation for $\alpha$-trees and other hierarchical structures is currently available.

## 3   Background

Let us now introduce some basic concepts to be used in the following sections. We will use the notations introduced in [3]. Let $I$ be a digital image and $E$ its definition domain. An image segmentation is a partition $P$ of $E$, that is a mapping $x \rightarrow P(x)$ from $E$ into $P(E)$ such that $\forall x \in E, x \in P(x)$ and $\forall x, y \in E$ either $P(x) = P(y)$ or $P(x) \cap P(y) = \emptyset$, with $P(x)$ indicating a set of $P$ containing $x \in E$.

Let us define $\pi(x \rightsquigarrow y)$ a path of length $N$ between any two elements $x, y \in E$, composed by a chain of pairwise adjacent elements $\langle x = x_0, x_1, ..., x_{N-1} = y \rangle$. We will consider here 4-adjacency between pixels, meaning that two pixels are adjacent if they share an edge. Let $d(x, y)$ be a predefined dissimilarity measure between attributes of $x$ and $y$. This measure can be defined, for instance, as the dissimilarity among pixel intensities, that is, contrast for grey level images.

Given these definitions, we could say that the hierarchical $\alpha$-tree representation is based on depicting an image through its $\alpha$-connected components [13] ($\alpha$-CCs), also $\alpha$-zones. For a given pixel $x$, its $\alpha$-zone is made up of all pixels reachable from $x$ through a path in which within its intermediary steps, $d(x_i, x_{i+1})$ is less or equal to a given $\alpha$. Let us denote the $\alpha$-zone of a given pixel $x$ as $\alpha - \mathcal{Z}(x)$. Let us observe that $\alpha$-zones define a partition or segmentation, i.e. $\bigcup_{x \in E} \alpha - \mathcal{Z}(x) = E$. It is possible to construct a tree of $\alpha$-zones, that is the $\alpha$-tree, by ordering them by inclusion relation. A zone covering the complete image is represented by the root of the tree.

## 4     Generation of the $CAdjF$, $\alpha$ and $\alpha^*$-trees

We present an extension of our previous works (see [7,8]) to generate the structure that allows an efficient construction of $\alpha$-trees, and other hierarchical structures that will be later introduced. The main notion presented in these previous works was the concept of Homological Spanning Forest (HSF). This concept is built by modeling the initial image as a special Abstract Cell Complex (ACC for short, see [6]). For the rest of the paper, let $I$ be a 2D digital image having $m \times n$ pixels and $q$ ordered levels of intensities.

Roughly speaking, an $HSF$ of $I$ is the set of two trees, denoted by $HST_{0,1}$ and $HST_{1,2}$, living at interpixel level within the self-dual cartesian square grid of $I$ and appropriately connecting all the interpixel elements without redundancy. These interpixel elements (also called cells) are the own pixels (having dimension 0), the edges between pixels (excepting those of the border of $I$) of dimension 1 and the corners between pixels of dimension 2 (excepting those of the border of $I$). In particular, if we denote by $\widetilde{HSF_{0,1}}$ a spanning tree of all the image pixels, $HSF_{0,1}$ is a subdivision of $\widetilde{HSF_{0,1}}$ in the sense that it has as nodes all the $m \cdot n$ pixels of $I$ (0-cells) and $(m \cdot n - 1)$ 1-cells connecting them. The $HSF_{1,2}$ is a tree whose nodes are all the $(m-1) \cdot (n-1)$ 2-cells of $I$ and the rest of 1-cells (concretely, $(m-1) \cdot (n-1)$ too) that are not included in $HSF_{0,1}$. Exhaustively applying operations of cell-pairing (coupling a 0-cell with 1-cell or a 1-cell with 2-cell) within these trees, we detect cells (called critical) that remain unpaired in some HSF-trees. Although the critical cells obviously depend on an specific cell pairing, they can be used as combinatorial representatives of integer homology classes.

An example of this (non-unique) $HSF$ representation is shown in Fig. 1. There is one critical 0-cell for each connected component (represented by purple triangles) and one critical 1-cell for each monochrome hole (represented by yellow arrows). However, $HSF$ can be simplified to just one $HST$ for binary images. In fact, this tree remains to be $\widetilde{HSF_{0,1}}$, and, then only 0-cells (which are image pixels with two possible colors) are contemplated for tree building. This tree can be divided into rooted sub-trees, with their root (called attractor) being detected when an edge "touches" two different colors. Such structure is shown in Fig. 2. This simplified representation implies a more efficient topological computation [10,11] and, from now on, it will be the underlying topological encoding for all the digital image structures used in this paper.

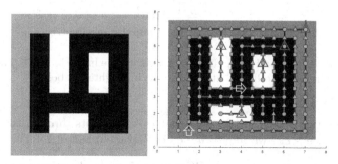

(a) A 3-color synthetic im-  (b) Complete $HSF$ of this image.
age.

**Fig. 1.** A 3-color synthetic image and its HSF. Circles: 0-cells; triangles: 1-cells; solid squares: 2-cells. $(0-1)$-tree: blue and red segments linking 0 and 1-cells; and $(1-2)$-tree: blue and green segments linking 1 and 2-cells. Critical 0-cells (representative elements of CCs): purple triangles. Critical 1-cells (representative elements of monochrome 1-holes): yellow arrows. (Color figure online)

The method presented here is based on building the adjacency trees $(AdjT)$ of a set of $q + 2$ contrast images of dimension $(2m + 1) \times (2n + 1)$ $I_c, \{c = -1, 0, 1, \ldots, q\}$, where $c$ runs over the dissimilarity values among pixels (whose minimum and maximum values are 0 and $q$ respectively) plus an additional trivial contrast image $I_{-1}$. For this purpose, we use the previous simplified $HSF$ framework for B/W images. The $AdjT$ offers a hierarchically and topologically consistent representation, modeling the nesting structure of spatial regions, where each node represents a connected component (CC) or region, and two nodes are adjacent if one of them is surrounded by the other (see [12]).

We design and implement here a parallel algorithm for computing those $AdjTs$ starting from a HSF representation of contrast binary images, so that they contain image information in terms of hierarchical representations (like the $\alpha$-tree and others). We consider here pixel intensity as dissimilarity measure, so that each $I_c$ is a binary image containing: background (BG) pixels as flat zones and foreground (FG) pixels as boundaries.

The computed set of $AdjT$, which conforms an adjacency forest, is called Contrast Adjacency Forest $(CAdjF)$. The $CAdjF$ includes another useful representation, called $\alpha^*$-tree, which is defined through an opposite concept to that of the $\alpha$-zone. Whereas this last is made up of all pixels reachable from a pixel, in the sense that there exists a path whose adjacent pixels do not exceed a certain contrast $c$, an $\alpha^*$-contour is composed of these pixel frontiers that impedes some

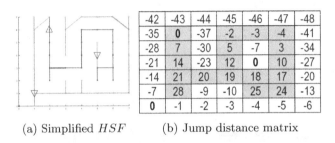

|     |     |     |     |     |     |     |
|-----|-----|-----|-----|-----|-----|-----|
| -42 | -43 | -44 | -45 | -46 | -47 | -48 |
| -35 | **0** | -37 | -2  | -3  | -4  | -41 |
| -28 | 7   | -30 | 5   | -7  | 3   | -34 |
| -21 | 14  | -23 | 12  | **0** | 10  | -27 |
| -14 | 21  | 20  | 19  | 18  | 17  | -20 |
| -7  | 28  | -9  | -10 | 25  | 24  | -13 |
| **0** | -1  | -2  | -3  | -4  | -5  | -6  |

(a) Simplified $HSF$          (b) Jump distance matrix

**Fig. 2.** Simplified $HSF$ and Jump distance matrix for the image in Fig. 1. The distance of each pixel is referred to its CC attractor (zero highlighted in bold).

path between two pixels, in the sense that this path cuts through two adjacent pixels that exceeds $c$. Two interesting cases become manifest for $I_c$ images:

a) An $\alpha^*$-contour can surround a BG region of an $I_c$, denoting a monochrome hole in its corresponding $\alpha$-zone of $I$.
b) A set of $\alpha^*$-contours can belong to a BG region. In this case, the longer this set is, the "weaker" its corresponding $\alpha$-zone is. In other words, it is more probable that the zone contains adjacent pixels with a high dissimilarity. This issue is efficiently computed using the proposed algorithms, allowing a fast identification of "bad" $\alpha$-zones for forthcoming applications (see Sect. 5).

We observe that the corresponding pixels of $I_c$ of the $\alpha$-zones plus those of the $\alpha^*$-contours define a partition or segmentation of $I_c$. Then, ordering $\alpha$-zones and $\alpha^*$-contours (more exactly their corresponding pixels) by inclusion relation, it is possible to construct the $\alpha$-tree, and the $\alpha^*$-tree.

Apart from these trees, our construction allows to compute at the same time (without any additional timing complexity) additional information of regions and contours, like areas and perimeters (see [10]), which might be used for further processing (see Sect. 5). In addition, and what is more important, $CAdjF$ is generated in a very efficient manner following our previous implementations discussed in [10,11]. Two important achievements are thus retained:

1) The parallel algorithm is achieved here through the proper conversion of color images into a set of binary contrast images $I_c$, and;
2) No processing step is done in a sequential manner. This allows to maintain the theoretical time complexity of the whole process near the logarithm of the width plus height of the image.

Generation of B/W contrast images $I_c$ from the original color image $I$ is done (for each intensity contrast $c$) as follows (see an example in Fig. 3). Every cell of $I$ (of any dimension) is transformed into a 0-cell of $I_c$, using the rules:

- Every 0-cell of $I$ is transformed into a BG pixel in $I_c$, meaning that the "interior" of a pixel is a flat zone.

- 1-cells of $I$ represent its contours; thus, if the two neighboring 0-cells of $I$ have an intensity dissimilarity bigger or equal than $c$, their corresponding $I_c$ pixels would be set to FG; BG otherwise.
- Finally, for each corresponding $I_c$ pixel of a 2-cell of $I$, only if its four 4-adjacent $I_c$ pixels were BG, it will be set to BG; FG otherwise. The BG of $I_c$ corresponds to 2-cells of $I_c$ having their 4-adjacent 0-cells identical, which means that the color area of $I$ is flat.

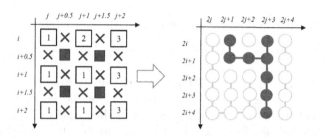

**Fig. 3.** Left: a fragment (9 pixels) of a color image. Numbers represent color intensities of the original image pixels (0-cells), crosses are 1-cells and solid squares 2-cells. Right: The corresponding B/W $I_c$ ($c = 0$) of this color image, including the HSF, depicted as lines.

According to the proposed framework, the parallel process for constructing the $CAdjF$ is divided into two main phases (Fig. 4).

1) *Generation of contrast images.* From the original image $I$, a set $I_c$ of contrast images are generated, according to the previous convention. For example, for grey level images, a set of 255+2 $I_c$ images can be generated fully in parallel, as there are no dependencies among these generations. If there were enough $PEs$, the timing order would be $O(1)$.

2) $HSF_c$ *computation.* For any previous $I_c$-images, their corresponding $HSF_c$s are computed in parallel. The results are a set of jump matrices $J_c$. At the same time, additional information for FG CCs (e.g. contour perimeters) and BG CCs (e.g. areas of flat zones) are also calculated. Each element of these matrices contains a jump distance to the corresponding CC attractor. We refer the reader to [10] for a detailed matrix-based description of this second phase.

3) Once the HSFs of contrast images are built, their $AdjTs$ are computed by simply following the pointers representing jump distances. In [10] a full example is described for a B/W image. In the present method, $AdjTs$ are extracted in the same manner, once the representative attractor lists of each $J_c$ are

completed. Besides, the set $J_c$ comprises the information of $\alpha$-tree as well as the $\alpha^*$-tree. The pseudocode for this phase is described in Algorithm 1.

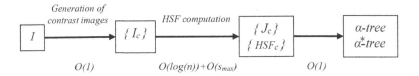

**Fig. 4.** Phases involved in the parallel $CAdjF$ generation. Complexity orders are shown below each stage.

To sum up, having enough $PEs$, the time order would be $O(log(n)) + O(s_{max})$, being $s_{max}$ defined in [10]. A summary of the previous phases and the generation of the set $I_c$ follows. Figure 5, Left shows a $8 \times 13$ synthetic image where each region is labelled with a letter and a number that represents its grey level. For completeness, we define a first contour image $I_{-1}$, which defines four contours for each pixel (trivial case, Fig. 5, Right). The only $I_c$ BG pixels come from $I$ 0-cells. Jump distance matrix $J_{-1}$ simply consists of the corresponding distances (for FG pixels) to the unique FG attractor (most right upper red dot), and a null distance for the inner BG pixels. Note that there is also a set of BG pixels in the image borders, in order to get a correct $AdjT$ representation. Thus, $I_{-1}$ $AdjT$ is composed of exclusively one FG node and as many BG nodes as pixels $I$ has.

Next $I_c$ images are shown in Fig. 6(a) for $c = 0$, and (B) for $c = 1$. In Fig. 6(a), there is a CC for each region of $I$, and a FG CC for each monochrome hole of $I$. In Fig. 6(b), those $I$ regions that share a border and have a grey difference of 1 are fused. In general, the higher the considered contrast, the lower the number of

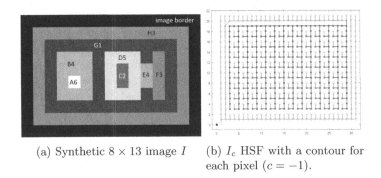

(a) Synthetic $8 \times 13$ image $I$      (b) $I_c$ HSF with a contour for each pixel $(c = -1)$.

**Fig. 5.** Synthetic $8 \times 13$ image $I$ (which has been surrounded by one pixel width additional borders) and its HSF. Green empty circles of $I_c$ are BG pixels; red solid dots of $I_c$ are BG pixels; Edges follows the same color convention. (Color figure online)

contour perimeter that persist and the number of BG zones that remain. Thus, subfigures 6c and 6d show the $I_c$ images for $c = 2$, and $c = 3$. Finally, for the highest existent contrast value in $I$ (in this case $c = 4$), the $I_c$ image results in a different trivial case: only one BG CC and only one FG CC (image border is considered to be out of $I$, and subfigure 6e shows $I_4$).

Once the complete set of $J_c$ has been obtained, it is straightforward to obtain the $\alpha$ and $\alpha^*$-trees, as the same linear addresses are used for all the $J_c$. We proceed in parallel for each attractor and each $J_c$ by simply looking at the same element in the previous $J_{c-1}$ The corresponding elements point to the same or to a different attractor. In the first case, no branch appears at the tree (e.g. region C2 for $\alpha = 0, 1, 2$ in Fig. 7a); in the second one, a link must be drawn (e.g. region fusion of E4F3E5 for $\alpha = 0$ to 1 in Fig. 7a). Similar examples for the $\alpha^*$-trees are depicted in Fig. 7b; in this case, there are contours that persist for different $\alpha$ values. Finally, all of them collapse into the tree root (trivial $c = -1$).

---

**Algorithm 1. [Generation of $\alpha$ and $\alpha*$-trees]**

**Input:** Number of FG,BG attractors $N_{FG}(c), N_{BG}(c)$. A set of global jump distance matrixes $\{J_c\}$
**Output:** $\alpha$ and $\alpha*$-trees

1: **for** $c = -1, 0, 1, 2, \ldots, (q-1)$ **do**
2:     $add\_ordered\_attr\_list(J_c, attr\_list_c, FG)$
3:     $add\_ordered\_attr\_list(J_c, attr\_list_c, BG)$ //Extracting the attractor lists from $J_c$. These lists are ordered by its linear addresses. Each entry in every $attr\_list$ contains: linear address, color, perimeter/area.
4: **end for**//Obtaining the $\alpha^*$-tree by adding a new field to every $attr\_list$
5: **for** $c = q-1, q-2, \ldots, 0$ **do**
6:     **for** $k = 1, 2, \ldots, N_{FG}(c)$ **do**
7:         $lin\_address = attr\_list_c(k).linear\_address$
8:         $prev\_lin\_address = J_{c-1}(lin\_address)$
9:         $attr\_list_c(k).\alpha^*\_pointer = binary\_search(\ prev\_lin\_address, attr\_list_{c-1})$
10:     **end for**
11: **end for**//Obtaining the $\alpha$-tree by adding a new field to every $attr\_list$
12: **for** $c = -1, 0, 1, 2, \ldots, (q-2)$ **do**
13:     **for** $k = N_{FG}(c) + 1, \ldots, N_{FG}(c) + N_{BG}(c)$ **do**
14:         $lin\_address = attr\_list_c(k).linear\_address$
15:         $next\_lin\_address = J_{c+1}(lin\_address)$
16:         $attr\_list_c(k).\alpha\_pointer = binary\_search(\ next\_lin\_address, attr\_list_{c-1})$
17:     **end for**
18: **end for**

128    F. Díaz-del-Río et al.

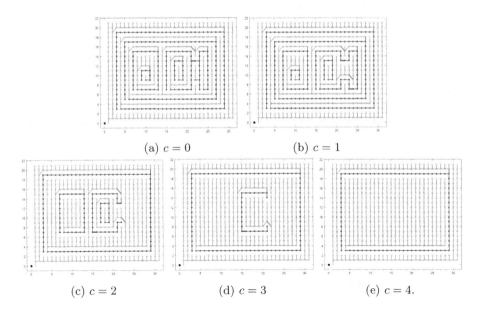

(a) $c = 0$     (b) $c = 1$

(c) $c = 2$     (d) $c = 3$     (e) $c = 4$.

**Fig. 6.** HSFs for the previous synthetic image; Since no contrast is bigger than 4 in (e), the HSF only contains one BG CC and one FG CC.

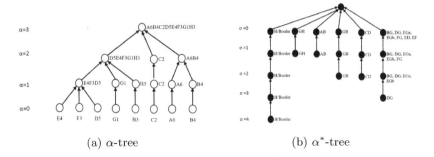

(a) $\alpha$-tree     (b) $\alpha^*$-tree

**Fig. 7.** Representation of the $\alpha$-tree and $\alpha^*$-tree

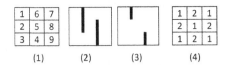

(1)     (2)     (3)     (4)

**Fig. 8.** (1) An image presenting chaining effect. (2) Perimeters for $I_0, I_1, I_2$. (3) Perimeters for $I_3$. (4) A chessboard image that does not present chaining effect.

## 5   Conclusions, Applications and Future Research

The Contrast Adjacency Forest is a hierarchical representation of a color digital image based on the intensity contrasts of its regions. The building of this Forest is done in a fully parallel manner with a theoretical computing time near the logarithm of the width plus the height of an image. This representation contains in turn another pair of trees ($\alpha$ and $\alpha^*$-tree), which are suitable for additional applications, while maintaining such an efficient computation timing. Moreover, they prevent some classical drawbacks that appears when working only with the $\alpha$-tree. One of the mayor drawbacks of $\alpha$-tree is the so-called *chaining effect* (see [4] for a deep discussion). This occurs when there are a set of adjacent regions with incremental intensities. Thus, the first level of this tree would join a big area that actually contains very different intensities. A classical example is given in Fig. 8 (1), where all its pixels would belong promptly to the first $\alpha$-zone. However, this problem can be detected by looking at the perimeters returned by the $\alpha^*$-tree. Figure 8 (2) and (3) show that other region contours must survive in $I_c$ for several levels of $c$. Conversely, for an image with a smaller intensity range (like the chessboard-like of Fig. 8 (4)), $\alpha^*$-tree perimeters will disappear in the next $I_c$. Therefore, inspecting the progression of perimeters with respect to $c$ would cut off artifacts of this chaining effect (in a negligible computing time), and without the need of computing the $\omega - tree$ (see [1]).

Implementation of the presented method is quite straightforward by using the algorithm presented in [10] (or its most enhanced version in [11]). Although an optimized code for the current proposal has not yet been written, the theoretical timing estimation for building the $CAdjF$ appears to be almost the same as that of [11] (if sufficient processing elements were available), due to the few changes with respect to the previous work that are required.

With respect to applications, our hierarchical representation contains a richer topological information than a unique tree. Thus, further processing can produce additional results. A proposal to be considered in the short term is the introduction of stronger conditions for the $I_c$ pixels to be considered as FG, that is, for the activation of the region contours. Additionally, more elaborated topological filters can be defined by extending our hierarchical representation.

**Acknowledgments.** This work was financed by Spanish MCINN and EU-FEDER funds through the research project Par-HoT (PID2019-110455GB-I00) and the VPPI of the US.

# References

1. Bosilj, P., Kijak, E., Lefèvre, S.: Partition and inclusion hierarchies of images: a comprehensive survey. J. Imaging **4**, 33 (2018)
2. Cousty, J., et al.: Hierarchical segmentations with graphs: quasi-flat zones, minimum spanning trees, and saliency maps. JMIV **60**(4), 479–502 (2018)
3. Havel, J., Merciol, F., Lefèvre, S.: Efficient schemes for computing $\alpha$-tree representations. In: Hendriks, C.L.L., Borgefors, G., Strand, R. (eds.) ISMM 2013. LNCS, vol. 7883, pp. 111–122. Springer, Heidelberg (2013). https://doi.org/10.1007/978-3-642-38294-9_10
4. Havel, J., Merciol, F., Lefèvre, S.: Efficient tree construction for multiscale image representation and processing. J. Real-Time Image Proc. **16**(4), 1129–1146 (2016). https://doi.org/10.1007/s11554-016-0604-0

5. You, J., Trager, S.C., Wilkinson, M.H.F.: A fast, memory-efficient alpha-tree algorithm using flooding and tree size estimation. In: Burgeth, B., Kleefeld, A., Naegel, B., Passat, N., Perret, B. (eds.) ISMM 2019. LNCS, vol. 11564, pp. 256–267. Springer, Cham (2019). https://doi.org/10.1007/978-3-030-20867-7_20

6. Kovalevsky, V.: Algorithms in digital geometry based on cellular topology. In: Klette, R., Žunić, J. (eds.) IWCIA 2004. LNCS, vol. 3322, pp. 366–393. Springer, Heidelberg (2004). https://doi.org/10.1007/978-3-540-30503-3_27

7. Molina-Abril, H., Real, P.: Homological optimality in discrete morse theory through chain homotopies. Pattern Recogn. Lett. **33**(11), 1501–1506 (2012)

8. Molina-Abril, H., Real, P.: Homological spanning forest framework for 2D image analysis. Ann. Math. Artif. Intell. **64**(4), 385–409 (2012)

9. Najman, L., Cousty, J., Perret, B.: Playing with kruskal: algorithms for morphological trees in edge-weighted graphs. In: Hendriks, C.L.L., Borgefors, G., Strand, R. (eds.) ISMM 2013. LNCS, vol. 7883, pp. 135–146. Springer, Heidelberg (2013). https://doi.org/10.1007/978-3-642-38294-9_12

10. Díaz del Río, F., Molina-Abril, H., Real, P.: Computing the component-labeling and the adjacency tree of a binary digital image in near logarithmic-time. In: Marfil, R., Calderón, M., Díaz del Río, F., Real, P., Bandera, A. (eds.) CTIC 2019. LNCS, vol. 11382, pp. 82–95. Springer, Cham (2019). https://doi.org/10.1007/978-3-030-10828-1_7

11. Diaz-del Rio, F., et al.: Parallel connected-component-labeling based on homotopy trees. Pattern Recogn. Lett. **131**, 71–78 (2020)

12. Rosenfeld, A.: Adjacency in digital pictures. Inform. Control **26**, 24–33 (1974)

13. Soille, P.: Constrained connectivity for hierarchical image partitioning and simplification. IEEE PAMI **30**(7), 1132–1145 (2008)

# Face Verification in Practice: The Case of Greek Artist Leonidas Arniotis

Nicolas Tsapatsoulis[1]([✉])[iD] and Katerina Diakoumopoulou[2]

[1] Cyprus University of Technology, Arch. Kyprianos 30, 4105 Limassol, Cyprus
nicolas.tsapatsoulis@cut.ac.cy
[2] National and Kapodistrian University of Athens, Athens, Greece
katdiak@theatre.uoa.gr

**Abstract.** In this paper we investigate a specific case of face verification: Given some confirmed photos and video frames of Leonidas Arniotis, a Greek artist of late 1800 and early 1900s, we have examined two photos, of very low resolution, of an unknown person that could be Leonidas Arniotis. The widespread of deep learning and the availability of ResNet-50 model, which was trained on VGGFace2 dataset, allowed us to apply transfer learning for face verification purposes. At the same time an alternative technique which is based on facial points matching was applied. The main aim of the paper is to show that despite the progress made in the fields of face recognition and face verification, actual systems that can be used by non-experts for examining real world cases, like the one we deal in the current paper, remain impractical. In the framework of the current work, we also examine and discuss, in a critical way, the effectiveness of transfer learning for real face verification cases through specific examples.

**Keywords:** Face verification · Deep learning · Transfer learning · Graph matching

## 1 Introduction

A few months ago, the co-author of this paper, Dr. Katerina Diakoumopoulou, a faculty member of the Department of Theatre Studies of the National and Kapodistrian University of Athens, contacted me to check whether two old photographs she found during her research about the Greek artist and performer Leonidas Arniotis are showing him or a different person. Some years had passed from the last time I was practically involved in the face verification research and my initial reaction was to consider that the progress in the field, especially with the widespread of deep learning, would allow an easy and quick investigation of the specific case. Unfortunately, it turned out that most of the progress made in the field remains in the papers and can be used only by technically skilled and familiar with the field people.

This paper reports the methodology we adopted to investigate the case (details can be found in Sect. 2) but the actual purpose of the current work

© Springer Nature Switzerland AG 2021
N. Tsapatsoulis et al. (Eds.): CAIP 2021, LNCS 13053, pp. 131–139, 2021.
https://doi.org/10.1007/978-3-030-89131-2_12

is to indicate that progress in one research field, such as computer vision, should be easily accessible and usable to scientist in other fields even if they come from a very different discipline, such as the theatre studies.. In summary: fewer papers and more practical systems are needed. To promote this effort we provide in Appendix A the Python code we used to investigate the specific case which, we strongly believe, could be easily applied by other scientists with a minimal knowledge of Python and absolutely no familiarity with computer vision research. Despite that, a critical view, through concrete examples, of the transfer learning method for face verification is also presented.

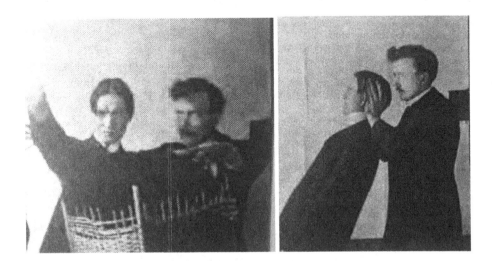

**Fig. 1.** Is the person shown at the right side of the photos Leonidas Arniotis?

## 2    Problem Statement

The problem we deal with in the current work can be summarized in one simple question: Is the person, shown at the right side of the photos in Fig. 1, Leonidas Arniotis? Leonidas Arniotis was a Greek artist and cultural personality of the early 20th century. According to some researchers in the field of theatre studies [1,2] he was the first Greek artist that participated in a silent movie at USA [3]. This fact caused increased interest among the researchers in Greek theatre studies who try to uncover as much information as possible for his life [4,5]. Thus, the question posed above should be answered with as much confidence as possible.

The query photos, shown in Fig. 1, were found in [6], a non-scientific textbook by (Professor) Leonidas, unknown further details, which lists in detail all the steps of the stage hypnosis. The writer-hypnotist-performer lists the secrets of his art and advises the budding hypnotists on locating the volunteers, subduing the audience, organizing their show, etc. Dr. Diakoumopoulou's first assumption

**Fig. 2.** Left: An advertising poster for the performance of Leonidas Arniotis at his theatre in Athens. Right: A photo of Leonidas Arniotis taken at 1908

was that (Professor) Leonidas and Professor Leonidas (Arniotis) may be the same person, who coexisted in Chicago, the place of publication of the book, at about the same time period. Throughout Arniotis' tour in the USA, he was never referred to as "Leonidas Arniotis" but as "Professor Leonidas". Leonidas (Arniotis) was also fascinated by the novelties of para-theatrical spectacles, which he used to experiment successfully. He was an inspirer of change, with powerful and intuitive abilities, he energetically expressed the spirit of the time, of the transition from the 19th to the 20th century and was a decisive figure in the introduction of world performing trends in the European and American scenes.

The available visual information to verify that the person shown in the query photos is Leonidas Arniotis comes from the low resolution video of Library of Congress [3] (see A7, B1-B3 in Fig. 3), from a poster photo for Arniotis' performance in his theatre at Athens (see Fig. 2, left), from a scanned photo of Leonidas Arniotis taken at 1908 found in the Internet (see Fig. 2, right) and from some low resolution photos taken from the article of E. Georgitsoyanni [5] (see A1-A3, A5 in Fig. 3). The main difficulties were the few confirmed visual examples of Arniotis and the low resolution of both examples and query images. The query images, in addition to low resolution were also heavily pixelized.

## 3   Methodology

In order to answer the research question of the current study we first searched for free to use online face verification systems/software. To our surprise no such system/software was located. This fact was extremely disappointing if we take into account that the literature on face recognition is extremely large with thousands of PhD dissertations, papers and books. Obviously, the main aim of the majority of the scientists working in the field is to publish and hopefully get citations rather than to solve real world problems. This is the reason that no literature review was included in the current paper: Lots of studies and mathematics but nothing for practical use. Some empirical studies [7] and online tutorials [8] provide much more help than sophisticated studies appeared in high impact journals and conferences.

The extremely low resolution of query images led us to go back to the very early days of face recognition/face verification and perform facial point matching as detailed in Sect. 3.2. On the other hand, we could not ignore the huge progress made in image classification and image analysis tasks with the advent of deep learning. As explained in Sect. 3.1, the lack of sufficient training data led us to the adoption of transfer learning as a second face verification approach. Verification is confirmed only is case both methods lead to the same, positive, result.

The main preprocessing step we followed for both methods is the manual cropping of the face area of similarly rotated images (this mainly refers to the photos taken from the video frames). In case automatic face detection and cropping is required the *MTCNN* method, introduced by Zhang *et al.* [9], can be used. A corresponding Python library, as indicated in the Appendix, is also available. Due to the low resolution of both query and target photos the *MTCNN* method could not be applied in our case. In addition, to the previous preprocessing step, the A1 and A4 photos (see Fig. 3) were flipped through the vertical axis crossing their middle.

## 3.1  Transfer Learning

The availability of very few training images led us to use transfer learning for face verification [10]. For that purpose, and following the recommendation by Cao *et al.* [11], we used the Resnet-50 architecture trained on the VGGFace2 dataset. That dataset contains 3.31 million images of 9131 subjects, downloaded using Google Image Search. The shown faces have large variations in pose, age, illumination, ethnicity and profession (e.g. actors, athletes, politicians).

The sample photos of our study, query and target ones, were first resized to 224 × 224 pixels to match the size of the VGGFace2 training images, and then they were converted to embeddings by using the pre-trained model. The Python Code in Appendix A can be used to reproduce the results precisely. The only requirement is to have the *keras* and *cv2* Python libraries installed. The similarity between the vector embeddings, composed of 2048 elements each, was obtained with the aid of the cosine coefficient between any pair vector embeddings. Since the cosine coefficient shows dissimilarity it was subtracted from 1 to be converted to similarity.

## 3.2  Facial Points Matching

The low resolution of both query and target photos did not allow us to use any automatic method for facial points localization [12]. Thus, nine facial protuberant points, which could be used to estimate basic facial characteristics (length and width of the face, size of eyes, mouth, nose and chin), were manually localized in the frontal photos (see for instance A5 in Fig. 3). For the profile photos

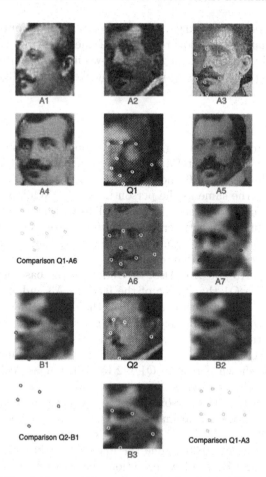

**Fig. 3.** Face verification via facial point matching

**Table 1.** Matching scores between query and target faces

|    | Q1    | Q2    | A1    | A2    | A3    | A4    | A5    | A6    | A7    | B1    | B2    | B3    |
|----|-------|-------|-------|-------|-------|-------|-------|-------|-------|-------|-------|-------|
| Q1 | -     | **0.904** | 0.282 | 0.203 | 0.190 | 0.142 | 0.239 | 0.106 | 0.211 | 0.282 | 0.353 | 0.266 |
| Q2 | **0.904** | -     | 0.256 | 0.176 | 0.166 | 0.141 | 0.203 | 0.101 | 0.191 | 0.276 | 0.324 | 0.235 |
| A1 | 0.282 | 0.256 | -     | 0.460 | 0.471 | 0.475 | **0.552** | 0.450 | 0.274 | 0.372 | 0.379 | 0.290 |
| A2 | 0.203 | 0.176 | 0.460 | -     | 0.579 | 0.534 | **0.611** | 0.520 | 0.428 | 0.497 | 0.518 | 0.461 |
| A3 | 0.190 | 0.166 | 0.471 | 0.579 | -     | 0.534 | **0.678** | 0.635 | 0.340 | 0.406 | 0.389 | 0.319 |
| A4 | 0.142 | 0.141 | 0.475 | 0.534 | 0.534 | -     | 0.534 | **0.700** | 0.379 | 0.455 | 0.450 | 0.392 |
| A5 | 0.239 | 0.203 | 0.552 | 0.611 | **0.678** | 0.534 | -     | 0.601 | 0.435 | 0.526 | 0.510 | 0.443 |
| A6 | 0.106 | 0.101 | 0.450 | 0.520 | 0.635 | **0.700** | 0.601 | -     | 0.414 | 0.459 | 0.451 | 0.404 |
| A7 | 0.211 | 0.191 | 0.274 | 0.428 | 0.340 | 0.379 | 0.435 | 0.414 | -     | 0.733 | 0.793 | **0.859** |
| B1 | 0.282 | 0.276 | 0.372 | 0.497 | 0.406 | 0.455 | 0.526 | 0.459 | 0.733 | -     | **0.928** | 0.821 |
| B2 | 0.353 | 0.324 | 0.379 | 0.518 | 0.389 | 0.450 | 0.510 | 0.451 | 0.793 | **0.928** | -     | 0.893 |
| B3 | 0.266 | 0.235 | 0.290 | 0.461 | 0.319 | 0.392 | 0.443 | 0.404 | 0.859 | 0.821 | **0.893** | -     |

only five points were used as shown, for instance, in B1 photo of Fig. 3. We should note again here that the very low resolution of query images did not allowed us to used additional points. Matching between two images was done by matching the corresponding point graphs as indicated by Weng *et al.* [13].

## 4   Results

The results are summarised in Fig. 3, for facial point matching, and in Table 1 for the transfer learning. A careful inspection of facial point matching between Q1 (first query photo) and A6 and A3 reveals that it cannot be verified that the person in Q1 is the same as the person in A6/A3. While the nose length is similar, there is a clear difference in the hairline which cannot be justified by the chronological difference between the time the photos were taken, while, also, the general head shape differs significantly. Assuming that the head is enclosed in a cylinder, the height of that cylinder is smaller for the face in Q1 than that of the faces in A3 and A6. Also, the radius of the base of that cylinder is larger for the face in Q1 than those of the faces in A3 and A6. The person in Q1 has smaller eyes and mouth compared to the person shown in A6/A3. The comparison between Q2 (second query photo) confirms the previous conclusions as well as the fact that the face of Leonidas Arniotis is longer that the face of the person shown in Q1/Q2. The previous conclusions were also numerically verified (probability of the shown person in Q1/Q2 to be Leonidas Arniotis $< 0.05$) by following the method proposed by Weng *et al.* [13].

The assumption that the person shown in Q1/Q2 is Leonidas Arniotis was also rejected by the transfer learning method. According to the matching scores (cosine similarity) shown in Table 1 the best matching target photo for Q1 is B2 with a similarity score 0.353 while the matching score between Q1 and Q2 is 0.904. Both Q1 and B2 are low resolution images with Q1 being also highly pixelized. Similarly, the best matching target photo for Q2 is also B2 which denotes once again the importance of low resolution compared to the facial characteristics. It is noted that B2 is a profile photo while Q1 is basically an enface photo.

As indicated above, the matching scores shown in Table 1 reveal that deep learning is highly affected by image resolution. The best matching scores were achieved among the faces taken from the video frames (A7, B1-B3) despite the differences in face orientation (3D rotation). The best matching scores among the independent training photos (A1-A6) ware achieved between A4 and A6 and A3 and A5. Both results agree with human interpretation and that shows the effectiveness of transfer learning, under the assumption of similar resolution.

## 5   Conclusion

One could say that the conclusion for this paper is straightforward: The person shown in the photos in Fig. 1 is not Leonidas Arniotis. However, some additional important conclusions can be drawn.

For specific face verification cases, like the one examined in the current study, manual intervention (for accurate extraction of protuberant facial points) and manipulation (photo registration and 3D rotation) is recommended. This is almost necessary whenever input (query) and/or training (confirmed) photos are low resolution ones. In that case traditional facial point matching may be the only reliable solution.

The second conclusion refers to the effectiveness of transfer learning for face verification. It appears that transfer learning can be applied for face verification but we must be very careful when comparing images of highly different resolutions. In that case, the learned embeddings seem to mainly capture global image characteristics rather than specific facial characteristics that can discriminate different persons. Despite that, deep learning models learned on the VGGFace2 dataset, to the surprise (and reservations) of the authors, perform quite well for face verification. Thus, transfer learning is an option when dealing with face verification, assuming that accurate face detection and registration is performed first.

## A    Python Code

```python
import cv2
import numpy as np
from scipy.spatial.distance import cosine
from mtcnn.mtcnn import MTCNN
from keras_vggface.vggface import VGGFace
from keras_vggface.utils import preprocess_input

def face_array(filename, required_size=(224, 224)):
    # load image from file
    pixels = cv2.imread(filename)
    # resize pixels to the model size
    image = cv2.resize(pixels, required_size)
    face_array = np.asarray(image)
    return face_array

def matching_score(query_embedding, target_embedding):
    # calculate cosine similarity between embeddings
    score = 1-cosine(query_embedding, target_embedding)
    return score

filenames = ["Query_01.jpg", "Query_02.jpg", "Arniotis_1897_a_A1.jpg",
    "Arniotis_1901_a_A2.jpg", "Arniotis_1902_a_A3.png",
    "Arniotis_1904_b_A4.png", "Arniotis_1908_a_A5.png",
    "Arniotis_1908_b_A6.png", "Arniotis_video_03_A7.png",
    "Arniotis_video_01_B1.png", "Arniotis_video_02_B2.png",
    "Arniotis_video_04_B3.png"]

keys = ["Q1","Q2","A1", "A2", "A3", "A4","A5","A6","A7","B1","B2","B3"]
```

```
>>> model = VGGFace(model="resnet50", include_top=False,
    input_shape=(224, 224, 3), pooling="avg")
>>> faces = [face_array(f) for f in filenames]
>>> samples = asarray(faces, "float32")
>>> samples = preprocess_input(samples, version=2)
>>> embeddings = model.predict(samples)
>>> MatchingScores={}
>>> for i in np.arange(len(keys)):
...     MatchingScores[keys[i]]={}
...     for j in np.arange(i+1,len(keys)):
...         MatchingScores[keys[i]][keys[j]] =
    matching_score(embeddings[i], embeddings[j])
...
>>> MatchingScores["Q1"]
{"Q2": 0.9040, "A1": 0.2816, "A2": 0.2028, "A3": 0.1902, "A4": 0.1424,
 "A5": 0.2390, "A6": 0.1064, "A7": 0.2108, "B1": 0.2817, "B2":
 0.3530, "B3": 0.2657}
```

# References

1. Diakoumopoulou, K.: Le roi de patience: the adventures course of Leonidas Arniotis in western scenes. The Scientific Yearbook, School of Philosophy, National and Kapodistrian University of Athens, vol. MD, pp. 335–356 (2013–2020). (in Greek)
2. Georgitsoyanni, E., Leonidas, A.: An important cultural personality of the early twentieth century. In: Proceedings of the First Local Congress of Laconian Studies, pp. 145–168. Athens, Greece (2002)
3. Library of Congress: Stealing a dinner (film/video). https://www.loc.gov/item/96519666/. Accessed 8 Aug 2021
4. Diakoumopoulou, K.: The theater of the Greeks in New York from the end of the 19th century until 1940, 1st edn. Kapa Publishing House, Athens, Greece (2020). (in Greek)
5. Georgitsoyanni, E.: An unknown verse newspaper of Greek Diaspora. In: Diaconu, M.A. (Ed.) Analele Universitatii "Stefan Cel Mare" Suceava, Seria Filologie, vol. XI, no. 1, pp. 45–64. ISSN: 15584–2886 (2005)
6. Leonidas (Professor): Stage Hypnotism - A Text Book Of Occult Entertainments. 1st edn. Bureau of Stage Hypnotism, Chicago (1901)
7. Georgakopoulos, T., Koutroumani, M., Moulias, T., Fidas, C: On the effectiveness of low-cost face recognition with deep learning. In: Proceedings of the 24th Pan-Hellenic Conference on Informatics (PCI'2020), pp. 57–60. ACM, Athens, Greece (2020). https://doi.org/10.1145/3437120.3437275
8. Brownlee, J.: How to Perform Face Recognition With VGGFace2 in Keras. https://machinelearningmastery.com/how-to-perform-face-recognition-with-vggface2-convolutional-neural-network-in-keras/. Accessed 8 Aug 2021
9. Zhang, K., Zhang, Z., Li, Z.: Joint face detection and alignment using multitask cascaded convolutional networks. IEEE Sign. Process. Lett. **23**(10), 1499–1503 (2016)

10. Liu, M., Zhang, P., Li, Q., Liu, J., Chen, Z.: LEFV: a lightweight and efficient system for face verification with deep convolution neural networks. In: Proceedings of the 3rd International Conference on Video and Image Processing (ICVIP'2019), pp. 222–227. ACM, Shanghai, China (2019). https://doi.org/10.1145/3376067.3376077
11. Cao, Q., Shen, L., Xie, W., Parkhi, O.M., Zisserman, A.: VGGFace2: a dataset for recognising faces across pose and age. In: Proceedings of the 13th IEEE International Conference on Automatic Face & Gesture Recognition (FG 2018), pp. 67–74. IEEE, Xi'an, China (2018). https://doi.org/10.1109/FG.2018.00020
12. Martinez, J.C.: Detecting Face Features with Python. https://livecodestream.dev/post/detecting-face-features-with-python/. Accessed 8 Aug 2021
13. Weng, R., Lu, J., Hu, J., Yang, G., Tan, Y-P.: Robust feature set matching for partial face recognition. In: Proceedings of the 2013 IEEE International Conference on Computer Vision (ICCV'2013), pp. 601–608. IEEE, Sydney, Australia (2013). https://doi.org/10.1109/ICCV.2013.80

# Object Recognition

# Spatio-Temporal Object Detection from UAV On-Board Cameras

Daniel Cores$^{(\boxtimes)}$ [iD], Víctor M. Brea [iD], and Manuel Mucientes [iD]

Centro Singular de Investigación en Tecnoloxías Intelixentes (CiTIUS) - Universidade de Santiago de Compostela, Santiago de Compostela, Spain
{daniel.cores,victor.brea,manuel.mucientes}@usc.es

**Abstract.** We propose a new two stage spatio-temporal object detector framework able to improve detection precision by taking into account temporal information. First, a short-term proposal linking and aggregation method improves box features. Then, we design a long-term attention module that further enhances short-term aggregated features adding long-term spatio-temporal information. This module takes into account object trajectories to effectively exploit long-term relationships between proposals in arbitrary distant frames. Many videos recorded from UAV on-board cameras have a high density of small objects, making the detection problem very challenging. Our method takes advantage of spatio-temporal information to address these issues increasing the detection robustness. We have compared our method with state-of-the-art video object detectors in two different publicly available datasets focused on UAV recorded videos. Our approach outperforms previous methods in both datasets.

**Keywords:** Object detection · Spatio-temporal features · CNN

## 1 Introduction

Object detectors precision has raised in recent years mainly fueled by the advances in Convolutional Neural Networks (CNNs). However, there are some scenarios that remain a huge challenge for state-of-the-art object detectors. Thus, videos recorded by on-board cameras mounted on Unmanned Aerial Vehicles (UAVs) are usually hard, mainly due to the high object density and the generally small object size. Moreover, camera movements might also increase the effect of motion blur that might degrade image quality at certain frames.

Traditional image object detectors are not designed to take into account temporal information available in videos. Therefore, the extended approach of applying a traditional object detector at frame level is suboptimal when it comes to video object detection. Spatio-temporal frameworks have been proposed to exploit spatio-temporal information to tackle occlusion and motion blur issues, generally increasing the detection precision. Still, most state-of-the-art video object detectors fail to effectively exploit spatio-temporal information when dealing with crowded images containing small objects.

© Springer Nature Switzerland AG 2021
N. Tsapatsoulis et al. (Eds.): CAIP 2021, LNCS 13053, pp. 143–152, 2021.
https://doi.org/10.1007/978-3-030-89131-2_13

This paper proposes a new spatio-temporal object detector architecture designed to overcome the main issues concerning object detection in videos recorded by cameras mounted on UAVs. Our implementation is based on a two stage object detector architecture. First, a short-term object aggregation method is implemented to exploit spatio-temporal information from the nearby frames. Then, shot-term enhanced box features are fed to an attention module that establishes long-term relations among object proposals in distant frames.

The main contributions of this work are:

– A new strategy to link object proposals in neighbouring frames. We avoid the use of short object tubelets to reduce the overhead of including spatio-temporal information. Instead, our Region Proposal Network (RPN) is fed with per frame anchor boxes as in the single image domain. Then, proposals associated with the same anchor in consecutive frames are linked.
– A new attention method to establish long-term proposal relationships. Our implementation takes into account object trajectories to update proposal positions. Therefore, at a given frame the attention module is fed with updated positions for each proposal instead of the original location in the corresponding frame. This makes possible to compare geometry features between proposals originally calculated in distant frames for the first time.
– We evaluate our method in two publicly available datasets. Video sequences in these datasets were recorded by UAVs with built-in cameras in different scenarios. We also compare our results with state-of-the-art video object detectors, proving that our approach achieves the best results.

## 2   Related Work

Single image object detectors follow two main approaches: two stage and one stage architectures. Two-stage object detectors [14] first generate object proposals, which are defined as regions with high probability of containing objects of interest. Then, the network head refines and classifies these proposals. One stage approaches [17] try to solve the detection problem without any proposal generator.

Using feature maps at different pyramid levels was first popularized by Feature Pyramid Network (FPN) [12]. Feature maps with different resolutions make the network robust against a wide range of object sizes. This idea was further developed in PANet [13] and EfficientDet [15].

Recently, the success of attention mechanisms in the natural language processing domain modeling different element dependencies [18] was implemented in the single image object detection [7]. It allows to establish relationships between object proposals to enhance box features.

The main approach to address the video object detection problem is to aggregate spatial features through time getting more robust feature maps. Several works have proposed to perform this aggregation at pixel level. Optical flow was first used by these methods to link features in the nearby frames [19,23]. As an alternative, the use of deformable convolutions was explored to identify these relationships [1]. Recurrent Neural Networks (RNN) have also been successfully applied to perform the pixel level aggregation in [20] by defining a new memory module that aggregates the spatio-temporal information. Motivated by the success achieved by attention mechanisms in the single image object detection domain, there have also been attempts to implement pixel level aggregation methods applying the same ideas [6].

As an alternative to pixel level aggregation, object level aggregation methods have also been implemented to effectively aggregate spatial information throughout time. These methods focus on areas of high probability of containing an object instead of aggregating spatial information from the whole image. Some spatio-temporal object detectors propose to link the per frame detection sets applying tracking algorithms [9,10]. As a follow on, [8] includes a Tubelet Proposal Network (TPN) that links object proposals instead of final detections. It exploits the generally large receptive field of CNNs to propagate static proposals throughout nearby frames, and adapts each proposal in the corresponding frame to the actual object position. This idea of object linking by means of short tubelet generation is further developed in [16]. In this case, authors designed a Cuboid Proposal Network (CPN) in which object tubelets are initialized as anchor cuboids, a spatio-temporal extension of the concept of anchor boxes defined in the single image domain. Anchor cuboids where also used in [3] as the first step for short-term feature aggregation. Moreover, this framework also includes a long-term object linking algorithm that reuses short-term tubelets to increase the robustness of the association process. Instead of relying on anchor cuboids to link proposals, we propose a new method based on anchor box linking that reduces the overhead in comparison with a single image object detector baseline.

Attention mechanisms have also proved to be useful to establish relationships between object proposals in different frames. Authors in [4] successfully extended the method described in [7] for single images. However, this spatio-temporal approach only exploits short-term information. Long-term information is added in [2], implementing a location free attention mechanism that only uses appearance features, ignoring geometry information such as object position and shape. Comparing object positions in distant frames is not meaningful to establish object relationships and adds noise to the linking process. Alternatively, we keep track of object trajectories in order to update proposal positions throughout time making possible to also exploit geometry features in the long-term.

## 3    Method

We propose a short- and long-term aggregation method that can be applied to two stage object detectors in order to take advantage of spatio-temporal information available in videos. Both short- and long-term aggregation stages take as input per frame object proposals calculated following the same strategy as the single image baseline. This reduces the overhead of including these techniques on traditional object detectors.

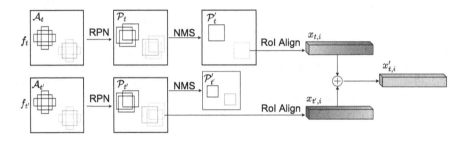

**Fig. 1.** Short-term aggregation process with one support frame $f_{t'}$.

Box proposal features at each reference frame $f_t$ are enhanced with features from nearby support frames $f_{t-N}, ..., f_{t-1}, f_t, f_{t+1}, ..., f_{t+N}$ by an object level aggregation method. Section 3.1 describes the short-term linking and aggregation strategy. A long-term spatio-temporal module (Sect. 3.2) is fed with short-term aggregated box features to establish long-term relationships and further improve object features.

Most previous works use spatio-temporal features to localize and classify the object. In contrast, in our implementation, spatio-temporal information is only used to boost the classification precision, as we argue that the most valuable information to localize the object comes from the current frame. Therefore, we use spatial information to localize the object and spatial and spatio-temporal information to classify each object. The final classification score is calculated as:

$$p = p_{tmp} + p_{spt}(1 - p_{tmp}) \tag{1}$$

being $p_{tmp}$ the classification score calculated with spatio-temporal features and $p_{spt}$ the score of the classification in the reference frame with just spatial information.

### 3.1 Short-Term Feature Aggregation

Our short-term aggregation method links proposals throughout the neighbouring frames and aggregates box features accordingly. Per frame object proposals are initialized as anchor boxes $\mathcal{A}_t = \{a_{t,i}\}_{i=1}^A$. Then, the proposal set $\mathcal{P}_t = \{p_{t,i}\}_{i=1}^A$ is calculated by an RPN modifying each anchor box to better fit the objects of interest. Each proposal $p_{t,i}$ consists of a bounding box $\mathbf{b}(p_i)$ and an objectness score $\mathbf{s}(p_i)$. Finally, spatially redundant proposals are removed applying Non-Maximum Suppression (NMS), getting the final proposal set $\mathcal{P}_t'$. This process is shown in Fig. 1.

For each reference frame $f_t$, we link proposals that come from the same anchor box in the same position for every supporting frame $f_{t'}$ in $\{f_{t-N}, ..., f_{t-1}, f_{t+1}, ..., f_{t+N}\}$. The high overlap in consecutive frames for the same object and the high field of view of CNNs make this lightweight linking strategy suitable for the short-term. However, since $|\mathcal{P}_t'| \leq |\mathcal{P}_t|$ due to the

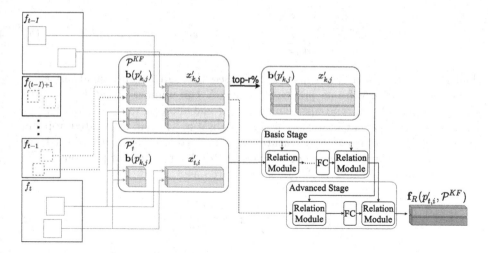

**Fig. 2.** Long-term aggregation strategy with one key frame $f_{t-I}$.

removed proposals, we link proposals in $\mathcal{P}'_t$ in the reference frame with proposals in $\mathcal{P}_{t'}$ in the supporting frames. Otherwise, proposals in $\mathcal{P}'_t$ and $\mathcal{P}_{t'}$ might not share the same anchors —see proposal associated with orange anchor and proposal associated with red anchor in Fig. 1 after NMS.

Box features are extracted for each proposal by the RoI Align method. Then box features that came from the same anchor box are aggregated (Fig. 1):

$$x'_{t,i} = \sum_{l=-N}^{N} \omega^s_{t+l,i}\, x_{t+l,i} \tag{2}$$

being $x'_{t,i}$ the output aggregated feature map calculated as a weighted sum of the per frame box feature maps $x_{t+l,i}$. The short-term aggregation weights $\omega^s_{t+l,i}$ are calculated as:

$$\omega^s_{t+l,i} = exp\left( \frac{x_{t,i}\, x_{t+l,i}}{|x_{t,i}||x_{t+l,i}|} \right) \tag{3}$$

normalizing the $\omega^s_{t+l,i}$ using a Softmax function to ensure that $\sum_{l=-N}^{N} \omega^s_{t+l,i} = 1$.

## 3.2 Long-Term Feature Aggregation

Although our anchor-based strategy provides a lightweight effective linking method in the short-term, it is not suitable for the long-term. The high overlap between nearby frames cannot be assumed in the long-term. Therefore, we design a new method based on attention mechanisms to link proposals from distant supporting key frames selected at a fixed interval $I$.

The attention module calculates $M$ relation features $\mathbf{f}_R^m$ given the support proposal set $\mathcal{P}^{KF}$ and proposals in the current frame $p'_{t,i}$:

$$\mathbf{f}_R^m(p'_{t,i}, \mathcal{P}^{KF}) = \sum_{k=1}^{K} \sum_{j=1}^{|\mathcal{P}'_k|} w_{t(i),k(j)}^m (W_V \, x'_{k,j}), \quad m = 1, ..., M \tag{4}$$

being $W_V$ a transformation matrix optimised through backpropagation. $\mathcal{P}^{KF}$ includes the per key frame proposals, being $K$ the number of key frames. We also include in $\mathcal{P}^{KF}$ proposals from current frame allowing to establish relationships also with current proposals. Each proposal $p'_{t,i}$ has an associated appearance feature $x'_{t,i}$ and geometry features $\mathbf{b}(p'_{t,i})$. Therefore, we use the short-term enhanced box features instead of the weaker RoI Align output of previous works [2,4]. The relation weight $w_{t(i),k(j)}^m$ is calculated as:

$$w_{t(i),k(j)}^m = \frac{g_{t(i),k(j)}^m \, exp(a_{t(i),k(j)}^m)}{\sum_q g_{t(i),q}^m \, exp(a_{t(i),q}^m)} \tag{5}$$

being $a_{t(i),k(j)}^m$ the appearance weight and $g_{t(i),k(j)}^m$ the geometry weight. The appearance weight is calculated as a normalized dot product:

$$a_{t(i),k(j)}^m = \frac{\langle W_H \, x'_{t,i}, W_Q \, x'_{k,j} \rangle}{\sqrt{d_h}} \tag{6}$$

where $W_H$ and $W_Q$ of Eq. 6, as well as $W_G$ in Eq. 7, are also learnt in the training process as $W_V$ (Eq. 4). $W_H$ and $W_Q$ project the appearance features in the reference frame and supporting key frames respectively, being $d_H$ the projected dimension.

Geometry weights are computed as:

$$g_{t(i),k(j)}^m = max\{0, W_G \, \mathcal{E}(\mathbf{b}(p'_{t,i}), \mathbf{b}'(p'_{k,j}))\} \tag{7}$$

where function $\mathcal{E}$ takes proposals bounding box definitions $\mathbf{b}(p')$ and embeds the vector $\left( log\left(\frac{|x_i - x_j|}{w_i}\right), log\left(\frac{|y_i - y_j|}{h_i}\right), log\left(\frac{w_j}{w_i}\right), log\left(\frac{h_j}{h_i}\right) \right)$ in a high dimensional representation following the method outlined in [18]. For features from key frames we do not use the original geometry features $\mathbf{b}(p'_{k,j})$, but a modified version $\mathbf{b}'(p'_{k,j})$ taking into account object trajectories —proposals with the same color in Fig. 2 belong to the same trajectory. We link proposals in consecutive frames reusing previously computed relation weights defining the association score between a proposal $i$ in one frame and a proposal $j$ in the next frame as:

$$\mathcal{S}_{i,j} = \mathbf{s}(p'_{\tau,i}) \, exp(\overline{w}_{\tau(i),k(j)}) \tag{8}$$

where $\overline{w}_{\tau(i),k(j)}$ is the average relation weight between proposal $i$ in frame $f_\tau$ and proposal $j$ in $f_k$. As we have previous relation weights already calculated, we can establish object trajectories from key frames to the previous frame $f_{t-1}$ maximising the association score $\mathcal{S}_{i,j}$ applying the Hungarian method [11]. Using this updated geometry features allows to compare proposal positions as if they were in consecutive frames rather than in arbitrary distant frames.

Finally, box features are calculated as the concatenation of $M$ relational features adding the result to the original appearance features:

$$\mathbf{f}_R(p'_{t,i}, \mathcal{P}^{KF}) = \mathbf{f}_R(p'_{t,i}, \mathcal{P}^{KF}) + concat[\{\mathbf{f}^m_R(p'_{t,i}, \mathcal{P}^{KF})\}^M_{m=1}] \qquad (9)$$

We stack a set of relation modules following an approach similar to [4]. Figure 2 shows this pipeline organized in *Basic* and *Advanced Stages*. The inputs to the *Basic Stage* are the key frame supporting proposals and the reference frame proposals $\mathcal{P}'_t$ that are iteratively improved. Then, the top r% proposals in $\mathcal{P}^{KF}$ are enhanced with the whole set $\mathcal{P}^{KF}$ as supporting proposals in the *Advanced Stage*. Finally, the second step of the *Advanced Stage* takes *Basic Stage* output and these enhanced proposals to calculate the final box features.

## 4   Experimental Results

### 4.1   Datasets

We evaluate our method in two publicly available datasets: Unmanned Aerial Vehicle Benchmark (UAVDT) [5] and VisDrone [21]. Both datasets are focused on videos recorded from on-board cameras mounted on UAVs. The UAVDT dataset contains 30 training videos and 20 testing videos recorded in urban areas with annotated objects belonging to one category: vehicles. The VisDrone dataset provides 56 training and 17 testing videos with annotations of 11 different object categories. Compared to UAVDT, the number of objects per frame is significantly higher in VisDrone with 25 and 85 objects per frame on average respectively.

### 4.2   Implementation Details

In our implementation, per frame features are extracted at different FPN levels using ResNeXt-101 as backbone with deformable convolutions [22] on *conv3*, *conv4* and *conv5*. The backbone is pre-trained in the ImageNet classification dataset.

To train our spatio-temporal network, we first train the single frame baseline, setting the base learning rate to $1.25 \times 10^{-3}$ for 45K iterations, and reducing it by *0.1 at 30 K and 40 K iterations. Then, we keep its weights frozen only training the spatio-temporal double head and the attention modules. For this spatio-temporal training, the initial learning rate is also set to $1.25 \times 10^{-3}$ for 15 K iterations, reducing it at 12 K iterations. Input images are resized keeping the shortest dimension bellow 540px for UAVDT and 720px for VisDrone.

Short-term support frames and long-term key frames are selected following different strategies in the training and testing stages. In the short-term case, instead of selecting $2N + 1$ consecutive frames $\{f_{t-N}, ..., f_{t-1}, f_t, f_{t+1}, ..., f_{t+N}\}$ for training, we randomly select two support frames in $(t - N, ..., t + N)$ for each reference frame. In testing, every video frame is processed sequentially making possible to reuse previous backbone calculations. However, in training

**Table 1.** Comparison with state-of-the-art spatio-temporal frameworks.

<table>
<tr><td colspan="4" align="center">(a) UAVDT</td><td colspan="4" align="center">(b) Visdrone.</td></tr>
<tr><td>Method</td><td>$AP^{@.5}$</td><td>$AP^{@.75}$</td><td>$AP^{@.5-.95}$</td><td>Method</td><td>$AP^{@.5}$</td><td>$AP^{@.75}$</td><td>$AP^{@.5-.95}$</td></tr>
<tr><td>FGFA [23]</td><td>57.6</td><td>25.6</td><td>28.9</td><td>FGFA [23]</td><td>30.7</td><td>11.8</td><td>14.1</td></tr>
<tr><td>RDN [4]</td><td>60.4</td><td>32.0</td><td>32.5</td><td>RDN [4]</td><td>31.5</td><td>11.7</td><td>14.4</td></tr>
<tr><td>MEGA [2]</td><td>59.4</td><td>30.7</td><td>31.7</td><td>MEGA [2]</td><td>31.8</td><td>11.7</td><td>14.5</td></tr>
<tr><td>Ours</td><td>**61.0**</td><td>**37.1**</td><td>**34.9**</td><td>Ours</td><td>**32.1**</td><td>**12.9**</td><td>**15.4**</td></tr>
</table>

we randomly select a fixed sized subsample of frames to reduce the effect of very large videos. Therefore, this optimization cannot be applied, increasing the training time when working with large $N$. In the long-term case, we follow a similar strategy in the training stage, randomly selecting two key frames from the complete video rather than evenly spaced key frames from previous frames. In our experiments we set $N = 5$.

We also report the performance of state-of-the-art video object detection frameworks in the same datasets. We use the implementations provided in [2]. To ensure a fair comparison, we keep the same parameters —apart from input image resolution— unchanged for both datasets.

### 4.3 Results

In this section we compare our framework with the state-of-the-art spatio-temporal object detectors in the selected datasets. The spatio-temporal methods included in the comparison are FGFA [23], RDN [4] and MEGA [2]. We report the Average Precision at different IoU levels for every dataset.

Although our method uses frames in advance in the short-term, long-term key frames are selected from previous frames. Therefore, our implementation can give the detection set with just a few frames of delay. That is the case for all the spatio-temporal approaches in the comparison except for MEGA [2]. In this case, key frames are randomly selected from the complete video. Thus, this method might not be suitable for certain applications in which using so many frames in advance is not possible.

Table 1 shows the results in the UAVDT and VisDrone datasets. Our method outperforms all the other methods in the UAVDT dataset (Table 1a) at every IoU level. It also shows that our approach not only gets better results but the difference is bigger as we set a more demanding IoU. Thus, the difference with the best spatio-temporal object detector is of 0.6% in $AP_{@.5}$ while in $AP_{@.75}$ it is of 5.1%. In the VisDrone dataset (Table 1b) our framework also improves the other methods in all the metrics. As in the previous case, the difference is more significant in $AP_{@.75}$ and $AP_{@.5-.95}$ with 1.2% and 0.9% over MEGA, the best spatio-temporal framework in this dataset.

# 5    Conclusions

We have proposed a new framework for spatio-temporal object detection that effectively exploits both short- and long-term information in videos recorded from UAVs on-board cameras. First, proposals are linked in the nearby frames allowing to aggregate short-term spatio-temporal information. Then, enhanced box features are further enriched by an attention stage that takes into account object trajectories to exploit geometry features.

Our framework outperforms state-of-the-art spatio-temporal object detectors in two publicly available datasets focused on videos recorded from UAVs. This proves the suitability of our method for this challenging real application.

**Acknowledgements.** This research was partially funded by the Spanish Ministry of Science, Innovation and Universities under grants TIN2017-84796-C2-1-R and RTI2018-097088-B-C32, and the Galician Ministry of Education, Culture and Universities under grants ED431C 2018/29, ED431C 2017/69 and accreditation 2016–2019, ED431G/08. These grants are co-funded by the European Regional Development Fund (ERDF/FEDER program).

# References

1. Bertasius, G., Torresani, L., Shi, J.: Object detection in video with spatiotemporal sampling networks. In: IEEE International Conference on Computer Vision (ICCV) (2018)
2. Chen, Y., Cao, Y., Hu, H., Wang, L.: Memory enhanced global-local aggregation for video object detection. In: IEEE Conference on Computer Vision and Pattern Recognition (CVPR), pp. 10337–10346 (2020)
3. Cores, D., Mucientes, M., Brea, V.M.: RoI feature propagation for video object detection. In: European Conference on Artificial Intelligence (ECAI) (2020)
4. Deng, J., Pan, Y., Yao, T., Zhou, W., Li, H., Mei, T.: Relation distillation networks for video object detection. In: IEEE International Conference on Computer Vision (ICCV), pp. 7023–7032 (2019)
5. Du, D., et al.: The unmanned aerial vehicle benchmark: Object detection and tracking. In: European Conference on Computer Vision (ECCV), pp. 370–386 (2018)
6. Guo, C., et al.: Progressive sparse local attention for video object detection. In: IEEE International Conference on Computer Vision (ICCV), pp. 3909–3918 (2019)
7. Hu, H., Gu, J., Zhang, Z., Dai, J., Wei, Y.: Relation networks for object detection. In: IEEE Conference on Computer Vision and Pattern Recognition (CVPR), pp. 3588–3597 (2018)
8. Kang, K., et al.: Object detection in videos with tubelet proposal networks. In: IEEE Conference on Computer Vision and Pattern Recognition (CVPR) (2017)
9. Kang, K., et al.: T-CNN: Tubelets with convolutional neural networks for object detection from videos. IEEE Trans. Circ. Syst. Video Technol. **28**(10), 2896–2907 (2017)
10. Kang, K., Ouyang, W., Li, H., Wang, X.: Object detection from video tubelets with convolutional neural networks. In: IEEE Conference on Computer Vision and Pattern Recognition (CVPR) (2016)

11. Kuhn, H.W.: The hungarian method for the assignment problem. Naval Res. Logist. Q. **2**(1–2), 83–97 (1955)
12. Lin, T.Y., Dollár, P., Girshick, R., He, K., Hariharan, B., Belongie, S.: Feature pyramid networks for object detection. In: IEEE Conference on Computer Vision and Pattern Recognition (CVPR) (2017)
13. Liu, S., Qi, L., Qin, H., Shi, J., Jia, J.: Path aggregation network for instance segmentation. In: IEEE Conference on Computer Vision and Pattern Recognition (CVPR), pp. 8759–8768 (2018)
14. Ren, S., He, K., Girshick, R., Sun, J.: Faster R-CNN: Towards real-time object detection with region proposal networks. In: Advances in Neural Information Processing Systems (NIPS) (2015)
15. Tan, M., Pang, R., Le, Q.V.: Efficientdet: Scalable and efficient object detection. In: IEEE Conference on Computer Vision and Pattern Recognition, pp. 10781–10790 (2020)
16. Tang, P., Wang, C., Wang, X., Liu, W., Zeng, W., Wang, J.: Object detection in videos by high quality object linking. IEEE Transactions on Pattern Analysis and Machine Intelligence (2019)
17. Tian, Z., Shen, C., Chen, H., He, T.: FCOS: Fully convolutional one-stage object detection. In: IEEE International Conference on Computer Vision (ICCV), pp. 9627–9636 (2019)
18. Vaswani, A., et al.: Attention is all you need. In: Advances in Neural Information Processing Systems, pp. 5998–6008 (2017)
19. Wang, S., Zhou, Y., Yan, J., Deng, Z.: Fully motion-aware network for video object detection. In: IEEE International Conference on Computer Vision (ICCV) (2018)
20. Xiao, F., Jae Lee, Y.: Video object detection with an aligned spatial-temporal memory. In: European Conference on Computer Vision (ECCV) (2018)
21. Zhu, P., Wen, L., Bian, X., Ling, H., Hu, Q.: Vision meets drones: A challenge. arXiv preprint arXiv:1804.07437 (2018)
22. Zhu, X., Hu, H., Lin, S., Dai, J.: Deformable convnets v2: more deformable, better results. In: IEEE Conference on Computer Vision and Pattern Recognition (CVPR), pp. 9308–9316 (2019)
23. Zhu, X., Wang, Y., Dai, J., Yuan, L., Wei, Y.: Flow-guided feature aggregation for video object detection. In: IEEE International Conference on Computer Vision (ICCV) (2017)

# Automatic Watermeter Reading
# in Presence of Highly Deformed Digits

Ashkan Mansouri Yarahmadi[(✉)] and Michael Breuß

Institute of Mathematics, Brandenburg Technical University, Platz der Deutschen
Einheit 1, 03046 Cottbus, Germany
{yarahmadi,breuss}@b-tu.de

**Abstract.** The task we face in this paper is to automate the reading
of watermeters as can be found in large apartment houses. Typically
water passes through such watermeters, so that one faces a wide range
of challenges caused by water as the medium where the digits are positioned. One of the main obstacles is given by the frequently produced
bubbles inside the watermeter that deform the digits. To overcome this
problem, we propose the construction of a novel data set that resembles
the watermeter digits with a focus on their deformations by bubbles. We
report on promising experimental recognition results, based on a deep
and recurrent network architecture performed on our data set.

**Keywords:** Underwater digit recognition · Sequence models ·
Connectionist Temporal Classification

## 1   Introduction

Automatic digit recognition is a standard but still challenging task, and it is
often considered as an application of scene text recognition in computer vision.
In practice, any supervised digit recognition algorithm must be invariant with
respect to the complexity of the environment and possible digit variations. The
underwater environment and the challenges that it introduces to pattern recognition tasks [10,16] is the setting of the application we consider in this work,
namely watermeter automation [4,11,15,19,20,22].

Mechanical watermeters are still the mainly used devices to measure water
consumption. They are commonly located in large tenements. The water passes
through such watermeters, and the digits are typically located in the water. Often
the water carries bubbles, also some dirt is common. Watermeters sometimes
receive low maintenance, making their digits hard to be read even for humans.
These issues may make the recognition of watermeter digits a challenging task.

For watermeter automation, we face a specific recognition problem expecting
a sequence of digits to convey a meaning, namely the volume of the consumed
water. As a major problem, bubbles inside the watermeter may result in deformation of digit appearance. This problem has to be tackled for image data that

© Springer Nature Switzerland AG 2021
N. Tsapatsoulis et al. (Eds.): CAIP 2021, LNCS 13053, pp. 153–163, 2021.
https://doi.org/10.1007/978-3-030-89131-2_14

can be easily acquired and transmitted, as this is relevant for technical realisation of watermeter automation using a stationary device. This setting introduces constraints on image resolution, and recognition must be robust with respect to available, working lighting.

The literature on watermeter automation can be divided into a few branches, namely those depending on segmentation based approaches [11,20] and deep learning based methods [15,19,22]. In the context of this paper let us especially refer to [22] where a sequence learning track of works [7,17,18] has been adopted to resolve the problem. However, these works rely on images of relatively high resolution, and the test data are not specifically tuned for dealing with strong digit distortions by bubbles, making the approaches not directly applicable for our automation approach. Let us stress explicitly, that the data set we propose in this work is much more challenging with respect to bubble distortions, compared to data used for learning in previous works. The main contribution of this paper put in relation to the previous approaches is *(i)* to propose the data set for learning to deal with strong bubble distortions, and *(ii)* to test the limits of currently available state-of-the-art neural networks approaches to deal with the bubble distortion problem that is a main obstacle in the application.

Among the literature, the segmentation based methods accomplish watermeter automation by first locating the digit segments from the image taken in different environmental complexities, later performing a classification on each segmented digit. One potential disadvantage of these methods is their dependency on user defined thresholds to segment and binarize the digits prior to the recognition phase.

In the other group of works various deep networks are adopted, namely *recurrent neural network* (RNN) [23], *fully convolutional sequence recognition network* (FCSRN) (CNN) [22] or a combined architecture of them, the *convolutional recurrent neural network* (CRNN) [18] along with the loss function *Connectionist Temporal Classification* (CTC) [1]. As for the latter, the main idea of combining (CRNN) and (CTC) is to optimize the CTC loss by a set of feature vectors, each representing a sequence of watermeter digits, obtained from the CRNN. The environmental complexities i.e., uneven lighting, bubble distortion etc., along with the digit variations are all embedded within the feature vectors.

We proceed in this paper by first elaborating on our setup that we use in Sect. 2 to sample a novel data set based on the standard MNIST data set [13]. We specifically focus on bubble deformations of digits and their impacts on recognition rate. We opt to maintain an acceptable recognition rate by training two deep learning based schemes CRNN [18] and FCSRN [22] in an underwater environment while real bubbles are introduced to distort the digits. The obtained results in this paper are based on the MNIST data set consisting of a collection of handwritten digits that we will highly distort by real bubbles produced by our physical setup. In Sects. 4 and 5, the adopted deep learning architectures along with a CTC loss function optimized based on our novel data set are explained. Finally, we present our results in Sect. 6.

## 2  Construction of Our Data Set

We established a physical setup to capture the deformed digits by bubbles. Our setup consists of a small air-pump, a transparent box, a camera and a monitor, where a plastic pipe carries the air from the pump and produces the bubbles inside a transparent box containing water. We located the transparent box on top of the monitor and showed the original MNIST digits resembling the watermeter digits on monitor area located under the box. A camera captures the distorted digits from a near distance. To have a stable setup, the monitor is horizontally located on a table and the camera captures the monitor from top. In next section, the obtained data set by our setup will be explained in more detail.

## 3  Data Set Preparation

We construct a data set, by taking any five adjacent digits from the MNIST data set and horizontally juxtapose them, so that they resemble the digits that appear on a watermeter. In total, 1856 number of such images are created based on the MNIST data set and deformed using our setup, few of which are shown in Fig. 1. Let us highlight some challenging aspects of the produced data set:

- A high deformation, destroying the digit patterns so that they are indeed not really readable (see the first row of Fig. 1)
- A high deformation, making some digits appear to be present twice (see middle row of Fig. 1)
- A realistic bubble deformation that warps the digits so that they are still readable (see the last row of Fig. 1)

**Fig. 1.** A small subset of highly deformed images captured by our setup. One notices that in all images at least two digits are deformed by bubbles. In specific, the deformations shown in first row make the digits hard to be read.

In contrast to the establishment of an ideal data set with a standard font that generally appears on watermeters, we intentionally opt to add such complexities in terms of digit deformation to the MNIST data set and train the adopted deep learning schemes [18, 22] as further will be explained in Sect. 4.

## 4  Deep Learning Schemes

We investigate the architectures of the two adopted deep learning schemes, namely CRNN [18] and FCSRN [22] in Subsects. 4.1 and 4.2.

## 4.1   The CRNN Approach

Proposed first by Shi et al. [18], the CRNN employs a convolutional, a recurrent and a transcription part. The convolutional part is constructed by adoption of the max-pooling and the convolutional layers from a standard CNN, while the fully-connected layers are eliminated. The convolutional part produces a set of feature vectors, called *feature sequence* that are integrated over time by the subsequent RNN layers. Specifically, each feature vector of the feature sequence corresponds to a rectangle region of the original image [14,18], and such rectangle regions in turn comprise the digits of the watermeter. In this way, the digit sequence of a watermeter are decoded from a spatial to a time domain using a RNN architecture. The adopted RNN in [18] is a *bidirectional long-short-term memory* (BLSTM) [3] that we further elaborate in coming paragraphs.

We start with *long-short-term memory* (LSTM) [5] as the building block of BLSTM. We assume that the convolutional part produces feature vectors $\mathcal{X} \in \mathbb{R}^{n \times b}$, with $n, b \in \mathbb{N}$ to be the feature vectors' dimensions and the batch size, respectively. In addition the LSTM has $q \in \mathbb{N}$ number of hidden units.

At a time step $t \in \mathbb{N}_0$, each LSTM cell shown as Fig. 2 accepts three numbers of inputs, the $\mathcal{X}\langle t \rangle$ as the feature vectors obtained at the time $t$ from the convolutional part and two others, namely $h^{\langle t-1 \rangle} \in \mathbb{R}^{q \times b}$ and $c^{\langle t-1 \rangle} \in \mathbb{R}^{q \times b}$, the so called the *hidden state* and *memory cell* both are already computed at the time $t - 1$. Here, $h^{\langle t-1 \rangle}$ is the activation result from the LSTM cell at the time $t - 1$ and $c^{\langle t-1 \rangle}$ carries some information from the memory cells corresponding to the time $t' < t$.

Let us have some observations on how the memory cell $c^{\langle t \rangle}$ (1) at time $t$ is computed by the following formula. A more precise look at (1) reveals that it partially depends on $\Gamma_f \odot c^{\langle t-1 \rangle}$ with $c^{\langle t-1 \rangle}$ being the memory cell at the previous time $t - 1$. Let us explain the term $\Gamma_f$ later and keep our focus on (1) via

$$c^{\langle t \rangle} = \Gamma_u \odot \tilde{c}^{\langle t \rangle} + \Gamma_f \odot c^{\langle t-1 \rangle} \tag{1}$$

with $\odot$ representing the elementwise vector multiplication. As (1) further shows, $c^{\langle t \rangle}$ also depends on $\tilde{c}^{\langle t \rangle}$ that itself is computed based on the feature vector $\mathcal{X}^{\langle t \rangle}$ and the previous hidden state $h^{\langle t-1 \rangle}$ as:

$$\tilde{c}^{\langle t \rangle} = \tanh\left( \mathcal{W}_c \times \left[ \left( h^{\langle t-1 \rangle} \right)_{q \times b} \middle| \left( \mathcal{X}^{\langle t \rangle} \right)_{n \times b} \right] + (b_c)_{q \times b} \right) \tag{2}$$

with $\times$ visualizing in this work standard matrix multiplication, and $b_c$ and $\mathcal{W}_c$ to be the corresponding bias respectively weight matrix.

In addition, (1) has two further terms $\Gamma_u$ and $\Gamma_f$ called the *update gate* and *forget gate* defined as

$$\Gamma_u = \sigma\left( \mathcal{W}_u \times \left[ \left( h^{\langle t-1 \rangle} \right)_{q \times b} \middle| \left( \mathcal{X}^{\langle t \rangle} \right)_{n \times b} \right] + (b_u)_{q \times b} \right) \tag{3}$$

and

$$\Gamma_f = \sigma\left( \mathcal{W}_f \times \left[ \left( h^{\langle t-1 \rangle} \right)_{q \times b} \middle| \left( \mathcal{X}^{\langle t \rangle} \right)_{n \times b} \right] + (b_f)_{q \times b} \right) \tag{4}$$

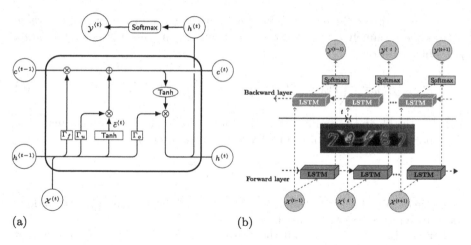

**Fig. 2.** (a) A graphical representation of the LSTM cell accepting the hidden state $h^{\langle t-1\rangle}$ and the memory cell $c^{\langle t-1\rangle}$ from the previous LSTM and the feature vector $\mathcal{X}^{\langle t\rangle}$ at the current time. As shown at the top of the diagram, the obtained hidden state $h^{\langle t\rangle}$ is converted to a probability distribution vector $\mathcal{Y}^{\langle t\rangle}$ as a result of its passage through a *softmax* function and later used as the input to the CTC loss function [1]. (b) A schematic representation of a BLSTM network [3] comprised of two recurrent LSTM layers, namely the forward and the backward layers, processing the data in two opposite directions. All interconnections among the LSTM nodes, the input feature vectors $\mathcal{X}$ and the output of the network $\mathcal{Y}$ are shown as dashed lines. The upper layer of LSTMs acts in backward and the lower one in forward pass. The flow of the error differentials in forward and the backward layers propagating in opposite directions are shown as blue and red. (Color figure online)

that are again based on the feature vector $\mathcal{X}^{\langle t\rangle}$ and the previous hidden state $h^{\langle t-1\rangle}$ with $b_u$, $b_f$, $\mathcal{W}_u$ and $\mathcal{W}_f$ to be the corresponding biases and weight matrices. Let us shortly conclude here, that the feature vector $\mathcal{X}^{\langle t\rangle}$ and the previous hidden state $h^{\langle t-1\rangle}$ are the essential ingredients used to compute $\tilde{c}^{\langle t\rangle}$, $\Gamma_u$ and $\Gamma_f$, that are all used to update the current memory cell $c^{\langle t\rangle}$ (1).

The motivation to use the *sigmoid function* $\sigma$ in structure of the gates shown in (3) and (4) is its activated range in $[0, 1]$, leading them in extreme cases to be fully on or off letting all or nothing to pass through them. In non-extreme cases they partially contribute the previous memory cell $c^{\langle t-1\rangle}$ and the on the fly computed value $\tilde{c}^{\langle t\rangle}$ to the current memory cell $c^{\langle t\rangle}$ as shown in (1).

In a bigger picture, let us visualize the role of the $\Gamma_u$ and $\Gamma_f$ gates concerning the memory cell $c^{\langle t\rangle}$. In Fig. 2, a direct line connecting $c^{\langle t-1\rangle}$ to $c^{\langle t\rangle}$ carries the old data directly from time $t-1 \to t$. Here, one clearly observes the $\Gamma_u$ and $\Gamma_f$ gates both are connected by $+$ and $\times$ operators to the passed line. They linearly contribute the current feature value $\mathcal{X}^{\langle t\rangle}$ and the adjacent hidden state $h^{\langle t-1\rangle}$ to the updating of the current memory cell $c^{\langle t\rangle}$. Meanwhile, $\Gamma_u$ shares its contribution through $\times$ operator with $\tilde{c}^{\langle t\rangle}$ to the passing line.

Finally, to make the current LSTM activated we need the memory cell value at the time $t$, namely $c^{\langle t \rangle}$, that we obtain from (1) and also the so called *output gate* obtained from

$$\Gamma_o = \sigma\left( \mathcal{W}_o \times \left[ \left( h^{\langle t-1 \rangle} \right)_{q \times b} \middle| \left( \mathcal{X}^{\langle t \rangle} \right)_{n \times b} \right] + (b_o)_{q \times b} \right) \tag{5}$$

with $\Gamma_o \in [0, 1]$, and $b_o$ and $\mathcal{W}_o$ to be the corresponding bias and weight matrices. The final activated value of the LSTM cell is computed by

$$h^{\langle t \rangle} = \Gamma_o \odot \tanh\left( c^{\langle t \rangle} \right). \tag{6}$$

Here, the obtained activated value $h^{\langle t \rangle}$ from (6) will be used as the input hidden state to the next LSTM cell at the time $t + 1$.

Let us also mention that all the biases $b_c, b_u, b_f, b_o \in \mathbb{R}^{q \times b}$ and the weight matrices are further defined as

$$\mathcal{W}_c := \left[ (\mathcal{W}_{ch})_{q \times q} \middle| (\mathcal{W}_{cx})_{q \times n} \right]^\top, \qquad \mathcal{W}_u := \left[ (\mathcal{W}_{uh})_{q \times q} \middle| (\mathcal{W}_{ux})_{q \times n} \right]^\top$$

$$\mathcal{W}_f := \left[ (\mathcal{W}_{fh})_{q \times q} \middle| (\mathcal{W}_{fx})_{q \times n} \right]^\top, \qquad \mathcal{W}_o := \left[ (\mathcal{W}_{oh})_{q \times q} \middle| (\mathcal{W}_{ox})_{q \times n} \right]^\top$$

leading both the $\tilde{c}^{\langle t \rangle}, c^{\langle t \rangle} \in \mathbb{R}^{q \times b}$.

In this work and similar to [18], a BLSTM [3] is used so that the contexts from both sides of a deformed digit are accounted. A schematic view of BLSTM is shown as Fig. 2 with two recurrent layers of LSTMs processing the data in two opposite directions. In addition, we follow [3] and use BLSTM network architecture as revealed in [18] with a stack of two LSTMs, except we increase the number of hidden units from 256 to 715, leading us to the obtained results.

## 4.2   The FCSRN Approach

The main motivation of Yang et al., [22] was to eliminate the need for the recurrent layers of the widely used CRNN that resulted to a reduction of training parameters and hence a lighter network with less computational time. The FCSRN is designed aiming to capture contextual information of watermeter images by deploying a sufficiently deep CNN along with two other temporal mapper and transcription CTC layers on top of it.

The residual blocks proposed in [6] are used to provide the deepness of the CNN part of the FCSRN capable of extracting the context information from the images. Next, the need for a recurrent layer is substituted by a temporal mapper to generate feature sequences before the transcription layer.

The temporal mapper consists of a convolution layer, a batch normalization layer [12], and a height normalization layer. The latter layer performs an average pooling over the 2D matrix obtained from its predecessor convolution and batch normalization layers converting their result to a one-dimensional sequential features, which are to be fed into the final transcription CTC layer [1].

# 5  The Connectionist Temporal Classification

As the next step, let us provide a mathematical basis on which, the CTC [1] transcripts the feature vectors obtained from the BLSTM to labels between 0 and 9. More specifically, we consider a set of labels defined as $\mathcal{L} = \{0, 1, \cdots, 9, \text{blank}\}$. Now, at each time step $t \in \mathbb{N}_0$ the obtained feature vector from BLSTM defined as $\mathcal{Y}^{\langle t \rangle} \in \mathbb{R}^{\|\mathcal{L}\|}$ is converted to a probability distribution that sums to one, using a softmax function (see Eq. (7)).

By considering all the time steps, one obtains a matrix of probabilities with each row to represent a label $l \in \mathcal{L}$ and each column to contain a probability distribution $\mathcal{Y}^{\langle t \rangle}$ obtained from the BLSTM. Each cell $(i, t)$ of the probability matrix conveys the probability occurrence of the label $l$ at the $i^{th}$ row and time $t$. The probability matrix is obtained by:

$$P(i, t \mid \mathcal{Y}) = exp(\mathcal{Y}_i^t) / \sum_{0 \leq j \leq t} exp(\mathcal{Y}_j^t)) \qquad (7)$$

With $\mathcal{T} \in \mathbb{N}$ to be the total number of time steps, any path connecting the matrix cells starting from $t = 0$ and ending at at $t = \mathcal{T} - 1$ is called an *alignment* $\pi^\kappa$ with $\kappa^{\text{th}} \in \mathbb{N}$.

An alignment $\pi^\kappa$ can include any possible repetition of labels including the blank and its probability. Given an input $\mathcal{X}$, it is obtained by

$$P(\pi^\kappa \mid \mathcal{X}) = \prod_{t=0}^{\mathcal{T}-1} P(\pi_t^\kappa, t \mid \mathcal{X}) \qquad (8)$$

with the product of the probability matrix cells at each time step comprising a particular alignment $\pi^\kappa$. Based on CTC [1], every alignment can always be described by its corresponding transcription $\mathcal{Z} = \text{“}\mathcal{Z}_0 \mathcal{Z}_1 \mathcal{Z}_2 \cdots \mathcal{Z}_c\text{”}$ after eliminating the repetitions and blanks [9], by knowing $\mathcal{Z}_{0 \leq c \leq \mathcal{T}-1} \in \{0, 1, \cdots, 9, \text{blank}\}$. For example, the alignment $\pi = \text{“blank, 2, 2, 1, 3, 3”}$ corresponds to the transcription $\mathcal{Z} = \text{“blank, 2, 1, 3”}$.

However, any particular transcription $\mathcal{Z}$ can be deduced from more than one alignment as there are as many possible alignments as different ways of separating labels with blanks. Let $\mathcal{G}(\cdot)$ be a function that maps an alignment $\pi^\kappa$ to its corresponding transcription $\mathcal{Z}$, that is $\mathcal{Z} = \mathcal{G}(\pi^\kappa)$. Then, the probability of a produced transcription $\mathcal{Z}$ reads

$$P(\mathcal{Z} \mid \mathcal{X}) = \sum_{\forall \kappa \mid \mathcal{G}(\pi^\kappa) = \mathcal{Z}} P(\pi^\kappa \mid \mathcal{X}). \qquad (9)$$

Finally, CTC [1] guides the training by directly minimizing the loss function

$$L_{CTC} = -\ln(P(\mathcal{Z}^* \mid \mathcal{X})) \qquad (10)$$

with $\mathcal{Z}^*$ to be the target transcription. Note that, since the *natural logarithm* is monotonically increasing, maximizing $P(\mathcal{Z}^* \mid \mathcal{X}) > 0$ is equivalent to minimizing its negative natural logarithm.

# 6   Results

To evaluate the efficiency of the adopted FCSRN and CRNN against our data set, we divided our 1856 number of images into two training and test parts each containing 1313 and 543 samples, respectively. In addition, almost one by third of the train samples are kept aside for the validation purpose. We trained the CRNN model by randomly drawing 2500 number of batches from train samples. The training of FCSRN is performed till 100 number of epochs, while the batch size in both cases was chosen to be 32 and a convergence of low validation and train errors was considered as the stopping criteria. Similar to [18] the automated mechanism introduced in ADADELTA [24] was adopted while training CRNN that needs no manual tuning of the learning rate. With this we evaluated the mean accuracy rate of 0.779 for FCSRN, and 0.9683 for CRNN, on unseen test part. Thereby, accuracy is defined as accuracy $= \mathcal{N}_c/\mathcal{N}_t$, where $\mathcal{N}_t$ and $\mathcal{N}_c$ are the total number and the correctly recognized number of images, respectively.

**Fig. 3.** A subset of our test data successfully recognized by both adopted approaches.

To have a better insight about the obtained results, let us have a look on Figs. 3 and Table 1, revealing some recognized and failed samples from the test set. At hand of Fig. 3 we illustrate that correct results are found for most test images featuring challenging bubble distortions as well as distortions that one may consider of lower to medium difficulty. Since the overall accuracy we obtain is quite high, this means we can confirm that we reach the objective of our approach.

As shown in Table 1, both methods interestingly fail to recognize some apparently easy samples not even deformed by bubbles (see the fourth row of Table 1), although many very highly distorted samples are read correctly. We believe, it is mostly the nature of the original MNIST samples relying on handwritten forms leading to the failure cases shown in the fourth row of Table 1. We conjecture that the many variations apparent in handwritten digits add upon the variations introduced by the bubbles, leading to these few misclassifications.

**Table 1.** Some of few cases from our test data set that are not recognized fully either by [18] or [22]. The cases are shown as two middle columns and their corresponding results on their sides. Each side of the table has three columns representing the real label, and the found results either by [22] and [18]. The struck out light blue and red color labels are used to show the failure of [22] or [18], respectively.

| [22] | Label | [18] | | | [18] | Label | [22] |
|---|---|---|---|---|---|---|---|
| 05726 | 05726 | 05766 | | | 95852 | 95832 | 95832 |
| 01239 | 01234 | 01239 | | | 47531 | 47931 | 47931 |
| 36-07 | 36497 | 36487 | | | 41718 | 41778 | 41778 |
| 928093 | 92809 | 92803 | | | 97199 | 97195 | 37195 |
| 67851 | 67853 | 67851 | | | 66611 | 66011 | 66011 |
| 24179 | 24075 | 24175 | | | 11081 | 11051 | 11081 |

## 7 Conclusion

With this work we demonstrated a significant step towards watermeter automation in a practically relevant setting. This is enabled by studying strong bubble distortions at hand of a novel, dedicated data set we introduced, combined with state-of-the-art neural network techniques. The deep features obtained from convolution layers considered on both sides of the digits, that are integrated over time and penalized by CTC loss, revealed an acceptable performance rate. In the current study (heading for academic publication) we did not include the mechanical digit designs available from our industrial partner Meine-Energie GmbH.

**Acknowledgements.** Authors would like to thank Meine-Energie GmbH and the financial support from Zentrale Innovationsprogramm Mittelstand (ZIM) over Arbeitsgemeinschaft industrieller Forschungsvereinigungen (AiF).

## References

1. Graves, A., Fernández, S., Gomez, F.: Connectionist temporal classification: labelling unsegmented sequence data with recurrent neural networks. In: Proceedings of the International Conference on Machine Learning, pp. 369–376 (2006)
2. Ali, S., Sakhawat, Z., Mahmood, T., Aslam, M.S., Shaukat, Z., Sahiba, S.: A robust CNN model for handwritten digits recognition and classification. In: IEEE International Conference on Advances in Electrical Engineering and Computer Applications, pp. 261–265 (2020)
3. Graves, A., Mohamed, A., Hinton, G.: Speech Recognition with Deep Recurrent Neural Networks. arXiv:1303.5778 (2013)

4. Gao, Y., Zhao, C., Wang, J., Lu, H.: Automatic watermeter digit recognition on mobile devices. In: Huet, B., Nie, L., Hong, R. (eds.) ICIMCS 2017. CCIS, vol. 819, pp. 87–95. Springer, Singapore (2018). https://doi.org/10.1007/978-981-10-8530-7_9

5. Hochreiter, S., Schmidhuber, J.: Long short-term memory. Neural Comput., 1735–1780 (1997)

6. He, K., Zhang, X., Ren, S., Sun, J.: Deep Residual Learning for Image Recognition. In: IEEE Conference on Computer Vision and Pattern Recognition (CVPR), pp. 770–778 (2016)

7. Liwicki, M., Graves, A., Fernández, S., Bunke, H., Schmidhuber, J.: A novel approach to on-line handwriting recognition based on bidirectional long short-term memory networks. In: Proceedings of the 9th International Conference on Document Analysis and Recognition, pp. 1–5 (2007)

8. Kayumov, Z., Tumakov, D., Mosin, S.: Combined convolutional and perceptron neural networks for handwritten digits recognition. In: 22th International Conference on Digital Signal Processing and its Applications, pp. 1–5 (2020)

9. Hwang, K., Wonyong Sung, W.: Character-level incremental speech recognition with recurrent neural networks. arXiv:1601.06581 (2016)

10. Ning Wang, N., Yuanyuan W., Er, M.J.: Review on deep learning techniques for marine object recognition: architectures and algorithms. Control Eng. Pract. (2020)

11. Liu, Y., Han, Y., Zhang, Y.: Image type water meter character recognition based on embedded DSP. arXiv:1508.06725 (2015)

12. Ioffe, S., Szegedy, C.: Batch normalization: accelerating deep network training by reducing internal covariate shift. arXiv:1502.03167 (2015)

13. LeCun, Y., Cortes, C., Burges, C.: MNIST handwritten digit database. http://yann.lecun.com/exdb/mnist/

14. Lei, Z., Zhao, S., Song, H., Shen, J.: Scene text recognition using residual convolutional recurrent neural network. Mach. Vis. Appl. **29**(5), 861–871 (2018). https://doi.org/10.1007/s00138-018-0942-y

15. Liao, S., Zhou, P., Wang, L., Su, S.: Reading digital numbers of water meter with deep learning based object detector. Pattern Recogn. Comput. Vis., 38–49 (2019)

16. Moniruzzaman, M., Islam, S.M.S., Bennamoun, M., Lavery, P.: Deep learning on underwater marine object detection: a survey. In: Blanc-Talon, J., Penne, R., Philips, W., Popescu, D., Scheunders, P. (eds.) ACIVS 2017. LNCS, vol. 10617, pp. 150–160. Springer, Cham (2017). https://doi.org/10.1007/978-3-319-70353-4_13

17. Rodriguez-Serrano, J.A., Perronnin, F., Meylan, F.: Label embedding for text recognition. In: Proceedings British Machine Vision Conference, pp. 5.1–5.12 (2013)

18. Shi, B., Bai, X., Yao, C.: An end-to-end trainable neural network for image-based sequence recognition and its application to scene text recognition. IEEE Trans. Pattern Anal. Mach. Intell. **39**(11), 2298–2304 (2017)

19. Suresh, M., Muthukumar, U., Chandapillai, J.: A novel smart water-meter based on IoT and smartphone app for city distribution management. In: 2017 IEEE Region 10 Symposium (TENSYMP), pp. 1–5 (2017)

20. Xiao-ping, R., Xian-feng, S.: A character recognition algorithm adapt to a specific kind of water meter. In: World Congress on Computer Science and Information Engineering, vol. 5, pp. 632–636 (2009)

21. Ye, Q., Doermann, D.: Text detection and recognition in imagery: a survey. IEEE Trans. Pattern Anal. Mach. Intell. **37** (2015)

22. Yang, F., Jin, L., Lai, S., Gao, X., Li, Z.: Fully convolutional sequence recognition network for water meter number reading. IEEE Access **7**, 11679–11687 (2019)

23. Yi, L., Ni, H., Wen Z., Liu B., Tao J.: CTC regularized model adaptation for improving LSTM RNN based multi-accent Mandarin speech recognition. In: 10th International Symposium on Chinese Spoken Language Processing, pp. 1–5 (2016)
24. Zeiler, M.D.: ADADELTA: an adaptive learning rate method. arXiv:1212.5701 (2012)

# HR-Crime: Human-Related Anomaly Detection in Surveillance Videos

Kayleigh Boekhoudt[1(✉)], Alina Matei[1], Maya Aghaei[2],
and Estefanía Talavera[1,3]

[1] University of Groningen, Groningen, The Netherlands
`k.j.boekhoudt@student.rug.nl`
[2] NHL Stenden University of Applied Sciences, Leeuwarden, The Netherlands
[3] University of Twente, Enschede, The Netherlands

**Abstract.** The automatic detection of anomalies captured by surveillance settings is essential for speeding the otherwise laborious approach. To date, UCF-Crime is the largest available dataset for automatic visual analysis of anomalies and consists of real-world crime scenes of various categories. In this paper, we introduce *HR-Crime*, a subset of the UCF-Crime dataset suitable for *human-related* anomaly detection tasks. We rely on state-of-the-art techniques to build the feature extraction pipeline for human-related anomaly detection. Furthermore, we present the baseline anomaly detection analysis on the HR-Crime. HR-Crime as well as the developed feature extraction pipeline and the extracted features will be publicly available for further research in the field.

**Keywords:** Forensics · Human-related anomaly detection · Surveillance videos

## 1 Introduction

The detection of anomalous events in videos is a challenging task due to the broad definition of the term 'anomaly', as well as insufficient annotated data. Despite this, there has been much research in the field of video surveillance anomaly detection in the past years [15]. Surveillance cameras are a widely used technology which aids law enforcement agencies in ensuring general public safety. Surveillance footage is also considered a reliable piece of forensic evidence when the anomalies captured on the footage are identified as crimes. However, due to the overwhelming amount of surveillance video data (usually, surveillance cameras transmit 24/7 live footage), there is an outstanding need for the automation of abnormality detection in such videos.

---

M. Aghaei and E. Talavera—Contributed equally.

© Springer Nature Switzerland AG 2021
N. Tsapatsoulis et al. (Eds.): CAIP 2021, LNCS 13053, pp. 164–174, 2021.
https://doi.org/10.1007/978-3-030-89131-2_15

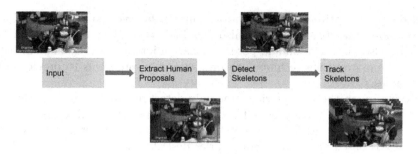

**Fig. 1.** Feature extraction pipeline of HR-Crime dataset. Given the frames of a video, we first extract human proposals using YOLOv3-spp [5]. Second, AlphaPose [3] is applied to detect body skeletons. Finally, PoseFlow [17] is used to track skeletons.

Human-related anomaly detection in surveillance videos, as a specific case of anomaly detection, is closely related to human activity detection that can be visually recognized as abnormal through body movement. In recent years, there have been many advances in the field of human pose (skeleton) estimation. Generally, there are two main types of frameworks used for pose detection. Two-step frameworks such as AlphaPose [3] use the top-down approach for pose detection. The idea is to first use an object detector to find people and then perform single-person pose estimation for each detected person. In contrast, methods that use the bottom-up approach to detect poses, first localize body parts and then group them into person instances [1,9].

There are advantages and disadvantages to these methods. Bottom-up methods feed the whole image to their architecture, which may impose limitations on the input image size. On the other hand, top-down methods crop and feed each individually detected human bounding boxes to their architecture. The disadvantages of the top-down method is that the keypoint detection performance depends on the quality of the bounding boxes and that the runtime is proportional to the number of people in the frame. Bottom-up approaches, on the contrary, do not have the issue of early commitment and runtime complexity. Cao et al. [1] suggests that AlphaPose [3] to be used for maximum accuracy, OpenPose [1] for maximum speed, and METU [9] for a trade-off between them.

Many efforts have also been made in recent years towards accurate human pose tracking. PoseTrack [8] and ArtTrack [6] introduced the multi-person pose tracking incorporating the idea of the part-based pose estimator DeeperCut [7] by extending spatial joint graph to spatio-temporal graph. First, the model generates for each frame, a set of detected keypoints and constructs the spatio-temporal graph. The model then solves an integer linear program to divide the graph into sub-graphs that correspond to skeleton trajectories of each person. These methods are also known as jointing schemes and are computationally heavy and not scalable to long videos. Top-down methods such as PoseFlow [17] are more scalable. The model starts by detecting human bounding boxes in every frame and extracts poses from each bounding box. The boxes are then tracked over the entire video in terms of similarity between pairs of boxes. These types of pose trackers are therefore also called Detect-And-Track methods. Pose-Flow [17] also takes motion and pose information into account by implementing a cross frame matching technique to propagate box proposals to previous and next frames.

Extending on the task of video anomaly detection, small progress has been made targeting the human-related anomaly detection plainly [2,4]. In [12], the authors proposed the MPED-RNN architecture for anomaly detection in surveillance videos based on skeleton trajectories described by local and global body movement. The proposed MPED-RNN follows an encoder-decoder architecture: the encoder learns close approximations of normal trajectory which are decoded with high accuracy; this implies that, when presented with abnormal trajectories, the encoder-decoder architecture obtains inaccurate reconstructions which results in high anomaly scores.

One reason for the small progress in human-related anomaly analysis might be the lack of human centered anomaly related datasets. Hence, the main contributions of this work are planned to target this shortage as following:

1. We introduce and make publicly available the Human-Related Crime dataset (HR-Crime) together with the annotations at the frame level.[1]
2. We present baseline results on HR-Crime intending to contribute to future research in the field of human-related anomaly detection.

The rest of the paper is organized as follows. In Sect. 2, we discuss our feature extraction pipeline for development of the HR-Crime dataset. In Sect. 3, we elaborate on the implementation details and discuss the obtained results. Finally, we draw conclusions in Sect. 4.

## 2    HR-Crime Dataset

As mentioned earlier, Morais et al. recently introduced the only work on human-related anomaly detection in surveillance videos [12]. Their introduced architecture, MPED-RNN, requires a defined set of features extracted from videos to detect the human-related abnormalities. In an attempt to provide the baseline results on HR-Crime, we opt for extracting the required features from the UCF-Crime [16] videos and only keep the relevant information out of it to build the HR-Crime dataset. In this section, we describe the followed steps to prepare the HR-Crime dataset.

[1] Dataset is publicly available at https://doi.org/10.34894/IRRDJE.

## 2.1   HR-Crime Statistics

The UCF-Crime dataset [16] consists of 950 real-world surveillance videos of anomalies, and 950 normal videos. The anomalies are divided into 13 categories: *Abuse, Arrest, Arson, Assault, Burglary, Explosion, Fighting, Road Accidents, Robbery, Shooting, Shoplifting, Stealing* and *Vandalism*. Duplicates may occur because some videos either have multiple anomalies or the anomaly may fall into more than one category. UCF-Crime dataset as is originally gathered to represent the *in-the-wild* nature of the crime scenes, at times lacks the required clarity in content even for human eyes. This comes in addition to the fact that only a subset of it is human-related. Hence, for further human-related anomaly analysis, we extracted HR-Crime out of UCF-Crime dataset using the following guidelines:

- Omitting videos of anomalous events that are not human-related. We refer to 'human-related' if the main performing subjects are human. Within this definition, dog abuse is not considered human-related.
- Excluding videos that do not have a clear view of the people at the scene.
- Ignoring videos with large crowds, as our goal is not to do crowd analysis which is essentially a different task than human behavior analysis.
- Ignoring videos longer than 100 min.

The resulted HR-Crime dataset consists of 789 human-related anomaly videos and 782 human-related normal videos. Examples are shown in Fig. 2. Table 1 shortly describes UCF-Crime and the newly proposed HR-Crime datasets. HR-Crime consists of 239 testing videos with annotation. Each video frame in this test set is annotated as normal or anomalous. As it can be observed, most categories consist mainly out of human-related videos. For instance, for *Shoplifting*, all the videos are human-related. In contrast, *Road accidents* has relatively the least number of human-related videos, which is expected as the people are mostly in cars, hence, not visible in the cameras.

Figure 3a compares the range and distribution of the video length in minutes for different categories. We observed that the video length varies for all categories. *RoadAccidents* has the smallest variability in length compared to the other categories. In contrast, videos from the categories *Shoplifting, Arrest, Fighting* and *Burglary* vary the most in length. However, the *Normal* category has the most number of videos that are longer than other videos of the same category. Inspecting the HR-Crime dataset, we realized that the longest *Normal* video lasts 93.62 min.

A comparison of the range and distribution of the number of tracked skeletons is shown in Fig. 3b. *Arson* varies the least in number of detected people. In contrast, *Arrest, Normal, Shoplifting* and *Fighting* range the most. After further analysis we realized that the *Normal* category has a video with a maximum of 1084 skeleton trajectories.

(a) Abuse

(b) Arrest

(c) Arson

(d) Assault

(e) Burglary

(f) Explosion

(g) Fighting

(h) Road Accidents

(i) Robbery

(j) Shooting

(k) Shoplifting

(l) Stealing

(m) Vandalism

(n) Normal

**Fig. 2.** From (a) to (n), example frames from HR-Crime: a man punches an older woman; the police escort a man; a person pours inflammable liquid on the ground; a man holds another man by his neck; two burglars steal an ATM; people run away from an explosion; a woman drags another woman by her hair; a car hits a child on a bicycle; a robber holds a knife; a shooting in an office; a man shoplifts a watch; a man hot-wires a motorcycle; a vandal writes on a garage door; a man walks down some stairs.

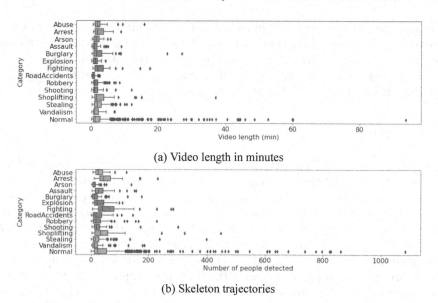

(a) Video length in minutes

(b) Skeleton trajectories

**Fig. 3.** Video length and number of skeleton trajectories distribution in HR-Crime.

**Table 1.** The first three rows display the number of videos, HR-videos and HR-test videos per category in UCF-Crime dataset, respectively. The number of anomalous and normal frames in HR-Crime for testing is shown in the bottom two rows. None of the *Abuse* videos is annotated with ground truth labels by the authors of [16].

| | Abuse | Arrest | Arson | Assault | Burglary | Explosion | Fighting | Road Accidents | Robbery | Shooting | Shoplifting | Stealing | Vandalism | Total anomalous | Total normal |
|---|---|---|---|---|---|---|---|---|---|---|---|---|---|---|---|
| Videos | 50 | 50 | 50 | 50 | 100 | 50 | 50 | 150 | 150 | 50 | 50 | 100 | 50 | **950** | **950** |
| HR-videos | 38 | 42 | 48 | 47 | 96 | 26 | 39 | 68 | 145 | 46 | 50 | 98 | 46 | **789** | **782** |
| Test HR-videos | 0 | 5 | 9 | 3 | 13 | 12 | 5 | 13 | 5 | 21 | 21 | 5 | 5 | **117** | **122** |
| Anomalous frames | 0 | 7820 | 8166 | 8520 | 16104 | 3097 | 4437 | 1233 | 3815 | 9314 | 7525 | 6007 | 2078 | **78116** | 0 |
| Normal frames | 0 | 25804 | 19722 | 18041 | 60420 | 31525 | 7855 | 10922 | 4512 | 65165 | 68609 | 13804 | 8999 | **335378** | **485227** |

## 2.2 Feature Extraction

The feature extraction pipeline starts with extracting human proposals from each frame of the video and extract skeletons from each proposal. As shown in Fig. 1, first, human body proposals are detected using YOLOv3-spp, a Dense Connection and Spatial Pyramid Pooling Based version of YOLOv3 [5]. Out of human body proposals, skeletons are retrieved employing AlphaPose [3]. Each skeleton consists of 17 keypoints representing body part locations. Skeletons are later tracked using PoseFlow [17] which uses FLANN and ORB descriptors to match two consecutive frames. The model we employed then uses tracked information in the last default 100 frames and using Hungarian algorithm [10] solves the bipartite matching problem for the current frame. PoseFlow uses Non-

Maximum Suppression just as AlphaPose to remove redundant trajectories and rematch disjoint pose flows. Given an input video, the skeletons are tracked over the frames to model the trajectory of each person appearing in a given video. The trajectories are later converted to CSV-files, which can be inputted to MPED-RNN human-based anomaly detector.

## 3  Experiments

To evaluate MPED-RNN, authors in [12] mainly used the HR-ShanghaiTech dataset [12]. This dataset originally does not contain ground-truth labels for human bounding boxes, skeletons or trajectories. Also, the feature extraction step on HR-ShanghaiTech is missing from the MPED-RNN pipeline provided by the authors. Therefore, we were unable to evaluate the feature extraction steps separately on the HR-ShanghaiTech. Thus, we propose to compare the performance of the pre-trained MPED-RNN on the trajectories obtained using our feature extraction pipeline against the trajectories provided by the authors. For completeness of the proposed dataset, we also include the baseline results of the MPED-RNN network applied on the skeleton trajectories of the HR-Crime.

### 3.1  Datasets

The HR-ShanghaiTech [12] consists of 101 human-related videos with anomalies such as running, jumping, riding a bicycle, etc. against the normality which is simply walking. HR-ShanghaiTech is a subset of ShanghaiTech dataset [11] consisting of 107 videos filmed by 12 cameras on the Shanghai Tech University campus.

Both the HR-ShanghaiTech test set [12] and UCF-Crime [16] test set are provided with frame-level ground truth labels by the authors indicating if the event is anomalous or normal. Table 1 shows that 239 videos of the UCF-Crime testing set are human-related (the sum of 117 anomalous and 122 normal videos). Only these videos are used for the evaluation since the remaining videos are not labelled at frame-level.

### 3.2  Results and Discussion

Following [12], we use the frame-level Receiver Operating Characteristic (ROC) curve and its corresponding Area Under (AUROC) to evaluate the performance of the methods on the HR-ShanghaiTech and HR-Crime datasets. A higher AUROC value indicates better performance.

*A) Pose extraction HR-Crime:* Figure 4 shows a few examples of skeletons extracted from HR-Crime using our feature extraction pipeline discussed in Sect. 2. As can be seen, the skeletons are reasonably accurate for higher quality videos and where the person is clearly in the camera view. However, for videos of lower quality or insufficient lighting, such as in Fig. 4b, the feature extraction pipeline fails to detect people and their poses.

*B) New baseline for HR-ShanghaiTech:* Authors of [12] made available 12 models, each trained separately on a camera subdivision of HR-ShanghaiTech. HR-Crime however, is not structured in a camera wise manner. Therefore to ensure further consistencies, we trained the MPED-RNN architecture, *de novo*, on the whole HR-ShanghaiTech training set from all the 12 cameras. For this training, we still used the trajectories provided by the authors. The model obtained from training on the entire HR-ShanghaiTech training set achieves a slightly lower performance in AUROC: 0.735 (see Table 2) compared to the 0.754 reported in [12], where 12 models are trained on the 12 camera subdivisions of HR-ShanghaiTech. This indicates that camera settings influence the complexity of the anomaly detection problem, at least when using MPED-RNN.

Moreover, as the authors of MPED-RNN did not provide detailed information on feature extraction steps from the videos, it is not possible to determine if feature extraction was purely done automatically or if human input was involved in refining the extracted features. This might be an important reason why using our feature extraction pipeline performs less accurately than the original trajectories given in [12] (0.534 AUROC score as compared to 0.735 AUROC score obtained by [12]).

*C) MPED-RNN on HR-Crime:* Our first approach to establish the HR-Crime baseline is to test the pre-trained MPED-RNN with the entire HR-ShanghaiTech training set (on trajectories provided by [12]), on the HR-Crime test set, without explicitly fine-tuning the model to the new domain. We report the performance on HR-Crime class-wise as well as on the entire test set. This shows how well the information learned from the HR-ShanghaiTech can generalize to other categories of crimes scenes.

The obtained results are presented in Table 2 and Table 3. They are reported based on the frame level reconstruction and prediction anomaly scores obtained by the MPED-RNN models. We observe that the AUROC scores are highest for videos of the type *Assault* (0.7487) and *Stealing* (0.7337). In contrast, *Arson* and *RoadAccidents* have the lowest AUROC scores, 0.4290 and 0.4171 respectively. These results indicate that the pre-trained MPED-RNN model can make promising predictions even on an unseen domain if the 'human' subjects are fairly present in committing the anomalies. This is also an indication of suitability of the proposed feature extraction pipeline.

*D) Fine-tuning MPED-RNN on HR-Crime:* The second approach for establishing the HR-Crime baseline is training the MPED-RNN architecture to the newly created HR-Crime. For this purpose, we train the MPED-RNN model *de novo* on the HR-Crime dataset. For completeness, we also propose to fine-tune the pre-trained MPED-RNN model on the HR-ShanghaiTech dataset, on HR-Crime. With this approach, we aim at closing the structural gap between the two datasets. The results are presented in Table 2. The model trained *de novo* on HR-Crime achieves 0.6030 AUROC performance which is explained by the increased complexity of the HR-Crime dataset as compared to HR-ShanghaiTech. Surprisingly, the fine-tuned model achieves a lower AUROC performance of 0.5879 as compared to the model trained *de novo*. We suspect, the information gain from

(a) Satisfactory feature extraction

(b) Unsatisfactory feature extraction

**Fig. 4.** Visual examples of skeletons (in red) obtained from HR-Crime videos using our feature extraction pipeline. The first row displays examples of satisfactory extractions from clear videos. The bottom row shows examples of unsatisfactory extractions.

**Table 2.** Baseline results for the HR-ShanghaiTech and HR-Crime datasets using MPED-RNN models.

| Dataset | AUROC |
|---|---|
| *B) New baseline for HR-ShanghaiTech* | |
| HR-ShanghaiTech | **0.7346** |
| *C) MPED-RNN on HR-Crime* | |
| HR-ShanghaiTech (pre-trained) [12] | 0.5346 |
| *D) Fine-tuning MPED-RNN on HR-Crime* | |
| HR-Crime (de novo) | **0.6030** |
| HR-ShanghaiTech (fine-tuned) | 0.5879 |

**Table 3.** Class-wise results for the HR-Crime dataset using the pre-trained MPED-RNN on HR-ShanghaiTech.

| Dataset | Crime class | AUROC |
|---|---|---|
| *C) MPED-RNN on HR-Crime* | | |
| HR-ShanghaiTech (pre-trained) [12] | Arrest | 0.5617 |
| | Arson | 0.4290 |
| | Assault | 0.7487 |
| | Burglary | 0.6790 |
| | Explosion | 0.4740 |
| | Fighting | 0.4847 |
| | Road accidents | 0.4171 |
| | Robbery | 0.6586 |
| | Shooting | 0.4900 |
| | Shoplifting | 0.6342 |
| | Stealing | 0.7337 |
| | Vandalism | 0.6396 |

the HR-ShanghaiTech model does not generalize well to the HR-Crime dataset. This emphasizes the complexity gap between the two datasets that is apparent when comparing anomalies such as running and jumping in HR-ShanghaiTech to the anomalous events in HR-Crime. Comparing to the results of the experiment (C), our fine-tuned model shows a slight increase in performance which might also suggest that the pre-training approach is relevant to consider when comparing two datasets with distinct structures.

# 4    Conclusion

In this work, we discussed the preparation steps to develop HR-Crime, and provided a baseline human-related anomaly detection analysis on it. The dataset as well as the feature extraction pipeline will be publicly available for further use by the community.

The results presented in Sect. 3 (C) show that the pre-trained MPED-RNN on HR-ShanghaiTech does not perform as well on HR-Crime compared to the performance achieved on HR-ShanghaitTech itself. We suspect this to happen due to the complexity gap between the two datasets as also has been observed in other domains [13] and [18]. HR-ShanghaiTech consists of videos shot on the same University campus. HR-Crime, on the other hand, is a collection of YouTube videos, where each video is filmed in a different location. Also, the types of anomalies differ greatly: HR-ShanghaiTech contains anomalous events such as *running* and *jumping*, while HR-Crime consists of real-world crime scenes with natural movements that are not staged. The quality of the videos also plays an important role in anomaly detection. The HR-ShanghaiTech videos are of high quality, while the HR-Crime videos range in quality and lighting. Thus, skeletons and trajectories are detected less accurately for HR-Crime.

Another factor that plays an essential role in the high number of false negatives for anomalous events is the frame-level evaluation. Each test video in HR-Crime is annotated with ground truth labels indicating the window of an anomalous event. These windows indicate the start and end frame of the event. As mentioned before, the HR-Crime dataset is composed of a complex set of videos. Therefore an anomalous event such as a *Burglary* can have multiple anomalous and normal movements in the same video. However, prediction and evaluation are made per frame. An alternative that we plan on exploring is to label the videos temporally and spatially to not only evaluate if a frame contains an anomalous event but also to find the area where it occurs as suggested in [14]. This is a more accurate way of evaluating anomalous events. However, it requires laborious work to annotate video frames manually. Future lines of research will also be dedicated to the categorical classification of the identified anomalies through the analysis of the descriptors of the movement of the human body.

# References

1. Cao, Z., Hidalgo, G., Simon, T., Wei, S.E., Sheikh, Y.: OpenPose: realtime multi-person 2D pose estimation using part affinity fields. IEEE Trans. PAMI (2019)
2. Emonet, R., Varadarajan, J., Odobez, J.M.: Multi-camera open space human activity discovery for anomaly detection. In: IEEE International Conference on AVSS (2011)
3. Fang, H.S., Xie, S., Tai, Y.W., Lu, C.: RMPE: regional multi-person pose estimation. In: IEEE International Conference on Computer Vision (2017)
4. Gong, M., Zeng, H., Xie, Y., Li, H., Tang, Z.: Local distinguishability aggrandizing network for human anomaly detection. Neural Netw. **122**, 364–373 (2020)

5. Huang, Z., Wang, J., Fu, X., Yu, T., Guo, Y., Wang, R.: DC-SPP-YOLO: dense connection and spatial pyramid pooling based yolo for object detection. Inf. Sci. (2020)
6. Insafutdinov, E., et al.: ArtTrack: articulated multi-person tracking in the wild. In: IEEE Conference on Computer Vision and Pattern Recognition (2017)
7. Insafutdinov, E., Pishchulin, L., Andres, B., Andriluka, M., Schiele, B.: DeeperCut: a deeper, stronger, and faster multi-person pose estimation model. In: Leibe, B., Matas, J., Sebe, N., Welling, M. (eds.) ECCV 2016. LNCS, vol. 9910, pp. 34–50. Springer, Cham (2016). https://doi.org/10.1007/978-3-319-46466-4_3
8. Iqbal, U., Milan, A., Gall, J.: PoseTrack: joint multi-person pose estimation and tracking. In: IEEE Conference on Computer Vision and Pattern Recognition (2017)
9. Kocabas, M., Karagoz, S., Akbas, E.: MultiPoseNet: fast multi-person pose estimation using pose residual network. In: Ferrari, V., Hebert, M., Sminchisescu, C., Weiss, Y. (eds.) ECCV 2018. LNCS, vol. 11215, pp. 437–453. Springer, Cham (2018). https://doi.org/10.1007/978-3-030-01252-6_26
10. Kuhn, H.W.: The Hungarian method for the assignment problem. Naval Res. Logistics Q., 83–97 (1955)
11. Liu, W., Luo, W., Lian, D., Gao, S.: Future frame prediction for anomaly detection-a new baseline. In: IEEE Conference on Computer Vision and Pattern Recognition (2018)
12. Morais, R., Le, V., Tran, T., Saha, B., Mansour, M., Venkatesh, S.: Learning regularity in skeleton trajectories for anomaly detection in videos. In: IEEE Conference on Computer Vision and Pattern Recognition (2019)
13. Quattoni, A., Torralba, A.: Recognizing indoor scenes. In: 2009 IEEE Conference on Computer Vision and Pattern Recognition, pp. 413–420. IEEE (2009)
14. Ramachandra, B., Jones, M.: Street scene: a new dataset and evaluation protocol for video anomaly detection. In: IEEE Winter Conference on Applications of Computer Vision (2020)
15. Ramachandra, B., Jones, M., Vatsavai, R.R.: A survey of single-scene video anomaly detection. IEEE Trans. Pattern Anal. Mach. Intell. (2020)
16. Sultani, W., Chen, C., Shah, M.: Real-world anomaly detection in surveillance videos. In: IEEE Conference on Computer Vision and Pattern Recognition (2018)
17. Xiu, Y., Li, J., Wang, H., Fang, Y., Lu, C.: Pose flow: efficient online pose tracking. arXiv preprint arXiv:1802.00977 (2018)
18. Zhou, B., Lapedriza, A., Khosla, A., Oliva, A., Torralba, A.: Places: a 10 million image database for scene recognition. IEEE Trans. Pattern Anal. Mach. Intell. **40**(6), 1452–1464 (2017)

# Sequence-Based Recognition of License Plates with Severe Out-of-Distribution Degradations

Denise Moussa$^{(\boxtimes)}$ [ID], Anatol Maier [ID], Franziska Schirrmacher [ID],
and Christian Riess [ID]

Friedrich-Alexander-Universität Erlangen-Nürnberg, Erlangen, Germany
denise.moussa@fau.de

**Abstract.** Criminal investigations regularly involve the deciphering of license plates (LPs) of vehicles. Unfortunately, the image or video source material typically stems from uncontrolled sources, and may be subject to severe degradations such as extremely low resolution, strong compression, low contrast or over- resp. underexposure. While LP recognition has a long history in computer vision research, the deciphering under such severe degradations is still an open issue. Moreover, since the data source is not controlled, it cannot be assumed that the exact form of degradation is covered in the training set.

In this work, we propose using convolutional recurrent neural networks (CRNN) for the recognition of LPs from images with strong unseen degradations. The CRNN clearly outperforms an existing conventional CNN in this scenario. It also provides an additional particular advantage for criminal investigations, namely to create top-$n$ sequence predictions. Even a low number of top-$n$ candidates improves the recognition performance considerably.

**Keywords:** License plate recognition · Forensics · Low-quality images

## 1 Introduction

Criminal investigations often include the examination of photo and video recordings that may serve as clue or evidence with probative value in a legal context. Forensic material might also contain the depiction of an escape vehicle or parts thereof. An important task then is the robust detection and recognition of the vehicle's license plate (LP). Unfortunately, such material regularly stems from sources of low quality, for example from cheap surveillance camera systems. In addition, environment based deterioration like motion blur or advert lighting can be challenging.

Most existing works on LP recognition assume high-quality images, i.e. photos that can also be deciphered by humans. Only few works address the task of

---

We gratefully acknowledge support by the German Federal Ministry of Education and Research (BMBF) under Grant No. 13N15319.

N. Tsapatsoulis et al. (Eds.): CAIP 2021, LNCS 13053, pp. 175–185, 2021.
https://doi.org/10.1007/978-3-030-89131-2_16

recognizing severely degraded LPs [2,7,11,14]. These works use standard CNN architectures. However, research on high-quality LPs showed improved performance by conducting a sequence analysis with the help of combined CNN and RNN architectures [10,15,16,18,20]. These types of networks exploit that LP character sequences usually follow rules which can be grasped by such architectures.

In this work, we propose such a sequence analysis for severely degraded LPs that are not perceptible to the human eye. Our adapted CRNN provides two essential benefits for criminal investigations. First, it performs very well on out-of-distribution degradations that were not part of the training set, which is a vital precondition for analyzing footage from unknown sources. Second, it provides top-$n$ predictions, which boosts the detection already for low $n$. Our specific contributions thus are:

1. We adapt the CRNN architecture by Shi *et al.* [15] for recognizing severely degraded LPs.
2. We show the effectiveness of the proposed method on real data, and evaluate its robustness on out-of-distribution samples on synthetic data.
3. We show that the proposed method outperforms existing work. Major additional improvements are obtained from the CRNN's top-$n$ predictions.

In Sect. 2, we describe previous approaches to LP recognition, particularly on low quality data. Section 3 presents the proposed architecture and data. In Sect. 4, we present the experimental protocol and results. Section 5 discusses our findings, and Sect. 6 concludes this work.

## 2   Related Work

Automatic license plate recognition (ALPR) is an active research topic, where most works focus on real-world image and video data of good quality that are captured from known cameras. These methods typically utilize a two stage process, consisting of LP detection and character recognition. Detection is often based on the YOLO real-time object detector [1,8,9,12,13,19]. Character recognition is modeled either as a classification task [1,8,9,19], or as a sequence labeling task via convolutional recurrent neural networks (CRNNs) [10,13,15,16,18,20]. Here, convolutional layers extract features from an image which is then reshaped into a sequence as input for recurrent layers. The resulting output matrix is then transformed to the final character sequence by a transcription layer using connectionist temporal classification (CTC) [5]. Contrary to CNNs, CRNNs are not limited to individual features for character predictions, but instead they operate on the whole sequence. Furthermore, CRNNs can predict sequences of arbitrary length without changes to the architecture.

However, ALPR on images that are degraded beyond human recognition has only received little attention so far. Agarwal *et al.* [2] propose a CNN to process LPs degraded by noise and very low resolution. Their method classifies two groups of three characters under several constraints on font style, character ratio,

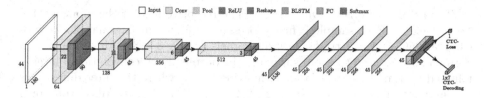

**Fig. 1.** Configuration of our adapted CRNN architecture

character width and foreground-background contrast. Lorch *et al.* [11] generalize their approach to LPs of five to seven characters without constraints on character properties. Their model uses seven output layers to achieve a per-character prediction for the whole input image. Kaiser *et al.* [7] analyze the impact of lossy compression on the performance of Lorch *et al.* [11]. The authors also study detection accuracy w.r.t. character position and the confusion of characters with similar shape. Recently, Rossi *et al.* [14] investigated cues for interpreting and explaining predictions for severely degraded LPs by adding a U-NET based denoiser prior to the recognition CNN. Hereby, the denoised output allows for a validation of the predictions.

All these previous works model degraded LP recognition by classifying each character independently [2,7,11,14]. However, as for ALPR on high-quality images, we argue that exploiting sequence information also improves recognition on strongly degraded LPs. We propose a CRNN architecture and compare its performance to the baseline method by Lorch *et al.* [11]. Our training data consists of synthetic Czech LPs subjected to compression, low resolution and Gaussian noise as employed by Kaiser *et al.* [7]. We provide an extensive robustness evaluation on degradations that are not part of the training set, namely underexposure, shot noise, salt and pepper noise, motion and defocus blur. We evaluate on real Czech LP images, showing the performance on mixed unseen degradations as expected in practice.

## 3  Methods

Here, we describe the proposed CRNN model, the pipeline for generating the synthetic training data and all degradation types for our training and test sets.

### 3.1  CRNN Architecture

Our CRNN model is based on the architecture by Shi *et al.* [15] which consists of three parts: a convolutional part for feature extraction, a recurrent part for sequence prediction, and a CTC layer for loss computation and sequence decoding. We adapt all hyperparameter values to fit our task formulation as described in the following text.

The architecture is shown in Fig. 1. The receptive field of the input is 44 × 180 × 1 pixels. Each sample is first processed by four convolutional blocks with 64, 128, 256, and 512 trainable filter kernels of size 3 × 3 with stride $z = 1$. Zero-padding is used to avoid shrinking the output. Each convolutional layer is followed by a max pooling layer with stride $z = 1$, where the filter dimensions per layer with increasing depth are $2 \times 2, 2 \times 2, 2 \times 1$, and $2 \times 1$. All convolutional blocks conclude with a ReLU activation followed by batch normalization.

The output of the convolutional part is reshaped as described by Shi et al. [15] to form a sequence of feature vectors along the columns of the input image. This enables the following bidirectional long short-term memory (BLSTM) [6] layers to sequentially process the feature map column by column. The four BLSTM layers are of depth 256, consisting of one forward and one backward LSTM of depth 128. Each layer uses dropout with probability 0.5. The resulting label sequence is $\mathbf{y} = [\mathbf{y}_0, \ldots, \mathbf{y}_T]$ with $T = 44$, where the 45 image columns are interpreted as positional dimensions in the sequence. This sequence is processed by a 45 × 37 fully connected layer, where the 37 columns encode the label characters, i.e., the 26 latin characters, the digits 0–9, and a blank. A softmax layer then yields a probability distribution over all 37 labels for each time step $t$. During training, the CTC loss is computed from the softmax output. During inference, CTC decoding is applied and the resulting prediction is returned.

The convolutional layers and BLSTM layers use Glorot (Xavier) uniform initialization for the kernel weights, and the bias is initialized with zeros. We apply the Adam optimizer with learning rate $\eta = 1\mathrm{e}{-}4$ and default parameters $\mu = 0.9$ and $\rho = 0.999$. Training and evaluation both use a batch size of 32. The training and validation data consists of 10 000 000 and 5 000 samples, respectively. Training is performed for one epoch, so that the model only processes each individual sample once. For the evaluation, we use test sets of 10 000 samples per run.

### 3.2   Generation of Synthetic Data Sets

To the best of our knowledge, no large-scale real world data exists with controlled degradations. Hence, we train the network on synthetic data. This allows to control degradation types and strengths for analyzing the impact of individual degradations. We generate Czech LPs to also evaluate our method on the real-world data set by Španhel et al. [17] (cf. Sect. 4.2).

We adapt the data generator by Lorch et al. [11] to Czech LP specifications, including the character ratio, character number, font type, different offsets and gap sizes [4]. Each LP consists of seven characters $c_n$, $0 \leq n \leq 6$, in groups of three and four characters separated by a gap with a sticker. For the first letter, we slightly deviate from the specification and only generate digits, since letters are very rare in practice. Position $c_1 \in \{A, B, C, E, H, J, K, L, M, P, S, T, U, Z\}$ specifies the region. Position $c_2$ can be any Latin character or digit. Positions $c_3, \ldots, c_6$ can only contain digits.

The pipeline for generating gray scale LPs is implemented as follows. First, random syntactically correct LP character strings are created with fonts, gaps and offsets within the specification range. Then, a background with random speckle is added to support the model generalization to real data. The font intensity is randomly selected while ensuring a minimum contrast to the background. The resulting image has a resolution of $120 \times 520$ pixels. Task-specific degradations are applied prior to nearest neighbor downsampling to a size of $44 \times 180$ pixels [11]. For network training we scale the intensities to $[0, 1]$.

### 3.3 Training Set Degradations

During training we use the union of the three types of image degradations from Lorch *et al.* [11] and Kaiser *et al.* [7]. These degradations include downsampling to extremely low resolution to simulate vehicles at a distance, the addition of additive Gaussian noise as general distortion, and the addition of JPEG compression. Note that for practical criminal investigations, further augmentations could be used. However, they generally have to operate on out-of-distribution data, where pictures stem from uncontrolled sources and suffer from all sorts and combinations of degradations. Hence, we argue that this selection approximates a minimum set of degradations that can be anticipated already at training time, while leaving sufficiently large room for unseen degradations to evaluate the method performance.

To each of the 10 000 000 training and 5 000 validation samples, each degradation is applied with a randomly chosen strength. Here, we use bicubic downsampling to create LPs with widths $w \in [20, 180]$ pixels, additive Gaussian Noise with a signal-to-noise ratio between original and distorted image of $SNR_{db} \in [-3, 20]$, and JPEG compression with quality factors $q \in \{5, \ldots, 95\}$.

### 3.4 Test Set Degradations

Real-world LP images from uncontrolled sources may exhibit degradations that are not covered by the training data. We hence create out-of-distribution degradations only used during testing.

**Underexposure** occurs at low-light acquisitions, which are of particular interest for criminal investigators. We simulate underexposure by multiplying a factor $c < 1$ to every pixel of an image.

**Shot Noise** is created within the camera, and has larger impact on low-light acquisitions. In the simulation, we synthetically underexpose the image and draw each final pixel value from a Poisson distribution with standard deviation $\lambda$ equal to the underexposed pixel value [3].

**Salt and Pepper Noise** is an impulse noise, randomly appearing as dark and bright pixels, typically caused by technical defects. We simulate this noise by randomly setting pixel values to 1 (salt) or 0 (pepper) with probability $p$.

**Motion Blur** from fast moving vehicles smears the intensities along the motion direction [3]. We simulate linear motion blur via convolution of the image with a box kernel of width $W$ in either horizontal or vertical direction.

**Defocus Blur** from defocused cameras is simulated by convolving the image with a symmetric 2-D Gaussian kernel with standard deviation $\sigma$.

| Underexp. | Shot Noise | Salt/Pepper | Hor. Motion | Vert. Motion | Defocus Blur |
|---|---|---|---|---|---|
| $c = 0.5$ | $c = 1.0$ | $p = 0.01$ | $W = 3$ | $W = 3$ | $\sigma = 1$ |
| $c = 0.25$ | $c = 0.01$ | $p = 0.1$ | $W = 7$ | $W = 7$ | $\sigma = 3$ |
| $c = 0.125$ | $c = 0.0025$ | $p = 0.5$ | $W = 15$ | $W = 15$ | $\sigma = 5$ |
| $c = 0.005$ | $c = 0.0001$ | $p = 0.8$ | $W = 35$ | $W = 35$ | $\sigma = 10$ |

**Fig. 2.** Exemplary synthetic samples with increasing level of degradation per row.

## 4    Evaluation

We report accuracies for the correct detection of whole LP sequences. The top-1 accuracy of the proposed method with best-path decoding [5] (CRNN) is compared to Lorch *et al.* [11] (CNN). We also report CRNN top-$n$ accuracies, which are not available for the CNN (cf. Sect. 5).

The CRNN top-$n$ predictions are obtained from beam search decoding with beam sizes $n \in \{3, 5, 10\}$. This beam search performs a breadth-first search with best-first strategy that explores $n$ label solutions per time step in a sequence.

### 4.1    Robustness Testing on Synthetic Out-of-Distribution Data

We evaluate the impact of each type of unseen degradation individually, except for shot noise, where the addition of Poisson noise comes with a reduction of exposure. Each individual unseen degradation parameter is evaluated using 10 000 test samples. Figure 2 shows example test samples with their associated degradation parameters.

**Underexposure.** We chose 15 levels of underexposure with $c \in 10^{-3} \cdot \{$ 0.1, 1, 2.5, 3.75, 4, 4.25, 4.5, 4.75, 5, 7.5, 10, 100, 125, 250, 500$\}$. The values are chosen adaptively during evaluation to densely cover regions with major accuracy variations. Figure 3a shows that the CRNN with best path decoding clearly outperforms the CNN. The CRNN robustly handles underexposure unless $c <$ 0.0075, while the CNN collapses for all $c \leq 0.25$. Beam search decoding does not improve performance over best path decoding.

**Shot Noise.** Since the standard deviation of shot noise is determined in dependence of the exposure, we re-use the exposure parameter $c$ and evaluate 18 adaptively chosen parameters $c \in 10^{-3} \cdot \{$0.1, 1, 2.5, 3, 3.25, 3.5, 3.75, 4.4, 4.25, 4.5, 4.75, 5, 10, 100, 125, 250, 500, 1000$\}$. Figure 3b shows the results. The CRNN model's performance using best path decoding outperforms the CNN. The CRNN accuracy is almost 1 for $c \geq 0.01$, and degrades steadily until $c = 0.003$. In contrast, the CNN performance drops sharply for $c \leq 0.5$.

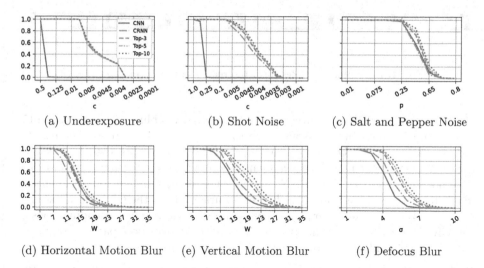

(a) Underexposure          (b) Shot Noise          (c) Salt and Pepper Noise

(d) Horizontal Motion Blur    (e) Vertical Motion Blur    (f) Defocus Blur

**Fig. 3.** Accuracy results of CNN and CRNN on synthetic test data sets. Detailed numerical results are available. (https://www.cs1.tf.fau.de/research/multimedia-security/code/.)

Compared to the previous experiment that only evaluates underexposure without noise, both models perform better. We assume that in this case, the additional Poisson noise slightly enhances the differences between the original pixel contrast. Beam search decoding leads to a further increase of the CRNN performance. This performance gain is already achieved with a beam width of $n = 3$, which indicates that the correct LP sequence is oftentimes only marginally missed in the top-1 prediction.

**Salt and Pepper Noise.** Salt and pepper noise is added with increasing probabilities $p \in \{0.01, 0.05, 0.075, 0.1, 0.25, 0.5, 0.65, 0.75, 0.8\}$ until the model accuracy drops to 0. Figure 3c shows the results. The CNN and the CRNN with best path decoding are very robust until $p \geq 0.25$, and performance gently degrades for higher noise levels. For $p \geq 0.1$, the CNN marginally outperforms the CRNN, but beam search decoding provides a major performance gain. Already, the top-3 accuracy improves the CRNN performance over the CNN. The top-10 predictions further increase accuracy over the CNN, most notably for $p = 0.5$ (0.8584 versus 0.2663) and $p = 0.65$ (0.2276 versus 0.1212).

**Horizontal Motion Blur.** We simulate 17 horizontal motion blur kernels with widths $W \in \{3, 5, 7, 9, 11, 13, 15, 17, 19, 21, 23, 25, 27, 29, 31, 33, 35\}$. Figure 3d shows the results. The CNN and the CRNN with best path decoding exhibit similar performance, with slightly better results for the CNN. Beam search decoding increases the performance of the CRNN already for $n = 3$. For beam width $n = 10$, the top-$n$ accuracy is on average 0.0458 higher than the CNN. In practice, this increases the chance of finding the correct LP, even though it has to be identified from 10 candidates.

(a)          (b)          (c)          (d)          (e)          (f)

**Fig. 4.** Exemplary samples form the real world data set *ReId* [17].

**Vertical Motion Blur.** To account for vertical motion blur, we use the same 17 motion blur kernels, but transpose each to flip it by ninety degrees. The results are shown in Fig. 3e. Overall, all accuracies are considerably higher, which is expected, as vertical motion does not smear across character boundaries, and also does not interfere with the CRNN's subdivision of the input into vertical slices. The CRNN achieves considerably higher accuracies than the CNN for all kernel sizes. For $W \geq 7$, the accuracy gently degrades. Beam search decoding boosts the CRNN performance. The average improvement over best path decoding is 0.0634, 0.0903 and 0.1260 for $n = 3$, $n = 5$ and $n = 10$.

**Defocus Blur.** The test data set is degraded by defocus blur with $1 \leq \sigma \leq 10$. The results are shown in Fig. 3f. The CRNN with best path decoding surpasses the CNN's performance. For $4 \leq \sigma \leq 6$, the accuracy declines. Beam search decoding provides a notable performance increase. With $n = 10$, the accuracy remains above 0.1 for $\sigma \leq 7$.

### 4.2 Performance on Real World Data

We use the *ReId* dataset by Špaňhel *et al.* [17] to test on low-quality real-world images from Czech LPs. The dataset consists of 76 412 images from video cameras on highway bridges. Approximately 99.67% of the samples show Czech LPs, the remaining 0.03% originate from other European countries. Example images are shown in Fig. 4.

We add an eighth output layer to the CNN to accommodate for the 8 characters of Czech LPs as described by Kaiser *et al.* [7]. The CRNN architecture is used without any changes regarding the architecture. Without retraining, the CNN accuracy is 0.6806, and the CRNN accuracy is only 0.1346, which indicates larger difficulties to generalize to this dataset. Beam search achieves top-$n$ accuracies of 0.2068, 0.2406 and 0.2849 for $n \in \{3, 5, 10\}$. The difficulties of both models to generalize is expected, even if most samples seem to be readable for human observers. The *ReId* dataset contains combined and unseen degradations like distortion and rotation. In addition, the LPs are not carefully aligned within the images.

Retraining the neural nets on the training part of the dataset of 105 924 images results in a significant improvement. The CNN achieves an accuracy of 0.9042, the CRNN achieves an accuracy of 0.9807 with best path decoding. The top-$n$ accuracies are even slightly higher with 0.9847, 0.9867 and 0.9891 with beam sizes $n \in \{3, 5, 10\}$.

# 5   Discussion

The results show that the proposed CRNN with best path decoding outperforms the CNN on most out-of-distribution degradation situations. When testing on synthetic data, the CRNN is superior for underexposure, shot noise, vertical motion blur and defocus blur. The CNN performs slightly better on salt and pepper noise and horizontal motion blur. The advantage of the CRNN becomes more apparent when investigating the benefit of top-3 and top-5 predictions, which always outperform the CNN by a large margin. Without retraining, the CNN generalizes better to real-world data with unseen degradations. However, when fine-tuning the networks, the CRNN again outperforms the CNN.

The possibility to perform top-$n$ predictions is particularly interesting for criminal investigations. For example, given 5 predictions, false candidates can be eliminated using additional knowledge like queries for registered LPs and the vehicle make and model. This benefit is only available for the CRNN: the CNN can only provide top-$n$ predictions per character, not per sequence. Converting such top-$n$ character predictions to reasonable top-$n$ sequences is a challenge in its own right. Furthermore, the CRNN can predict arbitrary numbers of characters on a license plate, while the CNN must be adapted to each length.

# 6   Conclusion

Forensic investigations can benefit from the possibility to decipher LP images with severe degradations from unknown sources. In this work, we propose sequence learning on such strongly degraded LP images. The proposed CRNN outperforms the CNN approach by Lorch et al. [11] and Kaiser et al. [7] by a large margin. A particular benefit of the CRNN are the top-$n$ most likely sequences. In many cases, the correct LP sequence is among the first few predictions. While the CRNN with only a single prediction already performs strongly, the top-$n$ for $n \in \{3, 5, 10\}$ considerably improve the results. In forensic practice, it is very reasonable to work with such a relatively small number of ranked predictions.

Future work may further investigate deeper into horizontal motion blur, and consider perspective distortions and rotation. It may also be interesting to investigate the CRNN on LPs from countries like Germany that impose richer syntactic sequence rules.

# References

1. Abdullah, S., Hasan, M.M., Islam, S.M.S.: YOLO-based three-stage network for Bangla license plate recognition in Dhaka metropolitan city. In: IEEE International Conference on Bangla Speech and Language Processing, pp. 1–6 (2018)
2. Agarwal, S., Tran, D., Torresani, L., Farid, H.: Deciphering Severely Degraded License Plates. Electronic Imaging 2017(7), 138–143 (2017)

3. Bovik, A.C.: Handbook of Image and Video Processing. Academic Press, Cambridge (2010)
4. Council of EU: Collection of Laws of the Czech Republic. No. 343/2014 (2014)
5. Graves, A., Fernández, S., Gomez, F., Schmidhuber, J.: Connectionist temporal classification: labelling unsegmented sequence data with recurrent neural networks. In: 23rd International Conference on Machine Learning, pp. 369–376 (2006)
6. Graves, A., Schmidhuber, J.: Framewise phoneme classification with bidirectional LSTM and other neural network architectures. In: IEEE International Joint Conference on Neural Networks, vol. 4, pp. 2047–2052 (2005)
7. Kaiser, P., Schirrmacher, F., Lorch, B., Riess, C.: Learning to decipher license plates in severely degraded images. In: Del Bimbo, A., et al. (eds.) Pattern Recognition. ICPR International Workshops and Challenges. ICPR 2021. Lecture Notes in Computer Science, vol. 12666. Springer, Cham (2021). https://doi.org/10.1007/978-3-030-68780-9_43
8. Laroca, R., Menotti, D.: Automatic license plate recognition: an efficient and layout-independent system based on the YOLO detector. In: Anais Estendidos do XXXIII Conference on Graphics, Patterns and Images, pp. 15–21. SBC (2020)
9. Laroca, R., et al.: A robust real-time automatic license plate recognition based on the YOLO detector. In: IEEE International Joint Conference on Neural Networks, pp. 1–10 (2018)
10. Li, H., Wang, P., Shen, C.: Towards End-to-End Car License Plates Detection and Recognition with Deep Neural Networks. IEEE Transactions on Intelligent Transportation Systems 20(3), 1126–1136 (2018)
11. Lorch, B., Agarwal, S., Farid, H.: Forensic reconstruction of severely degraded license plates. Electron. Imaging **2019**(5), 529-1 (2019)
12. Redmon, J., Divvala, S., Girshick, R., Farhadi, A.: You only look once: unified, real-time object detection. In: IEEE Conference on Computer Vision and Pattern Recognition, pp. 779–788 (2016)
13. Riaz, W., Azeem, A., Chenqiang, G., Yuxi, Z., Khalid, W., et al.: YOLO based recognition method for automatic license plate recognition. In: IEEE International Conference on Advances in Electrical Engineering and Computer Applications, pp. 87–90 (2020)
14. Rossi, G., Fontani, M., Milani, S.: Neural network for denoising and reading degraded license plates. In: Del Bimbo, A., et al. (eds.) Pattern Recognition. ICPR International Workshops and Challenges. ICPR 2021. Lecture Notes in Computer Science, vol. 12666. Springer, Cham (2021). https://doi.org/10.1007/978-3-030-68780-9_39
15. Shi, B., Bai, X., Yao, C.: An End-to-End Trainable Neural Network for Image-based Sequence Recognition and Its Application to Scene Text Recognition. IEEE Transactions on Pattern Analysis and Machine Intelligence 39(11), 2298–2304 (2016)
16. Shivakumara, P., Tang, D., Asadzadehkaljahi, M., Lu, T., Pal, U., Anisi, M.H.: CNN-RNN based method for license plate recognition. CAAI Transactions on Intelligence Technology 3(3), 169–175 (2018)
17. Špaňhel, J., Sochor, J., Juránek, R., Herout, A., Maršík, L., Zemčík, P.: Holistic recognition of low quality license plates by CNN using track annotated data. In: 14th IEEE International Conference on Advanced Video and Signal Based Surveillance, pp. 1–6 (2017)
18. Suvarnam, B., Ch, V.S.: Combination of CNN-GRU model to recognize characters of a license plate number without segmentation. In: 5th International Conference on Advanced Computing & Communication Systems, pp. 317–322 (2019)

19. Tourani, A., Shahbahrami, A., Soroori, S., Khazaee, S., Suen, C.Y.: A Robust Deep Learning Approach for Automatic Iranian Vehicle License Plate Detection and Recognition for Surveillance Systems. IEEE Access 8, 201317–201330 (2020)
20. Zhang, H., Sun, F., Zhang, X., Zheng, L.: License plate recognition model based on CNN+LSTM+CTC. In: Mao, R., Wang, H., Xie, X., Lu, Z. (eds.) Data Science. ICPCSEE 2019. Communications in Computer and Information Science, vol. 1059. Springer, Singapore (2019). https://doi.org/10.1007/978-981-15-0121-0_52

# Exploiting Spatio-Temporal Coherence for Video Object Detection in Robotics

David Fernandez-Chaves[1,2] , Jose Luis Matez-Bandera[1(✉)] ,
Jose Raul Ruiz-Sarmiento[1] , Javier Monroy[1] , Nicolai Petkov[2] ,
and Javier Gonzalez-Jimenez[1]

[1] Machine Perception and Intelligent Robotics group (MAPIR), Department
of System Engineering and Automation, Biomedical Research Institute of Malaga
(IBIMA), University of Malaga, Málaga, Spain
{davfercha,josematez,jotaraul,jgmonroy,javiergonzalez}@uma.es
[2] Johann Bernoulli Institute of Mathematics and Computing Science,
University of Groningen, Groningen, The Netherlands
n.petkov@rug.nl

**Abstract.** This paper proposes a method to enhance video object detection for indoor environments in robotics. Concretely, it exploits knowledge about the camera motion between frames to propagate previously detected objects to successive frames. The proposal is rooted in the concepts of planar homography to propose regions of interest where to find objects, and recursive Bayesian filtering to integrate observations over time. The proposal is evaluated on six virtual, indoor environments, accounting for the detection of nine object classes over a total of ∼7k frames. Results show that our proposal improves the recall and the F1-score by a factor of 1.41 and 1.27, respectively, as well as it achieves a significant reduction of the object categorization entropy (58.8%) when compared to a two-stage video object detection method used as baseline, at the cost of small time overheads (120 ms) and precision loss (0.92).

## 1 Introduction

The detection of the objects appearing in a sequence of images (i.e. a video) is of paramount importance for many applications, such as those involving mobile robots [4,8,17]. For this particular problem, the exploitation of the spatio-temporal information inherent in the sequence of images, is considered an important factor to boost the object detection performance [2,3,15].

Previous works have proposed the use of Spatio-Temporal Networks (STNs) such as tubelets-based [10,11,19] or memory-based approaches [1,20]. Yet, these techniques share a common drawback: they either use a fixed-length temporal window or apply a post-processing phase to the whole video sequence to integrate the observations over time. The latter prevents their use in real-time applications, like the ones relying on a mobile robot, as they require to take decisions upon the detected objects.

Multiple contributions have addressed these handicaps by including motion-guided propagation (MGP) algorithms such as object tracking networks [5,15] or

© Springer Nature Switzerland AG 2021
N. Tsapatsoulis et al. (Eds.): CAIP 2021, LNCS 13053, pp. 186–196, 2021.
https://doi.org/10.1007/978-3-030-89131-2_17

optical flow [10,12,21,22]. However, relying on visual information alone is prone to failures under challenging conditions like frames with motion blur, occlusions or appearance changes [10].

In this paper we propose an alternative method that, assuming knowledge about the camera motion between successive frames, leverages this information to enhance the detection of objects in a sequence of images. Concretely, we consider a typical two-stage object detection method consisting of a Region Proposal Network (RPN) that yields regions of interest where an object can be found, followed by an Object Classifier Network (OCN) that processes each region and returns a probability distribution over a given set of object classes for each one. Thus, the method outcome after processing each frame is a set of observations, each one corresponding to a region in the image, and their associated probability distributions. To provide temporal and spatial coherence to these results, our method introduces a motion-guided propagation model based on planar homography, obtained from the camera motion, to propagate previous observations to the frame being processed. Next, we perform a correspondence step that try to match the regions provided by the RPN in the frame $t$ with the previous propagated observations from $t-1$. In the case that an object observation becomes orphaned in the matching process (i.e. a detected object in frame $t-1$ is not proposed by the RPN in frame $t$), we propose it as a new region of interest. This results in an enhanced set of regions to be classified by the OCN. Finally, to provide further temporal coherence, the probability distributions of matched observations are integrated through a recursive Bayesian filter.

In order to evaluate the benefits of our proposals we have conducted multiple experiments over the robotic dataset Robot@VirtualHome [7]. We show that our combined method boosts video object detection by significantly increasing the recall (i.e. the number of unnoticed objects) while presenting a minor reduction of the precision and a very small time overhead.

## 2    Method Overview

Given a sequence of frames $\mathcal{F}_0, ..., \mathcal{F}_{t-1}, \mathcal{F}_t$, we propose a spatio-temporal object detection method that incorporates knowledge from frame $\mathcal{F}_{t-1}$ to frame $\mathcal{F}_t$. Specifically, for each new frame $\mathcal{F}_t$, we employ a two-stage detection pipeline (see Fig. 1). In a first phase, we rely on a region proposal network (RPN) to obtain regions of interest $B_t^i$, typically known as bounding boxes. These regions are rectangular boxes in the image whose enclosed pixels form an image patch $\pi_t^i$ where objects are expected to be found.

In a second phase, all image patches are evaluated by an object classifier, which yields a discrete probabilistic distribution $P(\mathbf{C}_t|\pi_t^i)$ over the considered set of objects class labels $\mathbf{C} = \{C^1, ..., C^N\}$.

It must be noticed that RPNs tend to predict multiple bounding boxes with different shapes and sizes for the same object. Thus, in this work we filter out redundant candidates by selecting the most appropriate one for each object. For this purpose, we employ a Non-Maximum Suppression (NMS) algorithm

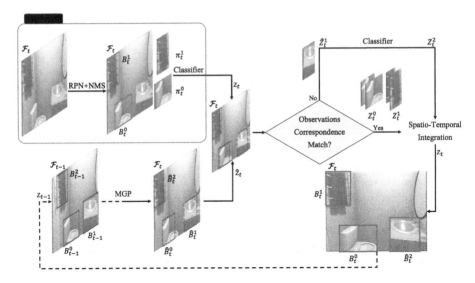

**Fig. 1.** Diagram showing the proposed method pipeline. Bounding boxes of the detected objects in frame $\mathcal{F}_{t-1}$ (in red) are projected to the next frame $\mathcal{F}_t$ (in blue) through a planar homography. Next, projected bounding boxes are matched with the new proposed bounding boxes given by the RPN. Black dashed line represents the feedback for the next iteration. The knowledge from both is temporally integrated to improve object detections in videos. (Color figure online)

for bounding boxes. Similarly, related to the classification probabilities of each image patch, we filter out candidates whose highest probability of belonging to an object class is lower than a given threshold, reducing false detections.

At this point, we define an observation $Z_t^i$ by the pair formed by a bounding box and the probability distribution resulting from the classification of its respective image patch: $Z_t^i = \{B_t^i, P(\mathbf{C}_t|\pi_t^i)\}$. Then, after obtaining the observations corresponding to the current frame $\mathcal{F}_t$, we compute the projections $\hat{\mathbf{Z}}_t$ of previous observations $\mathbf{Z}_{t-1}$ to propagate previous knowledge into the current frame (see Sect. 2.1). Subsequently, we carry out a correspondence step between projected observations $\hat{\mathbf{Z}}_t$ and new observations $\mathbf{Z}_t$ (see Sect. 2.2), and finally, we integrate both by applying a recursive Bayesian filter (see Sect. 2.3).

## 2.1 Motion-Guided Propagation Model

A MGP model allows us to propagate observations between frames by projecting the bounding box of each observation from one frame $B_{t-1}^i$ to the next $\hat{B}_t^i$ (see Fig. 1). In this work, we propose to transform the corner points which define each bounding box by means of a planar homography:

$$p_t = H p_{t-1} \tag{1}$$

where $p_t$ and $p_{t-1}$ are the homogeneous coordinates of the bounding box corners in two consecutive frames. The planar homography matrix $H$ is computed from the camera motion [9] as:

$$H = K \left( R - \frac{tn^T}{d} \right) K^{-1} \qquad (2)$$

where $R$ and $t$ are the rotation matrix and the translation vector of the camera between the two frames, and $K$ is the intrinsic camera matrix. $n$ and $d$ are the normal vector and the distance, respectively, to the 3D plane where the bounding box lies in the scene.

It must be emphasized that applying this planar homography transformation to the bounding boxes of the observations does not transform the objects themselves, because objects are not in a plane. However this transformation can be considered an approximate projection of the object observations. Moreover, for the specific case of mobile robotics, given that most robots are non-holonomic (i.e. their translation is only along the z-axis $t = [0, 0, t_z]$), we can consider that the camera translation between frames w.r.t. the distance to objects $d$ is sufficient small, thus $t_z/d \simeq 0$. Thus, $H$ is approximated as follows:

$$H = KRK^{-1} \qquad (3)$$

Upon projecting the bounding boxes of all previous observations, we disregard those that fall outside the image plane.

## 2.2 Correspondence Step and Region Proposal

For each new frame $\mathcal{F}_t$, we have a set of new observations $\mathbf{Z}_t = \{Z_t^1, ..., Z_t^J\}$ which we desire to integrate with previous observations $\mathbf{Z}_{t-1} = \{Z_{t-1}^1, ..., Z_{t-1}^I\}$. To this end, the MGP model (see Sect. 2.1) projects previous observations $\mathbf{Z}_{t-1}$ into the current frame $\hat{\mathbf{Z}}_t = \{\hat{Z}_t^1, ..., \hat{Z}_t^I\}$, where $\hat{Z}_t^i = \{\hat{B}_t^i, P(\mathbf{C}_t|\pi_{t-1}^i)\}$.

In this step, we perform a correspondence between $\mathbf{Z}_t$ and $\hat{\mathbf{Z}}_t$ to determine three possible outcomes: (i) an observation in $\mathbf{Z}_t$ refers to a possible new object, (ii) an observation in $\mathbf{Z}_t$ refers to a previously detected one; or (iii) a projected observation in $\hat{\mathbf{Z}}_t$ has not been detected in the current frame. To do so, we measure the similarity $s_{ij}$ between each pair of observations $(\hat{Z}_t^i, Z_t^j)$ as follows:

$$s_{ij}(Z_t^j, \hat{Z}_t^i) = \text{IoU}(B_t^j, \hat{B}_t^i) \qquad (4)$$

where $\text{IoU}(\cdot, \cdot)$ is the intersection over union function [16].

For each projected observation $\hat{Z}_t^i$, we select the pair $(Z_t^j, \hat{Z}_t^i)$ that maximizes the similarity function. Then, if the similarity is greater than a threshold $\mathcal{T}$, we integrate both observations by choosing the most recent bounding box $B_t^j$ and updating the probability distributions through a recursive Bayesian filter (see Sect. 2.3).

However, since observations in $t-1$ may not be proposed again by the RPN in $t$ (e.g. due to motion blur), projected observations $\hat{\mathbf{Z}}_t$ may be left alone, not matching with any new observation $Z_t^j$. It must be noticed that the latter does not implies that the object is not in the current frame, just that it is not proposed. To address this fact, we classify the image patch $\hat{\pi}_t^i$ associated to the projection of the previous bounding box $\hat{B}_t^i$ into the current frame $\mathcal{F}_t$, obtaining a new probability distribution $P(\mathbf{C}_t|\hat{\pi}_t^i)$. Next, we update the detection $\hat{Z}_t^i$ to $Z_t^j$, defining it with $\hat{B}_t^i$ and updating the probability distribution $P(\mathbf{C}_{t-1}|\pi_{t-1}^i)$ to $P(\mathbf{C}_t|\hat{\pi}_t^i)$ through a recursive Bayesian filter.

## 2.3   Bayesian Filtering over Object Class Labels

Seeking to capitalize on the temporal correlation inherent in the posterior distributions of matched observations along a sequence of images, we resort to a recursive Bayesian filter to estimate the accumulated belief over the object classes $Bel(\mathbf{C}_t) = P(\mathbf{C}_t|\pi_{1:t})$:

$$Bel(\mathbf{C}_t) \propto P(\pi_t|\mathbf{C}_t, \mathbf{C}_{1:t-1}) \sum_{n=1}^{N} P(\mathbf{C}_t|\mathbf{C}_{1:t-1}^n)Bel(\mathbf{C}_{t-1}^n) \tag{5}$$

where $P(\pi_t|\mathbf{C}_t, \mathbf{C}_{1:t-1})$ is the conditional density at time $t$, $N$ is the number of object classes, and $P(\mathbf{C}_t|\mathbf{C}_{1:t-1})$ is the transition probability. Assuming first order Markov properties, i.e. independence between object classes and between observations, we have $P(\mathbf{C}_t|\mathbf{C}_{1:t-1}) = P(\mathbf{C}_t|\mathbf{C}_{t-1})$ and $P(\pi_t|\mathbf{C}_t, \mathbf{C}_{1:t-1}) = P(\pi_t|\mathbf{C}_t)$. Thus, our accumulated belief is simplified to:

$$Bel(\mathbf{C}_t) \propto P(\pi_t|\mathbf{C}_t) \sum_{n=1}^{N} P(\mathbf{C}_t|\mathbf{C}_{t-1}^n)Bel(\mathbf{C}_{t-1}^n) \tag{6}$$

The transition probability function $P(\mathbf{C}_t|\mathbf{C}_{t-1})$ is the function that controls how the object classes evolve over time. We expressed this function as follows:

$$P(\mathbf{C}_t|\mathbf{C}_{t-1}) = \begin{cases} p_c\, s_{ij} & \text{if } \mathbf{C}_t = \mathbf{C}_{t-1} \\ \dfrac{1 - p_c\, s_{ij}}{N - 1} & \text{otherwise} \end{cases} \tag{7}$$

where $s_{ij}$ is the similarity score between the bounding boxes of both observations and $p_c$ is the probability that given two consecutive observations, the object class with maximum probability of both observations is the same. The latter value should be set with a higher probability in order to model the fact that in a video, two observations (with similar position, shape and size) from two consecutive frames have a high likelihood to be from the same object class.

Finally, note that the Bayesian filter requires the conditional density $P(\pi_t|\mathbf{C}_t)$, but the object classifier yields the posterior probability $P(\mathbf{C}_t|\pi_t)$. However, both probabilities are related through Bayes theorem as follows:

$$P(\pi_t|\mathbf{C}_t) \propto \frac{P(\mathbf{C}_t|\pi_t)}{P(\mathbf{C}_t)} \tag{8}$$

where $P(\mathbf{C}_t)$ is the marginal class probability. This probability encodes the probability of finding each object class in an environment, hence it is a prior that can be learned from experimental data. For example, in a household, objects such as *chairs* that are found in most rooms must have a greater probability than less common objects such as *microwaves* that are only typically found in kitchens.

# 3 Experiments

This section covers a set of comparative experiments aimed to evaluate the performance of the proposed method, and the contribution of each of its stages. Concretely, we present a comparison of the following incremental methods: i) B: baseline, ii) B + BF: including Bayesian filter, iii) B + BF + P: adding propagation without homography and iv) Our method: improving the previous one by using the motion-guided propagation model with homography.

## 3.1 Experimental Setup

To assess the performance of the proposed method we have conducted experiments with data from the state-of-the-art Robot@VirtualHome dataset [7]. This is a robotic dataset that includes sequences of images taken by a mobile robot while navigating through different virtual environments. In addition, the dataset provides the camera motion between frames and segmentation masks for the objects in the images.

We conducted experiments on six indoor environments from the dataset, which are composed by a total of 6, 929 frames with a resolution of $640 \times 480$ px. All images were captured by a frontal camera placed on the robot at a height of 1.59 m and $10°$ rotation in the pitch-axis.

## 3.2 Evaluation Metrics

To measure the performance of the competing methods we resort to three commonly used metrics: average precision (AP), recall (R) and F1-score [14]. Moreover, we consider an observation as right (i.e. a true positive) when its top-1 classification probability is greater than 0.5 and its associated object class matches the ground-truth label provided by the dataset. In addition, to evaluate temporal coherence, we compute the entropy of the probability distribution associated with each observation as a measure of uncertainty.

## 3.3 Implementation Details

The implementation of the proposed method has been carried out according to the following aspects:

- For the region proposal network, we rely on the DeepMask architecture with the weights from [13].
- To filter out multiple bounding boxes candidates for each object, we apply the NMS algorithm from [6].
- For the object classification stage, we used the state-of-the-art EfficientNet CNN with the pretrained model *EfficientNet-Lite4* [18]. This classifier yields a discrete probability distribution over the object classes from the ImageNet dataset, from which we considered 9 relevant indoor object types: *toilet, chair, bed, table, microwave, washbasin, closet, washer* and *burner*.

**Table 1.** Averaged metric results for each evaluated method over the 6 indoor environments. B: Baseline, BF: Bayesian Filter and P: Propagation (without homography). Our method is composed by the baseline, the bayesian filter and the motion-guided propagation model based on planar homography.

|            | Precision | Recall | F1-score | Entropy | Time (s) |
|------------|-----------|--------|----------|---------|----------|
| B          | 70.13%    | 19.66% | 30.13%   | 0.51    | **0.55** |
| B + BF     | **70.60%**| 19.72% | 30.26%   | 0.31    | 0.56     |
| B + BF + P | 63.90%    | 25.66% | 36.19%   | 0.31    | 0.61     |
| Our method | 64.73%    | **27.63%** | **38.16%** | **0.30** | 0.67  |

**Table 2.** Comparative results of propagating with/without planar homography facing different camera rotations.

|            | Rotation 10° |        |        | Rotation 15° |        |        |
|------------|--------------|--------|--------|--------------|--------|--------|
|            | AP           | R      | F1     | AP           | R      | F1     |
| B + BF + P | 62.87%       | 23.91% | 34.27% | 58.53%       | 25.60% | 34.97% |
| Our method | **67.60%**   | **27.37%** | **38.44%** | **72.96%** | **32.31%** | **43.83%** |

- Regarding the parameters of the proposed method, we set empirically the threshold $T$ as 0.3 and $p_c$ as 0.6, which control when there is a match between two bounding boxes and the transition probability of the Bayesian filter, respectively.
- All experiments have been carried out using a computer with an Intel Core i7-8750H processor at 2.20 GHz, a 16 GB DDR4 RAM memory at 1333 MHz, and a graphic card NVIDIA GeForce GTX 1070 with 8 GB of memory.

### 3.4   Experimental Results

Table 1 presents the average performance of the evaluated methods over the six tested environments. As can be seen, the baseline (first row) shows the second best precision with a 70.13% and the lowest processing time per frame (0.55 s). However, this method achieves the lowest recall (19.66%) and F1-score (30.13%), together with the maximum averaged entropy of the probability distributions (0.51). The inclusion of the Bayesian filter (second row) considerably decreases the averaged entropy a 58.8% w.r.t. the baseline, obtaining a value of 0.31, which implies the reduction of the uncertainty associated to the predicted classes.

A considerable performance improvement is appreciated when including the propagation (without planar homography) of previous observations (i.e. the position of bounding boxes in previous frames is preserved for next frames). In this case, the method boosts both recall and F1-score by a factor of 1.31 and 1.20 respectively, while increasing the processing time by 60ms and reducing precision by 6.23% w.r.t. baseline. The recall-precision trade-off is represented by the F1-score, which in this case shows an improvement of the performance.

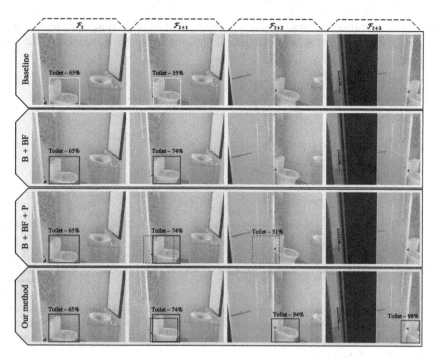

**Fig. 2.** Example frames where our method boost the video object detection performance during a robot rotation movement. Solid-line bounding boxes are proposed by the RPN. Dashed-line bounding boxes are projections of previous bounding boxes. The effect of Bayesian filter can be highlighted from $\mathcal{F}_{t+1}$ in advance. For the method B + BF + P can be seen how the bounding box is propagated inaccurately, so the *toilet* class probability decreases. In contrast, our method propagates more accurately the bounding box, so the observation of the *toilet* is kept and integrated over time. Note that for simplicity, we show only the object class with maximum probability.

Finally, the full pipeline where previous observations are propagated to next frames through planar homography yield the best results in terms of recall (27.63%), F1-score (38.16%) and average entropy (0.3). The recall enhancement reveals that the full pipeline improves object detection by proposing a considerable number of observations from previous frames that where unnoticed by the baseline, as shown in Fig. 2.

However, as can be seen in Table 1, the results between propagating with planar homography (Our method) and without (B + BF + P) is similar. This fact is due to the assumption made in the propagation model that only considers the rotation of the camera, so that when the robot only translates, both methods are equivalent. Since in our experiments only 12% of frames show important rotations, the planar homography effect is not highlighted. To analyze the performance impact of the planar homography, we evaluated both methods considering only consecutive frames exhibiting camera rotations larger than a certain angle. The obtained results are shown in Table 2, where we can observe that the higher rotations, the higher the benefit. For example, for 15° rotations, our method outperforms the propagation without planar homography by increasing a 14.43% precision, 6.81% recall and 8.86% F1-score.

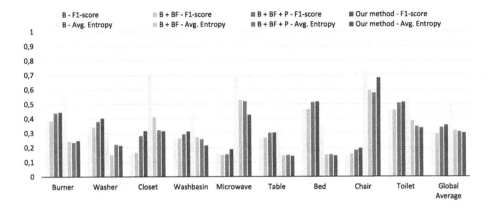

**Fig. 3.** F1-score (in blue) and entropy (in green). Results are obtained averaging over the 6 indoor environments, per object class and method. At the right, the global average for all object classes. Note that, for all cases, we desire a high F1-score but a low entropy. (Color figure online)

Finally, Fig. 3 illustrates the average F1-score and entropy results for each considered object class. Note that there is an inverse correlation between entropy and F1-score, as classes with higher entropy have lower F1-score, so their precision and recall are lower. This is mainly due to misclassification errors, such as classifying *chairs* as *tables*. The interested reader can see the proposed method in action in the following video: https://youtu.be/oNmGG3d0BM4.

## 4    Conclusions and Future Work

In this work, we have introduced a novel method to boost the detection of objects in a sequence of images given knowledge of the camera motion. Particularly, we have focused on the case of mobile robots operating in indoor environments. Our method uses a MGP model based on planar homography to spatially propagate observations from one frame to the next, allowing an efficient matching with new observations. Finally, a Bayesian filter is introduced to temporally integrate matched observations, yielding a posterior probability distribution or belief over the object classes.

Experimental validation has demonstrated how our proposal improves video object detection w.r.t. the baseline by increasing 8.03% F1-score and 7.97% recall, which implies that our method detect more objects than the baseline. Besides, our method reduces entropy by 58.8% on average, which proves the effect of the Bayesian filter by reducing the uncertainty about object classes over time. However, as drawbacks, the proposed method reduces the average precision by a factor of 0.92 w.r.t. the baseline due to the fact that also wrong detections are propagated over time.

In future work, we plan to extend this method to use a dynamic frame rate object detection based on the robot motion. Thus, each new frame will be taken after a certain robot movement, hence releasing resources such as the CPU and GPU while the view has little changes. In this way, we will reduce the computational cost, which is highly limited in robotics.

**Acknowledgements.** This work was supported by the research projects WISER (DPI2017-84827-R) and ARPEGGIO (PID2020-117057), the Spanish grant program FPU19/00704 and the UG PHD scholarship program from the University of Groningen.

# References

1. Bertasius, G., Torresani, L., Shi, J.: Object detection in video with spatiotemporal sampling networks. In: Ferrari, V., Hebert, M., Sminchisescu, C., Weiss, Y. (eds.) ECCV 2018, Part XII. LNCS, vol. 11216, pp. 342–357. Springer, Cham (2018). https://doi.org/10.1007/978-3-030-01258-8_21
2. Bosquet, B., Mucientes, M., Brea, V.M.: STDnet-ST: spatio-temporal ConvNet for small object detection. Pattern Recognit. **116**, 107929 (2021)
3. Chen, Y., Cao, Y., Hu, H., Wang, L.: Memory enhanced global-local aggregation for video object detection. In: IEEE/CVF CVPR, pp. 10337–10346 (2020)
4. Erol, B.A., Majumdar, A., Lwowski, J., Benavidez, P., Rad, P., Jamshidi, M.: Improved deep neural network object tracking system for applications in home robotics. In: Pedrycz, W., Chen, S.-M. (eds.) Computational Intelligence for Pattern Recognition. SCI, vol. 777, pp. 369–395. Springer, Cham (2018). https://doi.org/10.1007/978-3-319-89629-8_14
5. Feichtenhofer, C., Pinz, A., Zisserman, A.: Detect to track and track to detect. In: IEEE ICCV, pp. 3038–3046 (2017)
6. Felzenszwalb, P.F., Girshick, R.B., McAllester, D., Ramanan, D.: Object detection with discriminatively trained part-based models. IEEE Trans. Pattern Anal. Mach. Intell. **32**(9), 1627–1645 (2009)
7. Fernandez-Chaves, D., Ruiz-Sarmiento, J., Petkov, N., Gonzalez-Jimenez, J.: Robot@virtualhome, an ecosystem of virtual environment tools for realistic indoor robotic simulation (2021). submitted
8. Fernandez-Chaves, D., Ruiz-Sarmiento, J.R., Petkov, N., Gonzalez-Jimenez, J.: From object detection to room categorization in robotics (January 2020)
9. Hartley, R., Zisserman, A.: Multiple view geometry in computer vision (2000)
10. Kang, K., et al.: T-CNN: tubelets with convolutional neural networks for object detection from videos. IEEE TCSVT **28**(10), 2896–2907 (2017)
11. Kang, K., Ouyang, W., Li, H., Wang, X.: Object detection from video tubelets with convolutional neural networks. In: IEEE CVPR, pp. 817–825 (2016)
12. Li, H., Chen, G., Li, G., Yu, Y.: Motion guided attention for video salient object detection. In: IEEE/CVF ICCV, pp. 7274–7283 (2019)
13. Pinheiro, P.O., Collobert, R., Dollár, P.: Learning to segment object candidates. In: NIPS (2015)

14. Powers, D.M.: Evaluation: from precision, recall and f-measure to roc, informedness, markedness and correlation. arXiv preprint arXiv:2010.16061 (2020)
15. Ray, K.S., Chakraborty, S.: Object detection by spatio-temporal analysis and tracking of the detected objects in a video with variable background. J. Vis. Commun. Image Represent. **58**, 662–674 (2019)
16. Rezatofighi, H., Tsoi, N., Gwak, J., Sadeghian, A., Reid, I., Savarese, S.: Generalized intersection over union: a metric and a loss for bounding box regression. In: IEEE/CVF CVPR, pp. 658–666 (2019)
17. Ruiz-Sarmiento, J.R., Guenther, M., Galindo, C., Gonzalez-Jimenez, J., Hertzberg, J.: Online context-based object recognition for mobile robots. In: ICARSC (2017)
18. Tan, M., Le, Q.: EfficientNet: rethinking model scaling for convolutional neural networks. In: ICML, pp. 6105–6114. PMLR (2019)
19. Tang, P., Wang, C., Wang, X., Liu, W., Zeng, W., Wang, J.: Object detection in videos by high quality object linking. IEEE TPAMI **42**(5), 1272–1278 (2019)
20. Xiao, F., Lee, Y.J.: Video object detection with an aligned spatial-temporal memory. In: ECCV, pp. 485–501 (2018)
21. Zhu, X., Wang, Y., Dai, J., Yuan, L., Wei, Y.: Flow-guided feature aggregation for video object detection. In: IEEE ICCV, pp. 408–417 (2017)
22. Zhu, X., Xiong, Y., Dai, J., Yuan, L., Wei, Y.: Deep feature flow for video recognition. In: IEEE CVPR, pp. 2349–2358 (2017)

# Face and Gesture

# A Study of General Data Improvement for Large-Angle Head Pose Estimation

Jue Bai, Chenglei Peng$^{(\boxtimes)}$, Zhaoxu Li, Sidan Du$^{(\boxtimes)}$, and Yang Li$^{(\boxtimes)}$

Nanjing University, Nanjing 210046, China
{pcl,coff128,yogo}@nju.edu.cn

**Abstract.** Predicting Euler angles of head pose using end-to-end CNN from a single RGB image is a popular application in recent years. However, the existing methods ignored the information about the rotation order contained in the Euler angles, always following the traditional pitch-yaw-roll order. They also neglected the error sources from outlier samples with large-angle poses. We analyzed current shortcomings and made suggestions for improvement from the perspective of data distribution. We studied the influence of different rotation orders on the data distribution and showed choosing an appropriate rotation order to learn head pose can significantly optimize the data distribution and improve the prediction accuracy. Then a data enhancement method was proposed to increase the large-angle poses by rotating the 2D images randomly and solving the corresponding head poses, which can improve network performance on the large-angle poses. Evaluated on two popular networks and different datasets, our methods were proved to be effective and general.

**Keywords:** Head pose estimation · Euler angles · Large-angle poses · Data optimization · Data enhancement

## 1 Introduction

Head pose estimation is an important topic in the field of computer vision because of its wide-range applications. Head pose provides crucial clues for attention detection and behavior analysis, which can be applied to many scenarios, such as driver attention monitoring, understanding of social scene and human relationship.

There has been considerable research on estimating head pose from a single RGB image over the past 25 years. Historically, head pose is usually estimated by face alignment. Landmark-based methods firstly predict several facial landmarks [4–6] from the input image, then solve the projection relationship between these 2D landmarks and the assumed standard 3D face model to obtain head pose. However, this kind of approach is fragile and cumbersome, because it profoundly relies on the accuracy of the landmark detection. Dense face alignment methods [8, 9] reconstruct 3D face model by estimating the deformation parameters of the 3D morphable template, and the head pose is separated from several parameters. Multi-task learning methods [10, 11] predict multiple facial features simultaneously, including head pose, gender, expression, landmarks and age.

© Springer Nature Switzerland AG 2021
N. Tsapatsoulis et al. (Eds.): CAIP 2021, LNCS 13053, pp. 199–209, 2021.
https://doi.org/10.1007/978-3-030-89131-2_18

They put forward high requirements on the labels and calculations. Recently, methods [1, 7, 12–15] that directly regress the target angle values of the pose using end-to-end CNN have become popular and dominant because they are simple and effective. In this paper, we pay more attention to them.

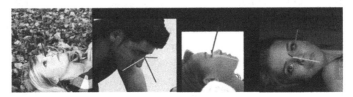

**Fig. 1.** Some samples with rare poses in AFLW2000 dataset [2]. The results are estimated by our improved model (YPR+R model in Sect. 4.3), which is based on the HopeNet [1].

We notice that the popular methods prefer Euler angles [1, 2, 7, 10–14] to represent and learn head pose with the advantages of simplicity and understandability, rather than quaternion [15] or rotation matrix [3]. However, they have always followed a tradition, using Euler angles in pitch-yaw-roll rotation order. No one paid attention to the information about rotation order contained therein. In fact, the same pose can be described by six Euler-angle combinations in different rotation orders, including pitch-yaw-roll, roll-yaw-pitch, yaw-pitch-roll, roll-pitch-yaw, yaw-roll-pitch and pitch-roll-yaw. So must the conventional pitch-yaw-roll order be the most appropriate? We challenge the tradition and study the different distribution of samples and the different effects on neural network learning under different rotation orders.

Also, the current methods [1, 7, 10–14] can estimate accurate results on the common poses close to the front face, but poorly adapt to some rare poses, as shown in Fig. 1. These samples are often the source of large errors, but previous methods have not paid attention. We find that the main reason for the prediction failure is the lack of such rare poses in the training dataset. Most of the methods have carried out the step of data enhancement. 300W-LP [2] was expanded by horizontal mirroring, [1, 7, 12] applied simply random cropping and random scaling. [13] suggested adjusting a proper margin for the bounding box of the detected faces. And the soft-label was proposed in [14], where each Euler angle of head pose is labeled as a Gaussian distribution rather than a single value. However, they all considered from the image itself or each Euler-angle label itself, having little grasp of overall situation of samples in the datasets, so they lacked specificity for the rare poses. We attempt to fill this gap and propose a new data enhancement method.

Aiming at these two shortcomings, we optimized and expanded the data distribution. Experiments on different network structures and datasets prove that our methods effectively improve head pose estimation accuracy, especially on large-angle poses.

## 2   Related Work

In the following, we introduce the related work about head pose estimation, including datasets, network and evaluation, on which our experimental settings during training and testing based.

### 2.1   Datasets

Currently the most popular datasets for head pose include 300W-LP [2], AFLW2000 [2] and BIWI [3]. 300W-LP is a synthetically generated dataset with 122,450 samples, twice the 61,225 samples by horizontal flipping. 300W-LP generates side views of original samples from 300W dataset through rotation and projection of the 3D models matching the 2D input images. Both AFLW2000 and BIWI are real-world datasets. AFLW2000 consists of the first 2,000 images whose labels are re-annotated for 3D face alignment from AFLW and these samples have various poses, backgrounds, illumination conditions, occlusion conditions and expressions. BIWI contains 24 videos of 20 subjects with 15,678 frames, which was recorded using Kinect under a controlled indoor environment. By convention [1, 7, 12–15], 300W-LP is generally used for training while AFLW2000 and BIWI are reserving for testing.

### 2.2   Networks

HopeNet [1] and FSA-Net [7] achieved state-of-the-art performance in the past three years and they were widely recognized and followed. Moreover, their network structures and regression losses are quite different.

HopeNet is a multi-loss network, which combines classification loss and regression loss. It uses ResNet50 as the convolutional backbone and adds three separate fully-connected layers after the backbone to respectively classify yaw, pitch and roll into one of 66 bins, each 3° as a bin. FSA-Net employs the soft stagewise regression and adds the feature aggregation module Capsule on their SSD-Net-MD, which harvests more spatial information. We follow their frameworks and training parameter settings, and adjust in details according to our experimental requirements.

### 2.3   Evaluation

Models of HopeNet and FSA-Net are all tested on the whole AFLW2000 dataset [2] and BIWI dataset [3]. And they follow the traditional evaluation criteria used in the previous methods [1, 7, 10–14], which is the mean absolute error of each Euler angle under pitch-yaw-roll order.

In our experiments, we follow their evaluation method. Note that the predicted angles in other rotation orders should be uniformly converted to pitch-yaw-roll order. And in order to verify the universality of our methods, we conduct experiments on two of the networks. Moreover, we pay more attention to large-angle poses, so we divide the samples of AFLW2000 into several parts according to their yaw values. The intervals are set as 30° in the yaw range of $[-90°, 90°]$. Then we also evaluate models on each subset.

# 3 Optimizing Data Distribution by Conversion of Rotation Orders

In this section, we show the importance of the rotation order of Euler angles on the data distribution and prediction accuracy.

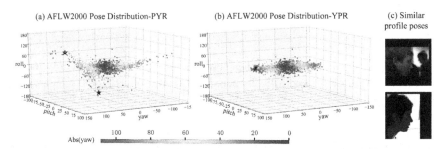

**Fig. 2.** The distributions of AFLW2000 dataset [2]. (a) under traditional pitch-yaw-roll order (PYR), and (b) under new yaw-pitch-roll order (YPR). The samples are colored according to the yaw values of Euler angles in pitch-yaw-roll order. The black stars represent the two profile poses in (c) that look extremely similar. They are far apart in PYR, but almost overlap in YPR.

## 3.1 Disadvantages of Traditional Pitch-Yaw-Roll Order

Representing head pose with Euler angles has a long history because they are intuitive and easy to understand. The currently popular datasets [2] and methods [1, 7, 10–14] have always followed the pitch-yaw-roll rotation order. Taking AFLW2000 dataset as an example, we study the spatial distribution of samples in Fig. 2 and focus on the area where large-angle poses are located.

Figure 2 (a) shows the distribution of samples under conventional pitch-yaw-roll rotation order, where the closer the absolute value of the yaw is to 90, the more scattered the samples are in the pitch and roll directions, resulting in large yaw often accompanied by large pitch and large roll. These samples labeled with the three large angles correspond to some profile poses, as the head images shown in Fig. 2 (c). Although they look extremely similar, they are distributed far apart in space. This imbalanced distribution increases the distance between the similar profile poses. The similar poses and their extremely different labels are difficult for networks to learn and predict, which causes large errors on such large-angle poses.

We believe this defectiveness is related to gimbal lock. It occurs when the rotation order is determined and the second gimbal is rotated at $\pm90°$. And the first and the third angle still counteract each other more as the second angle gets closer to 90°. Since there are many profile poses in AFLW2000 dataset, whose yaw values are around 90°, the disadvantages are clearly emerging in pitch-yaw-roll rotation order.

## 3.2 Study on Different Rotation Orders

As shown in Fig. 3, the different rotation orders describe the different rotation processes from the initial pose to the final pose. The different processes correspond to different values of Euler angles, thus changing the spatial distribution of samples.

In the shown coordinate system, X-axis points downward and the rotation angle around it is yaw. Similarly, Y-axis for pitch and Z-axis for roll. Three independent rotation matrices of rotating a certain angle around a certain axis can be determined as RX(yaw), RY(pitch) and RZ(roll).

$$RX(yaw) = \begin{bmatrix} 1 & 0 & 0 \\ 0 & \cos(yaw) & -\sin(yaw) \\ 0 & \sin(yaw) & \cos(yaw) \end{bmatrix}$$

$$RY(pitch) = \begin{bmatrix} \cos(pitch) & 0 & \sin(pitch) \\ 0 & 1 & 0 \\ -\sin(pitch) & 0 & \cos(pitch) \end{bmatrix}$$

$$RZ(roll) = \begin{bmatrix} \cos(roll) & -\sin(roll) & 0 \\ \sin(roll) & \cos(roll) & 0 \\ 0 & 0 & 1 \end{bmatrix} \tag{1}$$

Then the rotation matrix R representing the final head pose can be generated from and decomposed into Euler angles in different rotation orders.

$$R = RZ(roll_1) \cdot RX(yaw_1) \cdot RY(pitch_1) = RZ(roll_2) \cdot RY(pitch_2) \cdot RX(yaw_2) \tag{2}$$

In practice, we want to convert the Euler-angle labels of the datasets from pitch-yaw-roll order to yaw-pitch-roll and roll-pitch-yaw order. We choose pitch with the smallest range of variation as the second of the order to minimize the negative effect of gimbal lock, because it is hard and rare for people to face the ceiling (chin toward the camera) and face the floor (top of head toward the camera).

We can get R from the provided euler angles $pitch_1$, $yaw_1$, $roll_1$ as Formula (2). Take new yaw-pitch-roll order as example, due to our assumption that the range of pitch is between $-90°$ to $90°$, new pitch can be easily calculated by $pitch_2 = asin(-R[2][0])$. Then yaw whose range is between $-180°$ to $180°$ can be calculated by $\sin(yaw_2) = R[2][1]/\cos(pitch_2)$ and $\cos(yaw_2) = R[2][2]/\cos(pitch_2)$. The same goes for roll. The steps are based on the principle of Euler angle transformation [16].

Figure 2 (b) shows when the order is switched from pitch-yaw-roll to yaw-pitch-roll, the samples on both sides become more balanced and aggregated and the distance between the similar poses decreases. This optimization is particularly obvious in those profile poses with large yaw.

### 3.3 Results of Optimizing Data Distribution

According to the experimental settings in Sect. 2, we design comparative experiments based on HopeNet and FSA-Net. For each network, we use three combinations of Euler angles to learn head pose, that is traditional pitch-yaw-roll (PYR), new yaw-pitch-roll (YPR) and new roll-pitch-yaw (RPY). The PYR models re-implement the original models in their papers in our experimental environment, and they are benchmarks. All models are trained on 300W-LP dataset and evaluated on AFLW2000 dataset and BIWI dataset, and they all follow the same evaluation criteria. The results are shown in Table 1.

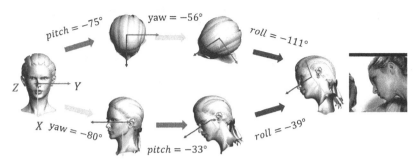

**Fig. 3.** Different processes from the same initial pose to the same final pose in different rotation order.

**Table 1.** Results of models learning head pose under different rotation orders

| Metrics | | AFLW2000 [2] | | | | BIWI [3] | | | |
|---|---|---|---|---|---|---|---|---|---|
| | | Yaw | Pitch | Roll | MAE | Yaw | Pitch | Roll | MAE |
| HopeNet [1] | Original | 6.92 | 6.64 | 5.67 | 6.41 | 4.81 | 6.61 | 3.27 | 4.90 |
| | PYR | 3.47 | 6.15 | 4.65 | 4.76 | 4.41 | 5.12 | 3.09 | 4.21 |
| | YPR | 3.39 | 5.73 | 4.33 | 4.48 | 4.28 | 4.73 | 3.27 | 4.09 |
| | RPY | 3.34 | 5.71 | 4.37 | 4.47 | 4.27 | 5.07 | 2.92 | 4.09 |
| F SA-Net [7] | Original | 4.50 | 6.08 | 4.64 | 5.07 | 4.27 | 4.96 | 2.76 | 4.00 |
| | PYR | 4.32 | 6.19 | 4.73 | 5.08 | 5.19 | 5.57 | 3.39 | 4.72 |
| | YPR | 4.15 | 6.20 | 4.78 | 5.04 | 4.70 | 5.84 | 3.34 | 4.63 |
| | RPY | 4.14 | 6.27 | 4.71 | 5.04 | 5.12 | 6.40 | 3.54 | 5.02 |

Obviously, the change of the rotation order, which is also the change of the data distribution, has a significant impact on prediction accuracy. Taking the models based on HopeNet as examples, YPR increase the accuracy by 6% on AFLW2000 and 3% on BIWI, compared with PYR.

We also find that changing the rotation order has more effects on HopeNet than on FSA-Net, and has different effects on the two datasets. This phenomenon may be related to the network structure and the type of the dataset. Different networks and datasets may fit different orders. Anyway, the rotation order of Euler angles is a point we should pay attention, because it determines how the data is distributed. Choosing an appropriate order is helpful to improve head pose estimation.

## 4   Data Enhancement by Random Rotation

In this section, a data enhancement method is proposed for the problem of data missing, which caused the poor prediction for some rare poses with large rotations.

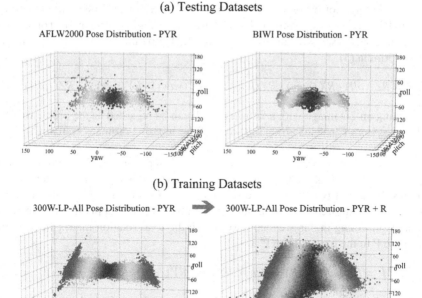

**Fig. 4.** The distributions of datasets under traditional pitch-yaw-roll rotation order. The two testing datasets AFLW2000 [2] and BIWI [3] are in (a), and the training datasets 300W-LP [2] before and after data enhancement are in (b). They are also colored according to yaw values.

## 4.1 Data Missing for Rare Poses

It can be observed that there are some outliers in the distribution of AFLW2000 and BIWI in Fig. 4 (a). Comparing them with the distribution of the original 300W-LP dataset (the left one in Fig. 4 (b)), we find that the training dataset lacks some outlier parts. These missing outliers correspond to some rare poses, such as lying down, upside down and taken from high view or low view. The problem of data missing causes the poor prediction. Naturally, we propose a new data enhancement method to make up for the missing parts. We rotate the head images by a random angle and figure out the corresponding poses. The right one in Fig. 4 (b) clearly shows that the simple rotation strategy effectively expands the data and makes the training dataset better fit the testing datasets. We believe that our method has robust scalability and can be used for various pose-related tasks, not just head pose.

## 4.2 Solution to the Head Pose of the Rotated Image

As shown in Fig. 5, assuming that the initial coordinate system $C_0$ consists of $X_0$-axis, $Y_0$-axis and $Z_0$-axis. $C_0$ describes the initial pose $P_0$ where $pitch_0 = 0$, $yaw_0 = 0$ and $roll_0 = 0$. And $pitch_0$, $yaw_0$, $roll_0$ respectively represent the angle that the current coordinate system rotates around $Y_0$-axis, $X_0$-axis and $Z_0$-axis. Similarly, the known pose $P$ of the original head image corresponds to C, X-axis, Y-axis and Z- axis. The rotation matrix R from $P_0$ to P is known or is constructed by Euler-angle labels in pitch-yaw-roll order. As a known condition, the same R can also be decomposed into Euler angles in roll-pitch-yaw order as Formula (3).

$$R = RZ(roll) \cdot RX(yaw) \cdot RY(pitch) = RX(yaw_1) \cdot RY(pitch_1) \cdot RZ(roll_1) \quad (3)$$

Then rotating an 2D image with a known pose P can be regarded as the problem of the coordinate system C rotates around Z0-axis of the initial coordinate system C0 in 3D space.

The solution can be split into the following three steps. Firstly, C should be rotated to a position where Z-axis coincides with Z0-axis, which is equivalent to the inverse operations of the last two of the three rotations from C0 to C in roll-pitch-yaw order. Then perform the desired rotation around Z0-axis by θ. Finally, apply the inverse of the step one. Connecting the above steps, we derive the total rotation matrix M from the known pose P to the rotated pose P':

$$M = RX(yaw_1) \cdot RY(pitch_1) \cdot RZ(\theta) \cdot RY(-pitch_1) \cdot RZ(-yaw_1) \quad (4)$$

In the end, we get the rotation matrix $R'$ from the initial pose $P_0$ to the rotated pose P' as Formula (5). Then $R'$ can also be decomposed into Euler angles in the rotation order we want.

$$R' = M \cdot R \quad (5)$$

### 4.3   Results of Data Enhancement

Based on the three models of HopeNet and the three models of FSA-Net in Sect. 3.3, we further verify the effect of data enhancement method on each model. We adopt exactly the same enhancement strategy R. R represents that the training dataset is enhanced to twice the original, and the angles of random rotation of the images follow Gaussian distribution with $\mu = 0$ and $\sigma = 30$. Table 2 shows that our data enhancement method improves the performance of each model basically, up to 10%. R fits the outliers of the testing datasets well and improves the generalization ability of the networks.

Furthermore, we compared the performance of the three models based on HopeNet on AFLW2000 in Fig. 6: PYR, YPR and YPR+R. The samples in AFLW2000 are divided into six subsets according to yaw values, every 30° of the yaw range of $[-90°, 90°]$ as one subset. It can be clearly seen the improvement of optimizing data distribution from PYR to YPR, and the improvement of enhancing dataset from YPR to YPR+R. And the comparison of PYR and YPR+R shows the combined effects of the two methods.

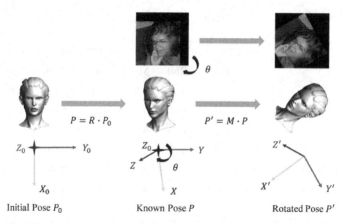

**Fig. 5.** Diagram of solving the corresponding head pose of the rotated image.

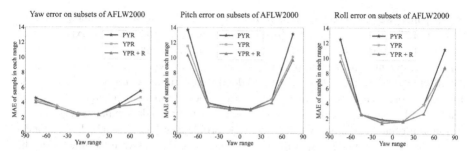

**Fig. 6.** Error comparison of three models on each of Euler angles on AFLW2000 dataset [2], blue for HopeNet [1] (PYR), orange for HopeNet (YPR) and green for HopeNet (YPR+R). The interval of subsets is set to 30° on the yaw range of [−90°, 90°].

**Table 2.** Results of models before and after data enhancement

| Metrics | | AFLW2000 [2] | | | | BIWI [3] | | | |
|---|---|---|---|---|---|---|---|---|---|
| | | Yaw | Pitch | Roll | MAE | Yaw | Pitch | Roll | MAE |
| HopeNet [1] | PYR | 3.47 | 6.15 | 4.65 | 4.76 | 4.41 | 5.12 | 3.09 | 4.21 |
| | PYR+R | 3.10 | 5.84 | 4.22 | 4.39 | 4.19 | 4.52 | 3.35 | 4.02 |
| | YPR | 3.39 | 5.73 | 4.33 | 4.48 | 4.28 | 4.73 | 3.27 | 4.09 |
| | YPR+R | 3.10 | 5.70 | 4.29 | 4.37 | 3.67 | 4.25 | 3.11 | 3.68 |
| | RPY | 3.34 | 5.71 | 4.37 | 4.47 | 4.27 | 5.07 | 2.92 | 4.09 |
| | RPY+R | 3.09 | 5.60 | 4.28 | 4.32 | 3.94 | 4.89 | 3.79 | 4.21 |

*(continued)*

**Table 2.** (*continued*)

| Metrics | | AFLW2000 [2] | | | | BIWI [3] | | | |
|---|---|---|---|---|---|---|---|---|---|
| | | Yaw | Pitch | Roll | MAE | Yaw | Pitch | Roll | MAE |
| FSA-Net [7] | PYR | 4.32 | 6.19 | 4.73 | 5.08 | 5.19 | 5.57 | 3.39 | 4.72 |
| | PYR+R | 3.95 | 5.65 | 4.05 | 4.55 | 4.52 | 5.28 | 3.61 | 4.47 |
| | YPR | 4.15 | 6.20 | 4.78 | 5.04 | 4.70 | 5.84 | 3.34 | 4.63 |
| | YPR+R | 3.74 | 5.74 | 4.13 | 4.54 | 4.34 | 4.78 | 3.48 | 4.20 |
| | RPY | 4.14 | 6.27 | 4.71 | 5.04 | 5.12 | 6.40 | 3.54 | 5.02 |
| | RPY+R | 3.79 | 5.80 | 4.13 | 4.57 | 4.65 | 4.86 | 3.62 | 4.38 |

## 5   Conclusion

In this paper, we discussed the facts of the poor prediction results of some large-angle poses from the perspective of data distribution, which was ignored by the existing methods. For the profile poses with large angles, we verified that the rotation order of Euler angles significantly affects the prediction accuracy. And we showed that according to the different distributions of the datasets under different rotation orders, selecting a more appropriate order can effectively improve the accuracy of models learning and predicting head pose. For outliers with rare poses in the distributions, a data enhancement method by random rotation was proposed to solve the problem of data missing. The expanded training dataset can better adapt to various head pose. Extensive experiments on different network structures and different datasets proved our methods achieve a general improvement. They can be universally applied to the existing and future methods.

**Acknowledgement.** We acknowledge the computational resources supported by High-Performance Computing Center of Collaborative Innovation Center of Advanced Microstructures, Nanjing University, and Nanjing Institute of Advanced Artificial Intelligence.

## References

1. Ruiz, N., Chong, E., Rehg, J.M.: Fine-grained head pose estimation without keypoints. In: 2018 IEEE/CVF Conference on Computer Vision and Pattern Recognition Workshops (CVPRW) (2018)
2. Zhu, X., et al.: Face alignment across large poses: a 3D solution. In: 2016 IEEE Conference on Computer Vision and Pattern Recognition (CVPR) (2016)
3. Fanelli, G., Dantone, M., Gall, J., Fossati, A., Van Gool, L.: Random forests for real time 3D face analysis. Int. J. Comput. Vis. **101**(3), 437–458 (2013)
4. Bulat, A., Tzimiropoulos, G.: How far are we from solving the 2D & 3D face alignment problem? (and a Dataset of 230,000 3D Facial Landmarks). In: IEEE International Conference on Computer Vision (2017)
5. Miao, X., et al.: Direct shape regression networks for end-to-end face alignment. In: 2018 IEEE/CVF Conference on Computer Vision and Pattern Recognition (2018)

6. Kowalski, M., Naruniec, J., Trzcinski, T.: Deep alignment network: a convolutional neural network for robust face alignment. In: 2017 IEEE Conference on Computer Vision and Pattern Recognition Workshops (CVPRW) (2017)

7. Yang, T.Y., et al.: FSA-net: learning fine-grained structure aggregation for head pose estimation from a single image. In: 2019 IEEE/CVF Conference on Computer Vision and Pattern Recognition (CVPR) (2020)

8. Zhu, X., Liu, X., Lei, Z., Li, S.Z.: Face alignment in full pose range: a 3D total solution. IEEE Trans. Pattern Anal. Mach. Intell. **41**(1), 78–92 (2019)

9. Feng, Y., Wu, F., Shao, X., Wang, Y., Zhou, X.: Joint 3D face reconstruction and dense alignment with position map regression network. In: Ferrari, V., Hebert, M., Sminchisescu, C., Weiss, Y. (eds.) Computer Vision – ECCV 2018. LNCS, vol. 11218, pp. 557–574. Springer, Cham (2018). https://doi.org/10.1007/978-3-030-01264-9_33

10. Ranjan, R., Patel, V.M., Chellappa, R.: HyperFace: a deep multi-task learning framework for face detection, landmark localization, pose estimation, and gender recognition. IEEE Trans. Pattern Anal. Mach. Intell. **41**(1), 121–135 (2019)

11. Kumar, A., Alavi, A., Chellappa, R.: KEPLER: keypoint and pose estimation of unconstrained faces by learning efficient H-CNN regressors (2017)

12. Zhou, Y., Gregson, J.: WHENet: Real-time Fine-Grained Estimation for Wide Range Head Pose (2020). https://arxiv.org/abs/2005.10353

13. Shao, M., et al.: Improving head pose estimation with a combined loss and bounding box margin adjustment. In: 2019 14th IEEE International Conference on Automatic Face & Gesture Recognition (FG 2019) (2019)

14. Liu, Z., et al.: Facial pose estimation by deep learning from label distributions. In: 2019 IEEE/CVF International Conference on Computer Vision Workshop (ICCVW) (2020)

15. Heng, W., et al.: QuatNet: quaternion-based head pose estimation with multiregression loss. Multimedia IEEE Transactions on (2018)

16. Pio, R.: Euler angle transformations. Automat. Control IEEE Trans. **11**(4), 707–715 (1966)

# Knight Tour Patterns: Novel Handcrafted Feature Descriptors for Facial Expression Recognition

Mukku Nisanth Kartheek[1,2]([✉]), Rapolu Madhuri[3], Munaga V. N. K. Prasad[1], and Raju Bhukya[2]

[1] Center for Affordable Technologies, Institute for Development and Research in Banking Technology, Hyderabad, Telangana, India
{mvnkprasad,kmnisanth}@idrbt.ac.in
[2] Department of Computer Science and Engineering, National Institute of Technology, Warangal, Telangana, India
raju@nitw.ac.in
[3] School of Computer and Information Sciences, University of Hyderabad, Hyderabad, Telangana, India

**Abstract.** Facial expressions are used frequently in the social interaction and are considered important as they can reflect the inner emotional states of an individual. Automatic Facial Expression Recognition (FER) systems aim at classifying the facial images into various expressions. To do this task accurately, better feature descriptors are to be developed to effectively capture the facial information. The main contribution of this paper is our novel local texture based feature extraction techniques, inspired by Knight tour problem namely Knight Tour Patterns (kTP and KTP). kTP extracts two feature values in the 3 x 3 overlapping neighborhood, whereas, KTP extracts three feature values in the 5 x 5 overlapping neighborhood. To the proposed methods, apart from binary weights, different weights (fibonacci, prime, natural, squares and odd) have been applied to further reduce the feature vector length. The extensive experiments have been performed on JAFFE, MUG, TFEID, CK+ and KDEF datasets with respect to both six and seven expressions in person independent setup. The proposed methods are compared with the standard existing variants of binary patterns to demonstrate the efficiency of the proposed methods.

**Keywords:** Chess game · Facial expressions · Feature extraction · Handcrafted features · Knight tour · Local descriptor

## 1 Introduction

Facial expressions are considered important in the social interaction, as they can reflect the inner emotional states of an individual. Also, they can compliment or contradict the information being conveyed through verbal words. The expressions such as fear, happy, sad, surprise, neutral, disgust and anger are commonly

N. Tsapatsoulis et al. (Eds.): CAIP 2021, LNCS 13053, pp. 210–219, 2021.
https://doi.org/10.1007/978-3-030-89131-2_19

used by the people, across all cultures and traditions [4]. Automatic recognition of facial expressions is essential today, as they have been incorporated in various real life applications such as human behaviour understanding, driver mood detection, robot control and animation etc. [6].

Traditional Facial Expression Recognition (FER) systems have three essential stages namely pre-processing, feature extraction and classification. The performance of an FER system is greatly impacted by the method employed for feature extraction, as extracting insignificant features would degrade the recognition accuracy, even after using the best classification techniques [6]. So, a feature extraction technique that could capture significant features from the facial images is essential. From the literature studies [6,7,19], texture descriptors have proven to be effective for capturing the minute changes in the facial appearances with respect to specific expressions. In this regard, novel local texture based approaches, kTP and KTP, inspired from the famous Knight tour problem are proposed for facial feature extraction. The proposed descriptors, kTP and KTP could capture distinctive facial information as the neighboring pixels are compared with the center pixel based on a Knight tour in a local neighborhood.

This paper is structured in the following manner: The related work in the field of FER has been summarized in Sect. 2. In Sect. 3, a brief summary of Knight tour problem is presented and the proposed feature descriptors, kTP and KTP are explained in detail. In Sect. 4, the experimental setup, the datasets considered, and the comparison of the proposed methods with the existing variants of binary patterns is reported. The concluding remarks are reported in Sect. 5.

## 2   Related Work

In FER system, the existing techniques in the literature are categorized into geometric feature and appearance feature based approaches [6]. The geometric feature based methods deal with the extraction of the locations of crucial components of face such as eyes, nose and mouth by encoding the Region Of Interest (ROI). Although, these geometric features represent facial geometry, they fail to capture specific local information such as ridges, changes in skin texture etc. The appearance feature based approaches are further classified into holistic and local based approaches [19]. The local based approaches are able to capture micro-level texture information such as specific skin changes, ridge details and minute characteristics that are relevant to various facial expressions [5]. These appearance based features can extract a detailed set of features which are noise resistant. The local based approaches are further classified into texture based and edge based approaches. Local Binary Pattern (LBP) [1], is the most widely used texture based feature descriptor for facial feature extraction, but it's feature representation capability is affected under random noises and illumination variations. In Local Directional Pattern (LDP) [2], the directions related to the top three responses from the eight obtained kirsch responses are encoded. Local Directional Number (LDN) [3] encodes both the directions of top negative and positive Kirsch response values to effectively capture facial information. In Local Directional Ternary Pattern (LDTerP) [4], ternary patterns are proposed for extracting the emotion related information.

Regional Adaptive Affinitive Pattern (RADAP) [6] uses multi-distance information for capturing the expression specific changes. In Local Directional Structural Pattern (LDSP) [5], the positional information of top two Kirsch mask responses is computed for extracting the structural information. Durga et al. [8] proposed LBP with adaptive window for extracting robust facial features, even in the presence of noise. Tuncer et al. [7] proposed Chess Pattern (CP) and extracted six features by considering the moves of Rook, Knight and Bishop in a 5 x 5 neighborhood. Shanthi et al. [19] proposed fusion of LBP and Local Neighborhood Encoded Pattern (LNEP) methods for analyzing the association among the adjacent pixels in a local neighborhood. Based on the studies performed as part of literature survey, the edge based feature descriptors are highly inconsistent in the presence of noise and they tend to generate unstable patterns in the smoother regions of an image. Recently, deep learning techniques such as Multibranch Cross Convolutional Neural Network (CNN) [15] and Residual Multi-task Learning (RMTL) [17], have shown promising results for facial expression recognition. But, those methods achieved better results at the cost of much training data and additional computational resources.

## 3  Proposed Methodology

### 3.1  Knight's Tour

Knight's Tour is defined as the series of moves taken by the Knight on the chessboard for visiting every square exactly once [9]. In a chess board, a Knight can move two squares horizontally and one square vertically or two squares vertically and one square horizontally. Finding the Knight tour is an instance of the Hamiltonian path problem in the graph theory. In a 5 x 5 chess board, the number of Knight tours depend on the position at which Knight starts, if it starts at the position (1, 1), then 304 Knight tours are possible. If it starts at position (3, 3), then 64 Knight tours are possible. If it starts at position (1, 2), then no knight tour is possible.

Drawing motivation from the Knight tour problem in graph theory, novel local texture based feature descriptors are proposed for facial feature extraction. kTP is proposed and implemented in the 3 x 3 neighborhood, whereas, KTP is proposed for feature extraction in the 5 x 5 neighborhood. There are many possibilities of Knight tours possible based on the starting index, as mentioned in Fig. 1 (a-b). Among those possibilities, one such possibility, where the Knight's move starting at the index (1, 1) and ending at the center pixel (3, 3) is chosen for feature extraction purpose.

### 3.2  kTP Feature Extraction

The Knight moves in a 3 x 3 neighborhood are considered as a basis for kTP's feature extraction. A 3 x 3 sample block is shown with indexes in Fig. 2(a) and

| (1,1) | (1,2) | (1,3) | (1,4) | (1,5) |
|---|---|---|---|---|
| (2,1) | (2,2) | (2,3) | (2,4) | (2,5) |
| (3,1) | (3,2) | (3,3) | (3,4) | (3,5) |
| (4,1) | (4,2) | (4,3) | (4,4) | (4,5) |
| (5,1) | (5,2) | (5,3) | (5,4) | (5,5) |

**(a)**

| 304 | 0 | 56 | 0 | 304 |
|---|---|---|---|---|
| 0 | 56 | 0 | 56 | 0 |
| 56 | 0 | 64 | 0 | 56 |
| 0 | 56 | 0 | 56 | 0 |
| 304 | 0 | 56 | 0 | 304 |

**(b)**

**Fig. 1.** (a) Indexes in a 5 x 5 block (b) Possibilities of 5 x 5 Knight tour, based on starting index

the pixels are numbered, which are used for feature extraction, as mentioned in Fig. 2(b). kTP extracts two feature values, namely $kTP_1$ and $kTP_2$. As, it is 3 x 3 neighborhood, the Knight can move only in neighboring pixel positions and the center pixel cannot be reached. Starting at index (1, 1) in a 3 x 3 neighborhood, the Knight can move in 'L' shape either in horizontal or in vertical direction. For feature extraction through $kTP_1$, from index (1, 1), initially, the Knight move in horizontal direction is considered. Generally, the neighboring pixels are compared with the center pixel, to capture discriminative information in a local neighborhood [6–8, 19]. Following the same, in the proposed methods, the pixels visited based on the Knight moves are sequentially compared with the center pixel as shown in Eq. (1) and shown in Fig. 2(c). The thresholding function for comparing subsequent pixels is shown in Eq. (2). Upon comparison, a 8 bit binary sequence is obtained, which is then multiplied with the weight matrix $(W_m)$, is shown in Eq. (3-4).

$$kTP_a = \{\sigma(b_4, b_9), \sigma(b_1, b_9), \sigma(b_6, b_9), \sigma(b_3, b_9), \sigma(b_8, b_9),$$
$$\sigma(b_5, b_9), \sigma(b_2, b_9), \sigma(b_7, b_9)\} \qquad (1)$$

$$\sigma(p, q) = \begin{cases} 1, & \text{if } p \geq q \\ 0, & otherwise \end{cases} \qquad (2)$$

$$kTP_1 = \sum(kTP_a. * W_m) \qquad (3)$$

$$m = \{\text{binary, fibonacci, prime, natural, squares, odd}\} \qquad (4)$$

$$kTP_b = \{\sigma(b_4, b_9), \sigma(b_7, b_9), \sigma(b_2, b_9), \sigma(b_5, b_9), \sigma(b_8, b_9),$$
$$\sigma(b_3, b_9), \sigma(b_6, b_9), \sigma(b_1, b_9)\} \qquad (5)$$

$$kTP_2 = \sum(kTP_b. * W_m) \qquad (6)$$

$$kTP = kTP_1 \cup kTP_2 \qquad (7)$$

**Table 1.** Different weights used for feature extraction

| Weights | Denoted by | Range | Max. | Length |
|---------|-----------|-------|------|--------|
| Binary | $W_{binary} = [1, 2, 4, 8, 16, 32, 64, 128]$ | 0–255 | 255 | 256 |
| Fibonacci | $W_{fibonacci} = [1, 1, 2, 3, 5, 8, 13, 21]$ | 0–54 | 54 | 55 |
| Prime | $W_{prime} = [2, 3, 5, 7, 11, 13, 17, 19]$ | 0–77 | 77 | 78 |
| Natural | $W_{natural} = [1, 2, 3, 4, 5, 6, 7, 8]$ | 0–36 | 36 | 37 |
| Squares | $W_{squares} = [1, 4, 9, 16, 25, 36, 49, 64]$ | 0–204 | 204 | 205 |
| Odd | $W_{odd} = [1, 3, 5, 7, 9, 11, 13, 15]$ | 0–64 | 64 | 65 |

**Fig. 2.** (a) Sample 3 x 3 block with indexes. (b) Sample 3 x 3 block with names given to neighboring pixels and center pixel. Numbering is given for sequence of pixels considered for feature extraction through (c) $kTP_1$ (d) $kTP_2$

In image processing applications, binary weights are mostly used for feature extraction. In this work, apart from binary weights, other weights such as fibonacci [18], prime, natural, squares and odd have been utilized for feature extraction. The different weights used for experimental evaluation are presented in Table 1. Max. in Table 1 denotes maximum value. For feature extraction through kTP$_2$, from index (1, 1), the Knight moves in vertical direction are considered, as shown in Fig. 2(d). So, the pixels visited based on the Knight moves are sequentially compared with the center pixel as shown in Eq. (5) and the binary sequence obtained is then multiplied with W$_m$ as shown in Eq. (6). Finally, both kTP$_1$ and kTP$_2$ are concatenated to form final feature vector kTP, as shown in Eq. (7). Thus, kTP considers discriminant information using Knight moves in both horizontal and in vertical directions.

### 3.3   KTP Feature Extraction

The Knight moves in a 5 x 5 neighborhood are considered as a basis for KTP's feature extraction. A 5 x 5 sample block is shown in Fig. 3(a). KTP extracts three feature values, namely KTP$_1$, KTP$_2$ and KTP$_3$. Staring from index (1, 1) in a 5 x 5 neighborhood, the Knight can move in all twenty five pixel positions. For the purpose of feature extraction through KTP, these twenty five pixels are divided into four groups. The first three groups contain eight pixels each, traversed by Knight moves sequentially, and the final group contains center pixel. Initially, for feature extraction through KTP$_1$, starting from index (1, 1) in a 5 x 5 neighborhood, the Knight moves in horizontal direction are considered. From there, the pixels covered by Knight moves are subsequently compared with the center pixel. For $KTP_1$, the first group of pixels, as shown in Eq. (8) and in Fig. 3(b), are compared with the center pixel, and the corresponding binary number thus obtained is multiplied with $W_m$, as shown in Eq. (9). Thus, $KTP_1$ covers horizontal and vertical neighbors in the 3 x 3 neighborhood and diagonal neighbors in the 5 x 5 neighborhood. For $KTP_2$, the second group, which contains next set of eight pixels as shown in Eq. (10) and in Fig. 3(c), covered by Knight moves, are then compared with the center pixel, and the corresponding binary number obtained is multiplied with $W_m$, as shown in Eq. (11). For $KTP_3$, the third group of eight pixels, as shown in Eq. (12) and in Fig. 3(d) are compared with the center pixel and the corresponding binary number obtained is multiplied with $W_m$, as shown in Eq. (13). Finally, all $KTP_1$, $KTP_2$ and $KTP_3$ are concatenated together to form the final feature vector KTP, as shown in Eq. (14). $\cup$ represents concatenation operation in Eq. (14).

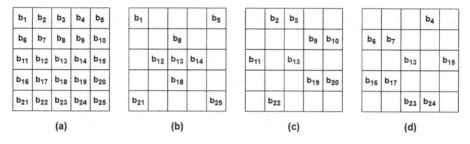

**Fig. 3.** (a). Sample 5 x 5 block. Pixels considered for feature extraction through (b) $KTP_1$ (c) $KTP_2$ (d) $KTP_3$

$$KTP_c = \{\sigma(b_1, b_{13}), \sigma(b_8, b_{13}), \sigma(b_5, b_{13}), \sigma(b_{14}, b_{13}), \sigma(b_{25}, b_{13}),$$
$$\sigma(b_{18}, b_{13}), \sigma(b_{21}, b_{13}), \sigma(b_{12}, b_{13})\} \qquad (8)$$

$$KTP_1 = \sum(KTP_c. * W_m) \qquad (9)$$

$$KTP_d = \{\sigma(b_3, b_{13}), \sigma(b_{10}, b_{13}), \sigma(b_{19}, b_{13}), \sigma(b_{22}, b_{13}), \sigma(b_{11}, b_{13}),$$
$$\sigma(b_2, b_{13}), \sigma(b_9, b_{13}), \sigma(b_{20}, b_{13})\} \qquad (10)$$

$$KTP_2 = \sum(KTP_d. * W_m) \qquad (11)$$

$$KTP_e = \{\sigma(b_{23}, b_{13}), \sigma(b_{16}, b_{13}), \sigma(b_7, b_{13}), \sigma(b_4, b_{13}), \sigma(b_{15}, b_{13}),$$
$$\sigma(b_{24}, b_{13}), \sigma(b_{17}, b_{13}), \sigma(b_6, b_{13})\} \qquad (12)$$

$$KTP_3 = \sum(KTP_e. * W_m) \qquad (13)$$

$$KTP = KTP_1 \cup KTP_2 \cup KTP_3 \qquad (14)$$

## 4   Experimental Analysis

For experimental analysis, five datasets namely Japanese Female Facial Expression (JAFFE) [10], Taiwanese Facial Expression Image Database (TFEID) [13], Multimedia Understanding Group (MUG) [11], Extended Cohn-Kanade (CK+) [12] and Karolinska Directed Emotional Faces (KDEF) [14] have been considered. The basic six expressions are anger, disgust, fear, happy, sad and surprise and neutral is considered as the seventh expression. For all the datasets, the experiments were performed both with respect to six and seven expressions. The information related to the number of subjects, number of images per expression, image format and size are presented in Table 2. CK+ database contains 593 image sequences captured from 123 subjects. In CK+ dataset, the images are stored in png format with size being 640 x 480 or 640 x 490. The threw apex frames from each sequence are selected for each expression class and the neutral expression images are selected from the onset of the image sequences.

**Table 2.** Information related to various datasets considered for experimental evaluation

| Dataset | Female subjects | Male subjects | Total subjects | Images per expression | Size | Format |
|---------|-----------------|---------------|----------------|-----------------------|------|--------|
| JAFFE | 10 | – | 10 | $\leq 4$ | 256 x 256 | tiff |
| MUG | 20 | 25 | 45 | 5 | 896 x 896 | jpg |
| TFEID | 20 | 20 | 40 | 1 | 480 x 600 | jpg |
| KDEF | 35 | 35 | 70 | 1 | 562 x 762 | JPEG |

For experimental evaluation, the number of images considered for each expression across datasets is reported in Table 3. For all the datasets, face detection is done using Viola Jones algorithm [16] and for maintaining an uniformity among all the datasets, all the images in the datasets have been resized into 120 x 120 image responses. Histogram equalization technique is then utilised for normalizing the illumination levels in an image. Then, the facial features are extracted using kTP and KTP and corresponding to kTP, two feature response maps are generated, whereas for KTP three feature response maps are generated. Each feature response is then partitioned into 'S' non-overlapping regions, where size of each block is H x H. The block size is empirically chosen as 8 i.e. (H=8) for all the datasets. For experimental evaluation, Person Independent (PI) scheme is adopted. As part of this scheme, leave one subject out policy, i.e. every time one subject is taken out from the training set and is included in the test set. This type of scheme is used in all the data sets except for CK+. For CK+ dataset alone, ten fold person independent cross validation scheme is adopted. The recognition accuracy is obtained by taking the average of accuracy obtained from each subject. For classification, a multi-class Support Vector Machine (SVM) with One-Versus-One (OVO) approach is utilized. SVM is chosen for experimental analysis as it the most widely used classifier in pattern recognition [6,8,19]. The experiments were performed using MATLAB R2018a software.

**Table 3.** Number of images considered for experimental analysis across datasets

| Database | Anger | Disgust | Fear | Happy | Neutral | Sad | Surprise | Total |
|---|---|---|---|---|---|---|---|---|
| JAFFE | 30 | 29 | 32 | 31 | 30 | 31 | 30 | 213 |
| TFEID | 34 | 40 | 40 | 40 | 39 | 39 | 36 | 268 |
| KDEF | 70 | 70 | 70 | 70 | 70 | 70 | 70 | 490 |
| CK+ | 135 | 177 | 75 | 207 | 369 | 84 | 249 | 1296 |
| MUG | 225 | 225 | 225 | 225 | 225 | 225 | 225 | 1575 |

**Table 4.** Recognition accuracy comparison of kTP using different weights

| Method | Six expressions | | | | | Seven expressions | | | | |
|---|---|---|---|---|---|---|---|---|---|---|
| | JAFFE | MUG | TFEID | KDEF | CK+ | JAFFE | MUG | TFEID | KDEF | CK+ |
| Binary | **62.28** | 86.88 | 92.92 | 83.81 | 91.23 | 58.52 | 81.02 | 93.57 | 80.82 | 87.03 |
| Fibonacci | 61.70 | **86.96** | 95.08 | **84.76** | **91.77** | 59.09 | **83.11** | 94.34 | **81.84** | 86.88 |
| Prime | 61.17 | 86.52 | 94.67 | 84.05 | 90.59 | 58.97 | 82.34 | 94.34 | 81.84 | 86.70 |
| Natural | 60.05 | 86.00 | 95.50 | 82.38 | 91.56 | **60.99** | 82.28 | 94.34 | 80.00 | 85.65 |
| Squares | 60.08 | 86.88 | 94.67 | 83.09 | 91.67 | 58.41 | 82.28 | 93.99 | 81.02 | **87.22** |
| Odd | 57.30 | 85.33 | **95.92** | 83.57 | 90.91 | 60.04 | 81.52 | **94.70** | 80.61 | 85.99 |

**Table 5.** Recognition accuracy comparison of KTP using different weights

| Method | Six Expressions | | | | | Seven Expressions | | | | |
|---|---|---|---|---|---|---|---|---|---|---|
| | JAFFE | MUG | TFEID | KDEF | CK+ | JAFFE | MUG | TFEID | KDEF | CK+ |
| Binary | **60.03** | 87.26 | 93.75 | 83.57 | **92.86** | 58.97 | 82.16 | 93.99 | 81.43 | 86.69 |
| Fibonacci | 59.41 | 87.11 | **95.00** | 83.81 | 92.20 | **59.47** | 81.08 | 94.34 | 81.22 | **86.86** |
| Prime | 60.00 | 87.26 | 94.92 | **84.05** | 92.43 | 58.50 | 82.98 | 93.93 | 81.84 | 86.57 |
| Natural | 59.51 | 87.04 | 94.50 | 82.86 | 91.55 | 58.09 | 82.79 | **95.00** | 80.61 | 85.82 |
| Squares | 58.82 | 86.82 | 94.08 | 83.81 | 92.64 | 57.97 | **83.11** | 93.93 | **82.04** | 86.69 |
| Odd | 59.93 | **87.55** | 94.50 | 82.38 | 91.77 | 57.45 | 82.35 | 94.28 | 81.22 | 86.15 |

For fair comparison, the existing variants of binary patterns such as LBP, LDP, LDN, LDTerP, LDSP, RADAP, CP and LBP+LNeP have been implemented in our environmental setup and correspondingly the recognition accuracy is reported. The proposed methods have been implemented with different weights and the results are tabulated in Table 4 for kTP and in Table 5 for KTP. For kTP in Table 4 and KTP in Table 5, for each dataset, the weight that had yielded the best recognition accuracy is highlighted in bold. In cases of tie, the method with least feature vector length is highlighted in bold. In Table 6, the comparison analysis of the proposed methods with the existing variants of binary patters is presented both with respect to six and seven expressions. From Table 6, the results demonstrated that the proposed methods outperformed the recent variants of binary patterns such as RADAP, LDSP, CP and LBP+LNeP. The experimental results indicate that kTP performed better than KTP in majority

**Table 6.** Comparison analysis with existing variants of binary patterns

| Method | Six expressions | | | | | Seven expressions | | | | |
|---|---|---|---|---|---|---|---|---|---|---|
| | JAFFE | MUG | TFEID | KDEF | CK+ | JAFFE | MUG | TFEID | KDEF | CK+ |
| LBP | 56.66 | 82.65 | 92.42 | 80.95 | 89.97 | 53.65 | 76.16 | 92.02 | 78.16 | 83.96 |
| LDP | 52.77 | 82.87 | 93.67 | 80.95 | 90.69 | 52.10 | 78.70 | 93.57 | 80.61 | 85.60 |
| LDN | 56.66 | 81.96 | 93.33 | 82.62 | 91.22 | 54.87 | 77.85 | 93.51 | 80.75 | 86.09 |
| LDTerP | 58.54 | 80.15 | 90.75 | 81.43 | 90.15 | 51.70 | 78.11 | 90.18 | 77.35 | 85.65 |
| LDSP | 56.70 | 85.19 | 94.50 | 82.38 | 91.54 | 52.49 | 80.63 | 93.15 | 80.61 | 84.19 |
| RADAP | 57.22 | 83.48 | 94.17 | 80.19 | 91.34 | 56.20 | 80.26 | 93.27 | 80.20 | 84.60 |
| CP | 58.74 | 86.23 | 92.92 | 84.04 | 91.34 | 58.50 | 81.26 | 93.27 | 81.43 | 85.94 |
| BP+LNEP | 61.29 | 86.52 | 93.00 | 83.57 | 92.21 | 59.04 | 81.45 | 93.27 | 81.84 | 86.30 |
| kTP | **62.28** | **86.96** | **95.92** | **84.76** | **91.77** | **60.99** | **83.11** | **94.70** | **81.84** | **87.22** |
| KTP | **60.03** | **87.55** | **95.00** | **84.05** | **92.86** | **59.47** | **83.11** | **95.00** | **82.04** | **86.86** |

of the cases, as observed from Table 6. Thus, kTP and KTP outperformed existing variants of binary patterns by capturing discriminative facial information by comparing pixels based on Knight moves in a local neighborhood.

## 5    Conclusion and Future Work

Novel local texture based feature extraction techniques, kTP and KTP, inspired by the Knight tour problem in graph theory, have been presented in this paper for facial feature extraction. kTP and KTP utilized Knight moves for comparing neighboring pixels with the center pixel in a local neighborhood. The proposed methods with different weights have been implemented on JAFFE, MUG, TFEID, CK+ and KDEF datasets with respect to both six and seven expressions. The experimental results demonstrated that the proposed method outperformed the standard existing variants of binary patterns. As a future work, research can be carried out on various weight approaches to choose the best weight. Also, novel light weight deep learning models can be developed for enhancing the overall recognition accuracy of FER systems.

## References

1. Shan, C., Gong, S., McOwan, P.W.: Facial expression recognition based on local binary patterns: a comprehensive study. Image Vis. Comput. **27**(6), 803–816 (2009)
2. Jabid, T., Kabir, M.H., Chae, O.: Robust facial expression recognition based on local directional pattern. ETRI J. **32**(5), 784–794 (2010)
3. Rivera, A.R., Castillo, J.R., Chae, O.O.: Local directional number pattern for face analysis: face and expression recognition. IEEE Trans. Image Process. **22**(5), 1740–1752 (2012)
4. Ryu, B., Rivera, A.R., Kim, J., Chae, O.: Local directional ternary pattern for facial expression recognition. IEEE Trans. Image Process. **26**(12), 6006–6018 (2017)
5. Makhmudkhujaev, F., Iqbal, M.T.B., Ryu, B., Chae, O.: Local directional-structural pattern for person-independent facial expression recognition. Turk. J. Electr. Eng. Comput. Sci. **27**(1), 516–531 (2019)

6. Mandal, M., Verma, M., Mathur, S., Vipparthi, S.K., Murala, S., Kumar, D.K.: Regional adaptive affinitive patterns (RADAP) with logical operators for facial expression recognition. IET Image Process. **13**(5), 850–861 (2019)

7. Tuncer, T., Dogan, S., Ataman, V.: A novel and accurate chess pattern for automated texture classification. Phys. A Stat. Mech. Appl. **536**, 122584 (2019)

8. Kola, D.G.R., Samayamantula, S.K.: A novel approach for facial expression recognition using local binary pattern with adaptive window. Multimedia Tools Appl. **80**(2), 2243–2262 (2020). https://doi.org/10.1007/s11042-020-09663-2

9. Shashikiran, B.S., Shaila, K., Venugopal, K.R.: Minimal block knight's tour and edge with LSB pixel replacement based encrypted image steganography. SN Comput. Sci. **2**(3), 1–9 (2021)

10. Zhang, Z., Lyons, M., Schuster, M., Akamatsu, S.: Comparison between geometry-based and gabor-wavelets-based facial expression recognition using multi-layer perceptron. In: Proceedings Third IEEE International Conference on Automatic Face and Gesture Recognition, pp. 454–459. IEEE (1998)

11. Aifanti, N., Papachristou, C., Delopoulos, A.: The MUG facial expression database. In: 11th International Workshop on Image Analysis for Multimedia Interactive Services WIAMIS 10, pp. 1–4. IEEE (2010)

12. Lucey, P., Cohn, J.F., Kanade, T., Saragih, J., Ambadar, Z., Matthews, I.: The extended cohn-kanade dataset (ck+): A complete dataset for action unit and emotion-specified expression. In: 2010 IEEE Computer Society Conference on Computer Vision and Pattern Recognition-Workshops, pp. 94–101. IEEE (2010)

13. Chen, L.F., Yen, Y.S.: Taiwanese facial expression image database. Institute of Brain Science, National Yang-Ming University, Brain Mapping Laboratory, Taipei (2007)

14. Goeleven, E., De Raedt, R., Leyman, L., Verschuere, B.: The Karolinska directed emotional faces: a validation study. Cogn. Emot. **22**(6), 1094–1118 (2008)

15. Shi, C., Tan, C., Wang, L.: A facial expression recognition method based on a multibranch cross-connection convolutional neural network. IEEE Access **9**, 39255–39274 (2021)

16. Viola, P., Jones, M.J.: Robust real-time face detection. Int. J. Comput. Vis. **57**(2), 137–154 (2004)

17. Chen, B., Guan, W., Li, P., Ikeda, N., Hirasawa, K., Lu, H.: Residual multi-task learning for facial landmark localization and expression recognition. Pattern Recogn. **115**, 107893 (2021)

18. Chandra Sekhar Reddy, P., Vara Prasad Rao, P., Kiran Kumar Reddy, P., Sridhar, M.: Motif shape primitives on fibonacci weighted neighborhood pattern for age classification. In: Wang, J., Reddy, G.R.M., Prasad, V.K., Reddy, V.S. (eds.) Soft Computing and Signal Processing. AISC, vol. 900, pp. 273–280. Springer, Singapore (2019). https://doi.org/10.1007/978-981-13-3600-3_26

19. Shanthi, P., Nickolas, S.: An efficient automatic facial expression recognition using local neighborhood feature fusion. Multimedia Tools Appl. **80**(7), 10187–10212 (2020). https://doi.org/10.1007/s11042-020-10105-2

# Exploiting Visual Context to Identify People in TV Programs

Thomas Petit[1,2(✉)], Pierre Letessier[1], Stefan Duffner[2], and Christophe Garcia[2]

[1] Institut National de l'Audiovisuel, Bry-sur-Marne, France
{tpetit,pletessier}@ina.fr
[2] Univ Lyon, INSA Lyon, LIRIS (UMR 5202 CNRS), Lyon, France
{thomas.petit,stefan.duffner,christophe.garcia}@liris.cnrs.fr

**Abstract.** Television is a medium that is implicitly highly codified. Every TV program has its own visual identity that is often rich in information; most of the time, a single frame extracted from a TV broadcast contains enough information for a human agent to determine the genre of the program, and sometimes even to predict who is likely to appear in it. Our goal is to exploit the visual context of TV programs to help identify the people appearing in them.

In this work, we introduce a new dataset of over 10 M frames extracted mainly from french TV programs and aired between 2010 and 2020. We also present an original approach for deep similarity metric learning in order to learn a descriptor that effectively captures the visual context of a TV program and helps to recognize the subjects appearing in the program.

**Keywords:** Dataset · Similarity measure · Visual context · Television

## 1 Introduction

Automatic facial recognition efficiency has increased considerably in the last decade and can now achieve impressive results. However, these state-of-the-art models may still make some mistakes on faces that are very hard to distinguish. In most cases, humans would not make the same mistakes as they would have access to much more information.

Among the additional information that the human brain uses to identify people, the visual context, i.e. all the visual information except for the face to identify, is particularly useful. We know, for example, that a human agent is able to achieve an accuracy score of 94.27% on the LFW protocol [3], which is a face verification protocol, when all faces have been masked [5], meaning using only the surrounding visual context.

We also know that the television is a very codified medium; given only a few static frames, a human is most of the time able to say from which kind of program they have been sampled, whether it is a sport match, a newscast, a political debate, and so on. We believe that this knowledge carries much information about the people possibly appearing in that program and could be used

© Springer Nature Switzerland AG 2021
N. Tsapatsoulis et al. (Eds.): CAIP 2021, LNCS 13053, pp. 220–230, 2021.
https://doi.org/10.1007/978-3-030-89131-2_20

to disambiguate the cases in which facial recognition systems fail. Our goal is to exploit the visual context to improve face retrieval and face verification in a dataset of TV programs.

In this paper, we present two contributions: 1) we introduce a new large-scale dataset of over 10 M images from TV programs aired between 2010 and 2020; 2) we propose a deep metric learning approach for visual context building an effective descriptor specific to TV. We experimentally show that this new descriptor can be used jointly with state-of-the-art face descriptors to improve the performances over a face verification task and a face classification task when such a visual context is available.

## 2  Related Work

Exploiting contextual information in order to improve facial recognition is an approach that has already been studied. However, as the available contextual information can be very specific to a given problem, the different approaches and solutions can differ a lot.

Some studies focused on exploiting a social context by identifying the relationships between the subjects or the events they appear in. This approach is particularly suitable for social networks where the relationships between the users are explicit [11] but have also been applied to other kinds of datasets such as movies [4] or TV shows [6].

Other papers chose not to limit the visual appearance of the subjects to their faces but also took advantage of their clothes by extracting features from different body parts and merging them together. This approach, which is particularly suited for person re-identification in a unique event, has been applied on photo albums [15] and on movies [4].

A different problem which is worth mentioning here because of its proximity with our approach is the genre classification for TV videos. The goal is to classify TV videos into a few different genres. Some models rely on automatically learned features, like Varghese et al. [12] classifying videos into different genres ("news", "entertainment" and "sport") using features learned on the SUN dataset [14]. Other models, on the other hand, use handcrafted features like Daudpota et al. [1] who rely on the number of scenes and quantify the motion of the subjects in order to classify videos as "talk shows" or "others".

Several datasets have already been proposed to deal with the scene categorization problem in a general setting. Two of them in particular are widely used: the SUN [14] and the Places365 dataset [17]. They contain a large number of indoor and outdoor scene categories. These scene categories are very diverse; Places365, for example, includes categories like "igloo", "synagogue" or even "stables". This large number of various categories is very interesting but does not make these datasets particularly suited to learn a visual descriptor of TV frames, as most categories are not related to TV programs.

## 3   Dataset

### 3.1   Motivation

Our goal is to be able to exploit the visual information in a video frame other than the facial appearances to help identify the people appearing on TV programs. We want to be able to extract continuous feature descriptors from video frames that carry information about the context of the program, and hence about the peoples appearing in those frames.

Existing datasets oriented towards context recognition have been designed in order to classify the images. Some datasets of locations images like SUN [14] or Places365 [17] are quite exhaustive in terms of labels, however they do not allow to capture the semantic proximity that can exist between two different classes, like between an airfield and an airport terminal, or between the ocean and a harbour. Also their distribution is quite different from what is to be expected in a dataset of TV frames. Some other datasets which are more TV specific only focus on classifying TV programs in a few classes like news, sports, music, and so on, but they fail at capturing the diversity within each of these classes and the semantic relationships that can exist between them.

### 3.2   Dataset Structure

We introduce the "Visual Context for TV Programs" dataset (VCTP), a dataset of 10,684,217 frames of TV programs aired between 2010 and 2020, mostly on the French TV, but not only. It is public and is completely available[1]. This dataset covers the diversity of visual contexts prone to appear on television with frames selected from a large number of TV programs of all sorts, such as news, sports, entertainment, talk shows, and so on. For legal reasons as well as practical reasons that will be detailed below, all the faces have been blurred in this dataset, so as to be unrecognizable. Figure 1 shows a few examples of frames from our dataset.

This dataset is unlabeled. However, it comes with a list of 4,362,818 pairs of frames where at least one individual appears on both frames.

## 4   Visual Context Metric Learning

The dataset has been built in order to be able to compute a continuous feature descriptor from a static image that captures its visual context and that can help identify the people depicted in it. To this end, we propose a deep metric learning approach and organize our dataset in triplets including one anchor, one positive element and one negative element, so that a similarity metric can be learned using the triplet loss or the TSML loss. This approach has been proved to be efficient for continuous visual descriptor learning [7], and we adapted it to specifically learn visual context as explained in the following.

---

[1] https://dataset.ina.fr/.

**Fig. 1.** Sample of the frames from our dataset. The visual contexts are various and reflect the diversity of the programs one can see on TV: news, entertainment, sport, weather forecast, and so on.

### 4.1 Triplet Formation

The difficulty lies in being able to define what makes a positive or a negative pair of frames. The purpose of this dataset is to help identify the persons appearing in the frames. Thus, we decided to rely on person identities to build our positive and negative pairs of frames, needed to form the (anchor, positive, negative) triplets.

**Positive Pairs.** We consider one pair of frames as positive context-wise if we are able to identify at least one person that appears in both frames. Given the impossibility to label manually all of the faces appearing in over 10M frames, we performed this automatically. We first detected all of the faces in the original frames of our dataset (not blurred) and computed the corresponding facial features descriptors. We then formed our pairs using a selective distance threshold between the faces to assert they do in fact belong to the one same person. Some examples are displayed on Fig. 2. The facial features model we used is a ResNet18 architecture trained on the VGGFace2 dataset. It achieves a 98.98% score on the LFW protocol [3].

**Negative Pairs.** A common and effective strategy in similarity metric learning setting is to focus on hard negative examples during training. For example, for facial features learning, comparing similar identities help differentiating them [7,9,10,13]. This often implies selecting negative pairs with similar embeddings.

**Fig. 2.** Examples of two positive pairs from our dataset.

Our problem, however, differs. If we can consider a pair as being positive when a common person appears in both frames, the absence of such a person is not enough to consider a pair as being negative. We might for example, sample two frames from the same program where no common people appears on both frames. We do not expect this pair to be considered as negative since the context is not expected to be any different within a unique program from one scene to another. The same can apply to two different programs with a very similar context but no common participant.

This make such an adversarial sampling very difficult to apply in our case as it could lead to sampling too many false negative pairs. For this reason, we decided to sample the negative elements of our triplets randomly and to rely on the large size and on the diversity of our dataset to make false negative pairs highly unlikely.

### 4.2  Model Learning

**Architecture.** To train our visual context model, we use a Resnet50 architecture [2] pre-trained on Places365 [17][2]. The last classification layer, with 365 nodes, is replaced with a 16-dimensional layer. The input of this network are $256 \times 256$ images.

**Loss Function.** The pretrained model is fine-tuned using the Triangular Similarity Metric Learning (TSML) loss [16]. This loss function is similar to the widely used triplet loss introduced in [7]. However, we observed that the performance using the TSML loss is slightly better. Hence, in this paper, we report only the TSML results.

**About the Face Blurring.** We mentioned earlier that all faces in our dataset have been blurred, in particular for legal reasons. It appears it is also a practical choice. A first model has been trained similarly using the same dataset on which faces had not been blurred. Its performances were satisfying; however, we noticed using some visualization techniques like the Smoothgrad algorithm [8] that this

---

[2] https://github.com/CSAILVision/places365.

model focuses primarily on the faces appearing on the images and not on the background as was desired (see Fig. 3). Moreover, its performances decreases when applied on frames where faces were blurred, which proves that it learned to recognize the faces as well as to recognize the visual context. This is not surprising given our triplet formation strategies, described above, where at least one person appears in both images of a positive pair. Blurring the faces in the dataset helped to largely avoid this issue.

**Fig. 3.** When using a variant of our dataset where faces are not blurred, the trained model focuses mainly on the actual faces and not on the surrounding context (left). This is not the case when trained on our dataset with blurred faces (right).

## 5    Experimental Evaluation

We split our dataset in three subsets:

- a training set, containing 4,357,969 positive pairs and 4,331,132 more elements to form the negative pairs of the triplets during training
- a validation set, with 2,456 triplets
- and a test set containing 2,393 triplets

After training our model on our training set, and using the validation set for early stopping, we evaluated it on our test set and compared it to other existing models.

### 5.1    Visual Context Metric Evaluation

To evaluate our model, we split our test set into 5 and use it to perform a 5-fold cross-validation to determine the best threshold to classify a pair as positive or negative, i.e. same or different context. The overall accuracy displayed in Table 1 is the average accuracy obtained over the 5 folds ± the standard deviation.

We compare our model with the pre-trained Places365 models. For these pre-trained models, we use either the 365-dimensional outputs of the classification layer or the 2048-dimensional output of the previous layer (which is the input of the classification layer itself).

**Table 1.** Average accuracy ± standard deviation with 5-fold cross-validation over our test set, for our model and for pre-trained Places365 models

| Model | Ours | Pl365 Resnet50 | Pl365 Resnet50 2048-d layer | Pl365 Densenet161 |
|-------|------|----------------|-----------------------------|-------------------|
| Acc. | **85.17 ± 1.46%** | 75.34 ± 0.68% | 76.72 ± 0.65% | 74.70 ± 0.68% |

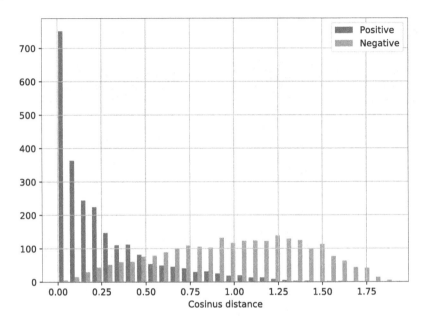

**Fig. 4.** Distributions of the distances of the positive and negative pairs of the test set computed with our visual context model.

Figure 4 shows the distribution of the cosine distances of the positive and negative pairs of the test set using our model. We can observe that the distribution of the negative pairs matches what would be expected from a random distribution uniformly distributed on the hyper-space. The distribution of the positive pairs, however, is much more concentrated towards low distance values.

## 5.2    Evaluation on a Face Verification Task of Doppelgangers

We evaluate the ability of our model to help recognize people when used jointly with facial features descriptors. In order to do this, we sample several face pairs to form a face verification task. The positive pairs are sampled in the same way as for the training set, i.e. with two face images of the same person. The negative pairs, however, have not been sampled randomly; we selected hard examples where both members of a pair are visually similar but are not the same person

**Fig. 5.** Example of doppelgangers pair used for the face verification task.

(see Fig. 5). All images have been sampled from TV programs that do not appear in the training, validation or test set introduced above. These face verification images are available with our dataset.

We use a total of 2922 pairs distributed into 2 splits. The first split is used to learn the best weight to combine the facial descriptors distances and the contextual descriptors distances and to learn the best threshold to classify pairs as positive or negative. These parameters are applied on the second split to get an accuracy score. The two splits are then swapped and this operation is repeated.

In Table 2 are displayed the average accuracy scores over the two splits. We observe that the combination of both facial and visual context descriptors achieves a better performance than the facial descriptors alone.

**Table 2.** Average accuracy over both splits of the doppelgangers verification task

| Input | Faces only | Context only | Faces + context |
|---|---|---|---|
| Accuracy | 85.87 ± 0.03 % | 65.86 ± 0.47% | **87.10 ± 0.17%** |

## 6 Qualitative Results

In order to illustrate how our model performs, Fig. 6 displays a few sample images and their nearest neighbors in our test set.

From these examples, we can see that frames from newscast, cartoons or weather forecasts are close to each other, respectively, even when coming from different TV channels.

**Fig. 6.** Sample images and their nearest neighbors in the test set. The queries are on the left column, and the nearest neighbors are then displayed from the closest ones on the left to the furthest on the right.

## 7    Conclusion

In this paper, we presented a new approach of leveraging visual context information in TV programs for person recognizing. We introduced VCTP, a new dataset of over 10 M frames from TV programs, that have been broadcast over an entire decade. It is, to our knowledge, the largest dataset available to learn a visual context descriptor that is specific to TV programs. We further present an original approach for visual context similarity metric learning specifically designed for identifying persons in TV programs. We show that our resulting neural network model can be used to effectively retrieve frames from semantically similar TV programs, and that it can be combined with state-of-the-art facial feature descriptors to improve the performance of a face verification task when such a visual context is available. We believe that the performance on the face verification tasks could be further improved with a suitable feature fusion strategy for facial descriptors and visual context descriptors.

# References

1. Daudpota, S.M., Muhammad, A., Baber, J.: Video genre identification using clustering-based shot detection algorithm. Sig. Image Video Process. **13**(7), 1413–1420 (2019). https://doi.org/10.1007/s11760-019-01488-3
2. He, K., Zhang, X., Ren, S., Sun, J.: Deep residual learning for image recognition. In: Conference on Computer Vision and Pattern Recognition, pp. 770–778 (2016)
3. Huang, G.B., Mattar, M., Berg, T., Learned-Miller, E.: Labeled faces in the wild: a database forstudying face recognition in unconstrained environments. In: Workshop on faces in'Real-Life'Images: Detection, Alignment, and Recognition (2008)
4. Huang, Q., Xiong, Y., Lin, D.: Unifying identification and context learning for person recognition. In: Proceedings of the Conference on Computer Vision and Pattern Recognition, pp. 2217–2225 (2018)
5. Kumar, N., Berg, A., Belhumeur, P.N., Nayar, S.: Describable visual attributes for face verification and image search. Trans. Pattern Anal. Mach. Intell. **33**(10), 1962–1977 (2011)
6. Petit, T., Letessier, P., Duffner, S., Garcia, C.: Unsupervised learning of co-occurrences for face images retrieval. In: International Conference on Multimedia in Asia, MMAsia 2020, ACM (2021)
7. Schroff, F., Kalenichenko, D., Philbin, J.: Facenet: A unified embedding for face recognition and clustering. In: Proceedings of the Conference on Computer Vision and Pattern Recognition, pp. 815–823 (2015)
8. Smilkov, D., Thorat, N., Kim, B., Viégas, F., Wattenberg, M.: Smoothgrad: removing noise by adding noise. arXiv preprint arXiv:1706.03825 (2017)
9. Smirnov, E., Melnikov, A., Novoselov, S., Luckyanets, E., Lavrentyeva, G.: Doppelganger mining for face representation learning. In: Proceedings of the International Conference on Computer Vision Workshops, pp. 1916–1923 (2017)
10. Smirnov, E., Melnikov, A., Oleinik, A., Ivanova, E., Kalinovskiy, I., Luckyanets, E.: Hard example mining with auxiliary embeddings. In: Proceedings Conference on Computer Vision and Pattern Recognition Workshops, pp. 37–46 (2018)
11. Stone, Z., Zickler, T., Darrell, T.: Autotagging facebook: social network context improves photo annotation. In: 2008 Computer Society Conference on Computer Vision and Pattern Recognition Workshops, pp. 1–8. IEEE (2008)
12. Varghese, J., Ramachandran Nair, K.N.: A novel video genre classification algorithm by keyframe relevance. In: Satapathy, S.C., Joshi, A. (eds.) Information and Communication Technology for Intelligent Systems. SIST, vol. 106, pp. 685–696. Springer, Singapore (2019). https://doi.org/10.1007/978-981-13-1742-2_68
13. Wang, C., Zhang, X., Lan, X.: How to train triplet networks with 100k identities? In: International Conference on Computer Vision Workshops, pp. 1907–1915 (2017)
14. Xiao, J., Hays, J., Ehinger, K.A., Oliva, A., Torralba, A.: Sun database: large-scale scene recognition from abbey to zoo. In: 2010 Computer Society Conference on Computer Vision and Pattern Recognition, pp. 3485–3492. IEEE (2010)
15. Zhang, N., Paluri, M., Taigman, Y., Fergus, R., Bourdev, L.: Beyond frontal faces: improving person recognition using multiple cues. In: Proceedings of the Conference on Computer Vision and Pattern Recognition, pp. 4804–4813 (2015)

16. Zheng, L., Idrissi, K., Garcia, C., Duffner, S., Baskurt, A.: Triangular similarity metric learning for face verification. In: 11th International Conference and Workshops on Automatic Face and Gesture Recognition (FG), vol. 1, pp. 1–7. IEEE (2015)
17. Zhou, B., Lapedriza, A., Khosla, A., Oliva, A., Torralba, A.: Places: a 10 million image database for scene recognition. Trans. Pattern Anal. Mach. Intell. **40**, 1452–1464 (2017)

# Foreground-Guided Facial Inpainting with Fidelity Preservation

Jireh Jam[1(✉)], Connah Kendrick[1], Vincent Drouard[2], Kevin Walker[2], and Moi Hoon Yap[1]

[1] Manchester Metropolitan University, Manchester, UK
jireh.jam@stu.mmu.ac.uk
[2] Image Metrics Ltd, Manchester, UK

**Abstract.** Facial image inpainting, with high-fidelity preservation for image realism, is a very challenging task. This is due to the subtle texture in key facial features (component) that are not easily transferable. Many image inpainting techniques have been proposed with outstanding capabilities and high quantitative performances recorded. However, with facial inpainting, the features are more conspicuous and the visual quality of the blended inpainted regions are more important qualitatively. Based on these facts, we design a foreground-guided facial inpainting framework that can extract and generate facial features using convolutional neural network layers. It introduces the use of foreground segmentation masks to preserve the fidelity. Specifically, we propose a new loss function with semantic capability reasoning of facial expressions, natural and unnatural features (make-up). We conduct our experiments using the CelebA-HQ dataset, segmentation masks from CelebAMask-HQ (for foreground guidance) and Quick Draw Mask (for missing regions). Our proposed method achieved comparable quantitative results when compare to the state of the art but qualitatively, it demonstrated high-fidelity preservation of facial components.

**Keywords:** Inpainting · Semantic · Foreground

## 1 Introduction

Image inpainting is an ongoing challenging research in computer vision. It is the art of reconstructing an image using algorithms powered by complex mathematical computations running in the background. Image inpainting is widely known as a restoration or editing technique commonly used by image/video

The authors would like to thank The Royal Society (Grant number: IF160006 and INF/PHD/180007). We gratefully acknowledge the support of NVIDIA Corporation with the donation of the Quadro P6000 used for this research.

© Springer Nature Switzerland AG 2021
N. Tsapatsoulis et al. (Eds.): CAIP 2021, LNCS 13053, pp. 231–241, 2021.
https://doi.org/10.1007/978-3-030-89131-2_21

Input        Ours        GT        Input        ours        GT

**Fig. 1.** Two Inpainted images (Ours) illustrate semantic understanding of our proposed model. The predictions of targeted regions show the ability of our model in realism preservation.

editing applications. Generative neural networks have shown greater ability to extract features over conventional (traditional) methods. The later usually use low level features to fill-in missing pixels by diffusion or match by exemplars to complete an inpainting task. The former use CNNs, capable of extracting high-quality textural and structural information that can fill in the missing contents by training a large scale dataset in a data-driven manner. The CNN model is known in literature to predict and understand an image structure without an explicit modelling of structures during the learning process [17].

Inpainting is not an easy task for ongoing learning-based models and have several limitations, some of which have been mentioned in Jam et al. [6]. One reason is the difficulty to propagate features from one area of the feature map to another using convolutional layers. This is because during convolutions, it is difficult to connect all locations within a feature map [15]. This problem is ongoing and numerous solutions have been attempted. For example Pathak et al. [15] tried to solve the problem by introducing fully-connected layers to directly connect all activation. Other models [5,11,12,17,18] have used different techniques with Liu et al. [11] introducing partial convolutions with hard mask updating and Yu et al. [18], gated convolutions with soft mask learning [18]. Though it has shown high understanding of the image structure there are still difficulties in solving problems with masks of arbitrary sizes, particularly in generating facial features with preserved realism of the inpainted regions. Facial features authenticate the face, thus a failure, incorrectly predicted or unnatural removal and replacement of a facial component will be easily detected by the audience (human). In this case, the face with such inpainted regions can be easily classed as invalid or determined as fake.

For these reasons described above, we propose the foreground guided image inpainting network. Our objective is to design and implement a model that has the capability to preserve the prominent features of the face with respect to various expressions and non-natural attributes as seen in Fig. 1. To instantiate the design, we assume that the foreground pixels reflect the background ones, which are readily available for disentanglement in latent space and are masked within the input image by the binary mask regions. The key point to consider from our assumption is that a foreground segmentation masks have a representation of disentangled pixels in latent space. Thus using a segmented mask manifold [13] will enable the CNN layers to propagate features with respect to facial attributes (natural and non-natural), pose and shapes.

## 2   Related Work

Pathak et al. [15] in 2016, proposed a deep learning method to solve the inpainting problem. Since its introduction, inpainting results have significantly improved over the years by numerous algorithms which have been documented in literature [1,6]. The advantage of these methods is its capability to utilize latent space given a large data of ground-truth images to learn from and hallucinate missing information from an input (masked image). This kind of learning and semantic understanding is particularly important to inpaint or restore images with natural and complex scenes. Iizuka et al. [2] improved on this method [15] by introducing a local and global discriminator. The use of two discriminators with this approach is to enforce local and global coherence of the inpainted region to the entire image. Based on literature, this method [2] still uses expensive post-processing (Poisson blending) on the generated image for realistic results.

### 2.1   Foreground Facial Inpainting Framework

Semantic scene understanding is an integral part of image inpainting because the hallucination of pixels to recover the damaged regions requires a semantic understanding of the global structure to the target region. The semantic segmentation map of a face can well represent the foreground of the image, where the binary mask is applied to create the damaged region. During hand inpainting, the painter takes into consideration the background pixels and tries to semantically draw a silhouette structure outlining the boundaries before colouring and linking the colour end-nodes or strokes to complete the damaged pixels, thus ensuring consistency with the entire image. Naturally, it is intuitive to consider that an occluded face will normally have two eye spots, a nose and a mouth. Based on this assumption, one can conclude that occlusion reasoning can improve the ability of CNNs to better estimate or hallucinate missing pixels regions created by the binary mask.

Schulter et al. [16] proposed to use a modified version of PSPNet [19] to conduct semantic foreground inpainting task. The network is designed to take two inputs (masked image and mask) based on a two pipeline encoder-decoder network where the reconstructed images are semantics and depth for visible and occluded pixels. This method is only limited to inpainting with semantic and depth. Lu et al. [14] introduced a max-pooling module and used semantic scene without foreground objects to conduct an inpainting task. The max-pooling module which is designed to fit within the encoder blocks takes an intermediate feature map, a foreground segmentation mask and binary mask as input to output an inpainted feature map. The limitation here is that sharing features between models can improve efficiency but degrade performance. Lee et al. [10] created the CelebAMask-HQ segmentation mask dataset as key intermediate representation of facial attributes and proposed a model that can flexibly manipulate these attributes with fidelity preservation. However, because GANs use a discriminator as the examiner, a direct supervision of an occluded region will not be possible if the ground-truth regions behind the binary mask are not available. Based on this assumption, we design our model with a discriminator that will judge the occluded regions to ensure that the inpainted region is realistic and semantically consistent with preserved realism.

Our proposed method uses foreground segmentation masks within a loss model but not through convolutions. Other models [14,16,17] apply the binary mask on the foreground masks, and passed through convolutions. The following sections describes our proposed facial inpainting framework and a new loss function that uses foreground mask to ensure fidelity preservation.

## 3    Architecture

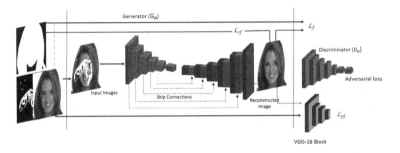

**Fig. 2.** Our proposed foreground-guided image inpainting framework with symmetric chain of convolutional and deconvolutional features. The foreground segmentation mask and masked image are the inputs to the network and parameters of the loss functions.

The design of our proposed network has an encoder-decoder, as the generator $(G_\theta)$ and a discriminator $(D_\theta)$, to achieve realistic results. The encoder architecture is based on [4] with the exception of the foreground mask and masked image as input. In the course of implementing the generator $(G_\theta)$, we make certain that the foreground mask is maintained and does not go through any convolutions throughout the training process. In order to obtain better average pixels during the backward pass, we utilise the foreground mask within the generator as an access mechanism for the loss. The masked image is downsampled to allow the network to learn latent representations of facial feature maps with weak supervision from the foreground mask. Specifically, we introduce a symmetric chain of convolutional and deconvolutional features, in which essential components of feature maps without corruption retrieved during convolutions are retained and incorporated inside the reconstruction unit.

## 3.1 Loss Function

To train our model, we introduce a new loss function based on $L_2$ and $L_1$ that takes into consideration foreground pixels to minimises the error between predicted $I_{pred}$ and ground-truth $(I_{gt})$ images. For a better understanding, we express the loss functions used within the generator as follows:

$$\mathcal{L}_{cF} = \frac{1}{N_{I_{gt}}}||M_F \odot (M_I - I_{pred})||_1 \tag{1}$$

$$\mathcal{L}_F = \frac{1}{N_{I_{gt}}}||M_F \odot (I_{gt} - I_{pred})||_2 \tag{2}$$

where $M_I$ is the input, and $N_{I_{gt}}$ is the number of elements in $I_{gt}$ in the shape height $(H)$, width $(W)$ and channel $(C)$, i.e. $N_{I_{gt}} = H * W * C$ and $\odot$ is the element-wise multiplication of the foreground mask $M_F$ with $I_{pred}$ and $I_{gt}$. These losses ensure preservation of luminance when computing the absolute difference between ground-truth image $(I_{gt})$ and the predicted image $(I_{pred})$.

$$\mathcal{L}_{pF} = \frac{1}{N_{I_{gt}}}||M_F \odot [\phi_i(M_I) - \phi_i(I_{pred})]||_2 \tag{3}$$

where $\phi_i$ is the feature map of the $i^ith$ layer of pre-trained VGG16 model. The $\mathcal{L}_{pF}$ uses the $M_F$ and intermediate features from a fixed VGG16 model [7] to compute the $L_2$ distance between ground-truth and predicted images.

For the discriminator, we adopt the Wasserstein GAN (WGAN) approach to measure the distance between predictions and the ground-truth.

$$\max_D V_{WGAN} = E_{x \sim p_r}[(D_\theta(I_{gt})] - E_{z \sim p_z}[D(G_\theta(I_{pred}))] \tag{4}$$

Equation 4 refers to the WGAN loss based on distributions of $I_{gt}$ (real) data and $I_{pred}$ (generated) data.

## 4 Training and Experiments

### 4.1 Datasets

The most commonly used publicly available datasets for facial image inpainting is the CelebA-HQ [8]. To create a damaged image or images with missing regions, a binary mask must be applied on the image to simulate the damaged. Usually this is done by an external dataset or function to create these masks regions. We made use of an external dataset namely Quick Draw Mask [3] resized to $256 \times 256$, with hole-to-image ratios ranging from 0.01 to 0.60. We use semantic segmentation masks from CelebAMask-HQ [10]. For the case of our model, we extract the skin and hair attributes, to form the foreground mask shown on Fig. 3 to compute our loss function.

**Fig. 3.** Images from CelebA-HQ [8] and segmentation masks of face and hair regions from CelebAMask-HQ [10] used as our foreground masks. The skin region without hair indicates the subject's hair is short or has no hair.

## 4.2   Method Comparison

Our proposed method compares quantitatively and qualitatively with the state-of-the-art methods.

- **Context encoder-decoder framework (CE)** [15] introduced the channel-wise fully connected layer . The channel-wise fully connected layer is designed to directly link all activation; thus enabling propagation of information within the activation of a feature map.
- **Partial Convolution (PConv)** [11] introduced convolutions with mask updating to alleviate the transfer of feature for irregular masks regions within convolutions.
- **Gated Convolution (GC)** [18] introduced gating mechanism that learns soft mask within convolutions to ease the transfer of features within convolutions. It is different from PConv in that the irregular mask is learned whereas in former, hard mask is updated in each step.
- **Ours** introduces semantic reasoning of features using a foreground mask within the network as a loss model. The key aspect here is that the foreground mask represents disentangled pixels of attribute features of the face. Thus semantic reasoning assists the convolutional layers to hallucinate pixels with fidelity preservation.

## 4.3   Implementation

We trained our model with the generator and discriminator loss defined in Sect. 3.1. We utilized a similar architecture to the one given in [4] and applied loss weights (coefficients) to the generator loss to get the results we obtained. Our goal was to guarantee that the generator gets penalised more severely during training by raising the loss weight of the foreground loss. This would allow the generator to learn structural and textural aspects, as well as an overall grasp of the semantic nature of the face region. We implement a foreground loss that further stresses consistency of predictions. This is accomplished by feeding the generator with a penalty on the background pixels using the foreground pixels in a backward pass, as shown in Fig. 2. We designed our network, and used the Keras libary with Tensorflow-backend to implement and train our model end-to-end. Our choice of dataset made us to follow the experimental settings by the state-of-the-art method [11] to split our data into 27K train and 3K test images. Our model is trained for 100 epochs with a learning rate of $10^{-4}$ in $G(z)$ and $10^{-12}$ in $D(x)$ using the Adam optimizer [9]. Our hardware condition limited us to a batch-size of 5 because of the deep nature of the network. We used GPU support (NVIDIA P6000) to conduct the full experiment from training to inference.

## 5 Results and Discussion

Here we evaluate the performances on predicted image, face/hair regions and discuss our experiment.

### 5.1 Quantitative Results

In real-life scenarios, the audience appreciate the visual quality of the blending between the inpainted and the original unmasked regions. However, in computer vision, we show quantitative to appreciate different approaches. We use the Mean Square Error (MSE), Mean Absolute Error (MAE), Frenchet Inception Distance (FID), Peak Signal to Noise Ratio (PSNR) and Structure Similarity Index Measure (SSIM), to quantify the performance against the state of the art ([11,15,18]). Table 1 shows the quantitative evaluation for the inpainted images with one of ours in bold.

**Table 1.** Quantitative comparison of various performance assessment metrics on 3,000 test images from the CelebA-HQ dataset. † Lower is better. ⊎ Higher is better.

| Performance assessment | | | | | | |
|---|---|---|---|---|---|---|
| Method | Author | MSE † | MAE † | FID† | PSNR ⊎ | SSIM ⊎ |
| CE | Pathak et al. [15] | 133.481 | 129.30 | 29.96 | 27.71 | 0.76 |
| PConv | Liu et al. [11] | 124.62 | 105.94 | 15.86 | 28.82 | 0.90 |
| GC | Yu et al. [18] | **102.42** | **43.10** | **4.29** | **39.96** | 0.92 |
| Ours | Foreground-guided | 194.86 | 57.38 | 9.63 | 34.35 | **0.92** |

The high values obtained for MSE, MAE and FID show poor performance of the model whereas lower values for these metrics indicate better performance. For clarity, we have included on the table † lower is better and ⊎ higher is better. PSNR and SSIM with higher values will indicate the prediction is closer to the ground-truth image, which will have a maximum score value of 1 for SSIM.

Our proposed method achieved the best SSIM score (tied with GC) and second performer in the majority of other metrics. This quantitative measures showed our method preserve the structure of the face. To further investigate, we perform quantitative measures on the foreground inpainted face and hair regions only, as shown on Table 2, with our proposed model outperformed the state-of-the-art models.

**Table 2.** Quantitative comparison of various performance assessment metrics on 3,000 test images from the CelebA-HQ dataset on Foreground inpainted regions. † Lower is better. ⊎ Higher is better.

| Performance assessment | | | | | | |
|---|---|---|---|---|---|---|
| Method | Author | MSE † | MAE † | FID† | PSNR ⊎ | SSIM ⊎ |
| CE | Pathak et al. [15] | 133.481 | 129.30 | 27.38 | 27.71 | 0.76 |
| PConv | Liu et al. [11] | 102.72 | 4.35 | 7.99 | 29.24 | 0.87 |
| GC | Yu et al. [18] | 29.14 | **1.47** | 2.23 | 35.33 | 0.95 |
| Ours | Foreground-guided | **26.01** | 2.58 | **1.19** | **37.38** | **0.96** |

## 5.2   Qualitative Results

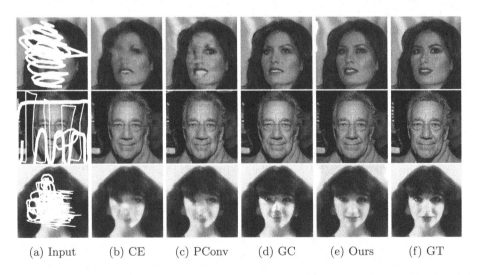

(a) Input        (b) CE        (c) PConv        (d) GC        (e) Ours        (f) GT

**Fig. 4.** Qualitative comparison of our proposed method with the state-of-the-art methods: (a) **Input masked-image**; (b) **CE** [15]; (c) **PConv** [11]; (d) **GConv**; (e) **Ours**; and (f) Ground-truth image.

In this section, we show visual comparison with our method compared with the state-of-the-art. Without bias and based on code availability, we used Pathak et al. [15] (**CE**), Liu et al. [11] (**PConv**), Yu et al. [18] (**GC**) to measure against our model. From Fig. 4, **CE** struggles with arbitrary hole-to-image mask regions and the generated image is blurry, while **PConv** and **GC** leave a bit of artefacts (best viewed when zoomed) on the generated image.

### 5.3 Semantic Inpainting with Fidelity Preservation

The qualitative results in Fig. 4 showed the performance of our model has great visual quality when compared to the state of the art. To further show reasonable semantic understanding of predictions, we showed that our model can fill-in high-level textural and structural information as seen in Fig. 4 where other methods have failed. As seen on the Fig. 1, the lip region on the image inpainted by our model is fully recovered, indicating a full semantic understanding of the image by putting a broader smile as compared to the original input. Furthermore, on Fig. 4, the earring, nose and eye regions are fully recovered with preserved realism with our model. This also show that our model has high semantic understanding of facial features when trained with the joint loss function. Thus semantic understanding of features in latent space significantly improves the visual quality of generated facial components, which is further supported by Fig. 5. When focuses on the face and hair regions only, the first row of Fig. 5 illustrates the ability of our method in predicting the missing eye region and the others show accurate prediction of mouth regions.

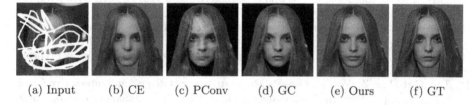

(a) Input      (b) CE      (c) PConv      (d) GC      (e) Ours      (f) GT

**Fig. 5.** Qualitative comparison of foreground inpainted regions with the state-of-the-art methods: (a) **Input masked-image**; (b) **CE** [15]; (c) **PConv** [11]; (d) **GConv**; (e) **Ours**; and (f) Ground-truth image.

## 6   Conclusion

In this paper, we introduced a method to inpaint missing region(s) within an image using foreground guidance. The results we obtained suggests the importance of foreground guidance training for the prediction of challenging corrupted patches on an image. We have shown how our model is able to predict and reconstruct plausible and realistic features with preserved realism of the faces.

Our model can produce high visual quality results that meets the objective of real-world in the wild scenarios. Further exploitation of foreground pixels is a promising ground-work for future inpainting task.

## References

1. Elharrouss, O., Almaadeed, N., Al-Maadeed, S., Akbari, Y.: Image inpainting: a review. Neural Process. Lett. 1–22 (2019)
2. Iizuka, S., Simo-Serra, E., Ishikawa, H.: Globally and locally consistent image completion. ACM Trans. Graph. (TOG) **36**(4), 107 (2017)
3. Iskakov, K.: Semi-parametric image inpainting. arXiv preprint arXiv:1807.02855 (2018)
4. Jam, J., Kendrick, C., Drouard, V., Walker, K., Hsu, G., Yap, M.: Symmetric skip connection wasserstein GAN for high-resolution facial image inpainting. In: Proceedings of the 16th International Joint Conference on Computer Vision, Imaging and Computer Graphics Theory and Applications - Volume 4: VISAPP, pp. 35–44 (2021). https://doi.org/10.5220/0010188700350044. ISBN 978-989-758-488-6, ISSN 2184-4321
5. Jam, J., Kendrick, C., Drouard, V., Walker, K., Hsu, G.S., Yap, M.H.: R-mnet: a perceptual adversarial network for image inpainting. In: Proceedings of the IEEE/CVF Winter Conference on Applications of Computer Vision, pp. 2714–2723 (2021)
6. Jam, J., Kendrick, C., Walker, K., Drouard, V., Hsu, J.G.S., Yap, M.H.: A comprehensive review of past and present image inpainting methods. Comput. Vis. Image Underst. 103147 (2020)
7. Johnson, J., Alahi, A., Fei-Fei, L.: Perceptual losses for real-time style transfer and super-resolution. In: Leibe, B., Matas, J., Sebe, N., Welling, M. (eds.) ECCV 2016. LNCS, vol. 9906, pp. 694–711. Springer, Cham (2016). https://doi.org/10.1007/978-3-319-46475-6_43
8. Karras, T., Aila, T., Laine, S., Lehtinen, J.: Progressive growing of gans for improved quality, stability, and variation. arXiv preprint arXiv:1710.10196 (2017)
9. Kingma, D.P., Ba, J.: Adam: A method for stochastic optimization. arXiv preprint arXiv:1412.6980 (2014)
10. Lee, C.H., Liu, Z., Wu, L., Luo, P.: Maskgan: towards diverse and interactive facial image manipulation. In: Proceedings of the IEEE/CVF Conference on Computer Vision and Pattern Recognition, pp. 5549–5558 (2020)
11. Liu, G., Reda, F.A., Shih, K.J., Wang, T.C., Tao, A., Catanzaro, B.: Image inpainting for irregular holes using partial convolutions. In: Proceedings of the European Conference on Computer Vision (ECCV), pp. 85–100 (2018)
12. Liu, X., Zou, Y., Xie, C., Kuang, H., Ma, X.: Bidirectional face aging synthesis based on improved deep convolutional generative adversarial networks. Information **10**(2), 69 (2019)
13. Liu, Z., Li, X., Luo, P., Loy, C.C., Tang, X.: Semantic image segmentation via deep parsing network. In: Proceedings of the IEEE International Conference on Computer Vision, pp. 1377–1385 (2015)
14. Lu, C., Dubbelman, G.: Semantic foreground inpainting from weak supervision. IEEE Robot. Autom. Lett. **5**(2), 1334–1341 (2020)
15. Pathak, D., Krahenbuhl, P., Donahue, J., Darrell, T., Efros, A.A.: Context encoders: feature learning by inpainting. In: Proceedings of the IEEE Conference on Computer Vision and Pattern Recognition, pp. 2536–2544 (2016)

16. Schulter, S., Zhai, M., Jacobs, N., Chandraker, M.: Learning to look around objects for top-view representations of outdoor scenes. In: Proceedings of the European Conference on Computer Vision (ECCV), pp. 787–802 (2018)
17. Xiong, W., et al.: Foreground-aware image inpainting. In: Proceedings of the IEEE/CVF Conference on Computer Vision and Pattern Recognition, pp. 5840–5848 (2019)
18. Yu, J., Lin, Z., Yang, J., Shen, X., Lu, X., Huang, T.S.: Free-form image inpainting with gated convolution. In: Proceedings of the IEEE International Conference on Computer Vision, pp. 4471–4480 (2019)
19. Zhao, H., Shi, J., Qi, X., Wang, X., Jia, J.: Pyramid scene parsing network. In: Proceedings of the IEEE Conference on Computer Vision and Pattern Recognition, pp. 2881–2890 (2017)

# Talking Detection in Collaborative Learning Environments

Wenjing Shi[1]([✉]), Marios S. Pattichis[1], Sylvia Celedón-Pattichis[2], and Carlos LópezLeiva[2]

[1] Image and Video Processing and Communications Lab, Department of Electrical and Computer Engineering, University of New Mexico, Albuquerque, NM, USA
{wshi,pattichi}@unm.edu
[2] Departtment of Language, Literacy, and Sociocultural Studies, University of New Mexico, Albuquerque, NM, USA
{sceledon,callopez}@unm.edu

**Abstract.** We study the problem of detecting talking activities in collaborative learning videos. Our approach uses head detection and projections of the log-magnitude of optical flow vectors to reduce the problem to a simple classification of small projection images without the need for training complex, 3-D activity classification systems. The small projection images are then easily classified using a simple majority vote of standard classifiers. For talking detection, our proposed approach is shown to significantly outperform single activity systems. We have an overall accuracy of 59% compared to 42% for Temporal Segment Network (TSN) and 45% for Convolutional 3D (C3D). In addition, our method is able to detect multiple talking instances from multiple speakers, while also detecting the speakers themselves.

**Keywords:** Talking detection · Video analysis · Majority voting system

## 1 Introduction

We study the problem of talking detection in collaborative learning environments. Here, our ultimate goal is to develop fast and reliable methods that can assist educational researchers analyze student participation in large video datasets.

Learning assessment relies heavily on the use of audio transcriptions that describe the interactions between the students and their facilitators. By identifying the video segments where a student is talking, educational researchers can then further analyze the nature of the interactions. For example, some students may stay quiet. Others may express themselves throughout the lessons. Ultimately, our computer-based system aims at aiding this type of analysis by

---

This material is based upon work supported by the National Science Foundation under Grant No. 1613637, No. 1842220, and No. 1949230.

N. Tsapatsoulis et al. (Eds.): CAIP 2021, LNCS 13053, pp. 242–251, 2021.
https://doi.org/10.1007/978-3-030-89131-2_22

identifying different talking patterns. However, for the purposes of this paper, we will only describe how to reliably detect students talking when the camera captures motions over their mouths.

We present an example of our collaborative learning environment in Fig. 1. We are interested in detecting talking activities for the group that is closest to the camera. The students that are farther away appear at a smaller scale and need to be rejected from further consideration. Students appear at different angles to the camera. Instead of talking, students can also be eating, laughing, or yawing, and these activities should not be confused with talking (e.g., see eating example in Fig. 1). In many cases, the mouths may not be visible to the camera. In such cases, talking detection is not possible without processing the audio of the video.

**Fig. 1.** A sample that contains multiple challenges for talking detection.

We develop a direct and fast approach to talking detection that avoids the need for large training datasets. First, we detect the heads and faces to include the mouth regions. Then, over the detected head or face regions, we compute optical flow vectors and project the log-magnitudes of the vectors to generate a single region-proposal image over each candidate speaker. We then use voting from a list of simple classifiers to classify each segment as a talking or a non-talking segment.

Our talking detection research extends prior research by our group. In [6,7] we introduced the use of multiscale AM-FM decompositions to detect student faces and the backs of the heads. In [9], the authors demonstrate the importance of using the instantaneous phase for face detection. In [8], we developed methods to identify possible group interactions through the use of AM-FM representations.

In [2], we developed an open-source system for detecting writing and typing over cropped video segments. In [1], the author developed a hand movement detection system. In [4], we used simple color-based object detection followed by classification of optical flow vectors to detect writing, talking, and typing over a very small number of cropped video segments.

There is also significant human activity detection research within the computer vision community. In [12], the authors developed the Temporal Segment Network (TSN) for video-based activity recognition. TSN describes a deep learning based approach to detect a diverse range of activities using ConvNets. In [10], the authors developed the C3D network that trains deep 3D convolutional networks on a large-scale supervised video dataset to detect a diverse range of different activities. More recently, [11] generates a new spatiotemporal convolutional block "R(2+1)D" to train CNNs for activity recognition.

Our approach avoids the need to train large, deep learning systems on human video activity detection. Our approach is very fast because it reduces talking detection to the classification of small proposal regions of the projected motion magnitudes over the students' faces or heads. It is ideally suited for our goal to process over 1,000 h of videos for talking detection. We also provide comparisons against TSN and C3D to demonstrate that our approach is much more accurate.

We organize the rest of the paper into three additional sections. In Sect. 2, we describe our proposed methodology. We then provide results in Sect. 3 and provide concluding remarks in Sect. 4.

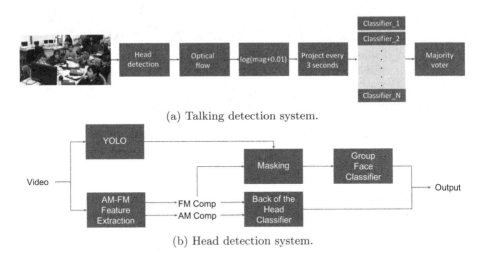

(a) Talking detection system.

(b) Head detection system.

**Fig. 2.** Group talking detection system.

## 2    Methodology

We present a system diagram of the entire system in Fig. 2(a). We also include
a block diagram for the head detection system in Fig. 2(b). In what follows, we
summarize the components of each system.

We use multiple methods to locate both faces and the backs of the heads
for the head detector. In the lower branch of Fig. 2(b), we show how we extract
AM-FM features using a 54-channel Gabor channel filterbank as described in [7]
and [6]. We use AM-FM components to locate the back of the head region. For
face detection, we use YOLO V3 [5]. We also use FM component classification
(LeNet) to reject background faces that are characterized by higher frequency
components since they are farther away from the camera.

**Fig. 3.**   Examples of input video frames and the 3-second projection images. The
top two rows show examples of talking video segments. The bottom two rows show
examples of non-talking video segments.

For each head detection, we produce 3-s video clip proposals for detecting
talking activities. Over these regions, we compute dense optical flow estimates
using Farneback's algorithm [3]. At each pixel, we evaluate $\log(\mathtt{mag}(i,j) + 0.01)$
where $\mathtt{mag}(i,j)$ represents the magnitude of each motion vector. Over each video

segment, we then compute the projection image as given by:

$$P(i,j) \sum_{\text{all frames} f} \log(\text{mag}_f(i,j) + 0.01).$$

We then train a variety of proposal region classifiers to differentiate between talking and non-talking activities.

We present example projection images in Fig. 3. From the examples, compared to projections of talking activities, it is clear that projections of non-talking activities are characterized by dark regions around the mouth regions.

For classifying the projected images, we consider simple classifiers. We considered a modified LeNet5, XGBoost, AdaBoost, decision tree, K-NN, quadratic discriminant analysis, and random forest classifier. Over the training set, we select the best three performing classifiers based on accuracy, AUC score, and F1 score, and then use a simple majority vote to combine them into a single system.

## 3    Results

We summarize our results into three subsections. First, we present results for our head detector in Sect. 3.1. Second, we present results for our head region video detection results in Sect. 3.2. Third, we present final results for the full system in Sect. 3.3.

### 3.1    Head Detection System Results

We summarize head detection results in Table 1. For training head detection, we selected 1,000 head examples and 1,200 non-face examples selected from 54 different video sessions. We then tested our head detector on four unseen videos as summarized in Table 1. We can see from the results that our proposed

**Fig. 4.** Results of head detection. True positives are bounded by green boxes. False positives are bounded by red boxes. False negatives are bounded by yellow boxes. (Color figure online)

5

approach achieved F1 scores that range from 0.81 to 0.87 over 905,550 labeled students.

Example detections are shown in Fig. 4. We can see from the example that our head classification system rejected all but one of the distant detections. Furthermore, we missed a single face due to occlusion.

**Table 1.** Results for student group detection over four videos. We present results over 905,550 labeled students. F1 scores are given for each video. The videos represent different student groups. TP refers to true positives. FP refers to false positives. FN refers to false negatives.

| Video | Labeled students | Detected students | TP | FP | FN | **F1** |
|---|---|---|---|---|---|---|
| V1 | 242,700 | 180,640 | 169,550 | 11,090 | 69,190 | 0.81 |
| V2 | 131,100 | 122,230 | 107,360 | 14,870 | 17,360 | 0.87 |
| V3 | 277,830 | 229,810 | 207,230 | 22,580 | 60,270 | 0.83 |
| V4 | 253,920 | 230,600 | 206,860 | 23,740 | 35,750 | 0.87 |

**Table 2.** Training dataset for talking detection. Video names include the cohort number and the level number (e.g., C3L1).

| Group ID | Cohort | Group | Date | Urban/Rural | Frame rate (fps) |
|---|---|---|---|---|---|
| 1 | C1L1 | D | May-04 | Rural | 60 |
| 2 | C1L1 | D | May-11 | Rural | 60 |
| 3 | C1L1 | C | May-02 | Urban | 60 |
| 4 | C1L1 | C | May-09 | Urban | 60 |
| 5 | C1L2 | A | Jun-22 | Rural | 60 |
| 6 | C2L1 | A | Mar-22 | Rural | 30 |
| 7 | C2L1 | A | Apr-19 | Rural | 30 |
| 8 | C2L1 | A | May-05 | Rural | 30 |
| 9 | C2L1 | A | May-10 | Rural | 30 |
| 10 | C2L1 | B | Mar-22 | Rural | 30 |
| 11 | C2L1 | D | Feb-23 | Rural | 30 |
| 12 | C2L1 | D | Mar-22 | Rural | 30 |
| 13 | C2L1 | A | Feb-20 | Urban | 30 |

## 3.2  Head Video Region Classification Results

In this section, we provide comparisons against single activity classifiers. For this purpose, we crop head regions and resize them to 100 × 100 pixels. For

**Table 3.** Validation dataset for talking detection. Video names include the cohort number and the level number (e.g., C3L1).

| Group ID | Cohort | Group | Date | Urban/Rural | Frame rate (fps) |
|---|---|---|---|---|---|
| 1 | C1L1 | B | Mar-02 | Rural | 30 |
| 2 | C1L1 | C | Mar-30 | Rural | 60 |
| 3 | C1L1 | C | Apr-06 | Rural | 60 |
| 4 | C1L1 | C | Apr-13 | Rural | 60 |
| 5 | C1L1 | E | Mar-02 | Rural | 60 |
| 6 | C2L1 | B | Feb-23 | Rural | 30 |
| 7 | C2L1 | C | Apr-12 | Rural | 30 |
| 8 | C2L1 | D | Mar-08 | Rural | 30 |
| 9 | C2L1 | E | Apr-12 | Rural | 30 |
| 10 | C2L1 | B | Feb-27 | Urban | 30 |
| 11 | C3L1 | C | Apr-11 | Rural | 30 |
| 12 | C3L1 | D | Feb-21 | Rural | 30 |
| 13 | C3L1 | D | Mar-19 | Urban | 30 |

**Table 4.** Head-based video region classification results.

| Methods | Accuracy | AUC Score | Precision | Recall | F1 | Confusion matrix |
|---|---|---|---|---|---|---|
| LeNet5 | 70% | 0.76 | 0.69 | 0.76 | 0.72 | 1785 960 / 702 2177 |
| XGBoost | 67% | 0.73 | 0.65 | 0.78 | 0.71 | 1549 1196 / 647 2232 |
| AdaBoost | 70% | 0.70 | 0.64 | 0.72 | 0.67 | 1557 1188 / 810 2069 |
| Decision tree | 59% | 0.59 | 0.60 | 0.60 | 0.60 | 1598 1147 / 1138 1741 |
| KNN | 68% | 0.74 | 0.68 | 0.71 | 0.70 | 1779 966 / 831 2048 |
| QDA | 61% | 0.71 | 0.82 | 0.30 | 0.44 | 2562 183 / 2026 853 |
| Random forest | 62% | 0.65 | 0.61 | 0.75 | 0.67 | 1354 1391 / 728 2151 |
| XGBoost+AdaBoost+ KNN | 79% | 0.77 | 0.69 | 0.72 | 0.70 | 1810 935 / 804 2075 |

our comparisons, each video segment is clipped at 3 s. We report results on two datasets. The first dataset is used for selecting the classifiers that are used in our majority classification system. We use a second dataset to assess the performance of the majority classifier on four videos that range from 11 to 24 min.

Table 5. Talking detection for long videos.

| Video | Duration | Person label | Ours | TSN | C3D |
|---|---|---|---|---|---|
| V1 | 23 min 45 s | Issac | 66% | 28% | 28% |
| | | Julia7P | 48% | 38% | 33% |
| | | Martina64P | 58% | 11% | 31% |
| | | Suzie66P | 44% | 11% | 7% |
| | | Bernard129P | 51% | 18% | 19% |
| | | Average | 53% | 21% | 24% |
| V2 | 11 min 20 s | Irma | 53% | 67% | 64% |
| | | Emilio25P | 68% | 21% | 14% |
| | | Herminio10P | 56% | 72% | 79% |
| | | Jacinto51P | 66% | 21% | 41% |
| | | Jorge17P | 60% | 53% | 43% |
| | | Juan16P | 62% | 39% | 35% |
| | | Average | 61% | 46% | 46% |
| V3 | 16 min 6 s | Kelly | 70% | 67% | 71% |
| | | Marta12P | 68% | 19% | 34% |
| | | Cindy14P | 74% | 23% | 74% |
| | | Carmen13P | 51% | 31% | 50% |
| | | Marina15P | 64% | 22% | 26% |
| | | Scott | 87% | 95% | 92% |
| | | Average | 69% | 43% | 58% |
| V4 | 23 min 45 s | Phuong | 58% | 71% | 58% |
| | | Jacob103P | 53% | 51% | 46% |
| | | Josephina104P | 42% | 63% | 47% |
| | | Juanita107P | 55% | 64% | 60% |
| | | Tina105P | 55% | 44% | 47% |
| | | Vincent106P | 45% | 43% | 40% |
| | | Average | 51% | 56% | 50% |
| | | Overall Average | 59% | 42% | 45% |

For training the proposed classification method and all other methods, we use 11,315 video clips extracted from 13 different video sessions, with a total of 27 students (see Table 2). For the validation set, we use 5,624 video clips extracted from 13 video sessions, with a total of 37 students (see Table 3). Table 4 summarizes the results from using different classifiers. We chose XGBoost, AdaBoost, and KNN for the voting system. Over our validation set, this combination gave the highest accuracy at 79%. For comparing our system against alternative approaches, we use four different videos as summarized in Table 5. From the results, our system gave an average accuracy of 59% compared to 42% for TSN and 45% for C3D.

**Fig. 5.** Example of talking detection on the original video.

### 3.3    Talking Activity Detection System

We present an example of the final system in Fig. 5. As shown in Fig. 5, our system detects who is talking and places a bounding box identifying the person talking. Furthermore, unlike single activity systems like TSN and C3D, we can detect multiple people talking at the same time.

## 4    Conclusion

We presented a new method for detecting students talking in collaborative learning environment videos. Our approach combines head detection with activity detection using a projection of motion vectors and a majority voting classification system. Our approach significantly outperformed single activity classification systems. Yet, our average accuracy at 59% suggests that there is still room for significant improvement. Our approach will also need to be further validated before it can be effectively used by educational researchers.

# References

1. Darsey, C.J.: Hand movement detection in collaborative learning environment videos (2018)
2. Eilar, C.W., Jatla, V., Pattichis, M.S., LópezLeiva, C., Celedón-Pattichis, S.: Distributed video analysis for the advancing out-of-school learning in mathematics and engineering project. In: 50th Asilomar Conference on Signals, Systems and Computers, pp. 571–575. IEEE (2016)
3. Farnebäck, G.: Two-frame motion estimation based on polynomial expansion. In: Bigun, J., Gustavsson, T. (eds.) SCIA 2003. LNCS, vol. 2749, pp. 363–370. Springer, Heidelberg (2003). https://doi.org/10.1007/3-540-45103-X_50
4. Jacoby, A.R., Pattichis, M.S., Celedón-Pattichis, S., LópezLeiva, C.: Context-sensitive human activity classification in collaborative learning environments. In: 2018 IEEE Southwest Symposium on Image Analysis and Interpretation (SSIAI), pp. 1–4. IEEE (2018)
5. Redmon, J., Farhadi, A.: Yolov3: An incremental improvement. arXiv preprint arXiv:1804.02767 (2018)
6. Shi, W.: Human Attention Detection Using AM-FM Representations. Master's thesis, the University of New Mexico, Albuquerque, New Mexico (2016)
7. Shi, W., Pattichis, M.S., CeledLón-Pattichis, S., LoLópezLeiva, C.: Robust head detection in collaborative learning environments using am-fm representations. In: IEEE Southwest Symposium on Image Analysis and Interpretation (in press, 2018)
8. Shi, W., Pattichis, M.S., Celedón-Pattichis, S., LópezLeiva, C.: Dynamic group interactions in collaborative learning videos. In: 2018 52nd Asilomar Conference on Signals, Systems, and Computers, pp. 1528–1531. IEEE (2018)
9. Tapia, L.S., Pattichis, M.S., Celedón-Pattichis, S., LópezLeiva, C.: The importance of the instantaneous phase for face detection using simple convolutional neural networks. In: 2020 IEEE Southwest Symposium on Image Analysis and Interpretation (SSIAI), pp. 1–4. IEEE (2020)
10. Tran, D., Bourdev, L., Fergus, R., Torresani, L., Paluri, M.: Learning spatiotemporal features with 3D convolutional networks. In: Proceedings of the IEEE International Conference on Computer Vision, pp. 4489–4497 (2015)
11. Tran, D., Wang, H., Torresani, L., Ray, J., LeCun, Y., Paluri, M.: A closer look at spatiotemporal convolutions for action recognition. In: Proceedings of the IEEE Conference on Computer Vision and Pattern Recognition, pp. 6450–6459 (2018)
12. Wang, L., et al.: Temporal segment networks: towards good practices for deep action recognition. In: Leibe, B., Matas, J., Sebe, N., Welling, M. (eds.) ECCV 2016. LNCS, vol. 9912, pp. 20–36. Springer, Cham (2016). https://doi.org/10.1007/978-3-319-46484-8_2

# Facial Recognition in Collaborative Learning Videos

Phuong Tran[1]($\boxtimes$), Marios Pattichis[1], Sylvia Celedón-Pattichis[2],
and Carlos LópezLeiva[2]

[1] Department of Electrical and Computer Engineering, University of New Mexico,
Albuquerque, NM 87106, USA
pnt204@unm.edu
[2] Department of Language, Literacy, and Sociocultural Studies,
University of New Mexico, Albuquerque, NM 87106, USA

**Abstract.** Face recognition in collaborative learning videos presents
many challenges. In collaborative learning videos, students sit around
a typical table at different positions to the recording camera, come and
go, move around, get partially or fully occluded. Furthermore, the videos
tend to be very long, requiring the development of fast and accurate
methods.

We develop a dynamic system of recognizing participants in collaborative learning systems. We address occlusion and recognition failures
by using past information about the face detection history. We address
the need for detecting faces from different poses and the need for speed
by associating each participant with a collection of prototype faces computed through sampling or K-means clustering.

Our results show that the proposed system is proven to be very fast
and accurate. We also compare our system against a baseline system
that uses InsightFace [2] and the original training video segments. We
achieved an average accuracy of 86.2% compared to 70.8% for the baseline system. On average, our recognition rate was 28.1 times faster than
the baseline system.

**Keywords:** Human front-face detection and recognition · Video
analysis

## 1 Introduction

We study the problem of face recognition in collaborative learning environments.
Our goal is to develop fast and accurate methods that can be used to quantify
student participation as measured by their presence in their learning groups.

This material is based upon work supported by the National Science Foundation under
Grant No.1613637, No. 1842220, and No. 1949230.

N. Tsapatsoulis et al. (Eds.): CAIP 2021, LNCS 13053, pp. 252–261, 2021.
https://doi.org/10.1007/978-3-030-89131-2_23

**Fig. 1.** Example of a collaborative learning group. We seek to recognize the students who are closer to the camera while ignoring students from all other groups.

Figure 1 represents an example of a collaborative learning group. A collaborative learning group is represented by the group of students closest to the camera. Background groups are not considered part of the collaborative group that we are analyzing. There is a possibility that students or facilitators move between groups. Thus, we need to recognize the current members of our group from a larger group of students.

A fundamental challenge of our dataset is that face recognition needs to work at a large variety of poses. As long as a sufficiently small part of the face is visible, we need to identify the student. As an example, in Fig. 1, the student on the front right with a white hoodie has his face mostly blocked. Furthermore, students may disappear or reappear because the camera moves, or the students take a break, or because they have to leave the group. Hence, there are significant video properties to our problem that are not present in standard face recognition systems.

As part of a collaborative project between engineering and education, our goal is to assist educational researchers in analyzing how students who join the program learn and facilitate the learning of other students. The problem of identifying who is crucial for assessing student participation in the project. Furthermore, the developed methods need to be fast. Eventually, we will need to apply our methods to approximately one thousand hours of videos that we need to analyze.

The standard datasets for face recognition use a database of front-facing images. The Labeled Faces in the Wild (LFW) dataset [3] contains more than 13,000 face images with various poses, ages, and expressions. The Youtube Face (YTF) dataset [5] contains around 3,500 videos with an average range of 181 frames/video from 1,600 different people. The InsightFace system [1] developed the use of Additive Angular Margin Loss for Deep Face Recognition (ArcFace) on a large-scale image database with trillions of pairs and a large-scale video dataset, and tested on multiple datasets with different loss function models (Arc-Face, Softmax, CosFace,..). InsightFace gave the best accuracies on LFW and YTF with 99.83% 98.02%. We adopt InsightFace as our baseline face recognition system because of their state-of-the-art performance.

We also provide a summary of video analysis methods that were developed specifically by our group for analyzing collaborative learning videos.

In [4], the authors introduced methods for detecting writing, typing, and talking activities using motion vectors and deep learning. In [6], the authors developed methods to detect where participants were looking at. In [7], the authors demonstrated that FM images with low-complexity neural networks can provide face detection results that can only be achieved with much more complex deep learning systems.

We provide a summary of the contributions of the current paper. First, we introduce the use of a collection of face prototypes for recognizing faces from different angles. Second, we apply multi-objective optimization to study the inter-dependency between recognition rate, the number of face prototypes, and recognition accuracy. Along the Pareto front of optimal combinations, we select an optimal number of face prototypes that provides for a fast approach without sacrificing recognition accuracy. Third, we use the past recognition history to deal with occlusions and, hence, support consistent recognition throughout the video. Compared to InsightFace [2], the proposed system provides for significantly faster recognition rates and higher accuracy.

We summarize the rest of the paper into three additional sections. In Sect. 2, we provide a summary of our methodology. We then provide results in Sect. 3 and concluding remarks in Sect. 4.

## 2    Methods

We present a block diagram of the overall system in Fig. 2. Our video recognition system requires a set of face prototypes associated with each participant. The video face recognition algorithm detects the faces in the input video and computes minimum distances to the face prototypes to identify each participant. To handle occlusion issues, the system uses past detection history.

### 2.1    Computation of Face Prototypes

We use two different methods to compute the face prototypes. First, we consider the use of K-means clustering to select a limited number of face prototypes from the training videos. Second, we consider a baseline approach where we use sparse sampling of the training videos to define the face prototypes. To achieve sparsity, we use one sample image per second of video. For our second approach, we used a video from Group D from urban cohort 2 level 1 (C2L1, Video 4) and Group E

---

**Algorithm 1:** Video Faces Recognition

---

**Input:**
> video: unlabeled video
> facePrototypes: list of images associated with each student pseudonym

**Output:**
> vidResult: store unique student identifiers and face locations along with face's landmarks per frame

**Local Variables:**
> ActiveSet and InactiveSet store unique student identifiers, face locations, totalAppearances,
>> totalFramesProcessed, continuousAppearances & distance.

**while** frame f in initial part of video
> ▷Detect and Recognize all faces initial duration
> **Detect** faces in f
> **Recognize** faces in f using minimum distance to facePrototypes
> **Update** vidResult

ActiveSet = []; InactiveSet = []; ▷Initialization
**while** face in all recognized faces
> **if** totalAppearances(face) / totalFramesProcessed(face) $>= 50\%$
>> **Add** face to ActiveSet
> **else:**
>> **Add** face to InactiveSet

**for** frame f in rest of video
> **Detect** faces in f
> **if** minor movement in detected face **then**     ▷Reuse face
>> **Reuse** face from ActiveSet
>> **Update** ActiveSet, vidResult with detected faces
> **else if** detected face found in InactiveSet **then**     ▷Update face
>> **Update** InactiveSet with detected face
>> **if** totalAppearances(face) / totalFramesProcessed(face) $>= 50\%$
>>> **Move** face to ActiveSet
>>> **Remove** face from InactiveSet
>>> **Update** ActiveSet, vidResult with detected faces
> **else**     ▷Possible new face
>> **Recognize** face in f using minimum distance to facePrototypes
>> **Update** InactiveSet with detected faces

> **for** face in ActiveSet
>> **if** face not found in all detected faces **then**
>>> **if** continuousAppearances $>=$ minAppearances **then**
>> ▷Occluded face
>>>> **Add** face to ActiveSet, vidResult
>>> **if** continuousAppearances $<$ minAppearances **then**
>> ▷Disappearing face
>>>> **Remove** face from ActiveSet
>>>> **Add** face to InactiveSet

> **for** all labels found in f     ▷Consistent assignment check
>> **if** same label exists
>>> **Set** label with larger distance to Unknown

---

Face prototypes for
each participant

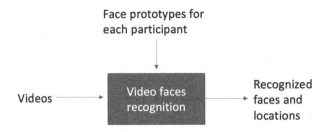

Videos ————→ Video faces ————→ Recognized
recognition      faces and
locations

**Fig. 2.** Block diagram for recognizing faces from videos. Each face is associated with a collection of face prototypes. The method computed face prototypes using video sampling or K-means clustering. K-means clustering is given here.

from C3L1 (Video 5), whereas the first approach tested on Group C from urban C1L1 (Video 1). Each sampled face is aligned and resized to $112 \times 112$.

We summarize the K-means approach in Fig. 2. We use K-means to cluster similar frames that appear when a student does not move very much. Hence, we expect that the centroids that result from the K-means algorithms would represent a small number of diverse face poses for each participant. To avoid unrealistic centroid images, we compute our face prototypes using the images closest to our cluster centroids. After finding a prototype image that is closest to the mean, we align and resize each prototype image to $112 \times 112$.

We use multi-objective optimization to determine the minimum number of face prototypes without sacrificing classification accuracy. We present our results for a representative video from group C, level 1, in Fig. 3. For the optimization, we use a log-based search by varying the number of face prototypes from $2^0$ to $2^{11}$. For K-means clustering, we see that the accuracy peaks at 79.8% for 1024 face prototypes, with a recognition rate of 4.8 s per frame. In this example, we only used one video to validate our approach. We expand the validation set to more videos as described in [8]. This process run on a personal Macbook Pro that ran Mac-OS with 2.3 GHz, 4-core, Intel i5 processors.

## 2.2    Video Faces Recognizer

We present the algorithm for video face recognition in Algorithm 1. The input is an unlabeled video and the `facePrototypes` that provides a list of images associated with each participant. The detected faces for each video frame are returned in `vidResult`. To address occlusion, the algorithm maintains the face recognition history in `ActiveSet` and `InactiveSet`.

First, for the first two seconds of the videos, we detect all participants in each video frame using MTCNN [9]. For each detected face, MTCNN computes five landmark points: two for the eyes, one for the nose, and two for the mouth corners. The face detector uses a minimum area requirement to reject faces that belong to another group. Thus, we reject smaller face detections that are part of another group or other false positives because they appear smaller in the video.

Second, we classify each detected face by selecting the participant that gives minimum distance to their associated prototypes stored in `facePrototypes`.

We use the initial face recognition results to initialize `ActiveSet` and `InactiveSet`. The faces that have been recognized in more than half of the frames are stored in the `ActiveSet`. The rest of them are stored in the `InactiveSet`. For each face detection, we use a dictionary to store: a pseudonym, location information, `totalAppearances` that stores the total number of frames where this face was detected, and `totalFramesProcessed` which represents the total number of frames processed since this face appeared for the first time. Hence, we use the `ActiveSet` to hold faces that appear consistently whereas `InactiveSet` contains faces that are still in doubt.

When a recognized face enters the `ActiveSet`, it gets a maximum value of 10 for its corresponding `continuousAppearances`. When a previously recognized face is missing, `continuousAppearances` gets decremented by 1. When a face re-appears, `continuousAppearances` is incremented until it reaches 10 again. We also set `minAppearances` to 5 as the minimum requirement on the number of prior continuous appearances for addressing occlusion issues. Thus, for each face in the `ActiveSet` that is not being detected in any frame, if `continuousAppearances` $\geq$ `minAppearances`, we declare the face as occluded, we mark it as present, and update `vidResult`. Else, if `continuousAppearances`

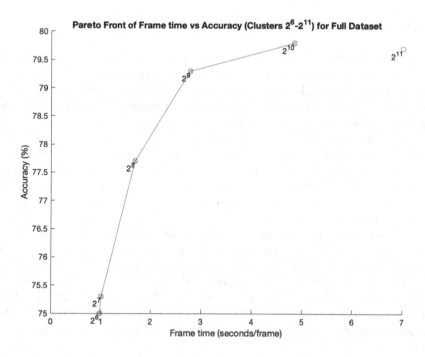

**Fig. 3.** Pareto front on the K-mean clustering results

< `minAppearances`, we declare the face as disappearing, and move it to the `InactiveSet`.

We thus process the rest of the `video` based on the following four cases:

(i) If a newly detected face corresponds to a minor movement of a prior detection, we keep it in the `ActiveSet`. This approach leads to a significant speedup in our face recognition speed.

(ii) If a newly detected face is in the `InactiveSet`, we update the `InactiveSet` with the new detection, and look at the ratio of `totalAppearances`/`totalFr- amesProcessed` to determine if it needs to move to the `ActiveSet`. Otherwise, the face stays in `InactiveSet`.

(iii) If a newly detected face does not belong to either set, then recognize it and move it to the `ActiveSet`.

(iv) If a face that belongs to the `ActiveSet` no longer appears, we consider the case for occlusion and that the participant has left the frame. As described earlier, we check `continuousAppearances` to determine whether to declare the face occluded or not.

Lastly, we do not allow the assignment of the same label to two different faces in the same frame. In this case, the face that gives the minimum distance is declared the recognized face while the other(s) are declared Unknown.

## 3   Results

We sampled twenty-four participants from our video dataset (11 boys and 13 girls). For training, we used 80% of the data for fitting and 20% for validation using different video sessions. From our video sessions, we randomly select short video clips of 5 to 10 s for training our video face recognizer. Overall, we use more than 200,000 video frames from 21 different video sessions. We have an average of about 10,000 image examples per participant. Furthermore, as the program lasted three years, the testing dataset used later on videos (e.g., later cohorts and different levels). For the testing dataset, we used seven video clips with a duration of 10 to 60 s. However, we do assume that we have trained for all of the students within the collaborative group. For reporting execution times, we use a Linux system with an Intel(R) Xeon(R) Gold 5118 CPU running @ 2.30 GHz with 16 GB Memory and Nvidia Quadro RTX 5000 GPU with 3072 Cuda cores.

We present face recognition accuracy results in Table 1 using said system. For InsightFace, we use all of the training video frames as face prototypes. From the results, it is clear that the proposed method is far more accurate than the baseline method. The difference in accuracy ranged from as low as 2% to as large as 25%. Out of 19 participants in these five videos, our method achieved higher or same accuracy in 17 cases. Overall, our method achieved 86.2% compared to 70.8% for the baseline method.

We present face recognition examples in Fig. 4. Figures 4(a) and 4(b) show results from the same video frame of Video 2. The baseline method recognized Javier67P (lower right in (a)) and Kenneth1P (white shirt with glasses in (a))

**Table 1.** Accuracy for Facial Recognition. Each video represents a different group session segment.

| Video | Duration | Person label | Ours | Insightface |
|---|---|---|---|---|
| 1 (Face prototypes using K-means) | 10 s | *Antone39W* | **36.5%** | 36.5% |
| | | *Jaime41W* | **86.7%** | 84.2% |
| | | *Larry40W* | **99.3%** | 98.3% |
| | | *Ernesto38W* | **96.5%** | 95.3% |
| | | **Average** | **79.8%** | 78.6% |
| 2 (Face prototypes using Sampling) | 10 s | *Chaitanya* | **95.3%** | 80.3% |
| | | *Kenneth1P* | **91%** | 83.1% |
| | | *Jesus69P* | **100%** | 100% |
| | | *Javier67P* | **100%** | 69.1% |
| | | **Average** | **96.5%** | 83.1% |
| 3 (Face prototypes using Sampling) | 60 s | *Chaitanya* | **80.0%** | 56.1% |
| | | *Kenneth1P* | **98.3%** | 61.5% |
| | | *Jesus69P* | **99.3%** | 96.3% |
| | | *Javier67P* | **80.6%** | 39.0% |
| | | **Average** | **89.5%** | 63.2% |
| 5 (Face prototypes using Sampling) | 10 s | *Melly77W* | **96.0%** | 59.7% |
| | | *Marisol112W* | **84.0%** | 60.5% |
| | | *Cristie123W* | 8.67% | **27.3%** |
| | | *Phuong* | **77.4%** | 21.4% |
| | | **Average** | **66.5%** | 42.2% |
| 5 (Face prototypes using Sampling) | 60 s | *Alvaro70P* | **96.4%** | 60.8% |
| | | *Donna112P* | **100%** | 99.8% |
| | | *Sophia111P* | 99.5% | **99.9%** |
| | | **Average** | **98.6%** | 86.8% |
| | | **Overall Average** | **86.2%** | 70.8% |

as Unknown, whereas our approach correctly identified all four participants. A second example for video 5 is presented in Figs. 4(b) and (e). The baseline method identified all three people correctly. However, the baseline method also detected and incorrectly claimed recognition of background participants that we did not train. Our proposed method used projection and small-area elimination to reject this false-positive recognition. A third example for video 4 is shown in Figs. 4(c) and (f). The baseline method only succeeded in recognizing Melly77W (pink sweater) and wrongly recognized Cristie123W (lower right) as Phuong, who is actually on the far left wearing glasses. Our method used history information to address the partial occlusion issue and correctly recognized Phuong who is in the far left of Fig. 4(f). Furthermore, our method rejected the wrong assignment of Phuong because it does not allow the assignment of the same identifier to two different faces. Instead, the wrong assignment was re-assigned to Unknown. A fourth example of our method is shown in Fig. 4(g). In Fig. 4(g), we can see

**Table 2.** Recognition time for facial recognition. Each video represents a different group session segment.

| Video | Duration | GT Faces | Insightface (seconds/frame) | Ours (seconds/frame) | Speedup factor |
|---|---|---|---|---|---|
| 1 | 10 | 4 | 9.91 | 2.8 | 3.5x |
| 2 | 10 | 4 | 9.96 | 0.8 | 12.5x |
| 3 | 60 | 4 | 15.8 | 0.3 | 52.7x |
| 4 | 10 | 4 | 10.1 | 0.9 | 11.2x |
| 5 | 60 | 3 | 18.2 | 0.3 | 60.7x |
|  |  | Average | 12.8 | **1.1** | 28.1x |

that our method works in occlusion cases. Herminio10P (dark blue polo, right) and Guillermo72P (blue T-shirt) were correctly recognized even though their faces were partial. We also present challenges in Figs. 4(h) and (i). In Fig. 4(h), Antone39W did not get recognized because he had his back facing the camera. In Fig. 4(i), Kirk28P was not recognized due to significant changes in appearance through time.

We present speed performance comparisons in Table 2. The baseline method required 9.9 to 18.2 s/frame whereas our proposed method required 0.3 to 2.8 s/frame. On average, the proposed method was 28.1× faster. Our speedups can be attributed to our use of a reduced number of face prototypes and the fact that we do not rerun the minimum distance classifier if there is little movement in the detected faces. For example, for 3 and 4, InsightFace took a very long time (more than ten seconds/frame) because it compared each participant against

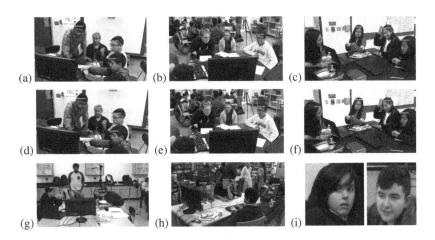

**Fig. 4.** Video face recognition results for three collaborative groups. The first row shows results from the use of InsightFace (baseline). The second row shows our results using the sampling method. In (g), we show successful detections despite occlusions. Results from the use of K-means clustering are shown in (h). Then, we show dramatic changes in appearance in (i).

(almost) ten thousand images. For 5, in addition to comparisons to about ten thousand images for the main group, InsightFace also had to compare against faces from the background groups. In comparison, our approach rejected the need to recognize background groups by applying a minimum face size constraint.

## 4    Conclusion

The paper presented a method for video face recognition that is shown to be significantly faster and more accurate than the baseline method. The method introduced: (i) clustering methods to identify image clusters for recognizing faces from different poses, (ii) robust tracking with multi-frame processing for occlusions, and (iii) multi-objective optimization to reduce recognition time.

Compared to the baseline method, the final optimized method resulted in speedy recognition times with significant improvements in face recognition accuracy. Using face prototype with sampling, the proposed method achieved an accuracy of 86.2% compared to 70.8% for the baseline system, while running 28.1 times faster than the baseline. In future work, we want to extend our approach to 150 participants in about 1,000 h of videos.

## References

1. Deng, J., Guo, J., Xue, N., Zafeiriou, S.: Arcface: additive angular margin loss for deep face recognition (2019)
2. Guo, J., Deng, J., An, X., Yu, J.: Deepinsight/insightface: State-of-the-art 2D and 3D face analysis project, July 2021. https://github.com/deepinsight/insightface
3. Huang, G.B., Ramesh, M., Berg, T., Learned-Miller, E.: Labeled faces in the wild: a database for studying face recognition in unconstrained environments. Tech. Rep. 07–49, University of Massachusetts, Amherst, October 2007
4. Jacoby, A.R., Pattichis, M.S., Celedón-Pattichis, S., LópezLeiva, C.: Context-sensitive human activity classification in collaborative learning environments. In: 2018 IEEE Southwest Symposium on Image Analysis and Interpretation (SSIAI), pp. 1–4 (2018). https://doi.org/10.1109/SSIAI.2018.8470331
5. Learned-Miller, G.B.H.E.: Labeled faces in the wild: Updates and new reporting procedures. Tech. Rep. UM-CS-2014-003, University of Massachusetts, Amherst, May 2014
6. Shi, W., Pattichis, M.S., Celedón-Pattichis, S., LópezLeiva, C.: Robust head detection in collaborative learning environments using am-fm representations. In: 2018 IEEE Southwest Symposium on Image Analysis and Interpretation (SSIAI), pp. 1–4 (2018). https://doi.org/10.1109/SSIAI.2018.8470355
7. Tapia, L.S., Pattichis, M.S., Celedón-Pattichis, S., Leiva, C.L.: The importance of the instantaneous phase for face detection using simple convolutional neural networks. In: IEEE Southwest Symposium on Image Analysis and Interpretation, SSIAI 2020, Albuquerque, NM, USA, 29–31 March 2020, pp. 1–4 (2020). https://doi.org/10.1109/SSIAI49293.2020.9094589
8. Tran, P.: Fast Video-based Face Recognition in Collaborative Learning Environments. Master's thesis, University of New Mexico (2021)
9. Zhang, K., Zhang, Z., Li, Z., Qiao, Y.: Joint face detection and alignment using multi-task cascaded convolutional networks. CoRR abs/1604.02878 (2016). http://arxiv.org/abs/1604.02878

# Guess the Age Contest

# Guess the Age 2021: Age Estimation from Facial Images with Deep Convolutional Neural Networks

Antonio Greco$^{(\boxtimes)}$ (iD)

Department of Computer Engineering, Electrical Engineering and Applied
Mathematics (DIEM), University of Salerno, Fisciano, Italy
agreco@unisa.it

**Abstract.** Guess The Age 2021 is an international contest meant for teams able to propose methods based on modern Deep Convolutional Neural Networks (DCNNs) for age estimation from facial images. In order to allow the teams to train effective models, the Mivia Age Dataset, including 575.073 images annotated with age labels, was provided as training set; it is among the biggest publicly available datasets of faces in the world with age annotations. The performance of the methods submitted by the teams have been evaluated on a test set of more than 150.000 images, different from the ones available in the training set; a new index, called AAR, which takes into account the age estimation accuracy, namely the average error, and the regularity, i.e. the standard deviation of the error, has been adopted for drawing up the final ranking. The BTWG team, winner of the contest, achieved an impressive AAR equal to 7.94, with a novel method demonstrating an impressive accuracy and regularity in facial age estimation.

**Keywords:** Contest · Age estimation · Convolutional neural networks

## 1 Introduction

Age estimation from face images [17] is nowadays a relevant problem in several real applications, such as digital signage [11], social robotics [19], business intelligence [13], access control [16] and minor privacy protection [10]. In the era of deep learning, many DCNNs for age estimation have been proposed, so effective to achieve performance comparable to those of humans [6]. To this concern, it is worth pointing out that the best methods use ensembles of DCNNs, making the obtained classifier not usable in real applications, as they require prohibitive computational resources not always available [2,18,20,22]; in addition, their training procedure is made complex by the plurality of neural networks and typically require huge training sets not simply collectable [1]. Finally, most of the methods are less accurate in the age estimation of children and elders, due to the lack of samples for these age groups [4]; therefore, the regularity of the DCNNs for age estimation is an aspect that should be further investigated. Within this framework, five years after the last competition on age estimation

© Springer Nature Switzerland AG 2021
N. Tsapatsoulis et al. (Eds.): CAIP 2021, LNCS 13053, pp. 265–274, 2021.
https://doi.org/10.1007/978-3-030-89131-2_24

[8,9], Guess The Age 2021 imposes the usage of a new huge unbalanced dataset, the MIVIA Age Dataset, restricts the competition to methods based on a single neural network and defines a novel performance metric, the Age Accuracy and Regularity (AAR) index. Having available a wide dataset, while in the previous competitions the number of images was less than 10,000, the teams were able to train novel DCNN architectures without using ensembles and to define innovative data augmentation strategies or training procedures for improving the accuracy and the regularity of their DCNN. The effectiveness of the proposed solutions have been evaluated by comparing the results on a large and challenging test set, so as the design choices in terms of network architecture, pre-training, data augmentation and learning procedure for obtaining methods accurate and regular.

## 2    Contest Task

In Guess the Age 2021 the goal of the teams is the training of a DCNN for age estimation from face images which achieves the best performance in terms of accuracy and regularity on the private test set. The teams had to respect two main constraints: i) they were allowed to use only the samples of the provided training set, namely the MIVIA Age dataset; ii) they were allowed to propose methods based on a single neural network and not on ensembles.

The MIVIA Age Dataset is composed of 575.073 images of more than 9.000 identities, got at different ages; in particular, they have been extracted from the VGGFace2 dataset [5] and annotated with age by means of a knowledge distillation technique [12], making the dataset very heterogeneous in terms of face size, illumination conditions, facial pose, gender and ethnicity. Each image of the dataset contains a single face, already cropped. Examples of images are depicted in Fig. 1.

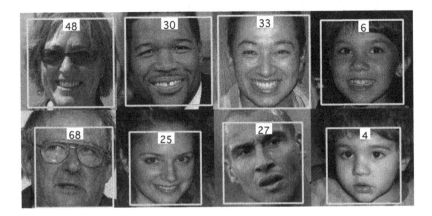

**Fig. 1.** Examples of face images taken from the MIVIA Age Dataset, whose age is estimated through a knowledge distillation technique [12].

The teams received a folder with all the images and a CSV file with the age labels of the training samples. The distribution of the dataset samples over the age is depicted in Fig. 2.

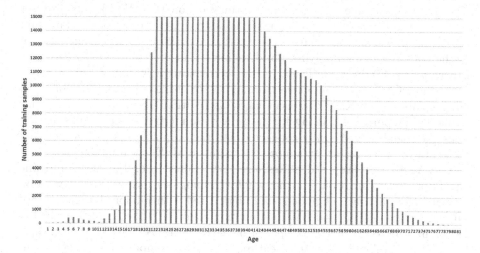

**Fig. 2.** Number of dataset samples (y-axis) over the age (x-axis). The teams had to train accurate and regular methods despite the unbalanced training set.

It is evident that the dataset is not balanced, since there are significantly less samples available for age groups under 20 and over 60; this is a standard problem that must be addressed when training a DCNN for age estimation. The teams had to deal with this imbalance without collecting samples from other dataset but only with augmentation techniques and/or specific learning procedure. To evaluate this aspect, the proposed methods were evaluated in terms of accuracy and regularity, as explained in Sect. 4. Thus, the winner of the contest was the team achieving a small but balanced age estimation error across all the age groups.

The teams downloaded the training samples and the corresponding age annotations from the website of the contest[1] and submitted their methods by following the detailed instructions provided on the website. The proposed approaches have finally been evaluated on a private test set of 169,372 images.

## 3 Methods

Before the deadline, 20 teams sent an official request for participating to the contest from all over the world: 9 from Europe, 5 from Asia, 4 from North America, 1 from South America and 1 from Africa. All the requests came from academia, except for one from a company. Finally, 7 teams submitted a valid

---

[1] http://gta2021.unisa.it/.

method to the contest, reported in alphabetic order: BTWG, CIVALab, GoF, GvisUleTeam, Levi, Pacific of Artificial Vision, VisionH4ck3rz. The approaches submitted by the teams are described in the following.

**BTWG** [3] used an EfficientNetV2-M, pre-trained for face recognition over MS-celeb-1M and fine tuned for age estimation on the MIVIA Age Dataset by decoupling the learning procedure in two steps: representation learning and classification. As a preliminary step, the team performed data augmentation on the training set by applying RandAugment and represented each age label as a gaussian distribution. Then, in the representation learning step they fine tuned the DCNN with the whole training set by using a custom loss function which combines the KL divergence (label distribution loss) and the L1 loss for regularization purposes. Finally, for the same reason in the classification stage the team fine tuned only the fully connected and the output layers with a balanced version of the training set by adopting a modified MSE loss function.

**CIVALab** [21] proposed a ResNeXt, pre-trained over ImageNet and fine tuned for age estimation on the whole training set pre-processed with z-normalization and face alignment and augmented with random horizontal flipping. The team defined a custom loss function inspired by the AAR, described in Sect. 4, in order to regularize the performance of the DCNN over the age groups. The obtained embedding of 2,048 features was given as input to a two-layer random forest (TLRF) with 100 trees for each layer, which acts as a regressor and returns the predicted age.

**GoF** modified a ResNet-50, pre-trained over ImageNet, with two additional fully connected layers and fine tuned it on the training set with a MSE loss function. The team did not perform data augmentation, but pre-processed the images by applying a canonical face alignment.

**GvisUleTeam** trained from scratch a SSR-Net with a MAE loss function. To reduce the imbalance of the training set, the team used StyleGANv2 and HRFAE to obtain at least 4,000 samples for minors and elders. In order to increase the representativeness, they also applied various data augmentation techniques, namely random masking, rotation and zoom.

**Levi** trained from scratch a DeepFace for age estimation (DeepAge), by removing the layer before the last for computational purposes. To reduce the imbalance of the training set, they used an autoencoder to obtain the additional samples for the less represented age groups, so as to collect 1,000 samples for them and 2,000 samples for each of the others. Crop, brightness, contrast, blur, grayscale, shift, scaling and rotation variations were also applied to augment the dataset.

**Pacific of Artificial Vision** [15] used a ResNet-50, pre-trained for face recognition over VGGFace2 and fine tuned for age estimation on a version of the training set extended through a custom Age Style GAN. The augmentation involved the less represented age groups ([0, 10], [11, 20], [61, 70], 70+), while a canonical face alignment was applied over all the training samples. A custom loss function, namely a combination between the mean variance and the cross entropy losses, was adopted to further regularize the performance over the age groups.

**VisionH4ck3rz** [7] applied data augmentation (random flip, zoom, rotation, brightness) only over the less represented age groups to obtain at least 8,000 samples for each age, by selecting only images bigger than $30 \times 30$ pixels. Then, they trained with this dataset and a MAE loss function an EfficientNet-B0, pre-trained over ImageNet, replacing the original output layer with a global average pooling, a batch normalization, a dropout and a single output neuron with linear activation.

The methods proposed by the teams are summarized in Table 1 in terms of DCNN, pre-training and regularization strategy.

**Table 1.** Methods submitted to the GTA contest.

| Team | DCNN | Pre-training | Regularization |
|---|---|---|---|
| BTWG | EfficientNetV2-M | MS-Celeb-1M | Custom loss |
| CIVA Lab | ResNeXt | ImageNet | Custom loss |
| GoF | ResNet-50 | ImageNet | None |
| GvisUleTeam | SSR-Net | From scratch | Augmentation |
| Levi | DeepFace | From scratch | Augmentation |
| Pacific of Artificial Vision | ResNet-50 | VGGFace-2 | Augm. and Custom loss |
| VisionH4ck3rz | EfficientNet-B0 | ImageNet | Augmentation |

From the analysis of the methods, it is possible to note that the teams addressed the main challenge of the contest, namely the regularization of the performance over the age groups, in two different ways, namely through data augmentation or by defining a custom loss function and/or learning procedure.

Four teams performed a data augmentation on the dataset to increase the number of samples of the less represented age groups; in particular, VisionH4ck3rz adopted a standard data augmentation, Levi an autoencoder and GvisUleTeam and Pacific of Artificial Vision used a GAN. This solution reduces but not completely solve the imbalance of the training set; this implies that the DCNNs, trained with these data, may be affected by the a priori distribution of the samples and, thus, not regular.

To this aim, other teams preferred the definition of a custom loss and/or learning procedure to consider the imbalance during the training. BTWG treated the problem as typically done for long tailed distributions [14], namely by dividing the training procedure in representation learning and classification; the first step was done with a custom loss, taking into account the absolute error and its standard deviation; the second step was performed with a balanced dataset, to regularize the results of the output layer over the age groups. CIVA Lab defined a custom loss function inspired by the AAR, the metric adopted for evaluating the performance over the test set; this choice is interesting, since the weights of the DCNN are optimized to solve the problem of finding a good trade-off between accuracy and regularity. The Pacific of Artificial Vision team combined the augmentation with a custom loss, which also takes into account the mean variance loss for regularizing the performance.

## 4   Evaluation Metrics

The methods proposed by the teams, trained on the set provided for the competition, were evaluated in terms of accuracy and regularity on a private test set; an index called Age Accuracy and Regularity ($AAR$) is introduced for taking into account accuracy and regularity in a single performance index.

In particular, the evaluation of the accuracy is carried out, as typically done in the literature, by means of the Mean Absolute Error ($MAE$) on the entire test set. If $K$ is the number of samples in the test and denoted $p_i$ the age prediction of a method for the i-th sample of the test set and the $r_i$ real age label, the absolute age estimation error on the i-th sample is:

$$e_i = |p_i - r_i| \tag{1}$$

Of course, the lower is the $MAE$ achieved by a method, the higher is its accuracy. According to the literature, the $MAE$ is computed as the average age estimation error over all the $K$ samples of the test set:

$$MAE = \sum_{i=1}^{K} \frac{e_i}{K} \tag{2}$$

The regularity over different age groups is measured through the standard deviation $\sigma$, according to the following rule:

$$\sigma = \sqrt{\frac{\sum_{j=1}^{8}(MAE^j - MAE)^2}{8}} \tag{3}$$

where:

 – $MAE^1$ is computed over the samples whose real age is in the range 1–10
 – $MAE^2$ is computed over the samples whose real age is in the range 11–20
 – $MAE^3$ is computed over the samples whose real age is in the range 21–30
 – $MAE^4$ is computed over the samples whose real age is in the range 31–40
 – $MAE^5$ is computed over the samples whose real age is in the range 41–50
 – $MAE^6$ is computed over the samples whose real age is in the range 51–60
 – $MAE^7$ is computed over the samples whose real age is in the range 61–70
 – $MAE^8$ is computed over the samples whose real age is in the range 70+

Therefore, the lower is the standard deviation $\sigma$ achieved by a method, the higher is its regularity.

The final score is the Age Accuracy and Regularity $AAR$ index, computed as follows:

$$AAR = max(0; 7 - MAE) + max(0; 3 - \sigma) \tag{4}$$

The $AAR$ index can assume values between 0 and 10, weighting 70% the contribution of $MAE$ (accuracy) and 30% the contribution of $\sigma$ (regularity). Methods which achieve $MAE \geq 7$ and $\sigma \geq 3$ obtain $AAR = 0$. A perfect method, obtaining $MAE = 0$ and $\sigma = 0$ achieve $AAR = 10$. Methods which achieve intermediate values of $MAE$ and $\sigma$ obtain intermediate values of $AAR$. The method which achieved the highest $AAR$ was the winner of the contest.

## 5 Results

The final ranking of guess the age 2021 is reported in Table 2. All the teams achieved excellent results, but the three on the top of the ranking were outstanding.

The winner of the contest is BTWG, which achieved an AAR equal to 7.94, combination of a remarkable accuracy ($MAE = 1.86$) and regularity ($\sigma = 0.20$). The second step of the podium is occupied by Pacific of Artificial Vision, which obtained a slightly lower AAR, equal to 7.55; the team achieved the best accuracy ($MAE = 1.84$) but a lower regularity ($\sigma = 0.61$). The CIVA Lab team ranks third, with an AAR equal to 6.97, result of $MAE = 2.05$ and $\sigma = 0.98$. In fourth position we find Levi ($AAR = 5.64$), also very regular ($\sigma = 0.93$) but less accurate ($MAE = 3.43$), followed shortly by VisionH4ck3rz ($AAR = 5.41$), more accurate ($MAE = 2.89$) but less regular ($\sigma = 1.70$). GoF ($AAR = 3.80$) and GvisUleTeam ($AAR = 3.69$) close the ranking, obtaining an accuracy comparable with Levi and VisionH4ck3rz ($MAE = 3.23$ and $MAE = 3.41$) but a substantially lower regularity ($\sigma = 2.97$ and $\sigma = 2.90$).

**Table 2.** Final ranking of Guess The Age 2021. According to the rules, the methods are ranked in descending order with respect to the AAR.

| Rank | Team | AAR | MAE | $\sigma$ |
|---|---|---|---|---|
| 1 | BTWG | 7.94 | 1.86 | 0.20 |
| 2 | Pacific of Artificial Vision | 7.55 | 1.84 | 0.61 |
| 3 | CIVA Lab | 6.97 | 2.05 | 0.98 |
| 4 | Levi | 5.64 | 3.43 | 0.93 |
| 5 | VisionH4ck3rz | 5.41 | 2.89 | 1.70 |
| 6 | GoF | 3.80 | 3.23 | 2.97 |
| 7 | GvisUleTeam | 3.69 | 3.41 | 2.90 |

In Table 3 a more detailed view of the MAE achieved by the teams over different age groups is reported; by looking at these results, we can further analyze the regularity of the proposed methods. It is possible to note that BTWG, winner of Guess The Age 2021, achieved a $MAE \leq 2.50$ for each age group; this observation denotes the impressive accuracy and regularity of the method, which also obtained the best absolute result in terms of $MAE^1$, $MAE^5$, $MAE^7$ and $MAE^8$. Pacific of Artificial Vision achieved the best $MAE^2$, $MAE^3$, $MAE^4$ and $MAE^6$ (and also the best $MAE$), but the method is not as regular as the one proposed by the BTWG team over the age groups $[1, 10]$ ($MAE^1 = 3.72$ vs $MAE^1 = 2.39$) and 70+ ($MAE^8 = 2.40$ vs $MAE^8 = 1.94$). CIVA Lab shows a trend that is quite similar to that of Pacific of Artificial Vision, with a slightly lower accuracy in the central age groups (from $MAE^2$ to $MAE^7$) and a more evident gap on the tails ($MAE^1$ to $MAE^8$), which implies a lower regularity. Levi achieved a comparable regularity with respect to the CIVA Lab team ($\sigma = 0.93$ vs $\sigma = 0.98$), but the average accuracy is significantly lower ($MAE = 3.43$ vs $MAE = 2.05$). Finally, the results achieved by VisionH4ck3rz, GoF and GvisUleTeam demonstrate that their methods are less regular, especially over the first and last age groups, while their accuracy is comparable with that of Levi on the others.

**Table 3.** Analysis of the MAE over the different age groups. The best results for each age group are highlighted in bold.

| Team | $MAE^1$ | $MAE^2$ | $MAE^3$ | $MAE^4$ | $MAE^5$ | $MAE^6$ | $MAE^7$ | $MAE^8$ |
|---|---|---|---|---|---|---|---|---|
| BTWG | **2.39** | 2.13 | 1.67 | 1.87 | **1.92** | 2.01 | **2.07** | **1.94** |
| Pacific of Artificial Vision | 3.72 | **2.08** | **1.60** | **1.83** | 1.98 | **1.90** | 2.18 | 2.40 |
| CIVA Lab | 4.84 | 2.45 | 1.87 | 2.05 | 2.10 | 1.94 | 2.44 | 3.67 |
| Levi | 5.54 | 2.35 | 3.15 | 3.69 | 3.87 | 3.21 | 3.04 | 4.55 |
| VisionH4ck3rz | 7.99 | 3.38 | 2.70 | 2.96 | 2.97 | 2.61 | 3.05 | 4.64 |
| GoF | 12.33 | 4.25 | 2.93 | 3.08 | 3.20 | 3.21 | 4.12 | 6.16 |
| GvisUleTeam | 12.07 | 4.49 | 3.19 | 3.29 | 3.44 | 3.20 | 3.84 | 6.92 |

## 6    Discussion

It is possible to observe that the methods based on a custom loss function and/or learning procedure, namely BTWG, Pacific of Artificial Vision and CIVA Lab are on the top of the ranking; therefore, this approach allows to regularize the performance over the age groups even using an unbalanced training set, keeping at the same time a high average accuracy. Among the methods, the one proposed by BTWG, inspired by a standard two-steps approach used for treating long tailed distributions, achieved a very good trade-off between accuracy and regularity; the general representation learned in the first step with the custom loss demonstrated its effectiveness and the fine tuning on a balanced training set allowed to achieve high accuracy and regularity. However, also the AAR inspired loss function proposed by CIVA Lab and the custom loss designed by Pacific of Artificial Vision proved to be valid solutions. BTWG and Pacific of Artificial Vision teams have also benefited from the use of a face recognition pre-training, which is known to be very effective for facial age estimation [6].

On the other hand, data augmentation only, without additional regularization strategies, is not sufficient for obtaining a DCNN that is both accurate and regular; this insight is evident by analyzing the results of Levi, VisionH4ck3rz and GvisUleTeam. However, the combination of data augmentation for balancing the training set with a learning procedure that optimizes both the accuracy (average age estimation error) and the regularity (standard deviation of the error) can be very effective, as demonstrated by the method proposed by Pacific of Artificial Vision.

## 7 Conclusion

Guess The Age 2021 compared 7 teams which proposed methods for estimating age from facial images. These approaches were based on a single DCNN, trained on the images of the MIVIA Age Dataset and designed to achieve regular performance across all the age groups despite a strongly unbalanced training set. BTWG team won this first edition of the contest by achieving an AAR equal to 7.94 with a method very accurate and regular thanks to the proposed learning procedure based on the decoupling in representation learning and classification. This idea, very effective for dealing with long tailed distributions, and other custom loss functions and novel data augmentation strategies proposed by the other teams, surely contributed to the advancement of research in the field of age estimation from facial images. The challenges are not over and certainly the scientific results that come out of this competition will give new ideas to researchers who want to try their hand at this topic.

## References

1. Antipov, G., Baccouche, M., Berrani, S.A., Dugelay, J.L.: Apparent age estimation from face images combining general and children-specialized deep learning models. In: Proceedings of of IEEE Conference on CVPR Workshops, pp. 96–104 (2016)
2. Antipov, G., Baccouche, M., Berrani, S.A., Dugelay, J.L.: Effective training of convolutional neural networks for face-based gender and age prediction. Pattern Recogn. **72**, 15–26 (2017)
3. Bao, Z., Tan, Z., Zhu, Y., Wan, J., Ma, X., Lei, Z., Guo, G.: LAE : long-tailed age estimation. In: Int. Conf. Comput. Anal. Images Patterns (2021)
4. Cao, D., Zhu, X., Huang, X., Guo, J., Lei, Z.: Domain balancing: face recognition on long-tailed domains. In: Proceedings of the IEEE/CVF Conference on Computer Vision and Pattern Recognition, pp. 5671–5679 (2020)
5. Cao, Q., Shen, L., Xie, W., Parkhi, O.M., Zisserman, A.: Vggface2: a dataset for recognising faces across pose and age. In: 2018 13th IEEE International Conference on Automatic Face & Gesture Recognition (FG 2018), pp. 67–74. IEEE (2018)
6. Carletti, V., Greco, A., Percannella, G., Vento, M.: Age from faces in the deep learning revolution. IEEE Trans. Pattern Analy. Mach. Intell. **42**(9), 2113–2132 (2020)
7. Castellano, G., Carolis, B.D., Marvulli, N., Sciancalepore, M., Vessio, G.: Real-time age estimation from facial images using yolo and efficientnet. In: International Conference on Computer Analysis of Images and Patterns (2021)

8. Escalera, S., et al.: Chalearn looking at people 2015: apparent age and cultural event recognition datasets and results. In: Proceedings of IEEE ICCV, pp. 1–9 (2015)
9. Escalera, S., et al.: Chalearn looking at people and faces of the world: face analysis workshop and challenge 2016. In: Proceedings of IEEE Conference on CVPR Workshops, pp. 1–8 (2016)
10. Fitwi, A., Yuan, M., Nikouei, S.Y., Chen, Y.: Minor privacy protection by real-time children identification and face scrambling at the edge. EAI Endorsed Trans. Secur. Safe. $7$(23), e3 (2020)
11. Greco, A., Saggese, A., Vento, M.: Digital signage by real-time gender recognition from face images. In: 2020 IEEE International Workshop on Metrology for Industry 4.0 & IoT, pp. 309–313. IEEE (2020)
12. Greco, A., Saggese, A., Vento, M., Vigilante, V.: Effective training of convolutional neural networks for age estimation based on knowledge distillation. Neural Comput. Appl. 1–16 (2021). https://doi.org/10.1007/s00521-021-05981-0
13. Greco, A., Saggese, A., Vento, M., Vigilante, V., et al.: Performance assessment of face analysis algorithms with occluded faces. In: Del Bimbo, A. (ed.) ICPR 2021. LNCS, vol. 12662, pp. 472–486. Springer, Cham (2021). https://doi.org/10.1007/978-3-030-68790-8_37
14. Kang, B., et al.: Decoupling representation and classifier for long-tailed recognition. arXiv preprint arXiv:1910.09217 (2019)
15. Lin, Y.H., Hsu, G.S.: Age-style augmentation for facial age estimation. In: International Conference on Computer Analysis of Images and Patterns (2021)
16. Osman, O.F., Yap, M.H.: Computational intelligence in automatic face age estimation: a survey. IEEE Trans. Emerg. Top. Comput. Intell. $3$(3), 271–285 (2018)
17. Punyani, P., Gupta, R., Kumar, A.: Neural networks for facial age estimation: a survey on recent advances. Artif. Intell. Rev. $53$(5), 3299–3347 (2019). https://doi.org/10.1007/s10462-019-09765-w
18. Rothe, R., Timofte, R., Van Gool, L.: Deep expectation of real and apparent age from a single image without facial landmarks. Int. J. Comput. Vis. $126$(2), 144–157 (2016). https://doi.org/10.1007/s11263-016-0940-3
19. Saggese, A., Vento, M., Vigilante, V.: MIVIABot: a cognitive robot for smart museum. In: Vento, M., Percannella, G. (eds.) CAIP 2019. LNCS, vol. 11678, pp. 15–25. Springer, Cham (2019). https://doi.org/10.1007/978-3-030-29888-3_2
20. Tan, Z., Wan, J., Lei, Z., Zhi, R., Guo, G., Li, S.Z.: Efficient group-n encoding and decoding for facial age estimation. IEEE Trans. PAMI $40$(11), 2610–2623 (2017)
21. Toubal, I.E., Lyu, L., Lin, D., Palaniappan, K.: Single view facial age estimation using deep learning with cascading random forests. In: International Conference on Computer Analysis of Images and Patterns (2021)
22. Uricar, M., Timofte, R., Rothe, R., Matas, J., Gool, L.V.: Structured output SVM prediction of apparent age, gender and smile from deep features. In: Proceedings of IEEE Conference on CVPR Workshops, pp. 730–738 (2016)

# Real-Time Age Estimation from Facial Images Using YOLO and EfficientNet

Giovanna Castellano◉, Berardina De Carolis◉, Nicola Marvulli,
Mauro Sciancalepore, and Gennaro Vessio$^{(\boxtimes)}$◉

Department of Computer Science, University of Bari "Aldo Moro", Bari, Italy
{giovanna.castellano,berardina.decarolis,gennaro.vessio}@uniba.it,
{n.marvulli1,m.sciancalepore20}@studenti.uniba.it

**Abstract.** Automatic age estimation from facial images is attracting increasing interest due to its many potential applications. Several deep learning-based methods have been proposed to tackle this task; however, they usually require prohibitive resources to run in real-time. In this work, we propose a fully automated system based on YOLOv5 and EfficientNet to perform face detection and subsequent age estimation in real-time. Also, to make the model more robust, EfficientNet was trained on the new MIVIA Age Dataset, released as part of a challenge. The results obtained in the contest are promising, and are strengthened by the lightness of the overall system which in fact is not only effective but also efficient.

**Keywords:** Computer vision · Age estimation · Convolutional neural networks · Face detection

## 1 Introduction

Age estimation aims to predict a person's age by analyzing face images. It is even a difficult task for humans and, as such, it has always been a challenging problem in Computer Vision [4,22]. An accurate age estimate from facial images would be beneficial for several real-world applications. For example, it can be useful in e-commerce applications to automatically suggest advertisements according to people's ages and show the content they are most likely to like, thus improving engagement [9]. Furthermore, in the field of safety and security, and in particular of human-computer interaction based on age, such systems can be used to prevent minors from browsing sensitive content [21]. Age estimation systems also prove effective when implemented on social robots, which typically take advantage of soft biometrics, including age, to show an empathic behavior. This is desirable in all contexts that require a natural interaction with humans, such as elderlycare [2] , museum guide [5], and so on.

The countless number of applications has brought great attention to age estimation systems; in fact, research in this field is very active both for the interest in its applications, but also for the great challenges that arise when

© Springer Nature Switzerland AG 2021
N. Tsapatsoulis et al. (Eds.): CAIP 2021, LNCS 13053, pp. 275–284, 2021.
https://doi.org/10.1007/978-3-030-89131-2_25

trying to solve this type of task [1]. The main challenges are related to the quality of the facial image, the different poses, orientations, occlusions, bad light conditions, and the presence of facial gadgets. The classical approaches to solving these problems are based on the manual extraction of features and generally consist of two different stages: one dedicated to the extraction of invariant and robust features that encode information on aging; the other dedicated to age estimation, using traditional machine learning algorithms (e.g., [11,13]). The disadvantages of the manual approach lie in the fact that the feature extraction process is closely related to the human experience and also requires a lot of effort. For these reasons, deep learning-based solutions for age estimation have begun to spread, thanks to their ability to build end-to-end age estimation systems, eliminating the need for any kind of manual feature engineering (e.g., [3,20]).

In this regard, it is worth underlining that the most promising methods proposed in the literature use complex architectures or ensembles of deep models, whose resulting classifiers are not usable in real applications, as they require prohibitive computational resources that are not always available. Furthermore, their training procedure, made even more complex by the plurality of neural networks to train, typically requires huge training sets that are not easy to collect. To address these issues, in this work we use a huge data set recently released, that is the MIVIA Age Dataset [10], and propose a method based on a single neural network, i.e. EfficientNet [26], to provide an effective and at the same time efficient model for age estimation suitable for real-time applications. In addition, to fully exploit the potential of the proposed model, it is combined with the lightweight YOLOv5 detector [15] to develop a fully automated face detection and age estimation framework.

This article accompanies our participation in the "Guess the Age" contest,[1] as part of CAIP 2021, in which the MIVIA Age Dataset was released and whose goal was to specifically design single network solutions.

The rest of this paper is structured as follows. Section 2 reviews related work. Section 3 describes the proposed method. Section 4 presents and discusses the experimental results. Section 5 concludes the paper.

## 2   Related Work

Early work attempting to solve the age estimation problem focused primarily on building robust sets of aging features, such as facial features and wrinkles [16], facial aging patterns [8] and biologically inspired features [13], taking into account different orientations and scales. General texture description features have also been exploited, such as Local Binary Patterns [11] and Gabor features [7]. Given the features extracted, age prediction is performed with a chosen learning algorithm, such as Support Vector Machines, Linear Discriminant Analysis, and so on. Further studies found that other traits, such as gender and ethnicity [6,12], can improve the overall performance. Age estimation can also be treated as a classification task rather than a regression task [17].

---

[1] http://gta2021.unisa.it/.

More recent works have begun to adopt techniques based on deep learning, some of which exploited rather complex architectures, such as the multi-scale architecture proposed in [29] and the tree-structured architecture proposed in [18]. Malli et al. [3] proposed an ensemble-based solution, training different deep models and then averaging their results to get the predicted age. Othmani et al. [20] recently showed that fine-tuning a state-of-the-art model, such as Xception or VGG16, on large age-related datasets, can improve predictive accuracy. While effective, these solutions are not always able to meet the stringent computational requirements of most critical real-time applications. With the aim to meet real-time requirements, in this work we propose a combination of lightweight models to provide not only an effective, but above all an efficient solution for real-time face detection and subsequent age estimation.

## 3    Proposed Method

The general framework was developed as a Web App, written in Python. The server side is built on the Flask library, which receives the image stream from the client and responds with a JSON file that contains the coordinates of the bounding box of the detected face, the confidence score and the age estimate. The core of the system is a two-stage process based on two different deep learning models. In the first stage, the images/frames streamed by the client are fed into a face detector based on the YOLOv5 architecture to extract face ROIs. In the second stage, an age estimation model based on the EfficientNet architecture runs to predict the age. These two steps are described in more detail in the following subsections. It should be noted that the system can operate in different modes, depending on the user's needs. It can perform inferences in real-time using a webcam, or in batch mode, feeding it with a single image, video or a folder with many of them.

### 3.1    Face Detection

To implement the face detector, we used YOLO ("You only look once"). YOLO is a family of single-shot object detection models, which aims to surpass demanding region-based detectors, in order to create lightweight but solid object detection systems capable of running on mobile or edge devices providing accurate performance in real-time [23]. The main idea of YOLO is to represent each image as a grid of $S \times S$ cells. If the center of an object falls within a cell, that same cell is the responsible for the object. Each cell of the grid predicts $B$ bounding boxes, assigning them confidence scores. Finally, non-maximum suppression is applied to clear overlapping or low-scoring boxes, given a certain threshold.

Among the different implementations of YOLO proposed in the literature, we adopted the latest Ultralytics implementation, namely YOLOv5 [15]. The adoption of YOLOv5, compared to other previous, yet powerful versions, is mainly due to its high versatility in the integration process and also to its lightweight structure that counts only 7.3M parameters. In fact, we have focused in particular on the lighter version, which is called YOLOv5s. The main difference between YOLOv5 and its predecessors is that it is implemented in PyTorch rather than being a fork of the original Darknet framework. In addition, some important improvements have been added, including self-learning bounding box anchors.

## 3.2   Age Estimation

To implement the age estimator, we used EfficientNet, a convolutional neural network that relies on AutoML and a so-called *compound coefficient* to uniformly scale its depth, width and resolution [26]. Unlike the conventional practice of arbitrary scaling these factors, in fact, the EfficientNet scaling method uniformly scales the width, depth and resolution of the network with a set of fixed scaling coefficients. The compound scaling method is motivated by the intuition that if the input image is large, the network needs more layers to increase the receptive fields and more channels to capture finer-grained patterns. EfficientNet currently achieves state-of-the-art performance across multiple benchmark datasets, but with an order of magnitude fewer parameters. The core EfficientNet-B0 network builds on the inverted residual blocks of MobileNetV2 [25], plus squeeze-and-excitation blocks. EfficientNet-B0 has been enhanced with the compound scaling method to achieve a family of models from B0 to B7. We chose EfficientNet-B0 to build our real-time age estimation model, as is the lightest, with 237 layers but only 5.3M parameters.

To adapt the model for the age estimation task, we removed the original classifier on top, replacing it with a global average pooling layer, a batch normalization layer, a dropout layer (with a small dropout rate of 0.2), and a single output neuron with linear activation.

## 4   Experiment

### 4.1   Datasets and Setting

YOLOv5 is a family of object detection architectures pre-trained on the COCO dataset. To fine-tune YOLOv5 for face detection, we used the Wider Face dataset [28] which includes 32,203 images, labeled in Pascal VOC format. We considered only a subset of 2200 images, which were selected excluding images with too small bounding boxes, i.e. in which the faces are not sufficiently large. To be used with YOLOv5, Pascal VOC labels (left, top, right, bottom) were converted to YOLO format (width, height, $x$ center, $y$ center). The dataset was split into a training set of 1600 images, a test set of 400 images and a validation set of 200 images. Fine-tuning was performed unfreezing the top 25 layers and using a learning rate of $10^{-2}$, a mini-batch size of 32 and the standard YOLO loss function.

To train the age estimator, we considered the MIVIA Age Dataset which is the main dataset of the "Guess the Age" contest. It consists of 575,073 images

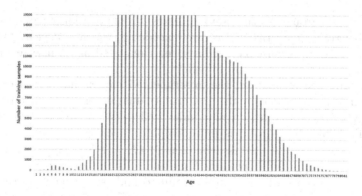

**Fig. 1.** MIVIA Age Dataset distribution by age (http://gta2021.unisa.it/).

of over 9,000 identities, obtained at different ages. It is worth mentioning that the MIVIA Age Dataset is among the largest publicly annotated datasets available on faces. Images were extracted from the VGGFace2 dataset and annotated with age using a "knowledge distillation" technique, making the dataset heterogeneous in terms of face size, lighting conditions, face pose, gender and ethnicity [10]. Each image in the dataset contains a single face, already cropped. Considering that most of the samples in the dataset are approximately 60 × 60 pixels, we decided to discard all images smaller than 30 × 30 pixels before training, in order to not damage the regression models. The distribution of the dataset samples by age is shown in Fig. 1. This distribution shows a strong imbalance between different ages, whit under-represented ages, at the tails of the distribution, counting only 2–10 images per age. To handle this imbalance, offline and online data augmentation techniques were applied. In particular, horizontal flipping, random zooming, rotation and brightness variation were used. To adapt EfficientNet to age estimation, the network was trained by fine-tuning the weights pre-trained on ImageNet on the MIVIA Age Dataset, unfreezing the top 20 layers. The Adam optimizer was used, with a learning rate of $10^{-4}$, a mini-batch size of 128, and the mean absolute error (described below) as a loss function. The dataset has been split into 80% for training and 20% for validation. To evaluate the effectiveness of the trained model, we submitted our model to the challenge organizers and they ran it on the private test set.

## 4.2 Metrics

Concerning face detection, we measured standard metrics commonly used in object detection tasks, i.e. precision, recall and average precision (AP). Precision is the ability of the method to detect *only* faces; in other words, it is the percentage of faces correctly detected over all detections. Recall is the ability of the method to find *all* faces; in other words, it is the percentage of faces correctly detected over all ground truth bounding boxes. Since precision-recall curves typically follow zigzag patterns, AP is also considered, which is basically the area under the precision-recall curve; it has been calculated at an intersection over union of 0.5.

Concerning age estimation, the experimented models have been evaluated using the metrics indicated by the challenge evaluation protocol: mean absolute error (MAE), regularity and a new index called *age accuracy and regularity* (AAR). The purpose of MAE is quite simple: it measures the mean absolute error of the age estimates and is defined as $MAE = \frac{1}{N}\sum_{i=1}^{N}|p_i - r_i|$, where $N$ is the test set size, $p_i$ is the predicted age and $r_i$ is the ground truth age. Due to the wide age range (1–70+), it is useful to understand whether the model performance is consistent across all age groups. For this reason, a regularity score is adopted. First, ages are divided into 8 categories (1–10, 11–20, 21–30, ...), then the MAE is calculated for each of them. Regularity is then defined as a standard deviation calculated with the rule $\sigma = \sqrt{\frac{\sum_{j}^{8}(MAE^j - MAE)^2}{8}}$, where $MAE^j$ is the MAE computed on the $j$-th age category. The smaller the standard deviation obtained with a method, the lower its regularity. Finally, to have a summary of these metrics, AAR is used, which is defined as $AAR = \max(0, 7 - MAE) + \max(0, 3 - \sigma)$. The AAR metric varies between 0 and 10, weighing 70% the MAE contribution and 30% the regularity contribution. A perfect method, achieving $MAE = 0$ and $\sigma = 0$, will therefore get $AAR = 10$.

## 4.3   Results

The overall system has been tested on a PC desktop with a Ryzen 5 3600 CPU and 32GB of RAM. Using YOLOv5s, face detection on the CPU takes 0.06 s (~16 fps). On Google Colab, with a Tesla T4, the inference time takes 0.009 s (~111 fps). As for EfficientNet, the neural network is capable of processing 76 facial images per second on the CPU, and 549 images on the GPU.

As for face detection with YOLOv5s, after convergence the model achieves the results reported in Table 1. We did not compare this version of YOLO with any other or any other object detection system, as the main focus of the challenge was age estimation. The model achieved a very high precision rate, at the expense of a lower recall, which could be due to the presence of many training samples containing groups of people, sometimes with hundreds of small faces per image. However, it should be noted that this drawback is largely mitigated by the very high detection rate, which allows the model to recover a face missed in a given frame in a subsequent frame.

As for age estimation, we compared EfficientNet-B0 with a custom baseline convolutional neural network (CNN), consisting of three convolutional layers (with an ascending depth of 96, 256 and 384 filters and a descending kernel size of $7 \times 7$, $5 \times 5$ and $3 \times 3$) and two fully-connected layers on top with a dropout in between. Moreover, we made a comparison with the popular ResNet50 [14]. The preliminary results obtained on the validation set are reported in Table 2. It can be seen that both EfficientNet and ResNet outperform the baseline model.

**Table 1.** Face detection results.

| Precision | Recall | AP |
|-----------|--------|-------|
| 94.6%     | 63.1%  | 67.6% |

**Table 2.** Comparison of age estimation models on our validation set.

| Model           | MAE  | Regularity | AAR  |
|-----------------|------|------------|------|
| Baseline CNN    | 4.13 | 0.75       | 5.12 |
| ResNet50        | 3.17 | 0.68       | 6.15 |
| EfficientNet-B0 | 2.50 | 0.70       | 6.80 |

**Table 3.** Age estimation challenge results.

| Model           | MAE  | Regularity | AAR  |
|-----------------|------|------------|------|
| EfficientNet-B0 | 2.89 | 1.70       | 5.41 |

They also show comparable regularity scores. However, although the regularity achieved by ResNet is slightly lower, EfficientNet shows a much better MAE. All in all, considering that EfficientNet is much more computationally efficient than ResNet, this allowed us to choose it for the participation in the challenge.

The results obtained on the competition private test set, reported in Table 3, are promising. The MAE obtained is slightly higher than that achieved in the preliminary evaluation on the validation set, indicating a small overfitting. Conversely, the regularity is much higher, indicating that the model is not stable across age groups. This could indicate that the data augmentation used to balance the dataset has not proved effective enough. To conclude our analysis, we compared the proposed method with existing deep learning-based methods proposed in the literature (see Table 4). As the challenge results are not yet publicly available at the time of writing, we have made the comparison with recent methods tested on other popular datasets, in particular FG-NET and MORPH. The comparison is less fair; however, at least we understand in what order of magnitude the error committed in the state-of-the-art is placed. Considering that state-of-the-art models do not fall below ~2 of MAE, that the MIVIA Age Dataset is an "in-the-wild" dataset, with noise and incorrectly labeled samples, and that the proposed method represents a very efficient solution compared to other methods, the results look pretty good.

Examples of application of the proposed system in real-time during the processing of the video stream of a simple webcam are shown in Fig. 2.

**Table 4.** Comparison with state-of-the-art methods based on deep learning. Only the MAE is compared, being the main metric used by previous works.

| Reference | Method | Dataset | MAE |
|---|---|---|---|
| Yi et al. [29] | Multi-scale CNN | MORPH | 3.63 |
| Wang et al. [27] | CNN + dimensionality reduction | FG-NET | 4.26 |
| Niu et al. [19] | Multi-output CNN | MORPH | 3.27 |
| Rothe et al. [24] | Fine-tuned VGG16 | MORPH | 2.68 |
| Othmani et al. [20] | Fine-tuned Xception | MORPH | 2.01 |
| *This work* | Fine-tuned EfficientNet | MIVIA Age | 2.89 |

**Fig. 2.** Examples of applications of the proposed system in real-time with a simple webcam. The real ages are 17, 23 and 23 from left to right respectively.

## 5 · Conclusion

In this work, we have presented our system based on YOLOv5 and EfficientNet that performs face detection and age estimation from facial images in a real-time two-step process. In particular, a version of EfficientNet, fine-tuned on the new, challenging MIVIA Age Dataset, proved to be quite effective in providing an acceptable age estimation on average. As a future work, we wish to experiment with more advanced balancing and data augmentation techniques to improve system stability.

## References

1. Al-Shannaq, A.S., Elrefaei, L.A.: Comprehensive analysis of the literature for age estimation from facial images. IEEE Access **7**, 93229–93249 (2019)
2. Buono, P., Castellano, G., De Carolis, B., Macchiarulo, N.: Social assistive robots in elderly care: exploring the role of empathy. In: 1st International Workshop on Empowering People in Dealing with Internet of Things Ecosystems, EMPATHY 2020, pp. 12–19 (2020)

3. Can Malli, R., Aygun, M., Kemal Ekenel, H.: Apparent age estimation using ensemble of deep learning models. In: Proceedings of the IEEE Conference on Computer Vision and Pattern Recognition Workshops, pp. 9–16 (2016)
4. Carletti, V., Greco, A., Percannella, G., Vento, M.: Age from faces in the deep learning revolution. IEEE Trans. Pattern Anal. Mach. Intell. **42**(9), 2113–2132 (2019)
5. Castellano, G., De Carolis, B., Macchiarulo, N., Vessio, G.: Pepper4Museum: towards a human-like museum guide. In: Proceedings of the AVI2CH Workshop on Advanced Visual Interfaces and Interactions in Cultural Heritage (2020)
6. Fujiwara, T., Koshimizu, H.: Age and gender estimations by modeling statistical relationship among faces. In: Palade, V., Howlett, R.J., Jain, L. (eds.) KES 2003. LNCS (LNAI), vol. 2774, pp. 870–876. Springer, Heidelberg (2003). https://doi.org/10.1007/978-3-540-45226-3_119
7. Gao, F., Ai, H.: Face age classification on consumer images with gabor feature and fuzzy LDA method. In: Tistarelli, M., Nixon, M.S. (eds.) ICB 2009. LNCS, vol. 5558, pp. 132–141. Springer, Heidelberg (2009). https://doi.org/10.1007/978-3-642-01793-3_14
8. Geng, X., Zhou, Z.H., Smith-Miles, K.: Automatic age estimation based on facial aging patterns. IEEE Trans. Pattern Anal. Mach. Intell. **29**(12), 2234–2240 (2007)
9. Greco, A., Saggese, A., Vento, M.: Digital signage by real-time gender recognition from face images. In: 2020 IEEE International Workshop on Metrology for Industry 4.0 & IoT, pp. 309–313. IEEE (2020)
10. Greco, A., Saggese, A., Vento, M., Vigilante, V.: Effective training of convolutional neural networks for age estimation based on knowledge distillation. Neural Comput. Appl. 1–16 (2021). https://doi.org/10.1007/s00521-021-05981-0
11. Gunay, A., Nabiyev, V.V.: Automatic age classification with LBP. In: 2008 23rd International Symposium on Computer and Information Sciences, pp. 1–4. IEEE (2008)
12. Guo, G., Mu, G.: Joint estimation of age, gender and ethnicity: CCA vs. PLS. In: 2013 10th IEEE International Conference and Workshops on Automatic Face and Gesture Recognition (FG), pp. 1–6. IEEE (2013)
13. Guo, G., Mu, G., Fu, Y., Huang, T.S.: Human age estimation using bio-inspired features. In: 2009 IEEE Conference on Computer Vision and Pattern Recognition, pp. 112–119. IEEE (2009)
14. He, K., Zhang, X., Ren, S., Sun, J.: Deep residual learning for image recognition. In: Proceedings of the IEEE Conference on Computer Vision and Pattern Recognition, pp. 770–778 (2016)
15. Jocher, G., et al.: ultralytics/yolov5: v5.0 - YOLOv5-P6 1280 models, AWS, Supervise.ly and YouTube integrations, April 2021. https://doi.org/10.5281/zenodo.4679653, https://doi.org/10.5281/zenodo.4679653
16. Kwon, Y.H., da Vitoria Lobo, N.: Age classification from facial images. Comput. Vis. Image Underst. **74**(1), 1–21 (1999)
17. Lanitis, A., Draganova, C., Christodoulou, C.: Comparing different classifiers for automatic age estimation. IEEE Trans. Syst. Man Cybern. Part B (Cybern.) **34**(1), 621–628 (2004)
18. Li, S., Xing, J., Niu, Z., Shan, S., Yan, S.: Shape driven kernel adaptation in convolutional neural network for robust facial traits recognition. In: Proceedings of the IEEE Conference on Computer Vision and Pattern Recognition, pp. 222–230 (2015)

19. Niu, Z., Zhou, M., Wang, L., Gao, X., Hua, G.: Ordinal regression with multiple output cnn for age estimation. In: Proceedings of the IEEE Conference on Computer Vision and Pattern Recognition, pp. 4920–4928 (2016)
20. Othmani, A., Taleb, A.R., Abdelkawy, H., Hadid, A.: Age estimation from faces using deep learning: a comparative analysis. Comput. Vis. Image Underst. **196**, 102961 (2020)
21. Pinter, A.T., Wisniewski, P.J., Xu, H., Rosson, M.B., Caroll, J.M.: Adolescent online safety: moving beyond formative evaluations to designing solutions for the future. In: Proceedings of the 2017 Conference on Interaction Design and Children, pp. 352–357 (2017)
22. Punyani, P., Gupta, R., Kumar, A.: Neural networks for facial age estimation: a survey on recent advances. Artifi. Intell. Rev. **53**(5), 3299–3347 (2020)
23. Redmon, J., Divvala, S., Girshick, R., Farhadi, A.: You only look once: unified, real-time object detection. In: Proceedings of the IEEE Conference on Computer Vision and Pattern Recognition, pp. 779–788 (2016)
24. Rothe, R., Timofte, R., Van Gool, L.: Dex: deep expectation of apparent age from a single image. In: Proceedings of the IEEE International Conference on Computer Vision Workshops, pp. 10–15 (2015)
25. Sandler, M., Howard, A., Zhu, M., Zhmoginov, A., Chen, L.C.: Mobilenetv 2: inverted residuals and linear bottlenecks. In: Proceedings of the IEEE Conference on Computer Vision and Pattern Recognition, pp. 4510–4520 (2018)
26. Tan, M., Le, Q.: Efficientnet: rethinking model scaling for convolutional neural networks. In: International Conference on Machine Learning, pp. 6105–6114. PMLR (2019)
27. Wang, X., Guo, R., Kambhamettu, C.: Deeply-learned feature for age estimation. In: 2015 IEEE Winter Conference on Applications of Computer Vision, pp. 534–541. IEEE (2015)
28. Yang, S., Luo, P., Loy, C.C., Tang, X.: Wider face: a face detection benchmark. In: Proceedings of the IEEE Conference on Computer Vision and Pattern Recognition, pp. 5525–5533 (2016)
29. Yi, D., Lei, Z., Li, S.Z.: Age estimation by multi-scale convolutional network. In: Cremers, D., Reid, I., Saito, H., Yang, M.-H. (eds.) ACCV 2014. LNCS, vol. 9005, pp. 144–158. Springer, Cham (2015). https://doi.org/10.1007/978-3-319-16811-1_10

# Single View Facial Age Estimation Using Deep Learning with Cascaded Random Forests

Imad Eddine Toubal$^{(\boxtimes)}$, Linquan Lyu, Dan Lin, and K. Palaniappan

Department of Electrical Engineering and Computer Science, University of Missouri,
Columbia, MO 65211, USA
itdfh@umsystem.edu

**Abstract.** The task of estimating a person's real age using unconstrained facial images has been actively studied in biometrics research.
We developed several deep learning architectures and supervision methods for facial age estimation and evaluate the impact of different pre-
processing and face alignment (or normalization) methods on the feature
embedding subspace. The proposed novel two-stage supervised learning
model utilizes ResNeXt as a backbone combined with a two-layer random forest (TLRF) to estimate age. Our deep architectures are trained
using a custom loss function to handle variations in gender, pose, illumination, ethnicity, expression and context, on the *VGG-Face2 MIVIA
Age Dataset* with over 575K images, as part of the Guess the Age (GTA)
contest. Surprisingly, face alignment using FANet during training did not
improve accuracy. We were able to achieve an Age Accuracy and Regularity score $AAR = 7.02$ with a variance $\sigma = 1.16$ using only ResNeXt.
The proposed ResNeXt+TLRF model improved age-class generalizability with a smaller variance of $\sigma = 0.98$ and a second best $AAR = 6.97$.

**Keywords:** Age estimation · Face recognition · Face verification · Face
alignment · Deepfakes · Deep learning · Random forest · Biological age

## 1 Introduction

Age estimation has many real-world applications including social robotic interaction, biometrics, demographics, business intelligence, online advertising, item
recommendation, identity verification, video surveillance, access control, human-
computer interaction, privacy and security, crowd behavior, law enforcement,
and many more [1–3]. Single facial image age prediction is highly challenging
[4–7], due to the variability in how individuals age based on their "ageotype"
[8]. Everyone ages at different rates and biological age is influenced by genetics,
diet, exercise, stress and environment. Moreover, visual cues about an individual's chronological age can vary due to pose, lighting, gender, scale, cosmetics,
accoutrements, race, height, weight, health, emotion, occlusion, etc. [1, 3, 9, 10].
Facial age feature embeddings can also be used to improve face recognition [11]
and distinguish between real and synthetic (Deepfake) faces [12].

© Springer Nature Switzerland AG 2021
N. Tsapatsoulis et al. (Eds.): CAIP 2021, LNCS 13053, pp. 285–296, 2021.
https://doi.org/10.1007/978-3-030-89131-2_26

In the field of facial age estimation, there is an absence of large, reliable annotated datasets due to the difficulty in establishing ground truth ages. The LAP 2016 dataset [13] is reliable but only contains 7,591 images. Large datasets, like IMDB-Wiki [14], CACD [15], and UTK [16] are annotated with the age information based on online web crawling and social networks, therefore, reliability is not guaranteed. Some of the datasets for face aging prediction (prediction of a person's appearance at a younger or older time period) do not have enough diversity because many pictures are from the same individual at different times; like the FG-NET [17] dataset which contains 1,002 images of only 82 people. MORPH Album 2 [18] is another longitudinal dataset that contains 55,134 images of 13,618 subjects, but with a limited age distribution that ranges between 16 to 77. The CAIP Guess the Age (GTA) Contest [19], uses the *VGG-Face2 MIVIA Age Dataset* [2]. It consists of 575,073 images of more than 9,000 identities, collected at different ages. The images are extracted from the VGGFace2 [20] and annotated with the person's age by means of a knowledge distillation technique [2]. The *VGG-Face2 MIVIA Age Dataset* is the most accurate facial age dataset currently available at this scale in terms of sample size and heterogeneity. Despite the lack of precise age data, several machine learning and data driven age estimation models have emerged [1]. DLDL-v2 (ThinAgeNet) [21] currently stands as the state-of-the-art on the MORPH Album 2 and ChaLearn 2015 and 2016 [22] datasets.

Guess the Age (GTA) Contest considers the biometric task of estimating a person's age using only their facial image as input [1,2]. Although there are over 575K age labeled images in the *VGG-Face2 MIVIA Age Dataset* covering gender, ethnicity, varying poses, scale and illumination, there is a high degree of age class imbalance. The four age groups covering, 1 to <20 and ≥60, the two youngest and two oldest groups (out of eight categories) constitute less than 10% of the data; the youngest and oldest age categories make up less than 1%.

In this paper, we propose a novel age estimation approach that uses a two-layer classification-plus-regression random forest trained on deep feature embeddings from the ResNeXt50 architecture [23]. We show that an ensemble of weak decision trees trained on deep features has smaller variance than a pure deep neural model with end-to-end optimization.

## 2    Deep Learning Methods for Age Estimation

### 2.1    Pre-processing

We used $z$-normalization to normalize the intensity value of the pre-cropped input face images. *VGG-Face2 MIVIA Age dataset* contains images with already cropped single faces, and hence a face detection step was not necessary.

Our experience with incorporating a face-alignment step using FANet produced mixed results [24]. FANet was used to estimate 68 facial key-points in the cropped face image. These extracted key-points are matched with a template (standard face pose) set of key-points to estimate the 2D alignment transformation matrix. We then apply this transformation to warp the original face image to realign the face. Sample results from this step are shown in Fig. 1.

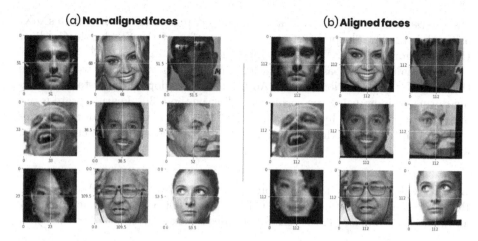

**Fig. 1.** Sample face-alignment using FANet [24] applied to face images from the *VGG-Face2 MIVIA Age Dataset*. Note that not all faces are warped when they are side profiles or have up-down tilts. Our final age estimates using ResNeXT+TLRF (vs actual) for these subjects from left to right and top to bottom are: 27 (27), 27 (30), 29 (29), 34 (35), 31 (31), 56 (57), 27 (29), 58 (59), 28 (28).

We evaluated the potential benefit of face-alignment since this can reduce the learning complexity for age estimation when faces are in similar poses. However, we found that face-alignment reduced the diversity in the training dataset which could lead to overfitting, and reduce the performance of deep neural networks. For this reason, we trained the deep neural models on non-aligned faces to ensure better generalizability. Although face-alignment of training images had limited benefit in our initial testing, several approaches are being studied to better incorporate face-alignment as a data augmentation approach to improve performance during inference.

## 2.2   ResNeXt CNN

**Architecture.** We use the ResNeXt architecture [23] for extracting feature descriptors due to its advantages over the classical ResNet architecture. ResNet uses residual blocks [25] that make use of sequential convolution layers with an added skip connection. This simple modification led to a breakthrough in performance when compared to classical CNNs (such as VGG [26]). The ResNeXt architectural insight was the notion of *cardinality*, that many parallel small convolutions are better than a single deep sequence of convolutions with wider kernels. This is done by using parallel convolution streams with fewer channels instead of a single sequential stream with more channels. Using the cardinality property, they experimentally demonstrated an improvement in accuracy on the ImageNet benchmark [27] by simply increasing the cardinality without adding more parameters. This is crucial when dealing with smaller class sizes where over-fitting is more likely.

**Hyper-parameters.** We train a single output regression version of ResNeXt using the Adam [28] optimizer that is a variation of the Stochastic Gradient Descent algorithm [29]. We use an initial learning rate $\alpha = 10^{-4}$. The model weight initialization is based on transfer learning with pre-trained weights from the ImageNet classification dataset. Additionally, we adopt warm restart scheduling during training using the cosine annealing method [30]. Learning rate is one of the most important hyper-parameters in training neural networks. For this reason, adaptively selecting a learning rate and/or scheduling are crucial for a more robust training [31–33].

**Loss.** We define a new loss function $\mathcal{L}_{AAR}$ inspired by the Age Accuracy and Regularity (AAR) metric from the GTA contest. For a set of predicted ages $\hat{\mathbf{y}}$ and real ages $\mathbf{y}$ of size $N$, the loss function equation is given as:

$$\mathcal{L}_{AAR}(\mathbf{y},\hat{\mathbf{y}}) = \gamma\mathcal{L}_1(\mathbf{y},\hat{\mathbf{y}}) + \lambda\sigma \tag{1}$$

where:

$$\mathcal{L}_1(\mathbf{y},\hat{\mathbf{y}}) = \frac{1}{N}\sum_{i=1}^{N}\ell_1(y_i,\hat{y}_i) \tag{2}$$

with:

$$\ell_1(y,\hat{y}) = \begin{cases} \frac{1}{2\beta}(y-\hat{y})^2, & \text{if } |y-\hat{y}| < \beta \\ |y-\hat{y}| - \frac{1}{2}\beta, & \text{otherwise} \end{cases} \tag{3}$$

and:

$$\sigma = \sqrt{\frac{1}{8}\sum_{j=1}^{8}[\mathcal{L}_1(y^j,\hat{y}^j) - \mathcal{L}_1(y,\hat{y})]^2} \tag{4}$$

where $y$ is the set of true ages, $\hat{y}$ is the set of predicted ages, $y^j$ and $\hat{y}^j$ are the true and predicted ages respectively that belong to $j^{th}$ age group. $\mathcal{L}_1$ is the smooth L1 norm (mean absolute error), $\sigma$ is a regularization term to reduce the model's sensitivity to the dataset imbalance. $\gamma$ and $\lambda$ are coefficients terms for two parts of the loss function. The loss parameters used in this work are $\gamma = 0.7$, $\lambda = 0.3$, and $\beta = 1.0$.

Note that there are two main differences between our loss function and the AAR metric. First, we use *smooth L1* distance $\ell_1$ as opposed to MAE. *Smooth L1* was proven less sensitive to outliers and less prone to exploding gradients [34,35]. Second, we do not clip $\mathcal{L}_1$ and $\sigma$ components to a maximum value; instead, we give them different weights to emphasize one over the other.

**Label Distribution Smoothing (LDS).** To tackle the challenge of age imbalance in the dataset, the Label Distribution Smoothing (LDS) method was evaluated [36]. LDS convolves a symmetric 1-D Gaussian smoothing kernel $k$ with the label distribution (histogram) $p(y)$ to produce a kernel-smoothed version that interpolates information of data samples with nearby labels. A symmetric kernel is a kernel that satisfies: $k(y+\Delta y) = k(y-\Delta y)$ and $\nabla_y k(y+\Delta y) + \nabla_y k(y-\Delta y) = 0, \forall y \in Y$. The smoothed label distribution, $p'(x)$, is a convolution between the distribution $p(y)$ and the kernel $k(y)$:

$$p'(y) = k(y) * p(y) \tag{5}$$

where $*$ is the convolution operator. The loss function is then reweighted by scaling the estimates with the inverse of the label frequency for each sample:

$$\mathcal{L} = \frac{1}{N} \sum_{i=1}^{N} \frac{\ell(y_i, \hat{y}_i)}{p'(\hat{y}_i)}. \tag{6}$$

### 2.3   Two-Layer Random Forest (TLRF)

ResNeXt takes an RGB input image $x_i$ and uses a series of convolutional blocks to produce a feature embedding of 2,048 dimensions $f_i \in \mathbb{R}^{2,048}$. It then uses a single-layer perceptron (fully connected neural regressor) with learned weights to make a final prediction of age, $\hat{y}_i \in \mathbb{R}$. We replace the neural regressor with our two-layer random forest (TLRF) combining classification-plus-regression to make a final prediction. In the first stage, TLRF uses ResNeXt features as input to the first layer (random forest classifier) to make a classification of the given sample's age group in the form of a probability vector $p_i(G) \in \mathbb{R}^8$ where:

$$G \in \{[1, 9], [10, 19], [20, 29], [30, 39], [40, 49], [50, 59], [50, 59], [60, +\infty]\}$$

We concatenate the 8-dimensional predicted probability vector for all eight of the age groups with the learned 2048-dimensional deep embedding feature vector $f_i$ into an augmented vector. We, then use that as input to the second random forest regressor layer in our TLRF. The final regression output is then rounded up to the nearest integer. A visual diagram of our approach is shown in Fig. 2.

Our experiments showed that TLRF improves the performance and stability of ResNeXt. For each layer of TLRF, we utilize a random forest of 100 decision trees trained in parallel on the ResNeXt embedding feature vectors, and each decision tree uses a maximum of 128 randomly selected features.

### 2.4   Training the Deep Architectures

**Dataset Split.** The *VGG-Face2 MIVIA Age Dataset* consists of 575,073 example cases [1,2]. We used 90% of this dataset (517,562) for training and the remaining 10% for evaluation (57,511). As the dataset is not uniformly distributed in terms of age, we sample 10% from each age group $j$ for evaluation; rather than 10% uniformly sampled across the entire set. We then divide the training data further into a training and validation split of 90% and 10% sizes respectively.

**Pre-processing.** Face images are normalized as explained in the pre-processing section. In addition, we resize the images to $224 \times 224$ resolution to match the expected input of ResNeXt network. Additionally, for better network stability, we normalize the age to range between 0 and 1.

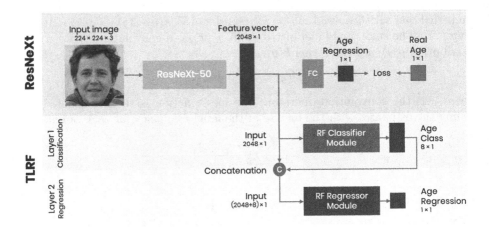

**Fig. 2.** Proposed ResNeXt+TLRF facial age estimation pipeline using ResNeXt-50 feature embedding vector with ImageNet transfer learning plus *VGG-Face2 MIVIA Age* training. A dual stage random forest estimates both class labels and age estimates.

**Data Augmentation.** For data augmentation, we use random horizontal flipping. Since our experiments showed that face-alignment hurts training, random rotations and distortions could also be applied in future work.

## 3    Experimental Results

In addition to the mean absolute error, we report the Age Accuracy and Regularity (AAR metric). GTA contest defined the AAR performance measure as:

$$\text{AAR} = max(0; 7 - \text{MAE}) + max(0; 3 - \sigma) \tag{7}$$

with a maximum score of 10; with $\sigma = \sqrt{\frac{1}{8}\sum_{j=1}^{8}(\text{MAE}_j - \text{MAE})^2}$ where MAE is the mean absolute error and $\text{MAE}_j$ is the mean absolute error for the $j^{th}$ age group. The mean average error (MAE) is given as $MAE = \frac{1}{N}\sum_i |y_i - \hat{y}_i|$, where $i$ is the sample index over all age categories. All evaluations are performed on the evaluation set that we described in Sect. 2.4 unless specified otherwise.

### 3.1    ResNeXt

A performance comparison of ResNet vs. ResNeXt in terms of MAE is given in the Table 1. Additionally, the table shows the difference in performance of our custom soft AAR loss compared to the mean squared error (MSE) loss $\mathcal{L}_{MSE}$ where, for a given batch of size $n$:

$$\mathcal{L}_{MSE} = \frac{1}{n}\sum_{i=1}^{n}||y_i - \hat{y}_i||^2 \tag{8}$$

Table 1 shows how using ResNeXt over its predecessor ResNet improves performance. Additionally, our custom AAR loss consistently improves the AAR metric in both networks. We can also note that LDS did not help in improving the performance; hence, we choose to move forward with ResNeXt trained using the AAR Loss. The LDS-trained ResNeXt network was trained using both MSE and AAR loss functions. The LDS-trained ResNeXt trained using AAR loss shows better performance.

**Table 1.** Accuracy comparison of ResNet, ResNeXt and ResNeXt with label distribution smoothing LDS using the evaluation data.

| Architecture | Loss | MAE₁ | MAE₂ | MAE₃ | MAE₄ | MAE₅ | MAE₆ | MAE₇ | MAE₈ | **MAE↓** | σ↓ | AAR↑ |
|---|---|---|---|---|---|---|---|---|---|---|---|---|
| ResNet | $\mathcal{L}_{MSE}$ | 1.74 | 1.94 | 1.58 | 2.00 | 2.05 | 1.83 | 1.77 | 1.94 | 1.87 ± 2.05 | 0.14 | 7.99 |
| | $\mathcal{L}_{AAR}$ | 1.79 | 1.96 | 1.47 | 1.83 | 1.94 | 1.77 | 1.69 | 1.99 | 1.75 ± 1.98 | 0.17 | 8.08 |
| **ResNeXt** | $\mathcal{L}_{MSE}$ | 2.11 | 1.85 | 1.53 | 1.95 | 2.02 | 1.81 | 1.72 | 1.93 | 1.82 ± 2.06 | 0.17 | 8.01 |
| | $\mathcal{L}_{AAR}$ | 1.91 | 1.89 | 1.46 | 1.80 | 1.93 | 1.72 | 1.74 | 1.78 | 1.73 ± 1.97 | 0.15 | 8.12 |
| ResNeXt (LDS) | $\mathcal{L}_{MSE}$ | 1.92 | 2.11 | 1.61 | 1.97 | 2.04 | 1.84 | 1.85 | 1.88 | 1.88 ± 2.06 | 0.15 | 7.98 |
| | $\mathcal{L}_{AAR}$ | 1.98 | 2.02 | 1.51 | 1.90 | 2.01 | 1.79 | 1.76 | 1.87 | 1.81 ± 2.05 | 0.17 | 8.03 |

### 3.2   Two-Layer Random Forest (TLRF)

**TLRF Classifier Module.** Although classifying a face's age group is an easier task than the exact age, it is still challenging due to age class imbalance. Table 2 shows the performance of the TLRF classifier module on our evaluation set. The F1 measure is much lower for underrepresented age groups due to lower recall.

**TLRF Regressor Module.** Several regression random forest topologies were evaluated against our proposed TLRF. First, a traditional regression random forest (RRF) was trained and evaluated with different number of trees using the ResNeXt 2048-dimensional feature descriptor. Then, we compare the single-layer random forest approach (RRF) to the proposed TLRF. Table 3 summarizes the RF ablation study experimental results using ResNeXt in combination with different RF configurations. For this part, a ResNeXt-50 was trained using MSE loss. The ResNeXt-50 residual deep network with a fully connected final regression layer performed well with an AAR of 8.01 on the held out evaluation set and 8.16 on the combined training and evaluation sets. Incorporating a random

**Table 2.** TLRF age group classifier module performance (using ResNeXt descriptor) on evaluation data. Support is the subset of data in each of the eight age categories used for evaluation.

| Age group | <10 | 10–19 | 20–29 | 30–39 | 40–49 | 50–59 | 60–69 | >69 | Overall |
|---|---|---|---|---|---|---|---|---|---|
| Precision | 0.85 | 0.75 | 0.87 | 0.83 | 0.82 | 0.83 | 0.82 | 0.85 | 0.83 |
| Recall | 0.63 | 0.58 | 0.89 | 0.83 | 0.83 | 0.84 | 0.77 | 0.54 | 0.83 |
| F1 | 0.72 | 0.66 | 0.88 | 0.83 | 0.82 | 0.84 | 0.80 | 0.66 | 0.83 |
| Support | 185 | 1960 | 14153 | 15001 | 13226 | 9341 | 3298 | 347 | 57,511 |

**Table 3.** Experimental results showing accuracy on *training+evaluation* (T+E) and *evaluation* (E) sets with different random forest learning methods (number of trees and number of layers). Last row ResNeXt+TLRF is our final result. RRF refers to Regression Random Forest. All ResNeXt networks were trained using the MSE loss.

| Method | MAE↓ | | $\sigma$ ↓ | | AAR↑ | |
|---|---|---|---|---|---|---|
| Dataset | T+E | E | T+E | E | T+E | E |
| ResNeXt | **1.35** ± 1.75 | **1.82** ± 2.06 | 0.14 | 0.17 | 8.16 | **8.01** |
| ResNeXt + RRF (64 trees) | 1.65 ± 1.57 | 1.90 ± 2.10 | 0.16 | 0.15 | 8.19 | 7.95 |
| ResNeXt + RRF (100 trees) | 1.66 ± 1.56 | 1.89 ± 2.09 | 0.15 | 0.15 | 8.20 | 7.96 |
| ResNeXt + RRF (200 trees) | 1.66 ± 1.56 | 1.89 ± 2.09 | 0.17 | 0.15 | 8.17 | 7.96 |
| ResNeXt + TLRF (2×100 trees) | 1.66 ± 1.56 | 1.88 ∓ 2.08 | **0.13** | **0.14** | **8.21** | 7.98 |

forest learning component improves the overall AAR accuracy using 100 trees to 8.20 on the combined training and evaluation sets and reduces AAR to 7.96 on the held out evaluation set. Increasing the number of trees to 200 did not improve performance on the evaluation set and decreased AAR performance to 8.17 on the combined T+E sets. *Using the two-layer classification plus regression random forest with the same ResNeXt-50 feature embedding vector results in the best AAR of 8.21 on the combined training and evaluation sets and improves the score to 7.98 comparing to traditional regression random forests.* This model also had the smallest class standard deviation ($\sigma$), on the held out evaluation set and the combined set.

### 3.3   Generalizability Performance Using the Withheld GTA Data

Based on the results described previously, we submitted the ResNeXt+TLRF as our single official submission to the GTA Challenge competition. After our official submission to the GTA contest, we continued to explore the generalization capability of the different architectures on the unseen hidden dataset with assistance from the MIVIA Lab at the University of Salerno.

Experimental results in Table 4 show that using the proposed custom AAR loss function consistently improves the generalizability of face estimation MAE accuracy in both our evaluation and the GTA hidden test set for all methods. ResNeXt trained using the AAR loss function has the highest AAR score of 8.12 on the heldout evaluation data and score of 7.02 on the hidden test set. The submitted ResNeXt+TLRF method also generalizes well on new unseen faces and has the lowest age group variance of 0.98. We notice that apart from the two underrepresented age groups ($MAE_1$ and $MAE_8$ with < 1.0% samples), the MAE scores are quite consistent between our evaluation split data and the GTA challenge's hidden test data. It is important to note that the standard deviation, $\sigma$, is more than eight times higher in the hidden dataset than the held out evaluation data due to larger deviations in $MAE_1$ and $MAE_8$. The lowest variation in the hidden or withheld data is the ResNeXt (MSE)+TLRF method, that we submitted to the GTA contest, and is italicized in Table 4.

**Table 4.** Results on the Guess the Age (GTA) contest hidden (or withheld) test dataset. Column labeled D indicates dataset used: T, for our separate evaluation set (see Sect. 2.4); H, for the unseen hidden GTA challenge test set.

| Method | D | MAE$_1$ | MAE$_2$ | MAE$_3$ | MAE$_4$ | MAE$_5$ | MAE$_6$ | MAE$_7$ | MAE$_8$ | MAE↓ | σ↓ | AAR↑ |
|---|---|---|---|---|---|---|---|---|---|---|---|---|
| ResNeXt (MSE) | T | 2.11 | 1.85 | 1.53 | 1.95 | 2.02 | 1.81 | 1.72 | 1.93 | 1.82 | 0.17 | 8.01 |
| ResNeXt (AAR) | T | 1.91 | 1.89 | 1.46 | 1.80 | 1.93 | 1.72 | 1.74 | 1.78 | **1.73** | 0.15 | **8.12** |
| ResNeXt (LDS MSE) | T | 1.92 | 2.11 | 1.61 | 1.97 | 2.04 | 1.84 | 1.85 | 1.88 | 1.88 | 0.15 | 7.98 |
| ResNeXt (LDS AAR) | T | 1.98 | 2.02 | 1.51 | 1.90 | 2.01 | 1.79 | 1.76 | 1.87 | 1.81 | 0.17 | 8.03 |
| ResNeXt + RF | T | 1.81 | 2.04 | 1.57 | 2.01 | 2.08 | 1.88 | 1.88 | 1.97 | 1.89 | 0.15 | 7.96 |
| *ResNeXt (MSE) + TLRF* | *T* | *1.89* | *1.92* | *1.57* | *2.01* | *2.08* | *1.87* | *1.87* | *1.92* | *1.88* | ***0.14*** | *7.98* |
| ResNeXt (AAR) + TLRF | T | 1.61 | 1.94 | 1.51 | 1.85 | 2.00 | 1.78 | 1.79 | 1.79 | 1.79 | 0.15 | 8.06 |
| ResNeXt (MSE) | H | 5.92 | 2.52 | 1.71 | 1.86 | 1.96 | 1.86 | 2.37 | 3.21 | 1.91 | 1.31 | 6.78 |
| ResNeXt (AAR) | H | 5.35 | 2.37 | 1.59 | 1.80 | 1.89 | 1.78 | 2.23 | 3.09 | **1.82** | 1.16 | **7.02** |
| ResNeXt (LDS MSE) | H | 5.87 | 2.63 | 1.86 | 2.03 | 2.02 | 1.85 | 2.07 | 2.60 | 2.00 | 1.26 | 6.74 |
| ResNeXt (LDS AAR) | H | 5.42 | 2.24 | 1.74 | 1.94 | 1.92 | 1.80 | 2.24 | 3.55 | 1.91 | 1.19 | 6.90 |
| ResNeXt + RF | H | 5.35 | 2.38 | 1.66 | 1.83 | 1.94 | 1.85 | 2.38 | 3.82 | 1.88 | 1.20 | 6.92 |
| *ResNeXt (MSE) + TLRF* | *H* | *4.84* | *2.45* | *1.87* | *2.05* | *2.10* | *1.94* | *2.44* | *3.67* | *2.05* | ***0.98*** | *6.97* |
| ResNeXt (AAR) + TLRF | H | 5.29 | 2.35 | 1.67 | 1.83 | 1.94 | 1.83 | 2.34 | 3.64 | 1.87 | 1.17 | 6.96 |

Additionally, using MSE loss, our TLRF method outperformed LDS. Although ResNeXt (AAR) without a TLRF module achieves a slightly better AAR score than ResNeXt+TLRF, it actually has a higher (worse) σ score, which indicates less generalizability across underrepresented age groups. Other methods of augmentation may help with enhancing the generalization capability of the architectures by pretraining with automatic face aging methods which provide a large amount of ground truth across age categories [37], selectively augmenting the lowest represented groups more, incorporating augmentation in feature space during the random forest training, etc.

## 4  Conclusions

Accurate unconstrained age estimation or categorization, using images or video, is useful in a number of applications including face recognition, age appropriate advertising and retail, venue access, detecting deep fakes, health and exercise monitoring, emotion analysis, forensics, privacy and security applications [38]. Our proposed two-stage supervised learning pipeline for facial age estimation using a ResNeXt deep learning stage followed by a two-layer random forest (TLRF) was able to estimate age with a mean absolute error of about 2 years across all eight age categories with a standard deviation of less than one year. Despite the significant class imbalance in the training data, we were able to achieve an AAR score of 6.97±0.98 (ResNeXt+TLRF) and 7.02±1.16 (ResNeXt) out of 10.0 on the hidden test data of the *VGG-Face2 MIVIA Age Dataset* as part of the Guess the Age (GTA) contest. The most challenging age categories are the youngest and oldest groups at the two extremes of the age distribution for which there was the least amount of training data (less than 1%). The experimental results demonstrate that a distribution adaptive (AAR) loss function is effective for training with class imbalance. Face alignment did not improve performance and test time data augmentation had limited benefit. For facial age estimation, an ensemble of weak learners trained on deep features is less sensitive to under-represented age groups compared to a purely deep neural regression model trained in an end-to-end fashion.

**Acknowledgments.** Research partially supported by U.S. National Science Foundation award 2114141, Army Research Laboratory cooperative agreement W911NF1820285 and Army Research Office DURIP W911NF-1910181. Any opinions, findings, and conclusions or recommendations expressed in this publication are those of the authors and do not necessarily reflect the views of the U.S. Government or agency.

# References

1. Carletti, V., Greco, A., Percannella, G., Vento, M.: Age from faces in the deep learning revolution. IEEE Trans. Pattern Anal. Mach. Intell. **42**(9), 2113–2132 (2020)
2. Greco, A.A., Vento, S.M., Vigilante, V.: Effective training of convolutional neural networks for age estimation based on knowledge distillation. Neural Comput. Appl. 1–16 (2021)
3. Abdolrashidi, A., Minaei, M., Azimi, E., Minaee, S.: Age and gender prediction from face images using attentional convolutional network. arXiv preprint arXiv:2010.03791 (2020)
4. Park, U., Tong, Y., Jain, A.K.: Age-invariant face recognition. IEEE Trans. Pattern Anal. Mach. Intell. **32**(5), 947–954 (2010)
5. Angulu, R., Tapamo, J.R., Adewumi, A.O.: Age estimation via face images: a survey. EURASIP J. Image Video Process. **2018**(1), 1–35 (2018)
6. Ranjan, R., et al.: Unconstrained age estimation with deep convolutional neural networks. In: Proceedings of the IEEE International Conference on Computer Vision Workshops, pp. 109–117 (2015)
7. Han, H., Otto, C., Liu, X., Jain, A.K.: Demographic estimation from face images: Human vs. machine performance. IEEE Trans. Pattern Anal. Mach. Intell. **37**(6), 1148–1161 (2015)
8. Ahadi, S., et al.: Personal aging markers and ageotypes revealed by deep longitudinal profiling. Nat. Med. **26**(1), 83–90 (2020)
9. Greco, A., Saggese, A., Vento, M., Vigilante, V.: A convolutional neural network for gender recognition optimizing the accuracy/speed tradeoff. IEEE Access **8**, 130771–130781 (2020)
10. Yolcu, G., Oztel, I., Kazan, S., Oz, C., Palaniappan, K., Lever, T.E., Bunyak, F.: Facial expression recognition for monitoring neurological disorders based on convolutional neural network. Multimed. Tools Appl. **78**(22), 31581–31603 (2019)
11. Wang, M., Deng, W.: Deep face recognition: a survey. Neurocomputing **429**, 215–244 (2021)
12. Lewis, J.K., et al.: Deepfake video detection based on spatial, spectral, and temporal inconsistencies using multimodal deep learning. In: IEEE Applied Imagery Pattern Recognition Workshop (AIPR), pp. 1–9 (2020)
13. Escalera, S., et al.: ChaLearn looking at people and faces of the world: face analysis workshop and challenge 2016. In: IEEE Conference on Computer Vision and Pattern Recognition Workshops, pp. 1–8 (2016)

14. Rothe, R., Timofte, R., Van Gool, L.: Deep expectation of real and apparent age from a single image without facial landmarks. Int. J. Comput. Vis. **126**(2), 144–157 (2018)
15. Chen, B.-C., Chen, C.-S., Hsu, W.H.: Cross-age reference coding for age-invariant face recognition and retrieval. In: European Conference on Computer Vision, pp. 768–783 (2014)
16. Zhang, Z., Song, Y., Qi, H.: Age progression/regression by conditional adversarial autoencoder. In: IEEE Conference on Computer Vision and Pattern Recognition pp. 5810–5818 (2017)
17. Lanitis, A., Taylor, C.J., Cootes, T.F.: Toward automatic simulation of aging effects on face images. IEEE Trans. Pattern Anal Mach. Intell. **24**(4), 442–455 (2002)
18. Rawls, A.W., Ricanek, K.: MORPH: Development and optimization of a longitudinal age progression database. In: European Workshop on Biometrics and Identity Management, pp. 17–24 (2009)
19. Guess The Age Contest 2021. https://gta2021.unisa.it/. Accessed 16 July 2021
20. Cao, Q., Shen, L., Xie, W., Parkhi, O.M., Zisserman, A.: VGGFace2: a dataset for recognising faces across pose and age. In: IEEE International Conference on Automatic Face & Gesture Recognition, pp. 67–74 (2018)
21. Gao, B.-B., Zhou, H.-Y., Wu, J., Geng, X.: Age estimation using expectation of label distribution learning. In: IJCAI, pp. 712–718 (2018)
22. Ponce-López, V., et al.: ChaLearn LAP 2016: first round challenge on first impressions - dataset and results. In: European Conference on Computer Vision Workshops, pp. 400–418 (2016)
23. Xie, S., Girshick, R., Dollár, P., Tu, Z., He, K.: Aggregated residual transformations for deep neural networks. In: IEEE Conference on Computer Vision and Pattern Recognition, pp. 1492–1500 (2017)
24. Bulat, A., Tzimiropoulos, G.: How far are we from solving the 2D & 3D face alignment problem? (and a dataset of 230,000 3D facial landmarks). In: IEEE International Conference on Computer Vision (2017)
25. He, K., Zhang, X., Ren, S., Sun, J.: Deep residual learning for image recognition. In: IEEE Conference on Computer Vision and Pattern Recognition, pp. 770–778 (2016)
26. Simonyan, K., Zisserman, A.: Very deep convolutional networks for large-scale image recognition. arXiv preprint arXiv:1409.1556 (2014)
27. Deng, J., Dong, W., Socher, R., Li, L.-J., Li, K., Fei-Fei, L.: ImageNet: a large-scale hierarchical image database. In: IEEE Conference on Computer Vision and Pattern Recognition, pp. 248–255 (2009)
28. Kingma, D.P., Ba, J.: Adam: a method for stochastic optimization. arXiv preprint arXiv:1412.6980 (2014)
29. Bengio, Y.: Practical recommendations for gradient-based training of deep architectures. In: Neural networks: Tricks of the Trade, pp. 437–478 (2012)
30. Loshchilov, I., Hutter, F.: SGDR: Stochastic gradient descent with warm restarts. arXiv preprint arXiv:1608.03983 (2016)
31. Xu, Z., Dai, A.M., Kemp, J., Metz, L.: Learning an adaptive learning rate schedule. arXiv preprint arXiv:1909.09712 (2019)
32. Schaul, T., Zhang, S., LeCun, Y.: No more pesky learning rates. In: International Conference on Machine Learning, pp. 343–351 (2013)
33. Zeiler, M.D.: ADADELTA: an adaptive learning rate method. arXiv preprint arXiv:1212.5701 (2012)
34. Girshick, R.: Fast R-CNN. In: IEEE International Conference on Computer Vision, pp. 1440–1448 (2015)

35. Philipp, G., Song, D., Carbonell, J.G.: The exploding gradient problem demystified-definition, prevalence, impact, origin, tradeoffs, and solutions. arXiv preprint arXiv:1712.05577 (2017)
36. Yang, Y., Zha, K., Chen, Y.-C., Wang, H., Katabi, D.: Delving into deep imbalanced regression. arXiv preprint arXiv:2102.09554 (2021)
37. Duong, C.N., et al.: Automatic face aging in videos via deep reinforcement learning. In: IEEE Conference on Computer Vision and Pattern Recognition, pp. 10013–10022 (2019)
38. Morris, J., Newman, S., Palaniappan, K., Fan, J., Lin, D.: Do you know you are tracked by photos that you didn't take: Location-aware multi-party image privacy protection. arXiv preprint arXiv:2103.10851 (2021)

# Age-Style and Alignment Augmentation for Facial Age Estimation

Yu-Hong Lin[1(✉)], Chia-Hao Tang[1], Zhi-Ting Chen[1], Gee-Sern Jison Hsu[1], Md Shopon[2], and Marina Gavrilova[2]

[1] National Taiwan University of Science and Technology, Taipei 10607, Taiwan
m10903430@mail.ntust.edu.tw
[2] University of Calgary, Calgary, AB T2N 1N4, Canada

**Abstract.** Facial age is an important soft biometric trait for better identification of a human subject. The development of a facial age estimation system requires a large collection of age-labeled data. However, the
imbalanced data distribution across age poses a major challenge to making a decent model to describe the variation of facial appearance caused
by age. The cross-age data imbalance can be observed in common facial
age datasets, for example, the MORPH [8], FG-NET [7] and the MIVIA
dataset [3] considered in the GTA Contest. It can be often seen that
insufficient data are provided for younger ages and senior ages, and the
insufficiency becomes worsened as the age moves close to both ends. To
deal with the data imbalance issues, many approaches implement various data augmentation schemes. In our approach, we propose a data
augmentation scheme built upon the Age-Style GAN (ASGAN), which
we propose for facial age regression and progression. In addition to the
ASGAN-based data augmentation, we leverage the mean-variance loss to
improve the age classification accuracy, and exploit face alignment as an
auxiliary scheme to augment the whole dataset with an aligned subset.
We conducted extensive experiments on the MIVIA dataset for verifying
the performance of our approach.

**Keywords:** Age estimation · Generative adversarial network · Facial
progression/rejuvenation

## 1 Introduction

Facial age estimation is an interesting topic in face analysis. It is considered
an important soft biometrics that helps to identify a core attribute of a face.
Due to the great success of deep learning approaches, a remarkable progress has
been made over recent years. However, the performances of most approaches are
affected by the cross-age data imbalance issues, which can be easily observed in
common benchmark datasets, for example, the MORPH [8], FG-NET [7] and the
MIVIA dataset [3] considered in the GTA Contest. The cross-age data number
distribution of the MIVIA is shown in Fig. 1. Relatively sufficient data are offered

© Springer Nature Switzerland AG 2021
N. Tsapatsoulis et al. (Eds.): CAIP 2021, LNCS 13053, pp. 297–307, 2021.
https://doi.org/10.1007/978-3-030-89131-2_27

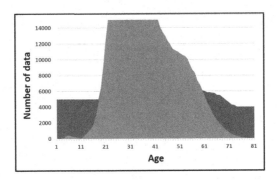

**Fig. 1.** The data distribution for age between 1 and 81 in the MIVIA dataset [3]. The orange part shows the original data distribution, and the blue parts show the ASGAN-based augmented data. (Color figure online)

for the age between 23 to 53; but the number of data drops substantially for age less than 18 and older than 58. A model developed upon this imbalanced data often leads to biased estimation. To address the data imbalance issue and design an age estimation solution, we propose a framework composed of the following three major modules: 1) the Age-Style Generative Adversarial Network (ASGAN) for the generation of the aged/rejuvenated face images to handle the data insufficiency at desired age intervals; 2) the Face Alignment Network (FAN) for the alignment of the faces to enhance the performance; and 3) the Age Estimator for learning from the augmented dataset to accurately estimate the age of a given face.

The proposed ASGAN (Age-Style GAN) is composed of an encoder-decoder generator and discriminators. The generator is trained to make the generated face appear with the required age traits and preserve the identity as of the input. Discriminators are trained to supervise the generation of the output faces and explores an age-level loss to enhance learning.

The Face Alignment Network (FAN) [1] is an off-the-shelf network constructed by stacking four HourGlass (HG) networks in which all bottleneck blocks were replaced by a set of hierarchical, parallel and multiscale blocks. We train the FAN on the 300W-LP dataset [11] to ensure the accuracy of the facial landmark localization. The age estimator is built on a ResNet-50 [4] and trained with the mean-variance loss and the cross-entropy loss to facilitate the age estimation.

Many approaches have been proposed in recent years for facial age estimation. The multi-stage features constraint learning explores a network structure designed to improve the discrimination between different age features [9]. Experiments on the CLAP dataset [2] demonstrate a impressive performance. Pan et al. [6] propose the mean-variance loss in their approach, leading to compelling and satisfying results on the MORPH Album II [8], FG-NET [7] and CLAP datasets.

Zeng et al. [10] propose a age label encoding method that simultaneously encodes both the ordinal information and the correlation between adjacent ages,

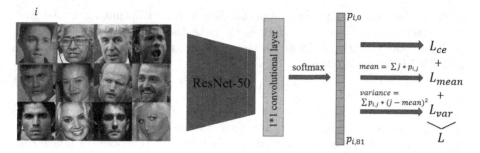

**Fig. 2.** The architecture of the facial age estimator with 3 losses considered at training, i.e., the cross-entropy loss $L_{ce}$, the mean loss $L_{mean}$ and the variance loss $L_{var}$.

and evaluate on the MORPH Album II, and CLAP databases. However, the aforementioned data imbalanced issues have not received sufficient attention. Our approach includes two data augmentation modules. One is developed to generate faces with appearance within a desired age boundaries so that we can augment the age segments of insufficient data. The other is made to align the faces so that the age-related facial features can be better learned.

The contributions of this work can be summarized as follows:

- A novel data augmentation approach is proposed for handling the common imbalanced facial age data issues.
- A facial age estimator network is verified on the MIVIA benchmark dataset with a competitive performance.

In the following, we first present our approach in Sect. 2, then the experimental setups in the Sect. 3, then the qualitatively and quantitative results in the Sect. 4, and then a conclusion to this study in Sect. 5.

## 2  Proposed Approach

Our approach has three modules, namely the facial age estimator network, the facial age data generator and the face alignment network. We first introduce the architecture and settings of the facial age estimator network in Sect. 2.1, followed by the age data generator made by the Age-Style GAN in Sect. 2.2, and then the face alignment network in Sect. 2.3.

### 2.1  Facial Age Estimator

The configuration of our facial age estimator network is shown in Fig. 2. We employ the ResNet-50 [4] as our backbone model, and utilize the mean-variance loss [6] and the cross-entropy loss as the overall objective function. The ResNet-50 network consists of 5 stages each with a convolution and identity block. We replace the fully connected layer to a 1 × 1 convolution layer with a softmax function which gives 81 predicated probability to the 81 output ages. The goal of this facial age estimator network is to make the predicted age as close as possible to the target age. To attain this goal, we consider the minimization of the following composite losses:

$$L = L_{ce} + \lambda_1 L_{mean} + \lambda_2 L_{var} \tag{1}$$

where $L_{ce}$ the cross-entropy loss, the combination of $L_{mean}$ and $L_{var}$ represents the mean-variance loss, and $\lambda_1$, $\lambda_2$ are the weighting of the loss function. During training, given a face $I$ as the input, the ResNet-50 model encodes the image $I$ to the predicted probability $p_{i,j}$, and we employ cross entropy loss $L_{ce}$ to measure the cross entropy between the ground truth $y$ and the prediction $p$

$$L_{ce} = \frac{1}{N} \sum_{i=1}^{N} -log p_{i,y_i} \tag{2}$$

where $N$ is the batch size, the subscript $i$ denotes the $i-th$ sample in the batch data, $y_i$ denotes the corresponding age label, and $p_{i,y_i}$ denotes the probability that sample $i$ belongs to the ground truth $y_i$. The mean loss $L_{mean}$ aims to penalize the difference between the mean of an estimated age distribution $m$ and the ground-truth age $y$. As such, it can be formulated as:

$$m_i = \sum_{j=1}^{K} j * p_{i,j} \tag{3}$$

$$L_{mean} = \frac{1}{2N} \sum_{1}^{N} (m_i - y_i)^2 \tag{4}$$

where $m_i$ is the mean of estimated age distribution, $j$ denotes the one-hot age label, and $p_{i,j}$ denotes the probability that sample $i$ belongs to the age class $j$ in the batch data. The variance loss $L_{var}$ is used to penalize the dispersion of an estimated age distribution, which can be computed as follows:

$$v_i = \sum_{j=1}^{K} p_{i,j} * (j - m_i)^2 \tag{5}$$

$$L_{var} = \frac{1}{N} \sum_{i=1}^{N} v_i \tag{6}$$

where $v_i$ is the variance of the estimated age distribution. Such a variance loss requires that an estimated distribution should be concentrated at a small range of the mean. This is helpful to obtain an accurate age estimation with a small confidence interval but a high confidence.

The combination of the cross-entropy loss and the mean-variance loss is designed to diminish the large fluctuations observed at early stage of training when using the mean-variance loss alone. Due to better training stability, we found that such a combination of losses also improves training convergence and efficiency.

## 2.2 Age Transfer Generative Adversarial Network

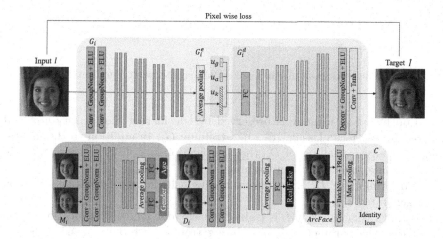

**Fig. 3.** The network structure of the Age-Style GAN.

The Age-Style GAN (ASGAN) is configured in Fig. 3. It is composed of $n$ triple networks denoted as $[T_0, T_1, ..., T_{n-1}]$ and a face feature extractor $C$. Each triple network $T_i$ consists of a generator $G_i$, a discriminator $D_i$ and a multitask classifier $M_i$, i.e., $T_i = [G_i, D_i, M_i]$. The face feature extractor $C$ warrants the identity consistency between the input and the generated output of $G_i$. The pixel-wise loss is made to maintain the similarity between the input and the generated output.

During training, give a face image $I$ as input and a target age $a_t$, the piecewise generator $G$ generates an output image $\hat{I} = G(I)$ that preserves the identity of $I$ and shows the age traits of the target age $a_t$. The $n$ triple networks $[T_i]_{i=0}^{n-1}$ are meant to characterize the facial appearance transformation across the $n+1$ age groups $[A_0, A_1, ..., A_n]$, where $A_i$ is a set of faces within a specific age span, and the ages contained in $A_i$ increase with $i$. The learning of the framework involves the following states and settings:

1. The piecewise generator $G$ is structured as a series of $n$ successive generators, i.e., $G = [G_0, G_1, ..., G_{n-1}]$. $G_i$ is trained for transforming between the age groups $A_i$ and $A_{i+1}$. Each $G_i$ consists of an encoder $G_i^e$ and a decoder $G_i^d$. Given an image $I_k$, the encoder $G_i^e$ is trained to encode $I_k$ into a latent vector $u_k = G_i^e(I_k)$, which is made disentangled of the age and gender through training. $u_k$ will be concatenated with an age code $u_a$ and a gender code $u_g$ to form $v_k = [u_k, u_a, u_g]$. The decoder $G_i^d$ is trained to decode $v_k$ to an image $\hat{x}_k = G_i^d(v_k)$ with the same identity as of $I_k$ and at the target age defined by the age code $u_a$. $u_a \in \mathbb{R}^2$ is meant to transform the age of $\hat{x}_k = G_i(I_k)$ between $A_i$ and $A_{i+1}$. The gender code $u_g$ keeps the gender consistency between input

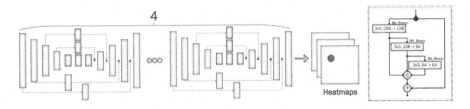

**Fig. 4.** The network structure of Face Alignment Network (duplicated from [1])

and output. The identity is preserved by considering the identity loss evaluated by the face classifier $C$ when training $G_i$. In addition to the identity loss, the adversarial loss of $D_i$, the classification loss of $M_i$ and the pixel-wise loss are all considered when training $G_i$.

2. The discriminator $D_i$ is trained to distinguish the real face images $I_k$ from the generated $\hat{I}_k$.
3. The multitask classifier $M_i$ is trained for age and gender classification. When updating the parameters in $M_i$ during training, we only consider the real data. When updating $G_i$ during training, we consider the classification loss computed from both the real and generated data.
4. The face feature extractor $C$ is formed by the feature embedding layers of a pretrained model which delivers a state-of-the-art performance for face verification. The feature loss between $I_k$ and $\hat{I}_k$ evaluated by $C$ is considered when training $G_i$.
5. The pixel-wise loss computes the pixel-to-pixel loss of the input $I_k$ and the output $\hat{I}_k$ images, the purpose is to preserve similarity between the input and output some variables, *e.g.*, the pose and illumination condition can be partially kept.

In summary, our framework composed from two parts, the loss function network $C$, and the successive generation networks $[T_i]_i$. The loss function network is made by the feature embedding layers of the networks trained for face recognition, and it is *not* updated during training, and used purely as a loss function that computes the difference between the input image $I$ and the generated image $\hat{I}$. The successive generation networks are designed to capture the successive transformation of the facial appearance across different age periods. The objective considered when training the successive generation networks includes the losses evaluated by the loss function networks.

### 2.3 Face Alignment Network

The network structure of the Face Alignment Network (FAN) is shown in Fig. 4. It is constructed on a stack of four HourGlass (HG) networks [5] to perform successive pooling and upsampling in order to improve the landmark localization. Instead of using the bottleneck block as the main building block for the HG (as in [5]), the FAN employs the residual block [4] for better accuracy.

The FAN is trained on the 300W-LP [11] to localize the 2D and 3D facial landmarks, respectively. We use the pre-trained FAN model from the official GitHub and obtain the 2D facial landmarks from each input image. The obtained 2D facial landmarks include sixty-eight points, and we utilize the midpoints of eyes and the right and left corners of the mouth for face alignment. The aligned face is used as the augmented data in our age estimator.

## 3  Experimental Setups

**Dataset.** The MIVIA Age Dataset [3] and the FFHQ dataset are considered in our experiments. The MIVIA Age Dataset is the training/validation set of the age estimator, which contains 575,073 images of around 9,000 individuals with ages from 1 to 81 years. We divided the dataset into eighty-one age groups with one-age interval, and employed 90% face images in each age group as the training data, and the remaining 10% as the validation data. The FFHQ dataset is the training set of the Age-Style GAN, which includes high-resolution (1024 × 1024) face images across age and gender.

**Pre-processing.** We used the Face Alignment Network [1] for the facial landmark detection. All faces were aligned to the eyes, and normalized in the fixed distance between the mouth and the center of both eyes. We have two kinds of normalized strategies: 1) For the age estimator, each image is normalized to 256 × 256 with fixed eye-mouth distance 86 pixels. 2) For Age-Style GAN, the normalized input image is 1024 × 1024 with fixed eye-mouth distance 334 pixels. Note that we use both aligned data and non-aligned data as training data. During training, the input image randomly crop to 0.875x in scale.

**Age Augmentation.** We used the Age-Style GAN to generate the augmented aged/rejuvenated images to balance the age distribution. We generated the augmented data into 4 ages groups, [0, 10], [11, 20], [61, 70], and [71]. The generated distribution is shown in Fig. 1, and the generated images can be visualized in Fig. 5. To be more precise, we randomly select 100,000 pictures of 20–30 years old to generate images under 20 years old and randomly select 50,000 of 40–50 years old to generate images over 50 years old and under 75 years old. The amounts of the generated images are listed as follows: 48,000 images belong to [0, 10], 26,981 images belong to [11, 20], 27,302 images belong to [61, 70], and 42,464 images belong to [71]. Due to the fact that the young and old faces are imbalanced, we only generate the aged/rejuvenated data which the age is less than 20 years old and greater than 61 years old.

**Training Settings.** The training was proceeded via the SGD optimizer with momentum 0.9, initial learning rate 0.0001, and batch size 64. We empirically set $\lambda_1 = 0.05$ and $\lambda_2 = 0.002$. For Age-Style GAN, we used Adam optimizer to train $G$ and $D$ at learning rate $2 * 10^{-4}$ and the batch size is 8. The implementation was on the Pytorch using a NVIDIA RTX3090 GPU with 24G memory.

## 3.1  Evaluation Metrics

We evaluate the performance with index called Age Accuracy and Regularity (AAR) which is specified in this competition. For AAR, we firstly compute mean absolute error (MAE), which is defined as the mean absolute error between the estimated age and ground-truth age. As such, the MAE can be calculated as follows:

$$MAE = \sum_{i=1}^{K} \frac{|p_i - y_i|}{K} \tag{7}$$

where $p_i$ is the estimated age and $y_i$ is ground-truth for $i - th$ sample, and $K$ is the number of samples in the test. Secondly, the regularity is calculated over the different age groups to measure the average standard deviation $\sigma$:

$$\sigma = \sqrt{\frac{\sum_{k=1}^{8}(MAE^k - MAE)^2}{8}} \tag{8}$$

where $MAE^k$ is computed over the samples whose real age is in the specified age group, $j \in \{0, 1, 2, \ldots 8\}$ denotes the different age group. We divide the data into 8 groups from 0 to 80 years old with 10 age intervals, which can be listed as follows: [1, 10], [11, 20], [21, 30], [31,40], [41, 50], [51,60], [61, 70], [70+]. The final score is the Age Accuracy and Regularity (AAR) computed as:

$$AAR = max(7 - MAE) + max(3 - \sigma) \tag{9}$$

The AAR index can assume values between 0 and 10, weighting 70% the contribution of MAE (accuracy) and 30% the contribution of $\sigma$ (regularity). A perfect method obtaining $MAE = 0$ and $\sigma = 0$ will achieve $AAR = 10$.

## 4  Experiments for Performance Evaluation

In this section, we conducted experiments to verify the effectiveness of data augmentation by using aligned data and age data. We show several augmented samples in Fig. 5, which give an insight of the comparison between the original images and augmented images. The first column from the left shows the original images, the second column from the left shows the aligned data made by FAN [1], column 3 to 6 visualize the aged/rejuvenated images made by Age-Style GAN. The age-progressed/regressive images not only shows the high-fidelity facial details, but also preserve the intrinsic identity information.

In the following, we have four training set setups: 1) ALI, which represents the aligned data only, 2) N-ALI, which represents the non-aligned data only, 3) ALI+N-ALI, which represents the combination of the aligned and the non-aligned data, 4) ALL, which represents the combination of the aligned, the non-aligned data and the age-augmented data.

The performances evaluated by AAR protocol are listed in Table 1, the ALI+N-ALI outperforms N-ALI and ALI settings, and the ALL setting shows

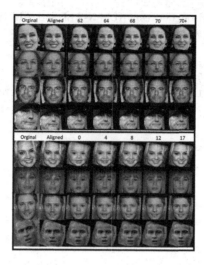

**Fig. 5.** The visualized results of the aligned images, and the age transform data made by Age-Style GAN.

**Table 1.** Comparison using different training data on AAR. The best two are ALI+N-ALI and ALL. Through our augmentation, we have a good performance in AAR results.

| Settings | AAR |
|---|---|
| N-ALI | **7.49** |
| ALI | **7.50** |
| ALI+N-ALI | **7.62** |
| ALL | **7.96** |

the best results. This indicates that the augmentations with both aligned and GAN-generated images improve the age estimation capability in our age estimator. Especially the age-augmented data, which shows more than 0.07 improvement of the age estimation rate.

The MAE performances are shown in Table 2, where the superscripts 1–8 in the top row refer to the eight age groups specified by the competition protocol. As expected, the improvements made by age augmented are clearly evident. The performances on $MAE^1, MAE^2, MAE^7$ and $MAE^8$ show 0.11 to 0.63 improvements, which again indicate the effectiveness of the age-augmented data.

We also show the final grade we obtained from Guess The Age Contest in Table 3, the result shows that we have great performance in the younger age group and elder age group.

**Table 2.** MAE comparison between ALI+N-ALI and ALL in different age group. $MAE^1$, $MAE^2$, $MAE^7$, and $MAE^8$ shows their progress after the age data augmentation

| Data | $MAE^1$ | $MAE^2$ | $MAE^3$ | $MAE^4$ | $MAE^5$ | $MAE^6$ | $MAE^7$ | $MAE^8$ |
|---|---|---|---|---|---|---|---|---|
| ALI+N-ALI | 4.17 | 1.96 | 1.34 | 2.0 | 1.92 | 1.74 | 2.20 | 3.80 |
| ALL | 3.54 | 1.87 | 1.35 | 2.0 | 1.92 | 1.75 | 2.06 | 3.27 |

**Table 3.** Result we obtained for the Guess the Age contest.

| $MAE$ | $MAE^1$ | $MAE^2$ | $MAE^3$ | $MAE^4$ | $MAE^5$ | $MAE^6$ | $MAE^7$ | $MAE^8$ | AAR |
|---|---|---|---|---|---|---|---|---|---|
| 1.84 | 3.72 | 2.08 | 1.6 | 1.83 | 1.98 | 1.9 | 2.18 | 2.4 | 7.55 |

## 5   Conclusion

We propose an approach for the estimation of facial age. The backbone of our approach is a ResNet [4] with the objective to minimize the mean-variance loss and cross-entropy loss. We explore the Age-Style GAN (ASGAN) to generate age-progressed and regressed images for a given face so that the data imbalance issue can be handled. We apply the Face Alignment Network (FAN) [1] to generate an additional set of the aligned data, and verify the advantages of using this additional aligned data with the original data for training. Experiments show that the performance of our approach can be considerably improved as all these ingredients work together.

## References

1. Bulat, A., Tzimiropoulos, G.: How far are we from solving the 2D & 3D face alignment problem? (and a dataset of 230,000 3D facial landmarks). In: ICCV (2017)
2. Escalera, S., et al.: ChaLearn looking at people and faces of the world: face analysis workshop and challenge 2016. In: CVPR Workshops (2016)
3. Greco, A., Saggese, A., Vento, M., Vigilante, V.: Effective training of convolutional neural networks for age estimation based on knowledge distillation. Neural Comput. Appl. (2021)
4. He, K., Zhang, X., Ren, S., Sun, J.: Deep residual learning for image recognition. In: CVPR (2016)
5. Newell, A., Yang, K., Deng, J.: Stacked hourglass networks for human pose estimation. In: Leibe, B., Matas, J., Sebe, N., Welling, M. (eds.) ECCV 2016. LNCS, vol. 9912, pp. 483–499. Springer, Cham (2016). https://doi.org/10.1007/978-3-319-46484-8_29
6. Pan, H., Han, H., Shan, S., Chen, X.: Mean-variance loss for deep age estimation from a face. In: CVPR (2018)
7. Panis, G., Lanitis, A., Tsapatsoulis, N., Cootes, T.F.: Overview of research on facial ageing using the FG-NET ageing database. IET Biom. (2016)

8. Ricanek, K., Tesafaye, T.: MORPH: a longitudinal image database of normal adult age-progression. In: 7th International Conference on Automatic Face and Gesture Recognition (FGR06) (2006)
9. Xia, M., Zhang, X., Weng, L., Xu, Y., et al.: Multi-stage feature constraints learning for age estimation. TIFS (2020)
10. Zeng, X., Huang, J., Ding, C.: Soft-ranking label encoding for robust facial age estimation. IEEE Access (2020)
11. Zhu, X., Lei, Z., Liu, X., Shi, H., Li, S.Z.: Face alignment across large poses: a 3D solution. In: CVPR (2016)

# LAE : Long-Tailed Age Estimation

Zenghao Bao[1,2], Zichang Tan[4,5], Yu Zhu[4,5], Jun Wan[1,2(✉)], Xibo Ma[1,2],
Zhen Lei[1,2,3], and Guodong Guo[4,5]

[1] CBSR&NLPR, Institute of Automation, Chinese Academy of Sciences,
Beijing, China
{baozenghao2020,jun.wan}@ia.ac.cn
[2] School of Artificial Intelligence, University of Chinese Academy of Sciences,
Beijing, China
{xibo.ma,zlei}@nlpr.ia.ac.cn
[3] Centre for Artificial Intelligence and Robotics, Hong Kong Institute of Science
and Innovation, Chinese Academy of Sciences, Beijing, China
[4] Institute of Deep Learning, Baidu Research, Beijing, China
[5] National Engineering Laboratory for Deep Learning Technology and Application,
Beijing, China
{tanzichang,zhuyu05,guoguodong01}@baidu.com

**Abstract.** Facial age estimation is an important yet very challenging
problem in computer vision. To improve the performance of facial age
estimation, we first formulate a simple standard baseline and build a
much strong one by collecting the tricks in pre-training, data augmentation, model architecture, and so on. Compared with the standard baseline, the proposed one significantly decreases the estimation errors. Moreover, long-tailed recognition has been an important topic in facial age
datasets, where the samples often lack on the elderly and children. To
train a balanced age estimator, we propose a two-stage training method
named Long-tailed Age Estimation (LAE), which decouples the learning
procedure into representation learning and classification. The effectiveness of our approach has been demonstrated on the dataset provided by
organizers of Guess The Age Contest 2021.

**Keywords:** Deep learning · Age estimation · Long-tailed recognition

## 1 Introduction

As one of the most concerning topics in facial analysis, age estimation remains
challenging for the uncontrolled nature of the aging process, a significant variance
among faces in the same age range, and a high dependency of aging traits on
a person. Since age estimation from face images is an inevitable problem in
several real applications, enhancing age estimation performance has also become
an urgent problem to be solved. In recent years, deep learning methods [5,10,
18,19,21], which automatically learn the effective image representations, have
gained many successes in facial age estimation.

---

Z. Bao and Z. Tan—Co-First Author.

However, the most promising methods [2, 10–12, 18, 19] use ensembles of DCNNs, making the obtained classifier not usable in real applications. These methods usually require prohibitive computational resources, complex training procedures caused by the plurality of neural networks, and substantial training sets, which are not simply collectible.

Motivated by this concern, we build a strong baseline based on a single neural network by collecting some efficient tricks in pre-training, model architecture, data augmentation, and so on. The strong baseline achieves impressive performance compared to the standard baseline. Nevertheless, the resulting estimator is still not a balance age estimator and usually shows poor performance in classes with fewer samples.

Unfortunately, existing methods for age estimation [5, 10, 21] still lack in long-tailed scenarios. The long-tail distribution of the visual world poses great challenges for deep learning-based classification models on how to handle the data imbalance problem. Inspired by the existing work [9], we decouple the learning procedure into representation learning and classification to train a balanced estimator.

In the representation learning stage, we obtain a robust feature extractor to distinguish different ages. Furthermore, in the classification stage, we freeze the model except for the FC layer and train the model on balanced MIVIA [6] dataset obtained by class-balanced sampling [15]. Moreover, we innovatively introduce Mean Square Error (MSE) loss into this stage for further narrowing down the standard deviation of different age groups. By applying this, we obtain a model that performs well at all ages.

To summarize, the main contributions are listed as follows:

– We collect some effective training tricks to build a strong baseline based on a single neural network, which effectively enhances age estimation performance.
– We propose a novel LAE method to deal with the age estimation in long-tailed scenarios. The resulting estimator performs well at all ages.
– Extensive experiments on MIVIA indicate the effectiveness of LAE.

## 2  Proposed Method

### 2.1  Overview

In our implementation, we break the neural network into two components, a feature extractor $\theta$ and a classifier $\psi$. The classifier consists of a linear layer and a softmax layer. Before explaining the proposed method in detail, we first define the key symbols. Assume we have an age dataset $D$. The $i$th sample in the $D$ is denoted by $(x_i, y_i, z_i)$, where $x_i$ denote the input image, $y_i$ denote the age label, and $z_i$ denote the label distribution. The label distribution of the sample is based on a typical Gaussian distribution, $i.e.$, $z_i^k = \frac{1}{\sqrt{2\pi}\sigma}exp(-\frac{(k-y_i)^2}{2\sigma^2})$ where $k \in [0, ..., 100]$ and standard deviation $\sigma$ is set to 1.

## 2.2    Standard Baseline

In this subsection, we provide a standard baseline used for comparison. During the training stage, the pipeline includes the following steps:

1. We initialize the ResNet18 [8] with pre-trained parameters on ImageNet [4] and change the dimension of the fully connected layer to K. And K is set to 101 in our experiments.
2. We resize each image into 224 × 224 pixels and each image is flipped horizontally with 0.5 probability.
3. Each image is decoded into 32-bit floating point raw pixel values in [0, 1]. Then we normalize RGB channels by subtracting 0.485, 0.456, 0.406 and dividing by 0.229, 0.224, 0.225, respectively.
4. Following the work [5], the network is trained with a KL divergence and $\ell_1$ loss. KL divergence is calculated by measuring the distance between label distribution $z_i$ and predicted age distribution $\hat{z}_i$, and $\ell_1$ loss aims to narrow the distance between the predicted age $\hat{y}_i$ and the ground truth label $y_i$. Specifically, the predicted age $\hat{y}_i$ is obtained by using an expectation regression on the softmax outputs.
5. SGD is adopted to optimize the model. The initial learning rate is set to be 0.005 and is decreased by 0.1 at the $20th$, $40th$, and $60th$ epoch. Totally there are 75 epochs.

## 2.3    Training Tricks

In this subsection, we introduce some effective tricks for training. After expanding all the tricks, the standard baseline becomes a strong baseline.

*Model Architecture:* Compared to the previous models, EfficientNetV2 [17] has a faster training speed and better parameter efficiency. In our submission, we use the EfficientNetV2-M as the backbone of the feature extractor.

*Pre-training:* Pre-training has a significant impact on the performance of an age estimator. Before training the network on age datasets, we pretrain the model on MS-celeb-1M [7], with only using identity labels. Following the work [20], which AM-softmax loss is employed as the loss function. In this way, a large number of face images are employed to enhance the network's discriminating ability with obtaining a good initialization.

*Batch Size:* The batch size also shows its impact on performance during training. Compared to 16, 64, and 128, keep 32 samples in one GPU shows the best performance. So the default batch size for us is 256 since we use 8 GPUs for training.

*Onecycle Scheduler:* Existing methods [5,18] for age estimation usually require many epochs to convergence, which undoubtedly brings a more significant time cost and occupation of computing resources. The existence of Onecycle [16] can make networks be trained much faster than before. In our case, it reduces the number of training epochs from the original 75 to 24.

*Data Augmentation:* As a data-space solution to the problem of limited data, data augmentation is capable of enhancing the size and quality of training datasets to avoid overfitting and make the resulting model more generalization. In our case, we applied data augmentation as follows: first, a random patch of the images is selected and resized to 224 × 224 with a random horizontal flip, followed by a color jitter, consisting of a random sequence of brightness, contrast, saturation, hue adjustments. Finally, RandAugment [3] is applied, and we set N = 2 and M = 9, where N denotes the number of transformations to apply, and M denotes the magnitude of the applied transformations.

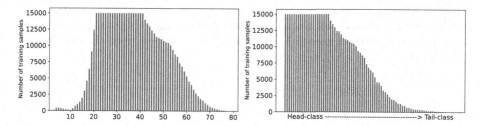

**Fig. 1.** The distribution of the dataset samples over the age is depicted on the left. The long-tailed distribution of the MIVIA is depicted on the right, sorted by the number of samples in class. Head-class denotes high-frequency class, and tail-class denotes low-frequency class. In practice, the number of samples per class generally decreases from head to tail classes.

## 2.4   Long-Tailed Age Estimation

The long-tail distribution of the visual world poses great challenges for deep learning-based classification models on how to handle the data imbalance problem [9,13]. As the result, the resulting model usually shows poor performance in classes with fewer samples. This phenomenon is reflected in most of the age datasets. As shown in Fig. 1, the age distribution of the MIVIA is imbalanced, in line with the premise of long-tailed recognition. Inspired by related research in the field of long-tailed recognition [9], we decouple the learning procedure into representation learning and classification to train a relatively balanced classifier, which performs well at all ages.

*Representation Learning Stage:* In this stage, we follow the pipeline of strong baseline for training a robust feature extractor to distinguish different ages. To this end, we finetune the model on the MIVIA training set. By feeding the feature maps into the classifier, we obtain the prediction distribution $\hat{z}_i^k$, which indicates the probability of classifying $x_i$ to age $k$. Then, we use KL divergence to measure the label distribution loss $L_{ld}$ between ground-truth label distribution $z_i^k = \frac{1}{\sqrt{2\pi}\sigma}exp(-\frac{(k-y_i)^2}{2\sigma^2})$ and the prediction distribution $\hat{z}_i^k$ [5]:

$$L_{ld} = \sum_{k=1}^{K} z_i^k log \frac{z_i^k}{\hat{z}_i^k} \qquad (1)$$

The predicted age $\hat{y}_i$ is obtained by using a expectation regression[14] on the output distribution. It can be denoted as $\hat{y}_i = \sum_{k=1}^{K} k\hat{z}_i^k$. Moreover, we employ a loss $L_{er}$ to further narrowing the distance between the predicted age label and the ground-truth label :

$$L_{er} = |y_i - \sum_{k=1}^{K} k\hat{z}_i^k| \qquad (2)$$

where $|\cdot|$ denotes $\ell_1$ loss.

Finally, we integrate all the above loss functions and train them simultaneously. Referring to the losses in Eq. 1, 2 as $L_{ld}, L_{er}$, respectively, then overall we optimize the feature extractor with $L_{fe}$:

$$L_{fe} = L_{ld} + \lambda L_{er} \qquad (3)$$

where $\lambda$ denotes the weight of $L_{er}$.

*Classification Stage:* To retrain the classifier without changing the parameters of the feature extractor, we freeze the model except for the FC layer and train on balanced MIVIA obtained by class-balanced sampling, which means each class has an equal probability of being selected. One can see this as a two-stage sampling strategy, where a class is first selected uniformly from the set of classes, and then an instance from that class is subsequently uniformly sampled [15].

Moreover, we innovatively introduce MSE loss into this stage for further narrowing down the standard deviation of different age groups. To this end, we optimize the classifier with $L_{cl}$:

$$L_{cl} = L_{ld} + (L_{er} - mae)^2 \qquad (4)$$

where *mae* denotes the mean absolute error over the validation set.

$$mae = \sum_{i=1}^{M} \frac{|y_i - \hat{y}_i|}{M} \qquad (5)$$

where $M$ is the total number of validating images, $y_i$ and $\hat{y}_i$ denote the ground-truth age and the predicted age, respectively. It is worth noting that the *mae* here results from the representation learning stage on the validation set.

## 3   Experiments

In this section, we first introduce the datasets and the evaluation metrics from our experiments. Then we provide implementation details for our LAE method, describe experimental setups, and discuss results.

## 3.1 Dataset

The MIVIA Age Dataset is composed of 575,073 images of more than 9,000 identities. Those images have been extracted from the VGGFace2 [1] dataset and annotated with age by means of a knowledge distillation technique, making the dataset very heterogeneous in terms of face size, illumination conditions, facial pose, gender, and ethnicity.

## 3.2 Metric

An index called Age Accuracy and Regularity (AAR) is introduced for taking into account accuracy and regularity:

$$AAR = max(0; 7 - MAE) + max(0; 3 - \sigma) \tag{6}$$

where MAE denotes the mean absolute error on the entire test set, and $\sigma$ is obtained by:

$$\sigma = \sqrt{\frac{\sum_{j=1}^{8}(MAE^j - MAE)^2}{8}} \tag{7}$$

where $MAE^j$ denotes the mae and is computed over the samples whose real age is in age group $j$. The details of age group are shown as below (Table 1).

Table 1. The details of the eight age groups.

| $MAE^1$ | $MAE^2$ | $MAE^3$ | $MAE^4$ | $MAE^5$ | $MAE^6$ | $MAE^7$ | $MAE^8$ |
|---------|---------|---------|---------|---------|---------|---------|---------|
| 1–10    | 11–20   | 21–30   | 31–40   | 41–50   | 51–60   | 61–70   | 71–81   |

## 3.3 Implementation Details

We use an SGD optimizer with a MultiStepLR scheduler over 18 epochs in the pre-training stage, with the milestones of [7, 14, 16]. Moreover, we use an SGD optimizer with a OneCycle schedule over 24 epochs and 8 epochs in the representation and classification stage. We set the base learning rate to 0.005 and 0.001, scaled linearly with the batch size (LearningRate = base × BatchSize/256). In addition, we use a global weight decay parameter of 5e−4. The default batch size is set to 256. According to the work [22], the images are aligned with five landmarks (including two eyes, nose tip, and two mouth corners). For a fair comparison, we fix the $\lambda = 1$ during all experiments.

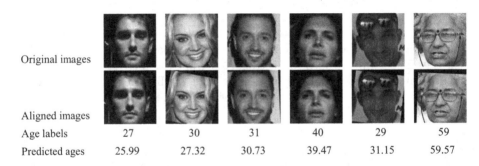

Original images

Aligned images

| Age labels | 27 | 30 | 31 | 40 | 29 | 59 |
| Predicted ages | 25.99 | 27.32 | 30.73 | 39.47 | 31.15 | 59.57 |

**Fig. 2.** Examples of apparent age estimation using LAE on MIVIA testing images.

### 3.4 Experimental Results

Since the test set is not available during the competition, we randomly divide the MIVIA into a training set and a validation set at a ratio of 4:1 to validate the effectiveness of the proposed methods. The result is shown as below. The standard baseline achieves 1.97 on MAE. Then, we add model architecture, pre-training, and data augmentation, respectively. The final strong baseline boosts more performance than other models. Finally, the bag of tricks makes the estimator achieves 1.71 on MAE and 7.18 on AAR. The results (such as in Fig. 2) shows that our proposed solution is able to predict the age of faces as well as people can or even better.

Moreover, the strong baseline is also the result of our representation learning stage. The estimator performs well at head-classes but shows poor performance at tail-classes. As a result, it also performs poorly on the $\sigma$ and the AAR. Then, we add the classification stage into the training procedure, and the final estimator shows the best performance on tail-classes, $\sigma$, and AAR on the MIVIA.

The results on test sets are provided by the organizers. And it is worth noting that the submission is trained on the whole MIVIA (Table 2).

**Table 2.** The performance of different models is evaluated on MIVIA. Baseline-S stands for the standard baseline introduced in Section 2.2. $MAE^1$ and $MAE^8$ stand for age groups consisting of tail-classes, and $MAE^3$ stands for head-classes. $*$ denotes the model is evaluated on the test set, and other models are all evaluated on the validation set. The best results on the validation set are in bold.

| Model | $MAE$ | $MAE^1$ | $MAE^3$ | $MAE^8$ | $\sigma$ | $AAR$ |
|---|---|---|---|---|---|---|
| Baseline-S | 1.97 | 7.16 | 1.61 | 3.45 | 1.93 | 6.10 |
| +model architecture | 1.93 | 6.47 | 1.59 | 2.99 | 1.65 | 6.42 |
| +pre-training | 1.78 | 5.09 | 1.45 | 2.73 | 1.33 | 6.89 |
| +data augmentation | 1.85 | 5.53 | 1.52 | 2.99 | 1.37 | 6.78 |
| Representation (Strong Baseline) | **1.71** | 4.66 | **1.40** | 2.59 | 1.11 | 7.18 |
| Classification | 1.89 | **2.69** | 1.62 | **2.11** | **0.37** | **7.74** |
| Submission$*$ | 1.86 | / | / | / | 0.20 | 7.94 |

# 4   Conclusions

In this paper, we first formulate a standard baseline and build a strong baseline by collecting the tricks in pre-training, model architecture, data augmentation, and so on. The bag of tricks significantly enhances the age estimation performance. The resulting estimator achieves the best performance on head-classes. Second, we propose an LAE method, which decouples the learning procedure into representation learning and classification, to obtain a more balanced estimator. The proposed method performs well at all ages, significantly outperforming the human reference.

**Acknowledgments.** This work was supported by the Chinese National Natural Science Foundation Projects #61961160704, #61876179, the External cooperation key project of Chinese Academy Sciences # 173211KYSB20200002, the Key Project of the General Logistics Department Grant No. AWS17J001, Science and Technology Development Fund of Macau (No. 0010/2019/AFJ, 0008/2019/A1 0025/2019/A-KP0019/2018/ASC).

# References

1. Cao, Q., Shen, L., Xie, W., Parkhi, O.M., Zisserman, A.: VGGFace2: a dataset for recognising faces across pose and age. In: 2018 13th IEEE International Conference on Automatic Face & Gesture Recognition (FG 2018), pp. 67–74. IEEE (2018)
2. Carletti, V., Greco, A., Percannella, G., Vento, M.: Age from faces in the deep learning revolution. IEEE Trans. Pattern Anal. Mach. Intell. **42**(9), 2113–2132 (2019)
3. Cubuk, E.D., Zoph, B., Shlens, J., Le, Q.V.: RandAugment: practical automated data augmentation with a reduced search space. In: CVPRW (2020)
4. Deng, J., Dong, W., Socher, R., Li, L.J., Li, K., Fei-Fei, L.: ImageNet: a large-scale hierarchical image database. In: 2009 IEEE Conference on Computer Vision and Pattern Recognition, pp. 248–255. IEEE (2009)
5. Gao, B.B., Zhou, H.Y., Wu, J., Geng, X.: Age estimation using expectation of label distribution learning. In: IJCAI, pp. 712–718 (2018)
6. Greco, A., Saggese, A., Vento, M., Vigilante, V.: Effective training of convolutional neural networks for age estimation based on knowledge distillation. Neural Comput. Appl., 1–16 (2021)
7. Guo, Y., Zhang, L., Hu, Y., He, X., Gao, J.: MS-celeb-1M: a dataset and benchmark for large-scale face recognition. In: Leibe, B., Matas, J., Sebe, N., Welling, M. (eds.) ECCV 2016. LNCS, vol. 9907, pp. 87–102. Springer, Cham (2016). https://doi.org/10.1007/978-3-319-46487-9_6
8. He, K., Zhang, X., Ren, S., Sun, J.: Deep residual learning for image recognition. In: CVPR, pp. 770–778 (2016)
9. Kang, B., et al.: Decoupling representation and classifier for long-tailed recognition. arXiv preprint arXiv:1910.09217 (2019)
10. Niu, Z., Zhou, M., Wang, L., Gao, X., Hua, G.: Ordinal regression with multiple output CNN for age estimation. In: CVPR (2016)
11. Othmani, A., Taleb, A.R., Abdelkawy, H., Hadid, A.: Age estimation from faces using deep learning: a comparative analysis. Comput. Vis. Image Underst. **196**, 102961 (2020)

12. Punyani, P., Gupta, R., Kumar, A.: Neural networks for facial age estimation: a survey on recent advances. Artif. Intell. Rev. **53**(5), 3299–3347 (2019). https://doi.org/10.1007/s10462-019-09765-w
13. Ren, J., et al.: Balanced meta-softmax for long-tailed visual recognition. arXiv preprint arXiv:2007.10740 (2020)
14. Rothe, R., Timofte, R., Van Gool, L.: DEX: deep expectation of apparent age from a single image. In: Proceedings of the IEEE International Conference on Computer Vision Workshops, pp. 10–15 (2015)
15. Shen, L., Lin, Z., Huang, Q.: Relay backpropagation for effective learning of deep convolutional neural networks. In: Leibe, B., Matas, J., Sebe, N., Welling, M. (eds.) ECCV 2016. LNCS, vol. 9911, pp. 467–482. Springer, Cham (2016). https://doi.org/10.1007/978-3-319-46478-7_29
16. Smith, L.N., Topin, N.: Super-convergence: very fast training of neural networks using large learning rates. In: Artificial Intelligence and Machine Learning for Multi-Domain Operations Applications, vol. 11006, p. 1100612. International Society for Optics and Photonics (2019)
17. Tan, M., Le, Q.V.: EfficientNetV2: smaller models and faster training. arXiv preprint arXiv:2104.00298 (2021)
18. Tan, Z., Wan, J., Lei, Z., Zhi, R., Guo, G., Li, S.Z.: Efficient group-n encoding and decoding for facial age estimation. IEEE TPAMI (2018)
19. Tan, Z., Yang, Y., Wan, J., Guo, G., Li, S.Z.: Deeply-learned hybrid representations for facial age estimation. In: IJCAI, pp. 3548–3554 (2019)
20. Wang, H., et al.: CosFace: large margin cosine loss for deep face recognition. In: Proceedings of the IEEE Conference on Computer Vision and Pattern Recognition, pp. 5265–5274 (2018)
21. Zeng, X., Huang, J., Ding, C.: Soft-ranking label encoding for robust facial age estimation. IEEE Access (2020)
22. Zhang, K., Zhang, Z., Li, Z., Qiao, Y.: Joint face detection and alignment using multitask cascaded convolutional networks. IEEE Signal Process. Lett. **23**, 1499–1503 (2016)

# Biometrics, Cryptography and Security

# Toward a Robust Shape and Texture Face Descriptor for Efficient Face Recognition in the Wild

Rahma Abed$^{(\boxtimes)}$, Sahbi Bahroun, and Ezzeddine Zagrouba

Laboratoire LIMTIC, Institut Supérieur d'Informatique, Université de Tunis El Manar, 2 Rue Abou Rayhane Bayrouni, 2080 Ariana, Tunisie
{rahma.abed,sahbi.bahroun}@isi.utm.tn, ezzeddine.zagrouba@uvt.tn

**Abstract.** Face recognition in complex environments has attracted the attention of the research community in the last few years due to the huge difficulties that can be found in images captured in such environments. In this context, we propose to extract a robust facial description in order to improve facial recognition rate even in the presence of illumination, pose or facial expression problems. Our method uses texture descriptors, namely Mesh-LBP extracted from 3D Meshs. These extracted descriptors will then be used to train a Convolution Neural Networks (CNN) to classify facial images. Experiments on several datasets has shown that the proposed method gives promising results in terms of face recognition accuracy under pose, face expressions and illumination variation.

**Keywords:** Face recognition · Mesh-LBP · Convolution neural networks · 3D morphable model

## 1 Introduction

Face recognition is the most effective technique and one of the most widely used biometrics for identifying and verifying people compared to voice, fingerprints, iris, retina, eye scanner, gait, ear and hand geometry [1]. However, face images suffer from several issues that could affect the achieved results, especially in an unconstrained environment. Such as facial expression, aging, accessories or even occlusion, low resolution, noise, illumination and pose variation [2]. Recently, several deep learning based face recognition methods was proposed [38]. These methods offer promising results in controlled environments. However, these results significantly decrease in real life scenarios.

In order to enhance face recognition results under these issues, two alternatives are offered. Face frontalization or robust face feature extraction. Face frontalization aim to produce a new face image, neutral and frontal, from the original image [3]. While robust face feature extraction extract a discriminative face representation using one or various face feature extractors. Nevertheless, these technique seems to be highly complex as the learning process requires a considerable amount of time and a large dataset for training [39].

© Springer Nature Switzerland AG 2021
N. Tsapatsoulis et al. (Eds.): CAIP 2021, LNCS 13053, pp. 319–328, 2021.
https://doi.org/10.1007/978-3-030-89131-2_29

For this purpose, we propose to use both face feature extraction and deep learning techniques in order to build a robust face recognition system. For this aim, we propose to use shape model and texture descriptor to obtain a robust face feature descriptor against facial expression, pose and illumination. Afterwards, we train a Convolution Neural Network (CNN) model for efficient facial recognition.

## 2    Related Works

Many face recognition algorithms still face difficulties when it comes to identify faces in large pose face images. These challenges have become a key factor that limit the effectiveness of face recognition in unrestricted environments [40].

Several techniques are used in order to enhance face recognition results. In this work, we focus on multi-modal 2D/3D and deep learning based methods. The multi modal techniques take benefit of the 3D face texture and the 2D face image descriptors to improve the recognition rate by considering the 3D face modeling as an intermediate step for 2D face recognition.

To deal with facial expressions issues, Abbad et al. [25] propose a 3D face recognition system based on feature extraction using geometric and local shape descriptors. Deng et al. [27] employed different features extraction based on local covariance operators. Zhang et.al [26] propose a data-free method for 3D face recognition using generated data from Gaussian Process Morphable Models (GPMM). Recently, Koppen et al. [31] propose a Gaussian mixture 3D morphable face model (GM-3DMM) that models the global population as a mixture of Gaussian subpopulations, each with its own mean, with shared covariance. These models are is constructed using Caucasian, Chinese and African 3D face data.

On the other hand, deep learning techniques train a deep model in order to predict the correct identity of the face image fed as input. FaceNet [36] use a deep convolutional network and maps a face images into a compact Euclidean space where distances correspond to a measure of face similarity. Parkhi et al. [19] fuse a very deep convolution neural network and the triplet embedding for building a robust face recognition system named VGG-faces. Wen et al. [18] propose a center loss function to estimate distance between images. Deng et.al [20] propose the measure of Deep Correlation Feature Learning (DCFL) for measure the correlation loss, which lead to create a large correlation between the deep feature vectors and their corresponding weight vectors in softmax loss. In correlation loss, it applies a weight vector in softmax loss as the prototype of each class.

In this work, we propose a new method based on fusing feature descriptors and 3D model with a neural network. We perform face feature extraction from a detected and aligned 3D face data using mesh-LBP. Indeed, the use of 3D data aim to reduce the impact of pose variation in facial image. In addition, when using mesh-LBP, we obtain a robust descriptor against pose, illumination and facial expression variation, which is not as expensive as generating new face image from a 3D model. Then, the obtained features will be fed into a neural network Face recognition. In our method we use raw images as our representation. We also provide a new CNN architecture through the use of the **locally connected layer**. This network will be trained on a very large labeled dataset.

# 3   Proposed Method

The proposed method is composed of three steps: Face detection and landmarks location, face feature extraction and CNN training. More details are shown in the following section.

## 3.1   Face Detection and Landmarks Location

In order to detect and crop facial region from images, we use the Dlib face detector [4]. As well as the detection, Dlib also performs face landmarks localization. This localization is very useful for extracting the most important facial structures from a face image. The Dlib face detector works as follows. First, the face detection and location. Then, the landmarks detection occurs. We highlight that the major facial areas to be labeled are the mouth, right eye and eyebrow, left eye and eyebrow, nose and jaw. The landmarks are provided as 68 point pairs (x, y) that correspond to the labeled facial areas.

## 3.2   Face Feature Extraction

Our method use 3D data obtained by the use 3D Morphable Face Models (3DMM) [5]. The 3D data could be used as an intermediate step to enhance 2D face recognition performance by modelling the difference in the texture map of the 3D aligned input and reference images. After that, we use the mesh-LBP [6] as a face feature extractor.

**3D Face Modelling:** We use the Surrey Face Model [5] for 3D face representation. These open source library provided includes methods to fit the pose and the shape of a model and perform face frontalization. This model is composed of two component: The first component is pose fitting. Given a set of 2D landmark locations and their correspondences in the 3D Morphable Model, the purpose is to estimate the pose of the face.

The second component consists of reconstructing the 3D shape based on the estimated camera matrix. The pose estimation and shape fitting process could be iterated in order to refine the estimates.

**Mesh-LBP:** The main advantage of the mesh-LBP is the fuse of geometric and appearance features extracted from 3D face models. In the standard LBP (2D-LBP) based face representation [7], we start by dividing the 2D face image into a grid of rectangular blocks, then an histograms of LBP descriptors are extracted from each block and concatenated in order to form a global description of the face.

To extend this workflow to the 3D face model, we need first to split the facial surface into a grid of regions. Then, we compute their corresponding histograms, and group them into a single structure.

The face descriptor construction process is illustrated in the Fig. 1

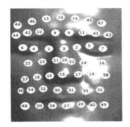

(a) The resulting 49 grid of points

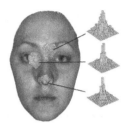

(b) Facet neighbor extraction

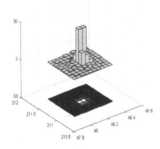

(c) Calculation of the multi-resolution mesh-LBP descriptor

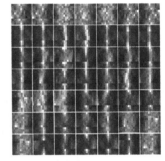

(d) Final face descriptor image

**Fig. 1.** Face image descriptor construction process

First, the plane formed by the nose tip and the two eyes inner-corner land-mark points is initially computed. In fact, the use of only these three landmarks is not arbitrary. But, these points are considered as the most accurate detectable landmarks on the face. Moreover, they are quite robust to facial expressions. Afterwards, the plane is tilted slightly, by a constant amount, to make it more aligned with the face orientation, and then we project this set of points on the face surface, along the plane's normal direction. The outcome of this procedure is an ordered grid of points, which defines an atlas for the facial regions that will divide the facial surface. The grid contain 49 points forming 7 × 7 constella-tion as shown in Fig. 1a. Once the grid of points has been defined, we extract a neighborhood of facets around each point of the grid. Each neighborhood can be defined by the set of facets confined within a geodesic disc or a sphere, centered at a grid point (Fig. 1b).

### 3.3   CNN Architecture and Training

We train our CNN in order to classify the face descriptor image created using mesh-LBP. In our work, we deal with a small neural network since we are dealing with images of face descriptors rather than images of faces. The proposed CNN, presented in Fig. 2.

**Fig. 2.** Architecture of the proposed CNN. The CNN is composed of two convolution layers (denoted by C1, C2), two fully connected layer (F1, F2), max-pooling layer(M) and a locally connected layer (L).

The size of the face descriptor image is $91 \times 91$ pixels. These images are fed to the our CNN. The first convolutional layer (C1) have 32 filters with size $11 \times 11$. The resulting 32 feature maps are then fed to a $3 \times 3$ max-pooling layer (M1) with a stride of 2, separately for each channel. Followed by another convolutional layer (C2) with 16 filters of size $9 \times 9$. The subsequent layers (L1) is a locally connected layer composed of 16 filter.

Finally, the last two layers, F5 and F6 are fully connected layers. These layers are able to capture correlations between distant face features. The output of the first fully connected layer (F1) in the network is used as our raw face representation feature vector throughout this paper. The output of the last fully-connected layer F2 is fed to a K-way softmax (where K is the number of classes) which produces a distribution over the class labels. It is important to mention the use of the ReLU [32] activation function after the convolution, locally connected and fully connected layer (except the last one L6). In addition, we use the cross-entropy loss in order to maximize the probability of the correct class (face id).

We train our architecture with around 500.000 images from the CASIA-WebFace [33], which contains 494,414 images of 10,575 subjects collected from the Internet. As a first experiment, we are working on face descriptor image, we use a smaller batch size of 200, and we train the network for 10 epochs over the whole data.

## 4   Experimental Results

In this section, we first present the datasets used in the experiment process. Then, we evaluate our method for face recognition against several challenges, including pose, illumination and face expression variation. Finally, we test our methods in various environments (controlled and crowded)

### 4.1    Datasets

In this evaluation, we use four datasets:

- **The CMU Multi-PIE face dataset** [8]: It contains more than 750,000 images of 337 people recorded in up to four sessions over the span of five months. Subjects were imaged under 15 viewpoints and 19 illumination conditions while displaying a range of facial expressions.
- **The Bosphorus dataset** [9]: It contains 4666 scans of 105 subjects scanned in different poses, action units, and occlusion conditions, Divided in multiple subsets corresponding to neutral and expressive: Anger, disgust, fear, happy, sad, surprise.
- **The LFW dataset** [10]: It consists of 13,323 web photos of 5,749 celebrities which are divided into 6,000 face pairs in 10 splits.
- **The YTF dataset** [11]: It collects 3,425 YouTube videos of 1,595 subjects (a subset of the celebrities in the LFW). These videos are divided into 5,000 video pairs and 10 splits and used to evaluate the video-level face verification.

### 4.2    Pose and Illumination-Invariant Face Recognition (PIFR)

The results presented in the Table 1, compares our method against other methods for Pose and illumination-invariant face recognition (PIFR). In other words, we evaluate face recognition while varying illumination and pose.

**Table 1.** Recognition rate (%) on the Multi-PIE dataset [8] across pose and illumination variations

| Method | $-45°$ | $-30°$ | $-15°$ | $+15°$ | $+30°$ | $+45°$ |
|---|---|---|---|---|---|---|
| DNN-CPF [28] | 73 | 81.7 | 98.4 | 89.5 | 80.4 | 70.3 |
| LNFF-LRA [29] | 77.2 | 87.7 | 94.9 | 94.8 | 88.1 | 76.4 |
| HPN [30] | 71.3 | 78.8 | 82.2 | 86.2 | 77.8 | 74.3 |
| U-3DMM [13] | 73.1 | 86.9 | 93.3 | 91.3 | 81.2 | 69.7 |
| ESO-3DMM [14] | 80.8 | 88.9 | 96.7 | 97.6 | 93.3 | 81.1 |
| GM-3DMM [31] | 84.3 | 89.4 | 97.4 | 99 | 96.8 | 92 |
| **Proposed Method** | **97.4** | **99.5** | **99.5** | **99.7** | **99.0** | **96.7** |

The state of the art method could be classified into two subsets. Deep learning based methods [28–30] and 3D based methods [13, 14, 31]. Our method outperform both deep learning and 3D based methods, and takes benefit from both technologies. By analyzing the results of the 3D based models [13, 14, 31], we could notice that the use of a 3DMM is well adapted to deal with extreme variations in pose and illumination. Besides, our method obtain much more interesting results, and this is more notable in right and left profile.

To conclude, we notice that the use of the mesh-LBP on 3D data are useful to provide a robust facial feature against illumination and pose.

## 4.3 Facial Expression Invariant Face Recognition

We tested our method on the Bosphorus dataset, which present seven variation in facial expressions. Results are presented in Table 2.

**Table 2.** Recognition rate (%) across facial expressions on the Bosphorus dataset

| Method | Neutral | Anger | Disgust | Fear | Happy | Sad | Surprise |
|---|---|---|---|---|---|---|---|
| Jingxin et al. [34] | – | 71.2 | 69.3 | 63.4 | 90 | 61 | 89 |
| Hariri et al. [22] | – | 86.25 | 85.25 | 81 | 93 | 79.75 | 90.50 |
| Sharma et al. [21] | 98.7 | 94.2 | 95.7 | 97.9 | 96.6 | 87.3 | 91.2 |
| Lei et al. [24] | 98.96 | 94.12 | 88.24 | 98.55 | 98.08 | 96.08 | 96.92 |
| Deng et al. [23] | 100 | 95.8 | 92.8 | 97.7 | 95.3 | 98.5 | 98.6 |
| Abbad et al. [25] | 100 | 95.77 | 88.41 | 81.41 | 88.68 | 96.97 | 92.96 |
| Zhang et al. [26] | 100 | 81.69 | 79.71 | 88.57 | 96.23 | 90.91 | 95.77 |
| Deng et al. [27] | 100 | 97.2 | 94.2 | 97.1 | 96.2 | 98.5 | 98.6 |
| Mesh-LBP [6] | 100 | 97.18 | 85.51 | 98.57 | 88.68 | 96.97 | 97.18 |
| Proposed Method | **100** | **97.18** | **96.75** | **100** | **97.63** | **98.88** | **100** |

Considering all results, we note that our method is more efficient than the state-of-the-art methods. In addition, the accuracy obtained for neutral emotion is always the highest and several methods achieve 100% accuracy since neutral face is the most common emotion. However, this accuracy decreases while varying facial expressions. Furthermore, disgust and sadness are measured with the lowest accuracy because these emotions are usually unpredictable.

On the one hand, when comparing our method and the Mesh-LBP, we observe that our results and those of the Mesh-LBP are competitive. Furthermore, our method achieves better results, in particular for the DISGUST and HAPPY emotions with an improvement of 10% and 8% respectively. This evolution is due to the learning process and the descriptors extracted from the 3D data

## 4.4 Face Verification

We evaluate our model against deep face recognition methods on LFW and YTF datasets. Results are presented in the two Tables 3a and 3b. the methods in Table 3a use face image generation for enhancing face recognition results. These methods provide good result, but it is still limited. This limitation is due mainly to the images used in the generation process or the recognition method used.

**Table 3.** Face verification ratio using the LFW and YTF datasets

| Method | Accuracy (%) |
|---|---|
| LFW-HPEN [12] | 96.25 |
| FF-GAN[16] | 96.42 |
| DED-GAN [17] | 97.52 |
| FI-GAN [35] | 98.3 |
| DA-GAN [15] | 99.56 |
| **Proposed method** | **99.59** |

(a) Face verification on the LFW dataset.

| Method | Accuracy (%) |
|---|---|
| Deep ID + [37] | 93.2 |
| FaceNet [36] | 95.12 |
| VGG-face [19] | 97.3 |
| Center loss [18] | 94.9 |
| DFCL [20] | 96.06 |
| **Proposed method** | **94.97** |

(b) Face verification on the YTF dataset.

Looking to Table 3b, our method do not achieve higher values such as [19, 20, 36]. But, improvement is always possible. Our method outperforms some of the well known deep learning method, and provide results that are concurrent to other methods.

## 5   Conclusion

Face recognition is considered as one of the most complex systems in the field of pattern recognition due to many constraints that are cased by face image appearance variation (accessories, occlusion, illumination, resolution).

In this paper, we propose to combine a 3D model-based alignment, an LBP descriptor constructed on the 3D mesh with a CNN model in order to predict facial identity. The obtained results are quite convincing. Thus, we could conclude that our method achieve higher rates compared to state of the art methods. While indicating that our method does not surpass some others. On the basis of the promising findings presented in this paper, work on the remaining issues is continuing and will be presented in future papers.

## References

1. Oloyede, M.O., Hancke, G.P., Myburgh, H.C.: A review on face recognition systems: recent approaches and challenges. Multimedia Tools Appl. **79**(37), 27891–27922 (2020)
2. Anwarul, S., Dahiya, S.: A comprehensive review on face recognition methods and factors affecting facial recognition accuracy. In: Proceedings of International Conference on Robotics and Intelligent Control ICRIC, pp. 495–514 (2020)
3. Yin, Y., Jiang, S., Robinson, J.P., Fu, Y.: Dual-attention GAN for large-pose face frontalization. arXiv preprint arXiv:2002.07227 (2020)
4. King, D.E.: Dlib-ml: a machine learning toolkit. J. Mach. Learn. Res., 1755–1758 (2009)
5. Huber, P., et al.: A multiresolution 3D morphable face model and fitting framework. In: Proceedings of the 11th Joint Conference on Computer Vision, Imaging and Computer Graphics Theory and Applications, pp. 79–86 (2016)

6. Werghi, N., Tortorici, C., Berretti, S., Del Bimbo, A.: Boosting 3D LBP-based face recognition by fusing shape and texture descriptors on the mesh. IEEE Trans. Inf. Forensics Secur. **11**(5), 964–979 (2016)
7. Wang, H., Hu, J., Deng, J.: Face feature extraction: a complete review. IEEE Access, 6001–6039 (2018)
8. Gross, R., Matthews, I., Cohn, J., Kanade, T., Baker, S.: Multi-pie. Image Vis. Comput. **28**(5), 807–813 (2010)
9. Savran, A., et al.: Bosphorus database for 3D face analysis. In: Schouten, B., Juul, N.C., Drygajlo, A., Tistarelli, M. (eds.) BioID 2008. LNCS, vol. 5372, pp. 47–56. Springer, Heidelberg (2008). https://doi.org/10.1007/978-3-540-89991-4_6
10. Huang, G.B., Mattar, M., Berg, T., Learned-Miller, E.: Labeled faces in the wild: a database for studying face recognition in unconstrained environments. In: Workshop on Faces in Real-Life Images: Detection, Alignment, and Recognition (2008)
11. Wolf, L., Hassner, T., Maoz, I.: Face recognition in unconstrained videos with matched background similarity. In: IEEE CVPR, pp. 529–534 (2011)
12. Zhu, X., Lei, Z., Yan, J., Yi, D., Li, S.Z.: High-fidelity pose and expression normalization for face recognition in the wild. In: Proceedings of the IEEE Conference on Computer Vision and Pattern Recognition, pp. 787–796 (2015)
13. Hu, G., et al.: Face recognition using a unified 3D morphable model. In: Leibe, B., Matas, J., Sebe, N., Welling, M. (eds.) ECCV 2016. LNCS, vol. 9912, pp. 73–89. Springer, Cham (2016). https://doi.org/10.1007/978-3-319-46484-8_5
14. Hu, G., et al.: Efficient 3D morphable face model fitting. Pattern Recognit. **67**, 366–379 (2017)
15. Yu, Y., Songyao, J., Joseph, P.R., Yun, F.: Dual-attention GAN for large-pose face frontalization. arXiv preprint arXiv:2002.07227 (2020)
16. Yin, X., Yu, X., Sohn, K., Liu, X., Chandraker, M.: Towards large-pose face frontalization in the wild. In: Proceedings of the IEEE International Conference on Computer Vision, pp. 3990–3999 (2017)
17. Hu, C., Feng, Z., Wu, X., Kittler, J.: Dual encoder-decoder based generative adversarial networks for disentangled facial representation learning. IEEE Access **8**, 130159–130171 (2020)
18. Wen, Y., Zhang, K., Li, Z., Qiao, Y.: A discriminative feature learning approach for deep face recognition. In: Leibe, B., Matas, J., Sebe, N., Welling, M. (eds.) ECCV 2016. LNCS, vol. 9911, pp. 499–515. Springer, Cham (2016). https://doi.org/10.1007/978-3-319-46478-7_31
19. Parkhi, O.M., Vedaldi, A., Zisserman, A.: Deep face recognition (2015)
20. Deng, W., Chen, B., Fang, Y., Hu, J.: Deep correlation feature learning for face verification in the wild. IEEE Signal Process. Lett. **24**(12), 1877–1881 (2017)
21. Sharma, S., Vijay, K.: Voxel-based 3D face reconstruction and its application to face recognition using sequential deep learning. Multimedia Tools Appl. (1–28) (2020)
22. Hariri, W., Tabia, H., Farah, N., Benouareth, A., Declercq, D.: 3D facial expression recognition using kernel methods on Riemannian manifold. Eng. Appl. Artif. Intell. **64**, 25–32 (2017)
23. Deng, X., Da, F., Shao, H.: Efficient 3D face recognition using local covariance descriptor and Riemannian kernel sparse coding. Comput. Electr. Eng. **62**, 81–91 (2017)
24. Lei, Y., Guo, Y., Hayat, M., Bennamoun, M., Zhou, X.: A two-phase weighted collaborative representation for 3D partial face recognition with single sample. Pattern Recognit. **52**, 218–237 (2016)

25. Abbad, A., Abbad, K., Tairi, H.: 3D face recognition: multi-scale strategy based on geometric and local descriptors. Comput. Electr. Eng. **70**, 525–537 (2018)
26. Zhang, Z., Da, F., Yu, Y.: Data-free point cloud network for 3D face recognition. arXiv, arXiv-1911 (2019)
27. Deng, X., Da, F., Shao, H., Jiang, Y.A.: Multi-scale three-dimensional face recognition approach with sparse representation-based classifier and fusion of local covariance descriptors. Comput. Electr. Eng. **85** (2020)
28. Yim, J., Jung, H., Yoo, B., Choi, C., Park, D., Kim, J.: Rotating your face using multi-task deep neural network. In: Proceedings of the IEEE Conference on Computer Vision and Pattern Recognition, pp. 676–684 (2015)
29. Deng, W., Hu, J., Wu, Z., Guo, J.: Lighting-aware face frontalization for unconstrained face recognition. Pattern Recognit. **68**, 260–271 (2017)
30. Ding, C., Tao, D.: Pose-invariant face recognition with homography-based normalization. Pattern Recognit. **66**, 144–152 (2017)
31. Koppen P, et al.: Gaussian mixture 3D morphable face model. Pattern Recognit. **74**, 617–628 (2018)
32. Dahl, G.E., Sainath, T.N., Hinton, G.E.: Improving deep neural networks for LVCSR using rectified linear units and dropout. In: IEEE International Conference on Acoustics, Speech and Signal Processing, pp. 8609–8613 (2013)
33. Yi, D., Lei, Z., Liao, S., Li, S.Z.: Learning face representation from scratch. arXiv preprint arXiv:1411.7923 (2014)
34. Jingxin, B., Yinan, L., Shuo, Z.: 3D multi-poses face expression recognition based on action units. In: International Conference on Information Technology and Computer Communications (2019)
35. Rong, C., Xingming, Z., Yubei, L.: Feature-improving generative adversarial network for face frontalization. IEEE Access **8**, 68842–68851 (2020)
36. Schroff, F., Dmitry, K., James, P.: FaceNet: a unified embedding for face recognition and clustering. In: Proceedings of the IEEE Conference on Computer Vision and Pattern Recognition (2015)
37. Taigman, M.L.Y., Yang, M.: Deep learning face representation from predicting 10,000 classes. In: IEEE Conference on Computer Vision and Pattern Recognition (CVPR), pp. 1891–1898 (2014)
38. Guo, G., Na, Z.: A survey on deep learning based face recognition. Comput. Vis. Image Underst. **189**, 102805 (2019)
39. Gui, J., Sun, Z., Wen, Y., Tao, D., Ye, J.: A review on generative adversarial networks: algorithms, theory, and applications. arXiv preprint arXiv:2001.06937 (2020)
40. Ning, X., Nan, F., Xu, S., Yu, L., Zhang, L.: Multi-view frontal face image generation: a survey. Concur. Comput. Pract. Exp. (2020)

# Automatic Gender Classification from Handwritten Images: A Case Study

Irina Rabaev[✉][iD], Marina Litvak[iD], Sean Asulin, and Or Haim Tabibi

Shamoon College of Engineering, 56 Bialik St. Be'er, 8410802 Sheva, Israel
{irinar,marinal,shonas,orita4}@ac.sce.ac.il

**Abstract.** Using a handwritten sample to automatically classify the writer's gender is an essential task in a wide range of areas, e.g., psychology, historical documents classification, and forensic analysis. The challenge of gender prediction from offline handwriting can be demonstrated by the relatively low (below 90%) performance of state-of-the-art systems. Despite a high interest within a broad spectrum of research communities, the published works in this area generally concentrate on English and Arabic languages. Most of the existing approaches focus on manual feature selection. In this work, we study an application of deep neural networks for gender classification, where we investigate cross-domain transfer learning with ImageNet pre-training. The study was performed on two datasets, the QUWI dataset, consisting of handwritten documents in English and Arabic, and a new dataset of documents in Hebrew script. We perform extensive experiments, analyze and compare the results obtained with different neural networks. We demonstrate that advanced deep-learning models outperform conventional machine learning approaches that were used in previous studies. We also compare the obtained results against human-level performance and show that the problem is challenging for non-experts.

**Keywords:** Gender classification · Offline handwriting analysis · Transfer learning · Deep neural network

## 1 Introduction

Handwriting gender classification is of great interest due to the broad range of areas it can be applied in, e.g., psychology, historical documents classification, and forensics [10,11,27]. Psychological studies of handwriting analysis have confirmed that gender classification can be made according to several significant differences in handwriting [10,11,27]. In general, while a female's handwriting tends to be more uniform, ordered, and has greater circularity, a male's handwriting tends to be more pointed, messy, and slanted.

With technological advances in image analysis and computer vision, manual handwriting analysis has become enhanced by automatic systems. The existing

---

I. Rabaev and M. Litvak—These authors contributed equally to this work.

N. Tsapatsoulis et al. (Eds.): CAIP 2021, LNCS 13053, pp. 329–339, 2021.
https://doi.org/10.1007/978-3-030-89131-2_30

automatic methods can be classified into two categories: (1) traditional machine learning techniques that require prior features selection and (2) methods that apply deep neural networks (DNNs), where features are learned within a network framework.

Many features were used for gender classification, including graphology features [9,16,26], textural features [1,9], geometric features [4], Cloud of Line Distribution (COLD) and Hinge features [8], and wavelet-based features [2]. Traditional machine learning algorithms include k-Nearest Neighbours (kNN) [9], support vector machine (SVM) [5,8], decision trees and random forests [26], Gaussian Mixture Models (GMM) [16], and combinations (ensembles) of several classifiers [1,2,4,9,17]. ICDAR competitions focusing on Gender Prediction from Handwriting [7,12] gathered researchers from around the world to compare between different techniques. All systems that participated in the competitions followed the standard approach of traditional machine learning, where feature extraction must be performed prior to the classification.

The serious disadvantage of traditional machine learning approaches is that they are strongly dependent on manual feature engineering, which in the case of handwriting analysis often requires expert knowledge. Therefore, in our study we decided to lean on the most advanced deep learning approaches, those designed for image processing and published recently (or during the last decade). The authors of [15] applied a CNN-based model with a relatively small number of layers. In [21], gender classification was performed using advanced CNNs, such as DenseNet201, InceptionV3, and Xception. In this work, we report a similar study but extended it to an additional language (Hebrew) and the most recent networks. In [28], an attention-based two-pathway densely connected convolutional network was proposed to identify the gender of a handwritten document. Transfer learning was applied in [19] to detect the writer's gender from scanned handwritten documents. The authors used two pre-trained CNNs, GoogleNet (InceptionV1) and ResNet, as fixed feature extractors. For the classification stage, they applied SVM. In [18], pre-trained CNNs have been employed as feature extractors to discriminate between male and female handwriting, while classification is carried out using a number of classifiers, with Linear Discriminant Analysis being the most effective. Both works, [19] and [18], performed feature extraction and classification separately, by different models. In our study, the analyzed documents are submitted as input to a network, and the same network provides their classes.

This paper has two main contributions. First, we present the results of a case study for gender classification from handwritten document images with multiple DNNs. Because DNNs require a vast amount of training data, we investigate an application of cross-domain transfer learning with ImageNet pre-training. We perform extensive experiments and analyze the results on two different datasets: a newly introduced Hebrew Gender (HHD_gender) dataset of handwritten documents in Hebrew script, and the QUWI dataset [3], which consists of documents in English and Arabic languages. Second, we establish baseline results for the HHD_gender. The original collection of scanned images was introduced in [20]. Here, we preprocess and annotate the dataset for the gender classification task. The preprocessed dataset can be downloaded from the Zenodo repository (https://zenodo.org/record/4729908#.YIvT7meJGhe). To the best of our knowledge, this is the first publicly available dataset in Hebrew script that can be used for gender classification. In addition, we compare the performances of the models against human-level performance on the HHD_gender dataset.

## 2   Case Study

The most successful recent image classification models are CNN-based. They show that shallow layers extract simple (low-level) features of an image, and deeper layers extract more complex (high-level) features. Thus, to make CNN more accurate, researchers mainly increase their depth by adding more layers. In this study we used the following models: VGGNet [22] (VVG16 and VGG19), ResNet [13], Inception [24] (Inception-v3 and Inception-ResNet-v2), Xception [6], DenseNet [14] (DenseNet121 and DenseNet169), NASNet [29], and Efficient-Net [25]. All the networks are pre-trained on ImageNet. For comparison, we also report the results for a simple CNN trained from scratch.

### 2.1   Datasets

The experimental study is performed on the HHD_gender dataset and the QUWI dataset, together containing documents written in three different languages.

The HHD_gender dataset is a subset of the HHD dataset introduced in [20]. It contains 819 handwritten forms written by volunteers of different educational backgrounds and ages, both native and non-native Hebrew speakers. Each participant voluntarily provided demographic information, such as date, gender, and age, written at the top of the form, and copied a text paragraph printed above the text field. There are 50 variations of the forms; each form contains a text paragraph with an average of 62 words. The forms were scanned in color at a resolution of 600 dpi. During the preprocessing, first, the handwritten paragraph was extracted using coordinates of the corresponding text box. Then, the ground truth labeling (male and female) was performed automatically, based on the number of foreground pixels in the corresponding field. Finally, the labels were proof-read manually. Documents that did not contain gender information (the participant preferred not to fill in personal information) were withdrawn from the dataset. This process yielded 368 forms written by males and 461 by females. Finally, the images were converted to grayscale since the color caries no important information for the gender classification. Examples of the processed images are illustrated in the top row in Fig. 1. For the experiments, the HHD_gender dataset was randomly subdivided into training (80%), validation (10%), and test (10%) sets.

The QUWI [3] dataset contains handwritten documents in Arabic and English languages. The documents were written by volunteers of different ages,

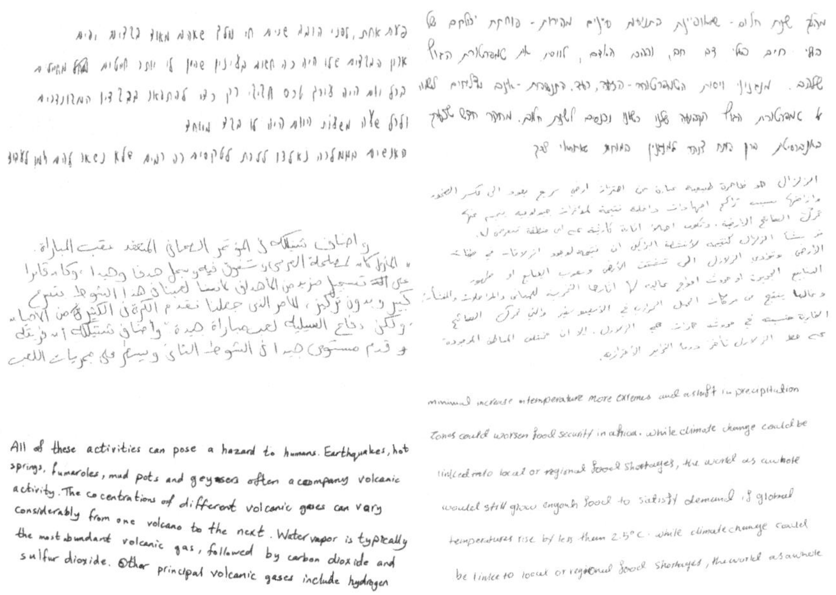

**Fig. 1.** Top row: Examples of the images from the HHD_gender dataset; male - left image, female - right image. Middle and bottom rows: Examples of the images from the QUWI dataset; male - left, female - right; different writers.

nationalities, and education levels. Each writer produced four handwritten documents: two in Arabic and two in English. One page in Arabic and one page in English contain the same text for all writers; the text on two other pages varies from writer to writer. Images are scanned with a 600 dpi resolution in JPG format. The middle and bottom rows in Fig. 1 illustrate the samples from the QUWI dataset.

The ICDAR 2013 and 2015 competitions on Gender Prediction from Handwriting [7,12] used a subset of the QUWI dataset. ICDAR 2013 dataset is composed of handwritten documents of 475 writers: 221 males and 254 females, and is divided into training (282 writers) and test (193 writers) sets. Three classification schemes were applied: training and testing on samples in Arabic, training and testing on samples in English, and training and testing on samples in both languages. ICDAR 2015 competition dataset is composed of documents written by 500 writers and is divided into training (300 writers), validation (100 writers), and test (100 writers) sets. This competition comprised four tasks: gender classification on Arabic handwriting; gender classification on English handwriting; gender classification using Arabic samples in training and English samples in testing; gender classification using English samples in training and Arabic samples in testing. Unfortunately, we were unable to get the dataset used in the ICDAR 2015 competition. However, we had access to the ICDAR 2013 dataset. Hence, we used it in our experiments. In order to create conditions as similar as

**Fig. 2.** Samples of the extracted patches; top row - the HHD_gender dataset, bottom row - the QUWI dataset.

possible to the conditions in the ICDAR 2015 competition, we randomly divided the 475 writers into training (300 writers), test (100 writers), and validation (75 writers) sets. This division is comparable to the division used in the ICDAR 2015 competition.

## 2.2 Experiment Settings

For the classification, we investigated ten architectures mentioned at the beginning of Sect. 2. We performed fine-tuning by replacing the last fully connected layer by fully connected layer with two neurons and freezing all other layers. The models were trained until convergence. We compared the results of all models with the results of a baseline system trained from scratch. This system was adopted from the Kaggle competition on image classification[1] – CNN with 11 (including two convolutional and consequent pooling) layers and 39257 parameters (39193 of them are trainable).

The networks were trained using patches extracted from each document image. The patches were extracted by moving a sliding window of size 400 × 400 pixels at a stride 200 pixels in vertical and horizontal directions. The patch size was chosen experimentally to include three to four text lines. Figure 2 illustrates the examples of the resulted patches from the QUWI and HHD_gender datasets.

In each experiment, the input images were resized to the input dimensions of the respective network. For prediction, the manuscript image was also cut into overlapping 400 × 400 pixels patches at a stride of 200 × 200 pixels, and each was classified. The resulting page-level classification was obtained by the majority voting scheme over all patches from the same page.

---

[1] https://www.kaggle.com/sujoykg/keras-cnn-with-grayscale-images/.

## 2.3  Results and Discussions

We applied the same models on both HHD_gender and QUWI datasets. For the QUWI dataset, we used the classification scenarios employed in ICDAR 2013 and 2015 competitions, as described in Sect. 2.1.

The HHD_gender column of Table 1 (left) contains the classification accuracy results for all models on the HHD_gender dataset. As can be seen, Xception provided the best accuracy. However, it consumes the largest number of epochs (40 vs. 15–20 for other models). EfficientNet and NasNet follow with the second best accuracy score.

We compared the results of all the models with the results of a baseline system - CNN with 11 layers. As can be seen, despite its considerably simpler structure and random initialization (the baseline is not pre-trained on ImageNet, in contrast to other models), its performance is comparable to the performance of the best models, even outperforming several networks—both VGGNets, both DenseNets, and Inception-v3. We explain this by a different nature of general pictures and handwriting images. As other studies show [23], pre-training on ImageNet is helpful when not enough training data is provided. However, in the case of the HHD_gender dataset, the training data we have is quite large, of high quality, and is sufficient for accurate learning (for moderate size CNN).

We have also experimented with various types of augmentation using the HHD_gender dataset, applying rotation between $-30$ to $30°$, scaling by a random factor from 0.8 to 1.2, and adding noise to the document. We experimented with these augmentation methods separately and in combination but did not observe any improvement in accuracy rates. Moreover, in some experiments, the augmentation actually harmed the performance. The most likely explanation for this outcome is that the HHD_gender dataset is consistent. Augmentation such as rotation did not help because the forms were aligned horizontally as a part of their preprocessing. Similarly, adding noise did not help because the test set includes clean images. Adding augmentation forced the network to learn examples that are not present in the test set, thereby wasting its predictive resources on irrelevant scenarios. Since augmentation did not improve the performance, the results with the augmentation are not presented in the paper.

We performed experiments on the QUWI dataset using both ICDAR 2013 and ICDAR 2015 settings, and compared the results against the top results from these competitions. All systems that participated in the competitions applied traditional machine learning with feature extraction performed prior to the classification. The ICDAR 2013 column of Table 1 (middle) contains the accuracy scores for the QUWI dataset splittings used in the ICDAR 2013 competition: (1) mono-script English handwriting, (2) mono-script Arabic handwriting, and (3) multi-script handwriting with both languages. In the mono-script experiments, training and testing were performed only on documents in one language; in the multi-script experiment, training and testing were run on handwriting documents in both languages[2]. The accuracy scores of all the models on the QUWI

---

[2] Because only LogLoss scores were reported in the ICDAR 2013 competition, the accuracy scores for the winning system were retrieved from [2].

**Table 1.** Models' performance on the HHD_gender and QUWI—ICDAR 2013 and 2015 splits—datasets.

| Models | HHD_gender | ICDAR 2013 | | | ICDAR 2015 | | | |
|---|---|---|---|---|---|---|---|---|
| | Hebrew | English | Arabic | Both | 2A | 2B | 2C | 2D |
| *Top ICDAR results* | – | *0.79* | *0.74* | *0.76* | *0.65* | *0.60* | *0.63* | *0.58* |
| Baseline | 0.81 | 0.52 | 0.61 | 0.56 | 0.61 | 0.62 | 0.65 | 0.52 |
| VGG16 | 0.79 | 0.70 | 0.59 | 0.65 | 0.56 | 0.67 | 0.64 | 0.51 |
| VGG19 | 0.74 | 0.69 | 0.66 | 0.67 | 0.55 | 0.60 | 0.60 | 0.52 |
| Xception | **0.85** | 0.75 | 0.68 | 0.68 | 0.64 | **0.75** | **0.66** | 0.55 |
| EfficientNet | 0.84 | 0.75 | **0.74** | 0.67 | **0.67** | 0.69 | 0.59 | 0.55 |
| Inception-ResNet-v2 | 0.81 | 0.71 | 0.65 | 0.75 | 0.65 | 0.68 | 0.64 | 0.54 |
| Inception-v3 | 0.77 | 0.73 | 0.69 | 0.71 | 0.61 | 0.74 | 0.70 | 0.54 |
| DenseNet121 | 0.74 | 0.68 | 0.69 | 0.69 | 0.61 | 0.71 | 0.64 | 0.51 |
| DenseNet169 | 0.74 | 0.71 | 0.66 | 0.67 | 0.63 | 0.72 | 0.62 | 0.50 |
| ResNet50 | 0.81 | 0.67 | 0.50 | 0.67 | 0.58 | 0.65 | 0.57 | 0.55 |
| NasNet | 0.84 | 0.60 | 0.64 | 0.66 | 0.66 | 0.74 | 0.62 | 0.55 |

dataset are lower than on the HHD_gender. We explain this by the smaller number of samples used in training in a mono-script setting, and a much more challenging scenario in the multi-script setting. Although the DNNs did not outperform the top results of the ICDAR 2013 competition, they achieved close results. EfficientNet has a clear advantage over the other systems in mono-script learning in both languages, except that Xception has the same score for English. Inception-ResNet-v2 has the best accuracy in multi-script gender detection.

The ICDAR 2015 column of Table 1 (right) shows the comparative results on the QUWI dataset, using the splitting ratios and scenarios as used in the ICDAR 2015 competition. The following scenarios were employed in the competition: (2A) Gender classification on Arabic writings; (2B) Gender classification on English writings; (2C) Gender classification using Arabic samples in training and English samples in testing; (2D) Gender classification using English samples in training and Arabic samples in testing. As can be seen, in 3 out of 4 scenarios Xception and EfficientNet outperform the best results from the ICDAR 2015 competition. As we mentioned in Sect. 2.1, we were unable to get the exact dataset used in the ICDAR 2015 competition. We used the ICDAR 2013 dataset, which is also the subset of the QUWI dataset, and created a split as applied in the ICDAR2015. Hence, we believe that our results obtained on this split can be fairly compared with the results from the ICDAR 2015 competition.

In general, we can see that two networks—Xception and EfficientNet—are the best-performing systems in most scenarios (except for the QUWI with mixed languages and cross-language classification using English samples in training and Arabic samples in testing). Their superiority can be explained by their advanced architectures. The Xception architecture has 36 convolution layers, which form a very strong basis for feature extraction from input handwritings. Because handwriting can be described by numerous features, the greater number of feature

**Table 2.** The results of human examiners on the samples from the HHD_gender dataset.

|  | # Participants | Accuracy |
| --- | --- | --- |
| Questionnaire 1 | 166 | 0.623 |
| Questionnaire 2 | 109 | 0.632 |
| Questionnaire 3 | 89 | 0.739 |
| Questionnaire 4 | 86 | 0.707 |
| Average over all questionnaires |  | 0.675 |

maps, which produce the greater number of features, is beneficial to our task. Also, inventors of the Xception model clearly showed the benefit of depthwise separable convolutions in neural computer vision architectures. EfficientNet's "secret" is in its synergy in scaling multiple dimensions together. The authors produced the theoretically optimal formula of "compound scaling" by an extensive grid search and used it to scale up the EfficientNet.

We also experimented with different combinations of ensembles of models. In each experiment, the final prediction was assigned using the majority voting over all components. Surprisingly, we found that the ensemble of models does not improve the classification results. We performed an error analysis and found that in most cases the networks gave incorrect predictions on the same documents. Because we were using the majority scheme over predictions by the networks, this resulted in lower classification rates compared to using the best single network. Interestingly, most human examiners have also wrongly classified the same documents on which the networks failed.

**Human-Level Performance.** To compare the models' performance to those of humans, we compiled four online questionnaires[3]. The questionnaires include 70 images from the HHD_gender dataset, divided into 18, 18, 17, 17 groups. Each participant can answer questions from one to four groups, using links from each questionnaire to the following one. Each participant was asked to classify the writer's gender, based on handwritten text samples. Upon completion, a participant can see the classification results. Comparing the results of human examiners, as presented in Table 2, with the results of automated classification from Table 1 (left), we can notice that the best deep-learning models have surpassed human-level performance. The possible limitation of this experiment is that the classification was carried by the general public. However, the results of the experiment show that the problem is challenging for non-experts, and the automatic classification system can be used in cases when an expert in handwriting analysis is unavailable.

---

[3] https://forms.gle/Ay7XV9CX61fkU6qt7.

# 3    Conclusions and Future Work

This paper reports the results of an extensive empirical case study for gender classification from offline handwritten images, performed on different datasets, with various deep CNNs designed for the image classification task. The aim of this study was an extensive investigation of the effect of cross-domain transfer learning with ImageNet pre-training for the gender classification task. We can conclude that advanced deep-learning models outperform conventional machine learning approaches used in previous studies, where features must be designed manually. Also, pre-training networks on a rich external dataset (ImageNet) has a positive effect on the gender classification task. For comparison, we also report the results for a simple CNN trained from scratch In addition, we established baseline results for a new dataset of handwritten images in Hebrew script, pre-processed and annotated with a writer's gender. The HHD_gender dataset is publicly available for the research community together with the partitions for the training and test sets. To the best of our knowledge, this is the first publicly available dataset in Hebrew script for a gender classification task.

We also show that the problem is challenging for non-experts, and that the automatic classification system can be used in cases when an expert in hand-writing analysis is unavailable. In the future, we intend to perform a similar experiment with a graphology expert.

# References

1. Ahmed, M., Rasool, A.G., Afzal, H., Siddiqi, I.: Improving handwriting based gender classification using ensemble classifiers. Expert Syst. Appl. **85**, 158–168 (2017)
2. Akbari, Y., Nouri, K., Sadri, J., Djeddi, C., Siddiqi, I.: Wavelet-based gender detection on off-line handwritten documents using probabilistic finite state automata. Image Vis. Comput. **59**, 17–30 (2017)
3. Al Maadeed, S., Ayouby, W., Hassaine, A., Aljaam, J.M.: QUWI: an Arabic and English handwriting dataset for offline writer identification. In: International Conference on Frontiers in Handwriting Recognition, pp. 746–751 (2012)
4. Al Maadeed, S., Hassaine, A.: Automatic prediction of age, gender, and nationality in offline handwriting. EURASIP J. Image Video Process. **2014**(1), 1–10 (2014). https://doi.org/10.1186/1687-5281-2014-10
5. Bi, N., Suen, C.Y., Nobile, N., Tan, J.: A multi-feature selection approach for gender identification of handwriting based on kernel mutual information. Pattern Recognit. Lett. **121**, 123–132 (2019)
6. Chollet, F.: Xception: deep learning with depthwise separable convolutions. In: Proceedings of the IEEE Conference on Computer Vision and Pattern Recognition, pp. 1251–1258 (2017)
7. Djeddi, C., Al-Maadeed, S., Gattal, A., Siddiqi, I., Souici-Meslati, L., El Abed, H.: ICDAR 2015 competition on multi-script writer identification and gender classification using 'QUWI' database. In: International Conference on Document Analysis and Recognition, pp. 1191–1195 (2015)

8. Gattal, A., Djeddi, C., Bensefia, A., Ennaji, A.: Handwriting based gender classification using cold and hinge features. In: International Conference on Image and Signal Processing, pp. 233–242 (2020)
9. Gattal, A., Djeddi, C., Siddiqi, I., Chibani, Y.: Gender classification from offline multi-script handwriting images using oriented basic image features (oBIFs). Expert Syst. Appl. **99**, 155–167 (2018)
10. Goodenough, F.L.: Sex differences in judging the sex of handwriting. J. Soc. Psychol. **22**(1), 61–68 (1945)
11. Hamid, S., Loewenthal, K.M.: Inferring gender from handwriting in Urdu and English. J. Soc. Psychol. **136**(6), 778–782 (1996)
12. Hassaïne, A., Al Maadeed, S., Aljaam, J., Jaoua, A.: ICDAR 2013 competition on gender prediction from handwriting. In: International Conference on Document Analysis and Recognition, pp. 1417–1421 (2013)
13. He, K., Zhang, X., Ren, S., Sun, J.: Deep residual learning for image recognition. In: Proceedings of the IEEE Conference on Computer Vision and Pattern Recognition, pp. 770–778 (2016)
14. Huang, G., Liu, Z., Van Der Maaten, L., Weinberger, K.Q.: Densely connected convolutional networks. In: Proceedings of the IEEE Conference on Computer Vision and Pattern Recognition, pp. 4700–4708 (2017)
15. Illouz, E., David, E.O., Netanyahu, N.S.: Handwriting-based gender classification using end-to-end deep neural networks. In: International Conference on Artificial Neural Networks, pp. 613–621 (2018)
16. Liwicki, M., Schlapbach, A., Bunke, H.: Automatic gender detection using on-line and off-line information. Pattern Anal. Appl. **14**(1), 87–92 (2011)
17. Maken, P., Gupta, A.: A method for automatic classification of gender based on text-independent handwriting. Multimedia Tools Appl., 1–30 (2021)
18. Moetesum, M., Siddiqi, I., Djeddi, C., Hannad, Y., Al-Maadeed, S.: Data driven feature extraction for gender classification using multi-script handwritten texts. In: International Conference on Frontiers in Handwriting Recognition, pp. 564–569 (2018)
19. Najla, A.Q., Suen, C.Y.: Gender detection from handwritten documents using concept of transfer-learning. In: International Conference on Pattern Recognition and Artificial Intelligence, pp. 3–13 (2020)
20. Rabaev, I., Kurar Barakat, B., Churkin, A., El-Sana, J.: The HHD dataset. In: International Conference on Frontiers in Handwriting Recognition, pp. 228–233 (2020)
21. Rahmanian, M., Shayegan, M.A.: Handwriting-based gender and handedness classification using convolutional neural networks. Multimedia Tools Appl., 1–24 (2021)
22. Simonyan, K., Zisserman, A.: Very deep convolutional networks for large-scale image recognition. arXiv preprint arXiv:1409.1556 (2014)
23. Studer, L., et al.: A comprehensive study of ImageNet pre-training for historical document image analysis. In: International Conference on Document Analysis and Recognition, pp. 720–725 (2019)
24. Szegedy, C., et al.: Going deeper with convolutions. In: Proceedings of the IEEE Conference on Computer Vision and Pattern Recognition, pp. 1–9 (2015)
25. Tan, M., Le, Q.: EfficientNet: rethinking model scaling for convolutional neural networks. In: International Conference on Machine Learning, pp. 6105–6114 (2019)
26. Topaloglu, M., Ekmekci, S.: Gender detection and identifying one's handwriting with handwriting analysis. Expert Syst. Appl. **79**, 236–243 (2017)
27. Upadhyay, S., Singh, J., Shukla, S.: Determination of sex through handwriting characteristics. Int. J. Curr. Res. Rev. **9**(13) 11 (2017)

28. Xue, G., Liu, S., Gong, D., Ma, Y.: ATP-DenseNet: a hybrid deep learning-based gender identification of handwriting. Neural Comput. Appl. **33**(10), 4611–4622 (2020). https://doi.org/10.1007/s00521-020-05237-3

29. Zoph, B., Vasudevan, V., Shlens, J., Le, Q.V.: Learning transferable architectures for scalable image recognition. In: IEEE Conference on Computer Vision and Pattern Recognition, pp. 8697–8710 (2018)

# Learning to Read *L'Infinito*: Handwritten Text Recognition with Synthetic Training Data

Silvia Cascianelli[(✉)] [iD], Marcella Cornia [iD], Lorenzo Baraldi [iD],
Maria Ludovica Piazzi, Rosiana Schiuma, and Rita Cucchiara [iD]

University of Modena and Reggio Emilia, Modena, Italy
{silvia.cascianelli,marcella.cornia,lorenzo.baraldi,marialudovica.piazzi,
rosiana.schiuma,rita.cucchiara}@unimore.it

**Abstract.** Deep learning-based approaches to Handwritten Text Recognition (HTR) have shown remarkable results on publicly available large datasets, both modern and historical. However, it is often the case that historical manuscripts are preserved in small collections, most of the time with unique characteristics in terms of paper support, author handwriting style, and language. State-of-the-art HTR approaches struggle to obtain good performance on such small manuscript collections, for which few training samples are available. In this paper, we focus on HTR on small historical datasets and propose a new historical dataset, which we call Leopardi, with the typical characteristics of small manuscript collections, consisting of letters by the poet Giacomo Leopardi, and devise strategies to deal with the training data scarcity scenario. In particular, we explore the use of carefully designed but cost-effective synthetic data for pre-training HTR models to be applied to small single-author manuscripts. Extensive experiments validate the suitability of the proposed approach, and both the Leopardi dataset and synthetic data will be available to favor further research in this direction.

**Keywords:** Handwritten text recognition · Historical documents · Synthetic data

## 1 Introduction

Transcribing ancient manuscripts is key in their conservation and valorization. Having searchable and easily accessible digital text will both ease scholars in their research activity and allow a broad lay public to read ancient texts (either by very famous authors and unknown people) without being experts in paleography and philology. AI-based techniques have already proven to be high-performing when it comes to recognizing patterns from visual inputs, and images of manuscripts make no exception [3,7]. In this context, state-of-the-art Handwritten Text Recognition (HTR) systems have shown remarkable performance when applied to both modern and historical manuscripts [1,6,12,18,23]. This is

N. Tsapatsoulis et al. (Eds.): CAIP 2021, LNCS 13053, pp. 340–350, 2021.
https://doi.org/10.1007/978-3-030-89131-2_31

allowed by the modeling capability of the deep convolutional and recurrent neural networks that constitute these systems, which, however, need a significant
quantity of data to train properly. In this respect, historical documents pose
critical challenges related to the historical period and geographic area in which
they were edited. Calligraphical handwriting has significantly changed over the
centuries, and many of the preserved more recent manuscripts have been written in the personal handwriting style of their authors. For this reason, HTR
systems trained on a specific handwriting style (or even on multiple handwriting
styles) can be ineffective when applied to manuscripts in a different style. Digital
libraries and archives can contain valuable manuscripts by historically and culturally important authors, which could be valorized and made available to the
large public by automatic transcription. However, such manuscripts can be in a
small quantity, making the training of HTR systems ineffective or even unnec-
essary. In this respect, strategies should be developed to enable high-quality
automatic transcription from few or none annotated training manuscripts.

To this end, we propose a new historical HTR dataset containing letters from
the famous Italian writer Giacomo Leopardi[1]. The dataset is relatively small and
poses the typical challenges of HTR for small but relevant document collections
preserved in historical libraries and archives. In particular, the paper support has
scratches and creases, there are stains and bleed-through ink, and the used language is early-seventeenth century Italian (thus, different from other languages
such as modern English, it is not sufficiently represented in standard language
corpora). The dataset is annotated at line-level, which is quicker and cheaper
to obtain compared to word-level annotation and allows gathering a fair number of training samples compared to paragraph-level or page-level annotation.
Moreover, line-level HTR systems are the most common in literature and can be
easily integrated into a transcription pipeline in conjunction with layout analysis and line-level segmentation. The dataset is used as a test bench for the task
of HTR on documents with limited training data and can be used for further
research. Moreover, to deal with the aforementioned task, we consider direct
transfer learning from a number of both modern and historical source datasets
and pre-training plus fine-tuning on a specifically designed synthetic dataset.

## 2   Related Work

An important factor for the development of efficient deep learning solutions is
the availability of big datasets. Here we review some of the most commonly used
western-characters datasets for line-level HTR. The most commonly used line-
level modern datasets are the IAM [16] and the RIMES [2] datasets. The former
is a collection of handwritten English sentences from the Lancaster-Oslo/Berge
(LOB) corpus [14], produced by approximately 40 different writers, for a total
of 10 373 lines. The latter contains free-layout letters handwritten by multiple

---

[1] Giacomo Leopardi (Recanati, 1798 - Naples, 1837) was an Italian philologist, writer,
and poet, considered to be one of the most relevant authors of the Italian Romanti-
cism literary current. *L'Infinito* (The Infinite) is one of his most known poems.

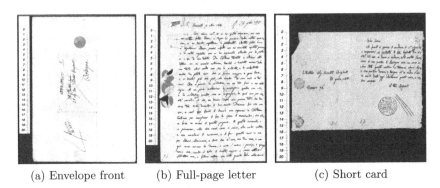

(a) Envelope front    (b) Full-page letter    (c) Short card

**Fig. 1.** Sample pages of the three categories considered for obtaining our devised Leopardi dataset.

authors in modern French, for a total of 12 111 lines. Among historical datasets, the largest and most commonly used line-level ones are those used for the International Conference on Frontiers of Handwriting Recognition 2014 and 2016 HTR challenges, namely the ICFHR14 [20] and ICFHR16 [21] datasets. The former consist of legal forms and drafts from the Bentham Papers collection [4], handwritten by the English philosopher Jeremy Bentham and his collaborators between mid-18th century and mid-19th century, for a total of 11 473 lines. The latter contains registers of the Bozen's Town Council's discussions from the Ratsprotokolle collection, handwritten by multiple writers from 1470 to 1805 in old German, for a total of 10 550 lines. Most of the available historical manuscript datasets are of small size. Among the most used there are those collected in the IAM-HisDB project [10]. These are the George Washington dataset, consisting of 656 lines from letters written in 18th century English by George Washington and one of his collaborators, the Parzival dataset [9], consisting of 4 477 lines of a Medieval German manuscript by two different writers, and the Saint Gall dataset [11], consisting of 1 410 lines from a single-writer 9th century Latin manuscript. Another interesting historical dataset is the Esposalles [19], a collection of 5 447 lines written in 17th century Catalan by a single writer. The number of lines in our presented Leopardi dataset is comparable to those of the aforementioned small historical datasets, is single-author and entirely in Italian.

A possible strategy to deal with HTR with small training sets is to apply data augmentation [17,18,26,27]. Typically, data augmentation consists of generic random distortions and color modifications. For big historical datasets, in [5], the authors demonstrated the benefits of carefully designed data augmentation. Another strategy is to apply transfer learning [1,12,13,15,25], *i.e.*, pretraining the HTR model on a big HTR dataset and fine-tuning it on the small training set of the dataset of interest. For HTR on small single-writer historical datasets, pretraining plus fine-tuning has been proven to be a more effective strategy than data augmentation [1]. Hence, in this work, we focus on this strategy. The dataset used for pretraining is, in general, one of the available benchmark ones. In [22],

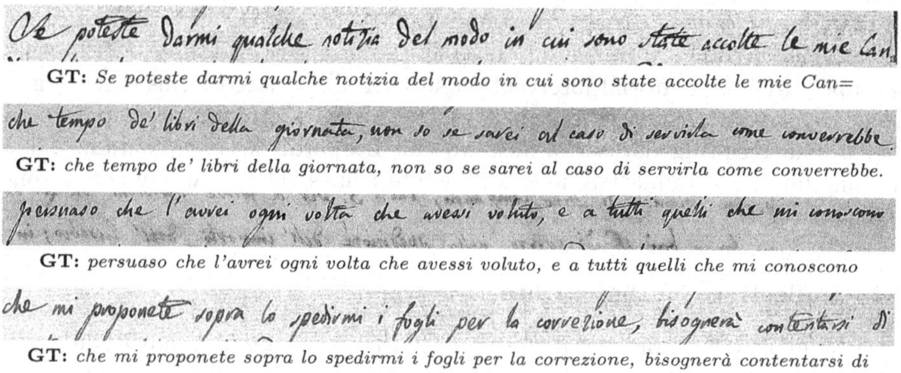

GT: *Se poteste darmi qualche notizia del modo in cui sono state accolte le mie Can=*

GT: *che tempo de' libri della giornata, non so se sarei al caso di servirla come converrebbe.*

GT: *persuaso che l'avrei ogni volta che avessi voluto, e a tutti quelli che mi conoscono*

GT: *che mi proponete sopra lo spedirmi i fogli per la correzione, bisognerà contentarsi di*

**Fig. 2.** Sample images and corresponding ground-truth (GT) transcription of the text lines contained in the collected Leopardi dataset.

instead, the authors used a synthetic dataset obtained by concatenating isolated handwritten Chinese characters to obtain synthetic text lines. Moreover, in [15], the authors proposed to pretrain a model on generic modern synthetic data and apply it to modern HTR data. Different from their approach, here, we carefully design synthetic data for pretraining a model for HTR on historical manuscripts.

## 3   Training HTR Models on Small Datasets

In this section, we present our Leopardi dataset and detail the semi-automatic procedure we propose for building a large quantity of synthetic training data. Moreover, we outline the HTR models considered for validating our approach.

### 3.1   Leopardi Dataset

To favor the research towards HTR systems able to work on historical documents even in the absence of large training datasets, we devise a new dataset consisting of a small collection of early 19$^{th}$ Century letters written in Italian by Giacomo Leopardi. The letters are preserved at the Estense Library in Modena, and their high-resolution scans are also available at its Digital Library[2]. In particular, there are 168 pages containing text in Giacomo Leopardi's handwriting, both letter bodies and envelope fronts.

For this study, the pages have been categorized in envelope fronts, full-page letters, and short cards (see Fig. 1). Half of the pages in each category have been used to obtain the training set (for a total of 84 pages), and the remaining pages in each category have been equally divided for obtaining the validation and test sets (both consisting of 42 pages). We manually segmented the pages at line level, with rectangular bounding boxes oriented to follow the line inclination. Each

---

[2] https://edl.beniculturali.it.

line has been manually transcribed and double-checked by experts. Note that we obtained diplomatic transcriptions (*i.e.*, the text is transcribed as it appears on paper, with no editorial intervention such as abbreviated forms extensions), where stroke-out text is transcribed as "#". Some examples are reported in Fig. 2. The resulting dataset, which we call Leopardi dataset, contains 1 303 training lines, 587 validation lines, and 569 test lines. The total number of non-*blank* characters in this dataset is 77.

### 3.2   Collecting Synthetic Data

Ancient manuscripts preserved in digital libraries are often organized in small collections authored by a single, culturally relevant author. This is also the case of the collection from which we obtained the Leopardi dataset. To deal with the training data scarcity of this scenario, we propose to semi-automatically generate synthetic data that closely mimic the real ones and can be used for training HTR models able to adapt easily to the real set.

In particular, we isolate two to four variants of Giacomo Leopardi's most used glyphs (*i.e.*, punctuation marks, typographic symbols, characters, and their ligatures) and combine them in a randomized font built with a professional tool. Then, we collect free e-books of Giacomo Leopardi's main prose works to better capture the author's writing style and language and split their text into lines of random length ranging from 6 to 10 words, as this is the typical length of the lines in the real dataset. Finally, we type the so obtained lines with the built font at different sizes, and we superimpose on the lines a piece of paper with no writes on it, from the same collection as the letters, to simulate the typical background of ancient documents. Some examples of text in the synthetic font in comparison with real Giacomo Leopardi's handwriting are reported in Fig. 3.

Note that isolating and transcribing a text line for the real Leopardi dataset took around 120 s. With our automatic procedure, we are able to generate arbitrarily big synthetic datasets in negligible time once the font is built. For this work, we obtain 111 465 text lines, 89 068 of which are used for training, and the remaining 22 397 for validation. The total number of non-*blank* characters in the synthetic dataset is 114. Furthermore, during the training with these text synthetic data, we apply random distortions to simulate variations in the shape of the handwritten characters and ink stains.

### 3.3   Baseline Models

Many state-of-the-art approaches for HTR work at line-level, *i.e.*, take as input an image representing a handwritten text line. The image is fed to a convolutional neural network to extract a sequence of visual feature vectors from the feature map of the last layer. In particular, the $C$-dimensional vectors of each of the $H$ rows of the $H \times W \times C$ feature map are stacked to obtain a sequence of $W$ feature vectors with $(H \cdot C)$-elements each. Each feature vector of the sequence corresponds to a region of the original image.

(a) Leopardi Real                           (b) Leopardi Synth

**Fig. 3.** Sample text parts from the real Leopardi dataset (a) and the corresponding text in the font and style used for obtaining the synthetic dataset (b).

The sequence is fed to a recurrent neural network that outputs, for each feature vector, the probability that the corresponding image region contains one of the characters in the charset, plus a special *blank* character meaning "no other characters". Finally, a decoding block outputs the final transcription by taking the most probable character at each timestep, removing duplicate characters not separated by a *blank*, and then removing the blanks. Such architectures are usually trained to maximize the Connectionist Temporal Classifier (CTC) probability of the transcribed sequence.

In this work, we consider two variants of this pipeline, commonly adopted as backbone for HTR systems, namely the method proposed by Shi *et al.* [23] for sequence recognition and that proposed by Puigcerver [18] for HTR. The first variant has a deeper convolutional part, while the second has a deeper recurrent part. Moreover, we consider two further variants of these models that employ Deformable Convolutions (DefConvs) [8] in place of standard convolutions in the convolutional part, as proposed in [6].

**Shi.** *et al.* **2016.** [23] In this variant, the convolutional part has the same architecture as VGG-11 [24] up to the sixth convolutional block, plus a $7^{th}$ one with a $2 \times 2$ kernel. Moreover, the receptive field of the $3^{rd}$ and $4^{th}$ max-pooling layers are rectangular $2 \times 1$ instead of $2 \times 2$, so that the resulting feature maps are wider and better reflect the height-width ratio of text-lines images. The recurrent part of this variant consists of a stack of two Bidirectional Long Short-Term Memory networks (BLSTMs).

**Puigcerver, 2017.** [18] In this variant, the convolutional part consists of five blocks containing a convolutional layer with $3 \times 3$ kernels, a Batch Normalization layer, and a LeakyReLU activation function. The convolutional layers at the $k = 1, ..., 5$ blocks have $16k$ filters, respectively. Moreover, a $2 \times 2$ max-pooling operation is applied to the output of the first three blocks. The recurrent part of this variant consists of a stack of five BLSTMs.

**Applying Deformable Convolutions.** [6] The mentioned variants use standard convolutions to represent the input image. In our recent work [6], we demonstrated the suitability of DefConvs to the HTR task due to the capability of their kernel to adapt to handwritten strokes and thus better deal with character variations in shape, scale, and orientation. In particular, the kernel grid of DefConvs is deformed depending on the processed input thanks to a set of learnable translation vectors, each applied to a separate element of the kernel grid. In this work, we further test the performance of DefConvs in the HTR task when trained on small historical datasets. For this reason, we replace the standard convolutional layers in the Shi *et al.* [23] and Puigcerver [18] variants with DefConvs layers. A DefConv layer is obtained by concatenating a standard convolutional layer in charge of learning the translation vectors and another convolutional layer in charge of learning the kernel weights.

## 4    Experimental Evaluation

In this section, we evaluate the performance of the considered HTR models when pretrained on the semi-automatically obtained synthetic data and then applied or fine-tuned on the presented Leopardi dataset. We compare our approach to pretraining on different datasets, both synthetic and real, and to training from scratch on the Leopardi dataset. The results are expressed in terms of the commonly used Character Error Rate (CER) and Word Error Rate (WER) scores.

### 4.1    Implementation Details

In the considered models, the output of the convolutional part is a $2 \times W \times 512$ tensor for the variants based on [23] and a $16 \times W \times 80$ tensor for those based on [18]. These are collapsed in a sequence of $W$ vectors of $1\,024$ and $1\,280$ elements, respectively. The BLSTMs have 512 hidden units each in the Shi *et al.* [23] variants and 256 in the Puigcerver [18] variants. The recurrent layers are separated by a dropout layer with dropout probability equal to 0.5.

When training from scratch or fine-tuning, we normalize the text line images between $-1$ and 1 and rescale them in height, keeping the original aspect ratio. In particular, the rescaled height is 60 pixels for the variants based on Shi *et al.* [23], 128 for those based on Puigcerver [18]. When pretraining, additionally to these pre-processing steps, we randomly alter the image brightness (with factor chosen between 0.5 and 5), its contrast (with factor chosen between 0.1 and 10), its saturation (with factor chosen between 0 and 5), and its hue (with factor chosen between $-0.1$ and 0.1), and apply Gaussian blur with size 5 and standard deviation randomly chosen between 0.1 and 2. Moreover, we randomly apply one of the following geometric distortions: random rotation between $-1°$ and $1°$, affine transformation randomly rotating the image between $-1°$ and $1°$ and randomly shearing it between $-50°$ and $30°$, or random homography.

When pretraining the models, we use batch size 16, while for fine-tuning and training from scratch, the batch size is 8. We use a learning rate of $10^{-4}$ in all experiments except for training from scratch the variants based on [18], where we use a learning rate equal to $3 \cdot 10^{-4}$. The proposed models have been trained using Adam as optimizer with $\beta_1 = 0.9$ and $\beta_2 = 0.999$, in combination with a scheduler that reduces the learning rate by a factor 0.1 when the CER on the validation set reaches a plateau. We train the models until the CER on the

**Table 1.** Performance of the considered models when pretrained on different real and synthetic datasets and directly applied to the Leopardi dataset test set.

|  | [23] | | [18] | | [23]+DefConv[6] | | [18]+DefConv[6] | |
|---|---|---|---|---|---|---|---|---|
|  | CER | WER | CER | WER | CER | WER | CER | WER |
| ICFHR14 | 47.2 | 102.7 | 59.7 | 120.1 | 77.8 | 112.4 | 103.9 | 147.1 |
| ICFHR16 | 76.0 | 129.8 | 79.1 | 111.0 | 83.1 | 109.3 | 86.9 | 144.6 |
| IAM | 46.5 | 92.9 | 68.0 | 96.4 | 60.4 | 97.5 | 74.4 | 98.9 |
| RIMES | 43.4 | 88.0 | 73.9 | 103.9 | 72.8 | 100.0 | 69.5 | 97.1 |
| Modern Leopardi Synth | 59.2 | 100.9 | 65.6 | 101.8 | 61.5 | 100.5 | 64.1 | 101.6 |
| **Leopardi Synth** | **35.9** | **86.4** | **38.5** | **93.9** | **40.2** | **92.1** | **36.3** | **94.0** |

validation set stops improving for 20 epochs in case of pretraining, 80 epochs in case of fine-tuning and training from scratch.

## 4.2  Experimental Results

First, we compare the performance of the four presented HTR models when pretrained on a big HTR dataset (source) and then directly applied to the test set of the devised Leopardi dataset (target). We consider both real benchmark datasets and synthetic datasets. In particular, the real datasets are the modern IAM and RIMES datasets and the historical ICFHR14 and ICFHR16 datasets, introduced in Sect. 2. The synthetic datasets are Leopardi Synth and Modern Leopardi Synth. Both are obtained by following the procedure explained in Sect. 3.2, the former by using the font inspired by Giacomo Leopardi's handwriting, the latter by using three freely available modern handwriting fonts. Note that the text, background, number of lines, and random transformations applied during training are the same for both these synthetic datasets. The results are reported in Table 1 and clearly show that directly applying models trained on the Leopardi Synth data allows reaching the lowest CER and WER on the real Leopardi dataset.

Further, we compare the performance of the considered models pretrained on the Leopardi Synth dataset and then fine-tuned on the 100% and 50% of the lines in the real Leopardi training, with the same models trained from scratch on the same quantity of real Leopardi training lines. The results are reported in Table 2, where we also report the results of the direct application of the models pretrained on Leopardi Synth for comparison. The benefits of pretraining are more evident in the case of fine-tuning on 50% of the training lines. In fact, in this case, the CER decreases by 1.8 and the WER of 4.1 on average, while in the case of fine-tuning on 100% of the training lines, the CER decreases by 0.8 and the WER of 3.1 on average.

**Table 2.** Experimental results of the considered models when pretrained on the Leopardi Synth dataset and then fine-tuned on different portions of the real Leopardi dataset, compared to their performance when trained from scratch on the same lines of the real Leopardi dataset.

| | [23] | | [18] | | [23]+DefConv[6] | | [18]+DefConv[6] | |
|---|---|---|---|---|---|---|---|---|
| | CER | WER | CER | WER | CER | WER | CER | WER |
| *Real Training Data: 0%* | | | | | | | | |
| **Leopardi Synth** | 35.9 | 86.4 | 38.5 | 93.9 | 40.2 | 92.1 | 36.3 | 94.0 |
| *Real Training Data: 50%* | | | | | | | | |
| Leopardi Real | 7.2 | 27.2 | 8.2 | 27.8 | 6.7 | 24.6 | 8.0 | 28.1 |
| **Leopardi Synth** | **5.7** | **22.1** | **5.7** | **21.6** | **6.1** | **23.0** | **5.3** | **20.3** |
| *Real Training Data: 100%* | | | | | | | | |
| Leopardi Real | 4.3 | 17.2 | 5.6 | 20.5 | 3.4 | 13.3 | 4.1 | 15.4 |
| **Leopardi Synth** | **3.8** | **14.3** | **3.8** | **14.3** | **3.2** | **12.7** | **3.3** | **12.8** |

## 5    Conclusion

In this paper, we explored line-level HTR on historical manuscripts when limited training data are available. To this end, we devised a newly collected dataset taken from letters authored by the Italian writer Giacomo Leopardi, which poses the typical challenges of small collections of handwritten historical documents. To deal with this scenario, we propose pretraining on a large quantity of synthetic data that reflect the real target manuscripts, which we built with a semi-automatic procedure, and fine-tuning on a portion of real data. The obtained experimental results demonstrate the suitability of the proposed approach for several HTR models, both in a direct transfer learning and a pretraining and fine-tuning scenario.

**Acknowledgments.** This work was supported by the "AI for Digital Humanities" project (Pratica Sime n.2018.0390), funded by "Fondazione di Modena", and by the "DHMoRe Lab" project (CUP E94I19001060003), funded by "Regione Emilia Romagna". We also thank Estense Digital Library for the support in the preparation of the Leopardi dataset.

## References

1. Aradillas, J.C., Murillo-Fuentes, J.J., Olmos, P.M.: Boosting offline handwritten text recognition in historical documents with few labeled lines. arXiv preprint arXiv:2012.02544 (2020)
2. Augustin, E., Carré, M., Grosicki, E., Brodin, J.M., Geoffrois, E., Prêteux, F.: RIMES evaluation campaign for handwritten mail processing. In: IWFHR (2006)
3. Baraldi, L., Cornia, M., Grana, C., Cucchiara, R.: Aligning text and document illustrations: towards visually explainable digital humanities. In: ICPR (2018)

4. Causer, T., Wallace, V.: Building a volunteer community: results and findings from transcribe bentham. Digit. Humanit. Q. **6** (2012)
5. Chammas, E., Mokbel, C., Likforman-Sulem, L.: Handwriting recognition of historical documents with few labeled data. In: DAS (2018)
6. Cojocaru, I., Cascianelli, S., Baraldi, L., Corsini, M., Cucchiara, R.: Watch your strokes: improving handwritten text recognition with deformable convolutions. In: ICPR (2020)
7. Cornia, M., Stefanini, M., Baraldi, L., Corsini, M., Cucchiara, R.: Explaining digital humanities by aligning images and textual descriptions. Pattern Recognit. Lett. **129**, 166–172 (2020)
8. Dai, J., et al.: Deformable convolutional networks. In: CVPR (2017)
9. Fischer, A., Frinken, V., Fornés, A., Bunke, H.: Transcription alignment of Latin manuscripts using hidden Markov models. In: Proceedings of the 2011 Workshop on Historical Document Imaging and Processing (2011)
10. Fischer, A., Keller, A., Frinken, V., Bunke, H.: Lexicon-free handwritten word spotting using character HMMs. Pattern Recogni. Lett. **33**(7), 934–942 (2012)
11. Fischer, A., et al.: Automatic transcription of handwritten medieval documents. In: VSMM (2009)
12. Granet, A., Morin, E., Mouchère, H., Quiniou, S., Viard-Gaudin, C.: Transfer learning for handwriting recognition on historical documents. In: ICPRAM (2018)
13. Jaramillo, J.C.A., Murillo-Fuentes, J.J., Olmos, P.M.: Boosting handwriting text recognition in small databases with transfer learning. In: ICFHR (2018)
14. Johansson, S., Leech, G.N., Goodluck, H.: Manual of information to accompany the Lancaster-Oslo/Bergen Corpus of British English, for use with digital computer. Department of English, University of Oslo (1978)
15. Kang, L., Riba, P., Rusiñol, M., Fornés, A., Villegas, M.: Pay attention to what you read: non-recurrent handwritten text-line recognition. arXiv preprint arXiv:2005.13044 (2020)
16. Marti, U.V., Bunke, H.: The IAM-database: an English sentence database for offline handwriting recognition. IJDAR **5**(1), 39–46 (2002)
17. Poznanski, A., Wolf, L.: CNN-N-gram for handwriting word recognition. In: CVPR (2016)
18. Puigcerver, J.: Are multidimensional recurrent layers really necessary for handwritten text recognition? In: ICDAR (2017)
19. Romero, V., et al.: The ESPOSALLES database: an ancient marriage license corpus for off-line handwriting recognition. Pattern Recognit. **46**(6), 1658–1669 (2013)
20. Sánchez, J.A., Romero, V., Toselli, A.H., Vidal, E.: ICFHR2014 competition on handwritten text recognition on transcriptorium datasets (HTRtS). In: ICFHR (2014)
21. Sanchez, J.A., Romero, V., Toselli, A.H., Vidal, E.: ICFHR2016 competition on handwritten text recognition on the READ dataset. In: ICFHR (2016)
22. Shen, X., Messina, R.: A method of synthesizing handwritten Chinese images for data augmentation. In: ICFHR (2016)
23. Shi, B., Bai, X., Yao, C.: An end-to-end trainable neural network for image-based sequence recognition and its application to scene text recognition. IEEE Trans. PAMI **39**(11), 2298–2304 (2016)
24. Simonyan, K., Zisserman, A.: Very deep convolutional networks for large-scale image recognition. In: ICLR (2015)
25. Soullard, Y., Swaileh, W., Tranouez, P., Paquet, T., Chatelain, C.: Improving text recognition using optical and language model writer adaptation. In: ICDAR (2019)

26. Voigtlaender, P., Doetsch, P., Ney, H.: Handwriting recognition with large multidimensional long short-term memory recurrent neural networks. In: ICFHR (2016)
27. Wigington, C., Stewart, S., Davis, B., Barrett, B., Price, B., Cohen, S.: Data augmentation for recognition of handwritten words and lines using a CNN-LSTM network. In: ICDAR (2017)

# Robust Watermarking Approach for 3D Multiresolution Meshes Based on Multi-wavelet Transform, SHA512 and Turbocodes

Malika Jallouli[1], Ikbel Sayahi[2(✉)], Anouar Ben Mabrouk[3,4], Mohamed Ali Mahjoub[1], and Chokri Ben Amar[2,5]

[1] LATIS Laboratory of Advanced Technology and Intelligent Systems, Université de Sousse, Ecole Nationale d'Ingénieurs de Sousse, 4023 Sousse, Tunisia
[2] Research Groups on Intelligent Machines Laboratory, Private National Engineering School of Monastir, University of Sfax, Monastir, Tunisia
[3] Department of Mathematics, Higher Institute of Applied Mathematics and Computer Science, University of Kairouan, 3100 Kairouan, Tunisia
[4] Department of Mathematics, Faculty of Science, University of Tabuk, Tabuk, Saudi Arabia
[5] College of Computers and Information Technology, Taif University, Taif, Saudi Arabia

**Abstract.** Since the 3D mesh security 3D mesh security has become intellectual property, 3D watermarking algorithms have continued to appear to secure 3D meshes shared by remote users. The originality of this approach is to insert copyright data in multiresolution domain using multi-wavelet transform which allowed us to significantly increase the size of the watermark. Our algorithm includes then two rounds of insertion where each one applies a different type of wavelet transform. The first one undergoes coefficients generated by Haar wavelet transform. As for the second iteration, it inserts data into coefficients resulting from Schauder wavelet transform. The watermark, which is a combination of the mesh description and source mesh signature (generated using SHA512) are encoded using a Turbo-code before being inserted into wavelet coefficients. Embedding data includes a transformation of these later to spherical coordinate system and a modulation steps. Finally watermarked mesh is reconstructed using inverse wavelet transform. The experimentation of our approach has shown a very high insertion rate due to the use of the hybrid insertion domain, while maintaining the mesh quality. Watermarked mesh and extracted data are obtained in real time. Our approach is also robust against the most popular attacks. Our results showed that the present approach improves the existing works.

**Keywords:** Multiwavelet transform · Turbocode · SHA512 · 3D multirolution meshes · Robustness · Invisibility · Insertion rate

© Springer Nature Switzerland AG 2021
N. Tsapatsoulis et al. (Eds.): CAIP 2021, LNCS 13053, pp. 351–360, 2021.
https://doi.org/10.1007/978-3-030-89131-2_32

# 1 Introduction

Since the last decade, 3D objects have been increasingly used in all domains. This wide range of application of 3D multiresolution meshes has made the protection of this type of data, frequently shared between remote users and saved in remote multimedia databases, an intellectual property.

To achieve this goal, efforts to develop 3D watermarking algorithms have continued to appear until today. Researchers have been trying to find the right compromise between the insertion rate, the invisibility and the robustness through the use of a wide variety of techniques. Despite all these improvements, 3D watermarking field still far from the level of maturity.

As a solution, we propose in this paper a new approach of 3D watermarking targeting 3D multiresolution meshes. Our approach is based on the use of multiwavelet to enhance invisibility while maintaining very high insertion rate, SHA512 to generate signature of the mesh source and turbocode to ensure robustness criteria. The originality of our approach may be resumed in the following points.

- The use of multiwavelet transfom to present the mesh in the multiresolution domain to guarantee invisibility and robustness against attacks and to enhance significantly the amount of information to be inserted.
- The use of turbocode to be able to extract correctly altered and even destroyed data from the watermarked and attacked meshes.
- The insertion of a grayscale image reflecting copyright information into the mesh. To enhance security, this image is encrypted using AES algorithm before being embedded.

# 2 Related Works

Sharing 3D meshes between remote users poses major security problems. Since these problems imposed themselves, efforts to propose adequate solutions have continued to appear until today. Indeed, to protect 3D meshes, several 3D watermarking approaches appeared. The main goal is to find the best compromise between watermark criteria: insertion rate, invisibility and robustness against attacks through the use of multitude techniques and tools. In order to classify these solutions, we consider the inserting domain as a criterion. The first kind being is approaches operating in the spatial domain, such as the approaches of Hitendra published in [4], Tsai et al. in [7] and Wang et al. in [5]. These approaches embed data either in the topological or in the geometric information. As for the second category, a transformed domain is used. Frequency domain [1–3,6,15] and multiresolution domain [8–11] are the most used domains. In this case data is inserted by modifying the frequency and multiresolutions coefficients. Notwithstanding the significant improvements brought by algorithms proposed over the last decade, digital watermarking field still suffers from deficiencies. This comes down, firstly, to the complexity to find the best compromise between watermark invisibility, high capacity and robustness which are contradictory (the increase of capacity causes either a deterioration of the mesh quality or reduces the level of robustness). Secondly, treating 3D multiresloution meshes is not an easy mission in comparing them with other types of meshes. This is justified by the sensitivity of handling this type of meshes which is due to the existence of the multi-resolution appearance in the 3D meshes.

## 3   Used Tools

### 3.1   SHA2 Algorithm

SHA-2 is a family of hashing functions that were designed by the US National Security Agency. It has six different variants (SHA-224, SHA-256, SHA-284, SHA-512, SHA-512/224 and SHA-512/256), which differ in proportion with the bit size used for encrypting data. Especially in this work, we work with SHA512 which is a hash algorithm based on non-reversible functions created specifically so that no decryption method exists, so it is inviolable. This algorithm includes three steps, namely:

- Input formatting: The input data to SHA512 must be a multiple of 1024 bits.
- Hash buffer initialization: To initialize buffers during the first iteration.
- Message Processing: Using addition and round operations for each bloc.

### 3.2   Multi-wavelet Transform

The proposed method in this paper is based on a combination of two different scaling functions (Haar and Schauder). The generated multiscale function is a new multiwavelet called Haar-Schauder Multiwavelet: the first function is the well known Haar wavelet based on the explicit $\varphi_1 = \chi_{[0\ 1[}$, the seconf one is based on Faber-Schauder wavelet based on $\varphi_2 = (1 - |x|)\chi_{[-1\ 1[}$ function which is a piecewise linear one.

The multiscaling function is giving by:

$$\phi(x) = \begin{pmatrix} \chi_{[0\ 1[} \\ (1 - |x|)\chi_{[-1\ 1[} \end{pmatrix} \tag{1}$$

Because of the compactness of Haar and schauder support, $H_l = 0$ whenever $|l| \geq 2$, thus

$$\phi = H_{-1}\phi_{1,-1} + H_0\phi_{1,0} + H_1\phi_{1,1}. \tag{2}$$

the values of $H_i$ are

$$H_{-1} = H_1 = \frac{1}{\sqrt{2}} \begin{pmatrix} 0 & 0 \\ 0 & 1/2 \end{pmatrix}, \ H_0 = \frac{1}{\sqrt{2}} \begin{pmatrix} 1 & 0 \\ 0 & 1 \end{pmatrix}. \tag{3}$$

The final multiwavelet mother function is:

$$\psi = G_{-1}\phi_{1,-1} + G_0\phi_{1,0} + G_1\phi_{1,1}. \tag{4}$$

where $G_l = (-1)^l H_{1-l}$.

## 3.3    Turbocodes

The effectiveness of error-correcting codes in the field of telecommunication lets us think vividly to use them for the recovery of altered watermarks. Especially in this paper, we use parallel turbo code. This new concept is similar to the notion of concatenated error-correcting codes since this is the concatenation of two convolutional codes separated by an interleaving block. Although this concatenation generates the doubling of the output information size, it remarkably enhances the ability of the model to correct errors that have occurred. Especially in this work, we focus on parallel concatenation.

A parallel turbo encoder step is executed before dissemination step to add control sequence to the original data. These sequences allow the correction of errors during the decoding phase. The parallel turbo encoder aims to encode the data simultaneously using two convolutional encoders. The result, as shown in Fig. 1 is in the form of three codewords. The final codeword (to be transmitted) is then the concatenation of these three.

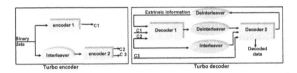

**Fig. 1.**  Parallel turbo encoder.

As for the turbo decoder, it aims to decode input data and correct any errors that have occurred. The output data from this decoder should be identical to that used as input for the encoder. The parallel turbo decoder architecture, as shown in Fig. 1, has two convolutional decoders working with the Viterbi algorithm, two interleaves and one deinterleave.

The interleave block is a required element in the diagram of a turbo code whose absence significantly affects its power. Indeed, this block allows swapping the data during their transition between the convolutional codes used so that two symbols close to the origin are as far as possible from each other which allow acting directly on the minimum distance of Hamming these codes. This allows in particular transforming an error involving grouped bits into an error distributed over the entire sequence.

## 3.4    LSB Mthod

LSB (Least Significant Bit) method is a steganographic process that applies the least significant bits of a sample of data to represent another one. In this paper, we used LSB method in order to insert data into 3D meshes especially by means of its spherical harmonics coefficients. Indeed, modifying, according to the information to be inserted, the bits of low weight of these coefficients ensure the invisibility of our watermarking system (see Fig. 2).

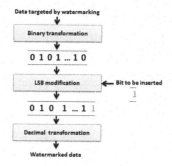

**Fig. 2.** LSB method.

# 4 Approach Description

Our watermarking scheme consists of inserting a watermark into a multi-resolution 3D mesh. The aim was to insert the mesh description as well as the mesh source signature in order to implement a system of copyright and indexing. The insertion phase is the first part of the watermarking diagram. It aims to insert the data into the mesh without altering its quality despite the high insertion rate. The application of treatments or attacks on this mesh must not alter the inserted data. As presented in Fig. 3, this phase involves preparing the watermark, host mesh and two iterations of watermarking.

Mesh preparation involves the application of a multi-wavelet transform to extract the wavelet coefficients targeted by the insertion. As for the preparation of the watermark, it consists in generating the digital signature of the source of the mesh and concatenating it with a description. The whole signal will be then transformed into a binary sequence before being encoded by a turbo encoder to generate the final codeword to be inserted into the mesh.

Once the host mesh and watermark are ready, two iterations of insertion will take place using the LSB method. Different modulation coefficients are used to eliminate the overlap between the inserted data.

Once the signal is received after a dissemination step, inserted data should be retrieved from the 3D multi-resolution mesh. To do it, the watermarked mesh undergoes a multiwavelet decomposition to extract wavelet coefficients. These Later go through two iterations of extraction, as shown in Fig. 3, to retrieve both parts of the already inserted data. A verification of integrity and copyright is done after decoding retrieved information using the parallel turbo decoder.

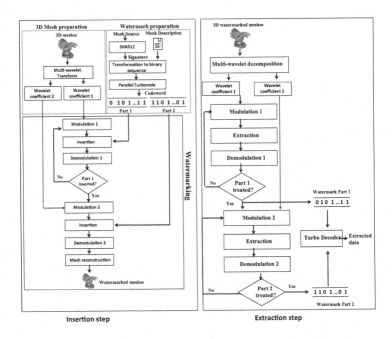

**Fig. 3.** Overview of our approach.

# 5   Results

The experimentation of our approach focuses on the following criteria:

- Insertion rate: it reflects the amount of information to be inserted into the mesh and will be measured using the number of bits.
- Invisibility: it refers to the influence of data insertion (gray-scale image in our case) on the quality of mesh that is measured in PSNR and MSQE.
- Robustness: it reflects the ability of our approach to retain data already inserted despite any treatment (or attack) applied to the watermarked mesh. The better the image is extracted, the more robust our algorithm is. To conclude on the robustness, the correlation metric is used.

## 5.1   Data Used for Tests

to test our approach, we use semi-regular multi-resolution meshes stored in DAT format files. In this category of files, 3D object is represented at different levels of details. It is in fact composed of a coarse mesh and more information to refine the coarse mesh to its finest levels version. Very few are the watermarking works manipulating files with this extension. This is due to the sensitivity of meshes having this structure. In this work, we watermarked multiresolution meshes of various sizes (Feline.dat with 258,046 Vertex, Horse.dat with112642 vertex, rabbit with 70658 vrtex, Banny with 34835 vertex and venus.dat with 40962 vertex). These objects are characterized by containing forms having very sensitive details. These latter are easily influenced by any treatment which threatens the invisibility criterion.

## 5.2  Invisibility and Insertion Rate Evaluation

To conclude on the effectiveness of a watermarking scheme, it was necessary to evaluate its invisibility and its insertion rate. The results of Mean SQuared Error(MSQE) and Peak Signal to Noise Ratio (PSNR) presented in Table 1 show that our algorithm have proven a high insertion rate (of the order of 500000 bits) while maintaining the quality of the mesh ($MSQE = 4.6 \times 10^{-8}$ and $PSNR = 134$). The high insertion rate is due to the use of double round of insertion which allows to double the amount of information to be inserted. In terms of MSQE value, it lies around $10^{-8}$. This low value, reflecting mesh quality conservation, is due to the transformation of the mesh in the multiresolution domain.

**Table 1.** Invisibility and insertion rate results

| Approaches | Insertion rate (bit) | MSQE | PSNR |
|---|---|---|---|
| [8] | 10650 | $0.2 \times 10^{-3}$ | – |
| [14] | 199 | $3.2 \times 10^{-5}$ | – |
| [9] | 250000 | $1,2 \times 10^{-6}$ | 126,35 |
| [10] | 337929 | $2 \times 10^{-7}$ | 131,3 |
| Our approach | 500000 | $4.6 \times 10^{-8}$ | 134 |

## 5.3  Robustness Evaluation

This section is devoted to evaluating the robustness of our algorithm against similarity transformation, noise addition, coordinate quantization, smoothing and compression attacks.

*Similarity Transformation Attack:* Which includes translation, rotation and uniform scaling. These treatments are frequently applied on watermarked meshes. Made experiments allow a correlation value equal to 1 when applying translation, rotation and uniform scaling to the watermarked meshes which justifies that our algorithm is robust against this kind of attacks.

*Noise Addition Attack;* To evaluate the robustness of our approach against this attack, we applied noise addition to watermarked meshes and tried to extract the inserted image. For each noise level, we calculate the correlation between original and extracted data. Values presented in Table 2 prove that our watermarking algorithm is robust against this attack since the correlation values are greater that 0.95(PSNR greater than 32) whatever the noise level. These results are enhanced in comparison with other recently published [5,10,12].

**Table 2.** Correlation values after Noise addition attack.

| Noise level | $10^{-3}$ | $10^{-4}$ | $10^{-5}$ | $10^{-6}$ | $10^{-7}$ |
|---|---|---|---|---|---|
| [5] | 0.05 | 0.3 | — | — | — |
| [12] | — | 0.99 | 1 | 1 | 1 |
| [10] | 0.57 | 0.9 | 1 | 1 | 1 |
| Our approach | 0.996 | 0.997 | 1 | 1 | |

*Smoothing Attack:* To evaluate the robustness of our approach against smoothing attacks, we varied the deformation factor and calculate every time the correlation between the inserted and extracted data. Results, as exposed in Table 3, that our system can extract the whole inserted data from a dfactor equal to $10^{-8}$. This result is enhanced in comparison with recent published results in [10–12,14].

**Table 3.** Correlation values due to smoothing attacks.

| dFactor | $10^{-7}$ | $10^{-8}$ | $10^{-9}$ | $10^{-10}$ |
|---|---|---|---|---|
| [11] | – | 0.18 | 0.31 | 0.43 |
| [14] | 0.4 | 0.5 | 0.8 | 1 |
| [12] | 0.9 | 1 | 1 | 1 |
| [10] | 0.8 | 0.92 | 1 | 1 |
| Our approach | 0.93 | 0.997 | 1 | 1 |

*Coordinate Quantization Attack:* To conclude the robustness of our algorithm against this attack, we opted to change the quantification level, and calculate each time the correlation between the inserted and extracted information. Obtained correlation (Table 4) is equal to 1 for a level of quantification greater than 5. These results, justified by the use of convolutional codes to retrieve the corrupted data, are very enhanced in comparison to those recently published [10, 12–14].

**Table 4.** Correlation values with applying coordinate quantization attacks.

| Quantization Level | 5 | 10 | 12 | 13 | 14 |
|---|---|---|---|---|---|
| [14] | – | 0.7 | 0.85 | – | – |
| [13] | – | 0.14 | 0.628 | 0.954 | 1 |
| [12] | 0.54 | 0.76 | 0.92 | 1 | 1 |
| [10] | 0.35 | 0.56 | 0.8 | 0.91 | 1 |
| Our approach | 0.84 | 0.91 | 1 | 1 | 1 |

*Compression Attack:* Which is often used to minimize the size of watermarked meshes before the transmission step. Compression must not alter nor deteriorate the inserted image. Results in Table 5, comprises a correlation value near or equals to 1 whatever the compression rate.

**Table 5.** Correlation values with applying compression attack.

| Bit/vertex | 0.5 | 1 | 1.5 | 2 | 2.5 | 3 |
|---|---|---|---|---|---|---|
| [13] | 0.34 | 0.4 | 0.6 | 0.89 | 0.9 | 1 |
| [12] | 0.56 | 0.79 | 0.83 | 0.9 | 0.56 | 1 |
| [10] | 0.42 | 0.6 | 0.78 | 0.9 | 1 | 1 |
| Our approach | 0.85 | 0.92 | 0.996 | 1 | 1 | 1 |

## 6  Conclusion

In this paper, we have presented a blind watermarking approach for 3D multi-resolution meshes based on the use of multi-wavelet transform, SHA512 algorithm, and turbo code. Our algorithm consists in transforming the host mesh to the multirsolution domain by applying multiwavelet transform. Each coefficient resulting from this transformation undergoes two iterations of insertion to be modified depending on the message to be inserted using the LSB method. Data to be inserted is composed of a signature generated using SHA512 algorithm and a mesh description. The whole data is coded using a parallel turbo encoder. Once all the information is inserted, mesh reconstruction takes. The watermarked mesh is then obtained.

Found results show clearly that our algorithm protects the mesh quality even with the insertion of a large amount of information due to the use of the multiwavelet. The application of various attacks (noise addition, coordinate quantization, smoothing, translation, rotation, uniform scaling and compression) to a watermarked mesh does not prevent the correct retrieval of inserted information. Obtained results are improved compared to the recently published works.

## References

1. Basyoni, L., Saleh, H.I., Abdelhalim, M.B.: Enhanced watermarking scheme for 3D mesh models. In: CIT 2015 The 7th International Conference on Information Technology, pp. 612–619 (2015). https://doi.org/10.15849/icit.2015.0107
2. Che, X., Gao, Z.: Watermarking algorithm for 3D mesh based on multi-scale radial basis functions. Int. J. Parallel Emergent Distribut. Syst. **27**(2), 133–141 (2011)
3. Geri, B.: A robust digital watermarking algorithm for three dimensional meshes. In: International Conference on Information Engineering for Mechanics and Materials, pp. 1105–1110 (2015)

4. Hitendra, G., Krishna, K.K., Manish, G., Suneeta, A.: Uniform selection of vertices for watermark embedding in 3-D polygon mesh using IEEE754 floating point representation. In: International Conference on Communication Systems and Network Technologies (2014)
5. Wang, J.T., Chang, Y.C., Yu, S.S., Yu, C.Y.: Hamming code based watermarking scheme for 3D model verification. In: International Symposium on Computer, Consumer and Control, pp. 1095–1098 (2014)
6. Lamiaa, B., Saleh, H.I., Abdelhalim, M.B.: Enhanced watermarking scheme for 3D mesh models. In: International Conference on Information Technology, pp. 612–619 (2015)
7. Tsai, Y.-Y.: An efficient 3D information hiding algorithm based on sampling concepts. Multimedia Tools Appl. **75**(13), 7891–7907 (2015). https://doi.org/10.1007/s11042-015-2707-1
8. Zaid, A.O., Hachani, M., Puech, W.: Wavelet-based high-capacity watermarking of 3-D irregular meshes. Multimedia Tools Appl. **74**(15), 5897–5915 (2014). https://doi.org/10.1007/s11042-014-1896-3
9. Sayahi, I., Elkefi, A., Ben Amar, C.: Blind watermarking algorithm for 3D multiresolution meshes based on spiral scanning method. In: International Journal of Computer Science and Information Security, vol 14, pp. 331–342 (2016)
10. Sayahi, I., Elkefi, A., Amar, C.B.: Join cryptography and digital watermarking for 3D multiresolution meshes security. In: Battiato, S., Gallo, G., Schettini, R., Stanco, F. (eds.) ICIAP 2017. LNCS, vol. 10485, pp. 637–647. Springer, Cham (2017). https://doi.org/10.1007/978-3-319-68548-9_58
11. Sayahi, I., Elkefi, A., Koubaa, M., Ben Amar, C.: Robust watermarking algorithm For 3D multiresolution meshes. In: International Conference on Computer Vision Theory and Applications, pp. 150–157 (2015)
12. Sayahi, I., Elkefi, A., Amar, C.B.: Crypto-watermarking system for safe transmission of 3D multiresolution meshes. Multimedia Tools Appl. **78**(10), 13877–13903 (2018). https://doi.org/10.1007/s11042-018-6721-y
13. Sayahi, I., Elkefi, A., Ben Amar, C.: A multi-resolution approach for blind watermarking of 3D meshes using scanning spiral method. In: International Conference on Computational Intelligence in Security for Information Systems, pp. 526–537 (2016)
14. XiaoYing, Y., Ruggero, P., Holly, R., Ioannis, I.: A 3D steganalytic algorithm and steganalysis-resistant watermarking. IEEE Trans. Visualizat. Comput. Graph. 1–12 (2016)
15. Zhou, X., Zhu, Q.: A DCT-based dual watermarking algorithm for three-dimensional mesh models. In: International Conference on Consumer Electronics, Communications and Networks, pp. 1509–1513 (2012)

# A Spherical Harmonics-LSB -quantification Adaptive Watermarking Approach for 3D Multiresolution Meshes Security

Ikbel Sayahi[2]([✉]), Malika Jallouli[1], Anouar Ben Mabrouk[3,4], Chokri Ben Amar[2,5], and Mohamed Ali Mahjoub[1]

[1] LATIS Laboratory of Advanced Technology and Intelligent Systems, Université de Sousse, Ecole Nationale d'Ingénieurs de Sousse, 4023 Sousse, Tunisie
[2] University of SFax, Research Groups on Intelligent Machines Laboratory, Private National Engineering School of Monastir, Monastir, Tunisia
[3] Department of Mathematics, Higher Institute of Applied Mathematics and Computer Science, University of Kairouan, 3100 Kairouan, Tunisia
[4] Department of Mathematics, Faculty of Science, University of Tabuk, Tabuk, Saudi Arabia
[5] College of Computers and Information Technology, Taif University, Taif, Saudi Arabia

**Abstract.** Since the release of the first 3D watermarking algorithm in the last decade, 3D meshes applying such an algorithm have been growing up with a diversity of techniques during the embedding of information into meshes. The main objective is always to secure data shared by remote users. The originality of the present work is issued from the use of spherical harmonics to transform the mesh to the frequency domain to be watermarked, and the entropy concept to estimate the optimal order of the reconstruction. Our algorithm includes three parts. The first is the data pre-processing based on a combination of a signature generated by the well-known Secure Hash Algorithm, and a mesh description, subject to a convolutional error correcting code. The second step is the mesh treatment, consisting in extracting spherical harmonics coefficients to be watermarked. Finally, the third part consists in inserting data into coefficients using LSB and quantification method, and next to reconstruct the watermarked mesh. The experimentation of our approach has shown a high insertion rate, while maintaining the mesh quality. It is also robust against the most popular attacks. Our results showed that the present approach improves the existing works.

**Keywords:** 3D multiresolution meshes · Entropy · Spherical harmonics · LSB method · Quantification method · Invisibility · Robustness · Insertion rate

© Springer Nature Switzerland AG 2021
N. Tsapatsoulis et al. (Eds.): CAIP 2021, LNCS 13053, pp. 361–370, 2021.
https://doi.org/10.1007/978-3-030-89131-2_33

# 1   Introduction

The protection of 3D meshes has become an intellectual property since these meshes began to be used in various fields, some of which require the transfer and ring of data such as industrial applications, movies production, games and medical visualization. Indeed, ring 3D meshes between remote users has spawned huge security problems, especially that digital copying does not entail any loss of quality. These problems have made the protection of data an intellectual property especially as legal protections are no longer sufficient to counter these digital abuses. As a result, digital watermarking has been announced as a solution to preserve the copyrights, and to reach document Integrity, mesh Indexation and medical Ethics.

Since the 3D mesh security problems imposed themselves, attempts to design watermarking algorithms targeting this data type have continued to grow up. Researchers have been trying to innovate their techniques to find the right compromise between insertion rate, invisibility, and robustness in order to remedy security problems. Notwithstanding all these improvements, 3D watermarking field still suffers from several defects.

To contribute to the security of 3D meshes, we propose in this paper a new 3D watermarking algorithm based on the combination of spherical harmonics, entropy, SHA algorithm and error correcting codes.

# 2   Related Works

Spatial watermarking approaches, such as [6], is the most evident watermarking scheme. Algorithms adopting this domain operate directly on the mesh by changing either the topological or the geometric information to hide the watermark. These approaches are simple and inexpensive in terms of time, which allows their use for real time applications to be easy, but they are not robust against attacks.

As for the algorithm operating in a transformed domain, the insertion must be preceded by a transformation step. The goal is to move from the spatial domain to another transformed one. The transformed domain can be either multi-resolution [11] or frequency [7]. In this case, hidden data does not target the topological and geometric information, but the coefficients resulting from applied transformations. In particular, frequency approaches opted to apply Fourier transform [1,7]. Unfortunately, spherical harmonics are not yet used in the field of 3D watermarking despite their performance proven in different areas. This can be justified by the complexity of applying spherical harmonics on 3D meshes known by their hypersensitivities and complexity. Otherwise, recent published results clearly showed that no perfect solution has been yet proposed [2,8,13,15].

As a solution, we propose, in this paper, a new approach of 3D watermarking based on spherical harmonics, the Secure Hash Algorithm (SHA) algorithm and error correcting code. The being objective is to insert a large quantity of information without affecting the mesh quality and to guarantee robustness against attacks applied to the watermarked mesh.

# 3   Used Techniques

## 3.1   Spherical Harmonic

Over the past decade, tools for acquiring and visualizing 3D models have become essential components of data processing in a number of disciplines, including medicine, chemistry, architecture, and entertainment. As a result, the need to be able to recover models from large databases has grown in importance.

Spherical Harmonics (SHs) are rotational invariant descriptors applied in modeling in order to reduce the dimensionality of the shape descriptor, and consequently to reduce both the storage space and the comparison time. These properties are essential for the implementation of interactive shape retrieval systems.

SHs represent a complete set of orthogonal functions defined on the surface of a sphere. This method originally used a radial representation limited to star-shaped surfaces. Brechbühler et al. solved this limitation by introducing the surface parameterization which decomposes a 3D surface into three orthogonal directions. This also makes it possible to establish a link between the SHs coefficients and the classical shape parameters.

The SHs basis element $Y_{l,m}$ presents several mathematical properties useful for modeling and pattern recognition,

- $S^2$ being a compact group, the Fourier transform is therefore represented by the Fourier coefficients with respect to the associated Legendre basis.
- The SHs form a complete set on the surface of the unit sphere.

These two properties permit to deduce the reconstruction formula for the surface to be modeled,

$$S(\theta, \varphi) = \sum_{l=0}^{\infty} \sum_{m=-l}^{l} S_{l,m} Y_{l,m}(\theta, \varphi). \tag{1}$$

where $S(\theta, \varphi)$ is the spherical representation of the 3D object to be modeled. The $S_{l,m}$ are the SHs coefficients calculated by analogy to the 2D Fourier coefficients as scalar products of the surface function with the basis elements $Y_{l,m}$,

$$S_{l,m} = \int_0^{2\pi} \int_0^{\pi} S(\theta, \varphi) \overline{Y_{l,m}}(\theta, \varphi) \sin\theta d\theta d\varphi. \tag{2}$$

For $l \in \mathbb{N}$, $m \in \mathbb{Z}$; $|m| \leq l$, $Y_{l,m}$ is defined by

$$Y_{l,m}(\theta, \varphi) = K_{l,m} P_{l,m}(cos\theta) e^{im\varphi}, \tag{3}$$

where

$$K_{l,m} = (-1)^m \sqrt{\frac{(2l+1)(l-m)!}{4\pi(l+m)!}} \tag{4}$$

and $P_{l,m}$ are the Legendre polynomials defined on $[-1, 1]$ by

$$P_{l,m}(x) = (-1)^m (1-x^2)^{\frac{m}{2}} \frac{d^m P_l(x)}{dx^m}. \tag{5}$$

## 3.2 Spherical Harmonics Entropy

In the theory of mathematical physics, entropy is a mathematical function based on probabilistic statistical theory that intuitively corresponds to the amount of information contained or provided by an information source.

The concept of entropy is originally linked to thermodynamics and initiated as Shannon's entropy. It is well known that the most common problem in modeling with SHs is determination of the optimal reconstruction order which represents the 'best' model closest to the initial surface.

For a process characterized by a number $N$ of states or classes of events, Shannon's entropy is initially expressed as:

$$ShE = - \sum_{i=1}^{N} p_i \log(p_i). \tag{6}$$

In [4], an SHs based entropy has been introduced by analogy to the SHE, by evaluating the information carried by the signal over its SHs coefficients or decomposition. Let

$$SHsEnt_L = - \sum_{l=0}^{L} SHsP(l) \log(SHsP(l)), \tag{7}$$

where

$$SHsP(l) = \frac{\sum_{|m| \leq l} |S_{i,m}|^2}{\sum_{l} \sum_{|m| \leq l} |S_{j,m}|^2}. \tag{8}$$

The $S_{i,m}$'s are effectively the SHs coefficient at the degree $i$ and order $m$, evaluated by analogy to the 2D Fourier coefficients.

A correlation between the entropy of the SHs decomposition and the SHs modeling is established to estimate in a precise and automatic way the optimal order of reconstruction without need to reconstruct the model at each iteration. The idea reposes on the extraction of the information (the probabilities) on the set of SHs coefficients instead of the original signal or its estimating reconstruction.

Therefore, at each iteration, the value of the entropy is estimated as the module of the coefficients the most close to the individual or the event or the value over the total energy. The optimal order is deduced when the entropy value is stabilized.

## 3.3 Convolutional Encoder

Error-correcting codes, widely used in digital data, have proven their performance in correcting transmission errors. This was one motivation to apply them in 3D digital watermarking. In particular, in the present work, we focused on convolutionnel error correction codes. The procedure of the application of these codes follows two steps.

A first step is known as convolutional encoder. It takes place as a prior step before inserting data into 3D multiresolution meshes, using trellis method which is a temporal representation of the encoder state machine. Each input sequence of the encoder corresponds to a single path in the trellis (and vice versa). At every instant, a transition is made according to the arrived bit. The generated binary sequence is called a code-word.

Once the data is received, a decoding step is required. The aim is to restore the initial information and correct any errors that have occurred. In our case, We will apply the Viterbi algorithm. This choice is justified by the ability of this algorithm to correct randomly distributed errors, as those errors due to attacks. To decode the extracted message, Viterbi algorithm searches the trellis for the most likely path based on the principle of maximum likelihood sequence.

## 4   Overview of the Proposed Approach

As already mentioned, we propose in this paper a new approach of 3D water-marking for multi-resolution meshes, which aims to enhance invisibility using spherical harmonics, reduce the number of harmonic coefficient to be water-marked, while keeping high insertion rate by combining LSB and quantification methods, and thus improve robustness against most popular attacks using con-volutional error correcting code. To achieve these objectives, an insertion and extraction steps should take place.

The purpose of the insertion step is to insert data into the mesh. This data relates to the source of the mesh as well as the description. The source of the mesh goes through the hash function SHA to get the signature. Next, it will be combined with the description. The whole signal will be then transformed into a binary sequence before being encoded by a convolutional encoder.

The mesh is transformed to the frequency domain using spherical harmonics entropy, in order to ensure that the insertion of data into the mesh does not deteriorate its quality. By using the entropy measure, the number of generated coefficients is limited to those used in the construction. Such a number or a set is estimated in advance. However, the greater the number of coefficients, the better the insertion rate is. In Fig. 1(sub-Figure A), we illustrated two iterations of insertion with different modulation coefficients to eliminate the overlap between the inserted data.

With regard to modification of harmonic coefficients during insertion, as already mentioned, two methods were used. The first one is LSB method, which consist in modifying the least significant bit of the coefficients according to the watermark bit. The second is a quantification step.

Once the signal is received after a dissemination step, inserted data should be retrieved from the 3D multi-resolution mesh. To do it, the watermarked mesh undergoes in a harmonic decomposition to extract harmonic coefficients. These Later go through two iterations of extraction, as shown in Fig. 1(sub-Figure B), to retrieve both parts of the already inserted data. A verification of integrity and copyright is done after decoding retrieved information using the convolutional decoder.

Sub-Figure A                    Sub-Figure B

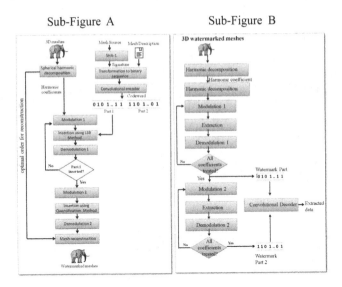

**Fig. 1.** Overview of our approach.

# 5   Results and Discussion

A watermarking algorithm is said to be effective if it allows the insertion of a significant rate of data while maintaining the quality of the mesh and ensuring the extraction of this data correctly in a rate of applied attacks. Apart from these evaluation metrics, we present in this paper a new result relating to the use of entropy which guarantees a huge gain in coefficients used when constructing the watermarked mesh.

## 5.1   Invisibility and Insertion Rate Evaluation

To conclude on the effectiveness of a watermarking scheme, it was necessary to evaluate its invisibility and its insertion rate. Indeed, the increase in the insertion rate leads to a deterioration in the mesh quality. The question then is to find the right compromise between these two criteria.

The results of Mean SQuared Error(MSQE) and Peak Signal to Noise Ratio (PSNR) presented in Table 1 show that our algorithm have proven a high insertion rate (of the order of 250000 bits) while maintaining the quality of the mesh ($MSQE = 0.5 \times 10^{-9}$ and $PSNR = 183.5$). The high insertion rate is due to the use of double round of insertion which allows to double the amount of information to be inserted. In terms of MSQE value, it lies around $10^{-9}$. This low value, reflecting mesh quality conservation, is due to the transformation of the mesh into the frequency domain.

**Table 1.** Invisibility and insertion rate results

| Approaches | Insertion rate (bit) | MSQE | PSNR |
|---|---|---|---|
| [9] | 10650 | $0.2 \times 10^{-3}$ | – |
| [15] | 199 | $3.2 \times 10^{-5}$ | – |
| [10] | 250000 | $1,2 \times 10^{-6}$ | 126,35 |
| [11] | 337929 | $2 \times 10^{-7}$ | 131,3 |
| Our approach | 250000 | $2.4 \times 10^{-9}$ | 183.5 |

## 5.2 Robustness Evaluation

Watermarked meshes, during dissemination step, may undergo in treatments, which may alter the information already inserted. These treatments are called attacks. A watermarked algorithm is said to be robust if it allows the preservation of the data despite attacks.

*Similarity Transformation Attack:* include translation, rotation and uniform scaling. Our approach allowed us to correctly extract all the information despite the application of these attacks on the watermarked mesh. Indeed, the correlation between the data inserted initially and those extracted is equal to 1 in the case of translation, rotation and uniform scaling. Our algorithm is then robust against similarity transformation attacks.

*Noise Addition Attack:* The application of this attack to a triangular mesh causes a random change in the coordinates of vertices. This change may alter and sometimes destroy the information already inserted into the mesh. We applied this attack to the watermarked meshes. Obtained results, as presented in Table 2, prove that our algorithm allowed us to correctly extract all the information from a noise level equal to $10^{-5}$. A correlation value is close to 0.9 for a higher noise level. These results, explained by the use of error correcting codes, are improved compared to existing works [6,11,13].

**Table 2.** Correlation values after Noise addition attack.

| Noise level | $10^{-3}$ | $10^{-4}$ | $10^{-5}$ | $10^{-6}$ | $10^{-7}$ |
|---|---|---|---|---|---|
| [6] | 0.05 | 0.3 | — | — | — |
| [13] | — | 0.99 | 1 | 1 | 1 |
| [11] | 0.57 | 0.9 | 1 | 1 | 1 |
| Our approach | 0.89 | 0.93 | 1 | 1 | 1 |

*Smoothing Attack:* This attack is applied to a mesh during its reconstruction to remove noise. To test the robustness of our algorithm against smoothing attack, we applied several tests on watermarked meshes. Each time, we vary the value of deformation factor (dFactor), and calculate the value of correlation. Results in Table 3 show that our correlation in very enhanced relative to other published correlation values such as [11–13,15].

**Table 3.** Correlation values due to smoothing attacks.

| dFactor | $10^{-7}$ | $10^{-8}$ | $10^{-9}$ | $10^{-10}$ |
|---|---|---|---|---|
| [12] | – | 0.18 | 0.31 | 0.43 |
| [15] | 0.4 | 0.5 | 0.8 | 1 |
| [13] | 0.9 | 1 | 1 | 1 |
| [11] | 0.8 | 0.92 | 1 | 1 |
| Our approach | 0.94 | 1 | 1 | 1 |

*Coordinate Quantization Attack:* This attack targets the vertex coordinates. It is usually applied during the compression of meshes. To conclude the robustness of our algorithm against this attack, we opted to change the quantification level, and calculate each time the correlation between the inserted and extracted information. Obtained correlation (Table 4) is equal to 1 for a level of quantification greater than 5. These results, justified by the use of convolutional codes to retrieve the corrupted data, are very enhanced in comparison to those recently published [11,13–15].

**Table 4.** Correlation values with applying coordinate quantization attacks.

| Quantization Level | 5 | 10 | 12 | 13 | 14 |
|---|---|---|---|---|---|
| [15] | – | 0.7 | 0.85 | – | – |
| [14] | – | 0.14 | 0.628 | 0.954 | 1 |
| [13] | 0.54 | 0.76 | 0.92 | 1 | 1 |
| [11] | 0.35 | 0.56 | 0.8 | 0.91 | 1 |
| Our approach | 0.92 | 1 | 1 | 1 | 1 |

*Compression Attack:* A 3D watermarking algorithm is said to be robust if it allows keeping the inserted information even in the presence of attacks as compression. To evaluate the robustness of our watermarking algorithm against this kind of attack, we applied compression to the watermarked meshes. Each time, we opted to change the compression rate, extract the inserted data and see if there are alterations. Table 5 summarizes our results which prove that our approach is more robust against this attack in comparison with other published approaches.

**Table 5.** Correlation values with applying compression attack.

| Bit/vertex | 0.5 | 1 | 1.5 | 2 | 2.5 | 3 |
|---|---|---|---|---|---|---|
| [14] | 0.34 | 0.4 | 0.6 | 0.89 | 0.9 | 1 |
| [13] | 0.56 | 0.79 | 0.83 | 0.9 | 0.56 | 1 |
| [11] | 0.42 | 0.6 | 0.78 | 0.9 | 1 | 1 |
| Our approach | 0.95 | 0.97 | 1 | 1 | 1 | 1 |

### 5.3 Impact of Spherical Harmonics Entropy

The new 3D spherical harmonics entropy was developed in [4], through which the order of reconstruction is defined in an automatic and precise manner without even resorting to the reconstruction of the spherical harmonic model at each iteration of the process.

**Table 6.** Impact of spherical harmonics entropy

| Object | Vertex number | Optimal order | Reconstruction coefficients |
|---|---|---|---|
| Feline | 250000 | 74 | 5625 |
| Venus | 40000 | 30 | 961 |
| Horse | 59540 | 35 | 1296 |
| Rabbit | 104288 | 51 | 2704 |

## 6 Conclusion

In this paper, we have presented a blind watermarking approach for 3D multiresolution meshes based on the use of spherical harmonics, SHA algorithm, and error correcting code. Our algorithm consists in transforming the host mesh to the frequency domain by applying spherical harmonics. Each coefficient resulting from this transformation undergoes two iterations of insertion to be modified depending on the message to be inserted using LSB and quantification method. Data to be inserted is composed of a signature generated using SHA algorithm and a mesh description. The whole data is coded using a convolutional encoder. Once all the information is inserted, mesh reconstruction takes place using an optimal order of coefficients already calculated. The watermarked mesh is then obtained.

The obtained results show clearly that our algorithm protects the mesh quality even with the insertion of a large amount of information compared to approaches existing in the literature. The application of various attacks (noise addition, coordinate quantization, smoothing, translation, rotation, uniform scaling and compression) to a watermarked mesh does not prevent the correct retrieval of inserted information.

As a perspective, we will apply encryption algorithm on the meshes and apply watermarking using other domains.

# References

1. Geri, B.: A robust digital watermarking algorithm for three dimensional meshes. In: International Conference on Information Engineering for Mechanics and Materials, pp. 1105–1110 (2015)
2. Hachicha, S., Sayahi, I., Elkefi, A., Amar, C.B., Zaied, M.: GPU-based blind watermarking scheme for 3d multiresolution meshes using unlifted butterfly wavelet transformation. Circuits Systems Signal Process. **39**(3), 1533–1560 (2019). https://doi.org/10.1007/s00034-019-01220-z
3. Jallouli, M., Zemni, M., Ben Mabrouk, A., Mahjoub, M.A.: Toward recursive spherical harmonics-issued bi-filters: Part I: theoretical framework. Soft. Comput. **23**(20), 10415–10428 (2018). https://doi.org/10.1007/s00500-018-3596-9
4. Jallouli, M., Belhaj khelifa, W., Ben Mabrouk, A., Mahjoub, M.A.: Toward recursive spherical harmonics issued Bi-filters: Part II: An Associated Spherical Harmonics Entropy for Optimal Modeling. Soft Computing (2019)
5. Jallouli, M., Zemni, M., Ben Mabrouk, A., Mahjoub, M.A.: Towards new multiwavelets: associated filters and algorithms. part 1: Theoretical Framework and Investigation of Biomedical Signals, ECG and Coronavirus Cases Soft Computing
6. Wang, J.T., Chang, Y.C., Yu, S.S., Yu, C.Y.: Hamming code based watermarking scheme for 3D model verification. In: International Symposium on Computer, Consumer and Control, pp. 1095–1098 (2014)
7. Lamiaa, B., Saleh, H.I., Abdelhalim, M.B.: Enhanced watermarking scheme for 3d mesh models. In: International Conference on Information Technology, pp. 612–619 (2015)
8. Malipatil, M., Shubhangi, D.C.: An efficient 3D Watermarking algorithm for 3D mesh models. In: 2020 Fourth International Conference on I-SMAC (IoT in Social, Mobile, Analytics and Cloud) (I-SMAC), Palladam, India, pp. 1–5 (2020)
9. Zaid, A.O., Hachani, M., Puech, W.: Wavelet-based high-capacity watermarking of 3-D irregular meshes. Multimedia Tools Appl. **74**(15), 5897–5915 (2014). https://doi.org/10.1007/s11042-014-1896-3
10. Sayahi, I., Elkefi, A., Ben Amar, C.: Blind watermarking algorithm for 3D multiresolution meshes based on spiral scanning method. Int. J. Comput. Sci. Inf. Securit. **14**, 1–342 (2016)
11. Sayahi, I., Elkefi, A., Amar, C.B.: Join cryptography and digital watermarking for 3D multiresolution meshes security. In: Battiato, S., Gallo, G., Schettini, R., Stanco, F. (eds.) ICIAP 2017. LNCS, vol. 10485, pp. 637–647. Springer, Cham (2017). https://doi.org/10.1007/978-3-319-68548-9_58
12. Sayahi, I., Elkefi, A., Koubaa, M., Ben Amar C.: Robust watermarking algorithm For 3D multiresolution meshes. In: International Conference on Computer Vision Theory and Applications, pp. 150–157 (2015)
13. Sayahi, I., Elkefi, A., Amar, C.B.: Crypto-watermarking system for safe transmission of 3D multiresolution meshes. Multimedia Tools Appl. **78**(10), 13877–13903 (2018). https://doi.org/10.1007/s11042-018-6721-y
14. Sayahi, I., Elkefi, A., Ben Amar, C.: A multi-resolution approach for blind watermarking of 3D :meshes using scanning spiral method. In: International Conference on Computational Intelligence in Security for Information Systems, pp. 526–537 (2016)
15. XiaoYing, Y., Ruggero, P., Holly, R., Ioannis, I.: A 3D steganalytic algorithm and steganalysis-resistant watermarking. IEEE Trans. Visualizat. Comput. Graph. 1–12 (2016)

# Authentication of Vincent van Gogh's Work

Lucas Oliveira David⬤, Helio Pedrini$^{(\boxtimes)}$⬤, Zanoni Dias⬤,
and Anderson Rocha⬤

Institute of Computing, University of Campinas, Campinas, Brazil
{lucas.david,helio,zanoni,anderson}@ic.unicamp.br

**Abstract.** Increasing digital art has, without a doubt democratized the access to art content to the public at large. It has had, however, resulted in an inadvertent growing number of forgeries and misinformation around art content. In this work, we employ convolutional network-based strategies to identify and classify art-related digital artifacts. Firstly, van Gogh paintings are used to explore and refine strategies capable of discriminating the brushstroke pattern of van Gogh. We achieve significant performance improvements over the VGDB-2016 dataset, while also increasing class-balanced accuracy when compared to previous results in the same set. In a second phase, we collect two new sets and perform cross-dataset evaluation to demonstrate that our solution generalizes well to painting recaptures with varying resolution, sizes and sources, while performing fairly well against unseen high-resolution scans of paintings. Finally, we propose a strategy for painting authentication that combines results of multiple recaptures.

**Keywords:** Machine learning · Computer image analysis · Authorship attribution · Painting analysis · Brushstroke analysis

## 1 Introduction

Nowadays, computer-assisted analysis of paintings has become a necessity with the advent of digital art, which is no longer displayed on occasional events, but spread at a massive scale across the web. In this vein, machine learning can be used to automatically organize and identify art content with respect to its provenance, aiding connoisseurs and enthusiasts alike in many distinct activities, such as art organization and categorization, provenance analysis, authorship and influence classification, and even serve as a verification step in the authorship attribution problem.

In the last decades, artwork and painting analysis has been frequently conducted using classic machine-learning and statistical methods. Image decomposition, dimensionality reduction and embedding methods, for instance, are often

Research funded by CAPES, CNPq, Microsoft Research Latin America and FAPESP (Grant #2017/12646-3).

employed when categorizing or visualizing art samples, as they focus on finding a meaningful representation from highly dimensional data [5,7]. Methods based on image filters are also often used to discern authorship. Examples of such are Scale-Invariant Feature Transform (SIFT), Gabor wavelet filters [4,9], Fisher Information [7] and combinations thereof using Genetic Programming [2] in paintings.

Going in a different direction, data-driven strategies with lower specialist-knowledge requirements are becoming more common with the great development of convolutional networks in the last decade. CNNs have been successfully employed to either extract features or directly analyze provenance of paintings, considering characteristics such as authorship [1,3], style [8] and media [10].

In this research, we set forth the objective of designing and deploying an approach to automatically extract discriminative features from large painting collections and learn specific nuances and attributes of a given painter, in order to distinguish one's work from the others' and to automatically attribute paintings of unknown authorship to the known classes. This process is known in the forensic literature as authorship attribution.

Our main contributions are: (a) we propose a classification pipeline based on CNNs that can be efficiently employed in a diverse set of authors without the resizing (and loss of information) of large paintings; (b) we present measurements and discussions around the extensibility of the proposed work in a cross-dataset scenario; and (c) we investigate the effect of combining predictions from multiple recaptures of a painting during its authentication process.

The remaining of this paper is organized as follows. Section 2 describes the strategies employed for the authentication of van Gogh's work. Section 3 describes the multiple datasets collected, as well as the experiments conducted on top of them. The results are presented in Sect. 4. Finally, we summarize our contributions in Sect. 5.

## 2    Methodology

Inspired by the many studies around the authentication of van Gogh's artwork, we opted to start ours here as well. We propose to sample few regions of interest from paintings and leverage pre-trained convolutional networks to train a Support Vector Machine authorship discriminator. We conduct a series of experiments over the VGDB-2016 dataset [3] and two newly collected sets (see Sect. 3). The remaining of this section describes in detail our solution to improve authentication over Vincent van Gogh's work.

### 2.1    Focusing on Important Regions of Paintings

While the fusion of patch predictions generated by a combination of CNN-based features and Support Vector Machines (SVM) proposed by Folego et al. [3] produced good results, it was also very resource demanding. During training, 54,092

**Fig. 1.** Examples of patches extracted from "White House at Night", by Vincent van Gogh, 1890 (left-most image). The remaining images represent four patches extracted with the **random** selection strategy.

non-overlapping patches were extracted from 264 paintings (approximately 205 patches per painting). The patches were then embedded using VGG19 trained over ImageNet and used to train an SVM binary model. The entire process took three hours in total, proving itself troublesome for even larger datasets, with more painters or paintings.

To tackle this problem, we highlight an interesting idea supported by art connoisseurs [6,7]: highly detailed regions in paintings are compositions of small and calculated corrections, rather than a fluid brushwork spontaneously created by an artist, which contains their signature. From this, we hypothesized that much of the authorship information could still be found in small subsections of the paintings, and the solution presented by Folego et al. [3] could therefore be improved by first sub-selecting a small set of patches that best represented the paintings.

In order to evaluate this, we re-apply the same classification strategy over VGDB-2016 dataset several times, reducing the amount of painting patches used during training and testing at each iteration. In each iteration, $k$ points are randomly chosen in the painting and $k$ non-disjointed patches centered on those points are extracted. It is expected from this procedure to comprise the most "unbiased" selection, resulting in a patch sample set with foreground/background, highly/low-detailed rate proportional to the original painting. Figure 1 illustrates examples of this strategy.

In addition to the random patch extraction procedure, two others were considered: (a) one that favored sampling patches from highly-detailed regions; and (b) one that favors smoother regions in the paintings. In both, the amount of detail in a region was defined by a probability map derived from the Canny Edge Detection algorithm. Both strategies have consistently resulted in worse accuracy compared to the truly random procedure, which we report in this paper.

## 2.2 Transfer Learning from ImageNet

Similarly to the classification strategy proposed by Folego et al. [3], we experiment with extracting features using frozen models pre-trained for the object classification over ImageNet, as well as *warm-starting* training with previously trained weights.

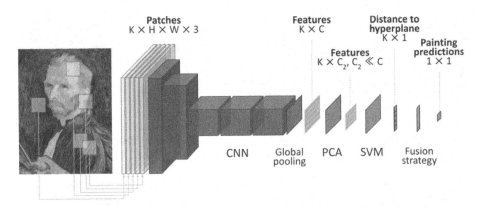

**Fig. 2.** Diagram of the proposed classification strategy.

Our classification strategy consists of sampling 50 patches of size $300 \times 300$ pixels from each of the paintings in the set. We adopt these numbers as they represent a reasonable tradeoff between the amount of brushstroke information retained and computing resources required to process it. These patches are encoded using a CNN trained over ImageNet into $d$-dimensional feature vectors. The set is further reduced with Principal Component Analysis (PCA), and used to train a Support Vector Machine (SVM) binary classifier. Grid search cross-validation is employed to tune the regularizing factor $C$, kernel function and class-balance strategy of the SVM. The architectures VGG19, InceptionV3, ResNet50, Xception and EfficientNet are employed as backbone networks. The diagram illustrated in Fig. 2 summarises our classifier.

Although brushstroke information was clear in patches from large paintings, high-level semantic features such as trees and houses were still visible in patches from smaller images. Concerned that this could add bias to the discriminator, we have also tested with a much smaller patch and network size. In this sense, 500 patches of shape $32 \times 32$ are extracted and used to train a DenseNet264 network from scratch until convergence. The CNN is then clipped at its final *Global Average Pooling 2D* layer, and used as the encoder in the classification pipeline previously described.

During evaluation, a painting-level prediction is obtained for each painting by fusing the predictions for all of its patches. We employ the fusion strategy **far** [3], where the most confident patch prediction is assigned to the whole painting.

### 2.3   Combining Recaptures

Inspired by the idea of patch fusion, we hypothesize that combining the classification of multiple recaptures of a same painting can increase the overall accuracy by fortifying the classifier against noise generated by diverging capturing conditions (e.g., illumination, saturation, equipment used). In order to demonstrate this, we collect a new dataset (RMP) consisting of multiple recaptures of paintings belonging to VGDB-2016/test. The most effective solution from Sect. 2.2 is

**Fig. 3.** Paintings in the UVGM dataset. From left to right: "Sunflowers" by Vincent van Gogh, 1889; and "Tulip Fields near The Hague" by Claude Monet, 1886.

used to classify each patch of each painting recapture. The hard-labels (*non-van Gogh* and *van Gogh*) of each recapture are then aggregated by their respective painting and the most frequent label is assigned to the painting.

Finally, while fusing recaptures can be used to measure the effect of multiple capture conditions over testing error, it is not sufficient to determine how much of the error can be attributed to the lack of variance in the training set. To understand this, multiple recaptures of each painting in the VGDB-2016/train were collected from various sources, and a new training set (RMP16/train) was formed by merging all training samples and their recaptures. The best scoring model described in Sect. 2.2 was re-trained over this new set and evaluated on VGDB-2016/test, RMP/test and the union of both (RMP16/test).

# 3 Cross-Dataset Experimental Setup

We first test the authentication strategies presented in Sect. 2 against VGDB-2016 [3] to compare with current literature. We report patch accuracy (ratio of patches correctly classified) and painting accuracy (ratio of paintings correctly classified after patch answers are fused). This set comprises 264 training images (99 van Gogh and 165 non-van Gogh) and 67 test images (25 van Gogh and 42 non-van Gogh). Images in this set represent high-quality captures of paintings with similar pixel density. More specifically, the average size of the samples in VGDB-2016/test is $3,115 \times 2,805$.

While VGDB-2016 presents similarly conditioned images, it is not reasonable to assume data will always be available in such a way. We collect two new datasets of paintings and perform cross-dataset testing over them. Although cross-dataset evaluation is not often employed in the literature, we consider of paramount importance to account for VGDB-2016 inherent bias and measure the extensibility of our solution over more realistic scenarios, with varying capturing conditions and sources. The first, *Unseen Paintings from the van Gogh Museum* (UVGM), consists of images of paintings retrieved from the van Gogh Museum website that do not appear in VGDB-2016. This set is composed of 34 van Gogh's paintings and 11 paintings by other artists somewhat related to van Gogh (Fig. 3). Samples were produced from high-quality scans of the paintings, resulting in high-resolution images (average of $6,000 \times 6,000$). An interesting question can be answered with this set: *how well does a model trained over VGDB-2016 generalize for unseen high-resolution scanned van Gogh's paintings?*

**Fig. 4.** Recaptures of "Landscape with Wheelbarrow" by Vincent van Gogh, 1883. The left-most image belongs to VGDB-2016, while the remaining three belong to RMP.

The second collected dataset, *Recaptures from Multiple Places* (RMP) comprises recaptures of paintings in VGDB-2016/test created under different capturing conditions, with various resolutions, pixel density and sources. They were retrieved using Google image search from a variety of sources that often employed informal capturing settings. For this reason, samples in this set were often smaller than $2000 \times 2000$. Being composed of 55 van Gogh recaptures and 85 recaptures from other artists (Fig. 4), this set is ideal to *understand the overall performance of the models on an unrestricted scenario*.

In an attempt to account for the difference in average painting sizes between the datasets, two sets of evaluation were performed: (a) no preprocessing was done to the images, and the models were tested over them as they were when retrieved; and (b) recaptures were resized so their largest dimension would match their counterpart in VGDB-2016. Unseen paintings were clustered into "vertical" and "horizontal", and resized so their largest dimension would match with the average dimension size among all paintings in VGDB-2016/test.

Finally, we opted to measure the solution efficacy over UVGM and RMP using *class-balanced accuracy* (or equivalently, *macro-recall*), in order to circumvent any bias caused by the class unbalance present in these datasets.

## 4   Results and Discussions

In this section, we present and discuss the results of the experiments previously described. They were organized to follow the same structure of Sect. 2.

### 4.1   Focus on Important Regions of a Painting

Patch and painting-level accuracy over VGDB-2016/test for different patches count is reported in Table 1a. Both scores increased (6.9 and 1.5% points, respectively) when limiting VGG19(fc2) SVM [3]'s input to only 50 patches (see first

**Table 1.** Patch accuracy and painting accuracy observed over the test set, considering (a) number of patches extracted; and (b) the classifier used.

| Count | Patch acc. | Painting acc. | Classifier | Patch acc. | Painting acc. |
|---|---|---|---|---|---|
| 205 [3] | 82.4% | 94.0% | VGG19 SVM [3] | 82.4% | 94.0% |
| 50 [3] | 89.3% | **95.5%** | FLGP [2] | - | 81.9% |
| 20 [3] | 87.9% | 91.0% | VGG19 SVM | 89.3% | 95.5% |
| 50 | **91.0%** | **95.5%** | Xception SVM | 89.0% | 94.0% |
| 20 | 89.7% | **95.5%** | Resnet50 SVM | 88.9% | 91.0% |
| 10 | 89.0% | 94.0% | InceptionV3 SVM | 91.0% | **95.5%** |
| 5 | 89.0% | 92.5% | DenseNet264 SVM | 87.0% | 91.0% |
| 2 | 87.0% | 91.0% | EfficientNetB3 SVM | 90.9% | 92.5% |
| 1 | 86.5% | 86.5% | EfficientNetB7 SVM | **91.3%** | 92.5% |

three lines in Table 1a). We attribute this to the data noise reduction by employing PCA, and the more comprehensive training procedure, which searched hyperparameters with Grid Search Cross-Validation. However, a degradation in accuracy becomes evident when further reducing patch count from 50 to 20, and six paintings are incorrectly identified. We observe a similar effect when considering our most promising model, based on InceptionV3 and SVM: both metrics decay after patch count is below 20 (see lines four through nine in Table 1a).

### 4.2 Transfer Learning from ImageNet

Results on transfer learning from ImageNet to the van Gogh attribution problem are presented in Table 1b. Any attempt to fine-tune large networks (such as InceptionV3) besides the last classifying layer resulted in overfitting and, later, test accuracy decrease. This is due to the large number of parameters/active units in contrast with the insufficient dataset size. This problem was not apparent when training the DenseNet264 model, as each painting in the train and test sets was subdivided into roughly 500 patches and sufficient data was present. Furthermore, more recent architectures, such as Xception and EfficientNetB7, were employed to extract features from the paintings, but consistently presented worse painting-level results than InceptionV3.

InceptionV3 SVM resulted in the best accuracy score over VGDB-2016/test, obtaining a 95.0% patch-level true positive rate, 87.0% patch-level true negative rate and 91.0% class-balanced accuracy. Combining patches improved the overall accuracy of the system to 100.0% painting-level true positive rate, 93.0% painting-level true negative rate and 96.5% class-balanced accuracy, that is, only three non-van Gogh's paintings were incorrectly attributed to van Gogh: 10500055, 18195595 and 10658644 (see Fig. 5). The first two are attributed to Paula Modersohn-Becker and Claude Monet respectively—authors closely related to Impressionism —, whereas the last example was created by the Post-Impressionist artist Ferdinand Hodler.

Finally, performance has significantly increased as we reduced patch count. The baseline (VGG19 SVM [3]) took 5 min and 36 s to embed all patches (using

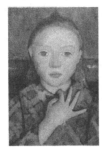

**Fig. 5.** Paintings in VGDB-2016/test that were incorrectly classified by our model in Table 1. From left to right: "Mdchenbildnis", Paula Modersohn-Becker, 1905; "The Palazzo Contarini, Venice", Claude Monet, 1908; and "Die Strasse nach Evordes", Ferdinand Hodler, 1890.

the maximum allowed batch size of 158), and approximately three hours to train. Meanwhile, InceptionV3 PCA SVM (using 50 random patches) has only taken 2 min and 15 s to embed (batch size of 362), and 18 min to train (where the best parameters found were the *rbf kernel* and $C = 10$). Evaluation time for both classifiers was negligible.

### 4.3  Evaluation over Unseen Paintings and Recaptures

Table 2a illustrates the effect of painting resizing before classification is applied. For UVGM, a slight decrease in patch accuracy (1.5% point) and increase in painting class-balanced accuracy (6.0% points) was observed. On the other hand, preprocessing samples in RMP results in the decrease of both metrics. We opted to continue our experiments without the resizing procedure, as it adds more processing without significant improvement over most observed metrics.

The results obtained over UVGM, RMP and RMP16 datasets for our best solution (InceptionV3 SVM) are reported in Table 2b. Firstly, we observe a significant decrease in both patch-level and painting-level accuracy over the UVGM dataset, when compared to VGDB-2016. An unbalanced true-positive and true-negative rates in all experiments indicated that the models have overfit onto VGDB-2016 dataset, as the *nvg* label becomes more likely to be predicted. However, our solution was able to generalize information from VGDB-2016 to some degree, obtaining a score of 66.0% in painting-level class-balanced accuracy score (which can be further improved by 6.0% points if images are resized beforehand). Recapture and painting accuracy are the same for UVGM, as this set does not contain any recaptures.

In RMP, our solution scored 78.5% of patch-level and 81.5% of recapture-level class-balanced accuracy. This could be explained by the fact that samples in RMP were closer in size and resolution to VGDB-2016, as well as being photographic captures of paintings, in opposite of UVGM's scans. We conclude that the model was able to fairly generalize information from VGDB-2016 onto this set of unrestricted samples.

**Table 2.** (a) Effect of painting preprocessing (Pre.) on patch accuracy (P. acc.) and painting accuracy (Acc.), when testing against UVGM and RMP datasets. (b) Patch (P. acc.), recapture (R. acc.) and painting (Acc.) class-balanced accuracy for UVGM, RMP and RMP16.

| Evaluation | Pre. | P. acc. | Acc. |
|---|---|---|---|
| UVGM | none | **65.5%** | 66.0% |
| | resize | 64.0% | **72.0%** |
| RMP | none | **78.5%** | **81.5%** |
| | resize | 77.5% | 79.5% |

| Training | Evaluation | P. acc. | R. acc. | Acc. |
|---|---|---|---|---|
| VGDB-2016 | VGDB-2016 | 91.0% | 96.5% | 96.5% |
| | UVGM | 65.5% | 66.0% | 66.0% |
| | RMP | 78.5% | 81.5% | 86.5% |
| | RMP16 | 82.4% | 86.2% | 92.5% |
| RMP16 | VGDB-2016 | 91.5% | 96.5% | 96.5% |
| | RMP | 78.5% | 82.5% | 86.5% |
| | RMP16 | 82.5% | 86.9% | 96.5% |

## 4.4 Combining Recaptures

Recapture fusion experiments are reported in the last column of Table 2b. When combining the classifications of multiple recaptures into a painting-level answer, we obtained a painting accuracy of 86.5% over RMP (an increase of 4.5% points). Furthermore, a class-balanced accuracy of 92.5% was achieved over RMP16 (when merging *VGDB-2016/test* and *RMP/test*). This indicates that combining the classifications of multiple captures of a given painting can further strengthen the model when deciding upon it.

After training over RMP16/train, patch accuracy increased by 0.5% point in VGDB-2016/test, while recapture-level accuracy stayed the same. The three incorrectly classified samples here are the same as the ones from VGDB-2016 (Fig. 5). This indicates that adding multiple recaptures during training can improve the system's overall accuracy in the original task, although it was not sufficient to correct our three *non-van Gogh* attributions in this case.

When evaluating the classifier trained over RMP16/train over RMP/test, recapture accuracy increased by 1.0% point. These results are very similar to the ones obtained when training exclusively over VGDB-2016. However, the difference between the true positive and true negative rate has decreased by 1.0% point; indicating a slight reduction in specificity.

Finally, the painting accuracy score of 96.5% was achieved over RMP16 (4.0% points higher than when training exclusively over VGDB-2016/train). This indicates training with multiple recaptures from multiple sources has a positive impact when classifying paintings originated from unrestricted capturing conditions. The incorrectly samples were once again the ones illustrated in Fig. 5.

## 5 Conclusions

In this work, we combined strategies for patch extraction, CNN-based features and answer fusion to create a machine-learning model capable of outperforming the literature results, while drastically reducing memory requirements and capable of fair generalization onto cross-domain datasets. More specifically, we achieved a 95.5% accuracy score and 96.5% class-balanced accuracy score in the original van Gogh data test set, while providing a speedup of 10 times on training time.

When cross-dataset testing our solution against recaptures extracted from multiple sources and unseen samples extracted from the van Gogh museum website, our best model scored a class-balanced accuracy of 81.5% and 72.0% respectively, effectively demonstrating its generalization capacity.

Finally, we found that combining the classification results of multiple recaptures of a single painting further improved the accuracy of the model over paintings captured on uncontrolled conditions, suggesting data-driven art analysis tools should not disregard the currently heterogeneous state-of-art data, but instead leverage these differences in order to build stability.

# References

1. Bar, Y., Levy, N., Wolf, L.: Classification of artistic styles using binarized features derived from a deep neural network. In: Agapito, L., Bronstein, M.M., Rother, C. (eds.) ECCV 2014. LNCS, vol. 8925, pp. 71–84. Springer, Cham (2015). https://doi.org/10.1007/978-3-319-16178-5_5
2. Bi, Y., Xue, B., Zhang, M.: An effective feature learning approach using genetic programming with image descriptors for image classification. IEEE Comput. Intell. Mag. 15(2), 65–77 (2020)
3. Folego, G., Gomes, O., Rocha, A.: From impressionism to expressionism: automatically identifying van Gogh's paintings. In: IEEE International Conference on Image Processing (ICIP), pp. 141–145 (2016)
4. Johnson, C.R., et al.: Image processing for artist identification. IEEE Signal Process. Mag. 25(4), 37–48 (2008)
5. Liu, H., Chan, R.H., Yao, Y.: Geometric tight frame based stylometry for art authentication of van Gogh paintings. Appl. Comput. Harmon. Anal. 41(2), 590–602 (2016)
6. Qi, H., Hughes, S.: A new method for visual stylometry on impressionist paintings. In: IEEE International Conference on Acoustics, Speech and Signal Processing (ICASSP), pp. 2036–2039 (2011)
7. Qi, H., Taeb, A., Hughes, S.M.: Visual stylometry using background selection and wavelet-HMT-based Fisher information distances for attribution and dating of impressionist paintings. Signal Process. 93(3), 541–553 (2013)
8. Sandoval, C., Pirogova, E., Lech, M.: Two-stage deep learning approach to the classification of fine-art paintings. IEEE Access 7, 41770–41781 (2019)
9. Shamir, L., Macura, T., Orlov, N., Eckley, D., Goldberg, I.: Impressionism, expressionism, surrealism: automated recognition of painters and schools of art. ACM Trans. Appl. Percept. 7, 8:1–8:17 (2010)
10. Yang, H., Min, K.: Classification of basic artistic media based on a deep convolutional approach. Vis. Comput. 36(3), 559–578 (2019). https://doi.org/10.1007/s00371-019-01641-6

# Segmentation and Image Restoration

# Anisotropic Diffusion-Based Enhancement of Scene Segmentation with Instance Labels

Ioannis Kleitsiotis[1,2]([✉]), Ioannis Mariolis[1], Dimitrios Giakoumis[1], Spiridon Likothanassis[1,2], and Dimitrios Tzovaras[1]

[1] Centre for Research and Technology-Hellas, Information Technologies Institute (CERTH/ITI), Thessaloniki, Greece
ioklei@iti.gr
[2] Large Scale Machine Learning and Cloud Data Engineering Lab, Computer Engineering and Informatics, University of Patras, Patras, Greece

**Abstract.** Many visual scene understanding applications, especially in visual servoing settings, may require high quality object mask predictions for the accurate undertaking of various robotic tasks. In this work we investigate a setting where separate instance labels for all objects under view are required, but the available instance segmentation methods produce object masks inferior to a semantic segmentation algorithm. Motivated by the need to add instance label information to the higher fidelity semantic segmentation output, we propose an anisotropic label diffusion algorithm that propagates instance labels predicted by an instance segmentation algorithm inside the semantic segmentation masks. Our method leverages local topological and color information to propagate the instance labels, and is guaranteed to preserve the semantic segmentation mask. We evaluate our method on a challenging grape bunch detection dataset, and report experimental results that showcase the applicability of our method.

**Keywords:** Anisotropic · Label diffusion · Label propagation · Semantic segmentation · Instance segmentation

## 1 Introduction

Vision-based understanding of complex natural scenes, e.g. in agricultural settings, can provide invaluable information for in-field robotic applications. With the success of deep learning frameworks for end-to-end object detection during the past years, new opportunities arise for more complete and robust field scene understanding. However, the biological entities which are needed to be considered for robotic applications are often highly complex. Especially in vineyards, the unstructured geometrical configuration of the vine plant parts which are more important for robotic applications, e.g. grape bunches, trunks, cordons

N. Tsapatsoulis et al. (Eds.): CAIP 2021, LNCS 13053, pp. 383–391, 2021.
https://doi.org/10.1007/978-3-030-89131-2_35

and shoots, lead to significant challenges for the state of the art object detection algorithms.

We are concerned with the instance segmentation problem, where the masks and instance labels for each countable object on the scene must be predicted. The caveat that motivates our method is that a semantic segmentation algorithm might predict object masks of higher quality than the corresponding masks from an instance segmentation algorithm. Therefore, our goal is the addition of instance labels to the higher fidelity semantic segmentation algorithm, with the guarantee that the original segmentation mask will be preserved. We formulate the 2D instance label enhancement problem of semantic segmentation as an anisotropic label diffusion process, taking inspiration both from the 3D label diffusion process presented in [25] and the generalization of label diffusion to the anisotropic case [13]. More specifically, our method leverages local pixel information to propagate all predictions from an instance segmentation algorithm intersecting with our semantic segmentation predictions, towards the remaining semantic segmentation predictions.

To the best of our knowledge, this is the first work to address the incorporation of instance labels in a deep semantic segmentation framework through the anisotropic diffusion of instance labels generated by a lower fidelity instance segmentation algorithm guided by topological and color information. We experimentally evaluate our results in a vineyard grape bunch setting using two representative state-of-the-art methods, PSPNet [31] for semantic segmentation and Mask R-CNN [11] for instance segmentation. We found PSPNet to achieve higher mask quality than Mask R-CNN in this setting, and thus, we preserved PSPNet predictions while simultaneously enhancing them with instance label information.

## 2   Related Work

Although several works combine semantic and instance segmentation for the task of panoptic segmentation [7,10,19,26,28], first described in [14], some works explicitly aim at mask improvement through the combination of the two tasks. The authors of [8] add an Atrous convolution segmentation head to Mask R-CNN to refine the predicted segmentation masks. In [24], a semantic segmentation U-Net [21] head is attached in Mask Scoring R-CNN [12] to facilitate mask prediction performance. The authors of [18] utilize a Bayesian setting to improve [16] with semantic segmentation masks from [23]. The authors of [9] present a novel Instance Mask Projection neural module that enhances segmentation mask prediction by projecting Mask R-CNN masks to the features of the semantic segmentation module. In [5] the authors improve the segmentation results of UNet in medical images first by estimating bounding boxes of anatomical structures with a connected components analysis, and afterwards by combining Mask R-CNN and UNet through a bounding box tracking-based approach. The tracking unfolds across 2D slices of the original Computed Tomography 3D volumes. The authors of [17] enforce consistency between semantic and instance segmentation masks prediction through a specialized loss construction. In [30], the authors add a semantic segmentation head in Mask R-CNN to uncover fine details in a crack detection setting. All the aforementioned works combine semantic and instance segmentation in a fusion setting, where it is assumed that the combination of the two tasks will facilitate the overall mask predictions. We on the other hand aim to preserve only the semantic segmentation masks, while simultaneously adding instance label information.

Two works that perform instance segmentation by applying the watershed transform on a semantic segmentation mask, and thus, like our method, retain the initial semantic segmentation mask quality, are [4] and [29]. In the first paper, the authors train a neural network to learn the energy basins of the watershed transform with an intermediate step of distance transform learning, and apply thresholds at predefined energy values to extract the object instances. The authors of the second work directly calculate the euclidean distance transform of the semantic segmentation output of a UNet [21] (based on the implementation found in [1]), and apply the watershed transform on it with markers provided by the centers of bounding boxes estimated by a modified Region Proposal Network (from Faster R-CNN [20]). Although these works preserve the semantic segmentation mask, the instance segmentation quality depends on the watershed transform performance, while our work aims at a modular design that permits the selection of an appropriate instance segmentation algorithm and offers controllable quality in instance label detection.

The work closest to ours is [3], where the authors combine the output of a semantic segmentation network with bounding boxes predicted by an object detector to perform instance segmentation. Their method retains semantic segmentation masks and assigns to the regions not covered by bounding boxes instance labels based on the mean field approximation of a CRF [15], which is a non-local [6] process. On the other hand, our method is mainly concerned with the utilization of instance mask predictions that have considerable overlap with the ground truth, i.e. each visible part of an object instance is covered by a coarse instance mask, and therefore does not aim to assign instance information in a global-scale, but smoothly propagate coarse predictions towards unlabeled pixels. The addition of anisotropic guidance to the diffusion process guarantees the prevention of possible "leakage" of instance label information between different instances.

## 3   Methodology

Let $L$ be the set of object instances occurring in an RGB image $I$ of width $W$ and height $H$, $M_I^l$ be the estimated mask from the instance segmentation algorithm for label $l \in L$, $M_S$ the mask predicted by the semantic segmentation algorithm, and $M_I$ the logical OR for all Mask R-CNN masks, i.e. $\vee_{l=0}^{|L|} M_I^l$. For each pixel $p_i \in M_S$ we find the set of its K-nearest neighbors based on the euclidean distance between the pixels, denoted as $KNN(p_i)$. We search for nearest neighbors only inside $M_S$, i.e. $p_j \in KNN(p_i) \Rightarrow p_j \in M_S$.

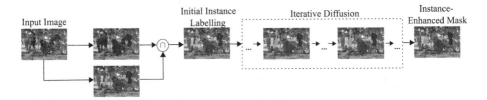

**Fig. 1.** The overall pipeline of our method: The intersection of the semantic segmentation and the instance segmentation outputs are combined to provide the initial instance labels, which are afterwards anisotropically diffused towards the remaining unlabeled pixels of the Semantic Segmentation output. The ∩ symbol signifies mask intersection.

We plan to propagate the instance labels predicted by the instance segmentation algorithm via anisotropic diffusion, towards the unlabeled pixels belonging to $M_S$ but not to $M_I$. To this end, we first define the set $z = \{z^l\}$ of label vectors $z^l \in \{0,1\}^{WH}$ with $l \in L$. We set the vector element $z^l(i)$ corresponding to pixel $p_i$ to be equal to 1 if $p_i \in M_I^j$, and zero otherwise. Then, we define the weighted graph $G = (P, E, W)$ with the set of nodes $P$ equal to the mask pixels $M_S$, edges $E \subset P \times P$ connecting the nodes and weights $W$ assigned to every edge. Each $z^l$ defines a function connecting the $i-th$ pixel/graph node $p_i$ with the value $z_i^l$ indicating whether $p_i$ belongs to instance label $l$ or not.

Let $|\cdot|_2$ denote the euclidean norm and $I(p_i)$ the RGB color value of pixel $p_i$. Then, the anisotropic graph laplacian $L^D(i)$ on graph node $i$ is defined as [13]:

$$L^D(i) = \left(\frac{1}{d_i}\sum_{j=1}^{n} w_{ij}q_{ij}\right) z_i^l - \frac{1}{d_i}\sum_{j=1}^{n} w_{ij}q_{ij}z_j^l \tag{1}$$

where $w_{ij}$ is the edge weight connecting nodes $i$ and $j$:

$$w_{ij} = \exp(\frac{|p_i - p_j|_2^2}{\sigma_d^2}) \cdot \exp(\frac{|I(p_i) - I(p_j)|_2^2}{\sigma_c^2}) \tag{2}$$

$d_i$ is the degree of node $i$:

$$d_i = \sum_{j=1}^{n} w_{ij} \tag{3}$$

and $q_{ij}$ is equal to:

$$q_{ij} = \exp(-\frac{w_{ij}(z_i^l - z_j^l)^2}{\sigma_a^2}) \tag{4}$$

where $\sigma_d$, $\sigma_c$ and $\sigma_a$ are the scale hyperparameters of the exponents.

Assuming a unit discretization interval, the Euler approximation for anisotropic diffusion on $G$ per instance label class is given by the following iterative update from step $t$ to step $t + 1$:

$$z_{t+1}^l \leftarrow z_t^l - L^D z_t^l \tag{5}$$

The total number of iterations is a hyperparameter - following [13], we first apply isotropic diffusion ($q_{ij} = 1$) for a small number of steps to decrease the number of iterations required for convergence. After the final iteration is completed for every instance $l$, we select the instance label $l_{p_i}$ of every initially unlabeled pixel $p_i$ to be equal to:

$$l_{p_i} = \arg\max_l(z^l) \tag{6}$$

A schematic overview of our method can be seen in Fig. 1.

## 4   Experimental Evaluation

Our method was tested on the publicly available Embrapa WGISD [22] dataset. Embrapa WGISD contains 137 RGB images with manually annotated instance segmentation masks of grape bunches. We follow the 88-22-27 training-validation-test images split used by the authors, with the same image resizing and augmentation strategies described in their paper. In our experiments, we found the Detectron2 [27] implementation of Mask R-CNN to produce superior results to the Matterport [2] implementation used in [22]. We trained both implementations of Mask R-CNN, and the implementation of PSPNet [33], [32], in an Nvidia Tesla K40m GPU, with the maximum available batch size and network backbone. The Detectron2 Mask R-CNN implementation was trained for 6000 iterations, the PSPNet implementation for 10000 iterations and the Matterport Mask R-CNN implementation for 6000 iterations. For our experiments, the instance segmentation masks from Mask R-CNN were predicted using the confidence value that maximized the (object detection) F-measure at 0.3 IoU of the validation set. In all frameworks, the default training parameters were kept.

We evaluate the mask quality of PSPNet and Mask R-CNN with total mask Grape Bunch IoU, total mask Background IoU (BG IoU) and per-pixel F-measure. We also include the F-measure metric reported in [22] for the Matterport Mask R-CNN implementation. The total scene masks for Mask R-CNN were derived by aggregating all predicted instance masks using the logical OR operator. The experimental results of Table 1 highlight the relevance of our method

**Table 1.** Results on Embrapa WGISD dataset

| Segmentation method | Grape Bunch IoU | BG IoU | F-measure |
|---|---|---|---|
| Matterport Mask R-CNN [22] | – | – | 0.889 |
| Matterport Mask R-CNN(Ours) | 0.792 | 0.979 | 0.884 |
| Detectron2 Mask R-CNN | 0.834 | 0.983 | 0.909 |
| PSPNet | **0.858** | **0.985** | **0.924** |

in this dataset, as the semantic segmentation algorithm predicts higher quality masks compared to the instance segmentation algorithm.

Therefore, we apply anisotropic diffusion-based instance label addition to the test set. Based on our experimental hyperparameter search, we utilized the 8 nearest neighbors and set $\sigma_d = 2$, $\sigma_c = 500$ and $\sigma_a = 0.1$. We also used the Detectron2 Mask R-CNN implementation to provide the initial instance labelling. In Table 2 we compare our method to a naive local algorithm that for each unlabeled pixel $p$, uses the label majority vote of the K nearest labeled neighbors to assign to $p$ an instance label. We refer to this baseline method as Majority Voting KNN (MV-KNN), and set the number of neighbors equal to 9. For labelled neighbors existing on Mask R-CNN mask overlaps, we select the contributing label randomly from one of the overlapping masks. We compare the methods using per-unlabeled-pixel average multi-class precision (Prec), recall (Rec) and F-measure. We found that our method produces adequate results even

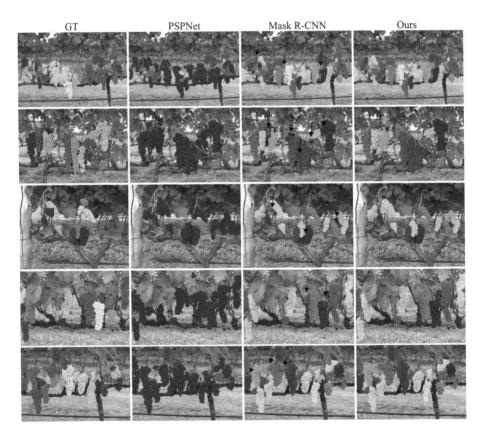

**Fig. 2.** PSPNet output enhancement with grape bunch instance label information. The columns from left to right depict: the ground truth instance segmentation labels, the PSPNet semantic segmentation output, the Mask R-CNN (Detectron2) instance segmentation results, and the results of our method.

for approximately 100 diffusion iterations, and reaches convergence with respect to the evaluation metrics at approximately 1000 iterations.

However, to have meaningful metrics, we remove the influence of wrong predictions from the semantic and instance segmentation algorithms. We remove the influence of object misclassification from Mask R-CNN by assigning to each pixel of the predicted instance segmentation masks the original ground truth instance labels - i.e., we still propagate from masks predicted by Mask R-CNN, but with instance labels given by the ground truth. Additionally, to disregard the effect of possible PSPNet mask inacacuracies, we calculate the metrics only on correct PSPNet mask estimations.

**Table 2.** Comparison of our method with the baseline

| Method | Prec | Rec | F-measure |
|--------|------|-----|-----------|
| MV-KNN | 0.841 | 0.907 | 0.843 |
| Ours | **0.904** | **0.911** | **0.893** |

Our method outperforms the baseline in all metrics, and achieves over 6% improvement in precision. Some qualitative results that highlight the effectiveness of our method can be seen in Fig. 2. The reader should notice that in the fourth column of Fig. 2 several Mask R-CNN instance masks have been improved. Regions from grape bunch masks that were improved by preserving PSPNet mask information have been noted with black arrows in the third column. The resolution of conflicts between adjacent bunch grape masks attempting to cover the same unclaimed PSPNet mask region, for example in the outermost right grape bunches (yellow and purple) in the second row, is guided by the local topological and color information in the diffusion process. It should be noted that the ground truth coloring of grape bunch masks is different from Mask R-CNN and our method, due to the fact that Mask R-CNN usually predicts a different number of instance masks, and in a different order.

## 5    Conclusion

An anisotropic diffusion-based instance labelling algorithm for semantic segmentation masks has been presented. Our method utilizes local distance and color cues to anisotropically propagate instance label information predicted by an instance segmentation algorithm towards mask pixels estimated by a semantic segmentation algorithm. The evaluation of our method in the Embrapa WGISD grape bunch instance segmentation dataset showcases the preservation of semantic segmentation mask quality. Our future work will concentrate on the fusion of RGB and depth information in the diffusion process to alleviate possible ambiguities in scene understanding originating from grape bunch instance segmentation misassignments. We also plan to evaluate our method on datasets of larger size and variability.

**Acknowledgements.** This work has been supported by the EU Horizon 2020 funded project namely: "BACCHUS (MoBile Robotic PlAtforms for ACtive InspeCtion and Harvesting in AgricUltural AreaS)" under the grant agreement with no: 871704.

# References

1. Nuset: A deep learning tool for reliably separating and analyzing crowded cells. https://github.com/yanglf1121/NuSeT
2. Abdulla, W.: Mask r-CNN for object detection and instance segmentation on keras and tensorflow (2017). https://github.com/matterport/Mask_RCNN
3. Arnab, A., Torr, P.: Bottom-up instance segmentation using deep higher-order crfs. ArXiv (2016)
4. Bai, M., Urtasun, R.: Deep watershed transform for instance segmentation. In: 2017 IEEE Conference on Computer Vision and Pattern Recognition (CVPR), pp. 2858–2866 (2017)
5. Bouget, D., Jørgensen, A., Kiss, G., Leira, H.O., Langø, T.: Semantic segmentation and detection of mediastinal lymph nodes and anatomical structures in CT data for lung cancer staging. Int. J. Comput. Assist. Radiol. Surg. **14**(6), 977–986 (2019). https://doi.org/10.1007/s11548-019-01948-8
6. Caye Daudt, R., Le Saux, B., Boulch, A., Gousseau, Y.: Guided anisotropic diffusion and iterative learning for weakly supervised change detection. In: Proceedings of the IEEE/CVF Conference on Computer Vision and Pattern Recognition (CVPR) Workshops, June 2019
7. Cheng, B., Collins, M.D., Zhu, Y., Liu, T., Huang, T.S., Adam, H., Chen, L.C.: Panoptic-deeplab: a simple, strong, and fast baseline for bottom-up panoptic segmentation. In: Proceedings of the IEEE/CVF Conference on Computer Vision and Pattern Recognition (CVPR), June 2020
8. Costea, A., Petrovai, A., Nedevschi, S.: Fusion scheme for semantic and instance-level segmentation. In: 2018 21st International Conference on Intelligent Transportation Systems (ITSC), pp. 3469–3475 (2018)
9. Fu, C.Y., Berg, T.L., Berg, A.C.: Imp: Instance mask projection for high accuracy semantic segmentation of things. In: Proceedings of the IEEE/CVF International Conference on Computer Vision (ICCV), October 2019
10. de Geus, D., Meletis, P., Dubbelman, G.: Panoptic segmentation with a joint semantic and instance segmentation network. ArXiv abs/1809.02110 (2018)
11. He, K., Gkioxari, G., Dollar, P., Girshick, R.: Mask r-CNN. In: IEEE International Conference on Computer Vision (ICCV), October 2017
12. Huang, Z., Huang, L., Gong, Y., Huang, C., Wang, X.: Mask Scoring R-CNN. In: CVPR (2019)
13. Kim, K.I., Tompkin, J., Pfister, H., Theobalt, C.: Context-guided diffusion for label propagation on graphs. In: 2015 IEEE International Conference on Computer Vision (ICCV), pp. 2776–2784 (2015)
14. Kirillov, A., He, K., Girshick, R., Rother, C., Dollár, P.: Panoptic segmentation. In: 2019 IEEE/CVF Conference on Computer Vision and Pattern Recognition (CVPR), pp. 9396–9405 (2019)
15. Krähenbühl, P., Koltun, V.: Efficient inference in fully connected CRFS with gaussian edge potentials. In: Shawe-Taylor, J., Zemel, R., Bartlett, P., Pereira, F., Weinberger, K.Q. (eds.) Advances in Neural Information Processing Systems, vol. 24. Curran Associates, Inc. (2011)

16. Li, Y., Qi, H., Dai, J., Ji, X., Wei, Y.: Fully convolutional instance-aware semantic segmentation (2017)
17. Liu, D., Zhang, D., Song, Y., Huang, H., Cai, W.: Panoptic feature fusion net: a novel instance segmentation paradigm for biomedical and biological images. IEEE Trans. Image Process. **30**, 2045–2059 (2021). https://doi.org/10.1109/TIP.2021.3050668
18. Pham, V., Ito, S., Kozakaya, T.: Biseg: simultaneous instance segmentation and semantic segmentation with fully convolutional networks. CoRR abs/1706.02135 (2017). http://arxiv.org/abs/1706.02135
19. Porzi, L., Rota Bulò, S., Colovic, A., Kontschieder, P.: Seamless scene segmentation. In: The IEEE Conference on Computer Vision and Pattern Recognition (CVPR), June 2019
20. Ren, S., He, K., Girshick, R., Sun, J.: Faster r-CNN: towards real-time object detection with region proposal networks. In: Cortes, C., Lawrence, N., Lee, D., Sugiyama, M., Garnett, R. (eds.) Advances in Neural Information Processing Systems, vol. 28. Curran Associates, Inc. (2015)
21. Ronneberger, O., Fischer, P., Brox, T.: U-Net: convolutional networks for biomedical image segmentation. In: Navab, N., Hornegger, J., Wells, W.M., Frangi, A.F. (eds.) MICCAI 2015. LNCS, vol. 9351, pp. 234–241. Springer, Cham (2015). https://doi.org/10.1007/978-3-319-24574-4_28
22. Santos, T.T., de Souza, L.L., dos Santos, A.A., Avila, S.: Grape detection, segmentation, and tracking using deep neural networks and three-dimensional association. Comput. Electron. Agricult. **170**, 105247 (2020)
23. Shelhamer, E., Long, J., Darrell, T.: Fully convolutional networks for semantic segmentation. IEEE Trans. Pattern Anal. Mach. Intell. **39**, 1 (2016)
24. Tian, Y., Yang, G., Wang, Z., Li, E., Liang, Z.: Instance segmentation of apple flowers using the improved mask r-CNN model. Biosys. Eng. **193**, 264–278 (2020)
25. Wang, B.H., Chao, W., Wang, Y., Hariharan, B., Weinberger, K.Q., Campbell, M.: Ldls: 3-D object segmentation through label diffusion from 2-D images. IEEE Robot. Automat. Lett. **4**(3), 2902–2909 (2019)
26. Wu, Y., Zhang, G., Gao, Y., Deng, X., Gong, K., Liang, X., Lin, L.: Bidirectional graph reasoning network for panoptic segmentation. In: The IEEE/CVF Conference on Computer Vision and Pattern Recognition (CVPR), pp. 9080–9089 (2020)
27. Wu, Y., Kirillov, A., Massa, F., Lo, W.Y., Girshick, R.: Detectron2 (2019). https://github.com/facebookresearch/detectron2
28. Xiong, Y., et al.: Upsnet: a unified panoptic segmentation network (2019)
29. Yang, L., et al.: Nuset: a deep learning tool for reliably separating and analyzing crowded cells. PLOS Computat. Biol. **16**(9), 1–20 (2020)
30. Zhang, Y., Chen, B., Wang, J., Li, J., Sun, X.: APLCNet: automatic pixel-level crack detection network based on instance segmentation. IEEE Access **8**, 199159–199170 (2020)
31. Zhao, H., Shi, J., Qi, X., Wang, X., Jia, J.: Pyramid scene parsing network. In: IEEE Conference on Computer Vision and Pattern Recognition (CVPR), pp. 6230–6239 (2017)
32. Zhou, B., Zhao, H., Puig, X., Fidler, S., Barriuso, A., Torralba, A.: Scene parsing through ade20k dataset. In: IEEE Conference on Computer Vision and Pattern Recognition (2017)
33. Zhou, B., et al.: Semantic understanding of scenes through the ade20k dataset. Int. J. Comput. Vis. (2018)

# Jigsaw Puzzle Solving as a Consistent Labeling Problem

Marina Khoroshiltseva[1,3]([✉]), Ben Vardi[4], Alessandro Torcinovich[1],
Arianna Traviglia[3], Ohad Ben-Shahar[4], and Marcello Pelillo[1,2]

[1] Università Ca' Foscari di Venezia, Venice, Italy
{m.khoroshiltseva,ale.torcinovich,pelillo}@unive.it
[2] European Centre of Living Technology, Venice, Italy
[3] Istituto Italiano di Tecnologia, Genoa, Italy
arianna.traviglia@iit.it
[4] Ben-Gurion University of the Negev, Beer Sheva, Israel
benva@post.bgu.ac.il, ben-shahar@cs.bgu.ac.il

**Abstract.** We explore the idea of abstracting the jigsaw puzzle problem as a *consistent labeling* problem, a classical concept introduced in the1980s by Hummel and Zucker for which a solid theory and powerful algorithms are available. The problem amounts to maximizing a well-known quadratic function over a probability space which we solve using standard relaxation labeling algorithms endowed with matrix balancing mechanisms to enforce one-to-one correspondence constraints. Preliminary experimental results on publicly available datasets demonstrate the feasibility of the proposed approach.

## 1 Introduction

Jigsaw puzzles were introduced in the1760s as children's games but despite their playful origins they can be encountered today in many application areas, such as image reconstruction, the reassembling of broken artifacts, shredded documents, etc. [4,6]. In its simplest form, what is now known as the *square jigsaw puzzle* problem consists of reordering a set of square pieces on a 2D grid in such a way as to form a perceptually coherent picture or, more formally, to find a permutation that encodes such a reordering. Although the problem is known to be NP-complete [5], it has attracted much attention in the past few years, employing computational schemes as varied as greedy algorithms, functional optimization and machine learning (e.g., [1–3,7,8,12,14,16,18]).

In this paper, we take a different route and explore the idea of abstracting the jigsaw puzzle problem as a *consistent labeling* problem, a class of problems widely studied in the computer vision and pattern recognition communities since the 1970s [9,15]. Attempts at formalizing the notion of a consistent labeling culminated in a seminal paper by Hummel and Zucker [10] who, motivated by the theory of variational inequalities, developed a formal theory of consistency that later turned out to have intimate connections with non-cooperative game

© Springer Nature Switzerland AG 2021
N. Tsapatsoulis et al. (Eds.): CAIP 2021, LNCS 13053, pp. 392–402, 2021.
https://doi.org/10.1007/978-3-030-89131-2_36

theory [11]. The theory generalizes classical (boolean) constraint satisfaction problems to scenarios involving "soft" compatibility measures and probabilistic (as opposed to "hard") label assignments. Within this framework, under a certain symmetry assumption, consistent labelings also turn out to be equivalent to local solutions of a linearly constrained quadratic optimization problem.

In our formulation, the jigsaw puzzle problem is viewed as the problem of finding a consistent labeling satisfying certain compatibility relations, with an additional requirement for one-to-one correspondences between the puzzle's tiles and their positions. We solve the problem using classical *relaxation labeling* algorithm which enjoys nice theoretical properties [13] and offers the advantage of avoiding *ad hoc* projections and problematic step size choices. To enforce the one-to-one constraints we endow the algorithm with two "matrix balancing" mechanisms, one based on the well-known Sinkhorn-Knopp procedure and the other inspired by von Neumann's method of alternating projections. Related to our work is the jigsaw puzzle problem formulation suggested by Andaló *et al.* [1], where a similar quadratic objective function is optimized with a different gradient-projection technique.

We conducted some preliminary experiments aimed at testing the plausibility of the proposed approach. We first show that in the presence of an ideal, or "oracle" compatibility measure, the "plain" relaxation labeling algorithm (that is, *without* enforcing one-to-one correspondence between pieces and locations) is always able to return perfect reconstruction results. We then show how performance deteriorates as we move away from this ideal setting, thereby demonstrating the necessity of the balancing operation. We conclude with experiments using real-world compatibilities on two publicly available (scaled) datasets, which show the feasibility of the proposed combined technique.

## 2    Relaxation Labeling for Consistent Labeling Problems

Suppose we are given a set of objects $B = \{b_1, \ldots, b_n\}$ and a set of labels $\Lambda = \{\lambda_1, \ldots, \lambda_m\}$, and our goal is to assign a label to each object in $B$. Numerous real-world problems, typically discrete in nature, can be abstracted in this way, where label assignments for object $b_i$ can be represented by a probability distribution $\mathbf{p}_i$ over all possible labels. Formally, $\mathbf{p}_i \in \Delta^m$, where

$$\Delta^m = \left\{ \mathbf{x} \in \mathbb{R}^m \mid x_\lambda \geq 0 \;\; \wedge \;\; \sum_{\lambda=1}^m x_\lambda = 1 \right\} \tag{1}$$

is the standard $m$-dimensional simplex and $p_{i\lambda}$ is the probability of object $b_i$ to "choose" label $\lambda$. Aggregating all $\mathbf{p}_i$, the vector $\mathbf{p} = [\mathbf{p}_1 \ldots \mathbf{p}_n]$ is a "soft" labeling assignment for all objects, residing in the multidimensional standard simplex $\Delta^{n \times m} = \Delta^m \times \cdots \times \Delta^m$, and thus may be represented as a labeling matrix of $n$ rows and $m$ columns.

An initial labeling assignment can originate from *local measurements* that capture the relevant features of individual objects when considered in isolation.

Such local measurements typically provide imperfect labeling assignments, a state of affairs that *relaxation labeling processes* seek to improve progressively. A major source of information that is utilized in such processes is *contextual information*, a prior that reflects the structure of the problem through compatibility relations about the assignment of labels in different objects. Contextual information is quantitatively expressed with a matrix of *compatibility coefficients* $\mathbf{R} = [r_{ij\lambda\mu}]$, where $r_{ij\lambda\mu}$ measures the strength of compatibility between the hypotheses "$b_i$ has label $\lambda$" and "$b_j$ has label $\mu$".

The compatibility model $\mathbf{R}$ is considered "contextual" because it naturally leads to measures of *contextual support*, i.e., how much the context supports the assignment of a particular label $\lambda$ to object $b_i$. The "context" in this case is considered the labels assigned to all *other* objects, and following the classic relaxation labeling theory [10] it is defined as

$$q_{i\lambda} = \sum_{j,\mu} r_{ij\lambda\mu} p_{j\mu}. \tag{2}$$

By properly weighting and combining the support of all labels at all objects, one can also quantify the average (or total) support of the assignment

$$A(\mathbf{p}) = \sum_{i,j} \sum_{\lambda,\mu} r_{ij\lambda\mu} p_{i\lambda} p_{j\mu}, \tag{3}$$

a measure termed *average local consistency* [10].

Using these tools, it remains to describe what labeling assignments should be the "desired" goal of relaxation labeling processes. To this end, Hummel and Zucker [10] defined a labeling assignment $\mathbf{p}$ to be *consistent* if for all $\mathbf{v} \in \Delta^{n \times m}$

$$\sum_\lambda^m p_{i\lambda} q_{i\lambda} \geq \sum_\lambda^m v_{i\lambda} q_{i\lambda} \quad \forall i = 1, \dots, n \tag{4}$$

and showed that if the matrix $\mathbf{R}$ is symmetric, then any (local) maximizer $\mathbf{p} \in \Delta^{n \times m}$ of $A(\mathbf{p})$ is consistent. Put differently, a labeling assignment $\mathbf{p}$ that maximizes the average local consistency $A(\mathbf{p})$ represents a consistent labeling. A process that relaxes a given inconsistent assignment towards a more consistent one (and with higher average local consistency) will intuitively care to increase $p_{i\lambda}$ when $q_{i\lambda}$ is high and decrease it when $q_{i\lambda}$ is low. Indeed, one of the best known update rules is defined by the following iterative procedure [13,15]:

$$p_{i\lambda}(t+1) = \frac{p_{i\lambda}(t) q_{i\lambda}(t)}{\sum_\mu p_{i\mu}(t) q_{i\mu}(t)} \quad \forall i, \lambda \tag{5}$$

where the nominator formalizes this intuition and the denominator projects the result to the multi-simplex. Importantly, this update rule does not require the problematic choice of a step size and theoretical analysis has proven that under non-negativity and symmetry conditions on $\mathbf{R}$ it is guaranteed to converge to a consistent labeling [13] (and thus locally maximizes the $A(\mathbf{p})$ term [10]).

Summarizing the discussion above, the relaxation labeling algorithm takes as input an initial labeling assignment, progressively updates it according to the update rule (that in turn is intimately related to the compatibility model $\mathbf{R}$), and converges to a consistent labeling. Ultimately, one may wish to set the initial labeling assignment in an informative way (i.e., in a way that reflects prior knowledge about the instance of the problem at hand). However, if no such knowledge is available, it is possible to initialize $\mathbf{p}(0)$ to the uniform probability mass function, or the barycenter of the multidimensional simplex, namely $p_{i\lambda}(0) = \frac{1}{m}$ for all $i$ and all $\lambda$.

# 3    Relaxation Labeling Algorithm for Puzzle Solving

We propose to cast jigsaw puzzle solving as a consistent labeling problem defined as above. Here, the set of objects $B$ represents the puzzle pieces, the labels $\Lambda$ are the relevant positions in the reconstruction plane, and the task is to assign a different position from $\Lambda$ to each puzzle piece from $B$. Note that in such an abstraction, the label-object representation can be easily exchanged to seek an assignment of a different piece to each possible position. In either case, not every assignment is admissible for puzzle solving, as one must seek a *permutation* matrix $\mathbf{p}$ that reorders the pieces to the correct positions.

While there is no guarantee that the relaxation labeling process always converges to the correct permutation matrix, under conditions of "ideal" compatibilities this is empirically the case, as is the observation that the average local consistency then assumes a *global* maximum (cf. Sect. 5.1).

When the relaxation algorithm is equipped with imperfect (noisy, or wrong) compatibilities, it may fail to recover a permutation. Indeed, the relaxation labeling update rule from Eq. (5) guarantees that $\mathbf{p}$ is a stochastic matrix (i.e., rows sum to 1) but does not enforce the same constraint for its columns. Therefore, the optimization process can converge to a consistent labeling that does not represent a permutation, leading to a solution where multiple pieces are assigned to the same position while other positions remain vacant. To alleviate this problem, we endow the relaxation process with matrix balancing steps that encourage convergence into a permutation matrix. Two such steps are explored:

*Sinkhorn-Knopp Balancing:* The Sinkhorn-Knopp (SK) algorithm [17] transforms a given non-negative square matrix to a related doubly stochastic matrix, with all rows and columns summing up to 1. This is done by alternately normalizing the rows and columns. Starting from an initial point $\mathbf{p}(0)$, the balancing is performed according to:

$$\mathbf{p}(t) = T_c(T_r(\mathbf{p}(t-1)))    \tag{6}$$

where $\mathbf{p}$ is a $n$-dimensional square matrix and $T_c$ and $T_r$ are respectively column- and row-wise normalization matrix operators. Under some assumptions one can show that the process converges to a doubly stochastic matrix. SK is incorporated in our algorithm as an additional balancing step applied after the update rule in each iteration.

*Alternating Projections:* Since the native relaxation labeling update rule normalizes the rows of the assignment matrix but not the columns, and since objects and labels in the puzzle solving abstraction are interchangeable (see above), it is tempting to switch the role of pieces (objects, rows) and positions (labels, columns), thereby switching between row and column normalization every step of the process. Computationally, this is done by alternately switching between Eq. (5) and the following update rule:

$$p_{i\lambda}(t+1) = \frac{p_{i\lambda}(t)q_{i\lambda}(t)}{\sum_j p_{j\lambda}(t)q_{j\lambda}(t)} \quad \forall i, \lambda \tag{7}$$

and keep doing so until convergence. In practice, we start this procedure only after $t$ steps, where only Eq. (5) is applied.

## 4    Compatibility Measure

A key component in all jigsaw puzzle solvers is a pairwise compatibility measure $C_{\mathcal{R}}(i,j)$ that quantifies the affinity between pieces $i$ and $j$ when placed adjacent to each other with spatial relationship $\mathcal{R} \in \{left, up, right, down\}$. This notion of compatibility can be extended naturally into a relaxation labeling compatibility after defining non-neighbor positions and self-comparison cases properly. We thus formalize $\mathbf{R}$ as follows:

$$r_{ij\lambda\mu} = \begin{cases} C_{\mathcal{R}}(i,j) & (i \neq j) \wedge (\lambda, \mu \text{ are adjacent locations in relation } \mathcal{R}) \\ 0 & \text{otherwise} \end{cases} \tag{8}$$

Clearly, $C_{\mathcal{R}}(i,j)$ can be measured in numerous different ways, as indeed discussed in many previous papers. While this choice is not central to our work, here we measure piece affinity by computing the dissimilarity between the abutting boundary pixels of two adjacent pieces. Even this particular approach can be implemented in many different ways, and here we adopt the improved Mahalanobis Gradient Compatibility (MGC) originally developed by Gallagher [7] and further improved by Son *et al.* [18], that considers both the color differences across pieces borders and the directional derivative differences along the borders.

Assuming for example that the two candidate pieces are positioned such that piece $i$ is placed to the left of piece $j$. We first define a dissimilarity measure $\Gamma_R(i,j)$:

$$\Gamma_R(i,j) = D_R(i,j) + D_L(j,i) + D'_R(i,j) + D'_L(j,i). \tag{9}$$

The first two terms, $D_R$ and $D_L$, penalize the changes in the pixel values across the boundary in the following way:

$$D_R(i,j) = \sum_{s=1}^{S} (\Lambda_R^{(ij)}(s) - E_R^{(ij)}(s)) V_{iR}^{-1} (\Lambda_R^{(ij)}(s) - E_R^{(ij)}(s))^{\top} \tag{10}$$

where $E_R^{(ij)}(s)$ is the expected change across the boundary, $\Lambda_R^{(ij)}(s)$ is the pixel intensity change across the boundary and $V_{iR}$ is a sample covariance calculated from samples $\{i(s,S) - i(s,S-1)), s = 1, 2, ..., S\}$, where $S$ is the length of the piece board. $D'_R$ and $D'_L$ are calculated in similar manner, replacing $i(u, v)$ with the directional derivatives $\delta(u, v) = i(u, v) - i(u-1, v)$. Please refer to [7,18] for additional information.

With the dissimilarities obtained, we next convert them to normalized compatibility values by (a) dividing them by the $K$ smallest dissimilarity and reflecting about 1, and (b) rectifying at zero as only positive scores are considered useful. Formally,

$$C_{\mathcal{R}}(i, j) = \max\left(1 - \frac{\Gamma_R(i, j)}{K_{min_{\mathcal{R}}}(i)}, 0\right) \tag{11}$$

where $K_{min_{\mathcal{R}}}(i)$ is the $K$-min value of the dissimilarity between all other pieces in relation $\mathcal{R}$ to piece $i$. The smaller the value of $K$, the more sparse $C_{\mathcal{R}}(i, j)$ becomes, leading to a sparser $\mathbf{R}$ matrix and, generally speaking, a more efficient relaxation labeling process.

To further sparsify the compatibility matrix, we adopt the *best buddies* concept from Pomeranz *et al.* [14]. We set the compatibility of any two best buddies to perfect compatibility (i.e., 1), and zero the compatibility values of all other non-best-buddy matches with respect to each of the two best buddies. We term this step the *sparsification* of the compatibility matrix, and experiment both with and without it.

# 5  Experimental Evaluation

## 5.1  Experiments with Oracle Compatibilities

In order to explore the effectiveness of our solver, we first tested the proposed algorithm using a synthetically generated ideal compatibility, dubbed *oracle compatibility* and defined as follows:

$$C_{\mathcal{R}}^{(oracle)}(i, j) = \begin{cases} 1 & \text{if } i, j \text{ are the correct neighbors in relation } \mathcal{R} \\ 0 & \text{otherwise} \end{cases} \tag{12}$$

We tested the relaxation labeling algorithm with this oracle compatibility on a puzzle of 540 pieces and examined its performance with and without balancing. All solvers have been executed with no-prior knowledge, i.e., using the barycenter of the standard multidimensional simplex as initial point. When used, we started the balancing algorithm after $t = 10$ iteration of relaxation labeling, to let the latter process first propagate the information without any constraint. We set the maximum number of iterations $T = 200$, without reaching it in none of the cases, meaning that the solvers always converged. Figure 1 shows the behavior of the average local consistency function along the iterations. The experiment demonstrates that each proposed strategy does reach a maximum and therefore a consistent labeling, which corresponded to the correct permutation solving the synthetic puzzle. As can be observed, endowing the procedure with either of the balancing components significantly expedited the convergence by forcing the optimization process towards doubly stochastic matrices early on.

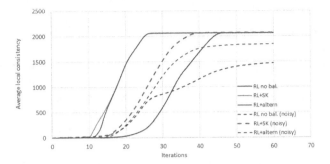

**Fig. 1.** The average local consistency over the relaxation labeling iterations with oracle compatibilities; solid lines - ideal oracle compatibility, dashed lines - "noisy" oracle compatibility with $\sigma = 0.02$.

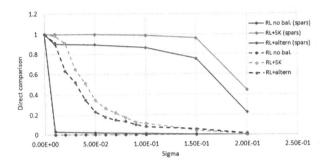

**Fig. 2.** Drop in accuracy of our solvers due to the perturbation of oracle compatibility; solid lines - results with sparsification, dashed lines - results without sparsification.

In real-world puzzles, however, it is of course difficult to guarantee an ideal oracle compatibility, so we verified the robustness of the proposed solvers by perturbing all coefficients with additive Gaussian noise $\epsilon \sim \mathcal{N}(0, \sigma^2)$ for increasing values of standard deviation $\sigma$, ranging in $(0, 0.1]$ for the experiments without the sparsification technique and in $(0, 0.2]$ for experiments with sparsification. In such cases, we applied the sparsification technique described in the previous section, setting $K = 5$. We assessed the performance of the three solvers using the *Direct Comparison* metric [2] which measures the ratio of pieces placed in correct position compared to the ground-truth. As Fig. 2 shows, the performance drops immediately unless balancing is incorporated. Moreover, with sparsification, the performance persists for much higher levels of noise, signifying the importance of this computational component. Such experiments show that the relaxation labeling scheme for consistent labeling is able to address the puzzle solving task quite effectively, and that the reliability of the compatibility function is a crucial aspect for the correctness of the solution.

## 5.2  Experiments with Natural Images

The quality of the compatibility computed for natural images depends on several factors that can be divided into two categories: the *image content*, that might make the assembling process particularly challenging, like the presence of repetitive patterns or large regions with homogeneous color, and the *puzzle size* that, when large, may lead to less informative pieces increasing the ambiguity in the compatibility computation. For these reasons, the compatibility measure should be sensitive enough to capture small differences between pieces. The dissimilarity measure that we chose for our procedure (cf. Section 4) is empirically demonstrated to be more reliable with respect to other measures proposed in the literature [18].

**Fig. 3.** Qualitative reconstruction performance of three images: (left) shuffled puzzles, (middle) results by SK balancing, (right) results by alternating projections. Purple areas represent vacant positions.

As dissimilarity measures incorporate more pictorial information for larger piece sizes, we tested the algorithm on the up-scaled versions of widely used datasets. Scaling was done by applying bicubic interpolation with a scale factor of 2, resulting in doubling the number of pixels involved in each dissimilarity computation, without changing the puzzle size. It should be noted that the quality of the obtained results, which is better when compared to the non-scaled results, is likely improved by the interpolation computation, which leaks information between pieces and thus raises the similarity of boundary pixels across neighboring pieces. Moreover, we emphasize that since the results were obtained for scaled datasets, they are not directly comparable with results obtained for the original datasets.

We tested the algorithm on the 20 scaled puzzles of 432 pieces from the *MIT dataset* presented by Cho *et al.* [2] and on the 20 scaled puzzles of 540 pieces from the *McGill dataset*, proposed by Pomeranz *et al.* [14]. In both datasets, piece size was scaled from 28 × 28 to 56 × 56 pixels, and the RGB color space was used in dissimilarity computations. All experiments refer to puzzles with known piece orientation. Both datasets are widely used as performance benchmarks and contain several images for which a good reconstruction is challenging. Some of the images contain horizontal and vertical lines that may be aligned with pieces edges and distort the compatibility; other images contain repetitive texture patterns (e.g., wall, grass) or homogeneous regions (e.g., sky, water) that may generate numerous false positive compatibilities.

Aside from the Direct Comparison metric, we adopt two other measures to assess solvers performance: the *Neighbor Comparison* metric [2] that measures the ratio of correctly assigned neighbors in the solution, and the *Perfect Reconstruction* metric [7] that is a binary indicator of whether all pieces are in the correct position.

As Table 1 shows, the relaxation labeling algorithm (with balancing) can handle real-world compatibilities and solve real puzzles in most cases. At the same time, the datasets contain some images that generate multiple false compatibilities that affect the quality of the solution obtained. Figure 3 shows one such problematic image where an admissible reconstruction was not obtained due to the presence of large white regions. Nevertheless, the main part of the puzzle is solved correctly. Analyzing the different versions of the puzzle solver it is evident that consistent labeling via relaxation labeling is a viable substrate for solving scaled natural image jigsaw puzzles, that however requires either highly predictive compatibility, or more realistically, the incorporation of balancing in the update rule. Empirically, both balancing methods we experimented with exhibited reliable performance, with SK reaching better performance than alternating projections.

**Table 1.** Reconstruction performance of puzzles from the MIT and McGill datasets (note that we used a scaled version of the original images; see text for explanation).

| Solvertype | MIT (scaled) | | | McGill (scaled) | | |
|---|---|---|---|---|---|---|
| | Direct | Neighbor | Perfect | Direct | Neighbor | Perfect |
| RL without balancing | 28% | 33% | 0/20 | 28% | 32% | 0/20 |
| RL with SK balancing | 91% | 95% | 15/20 | 98% | 99% | 15/20 |
| RL with alternating projections | 91% | 93% | 11/20 | 94% | 95% | 10/20 |

# 6   Conclusions and Future Work

In this work we have devised a new principled method to solve jigsaw puzzles, and presented a set of preliminary experiments attesting its plausibility. As a next step to further explore the potential of the proposed method, its known fragilities (such as with puzzles with homogeneous pieces) should be studied and addressed, so it can be compared to previous methods on non-scaled datasets. Moreover, a natural extension is enforcing the balancing step by directly embedding it in the update rule, devising optimization and relaxation labeling schemes more suitable for puzzle solving. As a further step, we are interested in devising new theoretical results pertaining the puzzle solving framework, as presented here, in the presence of regular (or almost regular) compatibility matrices. Finally, from the theoretical and practical results, it appears clear that the compatibility measure must be improved: to this end, we believe that the use of automatic feature extractors such as neural networks, with the recent advent of self-training techniques, represents an interesting branch of research to be explored.

# References

1. Andaló, F.A., Taubin, G., Goldenstein, S.: PSQP: puzzle solving by quadratic programming. IEEE TPAMI **39**(2), 385–396 (2017)
2. Cho, T.S., Avidan, S., Freeman, W.T.: A probabilistic image jigsaw puzzle solver. In: Proceedings CVPR, pp. 183–190 (2010)
3. Cruz, R.S., Fernando, B., Cherian, A., Gould, S.: Deeppermnet: visual permutation learning. CoRR abs/1704.02729 (2017)
4. Deever, A., Gallagher, A.: Semi-automatic assembly of real cross-cut shredded documents. In: Proceedings ICIP, pp. 233–236 (2012)
5. Demaine, E.D., Demaine, M.L.: Jigsaw puzzles, edge matching, and polyomino packing: connections and complexity. Graphs Comb. **23**(Suppl. 1), 195–208 (2007)
6. Derech, N., Tal, A., Shimshoni, I.: Solving archaeological puzzles. CoRR abs/1812.10553 (2018)
7. Gallagher, A.C.: Jigsaw puzzles with pieces of unknown orientation. In: Proceedings CVPR, pp. 382–389 (2012)
8. Gur, S., Ben-Shahar, O.: From square pieces to brick walls: The next challenge in solving jigsaw puzzles. In: ICCV, pp. 4029–4037 (2017)
9. Haralick, R.M., Shapiro, L.G.: The consistent labeling problem: part I. IEEE TPAMI **1**(2), 173–184 (1979)
10. Hummel, R.A., Zucker, S.W.: On the foundations of relaxation labeling processes. IEEE TPAMI **5**(3), 267–287 (1983)
11. Miller, D.A., Zucker, S.W.: Copositive-plus Lemke algorithm solves polymatrix games. Oper. Res. Lett. **10**, 285–290 (1991)
12. Paumard, M., Picard, D., Tabia, H.: Deepzzle: solving visual jigsaw puzzles with deep learning and shortest path optimization. CoRR abs/2005.12548 (2020)
13. Pelillo, M.: The dynamics of nonlinear relaxation labeling processes. J. Math. Imag. Vis. **7**(4), 309–323 (1997)
14. Pomeranz, D., Shemesh, M., Ben-Shahar, O.: A fully automated greedy square jigsaw puzzle solver. In: Proceedings CVPR, pp. 9–16 (2011)

402    M. Khoroshiltseva et al.

15. Rosenfeld, A., Hummel, R.A., Zucker, S.W.: Scene labeling by relaxation operations. IEEE Trans. Syst. Man Cybern. **6**, 420–433 (1976)
16. Sholomon, D., David, O.E., Netanyahu, N.S.: A generalized genetic algorithm-based solver for very large jigsaw puzzles of complex types. In: Proceedings AAAI, pp. 2839–2845 (2014)
17. Sinkhorn, R., Knopp, P.: Concerning nonnegative matrices and doubly stochastic matrices. Pacific J. Math. **21**(2), 343–348 (1967)
18. Son, K., Hays, J., Cooper, D.B.: Solving square jigsaw puzzle by hierarchical loop constraints. IEEE TPAMI **41**(9), 2222–2235 (2018)

# Single-Loss Multi-task Learning For Improving Semantic Segmentation Using Super-Resolution

Andreas Aakerberg[1(✉)], Anders S. Johansen[1], Kamal Nasrollahi[1,2],
and Thomas B. Moeslund[1]

[1] Visual Analysis and Perception, Aalborg University, Aalborg, Denmark
{anaa,asjo,kn,tbm}@create.aau.dk
[2] Research Department, Milestone Systems A/S, Brondby, Denmark

**Abstract.** We propose a novel means to improve the accuracy of semantic segmentation based on multi-task learning. More specifically, in our Multi-Task Semantic Segmentation and Super-Resolution (MT-SSSR) framework, we jointly train a super-resolution and semantic segmentation model in an end-to-end manner using the same task loss for both models. This allows us to optimize the super-resolution model towards producing images that are optimal for the segmentation task, rather than ones that are of high-fidelity. Simultaneously we adapt the segmentation model to better utilize the improved images and thereby improve the segmentation accuracy. We evaluate our approach on multiple public benchmark datasets, and our extensive experimental results show that our novel MT-SSSR framework outperforms other state-of-the-art approaches.

**Keywords:** Multi-task learning · Semantic segmentation · Super-resolution

## 1 Introduction

Semantic Segmentation (SS) is a widely studied computer vision problem that helps scene understanding by assigning dense labels to all pixels in an image. SS has several applications in fields such as autonomous driving, robot sensing, and similar tasks that require a semantic understanding with pixel-level localization. The accuracy of SS is highly correlated with the spatial resolution of the input images [23]. This is particularly prominent for segmentation of small objects, where High-Resolution (HR) is essential to obtain a high accuracy [10]. However, obtaining HR image data is not always possible. One possible solution is therefore to upsample Low-Resolution (LR) images as a pre-processing step. This can be done with classical interpolation-based methods, such as bicubic interpolation, or with the more recent deep-learning based Super-Resolution (SR) methods. The latter has shown to be the most effective in terms of restoring HR details from LR images [8,24]. Deep-learning based SR models are trained by minimizing the

© Springer Nature Switzerland AG 2021
N. Tsapatsoulis et al. (Eds.): CAIP 2021, LNCS 13053, pp. 403–411, 2021.
https://doi.org/10.1007/978-3-030-89131-2_37

loss, typically Mean Squared Error (MSE) loss, between the reconstructed HR image and the Ground-Truth (GT). Hence, these methods require paired LR/HR images for training. However, in the case of improving another computer vision task, such as SS, the objective and subjective quality of the super-resolved image is not necessarily the best metrics. Therefore, we hypothesize that by only using the segmentation loss, it is possible to optimize the SR model jointly, to produce super-resolved images that result in improved segmentation accuracy.

In this paper, we therefore propose a novel framework named Multi-Task Semantic Segmentation and Super-Resolution (MT-SSSR), for joint learning of SS and super-resolution as seen in Fig. 1. We use ESRGAN [24] and HRNet [22] respectively as SR and SS backbones, in our joint framework, and rely on a single loss for learning both models, namely the loss of the SS task. We evaluate our method on two different publicly available datasets, and present new State-of-the-Art (SoTA) results on both. In summary, the contributions of this paper are:

- A novel multi-task learning framework, which uses a single loss to improve the segmentation performance together with SR.
- Our method does not require LR/HR training image pairs for the SR model when jointly learning in the multi-task learning framework.
- We outperform SoTA SS methods on the challenging CityScapes and IDD-Lite datasets by respectively 4.2% and 2.2%, compared to the best existing published results.

## 2   Related Work

**Super-resolution:** Dong *et al.* [8] proposed the first deep-learning-based method for SR, which successfully learned to perform non-linear mapping from LR to HR images. Since then, most successful SR methods have been based on convolutional neural networks. One of the SoTA SR methods is ESRGAN [24], which uses a relativistic Generative Adversarial Network (GAN) with Residual-in-Residual Dense Block (RRDP). Besides improving Signal-to-Noise Ratio (SNR), or the perceptual quality of images, SR can also be used to assist other computer vision tasks to achieve better accuracy [7,14]. Recently, it has been shown that SR can improve optical character recognition accuracy by up to 15% [15] and object detection in satellite imagery by up to 30% [18].

**Semantic Segmentation:** A popular method to achieve SS is to use an encoder-decoder architecture [2,4,17] which encodes the input image to dense representational feature-maps and then decodes to regain spatial information [12,26]. Eff-UNet [3] utilizes Efficientnet [20] as an encoder and UNet [17] as a decoder, to achieve SoTA performance the IDD-Lite dataset [13]. DeeplabV3 [5] uses atrous convolutions and skip-connections for decoding. ERFNet [16] uses deconvolutional layers, combined with a non-bottleneck-1d layer to reduce computational cost. PSPNet [27] proposes a spatial pyramid pooling layer that gathers information by pooling over an increasingly smaller region of the image, then fusing those feature-maps with the original feature-map. Unlike the previously mentioned methods, HRNet [22], aims to retain as much of the resolution of the input image, by combining a HR branch with parallel LR branches to achieve representational information, and subsequently fusing the information from all branches before the final layer. Segmentation models are often optimized using cross-entropy loss, which is a per-pixel evaluation. In [28], Region Mutual Information (RMI) loss is proposed, which utilizes neighboring pixels in a statistical approach, allowing the model to adjust the loss based on how difficult the prediction is, resulting in an overall improvement in accuracy [28].

**Multi-task Learning:** Multi-task learning has proven to be effective for different computer vision problems, when multiple tasks need to be solved at once. By jointly learning multiple related tasks, the performance of the individual tasks can be further improved, compared to learning them separately. In [9], multi-task learning is used to jointly learn image segmentation and depth estimation. In [25] it is proposed to use two GAN for joint de-noising and SR. In [11] a network that can perform a selection of tasks with the same weights is proposed. This is done with task-specific feature modulation, and residual adapters to adjust the forward pass. The work most closely related to ours is DSRL proposed in [23], where multi-task learning is used to jointly learn SR and SS. As the main purpose of multi-task learning in [23] is to improve the encoder of the segmentation model, the SR is considered an auxiliary task that is removed at test time. A key difference in our approach is that we use our SR model to upsample the input images during both training and testing. Additionally, we use the segmentation loss for optimizing our SR model, while [23] uses MSE, which requires a HR ground truth version of the input images for supervised learning.

## 3   The Proposed Framework

While the use of SR has shown to improve the performance of other vision tasks, experiments show that traditional SR metrics cannot be used as full proxies to recover all the lost details [7]. We postulate that using traditional SR metrics as auxiliary loss for multi-task learning, serves to optimize the model on some implicit assumptions rather than a global optimum for the entire system. We therefore propose using the segmentation task's loss for improving the performance of the SR task as well.

The block diagram of our proposed method, MT-SSSR, is shown in Fig. 1. By jointly training both models using the segmentation loss, we remove the need for LR/HR image pairs during training. This makes our method applicable to real-world applications where such data are not available. The SR backbone in our framework is built upon the RRDB generator from ESRGAN [24]. Hence, we do not perform traditional Generative Adversarial Network (GAN) training with ESRGAN, and instead replace all pixel and feature-based loss functions with our task loss. For SS it is vital to have a high spatial resolution to accurately segment the contents of an image. Hence, we chose HRNet [22] as the backbone architecture. Other than replacing the Online Hard Example Mining (OHEM) cross-entropy loss [19] with RMI loss, we do not modify the HRNet architecture further.

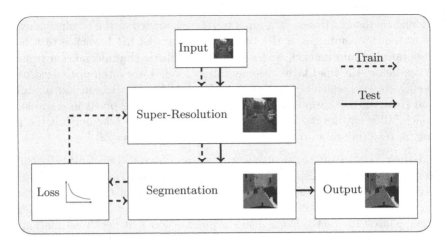

**Fig. 1.** Our proposed framework, MT-SSSR. Dashed and full lines represent training and testing phases, respectively. The SR model learns to upsample and enhance the input image based on the segmentation task loss. The segmentation model uses the same loss to improve the accuracy of its prediction.

## 4    Experiments and Results

### 4.1    Datasets

The IDD dataset [21] contains driving scenes in unstructured environments, including both urban and rural scenes. In our experiments we use the IDD-Lite dataset [13] which is a sub-sampled version of the IDD dataset. The IDD-Lite dataset contains pixel annotations for 1404 training, 204 validation, and 408 test images, respectively. The dataset has a resolution of $320 \times 227$ pixels and contains 7 classes. Ground truth labels are only publicly available for the training and validation images.

The CityScapes dataset [6] contains driving scenes from 50 different cities recorded across several months. The dataset contains finely annotated semantic maps for 2975 training, 500 validation, and 1525 test images, respectively, which have a resolution of $2048 \times 1024$ pixels. Following [23], we sub-sample the CityScapes dataset to $1024 \times 512$ pixels. There are 19 classes to be segmented. We report our results on the test set, based on submission to the CityScapes Online Server.

### 4.2    Implementation Details

For both our experiments on CityScapes and IDD-Lite, we initialize the segmentation backbone with weights pre-trained on CityScapes training data. For the SR backbone, we use transfer-learning by pre-training the model on generic LR/HR image pairs before the model is used in the multi-task framework. For this, we use the DF2K dataset, which is a merge of DIV2K [1] and Flickr2K

[24], and use bicubic interpolation to downsample the HR images. We denote the pre-trained SR model as $SR_{ST}$ (Super-Resolution$_{Single-Task}$).

For our experiments on CityScapes, we use the sub-sampled images, but test against the full-resolution labels by upsampling our predictions with bilinear interpolation. For our experiments on IDD-Lite we train at the native resolution training images and labels, and test against $256 \times 128$ pixel labels according to [13]. We experiment with both $\times 2$ and $\times 4$ upsampling in our MT-SSSR framework.

**Training Setup:** Due to memory constraints, we use a cyclic approach for training our MT-SSSR framework, where we alternate between training on patches and the full image. For patch training, we randomly crop $128 \times 128$ pixel LR patches from the training images and update both the weights of the SR and the SS model. When training on the full image, we only update the weights of the SS model.

We train all our models using gradient-descent with a mini-batch size of 12 on four V100 GPUs using a learning rate of 0.001 with an exponential decay ($lr \times \frac{iter_{cur}}{iter_{max}}^{0.9}$) trained until convergence. For the segmentation models we additionally use momentum (0.9) and weight decay (0.0005).

### 4.3  Results

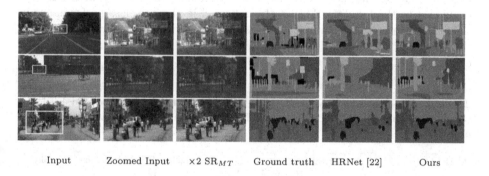

| Input | Zoomed Input | $\times 2\ SR_{MT}$ | Ground truth | HRNet [22] | Ours |

**Fig. 2.** Comparison of segmentation results on CityScapes (rows 1,2) and IDD-Lite (row 3). The three first columns show the input image together with a zoomed-in crop of the input and super-resolved image respectively. The last three columns show the differences between the ground truth, HRNet [22] (baseline), and our best performing model respectively. Noticeable differences include; distant streetlights, poles and signs in row 1, traffic poles, and people in row 2, and distant poles and people in row 3.

**Results on CityScapes:** Table 1 shows the segmentation accuracy on CityScapes. We include results for experiments with $1024 \times 512$ resolution input images and $\times 2$ upsampling of these. Most noticeably, our MT-SSSR framework provides 4.2% improvement over the current SoTA [23] and 3.6% improvement over the HRNet baseline [22] on the test set. As seen in the qualitative comparison in Fig. 2, our jointly trained SR model enhances sharpness and details of the input images, which in turn helps the segmentation model to better segment smaller distant objects, compared to the baseline.

Table 1. Quantitative segmentation results on CityScapes.

| Method | Scale factor | Val. (%) | Test (%) |
|---|---|---|---|
| DeepLabV3+ [5] | Native | 70.0 | 67.1 |
| PSPNet [27] | Native | 71.5 | 69.1 |
| HRNet [22] | Native | 77.3 | 75.4 |
| DSRL [23] | ×2 SR$_{MT}$ | 75.7 | 74.8 |
| **MT-SSSR (ours)** | ×2 SR$_{MT}$ | **80.3** | **79.0** |

**Results on IDD-Lite:** The segmentation accuracy on IDD-Lite reported in Table 3 shows that the performance increases with the upsampling factor in our MT-SSSR. In particular, our method with ×4 upsampling provides 2.5% improvement compared to the current SoTA [3] and 6.9% improvement over the baseline HRNet [22]. In the qualitative segmentation results in Fig. 2, it can be seen that our method more accurately segments fine details in the image, compared to the baseline. This is also reflected in the per-class performance in Table 2. An interesting example can be seen for the triangular part of the pole in the upper left corner (row three), where our method can label the sky correctly, even though this is mislabeled in the GT.

Table 2. Per-class accuracy on IDD-Lite. Compared to the baseline and Eff-UNet our method improves significantly on small objects such as living things and roadside objects.

| Method | Drivable | Non drivable | Living things | Vehicles | Roadside objects | Far objects | Sky |
|---|---|---|---|---|---|---|---|
| HRNet + RMI | 94.78 | 43.16 | 51.10 | 77.80 | 51.93 | 75.97 | 94.72 |
| Eff-UNet [3] | 94.86 | **50.12** | 61.96 | 81.31 | 54.99 | 77.54 | 95.55 |
| **MT-SSSR (ours best)** | **95.07** | 47.69 | **68.50** | **85.97** | **59.01** | **80.91** | **96.66** |

### 4.4 Ablation Study

**Effect of Upsampling and RMI-loss:** We investigate the effect of SR and RMI-loss on the CityScapes and IDD-Lite datasets. As seen in Table 4 and 5, RMI-loss improves slightly over using OHEM-loss in the baseline HRNet on

**Table 3.** Quantitative segmentation results on IDD-Lite.

| Method | Scale factor | Val. (%) |
|---|---|---|
| DeepLabV3+ [5] | Native | 64.3 |
| ERFNet [16] | Native | 66.1 |
| HRNet [22] | Native | 69.4 |
| Eff-UNet [3] | Native | 73.8 |
| MT-SSSR (ours) | ×2 $SR_{MT}$ | 74.1 |
| **MT-SSSR (ours)** | **×4 $SR_{MT}$** | **76.3** |

both datasets. Furthermore, naively upsampling the input images with ×2 bicubic interpolation also improves the performance slightly. However, when using ×4 upsampling with bicubic interpolation on the IDD-Lite dataset, the accuracy drops 2.3% below baseline. Using images upsampled in a pre-processing step with the pre-trained single-task SR model, $SR_{SR}$, together with HRNet + RMI, provides 0.7 and 1.3% improvement over the baseline on CityScapes and IDD-Lite, respectively. When combining RMI-loss and SR in our multi-task framework we improve the performance by 3.6% and 6.9% for the CityScapes and IDD-Lite datasets, respectively.

**Inference Time:** We compare our method in terms of inference time against the baseline model on the CityScapes dataset, on a V100 GPU. The inference time is 101 ms and 1888 ms per image for the baseline HRNet and MT-SSSR, respectively. The inference time of HRNet at the increased resolution alone is 592 ms per image. This means that the increased performance comes at a significant computational cost. However, no particular efforts has been made in order to optimize the inference time.

**Table 4.** The effect of RMI-loss and SR on segmentation accuracy on the CityScapes dataset. $MT$ and $ST$ denote multi-task and single-task, respectively.

| Method | Scale factor | Val. (%) |
|---|---|---|
| HRNet [22] | Native | 77.3 |
| HRNet + RMI | Native | 77.4 |
| HRNet + RMI | ×2 Bicubic | 78.0 |
| HRNet + RMI | ×2 $SR_{ST}$ | 78.1 |
| **MT-SSSR (ours)** | **×2 $SR_{MT}$** | **80.3** |

**Table 5.** The effect of RMI-loss and SR on segmentation accuracy on the IDD-Lite dataset. $_{MT}$ and $_{ST}$ denote multi-task and single-task, respectively.

| Method | Scale factor | Val. (%) |
|---|---|---|
| HRNet [22] | Native | 69.4 |
| HRNet + RMI | Native | 69.9 |
| HRNet + RMI | ×2 Bicubic | 70.9 |
| HRNet + RMI | ×4 Bicubic | 67.1 |
| HRNet + RMI | ×2 SR$_{ST}$ | 71.2 |
| MT-SSSR (ours) | ×2 SR$_{MT}$ | 74.1 |
| **MT-SSSR (ours)** | **×4 SR$_{MT}$** | **76.3** |

## 5 Conclusion

In this paper, we propose a novel framework for SS based on multi-task learning with super-resolution. The super-resolution model learns to enhance the input images such that they become more suitable for the SS model, while the segmentation model jointly learns to predict more accurate segmentation maps. Our experimental results show that our proposed system outperforms existing SoTA SS methods significantly on the challenging CityScapes and IDD-Lite datasets.

**Acknowledgements.** This work was partially supported by the Milestone Research Programme at Aalborg University (MRPA) and Danmarks Frie Forskningsfond (DFF 8022-00360B).

## References

1. Agustsson, E., Timofte, R.: Ntire 2017 challenge on single image super-resolution: dataset and study. In: CVPR (2017)
2. Badrinarayanan, V., Kendall, A., Cipolla, R.: Segnet: a deep convolutional encoder-decoder architecture for image segmentation. IEEE Trans. Pattern Anal. Mach. Intell. **39**(12), 2481–2495 (2017)
3. Baheti, B., Innani, S., Gajre, S., Talbar, S.N.: Eff-unet: a novel architecture for semantic segmentation in unstructured environment. In: CVPR, pp. 358–359 (2020)
4. Chen, L.C., Papandreou, G., Kokkinos, I., Murphy, K., Yuille, A.L.: Deeplab: semantic image segmentation with deep convolutional nets, atrous convolution, and fully connected crfs. IEEE Trans. Pattern Anal. Mach. Intell. **40**(4), 834–848 (2017)
5. Chen, L.C., Zhu, Y., Papandreou, G., Schroff, F., Adam, H.: Encoder-decoder with atrous separable convolution for semantic image segmentation. In: ECCV, pp. 801–818 (2018)
6. Cordts, M., et al.: The cityscapes dataset for semantic urban scene understanding. In: CVPR, pp. 3213–3223 (2016)
7. Dai, D., Wang, Y., Chen, Y., Van Gool, L.: Is image super-resolution helpful for other vision tasks? In: WACV, pp. 1–9 (2016)

8. Dong, C., Loy, C., He, K., Tang, X.: Image super-resolution using deep convolutional networks. IEEE Trans. Pattern Anal. Mach. Intell. **38**(2), 295–307 (2016)
9. Jha, A., Kumar, A., Pande, S., Banerjee, B., Chaudhuri, S.: MT-UNET: a novel u-net based multi-task architecture for visual scene understanding. In: ICIP, pp. 2191–2195 (2020)
10. Kampffmeyer, M., Salberg, A.B., Jenssen, R.: Semantic segmentation of small objects and modeling of uncertainty in urban remote sensing images using deep convolutional neural networks. In: CVPR-W, pp. 1–9 (2016)
11. Maninis, K.K., Radosavovic, I., Kokkinos, I.: Attentive single-tasking of multiple tasks. In: CVPR, pp. 1851–1860 (2019)
12. Minaee, S., Boykov, Y., Porikli, F., Plaza, A., Kehtarnavaz, N., Terzopoulos, D.: Image segmentation using deep learning: A survey. arXiv preprint (2020)
13. Mishra, A., Kumar, S., Kalluri, T., Varma, G., Subramaian, A., Chandraker, M., Jawahar, C.V.: Semantic segmentation datasets for resource constrained training. In: NCVPRIPG, vol. 2, p. 6 (2020)
14. Na, B., Fox, G.C.: Object classifications by image super-resolution preprocessing for convolutional neural networks. ASTESJ **5**(2), 476–483 (2020)
15. Robert, V., Talbot, H.: Does super-resolution improve OCR performance in the real world? ICIP, a case study on images of receipts. In: 2020 IEEE International Conference on Image Processing (ICIP), pp. 548–552 (2020)
16. Romera, E., Alvarez, J.M., Bergasa, L.M., Arroyo, R.: Erfnet: efficient residual factorized convnet for real-time semantic segmentation. T-ITS **19**(1), 263–272 (2018)
17. Ronneberger, O., Fischer, P., Brox, T.: U-net: convolutional networks for biomedical image segmentation. In: Navab, N., Hornegger, J., Wells, W.M., Frangi, A.F. (eds.) MICCAI 2015. LNCS, vol. 9351, pp. 234–241. Springer, Cham (2015). https://doi.org/10.1007/978-3-319-24574-4_28
18. Shermeyer, J., Van Etten, A.: The effects of super-resolution on object detection performance in satellite imagery. In: CVPR-W (2019)
19. Shrivastava, A., Gupta, A., Girshick, R.: Training region-based object detectors with online hard example mining. In: CVPR, pp. 761–769 (2016)
20. Tan, M., Le, Q.V.: Efficientnet: rethinking model scaling for convolutional neural networks. In: ICML, pp. 6105–6114 (2019)
21. Varma, G., Subramanian, A., Namboodiri, A.M., Chandraker, M., Jawahar, C.V.: IDD: a dataset for exploring problems of autonomous navigation in unconstrained environments. In: WACV, pp. 1743–1751 (2019)
22. Wang, J., et al.: Deep high-resolution representation learning for visual recognition. TPAMI (2019)
23. Wang, L., Li, D., Zhu, Y., Tian, L., Shan, Y.: Dual super-resolution learning for semantic segmentation. In: CVPR, pp. 3774–3783 (2020)
24. Wang, X., et al.: Esrgan: enhanced super-resolution generative adversarial networks. In: ECCV, vol. 38, pp. 295–307 (2019)
25. Yuan, Y., Liu, S., Zhang, J., Zhang, Y., Dong, C., Lin, L.: Unsupervised image super-resolution using cycle-in-cycle generative adversarial networks. In: CVPR (2018)
26. Zhao, B., Feng, J., Wu, X., Yan, S.: A survey on deep learning-based fine-grained object classification and semantic segmentation. Int. J. Autom. Comput. **14**(2), 119–135 (2017). https://doi.org/10.1007/s11633-017-1053-3
27. Zhao, H., Shi, J., Qi, X., Wang, X., Jia, J.: Pyramid scene parsing network. In: CVPR (2017)
28. Zhao, S., Wang, Y., Yang, Z., Cai, D.: Region mutual information loss for semantic segmentation. In: NIPS (2019)

# Deep Fisher Score Representation
# via Sparse Coding

Sixiang Xu[✉], Damien Muselet, and Alain Trémeau

Laboratoire Hubert Curien UMR 5516, 42023 SAINT-ETIENNE, France
{sixiang.xu,damien.muselet,alain.tremeau}@univ-st-etienne.fr

**Abstract.** Fisher Score has been shown to be accurate global image features for classification. Most of time, it is based on a Gaussian mixture model (GMM). Nevertheless, recent studies show that GMM does not fit well high dimensional data such as the ones extracted by deep convolutional networks. In this paper, we propose to resort to a sparse representation of the centers of the Gaussian functions in order to better cover the high dimensional feature space. This solution has already been used in a framework constituted by independent and off-the-shelf modules and the contribution of this paper is to embed these steps in an end-to-end deep neural network so that all the modules work together for the sole purpose of improving classification performance. Experimental results show that this solution clearly outperforms many alternatives in the context of material, indoor scenes or fine-grained image classification.

**Keywords:** Fisher score · Sparse coding · Orderless pooling · Classification

## 1 Introduction

Deep neural networks have emerged as an essential solution for performing classification tasks. In these networks, convolutional layers extract accurate local features that are pooled to a local feature vector which is sent to fully connected layers for classification. The first networks neglected the pooling step and directly sent the set of local features in the dense layers [20], while the series of ResNet apply a global average pooling to decrease the dimension of the global feature vector and hence reduce the number of parameters of the network [8]. Orderless pooling was widely used before convolutional neural networks (CNN) with the bags of visual words (BOW) [12], VLAD [10] or Fisher Vectors [21] and has shown to provide good results when applied to CNN features [4,6]. Among them, the Fisher Vectors (FV) were the most promising because they generalize the VLAD and BOW. The main idea of FV is to model the distribution of the training data with a Gaussian mixture and to characterize each data point with the derivatives over the model parameters. This coding approach is referred as Gaussian Mixture Model based Fisher Vector Coding(GMMFVC). Nevertheless, a Gaussian Mixture Model (GMM) seems not to be well adapted to the deep local features since they are lying in a very high dimensional space and require

© Springer Nature Switzerland AG 2021
N. Tsapatsoulis et al. (Eds.): CAIP 2021, LNCS 13053, pp. 412–421, 2021.
https://doi.org/10.1007/978-3-030-89131-2_38

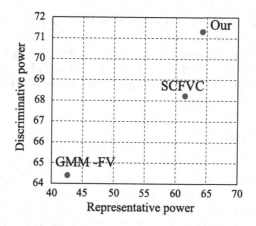

**Fig. 1.** Discriminative power and representative power of the Gaussian Mixture Model (GMM), the Off-the-shelf Sparse Coding solution (SCFVC) proposed in [15] and our solution. See text for details.

to many Gaussians to be accurately modeled [15]. Liu et al. proposed a smart solution to overcome this problem which consists in sampling the center of each Gaussian from a subspace and therefore benefiting from an infinite number of Gaussians to fit the data distribution [15]. The authors show that this problem can be solved by a classical sparse coding method. Unfortunately, their approach can not take advantage of the main interest of the CNN, i.e. training end-to-end the feature extraction, the pooling and the classification layers. In this paper, we propose a solution to embed all these modules in a deep CNN that can be trained end-to-end. This way, we take advantage of the sparse coding solution of [15] to improve the representative power of our model (compared to the classical GMM) thanks to an infinite number of Gaussians and we also improve the discriminative power (over [15] and GMM) of the different elements (subspace bases and sparse codes) thanks to the end-to-end training.

For illustration, Fig. 1 displays the representative and discriminative powers of the GMMFVC, the Off-the-shelf Sparse Coding solution (SCFVC) proposed in [15] and our solution. These values are evaluated on the MIT indoor dataset [18] with AlexNet [11]. The representative power is evaluated as $100 - d$, where $d$ is the average distance between the data points and their respective nearest Gaussian center. The discriminative power is the classification accuracy of the method. This Figure clearly shows that inserting the sparse coding and Fisher vector extraction in the network allows to improve both criteria.

The classical sparse coding problem presented in [15] is a regression with $L_1$ norm regularization (called LASSO regression). Using proximal gradient descent, it can be solved with an iterative algorithm with soft-thresholding, called ISTA [5]. Gregor and Lecun have proposed in [7] to approximate this solver with an unfolded module (LISTA) that can be inserted in a deep network. In this paper, we use LISTA to learn a discriminative dictionary and to extract an adapted sparse code for each input data. These dictionary and sparse code allow us to evaluate the corresponding Fisher vector that is the input of the classification layers. By backpropagating the gradient of the classification loss, we are able to make all these modules (local feature extraction, LISTA, Fisher Vector and classification) collaborate with the sole objective of improving the performance of the classification task. Experimental tests on three different datasets and three different backbone architectures show that our solution outperform many alternatives.

## 2   Related Works

Orderless pooling was widely used before the emergence of the CNN-based solutions. The most popular approaches were based on bags of visual words (BOW) [12], VLAD [10] or Fisher Vectors [21]. Inspired by these early methods, some works have evaluated the Fisher vectors or VLAD from deep features for texture or image classification [4,6]. They show improvements over the SIFT-based counterparts but, in their workflow, the dictionary or Gaussian mixture model are learned independently from the deep features and from the classifier, leaving a large margin of progression.

Thus, the next works have focused on embedding orderless pooling in deep networks to allow end-to-end training. Passalis and Tefas have inserted a Bag-of-Features pooling in deep neural networks thanks to radial basis function neurons [17]. The output of the pooling module is a histogram of the visual words ($0^{th}$ order statistic) learned on the training set.

Instead of counting the occurrences of the visual words in one image, VLAD-based approaches aggregate the residuals between the local features and their nearest visual words ($1^{st}$ order statistic). NetVLAD is the first network that solves this task with an end-to-end training [1] and is later improved by Zhang et al. with Deep Ten [26]. It has been show that first order statistics are more accurate to characterize images in classification tasks and the Fisher vectors go further by using first and second order statistics. Deep FisherNet is an embedded implementation of the GMM Fisher vector [22]. [14] introduces NetFV which extends NetVLAD by appending the second order statistics. The main disadvantage of all these approaches is that they rely on a limited number of codewords or Gaussian centers, which prevents accurate modeling of the data distribution in the high-dimensional deep feature spaces [15].

One interesting solution to cope with this problem has been proposed by Li et al. [13]. The authors compute Fisher vectors from a mixture of factor analyzers (MFA), instead of the classical GMM. Their solution is embedded in a deep network which is trainable end-to-end. The idea of MFA is to approximate the data manifold by low dimensional linear spaces and, in this sense, is similar to the idea of sparse coding [15]. Nevertheless, even if the MFA module is embedded in a deep network, the authors show that an accurate initialization of the weights of the network is required to obtain good performance. This initialization consists in running an Expectation-Maximization algorithm on the set of local features that have to be saved in memory. Furthermore, it appears that this second order representation requires high computation costs, high number of parameters to learn and occupies a very large memory space (500k dimensions which is more than the image itself) [9].

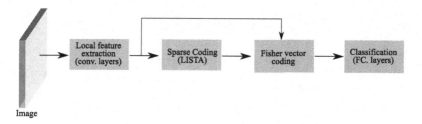

Image

**Fig. 2.** Workflow of the proposed solution.

Another group of second-order pooling works is based on bilinear coding, such as BCNN [14] which is also an end-to-end trainable network and aggregates feature vectors by sum-pooling their outer products. Since this pooled representation always has cumbersome size, SMSO [25] proposes to compress the bilinear pooled features and improves the classification performance.

Our method is inspired by the work of Liu et al. [15], detailed in the next section,. More recently, they have also proposed an improved version of their work in [16], called HSCFV. It uses two dictionaries to code input features and consequently, doubles dimension size of the Fisher vector. Nevertheless, their approach is not embedded in a deep CNN for end-to-end training.

Our method combines all the benefits of these previous solutions: it is embedded in an end-to-end trainable network, it samples an infinite number of Gaussian centers from a learned subspace and it does not require any heavy computation or storage to initialize the weights.

## 3   Deep Sparse Coding Fisher Vector

Figure 2 illustrates the complete workflow of our solution whose successive steps are detailed in the next sections.

### 3.1   From Subspace Sampling to Sparse Coding

In order to increase the number of Gaussians that model the distribution of the data, we take advantage of the idea from [15] that sample the Gaussian mean vectors in a subspace spanned by a set of bases. Each mean vector is coded in this "dictionary" $B$ with a code $u$ drawn from a zero-mean Laplacian distribution (to enforce sparsity). Then each local feature vector $x$ extracted from the images and associated with the code $u$ is drawn from a Gaussian distribution $\mathcal{N}(Bu, \Sigma)$ centered on $Bu$. Figure 3 illustrates the interest of this approach.

Then, assuming a constant and diagonal covariance matrix as $\sigma$ and using pointwise maximum to approximate the integral of the distribution, Liu et al. show that the logarithm of the likelihood of $x$ can be estimated as [15]:

$$log(P(x|B)) = \min_u \frac{1}{\sigma^2}||x - Bu||_2^2 + \lambda||u||_1, \qquad (1)$$

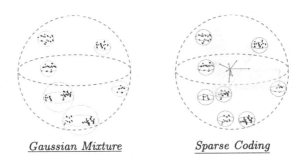

*Gaussian Mixture*          *Sparse Coding*

**Fig. 3.** Some data in a high dimensional space (illustrated by the sphere). Left: With GMM the data distribution is not well fitted because of the limited number of Gaussians. Right: With Sparse Coding, the Gaussian centers are coded sparsely in an adapted basis (green arrows) allowing to create unlimited number of Gaussians and so to fit better the data distribution. The sparsity is illustrated by the low number of basis required to code each center position (lines, planes or parallelograms). (Color figure online)

where $\lambda$ is the scale parameter of the Laplacian distribution of $u$.

Interestingly, this equation represents the classical problem of sparse coding. Liu et al. proposed to use an off-the-shelf sparse coding solver to learn the dictionary $B$ and infer the code $u$ [15]. Obviously, making use of such independent solver is a good solution to minimize the reconstruction error of $x$ with a sparse code, but it neglects the main goal which is to improve the performance of the classification task.

Hence, we propose in the next section to embed a sparse coding module in a deep neural network that is trained end-to-end. The main advantage of such an approach is that it is learning a dictionary and sparse codes that are accurate to discriminate the different categories in the current dataset.

### 3.2   Embedding Sparse Coding with LISTA

Our aim is to find a solution for the following equation:

$$\min_{u} f(u) + \lambda ||u||_1 \tag{2}$$

where $f(u) = ||x - Bu||_2^2$, $x$ is a data point, $B$ the dictionary and $u$ the sparse code of $x$.

One way to solve this equation is to resort to an Iterative Shrinkage/Thresholding Algorithm (ISTA) [5] that iteratively approximates the solution with:

$$u_k = \mathcal{T}_{\lambda t_k}(u_{k-1} - t_k \nabla f(u_{k-1})), \tag{3}$$

where $\mathcal{T}_\alpha$ is a component-wise vector shrinkage function such that $[\mathcal{T}_\alpha(v)]_i = (|v_i| - \alpha)_+ sign(v_i)$, $t_k$ is the step size at iteration $k$ and $\nabla$ is the gradient operator.

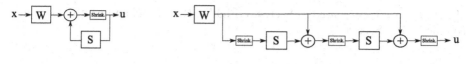

*ISTA block diagram*          *Learned ISTA block diagram*

**Fig. 4.** Block diagrams of ISTA and LISTA. LISTA is an unfolded version of ISTA (2 iterations here).

Evaluating the gradient of $f(u)$ defined above, we get:

$$u_k = \mathcal{T}_{\lambda t_k}(u_{k-1} - 2t_k B^T(Bu_{k-1} - x)),$$
$$= \mathcal{T}_{\lambda t_k}((I - 2t_k B^T B)u_{k-1} + 2t_k B^T x),$$
$$= \mathcal{T}_{\lambda t_k}(Su_{k-1} + Wx),$$

where $S = I - 2t_k B^T B$ and $W = 2t_k B^T$.

As mentioned in [7], this equation can be illustrated as a recurrent block diagram as in Fig. 4, left. Fortunately, Gregor and Lecun proposed a fast approximation of ISTA called Learned ISTA (LISTA) [7]. This is an unfolded version of ISTA with a fix number of iterations and that can be plugged into a neural network to provide a sparse code (see Fig. 4, right). Embedding this LISTA module in our CNN is a smart solution to learn a dictionary and sparse codes that help to discriminate between the categories of the current task.

### 3.3   Dictionary Based Fisher Coding

When a classical GMM is used to model the data distribution, the Fisher code is based on the partial derivatives of the posterior probabilities with respect to the weights, the mean and the standard-deviation parameters of the model [21]. In our case, the model is based on a learned dictionary and we use a particular Fisher coding, as in [15], evaluated as the partial derivative of the log probability of the local features with respect to the dictionary itself:

$$\frac{\partial log(P(x|B))}{\partial B} = \frac{\partial \frac{1}{\sigma^2}||x - Bu^*||_2^2 + \lambda||u^*||_1}{\partial B} = (x - Bu^*)u^{*T}, \qquad (4)$$

where $u^* = argmax_u P(x|u, B)P(u)$ (see [15] for details).

This module is very easy to insert in our deep network and provides the pooled features from the input image. These features are then sent to the last fully connected layers for classification. All these modules are constituting our CNN which can be trained end-to-end (see Fig. 2).

## 4   Experiments

In this section, we are running experimental tests on different datasets and compare our results with those of many alternatives. The datasets and their respective experimental settings are detailed in Sects. 4.1 and 4.2. The training strategy of our network is presented in Sect. 4.3. Finally, the results and comparisons are commented in Sect. 4.4.

### 4.1  Datasets

In order to show the versatility of our solution for image classification tasks, we run experiments on three datasets, which vary between tasks and scales. Note that we always make use of official training-test splits released with the datasets.

MINC-2500 [2] is a large-scale material dataset containing 23 commonly-seen material categories, such as water, wood or paper. There are in total 2,500 images per category among which 2,350 are used for training. MIT Indoor 67[18] is a medium but widely-accepted benchmark for indoor scene classification task with 67 indoor categories and 100 images in each category. 80 images per category are used for training. CUB-200-2011[23] consists of 11,788 images with 200 bird species and is always considered as a fine-grained classification dataset because inter-class difference between bird species is very subtle.

### 4.2  Experimental Settings

Depending on the tested dataset, we use different backbones for fair comparison with other works. Our deep pooling module (DPM) is constituted by a $1 \times 1$ convolution layer, a LISTA module with two iterations (see Fig. 4) and the Fisher encoding layer. Then the last layer is a fully connected layer with softmax activation for classification. The loss is the classical cross-entropy.

When testing on MIT-67 and CUB-200 2011 datasets, we follow the settings adopted by the state of the art methods [14,25]. The input image size is 448x448 and the backbone networks are either the pretrained VGG-D (a.k.a VGG-16) or Alexnet. Our DPM is plugged on the last convolutional layer for VGG-D and on the Fc6 layer for Alexnet. The $1 \times 1$ convolutional layer in our DPM does not change the input feature size and the sparse code in LISTA has 100 elements.

For the tests on MINC-2500, the network backbone is the pretrained ResNet-50 [8]. The $1 \times 1$ convolutional layer in our DPM reduces the input feature size to 128 and the provided sparse code in LISTA has 32 elements. While training, we follow the data augmentation settings of [24]: the input image is resized to $256 \times 256$, 8% to 100% of the area of the of image is cropped with a random aspect ratio between $\frac{3}{4}$ and $\frac{4}{3}$ and the crop is resized to $224 \times 224$. 50% chance horizontal and vertical flip is applied. At test time, we use central crop of 224x224 as input.

### 4.3  Training Details

For training our network, three consecutive steps are conducted. First, we run a PCA on a small subset of feature vectors (around 10,000) extracted from the backbone outputs and initialize the $1 \times 1$ convolutional layer of our DPM with these PCA parameters. Second, inspired by [3], we apply a warming-up

**Table 1.** Comparison of the classification accuracy (%) with closed-related alternatives on three datasets and three backbone architectures.

| | Approaches | MIT AlexNet | MIT VGG16 | CUB AlexNet | CUB VGG16 | MINC ResNet50 |
|---|---|---|---|---|---|---|
| Off-shelf | Baseline | 58.4 [19] | | 53.3 [19] | 60.4 [14] | |
| | GMMFVC | 64.3 [15] | 72.6$^a$ [16] | 61.7 [15] | 70.1$^a$ [16] | |
| | SCFVC | 68.2 [15] | 77.6$^a$ [16] | 66.4 [15] | 77.3$^a$ [16] | |
| | HSCFVC | | 79.5$^a$ [16] | | 80.8 [16] | |
| End-to-End | Baseline | | 64.51 [25] | | 70.4 [14] | 79.1 [25] |
| | Deep Ten | | | | | 80.4 [24] |
| | NetVLAD | | | | 81.9 [14] | |
| | NetFV | | 78.2 [14] | | 79.9 [14] | |
| | FisherNet | | 76.4 [13] | | | |
| | MFAFVNet | 69.89$^b$ [13] | 78.01$^b$ [13] | | | |
| | B-CNN | | 77.6 [14] | | 84.0 [14] | 79.05 [25] |
| | SMSO | | 79.45 [25] | | **85.01**[25] | 81.3 [25] |
| | Our | **70.3** | **80.22** | **73.4** | 84.28 | **81.5** |

$^a$ These methods were trained with VGG19 (not VGG16) with 2 scales, whereas the other approaches from the column are trained with a single scale. $^b$ Since MFAFVNet works on patches and not on images, we have selected in [13] the results provided with the nearest patch scale from our settings (160 × 160).

process that consists in training our DPM and FC layer (while the backbone is frozen) with an objective function which is the sum of the cross-entropy loss and the sparse coding loss (see Eq. (1)). Finally, the whole network is fine-tuned end-to-end under the supervision of the sole cross-entropy loss.

For training, we use stochastic gradient descent as optimization algorithm with a mini-batch size of 64, a weight decay of $5e^{-4}$ and a momentum of 0.9. The learning rate is 0.004 during the warming-up. During the end-to-end finetuning, it starts from 0.004 and is divided by 10 when the training loss meets a plateau.

## 4.4 Results

The top-1 classification accuracy of our approach and many alternatives are resumed in Table 1. The results of the related works are extracted from different papers that are referenced in this table. Note that our CNN is trained on single-scale images while many state-of-the-art approaches are training on multi-scales, so we have carefully selected the results that allows fair comparisons, even if some results in Table 1 are from multi-scale training.

The methods called 'Off-the-shelf' use independent modules that are not fine-tuned together while the 'Finetuned' group contains approaches that use end-to-end trainable networks. We notice that the results provided by fine-tuned networks overall outperform those of the Off-the-shelf solutions. This shows that it is always better to make the modules work together to optimize the same loss instead of independently optimizing them. Also our approach is built upon SCFVC which produces more discriminant second-order pooled features than the classical Fisher vector or VLAD. The proposed smart combination of these two advantages make our method outperform most of the alternatives for all the datasets and backbones.

## 5    Conclusion

Fisher vectors are very accurate features for classification but require many Gaussians when applied on high-dimensional deed features. One way to cope with this problem is to code sparsely the Gaussian centers in an adapted basis in order to increase the number of available Gaussians and better fit the data distribution. In this paper, we have shown that this coding can be embedded in a deep network allowing to adapt the basis and sparse code such that they optimize the classification performance. We have also proposed a training strategy that can easily and quickly initialize the network parameters before finetuning. With the support of the end-to-end learning and a powerful Fisher score representation, our method outperforms many alternatives on three different datasets.

## References

1. Arandjelović, R., Gronat, P., Torii, A., Pajdla, T., Sivic, J.: Netvlad: CNN architecture for weakly supervised place recognition. In: IEEE Conference on Computer Vision and Pattern Recognition (CVPR), pp. 5297–5307 (2016)
2. Bell, S., Upchurch, P., Snavely, N., Bala, K.: Material recognition in the wild with the materials in context database. In: Computer Vision and Pattern Recognition (CVPR), pp. 5297–5307 (2015)
3. Branson, S., Van Horn, G., Belongie, S., Perona, P.: Bird species categorization using pose normalized deep convolutional nets. arXiv preprint arXiv:1406.2952 (2014)
4. Cimpoi, M., Maji, S., Vedaldi, A.: Deep filter banks for texture recognition and segmentation. In: Proceedings of the IEEE Conference on Computer Vision and Pattern Recognition, pp. 3828–3836 (2015)
5. Daubechies, I., Defrise, M., Mol, C.: An iterative thresholding algorithm for linear inverse problems with a sparsity constraint. Comm. Pure Appl. Math. **57**, 1413–1457 (2004)
6. Gong, Y., Wang, L., Guo, R., Lazebnik, S.: Multi-scale orderless pooling of deep convolutional activation features. In: Fleet, D., Pajdla, T., Schiele, B., Tuytelaars, T. (eds.) ECCV 2014. LNCS, vol. 8695, pp. 392–407. Springer, Cham (2014). https://doi.org/10.1007/978-3-319-10584-0_26
7. Gregor, K., LeCun, Y.: Learning fast approximations of sparse coding. In: Proceedings International Conference on Machine learning (ICML 2010) (2010)
8. He, K., Zhang, X., Ren, S., Sun, J.: Deep residual learning for image recognition. In: The IEEE Conference on Computer Vision and Pattern Recognition (CVPR), June 2016

9. Jacob, P., Picard, D., Histace, A., Klein, E.: Efficient codebook and factorization for second order representation learning. In: Proceedings International Conference on Learning Representations (ICLR) (2019)

10. Jégou, H., Perronnin, F., Douze, M., Sánchez, J., Pérez, P., Schmid, C.: Aggregating local image descriptors into compact codes. IEEE Trans. Pattern Anal. Mach. Intell. (TPAMI) **34**(9) (2012)

11. Krizhevsky, A., Sutskever, I., Hinton, G.E.: Imagenet classification with deep convolutional neural networks. Adv. Neural Inf. Process. Syst. **25**, 1097–1105 (2012)

12. Lazebnik, S., Schmid, C., Ponce, J.: Beyond bags of features: Spatial pyramid matching for recognizing natural scene categories. In: IEEE Computer Society Conference on Computer Vision and Pattern Recognition (CVPR 2006), vol. 2, pp. 2169–2178 (2006)

13. Li, Y., Dixit, M., Vasconcelos, N.: Deep scene image classification with the mfafvnet. In: Proceedings of the IEEE International Conference on Computer Vision, pp. 5746–5754 (2017)

14. Lin, T.Y., RoyChowdhury, A., Maji, S.: Bilinear convolutional neural networks for fine-grained visual recognition. IEEE Trans. Pattern Anal. Mach. Intell. **40**(6), 1309–1322 (2017)

15. Liu, L., Shen, C., Wang, L., Hengel, A.v.d., Wang, C.: Encoding high dimensional local features by sparse coding based fisher vectors. In: Advances in Neural Information Processing Systems(NIPS) (2014)

16. Liu, L., et al.: Compositional model based fisher vector coding for image classification. IEEE Trans. Pattern Anal. Mach. Intell. **39**(12), 2335–2348 (2017)

17. Passalis, N., Tefas, A.: Learning bag-of-features pooling for deep convolutional neural networks. In: 2017 IEEE International Conference on Computer Vision (ICCV), pp. 5766–5774 (2017)

18. Quattoni, A., Torralba, A.: Recognizing indoor scenes. In: 2009 IEEE Conference on Computer Vision and Pattern Recognition, pp. 413–420. IEEE (2009)

19. Sharif Razavian, A., Azizpour, H., Sullivan, J., Carlsson, S.: Cnn features off-the-shelf: An astounding baseline for recognition. In: Proceedings of the IEEE Conference on Computer Vision and Pattern Recognition (CVPR) Workshops, June 2014

20. Simonyan, K., Zisserman, A.: Very deep convolutional networks for large-scale image recognition. In: Proceedings International Conference on Learning Representations (ICLR 2015) (2015)

21. Sánchez, J., Mensink, T., Verbeek, J.: Image classification with the fisher vector: theory and practice. Int. J. Comput. Vis. **105** (2013)

22. Tang, P., Wang, X., Shi, B., Bai, X., Liu, W., Tu, Z.: Deep fishernet for image classification. IEEE Trans. Neural Netw. Learn. Syst. **30**(7), 2244–2250 (2019)

23. Wah, C., Branson, S., Welinder, P., Perona, P., Belongie, S.: The Caltech-UCSD Birds-200-2011 Dataset. Tech. Rep. CNS-TR-2011-001, California Institute of Technology (2011)

24. Xue, J., Zhang, H., Dana, K.: Deep texture manifold for ground terrain recognition. In: Proceedings of the IEEE Conference on Computer Vision and Pattern Recognition, pp. 558–567 (2018)

25. Yu, K., Salzmann, M.: Statistically-motivated second-order pooling. In: Proceedings of the European Conference on Computer Vision (ECCV), pp. 600–616 (2018)

26. Zhang, H., Xue, J., Dana, K.: Deep ten: Texture encoding network. In: Proceedings of the IEEE Conference on Computer Vision and Pattern Recognition, pp. 708–717 (2017)

# D-LSD: A Distorted Line Segment Detector for Calibrated Images

David Zuñiga-Noël, Francisco-Angel Moreno$^{(\boxtimes)}$, and Javier Gonzalez-Jimenez

Machine Perception and Intelligent Robotics Group (MAPIR), Department of System Engineering and Automation, University of Malaga, Malaga, Spain
{dzuniga,famoreno,javiergonzalez}@uma.es

**Abstract.** In this paper, we present an algorithm for the detection of line segments directly on the original, distorted images captured by calibrated wide-angle, fisheye and omnidirectional cameras. Distorted line segments are detected as convex polygonal chains of connected straight lines and then validated as the projection of 3D lines. This last validation step is our main contribution, which is formulated in a generic way in order to allow the detection of line segments from calibrated central projection vision systems and without requiring the rectification of the whole image. We evaluate our method with real images from a publicly available dataset and compare it with state-of-the-art alternatives, achieving comparable line detection performance without requiring image rectification. Additionally, we provide an open source reference implementation.

## 1 Introduction

Typical computer vision techniques rely on point image features to perform, for example, visual SLAM [19], camera motion estimation [20], place recognition [3] or object recognition [8], among many others. However, higher level geometric primitives, such as lines, are gaining growing importance in recent years, as they provide a set of advantages, specially in terms of reliability. These include their higher robustness against illumination changes in the image, as well as their natural presence in human-made environments [25]. Not only that, unlike point features, lines can be found even in images from low-textured environments, which is known to be one of the main issues of geometric computer vision techniques. This problem can be partially mitigated by employing fish-eye or omnidirectional cameras, which provide wider Field-of-View (FoV), hence covering larger areas of the environment and consequently reducing the probability of capturing low-texture areas, but it still remains an issue.

The benefits that line features provide have been exploited recently for the development of new systems employing them either as their main source of information or at least complementary to point features [5,6,14,15,17]. Nevertheless, detecting and managing line features is more costly than using their point counterpart, specially in wide FoV cameras where distortion is significantly larger than in standard perspective cameras, causing that straight lines in the environment are no longer projected as straight 2D lines on the images. To avoid

N. Tsapatsoulis et al. (Eds.): CAIP 2021, LNCS 13053, pp. 422–431, 2021.
https://doi.org/10.1007/978-3-030-89131-2_39

this, the images need to be rectified [11] in a process that presents two main issues: (i) it is computationally expensive, and (ii) the maximum effective FoV after rectification is reduced, in practice, to about 130° [7] instead of the original ~180° FoV for fish-eye and up to 360° for omnidirectional cameras. Our proposal provides a solution to these two problems.

In this paper, we present D-LSD (Distorted Line Segment Detector), the first line segment detector that enables direct detection of distorted lines from non-rectified images. We formulate the distorted line detection problem under the mild assumption of a calibrated central projection system, resulting in a very efficient line detector capable of handling from pinhole to omnidirectional camera projection models. We evaluate our approach with publicly available real images and compare the execution time and detection rates against state-of-the-art straight line detection methods on rectified images.

## 2    Related Work

The most popular line segment detector is LSD [16], by Grompone von Gioi *et al.* The LSD algorithm works by grouping pixels with the same gradient direction and validating lines as rare events in the *a contrario* model, according to the Helmholtz principle [10]. This method gained popularity as one of the first line detectors capable of operating in real-time.

Alternatively, in [1], Akinlar and Topal propose to detect lines from a continuous, 1 px-wide chain of edge pixels by least squares line fitting. These high quality edges are detected from their proposed Edge Drawing [23] algorithm. This approach, termed *EDLines*, results in a very efficient line detection algorithm (about one order of magnitude faster than LSD). A similar approach, named CannyLines, is proposed in [18] by Lu *et al.* where lines are detected directly on the edge map extracted by their parameter-free Canny operator.

Following a different approach, Cho *et al.* propose in [9] a new line segment detector exploiting the properties of digitalized lines. In this work, anchor points (*i.e.* peaks in the gradient map) are connected horizontally or vertically only, creating what the authors call *linelets*. Then these linelets are grouped into line segments according to some rules derived from the digitalization properties and validated from a probabilistic perspective. Recently, Zhang *et al.* proposed AG3line [24], which detects line segments by actively grouping anchor points. Finally, the detected lines are validated according to the density of anchors and the alignment of the gradient magnitudes.

Unlike our proposal, all these methods operate only in rectified images and cannot find straight lines in distorted images. In this work, we rely on the efficient Edge Drawing [23] algorithm for continuous edge segmentation and exploit the fact that distorted lines are locally straight to fit 2D line segments, similar to the EDLines [1] approach. Then, connected 2D line segments forming a smooth convex curve are grouped and validated as being the projection of a 3D line, according to the calibrated intrinsic parameters of the camera.

## 3    Background

The mapping of a 3D point $x \in \mathbb{R}^3$ to image coordinates $u \in \Omega \subset \mathbb{R}^2$ is characterized by the projection function $\pi : \mathbb{R}^3 \to \Omega$. In this work, we consider central projection cameras in which all light-rays pass through a single point in space: the projection (or optical) center of the camera. This includes both dioptric and catadioptric cameras.

In general, lines are projected as conic sections in any radially distorted image. Svoboda and Pajdla [22] showed that lines are imaged as conic sections in catadioptric systems. Accordingly, Barreto [4] showed that this is also true for perspective cameras with radially symmetric distortion following the division model [13]. Here, we only assume that lines are imaged as smooth convex curves, *i.e.* its curvature is either always non-negative or always non-positive, up to a *smoothness* threshold $\theta \in \mathbb{R}^+$ (see Fig. 1). Note that this is a typical assumption used, for example, to find circles [2] or ellipses [21].

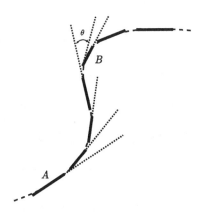

**Fig. 1.** Curves are approximated in a piecewise linear fashion, *i.e.* as polygonal chains. The polygonal chain starting at segment $A$ breaks both the convexity and smoothness assumptions at $B$. Therefore, a new polygonal chain candidate starts at $B$.

Finally, under the central projection assumption, the two endpoints $x_1, x_2 \in \mathbb{R}^3$ defining a three-dimensional line, along with the center of projection, define a plane with normal vector $n \in \mathbb{R}^3$ (see Fig. 2). This fact, along with the inverse of the projection function $\pi^{-1} : \Omega \to \mathbb{R}^3$ will be used to generate a model of the observed curve. Note that the depth of a 3D point is lost during the projection process, thus $\pi^{-1}$ can only recover its direction.

## 4    Algorithm Description

D-LSD operates in 4 main steps as follows. First, a set of continuous edges are extracted from the intensity image. Subsequently, smooth convex curves are

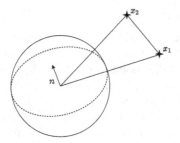

**Fig. 2.** In a central projection system, a 3D line and the center of projection form a plane. This plane intersects the unit sphere in the dotted circle. The line segment is thus an arc on the unit sphere.

extracted as polygonal chains from connected edges. A model of a 3D line is then extracted by means of a least squares minimization from the pixels on the curve and, finally, such curve is validated as a distorted line according to its reprojection error in the image.

## 4.1   Edge Detection

We rely on the Edge Drawing (ED) algorithm by Topal and Akinlar [23] for edge detection, since it is a very efficient method to extract connected, 1 px-wide chains of edge pixels. In summary, this algorithm works through these steps:

1. The image gradient magnitude and direction is computed at each pixel from a smoothed version of the input image.
2. Pixels with local maximum gradient are selected. These pixels, known as *anchors*, correspond to edge elements with a very high probability.
3. Finally, anchors are connected using the neighbor's gradient magnitude and direction, following gradient maximum values.

## 4.2   Polygonal Chain Extraction

Smooth convex curves are then extracted from continuous edge segments in two steps. First, straight lines are extracted from the edge segments, similar to the line segment extraction method EDLines [1]. Essentially, we fit a straight line to the segments under a least squares approach and then pixels are added one by one from the connected edge segment until the error exceeds a given threshold. When no more pixels can be added for that threshold, a new line is initialized and the process is repeated with the remaining pixels.

Finally, once straight lines have been extracted, they are grouped into polygonal chains according to the smoothness and convexity assumptions. Starting from a line segment, consecutive line segments are added to the group as long as the angle between them is below a certain threshold and the whole group shares the same turn direction (refer to Fig. 1). This builds a candidate curve.

## 4.3    Model Generation

Given a set of pixels from a candidate curve, in this step we want to extract a model of its corresponding 3D line in a least squares sense.

As stated in Section 3, the points from a 3D line, along with the camera's center of projection, all lie in a plane. Therefore, in this step, we are interested in estimating the the parameters of such plane.

A plane is described by the unit normal vector $n \in \mathbb{R}^3$ and its distance to the origin $D \in \mathbb{R}$. This way, the point-to-plane distance can be simplified to

$$d_n(x) = x \cdot n + D \qquad (1)$$

Setting the center of projection coincident to the origin makes $D = 0$, and then the least squares solution to the plane parameters, in terms of the point-to-plane distance, is given by:

$$n^* = \underset{n}{\arg\min} \sum_{u \in \mathcal{C}} \left\| \pi^{-1}(u) \cdot n \right\|^2$$
$$\text{subject to } \|n\| = 1 \qquad (2)$$

where $\pi^{-1}$ is the inverse projection function, for all pixels $u \in \Omega$ in the segmented curve $\mathcal{C}$.

Note that (2) is a quadratic system with a quadratic constraint and, thus, it can be expressed compactly in matrix form as:

$$n^* = \underset{n}{\arg\min} \ n^\top M n$$
$$\text{subject to } n^\top I_{3\times3} n = 1 \qquad (3)$$

where $M$ is the symmetric matrix

$$M = \sum_{u \in \mathcal{C}} \pi^{-1}(u)\left(\pi^{-1}(u)\right)^\top \qquad (4)$$

We solve this constrained optimization problem in closed form using the method of Lagrange multipliers as follows. Considering the Lagrangian:

$$\mathcal{L}(n) = n^\top M n + \lambda(n^\top I n) \qquad (5)$$

the necessary conditions for optimality are then:

$$\frac{\partial \mathcal{L}(n)}{\partial n} = 2n^\top (M + \lambda I) = 0^\top \qquad (6)$$

Disregarding the trivial solution, the $3 \times 3$ matrix $M + \lambda I$ must be singular in order to satisfy (6). Thus, we solve for the values of $\lambda \in \mathbb{R}$ that make

$$\det\left(M + \lambda I\right) = 0 \qquad (7)$$

This is a polynomial expression in $\lambda$ of degree 3, for which a closed form solution exists. This is the characteristic polynomial, and the roots correspond to the eigenvalues of $M$. Finally, the solution to the original problem can be extracted from the kernel of $M + \lambda I$.

Up to 3 solutions satisfy equation (6), so we choose as the optimal solution the one with the lowest cost, given by $n^\top M n$.

**4.4   Geometric Validation**

Finally, once we have a model of the 3D line, we geometrically verify if it corresponds to the observed curve as follows. Given a pixel $u$ of the curve $\mathcal{C}$, we get the direction vector of the corresponding light-ray and project it to the plane model of the line estimated as explained above. The projected vector on the plane is finally re-projected to the image using the projection function $\pi$. Thus, we say that a curve is the projection of a 3D line, within a certain threshold $\rho$, if, for all segmented pixels of the curve, their re-projection fall within a $\rho$-radius circle around the source pixels, measured in image coordinates:

$$\left\| u - \pi\big(x - (x \cdot n)n\big) \right\| \leq \rho, \quad \forall u \in \mathcal{C} \tag{8}$$

where $x = \pi^{-1}(u)$ and $n$ is the normal vector of the fitted plane. It is worth noticing that, for computational efficiency reasons, only the endpoints of the 2D line segments forming the polygonal chain are verified.

# 5   Experimental Evaluation

We have evaluated D-LSD with real images from the TUM mono dataset [12], comparing it with the fastest state-of-the-art line segment detectors: LSD [16], EDLines [1] and AG3line [24]. For a fair comparison, we have used the original authors' C++ implementations[1]. All the experiments were conducted on an Intel Core i7-7700HQ CPU with 16 GB of RAM and on a Linux-based OS.

The TUM monocular dataset is tailored for the evaluation of visual odometry and SLAM systems. In this evaluation, we focus on the specific wide_whitePaper calibration sequence, which contains 800 images showing two sheets of white paper on top of a dark table. This sequence is particularly interesting since long and high contrast line segments are observed along the whole sequence from different points of view. A wide-angle camera was used to record this sequence, having 148° × 122° non-rectified field of view. The camera parameters, as provided with the dataset, are calibrated using the pinhole projection with the FoV [11] distortion model. Finally, the camera has a global shutter CMOS sensor with 1280 px × 1024 px resolution, recording frames at a fixed rate of 10 fps.

In order to test the other methods, we first rectify the raw images using the tools provided with the dataset[2] in crop mode, which keeps as much pixels from the original image as possible but without adding any black borders (see Fig. 3). We set the output image resolution to match the original 1280 px × 1024 px for a fair comparison between the methods using rectified images and D-LSD. The other evaluated methods are then applied to the rectified images keeping their default parameters. In turn, for D-LSD, we have set the smoothness threshold to $\theta = \frac{\pi}{16}$ and the reprojection error for line validation to $\rho = 4$ px. Additionally, small (less than 25 px) single straight line polygonal chains are omitted.

---

[1] The reference implementation of D-LSD as well as the others' used for evaluation are publicly available at: https://github.com/dzunigan/line_detection.
[2] https://github.com/tum-vision/mono_dataset_code.

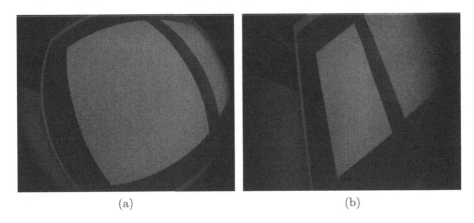

(a)                                                      (b)

**Fig. 3.** Original (3a) and rectified (3b) images from the `wide_whitePaper` sequence of the TUM monocular dataset [12].

We have measured the D-LSD performance with the *recall* value, computed as the ratio of the number of line segments found in the distorted image by D-LSD w.r.t. the number of segments in the image, as given by any of the state-of-the-art methods on the rectified image. Thus, a maximum value of 100 % would tell us that all the line segments detected in the rectified image have been recovered with D-LSD. A correspondence between rectified and distorted lines is set if at least 90 % of the rectified line falls within 4 px of a distorted line detected by D-LSD. We omit small line segments from the evaluation since their detection is highly affected by the internal parameters of each algorithm. However, the length in pixels of the same line segment is different in rectified and non-rectified images. Thus, we set the minimum line length threshold in terms of the angle between the light-rays of the endpoints of a line, which does not depend on the actual projection function. In this way, we can discard the same small segments for all the evaluated methods. The length threshold is represented as a percentage of the vertical FoV.

The recall rates for the whole `wide_whitePaper` sequence and for different values of the minimum line length threshold are shown in Fig. 4. The results of the experiment show that most of the long lines (about 21° and above) are detected by D-LSD, while it struggles to detected smaller lines. This is, in part, because of some internal thresholds of D-LSD that are expressed in pixels and thus are not equivalent when using rectified images. The total number of line segments detected by each algorithm along with the average execution time are reported in Table 1. Only line segments with length above 25 % minimum length threshold (*i.e.* 61° and above) are taken into account. It is important to highlight that one of the advantages of using D-LSD is that it can detect a larger number of the long lines than the rest of the methods, since it uses the original non-rectified images with wider FoV. Not only that, our proposal is the fastest detector, even without taking into account the previous rectification step needed by the others (first column in Table 1).

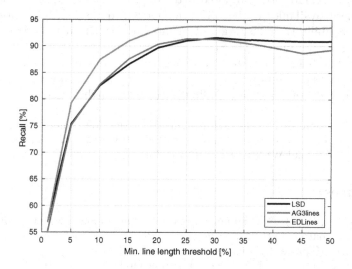

**Fig. 4.** D-LSD recall ratio compared to state-of-the-art line segment detectors on rectified images from the `wide_whitePaper` sequence.

**Table 1.** Total number of line segments detected in the `wide_whitePaper` sequence at 25 % length threshold and average execution time (with standard deviation) measured in milliseconds.

|            | Rectification [12] | LSD [16]    | AG3line [24] | EDLines [1] | D-LSD      |
|------------|--------------------|-------------|--------------|-------------|------------|
| Total lines | –                 | 6654        | 5868         | 6273        | 7186       |
| Exec. time | 7.32 (1.64)        | 38.8 (2.84) | 20.2 (2.70)  | 12.9 (3.85) | 12.4 (3.92) |

## 6 Conclusions

In this work, we have presented a new line segment detector for calibrated images that works directly on the original, non-rectified image. An open source C++ implementation of our algorithm is available at https://github.com/dzunigan/line_detection.

Our approach, coined D-LSD, relies on the efficient Edge Drawing [23] algorithm for edge detection. Edge pixels are then grouped into polygonal chains, representing smooth convex curves. Finally, the segmented curves are validated as the projection of a 3D line by fitting a plane that includes the projection center and the light-rays passing through the curve pixels. This plane fitting problem is formulated as a quadratically constrained quadratic optimization problem, which is solved in closed form using the method of Lagrange multipliers. Our method is general enough to handle any central projection system: from wide-angle to omnidirectional cameras. We have evaluated the proposed detector with images captured by a wide-angle camera available in the TUM monocular dataset [12], comparing its detection capabilities against state-of-the-art line segment detectors on rectified images. In the experiments, D-LSD shows comparable performance for non-short segments while being the fastest approach and without requiring any previous image rectification. We believe D-LSD could be of much interest for demanding real time applications that rely on line features for further image analysis.

**Acknowledgements.** This research was funded by the Government of Spain and the European Regional Development's funds (FEDER) under the projects ARPEGGIO (PID2020-117057) and WISER (DPI2017-84827-R).

# References

1. Akinlar, C., Topal, C.: EDLines: a real-time line segment detector with a false detection control. Pattern Recogn. Lett. **32**(13), 1633–1642 (2011). https://doi.org/10.1016/j.patrec.2011.06.001
2. Akinlar, C., Topal, C.: EDCircles: a real-time circle detector with a false detection control. Pattern Recogn. **46**(3), 725–740 (2013). https://doi.org/10.1016/j.patcog.2012.09.020
3. Angeli, A., Filliat, D., Doncieux, S., Meyer, J.A.: Fast and incremental method for loop-closure detection using bags of visual words. IEEE Trans. Robot. **24**(5), 1027–1037 (2008). https://doi.org/10.1109/TRO.2008.2004514
4. Barreto, J.P.: A unifying geometric representation for central projection systems. Comput. Vis. Image Underst. **103**(3), 208–217 (2006). https://doi.org/10.1016/j.cviu.2006.06.003
5. Briales, J., Gonzalez-Jimenez, J.: A minimal closed-form solution for the perspective three orthogonal angles (P3oA) problem: application to visual odometry. J. Math. Imaging Vis. **55**(3), 266–283 (2015). https://doi.org/10.1007/s10851-015-0620-x
6. Briales, J., Gonzalez-Jimenez, J.: A minimal solution for the calibration of a 2D laser-rangefinder and a camera based on scene corners. In: 2015 IEEE/RSJ International Conference on Intelligent Robots and Systems (IROS), pp. 1891–1896 (2015). https://doi.org/10.1109/IROS.2015.7353625
7. Caruso, D., Engel, J., Cremers, D.: Large-scale direct SLAM for omnidirectional cameras. In: 2015 IEEE/RSJ International Conference on Intelligent Robots and Systems (IROS), pp. 141–148 (2015). https://doi.org/10.1109/IROS.2015.7353366
8. Cheng, G., Han, J.: A survey on object detection in optical remote sensing images. ISPRS J. Photogrammetry Rem. Sens. **117**, 11–28 (2016). https://doi.org/10.1016/j.isprsjprs.2016.03.014
9. Cho, N., Yuille, A., Lee, S.: A novel linelet-based representation for line segment detection. IEEE Trans. Pattern Anal. Mach. Intell. **40**(5), 1195–1208 (2018). https://doi.org/10.1109/TPAMI.2017.2703841
10. Desolneux, A., Moisan, L., Morel, J.M.: Edge detection by Helmholtz principle. J. Math. Imaging Vis. **14**(3), 271–284 (2001)
11. Devernay, F., Faugeras, O.: Straight lines have to be straight. Mach. Vis. Appl. **13**, 14–24 (2019). https://doi.org/10.1007/PL00013269

12. Engel, J., Usenko, V., Cremers, D.: A photometrically calibrated benchmark for monocular visual odometry. arXiv e-prints p. arXiv:1607.02555 (2016)
13. Fitzgibbon, A.W.: Simultaneous linear estimation of multiple view geometry and lens distortion. In: Proceedings of the 2001 IEEE Computer Society Conference on Computer Vision and Pattern Recognition. CVPR 2001, vol. 1, pp. 1 (2001). https://doi.org/10.1109/CVPR.2001.990465
14. Gomez-Ojeda, R., Briales, J., Gonzalez-Jimenez, J.: PL-SVO: Semi-direct monocular visual odometry by combining points and line segments. In: 2016 IEEE/RSJ International Conference on Intelligent Robots and Systems (IROS), pp. 4211–4216 (2016). https://doi.org/10.1109/IROS.2016.7759620
15. Gomez-Ojeda, R., Moreno, F., Zuñiga-Noél, D., Scaramuzza, D., Gonzalez-Jimenez, J.: PL-SLAM: a stereo SLAM system through the combination of points and line segments. IEEE Trans. Robot. 35(3), 734–746 (2019). https://doi.org/10.1109/TRO.2019.2899783
16. Grompone von Gioi, R., Jakubowicz, J., Morel, J., Randall, G.: LSD: A fast line segment detector with a false detection control. IEEE Trans. Pattern Anal. Mach. Intell. 32(4), 722–732 (2010). https://doi.org/10.1109/TPAMI.2008.300
17. Lee, J.H., Zhang, G., Lim, J., Suh, I.H.: Place recognition using straight lines for vision-based SLAM. In: 2013 IEEE International Conference on Robotics and Automation, pp. 3799–3806 (2013). https://doi.org/10.1109/ICRA.2013.6631111
18. Lu, X., Yao, J., Li, K., Li, L.: CannyLines: a parameter-free line segment detector. In: 2015 IEEE International Conference on Image Processing (ICIP), pp. 507–511 (2015). https://doi.org/10.1109/ICIP.2015.7350850
19. Mur-Artal, R., Montiel, J.M.M., Tardós, J.D.: ORB-SLAM: a versatile and accurate monocular SLAM system. IEEE Trans. Robot. 31(5), 1147–1163 (2015). https://doi.org/10.1109/TRO.2015.2463671
20. Nistér, D., Naroditsky, O., Bergen, J.: Visual odometry. In: Proceedings of the 2004 IEEE Computer Society Conference on Computer Vision and Pattern Recognition, 2004. CVPR 2004, vol. 1, pp. 1. IEEE (2004)
21. Pătrăucean, V., Gurdjos, P., Grompone von Gioi, R.: Joint a contrario ellipse and line detection. IEEE Trans. Pattern Anal. Mach. Intell. 39(4), 788–802 (2017). https://doi.org/10.1109/TPAMI.2016.2558150
22. Svoboda, T., Pajdla, T.: Epipolar geometry for central catadioptric cameras. Int. J. Comput. Vis. 49, 23–37 (2002). https://doi.org/10.1023/A:1019869530073
23. Topal, C., Akinlar, C.: Edge drawing: a combined real-time edge and segment detector. J. Vis. Commun. Image Rep. 23(6), 862–872 (2012). https://doi.org/10.1016/j.jvcir.2012.05.004
24. Zhang, Y., Wei, D., Li, Y.: AG3line: active grouping and geometry-gradient combined validation for fast line segment extraction. Pattern Recogn. 113, 107834 (2021). https://doi.org/10.1016/j.patcog.2021.107834
25. Zuñiga-Noël, D., Jaenal, A., Gomez-Ojeda, R., Gonzalez-Jimenez, J.: The UMA-VI dataset: Visual-inertial odometry in low-textured and dynamic illumination environments. Int. J. Robot. Res. 39(9), 1052–1060 (2020). https://doi.org/10.1177/0278364920938439

# Efficient Data Optimisation for Harmonic Inpainting with Finite Elements

Vassillen Chizhov$^{(\boxtimes)}$ and Joachim Weickert

Mathematical Image Analysis Group, Faculty of Mathematics and Computer Science, Campus E 1.7, Saarland University, 66041 Saarbrücken, Germany
{chizhov,weickert}@mia.uni-saarland.de

**Abstract.** Harmonic inpainting with optimised data is very popular for inpainting-based image compression. We improve this approach in three important aspects. Firstly, we replace the standard finite differences discretisation by a finite element method with triangle elements. This does not only speed up inpainting and data selection, but even improves the reconstruction quality. Secondly, we propose highly efficient algorithms for spatial and tonal data optimisation that are several orders of magnitude faster than state-of-the-art methods. Last but not least, we show that our algorithms also allow working with very large images. This has previously been impractical due to the memory and runtime requirements of prior algorithms.

**Keywords:** Inpainting · Image reconstruction · Finite element method

## 1 Introduction

In recent years, alternatives to transform-based compression have been proposed under the name inpainting-based compression; see e.g. [2,6,8,9,11,13,17,19,20, 29]. During encoding, these approaches store an optimised subset of the image data (e.g. 5% of all pixels), the so-called *inpainting mask*. In the decoding phase, they reconstruct an approximation of the original image from the mask data with the help of an inpainting process. Inpainting-based methods have been able to qualitatively outperform widely used codecs such as JPEG and JPEG2000; see e.g. [29]. Two of the simplest inpainting methods are based on linear spline approximation over triangle meshes [1,9,10,22] and on discretisations of the Laplace equation [21] (also called *homogeneous diffusion inpainting* or *harmonic inpainting*) with the finite difference method (FDM). Although these approaches are relatively simple, they can achieve very good quality if the inpainting data are carefully optimised [4,9,13,21,25]. Their quality also exceeds the one reported for recent neural network approaches for sparse inpainting [7].

Unfortunately, the data optimisation during the encoding phase is typically costly both in terms of memory and runtime. It consists of two problems: spatial

This project has received funding from the European Research Council (ERC) under the European Union's Horizon 2020 research and innovation programme (grant agreement No 741215, ERC Advanced Grant INCOVID).

© Springer Nature Switzerland AG 2021
N. Tsapatsoulis et al. (Eds.): CAIP 2021, LNCS 13053, pp. 432–441, 2021.
https://doi.org/10.1007/978-3-030-89131-2_40

optimisation and tonal optimisation. The spatial optimisation problem aims at finding the optimal locations on the image grid for the set of pixels to be stored. This is a hard combinatorial minimisation problem that requires efficient heuristics. In contrast, the tonal optimisation problem consists of modifying the grey values (or colour values) of the stored data. While this is a least squares problem, it can require large computational and memory resources [12,14,21]. This precludes previous tonal optimisation methods for harmonic inpainting from being applied to very large images.

Artifacts constitute another problem. Linear spline inpainting may suffer from conspicuous structures of the triangle mesh, and FDM-based harmonic inpainting typically exhibits logarithmic singularities at the stored pixels.

**Our Contributions.** The goal of our paper is to address the above-mentioned problems by introducing three improvements of high practical relevance:

1. We propose to implement harmonic inpainting with a finite element method (FEM) based on adaptive triangulation. Compared to finite differences on the pixel grid, its adaptivity allows to achieve better quality in lower time. Interestingly, this also alleviates the logarithmic singularities that are characteristic for the finite difference solution.
2. We devise a computationally efficient spatial optimisation strategy which scales better and is multiple orders of magnitude faster than current state-of-the-art approaches without compromising reconstruction quality.
3. We propose a computationally and memory efficient algorithm for tonal optimisation. Its runtime and memory requirements scale much more favourably with the image resolution compared to previous state-of-the-art approaches. This allows us to handle also very large images, which has been problematic for previous tonal optimisation approaches for harmonic inpainting.

**Related Work.** Finite elements have been successfully used for PDE models for image denoising [3,18,27] and restoration [5,32]. However, to our knowledge they have not been applied to PDE-based image approximation from sparse data.

Various spatial optimisation strategies have been proposed for inpainting-based compression. Mainberger et al. [21] introduced a probabilistic sparsification approach that selects a subset of pixels to be removed at each iteration. A subsequent nonlocal pixel exchange step relocates pixels probabilistically and keeps only relocations that decrease the error. The dithering-based densification strategy of Karos et al. [17] iteratively adds a fraction of the target pixels by halftoning an inpainting error image. The Voronoi densification of Daropoulos et al. [8] constructs a Voronoi diagram from the currently stored pixel data and inserts a new pixel in the cell with the highest error at each iteration. Our approach combines the ideas of densification with an error map [17] and a partitioning of the domain [8]. However, we use the tessellation already available from the FEM mesh. In our case this is a Delaunay triangulation which is dual to a Voronoi tessellation and avoids storing the mesh connectivity.

Tonal optimisation approaches can be split into two categories: methods that explicitly compute the dense solution for the inpainting, and iterative descent-based strategies. The former ones include inpainting echoes [20], LSQR relying on an LU factorisation [14], and Green's functions [15]. Their memory requirements scale quadratically in the number of mask points or image pixels. This makes them inapplicable for larger images. The second category includes gradient descent methods [12,15], quasi-Newton techniques such as L-BFGS [6], and primal-dual algorithms [14]. Our approach falls in this category and is very efficient by using nested conjugate gradient iterations [28].

**Outline.** In Sect. 2 we discuss the mathematical formulation of harmonic inpainting and the application of FEM to it. Then we describe our spatial optimisation approach in Sect. 3 and our tonal optimisation algorithm in Sect. 4. We present our results in Sect. 5, and we conclude the paper with some potential avenues for future research in Sect. 6.

# 2    FEM for Harmonic Inpainting

In this section we introduce the mathematical formulation for harmonic inpainting in the continuous setting and then motivate the choice of an FEM discretisation over an FDM discretisation. Additionally, we describe how the FEM mesh is constructed and how the solution is interpolated to all image pixels.

## 2.1    Continuous Formulation of Harmonic Inpainting

We use harmonic inpainting to construct an approximation of the original image given a sparse subset of the image data. Let us consider a continuous greyscale image $f : \Omega \to \mathbb{R}$ on some rectangular image domain $\Omega$. Rather than storing $f$ on the entire domain $\Omega$, we only specify values on a *data domain* $K \subset \Omega$ (the so-called *mask pixels* in a discrete setting). In the remaining domain $\Omega \setminus K$, we fill in missing values by solving the Laplace equation with reflecting boundary conditions on $\partial\Omega$:

$$-\Delta u(\boldsymbol{x}) = 0, \quad \boldsymbol{x} \in \Omega \setminus K, \tag{1}$$

$$u(\boldsymbol{x}) = g(\boldsymbol{x}), \quad \boldsymbol{x} \in K, \tag{2}$$

$$\partial_n u(\boldsymbol{x}) = 0, \quad \boldsymbol{x} \in \partial\Omega, \tag{3}$$

where $\boldsymbol{n}$ is normal to $\partial\Omega$. In order to improve the approximation quality of $u$ w.r.t. $f$, one optimises the shape of the data domain $K$ under some size constraint *(spatial optimisation)* and the corresponding grey values $g$ within $K$ *(tonal optimisation)*. In the discrete setting, $\boldsymbol{f}$, $\boldsymbol{g}$, and $\boldsymbol{u}$ are vectors instead of functions.

## 2.2    FEM Formulation

Finite difference methods (FDM) [24] and finite element methods (FEM) [16] are two classes of numerical techniques used to solve differential equations. FDM is often applied on a regular and equidistant grid (the pixel grid for digital images), while FEM is well-suited for data on adaptive meshes. Therefore, the number of unknowns for the FDM method grows rapidly with the image resolution, while one has fine control over the number of unknowns in FEM by means of the construction of the underlying mesh. This flexibility naturally suggests using an adaptive lower resolution FEM mesh with fewer unknowns in order to speed up the inpainting compared to FDM.

Our FEM formulation relies on a triangle mesh; see Figure 2, right. Every mask pixel is a vertex in this mesh, and a subset of the remaining non-mask pixels are chosen as unknowns, depending on how many unknowns are required or on the runtime constraints. We call this subset the *unknown vertices*. If all non-mask pixels were chosen as unknown vertices, then the standard (5-point stencil) FDM discretisation of the Laplace equation would be recovered. Once the vertices for the mesh have been determined, a Delaunay triangulation is constructed from the point set formed by the vertices [26]. The Delaunay property of maximising the minimum angle in the triangulation is desirable, since it provides guarantees regarding the optimality of the resulting condition number for the matrices involved in the inpainting and tonal optimisation [30]. Furthermore, this frees us from storing any connectivity, since the mesh can be reconstructed only from the mask pixels and unknown vertices [26].

We consider a *linear* FEM method: The reconstructed image is linear within each triangle of the aforementioned mesh and continuous at edges and vertices. At each mask pixel the corresponding stored grey value is prescribed, while the values at the unknown vertices are found by solving the linear system arising from the FEM formulation. Each unknown corresponds to an unknown vertex. We typically choose as many unknown vertices as we have mask pixels. For further technical details on FEM, we refer to the standard literature [16]. Given a Delaunay mesh with at least one mask pixel, the system matrix is symmetric and positive definite. Thus, we can use the conjugate gradient method [28] in order to approximate the solution. Finally, the solution is linearly interpolated within each triangle for the remaining non-mask pixels which do not correspond to vertices in the mesh.

## 3    Spatial Optimisation

Our spatial optimisation algorithm is based on a novel coarse-to-fine error map densification strategy that combines concepts from an error map dithering [17] and a Voronoi densification algorithm [8]. The main idea is to introduce $m$ mask pixels over $n$ iterations, where each iteration requires a single inpainting.

To this end, we have investigated many strategies, and we now describe the one which has produced the best results. Most importantly, we have found that the error map must be considered at a locally adaptive scale that reflects the mesh structure as a function of the mask pixel density. In each iteration we introduce $\frac{m}{n}$ of all mask pixels. In the very first iteration we distribute all unknown vertices uniformly at random on the image grid, and introduce the first $\frac{m}{n}$ mask pixels also uniformly at random. In each subsequent iteration, we compute the inpainted image $u$ from the current mesh, and its error map $e_i = (u_i - f_i)^2$ in each pixel $i$. Afterwards we evaluate the total $L_2$ error in each triangle. We insert a single mask pixel in each triangle, in descending order of the $L_2$ error. The position of the mask pixel within a triangle is chosen to be at the empty location with the largest pointwise error.

This procedure ensures that the inserted mask points are adapted to the evolving FEM mesh, which is the main advantage over previous approaches [8,17]. Generally, the more iterations/inpaintings $n$ are allowed, the higher the quality of the mesh is for the purpose of approximating $f$. Practically useful numbers range between $n = 10$ and $n = 100$.

## 4    Tonal Optimisation

Let the grey values in the $m$ optimised mask pixels be given by a vector $g \in \mathbb{R}^m$. Then the corresponding inpainting result $u$ can be written formally as $u = Bg$, where the matrix $B$ is dense and depends only on the mesh and the enumeration of the vertices. It also includes the discussed interpolation from Sect. 3 for image pixels that are not vertices in the mesh. The goal of the tonal optimisation problem is to find the grey values $g^*$ that give the best reconstruction $u^* = Bg^*$:

$$g^* = \underset{g \in \mathbb{R}^m}{\arg \min} \|Bg - f\|_2^2 . \tag{4}$$

Since this is a linear least squares problem, its solution is given by the linear system of equations (the so-called normal equations):

$$B^T B g = B^T f. \tag{5}$$

A straightforward approach to solve the normal equations would compute $B$ explicitly. Unfortunately, this would require memory that scales *quadratically* in the number of pixels. This becomes unfeasible for very large images.

As a remedy, we exploit the fact that $B$ is formed as the product of a sparse matrix (interpolation) and the inverse of a sparse matrix (Laplace equation). This means that the required memory for our optimisation scales *linearly* in the number of pixels. We achieve this by applying a nested conjugate gradient solver to (5). The inner iterations are effectively solving inpainting problems due to the Laplace equation instead of inverting the matrix from the FEM formulation explicitly. The outer iterations optimise the grey value vector $g$.

Interestingly, our approach results not only in a better memory scaling: Also its runtime is much lower than the inpainting echo approach [21], and it is also faster than alternative tonal optimisation techniques [12,15] for usual mask densities.

## 5    Experiments

Figure 1 displays the results of our FEM approach for three classical test images that are popular for sparse harmonic inpainting: *trui*, *walter*, and (a 256 × 256

original image *trui*          original image *walter*          original image *peppers*

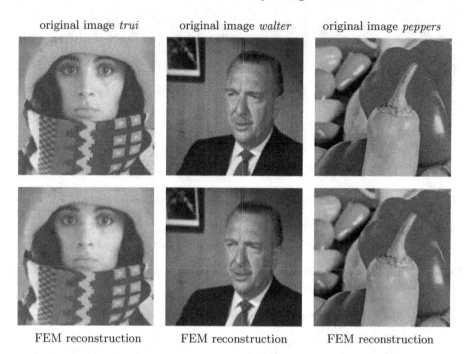

FEM reconstruction          FEM reconstruction          FEM reconstruction

**Fig. 1.** FEM reconstructions for *trui*, *walter*, and *peppers* with 4% density and $n = 100$.

crop of) *peppers*. We see that even at a low mask density of 4%, the reconstructions are fairly convincing. A quantitative analysis in terms of the mean squared error (MSE) is presented in Table 1, where we also compare our densification methods against the probabilistic sparsification results of Hoeltgen et al. [12]. We observe that our algorithms achieve a consistently better quality. When we apply tonal optimisation after the spatial optimisation, the MSE decreases further by about one third. Sometimes tonal optimisation can even fully compensate suboptimal spatial optimisation, as can be seen for the *peppers* image.

**Table 1.** MSE comparisons at 4% density without and with tonal optimisation (TO).

| Method | *trui* | | *walter* | | *peppers* | |
|---|---|---|---|---|---|---|
| | no TO | with TO | no TO | with TO | no TO | with TO |
| Prob. spars. ($q = 10^{-6}$) | 66.11 | 36.04 | 32.96 | 19.24 | 44.85 | 28.58 |
| Ours ($n = 10$) | 44.62 | 30.07 | 19.09 | 12.62 | 43.20 | 29.83 |
| Ours ($n = 30$) | 40.58 | 28.21 | 16.35 | **11.09** | 38.37 | **28.11** |
| Ours ($n = 100$) | **37.60** | **26.62** | **15.92** | 11.21 | **36.68** | 28.85 |

  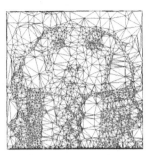

FDM, MSE=36.04          FEM, MSE=26.62          Delaunay triangulation

**Fig. 2.** Comparison between FDM with probabilistic sparsification (left) and FEM with densification (middle), both at 4% density and tonally optimised. The FEM result does not suffer from the pronounced singularities on the scarf and face present for FDM. Right: Delaunay triangulation used for the FEM method.

**Table 2.** Runtime scaling with resolution (in seconds) of our spatial optimisation and tonal optimisation with $n = 10$ at a density of 4%.

| Image size | $64 \times 64$ | $128 \times 128$ | $256 \times 256$ | $512 \times 512$ | $1024 \times 1024$ |
|---|---|---|---|---|---|
| Spatial optimisation | 0.01 | 0.03 | 0.11 | 0.49 | 2.07 |
| Tonal optimisation | 0.03 | 0.14 | 0.53 | 2.96 | 12.77 |

In terms of runtime for the spatial optimisation, a probabilistic sparsification of a $256 \times 256$ image with the parameters from [12] on a Ryzen 4800H CPU takes about 10 min, while our FEM densification needs only 0.3 s. This shows that our method is 1800 times faster. This factor grows rapidly with the image size: For $512 \times 512$ images, it is already 10,000 (4 h versus 1.3 s). The complexity of the optimisation is $\mathcal{O}(nq\sqrt{k})$, where $n$ is the number of iterations, $k$ is the condition number of the matrix, $q$ is the number of non-zero entries in the matrix (at most $6\times$ the number of vertices of the FEM mesh).

Our tonal optimisation algorithm is also several orders of magnitude faster, requiring 0.3 s for a $256 \times 256$ image. The reported runtimes from Hoeltgen et al. [12] on a Xeon 3.2 GHz CPU vary between 77 s and 458 s for the different algorithms discussed there. The tonal optimisation has a time complexity of $\mathcal{O}(q\sqrt{k_2}\sqrt{k})$, where $k_2$ is the condition number of the tonal optimisation matrix. Additionally, previous methods relying on QR or LU factorisations [14] require memory that grows quadratically in the number of mask pixels. In contrast, our algorithm's memory requirements grow linearly in the number of image pixels ($12q + 32v$ bytes, where $v$ is the number of vertices in the FEM mesh). Thus, it can be applied to much larger images.

In Fig. 2, we juxtapose FEM method with densification to the FDM approach with probabilistic sparsification, both in the tonally optimised case. We observe that the FEM technique does not suffer from the pronounced singularities around mask pixels. These artifacts can be explained by the logarithmic singularities of

original image saomiguel                    FEM reconstruction

**Fig. 3.** Left: A richly textured colour image of size $4896 \times 3264$ amounting to ca. 16 million pixels. Photo: J. Weickert. Right: Our FEM reconstruction with $n = 30$ iterations, 10% mask density, and $L_1$ optimisation.

the Green's functions in the continuous harmonic inpainting model; see [23] for more details. Our FEM approach with linear approximations within each triangle handles them more gracefully.

Table 2 reports scaling results for the spatial and tonal optimisation steps of our FEM method. We see that it scales almost linearly with the number of image pixels. The slight deviations from an ideal linear scaling are caused by the conjugate gradient solver: Large images lead to a higher condition number of the linear systems, such that the conjugate gradient method needs a few more iterations [28].

Finally, Fig. 3 illustrates that our approach can also reconstruct large and richly textured colour images with very high perceptual quality. Extending the method to colour images is straightforward. In order to achieve highest visual fidelity, we have followed [31] and optimised the $L_1$ error instead of the $L_2$ one.

## 6    Conclusions and Future Work

Our paper is the first one that considers finite elements for inpainting-based image compression. We have seen that they offer a much higher efficiency due to their better adaptivity to the image structure. Moreover, our algorithms have substantially better scaling properties than previous approaches. This allows to apply them to much larger images, which is an important issue for bringing inpainting-based compression into practical applications.

In our ongoing work, we are studying options to increase the efficiency of our approach even further and to extend it to other PDEs and the compression of data on manifolds.

## References

1. Adams, M.: A highly effective incremental/decremental Delaunay mesh generation strategy for image representation. Sig. Process. **93**(4), 749–764 (2013)

2. Andris, S., Peter, P., Mohideen Kaja Mohideen, R., Weickert, J., Hoffmann, S.: Inpainting-based video compression in FullHD. In: Elmoataz, A., Fadili, J., Quéau, Y., Rabin, J., Simon, L. (eds.) SSVM 2021. LNCS, vol. 12679, pp. 425–436. Springer, Cham (2021). https://doi.org/10.1007/978-3-030-75549-2_34

3. Bänsch, E., Mikula, K.: A coarsening finite element strategy in image selective smoothing. Comput. Vis. Sci. **1**, 53–61 (1997)

4. Bonettini, S., Loris, I., Porta, F., Prato, M., Rebegoldi, S.: On the convergence of a linesearch based proximal-gradient method for nonconvex optimization. Inverse Problems 33(5) (Mar 2017), article 055005

5. Boujena, S., Bellaj, K., Gouasnouane, O., Guarmah, E.: An improved nonlinear model for image inpainting. Appl. Math. Sci. **9**(124), 6189–6205 (2015)

6. Chen, Y., Ranftl, R., Pock, T.: A bi-level view of inpainting-based image compression. In: Kúkelová, Z., Heller, J. (eds.) Proc. 19th Computer Vision Winter Workshop. Křtiny, Czech Republic, Feburary 2014

7. Dai, Q., Chopp, H., Pouyet, E., Cossairt, O., Walton, M., Katsaggelos, A.: Adaptive image sampling using deep learning and its application on X-ray fluorescence image reconstruction. IEEE Trans. Multimedia **22**(10), 2564–2578 (2020)

8. Daropoulos, V., Augustin, M., Weickert, J.: Sparse inpainting with smoothed particle hydrodynamics. arXiv:2011.11289 [eess.IV] (2020)

9. Demaret, L., Dyn, N., Iske, A.: Image compression by linear splines over adaptive triangulations. Sig. Process. **86**(7), 1604–1616 (2006)

10. Distasi, R., Nappi, M., Vitulano, S.: Image compression by B-tree triangular coding. IEEE Trans. Commun. **45**(9), 1095–1100 (1997)

11. Galić, I., Weickert, J., Welk, M., Bruhn, A., Belyaev, A., Seidel, H.-P.: Towards PDE-based image compression. In: Paragios, N., Faugeras, O., Chan, T., Schnörr, C. (eds.) VLSM 2005. LNCS, vol. 3752, pp. 37–48. Springer, Heidelberg (2005). https://doi.org/10.1007/11567646_4

12. Hoeltgen, L., et al.: Optimising spatial and tonal data for PDE-based inpainting. In: Bergounioux, M., Peyré, G., Schnörr, C., Caillau, J.P., Haberkorn, T. (eds.) Variational Methods in Imaging and Geometric Control, pp. 35–83. De Gruyter, Berlin (2017)

13. Hoeltgen, L., Setzer, S., Weickert, J.: An optimal control approach to find sparse data for laplace interpolation. In: Heyden, A., Kahl, F., Olsson, C., Oskarsson, M., Tai, X.-C. (eds.) EMMCVPR 2013. LNCS, vol. 8081, pp. 151–164. Springer, Heidelberg (2013). https://doi.org/10.1007/978-3-642-40395-8_12

14. Hoeltgen, L., Weickert, J.: Why does non-binary mask optimisation work for diffusion-based image compression? In: Tai, X.-C., Bae, E., Chan, T.F., Lysaker, M. (eds.) EMMCVPR 2015. LNCS, vol. 8932, pp. 85–98. Springer, Cham (2015). https://doi.org/10.1007/978-3-319-14612-6_7

15. Hoffmann, S.: Competitive image compression with linear PDEs. Ph.D. thesis, Department of Computer Science, Saarland University, Saarbrücken, Germany (2016)

16. Johnson, C.: Numerical Solution of Partial Differential Equations by the Finite Element Method. Dover, New York (2009)

17. Karos, L., Bheed, P., Peter, P., Weickert, J.: Optimising data for exemplar-based inpainting. In: Blanc-Talon, J., Helbert, D., Philips, W., Popescu, D., Scheunders, P. (eds.) ACIVS 2018. LNCS, vol. 11182, pp. 547–558. Springer, Cham (2018). https://doi.org/10.1007/978-3-030-01449-0_46

18. Kačur, J., Mikula, K.: Solution of nonlinear diffusion appearing in image smoothing and edge detection. Appl. Numer. Math. **17**, 47–59 (1995)

19. Liu, D., Sun, X., Wu, F., Li, S., Zhang, Y.Q.: Image compression with edge-based inpainting. IEEE Trans. Circ. Syst. Video Technol. **17**(10), 1273–1286 (2007)
20. Mainberger, M., Bruhn, A., Weickert, J., Forchhammer, S.: Edge-based compression of cartoon-like images with homogeneous diffusion. Pattern Recogn. **44**(9), 1859–1873 (2011)
21. Mainberger, M., et al.: Optimising spatial and tonal data for homogeneous diffusion inpainting. In: Bruckstein, A.M., ter Haar Romeny, B.M., Bronstein, A.M., Bronstein, M.M. (eds.) SSVM 2011. LNCS, vol. 6667, pp. 26–37. Springer, Heidelberg (2012). https://doi.org/10.1007/978-3-642-24785-9_3
22. Marwood, D., Massimino, P., Covell, M., Baluja, S.: Representing images in 200 bytes: compression via triangulation. In: Proceedings 25th IEEE International Conference on Image Processing, pp. 405–409, October 2018
23. Melnikov, Y.A., Melnikov, M.Y.: Green's Functions: Construction and Applications. De Gruyter, Berlin (2012)
24. Mitchell, A.R., Griffiths, D.F.: The Finite Difference Method in Partial Differential Equations. Wiley, Chichester (1980)
25. Ochs, P., Chen, Y., Brox, T., Pock, T.: iPiano: inertial proximal algorithm for nonconvex optimization. SIAM J. Imaging Sci. **7**, 1388–1419 (2014)
26. Preparata, F.P., Shamos, M.I.: Computational Geometry: An Introduction. Texts and Monographs in Computer Science, Springer, New York (1985)
27. Preußer, T., Rumpf, M.: An adaptive finite element method for large scale image processing. In: Nielsen, M., Johansen, P., Olsen, O.F., Weickert, J. (eds.) Scale-Space 1999. LNCS, vol. 1682, pp. 223–234. Springer, Heidelberg (1999). https://doi.org/10.1007/3-540-48236-9_20
28. Saad, Y.: Iterative Methods for Sparse Linear Systems. SIAM, Philadelphia, second edn (2003)
29. Schmaltz, C., Peter, P., Mainberger, M., Ebel, F., Weickert, J., Bruhn, A.: Understanding, optimising, and extending data compression with anisotropic diffusion. Int. J. Comput. Vis. **108**(3), 222–240 (2014)
30. Shewchuk, J.: What is a good linear element? Interpolation, conditioning, and quality measures. In: Chrisochoides, N. (ed.) Proceedings of the 11th International Meshing Roundtable, IMR 2002, Ithaca, New York, USA, 15–18 September 2002, pp. 115–126, January 2002
31. Sinha, P., Russel, R.: A perceptually based comparison of image similarity metrics. Perception **40**(11), 1269–1281 (2011)
32. Theljani, A., Belhachmi, Z., Kallel, M., Moakher, M.: A multiscale fourth-order model for the image inpainting and low-dimensional sets recovery. Math. Meth. Appl. Sci. **40**(10), 3637–3650 (2016)

# Author Index

Printed in the United States
by Baker & Taylor Publisher Services